Democracy's Heartland

Praise for the Book

'*Democracy's Heartland* stands out for its unique regional perspective and scholarly depth. It powerfully captures South Asia's democratic journey – including Bhutan's own unique transition – its challenges, aspirations and global relevance. A truly important work.' – **Tshering Tobgay, Prime Minister of Bhutan**

'With his unparalleled experience and knowledge of democratic processes, Dr Quraishi has written a book on democracy in South Asia that explains both the difficulties and the persistent attractions of and striving for democracy in the sub-continent. A must-read for South Asians and all those interested in the progress of democracy and human welfare. – **Shivshankar Menon, former National Security Advisor, India**

'There can be no one as qualified as Dr S.Y. Quraishi, a former Chief Election Commissioner of India, to offer a comprehensive study of democracy in South Asia. His unparalled scholarship and his experience in managing the most ambitious electoral exercise in India, shine through the pages of this remarkable book. *Democracy's Heartland* will serve as an indispensable reference work on the subject.' – **Shyam Saran, former Foreign Secretary, India**

'Rich in detail and regional wisdom, *Democracy's Heartland* skilfully examines the foundations and fault lines of South Asian democracies. Its insights echo Sri Lanka's democratic journey and make it a valuable addition to the discourse of our time.' – **Mahinda Deshapriya, former Chairman of the Election Commission of Sri Lanka**

'As Bhutan's first Chief Election Commissioner, I drew heavily on India's electoral model. *Democracy's Heartland* captures, with clarity and depth, the strengths and struggles of South Asia's democracies – insights that will resonate across the region. An essential read.' – **Dasho Kunzang Wangdi, former Chief Election Commissioner of Bhutan**

'Having seen the Maldives rise, falter and recover, I recognize in *Democracy's Heartland* a rare and timely work. Dr Quraishi distils South Asia's democratic

struggles and aspirations with insight that speaks directly to our own journey.
– Fuwad Thowfeek, former Chief Election Commissioner of the Maldives; Ambassador to Thailand

'A deeply engaging and thoughtful study, *Democracy's Heartland* offers a unique insight into the electoral and democratic dynamics of South Asia. Its reflections echo Nepal's own democratic struggles and aspirations – making it an important work for scholars, practitioners and citizens alike.' – **Neel Kantha Uprety, former Chief Election Commissioner of Nepal**

'At a time when democracy in Bangladesh and across South Asia is under strain, Dr S.Y. Quraishi's *Democracy's Heartland* shines as a beacon of clarity and hope. His wisdom, drawn from deep experience, offers direction in an era of uncertainty. This book is not just timely – it's necessary.' **– Prof. Abed Ali, Chairman, Election Monitoring Forum, Bangladesh; Peace Ambassador (South Asia), United Nations Peace Ambassador Foundation**

'Too often, South Asian countries are viewed in isolation. S.Y. Quraishi breaks that mold with a sweeping, comparative exploration of democracy across the region. An essential resource for students, scholars and curious readers alike.' – **Milan Vaishnav, Director and Senior Fellow, South Asia Program, Carnegie Endowment for International Peace**

'At a time when the world watches with amazement at "mothers of parliaments" and "cradles of democracy" struggle to deliver the ideals of democracy in world of social media, it is important to hear from the part of the world which practices it at scales unimaginable to the Athenians. Conceived during Dr Quraishi's fellowship engagement at King's College London, Democracy's Heartland exemplifies scholarship that bridges theory and practice – and marks a shift perhaps in where the new inspiration for democratic ideals will come from. This text should appeal to scholars and students of political sciences and democracy, but should also capture the attention of engaged citizens all over.' – **Prof. Shitij Kapur, Vice-Chancellor and President, King's College London**

'Written by someone who has devoted a career to the service of democracy, *Democracy's Heartland* offers invaluable insight into the practice and future of democracy in South Asia. As Dr Quraishi eloquently argues, this is a region – home to 40 per cent of the world's democratic citizens – that is a crucible for the global future of democracy in an age of democratic backsliding.' – **Prof. Louise Tillin, Director, King's India Institute**

Democracy's Heartland

Inside the Battle for Power in South Asia

S.Y. Quraishi

JUGGERNAUT BOOKS
C-I-128, First Floor, Sangam Vihar, Near Holi Chowk, New Delhi
110080, India

First published by Juggernaut Books 2025

10 9 8 7 6 5 4 3 2 1

P-ISBN: 9789353455828
E-ISBN: 9789353452216

Typeset in Adobe Caslon Pro by R. Ajith Kumar, Noida

Printed at Thomson Press India Ltd

To those who lit the first spark –
FICCI and King's College London –
for believing in an idea before it became a book

Contents

Acknowledgements

In 2015, Alwyn Didar Singh, the then secretary general of the Federation of Indian Chambers of Commerce & Industry (FICCI), extended a fellowship opportunity at King's College London, at its India Institute during a conversation at the Delhi Golf Club. The offer was generous and open-ended – I was to choose a topic of interest, conduct research at King's College, write a paper and deliver a few public lectures. I proposed 'Democracy and Electoral Challenges in South Asia' – a theme that Alwyn approved immediately, pending the concurrence of the India Institute. The Institute, under the leadership of Sunil Khilnani, welcomed the idea. While he initially suggested narrowing the scope to one or two countries, I felt a broader comparative approach would better reflect the region's complex democratic trajectories, about which very little is known. We agreed to focus on the eight countries of the SAARC region.

I owe special thanks to the FICCI and King's College London not just for their institutional support but for inspiring the very idea of this work. It is only fitting that this book is dedicated to them. I am especially grateful to Naina Lal Kidwai, the then president of the FICCI, for reposing her trust in me.

Though the original fellowship lasted just a couple of months, it planted the seed for this book. The research could not be completed within that time frame, but I returned with the conviction that the subject merited not merely an academic paper, but a full-length book.

The journey since then has been long and frequently interrupted. Over the years, I worked intermittently on the manuscript, assisted by a series of young and gifted research assistants. The delays were entirely mine – as I often redirected their efforts to support my newspaper columns and public commentary. Despite many promising starts, the book remained unfinished. Nonetheless, I gratefully acknowledge the contributions of the many research assistants who worked with me over the years – Shruti Slaria, Shivanshi Asthana, Tripti Jain, Nikita Singh and Ushmayo Bhattacharya – and whose dedication, even when brief, helped shape this book.

The turning point came when Abhishek Matta, an Oxford-educated scholar of exceptional intellect and discipline, joined me. Abhishek brought structure, analytical clarity and unwavering focus to a project that had long remained scattered. Even though I could not shield him entirely from other assignments, he remained committed to the manuscript's completion. When I finally curtailed my media engagements to focus on the book, the end came into view. Without Abhishek's contributions, this book would likely still be a work in progress.

I am deeply grateful to Swati Chopra, editorial director at Juggernaut Books, who had previously published three of my books – *The Great March of Democracy*, *The Population Myth* and *India's Experiment with Democracy* – with Penguin and HarperCollins. Swati understands my writing rhythm and idiosyncrasies better than most, making the publishing process refreshingly smooth. I was delighted when she offered to publish this volume at Juggernaut. My thanks to the entire team at Juggernaut Books for embracing the book.

My thanks also go to the copy editor Padmini Smetacek, the proofreader Sagareeka Pradhan and the book cover designer Harpreet Padam and Lavanya Asthana, Unlike Design Co., whose skill and care have shaped the final form of this work.

Above all, I wish to express my heartfelt gratitude to my wife, Ila Sharma, former election commissioner of Nepal (2013–19). Her professional journey has paralleled mine in uncanny ways. Her perspective – both as a South Asian election official and a thoughtful observer – has enriched this project immeasurably.

Finally, to you – the reader – thank you for picking up this book. It is your curiosity about democracy in South Asia that gives meaning to the years of work behind these pages. In a lighter vein, I commend your superb judgement in choosing it! I hope this labour of love informs, provokes and engages you in equal measure.

Foreword

Writing this foreword is an honour for me. The author of this book, Dr S.Y. Quraishi, is a man of integrity and wisdom, with a lifelong commitment to public service, and to the type of reasoned public debate that has become rare in our increasingly embittered democracies. Moreover, as a former Chief Election Commissioner of India, he is a towering figure in the electoral world. It was thus that I met him and came to admire him. I had the privilege of tapping into his profound knowledge of and commitment to democracy when he was part, for nearly a decade, of the International IDEA's Board of Advisers. The reverence for democratic institutions and values that he brought to our organization also infuses every page of this volume.

This assignment is also an honour because *Democracy's Heartland: Inside the Battle for Power in South Asia* is an important and timely book. As the author points out, South Asia has been unduly neglected in the literature on democratic development. I can attest to the fact that, for example, in the exceptionally prolific literature on democratic transitions in my part of the world, Latin America, one would be hard pressed to find any mention of the exceptionally rich, diverse, oscillating, often troubled, democratic experience of a region that today is home to one fourth of humanity, the world's largest democracy, and some of the most vibrant polities anywhere. It is remarkable that not even the improbable success of democracy in India, which harbours crucial lessons for other emerging democracies in the developing world, has been systematically interrogated in a comparative way.

This is the glaring gap in our knowledge that this book sets out to correct. Doing so is urgent for many reasons, not least the certainty that, at a time of rapid geopolitical change, South Asia, and particularly India, is set to play a pivotal role in global affairs in the future. Like few other regions, South Asia today embodies the promise and perils of democracy in the world. As I write, two of the world's most promising, if uncertain, democratic turnarounds are taking place in Bangladesh and Sri Lanka, while intense debates continue to rage about the recent trajectory of democratic institutions in India, a story with enormous potential implications for the global fate of democracy.

This book is kaleidoscopic in nature. It touches on the myriad issues that have defined the vastly divergent trajectory of democratic institutions in the eight South Asian countries, ranging from the vibrancy of democracy in India to the tragedy of state collapse in Afghanistan. Yet, if there is one theme that emerges from this complex picture, it is that of the limits of electoral democracy. Even in those cases where democracy has failed to gain a steady hold – Pakistan, Bangladesh, clearly Afghanistan – a lot of faith has been placed on the power of elections to singlehandedly make democracy blossom on barren land. Over the past several decades, both electoral practices and the prominent role of electoral authorities have been a persistent presence in nearly every country in South Asia, to a much greater extent than could be inferred from the region's checkered political history. The citizens' dogged demand for democratic elections is, no doubt, a piece of good news in South Asia. But the truth remains that this demand has, more often than not, ended in bitter disappointment. The region shows that democracy will live dangerously where ethnic and religious tensions, military influence, corruption, oligarchic political mores and, above all, widespread forms of social exclusion are left to fester. This is true even in India, where elections are truly awe-inspiring events, and adherence to foundational democratic values, like constitutionalism, is part of the national identity. Essential though they are, elections are merely the instant gratification element of democracy. Democracy's robustness, longevity and success require deeper and much longer commitments to the task of distributing power in society and keeping it accountable. Fidelity to a notion of limited political power, where the state's legitimate sphere of action is constrained by citizens' rights and the law, is the secret sauce of democratic success, if there's one. At their best, elections can help a citizens' democracy to emerge over time, but they cannot singlehandedly bring it to life.

The reading of this book makes clear that South Asia is a good place to unpack the complex links between democracy and development, an issue that should be carefully considered by anyone involved in the endeavour of measuring democratic performance around the world, as International IDEA is. In this volume, Dr Quraishi emerges as a crucial voice in the defence of exercises to monitor democratic performance, albeit not in an uncritical way. I can attest to the impatience that I have encountered in some of my interlocutors in the developing world with regards to these global measuring exercises. While some of that impatience may well be self-serving, a lot of it points to legitimate questions. Should we measure the performance of democratic institutions in Sweden or Denmark with the same yardsticks as in Sri Lanka or Bangladesh, knowing the overwhelming pressures created by the need to respond to high levels of poverty and social exclusion? How can we make our notion of democracy, and our way to measure it, more sensitive to development pressures?

In my travels with International IDEA, including in South Asia, I've come across good and bad ways to think about the relationship between democracy and development. One bad way, for example, is to see the checks and balances at the heart of democracy as an encumbrance for development. Should developing countries be entitled to cut some corners in terms of individual rights as an acceptable price for collective wellbeing? Perhaps. But one should be aware that, sooner or later, that abstract principle leads to very thorny decisions. Should building an important dam entail the price of running roughshod over the rights of an indigenous community? Should the fight against rampant crime, even when welcomed by society, justify obliterating due process and habeas corpus for those apprehended by the authorities, as it is happening today in Nayib Bukele's El Salvador? There are no obvious answers to these questions. There is only the real danger that once a government starts playing fast and loose with individual or collective rights in the name of lofty objectives, citizens may well end up with a government that they cannot get rid of. Sooner or later, the degradation of the rule of law begets the degradation of the other foundational components of democracy, especially free and fair elections.

Yes, our methods to measure democratic performance should be sensitive to development imperatives. The obvious way to do this is by reminding ourselves of the indivisibility of the corpus of fundamental rights that are the lifeblood of citizenship and democracy. Our measurement tools should shed the presumption that they prize civil and political rights above everything. They should state, loud and clear, as we do at International IDEA, that access to and the protection of social, economic and cultural rights are just as important for democracy as the achievement of civil and political rights. We should also be less judgemental about the developing countries' *current level* of democratic performance and focus more on the *trends* evinced by their performance. Where a country stands in comparison to Sweden or Denmark should matter less than the direction in which it is moving. When we measure the quality of democracy, more patience and less finger-wagging is the way to go. After all, it took the United States two centuries to grant full access to civil and political rights to African Americans, and nine centuries for Europe to move from a parliament of nobles to one elected by universal suffrage. These things take time.

Today there are legitimate concerns about the trends of democratic performance in South Asia, and Dr Quraishi pulls no punches about this. Yet, I also see grounds for optimism. The recent cases of Sri Lanka and Bangladesh, where two semi-authoritarian regimes were removed from power by large civic movements in which young people featured prominently, are signs that the demand for democracy remains vigorous in the region. At the same time, despite the real challenges to civil liberties and the breathless headlines of the past few years, the 2024 Indian election makes it is very difficult to claim now that the country is anything other than a solid democracy. The fact that in the world's most populous country, courts protected opposition leaders, electoral authorities went unperturbed about their tasks, citizens held the government to account and the results were accepted immediately by all political actors should count as a bright spot in an otherwise bleak global landscape.

And then there is the headway that South Asia is making when it comes to political inclusion. This I have witnessed directly. One of my most unforgettable memories of the past few years involves a meeting in 2023 with a group of local women councillors in the outskirts of Janakpur, Nepal, who were part of one of International IDEA's programmes to make local governments more inclusive. Under a blazing sun, those impressive women proudly told me that their election had enabled them to refocus the priorities of their local council towards supporting education and preventing domestic violence, which we can safely assume would not be the priorities of a male-dominated council. That's what a citizens' democracy inching forward amidst immense challenges looks like.

I could go on sharing the many reflections elicited by this book. I could, for example, delve into the myriad proposals that Dr Quraishi puts forward in every chapter to bring South Asia closer to democracy's ideals. Moreover, I could unpack his very worthy proposal to create a Regional Forum for Strengthening Democracy in South Asia and Southeast Asia, as a venue for regional and international cooperation to support democracy. But I'll stop here. For now, it suffices to say that this is an indispensable volume for anyone who cares about South Asia or democracy. It is, simultaneously, a source of information on the recent political history of South Asia, a critical survey of the democratic trajectory of all the countries in the region, and an overview of how some of the key democratic challenges of our time manifest themselves in South Asia and what can be done about them. Most of all, this book is a kind of political testament that reveals its author's deep respect for democracy and, as the great Albert Hirschman would have it, his bias for hope. I cannot recommend this work enough, hoping that it will achieve the wide readership it deserves.

Dr Kevin Casas-Zamora
Secretary General, International IDEA
Stockholm, July 2025

Introduction

Reframing the Democratic Narrative in South Asia

A striking paradox in contemporary global discourse on democracy is the relative marginalization of South Asia as a collective democratic space. Despite the region encompassing nearly a quarter of the world's population and 40 per cent of the world's democracy, and also hosting some of the most complex and enduring democratic practices, it remains under-represented in comparative democratic scholarship. When South Asia is referenced, it is often through a narrow lens – centred almost exclusively on India. This tendency – while perhaps understandable given India's demographic magnitude, economic weight and geopolitical standing – has resulted in a lopsided portrayal of the region's political realities.

In numerous international conferences and academic forums – particularly in the United Kingdom (UK) and the United States (US) – this imbalance has been palpable. Colleagues and participants from other South Asian nations, including Pakistan, Bangladesh, Sri Lanka, Nepal, Bhutan and the Maldives, have frequently expressed frustration at being relegated to the periphery of discussions ostensibly focused on the region as a whole. Their democratic trajectories, institutional innovations and political struggles are often overlooked or treated as secondary to the Indian experience. Even within Western universities that house departments of South Asian studies there exists a persistent institutional bias wherein research, syllabi and public engagement initiatives overwhelmingly centre on India. This intellectual asymmetry distorts our understanding of South Asia's democratic landscape, and risks reinforcing simplistic narratives that fail to capture the region's rich political diversity.

This book is, in part, a response to that gap. It seeks to broaden the analytical frame and contribute to a more inclusive and balanced discourse on democracy in South Asia. By examining the political developments, electoral processes, institutional challenges and civic engagements across all South Asian countries, the book aims to illuminate the region's democratic pluralism. Each country's experience offers unique insights into the possibilities and perils of democratization in postcolonial, multi-ethnic and often economically constrained contexts.

In reframing the narrative, the objective is not to diminish India's significance, but rather to situate it within a broader regional context – one that recognizes the interdependencies, contrasts and shared challenges that define South Asia's political fabric. Ultimately, the aim is to foster a more equitable and nuanced understanding of the region's democratic evolution, and to highlight voices and experiences that have too often been sidelined in global and regional analyses.

South Asia, a region encompassing just eight countries – Afghanistan, Bangladesh, Bhutan, India, the Maldives, Nepal, Pakistan and Sri Lanka – is home to nearly 2 billion people. Collectively, these nations constitute the largest and most dynamic hub of democratic life on the planet. Despite this astonishing demographic and political significance, the region not only remains underappreciated in global discourses on democracy but is also especially under-supported by Western powers and international funding agencies that otherwise advocate the global promotion of democratic values.

What has been missing is an intentional, long-term investment in democratic deepening and institutional strengthening in the region. This oversight is particularly troubling at a time when authoritarianism is not only resurging but becoming increasingly exportable. China, South Asia's powerful neighbour, has systematically offered an alternative political model – centred on state-led capitalism, surveillance governance and political centralization – that poses a direct ideological and economic challenge to democracy. In contrast, South Asia, with all its democratic deficits, still embodies the idea that pluralism and representation are possible even in conditions of poverty, inequality and deep social diversity. By investing in the resilience of South Asian democracies, the global community would not simply aid regional stability, it would also shore up a vital bulwark against the spread of authoritarian governance and defend the normative space for democratic experimentation outside the Western context.

The idea for this book emerged from the recognition of this paradox: South Asia, though often marginalized in global narratives about democratic progress and innovation, offers one of the richest, most diverse and most instructive labouratories for democratic practice anywhere in the world. Across its many linguistic, religious, ethnic and political landscapes, democracy in South Asia has been remarkably resilient, even if often contested, fragile or incomplete.

While the literature on democratic backsliding in the West is expanding rapidly, and while Eastern Europe, Latin America and Sub-Saharan Africa receive sustained scholarly and institutional attention, South Asia's vibrant democratic cultures are either misunderstood or reduced to simplistic binaries – fragile or flawed, resilient or chaotic – besides being India-centric. These narratives fail to grasp the region's remarkable democratic endurance and its unique contributions to the global evolution of participatory governance. However, these complex and layered democratic processes are rarely the focus of international funding agencies or Western research institutions.

The bulk of global democracy assistance bypasses South Asia or remains narrowly focused on issues like election observation, legal reform or women's empowerment, in isolation from broader political ecosystems. South Asian democracies are often expected to follow the rules and standards set by Western democracies, but without the kind of funding, support or guidance that helped many of those countries build their systems in the first place.

This underinvestment is shortsighted. The democratic future of nearly 2 billion people – and with it the stability and moral authority of the global democratic project – cannot be taken for granted. South Asia is too significant to be ignored, too diverse to be flattened and too instructive to be overlooked. Its experiments with federalism, affirmative action, caste and gender representation, youth voting, and digital campaigning offer lessons that extend well beyond the region. Its challenges – majoritarianism, populism, democratic backsliding and identity politics, among others – mirror those of established democracies, albeit under different conditions.

This is also a book that insists on hope. Despite myriad challenges – from entrenched patriarchy to deep economic inequality, from religious polarization to institutional weakness – people across South Asia continue to place their faith in the promise of democracy. They vote in enormous numbers, hold their governments to account, challenge exclusionary norms, and demand dignity and justice. This persistent democratic energy, especially in the face of adversity, is perhaps South Asia's greatest gift to the world.

Why a Book on South Asia?

No other region on earth hosts such a vast and diverse democratic public. Whether democracy retains its global relevance, or recedes into a Western and elite preoccupation, depends significantly on the trajectories unfolding in South Asia.

However, South Asia is not simply a statistical marvel. It is a living labouratory of democratic experiments where representation is tested amid poverty, pluralism and persistent institutional fragility. The region houses India – the world's largest democracy and the most populous country – and the Maldives, one of its smallest and most climate-vulnerable republics. It contains two nuclear powers (and a third in the form of China as an immediate neighbour), multiple secessionist movements, and a legacy of colonial extraction and partition that still shapes political contestations. Despite these fractures, South Asia is where hundreds of millions vote regularly, where constitutions are rewritten and debated in public squares, and where democratic backsliding sparks protest, litigation and resistance – not just acquiescence.

Its contradictions are dense. This is a region with the largest youth population in the world, yet also has the highest levels of youth unemployment.[1] It is where women turn out to vote in record numbers but rarely see proportional representation in parliaments.[2] It is where digital connectivity is rising sharply, even as Internet shutdowns are normalized tools of state control.[3] The region's democratic potential is immense but so are its democratic tensions.

What makes South Asia globally consequential is not just its demographic scale or electoral frequency, but its democratic dilemmas that are writ large: Can democracy survive in conditions of economic inequality and cultural polarization? Can democratic institutions constrain executive power in fragile states? Can deeply hierarchical societies produce genuinely egalitarian political orders? These are not South Asian questions alone – they are global questions, and South Asia offers the most concentrated and consequential site of their contestations.

As 40 per cent of ballots cast globally over the next two decades will be from a South Asian voter, the democratic choices made here – by governments, courts, citizens and movements – will reverberate across international norms, alliances and expectations. A democratic reversal in this region would recalibrate global indices, embolden autocrats elsewhere and further fracture the post-war democratic consensus. Conversely, democratic renewal in South Asia could provide the most compelling proof that democracy remains viable, adaptive and morally necessary even under the most challenging conditions.

This book takes that challenge seriously. As discussed, it begins with the premise that South Asia is not peripheral to the global story of democracy – it is central to it. And therefore, to track its electoral systems, its institutional evolutions, its legal innovations and its civic movements is not merely a regional study but a global imperative.

Over the years, there have been some books that sought to address the region of South Asia as a whole, most importantly, Susan Wadley's *South Asia in the World*[4] and Sugata Bose and Ayesha Jalal's *Modern South Asia: History, Culture, Political Economy*[5]. Even if there are some convergences I share with these books, there are, nonetheless, very marked divergences in methodology, approach, scope and style.

Ultimately, the key divergence between the three volumes lies primarily in their disciplinary orientation and methodological approach. Wadley's volume adopts an ethnographic, micro-level methodology, grounded in localized case studies and detailed cultural narratives. Bose and Jalal's volume takes on a historical and political account but is mostly restricted to the region of the Indian subcontinent. In contrast, my book takes a distinctly comparative and institutionally oriented approach, characterized by systematic political analysis structured around democratic governance, electoral integrity and policy-oriented assessments.

Wadley's book delves into selected cultural and social phenomena through illustrative ethnographic vignettes – such as marriage customs in South India, transgender activism in Pakistan or forest management practices in Rajasthan – highlighting localized intricacies and social dynamics. In sharp contrast, my methodological strategy systematically encompasses every single South Asian country individually – India, Pakistan, Sri Lanka, Bangladesh, Afghanistan, Nepal, Bhutan and the Maldives – in dedicated country profiles – a comprehensive coverage often absent in broader regional analyses, including Wadley's and Bose and Jalal's. Moreover, the thematic sections in this book offer rigorous comparative insights across these countries on key governance-related issues such as political financing, voter education, electoral technologies and inner-party democracy, providing readers with region-wide analytical depth rarely achieved in existing literature on South Asia.

In contrast to both the books, moreover, the aim of this book is to deliver comprehensive, comparative political analysis and concrete proposals aimed explicitly at institutional and electoral reform.

How Have the Member Countries Fared?

India, the largest democracy in the world by population, held its first general elections in 1951–52, defying contemporary Western scepticism about the viability of liberal democracy in a poor, largely illiterate and highly diverse post-colonial state. Bangladesh, also born out of a liberation struggle, has oscillated between democratic and authoritarian governance but has seen robust voter participation and a unique pattern of female leadership. Nepal has made a remarkable transition from monarchy to federal democracy, while Pakistan continues to negotiate the role of civilian governance in the face of entrenched military influence. Afghanistan has struggled to build a democratic state amid persistent conflict, while Sri Lanka, Bhutan and the Maldives each present distinct democratic stories marked by both innovation and instability.

What binds these disparate trajectories together is not a uniform commitment by governments, but a deeper, more enduring belief among the people of South Asia in the promise of democracy. Across regimes that have veered between authoritarianism and electoralism – whether in the shadow of the Taliban in Afghanistan, under military tutelage in Pakistan or through volatile transitions in the Maldives – the popular desire for electoral legitimacy, constitutional rule and accountable governance has remained strikingly resilient. This persistent civic aspiration – forged despite poverty, inequality, sectarian violence and political repression – merits not only sustained scholarly attention but also genuine international solidarity and support.

Yet, South Asia has long remained peripheral in the eyes of Western donors, multilateral institutions and democracy-promotion foundations. The bulk of democracy assistance funding and academic attention continues to be directed toward Eastern Europe, Latin America and parts of Africa. South Asia is often viewed through a narrow security or development lens, with democracy being treated as either a backdrop or a collateral concern. This persistent underinvestment reflects a larger failure to appreciate the region's critical role in shaping the future of democratic norms and practices globally.

There are structural and ideological reasons behind this neglect. For one, the region's democratic evolution does not fit neatly into Western models. South Asian democracies are often noisy, turbulent and unpredictable. Their institutions are sometimes weak; corruption is endemic; and majoritarianism, clientelism and populism remain persistent challenges. However, these characteristics are not unique to South Asia – they are increasingly visible in the democracies of the West as well. The reluctance to treat South Asia as a legitimate site of democratic experimentation reveals a lingering bias that equates democracy with Western political genealogy and institutional design.

Moreover, South Asian democracies have often crafted indigenous frameworks of democratic functioning that prioritize participation, inclusion and negotiation over procedural orthodoxy. The region has pioneered models such as caste-based reservations, *panchayati raj* institutions, decentralized governance, public interest litigation and gender quotas in local elections – innovations that offer valuable lessons for democratic deepening in other parts of the world. South Asia also offers a striking diversity of electoral systems, federal arrangements, civil society formations and media ecologies, providing a rich terrain for comparative analysis among these issues.

This book seeks to respond to this gap in scholarly and policy attention. It brings together thematically structured essays that analyse key pillars of democratic life in South Asia: electoral systems and representation, political finance, gender and inclusion, criminalization of politics, status of religious and ethnic minorities, civil society and youth involvement, judicial independence, executive–legislative relations, and the general trend of democratic backsliding in the region. It features critical assessments of constitutional frameworks, legal innovations, voter behaviour, identity politics, and the role of religion and ethnicity in shaping democratic participation. Throughout, the book foregrounds the lived realities of democracy in South Asia, combining rigorous empirical research with normative reflections.

The SAARC – The Regional Dream That Faltered

No serious study of democracy in South Asia can afford to ignore the institutional framework that was envisioned to bind its nations together: the South Asian Association for Regional Cooperation (SAARC). The SAARC emerged in 1985 as a formal attempt to realize the promise of regionalism.[6] Modelled loosely after other regional blocs such as ASEAN and the European Union (EU), it was born out of a recognition that South Asia's shared history, porous borders and interlinked socio-economic challenges required collective solutions, not merely national ones.[7]

The official declaration that led to the SAARC's formation came in December 1985 in Dhaka, Bangladesh. The seven founding countries – Bangladesh, Bhutan, India, the Maldives, Nepal, Pakistan and Sri Lanka (later joined by Afghanistan in 2007) – adopted the SAARC Charter with ambitions that were as lofty as they were necessary: to promote peace, stability and prosperity through regional cooperation.[8] They pledged to collabourate on issues ranging from poverty alleviation to education, from health to environmental sustainability, and from cultural exchange to economic integration. Crucially, the SAARC Charter avoided addressing bilateral disputes, in particular the India–Pakistan rivalry, in the hope that political disagreements would not derail the developmental agenda.[9]

Despite this high-minded vision, the SAARC was constrained from the outset by the very geopolitical realities it sought to transcend. The region's asymmetrical power distribution, particularly India's outsized economic and political dominance – accounting for over 70 per cent of SAARC's GDP – generated suspicion among its smaller neighbours.[10] Moreover, the adversarial relationship between India and Pakistan has proven to be a chronic roadblock. Their animosities have not only poisoned bilateral relations but also repeatedly stymied the SAARC's potential as a collective platform. The last SAARC summit was held in Kathmandu in 2014. Since then, summits have been indefinitely postponed, most notably following the 2016 Uri attack and India's subsequent boycott of the Islamabad summit.

And yet, the SAARC was not without its achievements. It facilitated the establishment of institutions like the SAARC Development Fund, the South Asian University and the SAARC Disaster Management Centre. It catalysed initiatives on women's empowerment, child health and food security. Its conventions on combating terrorism and drug trafficking, while limited in enforcement, laid down common legal frameworks.[11] The South Asian Free Trade Area (SAFTA), though poorly implemented, represented a step toward economic integration. Still, these victories were sporadic and largely symbolic. Intraregional trade continues to hover around a mere 5 per cent, a dismal figure when compared to ASEAN's 25 per cent.[12] Visa regimes remain restrictive, cultural exchange is minimal and the organization suffers from weak institutional architecture, lacking both the political will and the bureaucratic capacity to enforce its mandates.

The broader tragedy of the SAARC lies not just in its ineffectiveness, but in its missed opportunity. The region's most urgent problems – climate change, health pandemics, energy insecurity, youth unemployment and digital misinformation – are transnational in character and cannot be addressed by states acting in isolation.[13] The SAARC was envisioned to provide precisely this kind of regional scaffolding. Its failure to do so has left a vacuum now increasingly filled by bilateral tensions and extra-regional powers.[14] Yet, paradoxically, this very failure underscores its necessity. If democracy is to be revitalized in South Asia, it will require not only national reforms but also renewed regional cooperation. A reimagined SAARC – one that is depoliticized, people-centric and democratically accountable – may yet serve as the platform for such a future.

In what follows, this book turns to the contemporary state of democracy in the SAARC countries – measured, compared and critiqued through the lens of global democratic indices. But it does so with the understanding that South Asia is more than a sum of its parts. Its democratic journey must be understood in concert, not isolation.

Witnessing Democracies: A Comparative Global Vantage

Over the past several years, my work in the domain of electoral democracy has taken me across borders – from the snow-lined polling booths of Nepal to the rural heartlands of Pakistan, from election headquarters in Colombo to civic forums in Nairobi, Maputo and Abuja. I have served as an election observer not only within the South Asian region, but also in democracies as varied as Kenya and Nigeria, Mozambique, and the UK. These experiences have offered more than institutional insight; they have been encounters with the plural textures of democratic life: the quiet dignity of first-time voters, the logistical choreography of large-scale electoral machinery and the political undercurrents that shape how citizens trust, fear or challenge the ballot. Each country offered its own answer to the democratic question, and cumulatively, these journeys endowed me with a comparative lens through which to examine South Asia's electoral landscape – not as an isolated case, but as part of a global continuum of aspiration and contestation.

This book, while centred on the SAARC region, is profoundly shaped by those broader observations. The comparative vantage has allowed me to see more clearly what is exceptional, endangered or instructive about democracy in South Asia. Why do countries with similar colonial legacies diverge so radically in democratic endurance?

Why do some electoral commissions win the public's trust while others remain beholden to power? Why do youth rise up in protest in one context and retreat into apathy in another? My visits to countries across Africa, Europe and North America were not digressions from a South Asian inquiry – they were prisms that refracted its complexity. This book, then, is both regional in its scope and global in its sensibility, grounded in the belief that to understand democracy in South Asia is also to engage with democracy everywhere – as a promise, a process and a struggle still unfolding.

Fieldnotes from the Frontlines: Sri Lanka and Pakistan

One of the most vivid memories I carry from my years observing elections across the region is from Sri Lanka in November 2015. It was a country still walking the tightrope between past authoritarianism and future possibility. I had been invited to lead a delegation of twenty-three members from the Association of Asian Election Authorities (AAEA), and over four days, I travelled more than 1,200 km through former war-torn provinces in the north, from Jaffna to Mullaitivu, watching the machinery of democracy click, creak and somehow function.

At the time, Sri Lanka's election commission had technically been abolished as an independent constitutional body, reduced to a mere government department, that too under a dictator. And yet, its commissioner, Mahinda Deshapriya, refused to let that institutional weakening paralyse the conduct of the vote. Civil society groups like People's Action for Free and Fair Elections (PAFFREL) and Centre for Monitoring Election Violence (CMEV) were loud, organized and fearless. Rumours of military roadblocks and voter intimidation circulated widely. But on polling day, not a single army checkpoint blocked our path. 'Send the maximum number of observers to the north,' Deshapriya had urged me days earlier, almost pleading. I now believe that our presence – especially in areas most vulnerable to voter suppression – may have altered the script through voter confidence.

The most unforgettable moment came just hours after the polls closed. As results were being declared live on national television, Deshapriya stood beside the incoming president and prime minister (PM), holding up my book *An Undocumented Wonder: The Making of the Great Indian*

Election. He quoted Gopal Gandhi's line from the foreword of the book – 'Among the many great things that India has, three are most important: the Taj Mahal, Mahatma Gandhi, and an electoral democracy' – and said he hoped Sri Lanka might one day match India not only in holding elections, but in empowering the institutions that safeguard them. It was a moving moment, not for personal reasons alone but because it reminded me that the Indian electoral model, despite its many flaws, still held aspirational power across the region.

The results themselves were dramatic: the powerful Rajapaksa political dynasty was defeated by Maithripala Sirisena, a former ally turned challenger. It was one of those rare transitions in South Asia where an entrenched regime was unseated not by revolution or collapse, but through the silent will of the ballot. In hindsight, that election became a test case in this book's central concern with how electoral institutions, when bolstered by civic vigilance and international observation, can restrain majoritarianism and restore credibility even in post-conflict, illiberal contexts. For our broader reflections on civil–military relations, electoral oversight and the reconstruction of institutional legitimacy across the SAARC countries, Sri Lanka's 2015 moment remains an enduring and instructive case.

Later, I was in Pakistan for the 2018 general elections, this time as a member of the Commonwealth Observer Group led by Nigeria's former head General Abdulsalami Abubakar. It was a historic moment – the second time in Pakistan's turbulent history that a civilian government handed over to another civilian government after completing a full term. But even as the handover looked smooth on paper, the air in Islamabad and Lahore was thick with euphemism. No one mentioned the army directly. Instead, people spoke of the 'establishment', the '*khalai makhlooq* (people from space)', the 'angels' and even the 'agriculture department'. There were murmurs of journalists being silenced, party candidates pressured to withdraw and court cases timed with uncanny precision. When we met media professionals, one of them shrugged and said, 'We have learnt how to censor ourselves. It's safer.'

And yet, as the days unfolded, we saw another side of the picture: women voting in tribal areas for the first time, thanks to a new rule that invalidated any result where less than 10 per cent of female voters turned out. Political parties ran special enrolment drives. Women-only polling stations – staffed entirely by women – popped up even in Khyber Pakhtunkhwa. Despite real threats in places like Balochistan, the day itself passed peacefully. The Election Commission of Pakistan had more power than ever before: to discipline officials, to make rule and to deregister political parties. But it still struggled with transparency, especially during the counting, when result forms weren't distributed or pasted publicly. Even the result transmission system collapsed. One minister quipped, 'Blame the British. Their app failed.'

The results, which saw Imran Khan's PTI (Pakistan Tehreek-e-Insaf) sweep into power, were met with celebration by some and with deep suspicion by others. And that ambiguity – between democratic advance and democratic manipulation – is, in some ways, quintessentially South Asian. Pakistan's 2018 election illustrated both the strides and limits of reform: a legal framework stronger than ever, but still vulnerable to extra-electoral influence. What it taught me – and what this book takes seriously – is that in many SAARC countries, democratic transitions are not always about clean breaks or grand moments of rupture. They are more often about slow, uneven shifts where legal reform jostles with latent power, where electoral commissions may grow sharper teeth but still lack the bite, and where civil society becomes the buffer between what is promised and what is practised.

Nepal and Myanmar: Between Blueprint and Reality

If Sri Lanka's 2015 polls offered a lesson in how democratic institutions can reassert themselves after institutional erosion, then Nepal's elections in late 2017 gave a glimpse into what it looks like when a fledgling democratic order begins to breathe on its own. I was in Kathmandu during the final phase of voting as part of an observer delegation drawn from across South Asia. What I witnessed was not just an election but a kind of civic rite – calm, orderly and quietly determined. After years of political volatility, street agitation and constitutional wrangling, Nepal was conducting simultaneous elections to both the federal parliament and the newly created provincial assemblies under the 2015 Constitution. That this was the country's second major election in just seven months (the earlier being for local governments) spoke to an electoral machinery that, though still young, had begun to find its rhythm.

I visited several polling booths in both urban and hilly areas. There were no frills, no loudspeakers or garlands or processionals, just long queues of voters – many elderly, many first-timers – waiting with stoic patience. Despite high rates of illiteracy, voters had little difficulty handling multiple ballot papers, thanks to a modest but effective voter education campaign. In one village, I watched an old man leaning on a stick, carefully inspect all three ballots – the FPTP (first-past-the-post) system and proportional representation papers for both tiers – and then slip them into separate boxes with deliberation. The symbolism was hard to miss: a fractured, post-conflict society trying to stitch itself together through the act of voting.

That Nepal's voters were able to embrace a complex new system – combining direct and proportional representation – suggests a degree of democratic maturity often overlooked in regional assessments. The Left alliance, which went on to sweep the polls, campaigned on promises of stability and economic revival. Whether it delivered on those promises is a question that continues to animate political debate in Nepal. But for this book's purposes, Nepal's 2017 election is important for another reason: it reflects the promise and pitfalls of federalism in South Asia, where newly devolved structures coexist with unresolved ethnic and regional tensions. Madhesi protests, the ambiguity over provincial boundaries and the still-unformed National Assembly all point to the fragility of what has been achieved. Yet, it also shows how the electoral process itself – if credible and inclusive – can serve as a slow, imperfect blueprint for peace-building in deeply plural societies.

From Nepal's hopeful ballot to Myanmar's (previously Burma) fraught one, the arc of the region bends unevenly. I travelled to Yangon in late 2015 to observe what was then being hailed as Myanmar's first truly open national election in decades. On paper, the enthusiasm was palpable: over 6,000 candidates from ninety-one parties, 40,000 polling booths, and a swelling wave of expectation surrounding Aung San Suu Kyi and her National League for Democracy (NLD). But the optimism was laced with unease. At one meeting, a local activist told me, 'We're voting under the shadow of ghosts,' – referring to the country's long history of military surveillance, voter suppression and ethnic exclusion. The Election Commission itself had admitted it could only vouch for 30 per cent accuracy in the voter rolls. And worse, nearly a million Rohingya Muslims had been stripped of their voting rights altogether.

At one polling centre outside the Rakhine region, I met an elderly woman who said she had walked two hours to vote 'because last time, I wasn't allowed'. But the deeper irony of that election lay not in who voted, but in who couldn't. Rohingya candidates were disqualified en masse. No Muslim was fielded by the NLD. Suu Kyi, once the emblem of global democratic hope, maintained a studied silence. It was a silence many of us from South Asia recognized: the silence of 'electoral necessity'. It raised a question central to this book – can electoral democracy in the region survive without confronting the exclusions it enables? Myanmar's 2015 election marked a step forward, yes, but one that left many – especially the displaced, the stateless and the disenfranchized – outside its moral boundary.

Even the constitutional architecture betrayed deep institutional entrenchment. A quarter of all parliamentary seats remained reserved for the military. The presidency remained barred to Suu Kyi due to her family's foreign citizenship. The military retained its veto on any constitutional amendment. Yet, for a country that had been under direct military rule for over fifty years, the very act of holding an election with independent observers, vibrant campaigning and a large voter turnout was a symbolic rupture. Myanmar's story, unlike Nepal's, was not about democratic consolidation but about the fragility of transitional states where formal rituals of democracy outpace structural reform. For South Asia as a whole, it remains a cautionary case: a free vote is not always a free polity.

Nigeria, Kenya and Mozambique: Watching Democracy Hold Its Breath

In early 2019, I found myself in Abuja, observing Nigeria's sixth general election since its return to democracy two decades earlier. It was an election bloated with promise, tension and disarray – everything that tends to characterize a large, diverse, postcolonial democracy trying to square its plural realities with institutional form. With ninety-one political parties and seventy-three presidential candidates on the ballot, Nigeria, at first glance, felt like a theatre of democratic abundance. But beneath that surface, it was a story riddled with logistical collapse, voter fatigue and fragile trust. The night before polling, six hours before voting was to begin, the election was postponed by a week due to a breakdown in logistics. The frustration across the country was palpable, and the economic losses were estimated in the billions. That week-long delay never quite healed.

I visited polling booths in both urban centres and semi-rural fringes. Many opened hours late. Ballot secrecy was often compromised. In some places, the biometric smart card readers failed en masse. Voter turnout plummeted to 35 per cent – the lowest in Nigeria's democratic history. Yet, what struck me most was the split reality: while international observers commended the electoral commission's neutrality, many voters I spoke to felt something essential had frayed. 'It's not the rigging,' one man said quietly outside a polling centre in Lagos, 'it's the feeling that we don't matter enough to get it right.' That stayed with me.

And yet, despite its chaos, Nigeria's election offered insights into electoral transitions in states where democratic infrastructure exists in uneasy proximity to elite power and fragile state capacity. Muhammadu Buhari's re-election was contested but held. The electoral commission (Independent National Electoral Commission) was formally powerful and independent, yet visibly overstretched. For the SAARC region – particularly countries grappling with youth apathy and turnout drops – Nigeria is a mirror. It reminds us that legitimacy does not arise from formal autonomy alone; it must be seen, felt and trusted by those who vote. In this, India and Nigeria – both continental democracies – have much to learn from each other, not least in how to preserve scale without eroding credibility.

A few years earlier, in 2013, I had travelled to Kenya, where the stakes were far more visceral. The last national election in 2007 had ended in catastrophe – violence that killed over 1,300 people and displaced more than half a million. This time, the mood was sober, near-reverent. The queues at polling stations began at 4.00 a.m., hours before the booths opened. 'We want to vote before anything goes wrong,' a young man told me. Our driver nodded in agreement. People feared violence might erupt again in the afternoon, so they came early. Though the fear did not materialize, the trauma of 2007 hung like mist over the long lines. Kenya had collectively resolved that it would not slip again.

The new Independent Electoral and Boundaries Commission had worked hard to earn public trust, including by drawing on international partnerships. I had earlier hosted a delegation of Kenyan commissioners in India. They studied our systems closely, fascinated by how our electoral machinery held together across impossible terrain. Now in Nairobi, I watched them attempt to reproduce that scaffolding – six simultaneous elections, six ballot boxes, colour-coded lids and biometric systems. It was a staggering logistical operation. Some elements failed, particularly the voter identification technology and the result transmission system, which collapsed during the count. But the will to get it right was unmistakable.

The patience of Kenyan voters was astonishing. I remember one woman, waiting in the sun for nearly seven hours, telling me, 'If I leave, who will vote for my children's peace?' One major logistic blunder created chaos – families were split up to join different alphabetical queues, with the umbrella going with one member and the water bottle with another in separate lines. The counting took five anxious days. Uhuru Kenyatta won – just barely – crossing the 50 per cent threshold by a whisker. Raila Odinga challenged the result in court. The nation held its breath. And when the Supreme Court eventually upheld the result, Odinga conceded and called for peace.

The lesson Kenya offered was simple but sobering: elections can restore public faith, but only if their administrative spine is strong enough to bear the weight of national trauma. Even well-intentioned reforms can falter under technological strain and public expectation. For the SAARC region, particularly in post-conflict or identity-fractured societies, Kenya serves as a valuable case which shows that peace, participation and procedural legitimacy must move together or not at all.

A year later, in October 2014, while Maharashtra and Haryana queued up to vote in their own assembly elections, I found myself nearly 7,000 km away, watching another kind of democratic exercise unfold – this time in Mozambique. I had joined the Commonwealth Observer Group, a fourteen-member team led by the former PM of the Bahamas, with participants from five continents and nearly every corner of the old empire. The sun, I remember thinking as I flew in over Maputo, may have set on the British empire, but it still rises with democratic hope in the Commonwealth.

Mozambique was one of Africa's more hopeful stories back then: from civil war to economic turnaround, propelled by discoveries of offshore gas and new mineral wealth. And yet, even with its relatively clean democratic record, the election process felt precarious – like a tightrope strung across a ravine of mistrust. The ruling party, FRELIMO (Frente de Libertação Moçambique; Mozambique Liberation Front), still dominant since independence, faced a fractured opposition: RENAMO (Resistência Nacional Moçambicana; Mozambican National Resistance), a former rebel group turned political party whose leader, Afonso Dhlakama, had contested (and rejected) the outcome of every single election since 1994; and the newer Mozambique Democratic Movement, a breakaway faction hoping to disrupt the old binary.

Election day itself was calm, festive even. Voters queued patiently outside school buildings and temporary booths. Teachers ran the polling stations, joined by three party agents representing the major political factions – a practice designed to improve transparency but not without its own tensions. Ballots were counted immediately after polls closed, but that was only the beginning of a long and unwieldy process. From the polling station to the district centre, then onward to the provincial and national levels, the tabulation process crawled through several bureaucratic stages. As results slowly percolated up to Maputo, speculation filled the void. It was, in many ways, an election run in good faith but not in good time.

What impressed me was not the machinery but the human texture of the process. Women and youth were visibly present – not just as voters, but as candidates, volunteers and civil society actors. The Youth Parliament, despite its slightly misleading name, was an energetic NGO that had mobilized young people to engage with politics beyond the ballot. Like India, Mozambique is demographically young, and while the turnout remained modest at just under 50 per cent, the symbolic presence of these groups mattered. It was one of those elections where the ritual itself – of being seen to vote and seen to participate – seemed to matter as much as the outcome.

But the process was not without flaws. Nearly 5.5 per cent of ballots were left blank, and over 3 per cent were declared invalid – a reminder of how much work still remains in voter education. The media, too, seemed subdued. Self-censorship was a term we heard often – less from coercion than from fatigue or financial pressure. 'We report,' one journalist told me, 'but we've learnt when not to ask questions.' And while the electoral commission deserved credit for its openness – it had invited nearly 6,000 observers, including 350 international ones – trust remained fragile. Dhlakama, predictably, rejected the result again.

For the SAARC region, Mozambique offers a quiet but valuable analogy. Here is a country emerging from armed conflict, seeking legitimacy not through dramatic revolutions but through procedural repair – something Nepal, Sri Lanka and even parts of India can resonate with. Mozambique reminds us that electoral democracy, especially in post-conflict societies, does not always roar; sometimes, it murmurs its way forward, balancing ritual with risk. And it reminds us too that democratic trust is not won once but earned over and over again – with every line marked on a ballot, every hand raised in a count and every peaceful morning after.

The UK: A Smaller Mirror, A Sharper Contrast

After journeys through elections across South Asia and Africa, the UK presented a different tempo altogether – quieter, neater, almost reticent. In May 2015, I found myself walking through the polling stations of rural England, observing the UK general election alongside a diverse group of international delegates – former election commissioners, journalists and academics. It was the first election held under the Fixed-Term Parliaments Act, and while the contest itself had drawn significant global attention, my focus – as always – was on the scaffolding: how the election was managed, structured and experienced. Two of the three constituencies I visited later sent successive PMs to Downing Street – David Cameron and Theresa May.

At first glance, the UK's electoral model is familiar to South Asia: FPTP, single-member constituencies and direct election to the lower house. But the scale is radically different. The UK electorate is about the size of the Indian state of Rajasthan, and yet the House of Commons has

650 members of parliament (MPs), compared to the 543 in the Indian Lok Sabha. On average, a UK MP represents just 70,000 constituents; in India, Pakistan or Bangladesh, that number easily stretches into the millions. What this disparity creates is not merely a difference of magnitude but one of logistical philosophy. The UK's elections are, by design, low-key: no identity proof is required, no fingers are inked and no security is posted at polling stations. The assumption is that democratic trust need not be policed.

Nevertheless that very simplicity also invites scrutiny. In the UK, ballot papers can run out – as they did in London in both the 2010 and 2015 elections. Voting continues to rely entirely on paper, with no serious momentum for electronic voting. By contrast, India has used electronic voting machines (EVMs) since 1998, and several other South Asian countries have initiated or explored pilot models for technological upgrades. The UK's aversion to reform may signal stability, but it can also suggest inertia. Meanwhile, the clamour for online or Internet voting – a new frontier – has begun to stir in both the UK and in parts of the SAARC region, particularly among diasporic voters and younger constituencies.

Importantly, the UK model is not without distortion. The same FPTP system that routinely under-represents smaller or regionally dispersed parties in Bangladesh and India also drew criticism in the UK. A national referendum to replace it with a preferential voting system failed in 2011, but it did raise enduring questions about majoritarian bias and democratic fairness – questions that are equally pressing across the SAARC countries. In Nepal and Sri Lanka, proportional representation systems have been adopted precisely to address such distortions. In Bhutan, even the sequencing of parties is designed to promote a broader political consensus. In that sense, South Asia's electoral innovations reflect not deficit but design, in response to the urgent pluralisms of the region.

I began with post-war Sri Lanka and post-conflict Nepal, moved through fragile democratic transitions in Pakistan and Myanmar, and then reflected on African lessons in Nigeria, Kenya and Mozambique. The UK offers not a superior model, but a useful contrast: a smaller mirror in which to view the scale, volatility and inventiveness of South

Asian democracy. What the UK's elections reveal is not how we fall short, but how we have adapted a shared institutional heritage to far more complex and conflict-ridden contexts. The real story, as this book argues, lies not in replicating Westminster but in surpassing its assumptions. And that, South Asia is already well underway in doing.

Looking Out to Look Within

Despite references to Africa and the UK, this book is firmly rooted in South Asia. Its scope, data and argumentation revolve around the eight SAARC countries, whose democratic trajectories – though interlinked by geography and history – have diverged in startling ways. And yet, it was essential to begin with these field-notes from beyond the region – not as digressions, but as vantage points. Observing elections in Kenya or the UK, in Nigeria or Myanmar, has not taken me away from South Asia – it has brought me back to it with a clearer eye. These comparative encounters have sharpened my understanding of what is distinctive, urgent and instructive about electoral democracy in the subcontinent.

South Asia does not exist in isolation. Its democracies are informed by legacies of Westminster and shaped by pressures that resonate across the Global South: contested institutions, youth bulges, identity politics, logistical burdens and civic innovations. By looking outwards – towards fragile transitions, inherited systems and resilient electorates – I have found a fuller vocabulary to speak of the region's democratic dilemmas. These international reflections serve, then, not as detours, but as preludes. They prepare the ground for what follows: a closer, deeper examination of democracy as it unfolds, frays, reforms and re-imagines itself within and across the SAARC nations.

If this section ventures beyond SAARC boundaries, it is only to better illuminate what lies within – not to elevate external models. Rather, these comparative glimpses reveal that South Asia lacks neither democratic ambition nor electoral creativity. From Nepal's hybrid electoral designs and Bhutan's consensus-driven model, to Bangladesh's voter-registration advances and India's robust voter-education drives, SAARC countries exemplify democratic resilience. By placing global contexts at the outset, the aim is not external validation, but a recognition of South Asia's place within a complex, interconnected democratic landscape. It is only by looking out, occasionally, that one can look within more honestly. The chapters that follow return squarely to the SAARC region; but they do so with a clearer sense of context, and a deeper commitment to understanding what democracy means and what it demands across our part of the world.

The Structure of the Book

The book follows a twin approach. In one section, there is a separate chapter on each country, profiling the birth and evolution of democracy in it and the current challenges. This is meant for the ease of the readers who are focused on a particular country. Another section, instead of taking a country-by-country approach, follows a thematic structure allowing for cross-national comparisons and insights into common trends, as well as divergences within the region. It also reflects my belief that democracy is not merely about elections or institutional design – it is about the values, cultures, practices and everyday negotiations that sustain (or erode) democratic life.

In assembling this volume, I have drawn from a wide range of disciplines – political science, law, sociology, economics, history, media studies and development studies – recognizing that democracy is a multidimensional phenomenon. The book is a mix of opinions of seasoned scholars and emerging voices from within the region and beyond, ensuring that the volume combines intellectual depth with fresh perspectives.

The West's democratic crisis – marked by declining trust, polarization, misinformation and populist authoritarianism – should prompt a serious rethinking of where to look for democratic resilience. South Asia, with all its contradictions and challenges, has a compelling case to make. It is a region where democracy continues to inspire mass participation, where elections mobilize hundreds of millions of voters, where protests can still shake regimes and where civil society struggles persist in the face of adversity. It is time the world took serious note of this democratic vitality.

Finally, this volume is also a call for solidarity. The countries of the region have to learn from each other with the established democracy like India playing a lead role of experience sharing and hand holding.

In this context, the Forum of Election Management Bodies of South Asia (FEMBoSA) stands out as a uniquely relevant and timely initiative. Unlike the SAARC, which remains hamstrung by geopolitical tensions and the paralysis of inter-state diplomacy, FEMBoSA is not a political entity but a professional and functional association of independent election commissions. This institutional independence has allowed it to remain active, credible and collabourative, even when the broader regional architecture has faltered. FEMBoSA's work – ranging from peer-to-peer learning and joint capacity-building efforts to knowledge-sharing on electoral innovations and inclusion strategies – has quietly but steadily reinforced the foundations of electoral democracy across the region. At a time when formal political cooperation among South Asian nations is under strain, the continuity and relevance of FEMBoSA demonstrates that democracy-building can, and indeed must, be insulated from the vagaries of political relationships. Its durability also underscores the potential of South Asia's electoral institutions to not only learn from each other, but to collectively advance the democratic project, even in the absence of a robust inter-governmental framework.

South Asia's democratic destiny is not the region's burden to bear alone. It should concern all who care about democracy in the twenty-first century. The region demands more scholarly engagement, more inclusive narratives and greater material support from global democracy stakeholders. Investing in South Asia's democratic future is not charity – it is an urgent necessity for the global democratic project.

I also hope that this work will serve not only as a scholarly resource but also as a ready-to-consult reference book. I also hope this handbook will serve as a catalyst for further research, debate and action – rooted in the understanding that democracy in South Asia is not an anomaly but an essential part of the global story.

The coming section explores the institutional and historical foundations of democracy in the respective countries of the region. They examine how South Asian democracies were shaped by colonial legacies, constitutional choices and early post-independence experiments in representation, rights and state-building. This historical lens is crucial – not merely to explain present crises, but to recover the aspirations and architecture that once animated democratic life across the subcontinent.

Part I

Country Profiles

1

India: The Democratic Colossus

In August 1947, the British Empire formally relinquished its hold over India, granting independence to the region but dividing it into two sovereign states: India and Pakistan. This Partition marked the culmination of a long and complex political journey, deeply intertwined with the legacies of colonial rule and the aspirations of diverse communities.

India had been the centrepiece of the British Empire since 1858, following the dissolution of the East India Company in the aftermath of the Revolt of 1857. This revolt, a watershed moment in Indian history, underscored widespread discontent with Company rule, leading to the transfer of authority to the British Crown.[1] Over subsequent decades, debates over self-governance gained momentum, with legislative milestones such as the Indian Councils Act of 1909 and the Government of India Act of 1919 introducing limited measures of Indian representation.[2] By 1935, another Government of India Act proposed a framework for provincial autonomy under a dominion status, envisaging a confederal structure with strong provinces and princely states, and a central government limited to defence, foreign affairs and currency. However, the scheme faltered due to resistance from the princely states, leaving its vision unrealized.[3]

The onset of World War II further strained relations between British and Indian political leadership. When Britain declared war on Germany in 1939, it unilaterally committed India to the conflict without consulting its leaders, prompting the resignation of Congress ministries in protest. Amid wartime pressures, the Cripps Mission of 1942 sought to secure Indian cooperation by proposing post-War self-rule. However, its terms were rejected by both the Indian National Congress and the All-India Muslim League, leading to the Quit India Movement and widespread detentions of Congress leaders until the War's end.[4]

With the Labour Party's electoral victory in Britain in 1945, a renewed commitment to Indian independence emerged. Provincial elections in 1946 revealed polarized political allegiances: the Congress dominated in general constituencies, while the Muslim League secured all Muslim-reserved seats, solidifying its demand for a separate Muslim homeland. The Cabinet Mission of 1946 proposed a united India, with grouped provinces exercising autonomy, but this plan failed to reconcile the diverging aspirations of the Congress and the League. By 1946, tensions erupted violently during Direct Action Day, called by Muhammad Ali Jinnah, resulting in communal riots that claimed thousands of lives.[5]

The roots of the demand for Pakistan were laid in the early twentieth century: Allama Iqbal first articulated the idea of a Muslim state, while Choudhry Rahmat Ali coined the term 'Pakistan'. The Lahore Resolution of 1940, endorsed by Jinnah, crystallized the League's call for a separate nation. By 1947, with an interim government struggling to function amid discord, the last British Viceroy, Lord Mountbatten, advanced the Partition plan, drawing upon earlier proposals from the Cabinet Mission.[6]

The Partition plan, announced in June 1947, divided British India along religious lines. Punjab and Bengal, with near-parity between Muslim and non-Muslim populations, were partitioned through the intervention of the Radcliffe Commission, chaired by Cyril Radcliffe. The hastily drawn borders, decided without prior consultation with local populations, ignited unprecedented violence and mass displacements. Entire communities were uprooted as communal hatred engulfed regions, particularly Punjab and Bengal. Millions fled their ancestral homes: Hindu and Sikh families moved from areas allotted to Pakistan, while Muslims migrated from India, creating refugee crises on both sides.[7]

Partition: Freedom and Fracture

The founding leaders of India were resolute in their vision of establishing a democratic state when the nation attained independence in 1947. This commitment to democracy, however, was neither predetermined nor assured, particularly in the aftermath of the unprecedented upheaval caused by the Partition.

The human toll was staggering: estimates suggest that up to 20 million were displaced, and deaths ranged from 200,000 to over a million. The violence inflicted unspeakable suffering, with women and children bearing the brunt of abductions, assaults and killings. The Partition remains one of the most transformative and traumatic events in the history of the Indian subcontinent. The enduring legacy of this division continues to shape the political, social and cultural fabric of South Asia.

The creation of a democratic polity was further challenged by the profound and complex realities of Indian society. Deeply entrenched social divisions, endemic poverty and low levels of literacy posed formidable obstacles, defying the conditions that many scholars have traditionally deemed essential for the successful establishment and sustainability of democracy. Yet, despite these adverse circumstances, the Indian leadership embarked on a path to construct a political system that would uphold the principles of inclusivity, representation and self-governance, laying the foundation for a democratic experiment of unprecedented scale and complexity.[8]

The Early Years

In May 1952, the MPs of India's first Lok Sabha convened to elect its inaugural speaker. The Congress, commanding a clear majority in the house, nominated G.V. Mavalankar, who had previously served as the speaker since 1946. His opponent was Shankarrao Shantaram More, a first-time parliamentarian. Acknowledging the customary graciousness of parliamentary traditions, More cast his vote for Mavalankar, stating, 'In the best traditions of Parliament, a gracious custom prevails by which where two candidates are proposed for the Speakership, each candidate votes for the other candidate. I have observed that custom by voting for you."[9]

Upon his election, Mavalankar recognized the gravity of his role as the first speaker of a newly independent republic. In his address to the assembly, he observed, 'Parliamentary life has only recently begun in our land, and it is yet a tender plant that requires delicate and careful handling – and if I may say so, careful nursing. It is, therefore, the special responsibility of this Parliament to set up sound and healthy traditions, as whatever we do now is more likely to be a precedent for all times to come.'[10]

The Constituent Assembly

The development of modern legislative institutions in India is steeped in historical complexity. The increasing demand for self-government during the colonial period necessitated the creation of a bicameral national Dominion Legislature under the Government of India Act of 1919. While this pre-Independence legislature had limited powers, serving primarily as a platform for critiquing colonial policies, it nonetheless marked a significant step in India's democratic evolution. This body ceased to exist following Independence, with its functions subsumed by the Constituent Assembly.

The Constituent Assembly, tasked with framing the Constitution, initially faced the challenge of balancing dual responsibilities: drafting a foundational document while serving as the Dominion Legislature. On 29 August 1947, the Assembly resolved to distinguish between these roles, setting aside separate days or sittings for constitution-making and legislative duties. The Central Hall of Parliament became the venue for drafting the Constitution, while legislative sessions were convened in the Lok Sabha chamber under the title of the Constituent Assembly (Legislative).

Presiding over this dual enterprise were G.V. Mavalankar, as speaker of the legislative sessions, and Rajendra Prasad, as chair of the constitution-framing process. Prasad, who was also a minister, frequently responded to parliamentary questions in his legislative capacity.

The Constituent Assembly first met in its legislative role in November 1947, a time of national turmoil marked by the human and social upheaval of Partition. The massive influx of refugees and outbreaks of communal violence underscored the fragile state of the newly independent nation. Against this backdrop, Mahatma Gandhi travelled to Delhi to promote communal harmony. In January 1948, Gandhi undertook a fast unto death to quell the violence – an act that surprised both his colleagues and government leaders. His assassination by Nathuram Godse on 30 January 1948 plunged the nation into mourning.

When the Assembly reconvened on 2 February, Speaker Mavalankar opened the proceedings with a solemn acknowledgement: 'We are meeting today under the shadow of a double calamity – the sad demise of the tallest leader of our age, who has led us from slavery to independence, and the reappearance of the cult of political violence in our country.'[11] After paying heartfelt tributes to Gandhi, the Assembly adjourned for the day.

From late 1947 to 1949, the Constituent Assembly operated in its dual capacities, meeting for 104 days in 1948 and extending its sessions over six months in 1949.[12] During their time in Delhi, members resided in repurposed military barracks previously occupied by American troops during World War II. Renamed the Constitution House, this complex became the hub of political activity, hosting legislative deliberations and Congress meetings.

On 26 November 1949, the Constituent Assembly formally adopted a comprehensive written Constitution, a document that has guided India's political destiny for over seven decades. India's founding document came into force on 26 January 1950, marking the end of the Assembly's constitution-making role and its transition into a provisional Parliament, setting the stage for India's enduring democratic experiment.

The republic envisioned by this Constitution came into being on 26 January 1950. At the time of its commencement, the Constitution of independent India contained 395 articles divided into twenty-two parts and eight schedules. It laid out a comprehensive catalogue of fundamental rights and an extensive set of Directive Principles of State Policy, which the state is enjoined to promote. Over the decades, the Constitution has undergone significant amendments – ninety-seven in number as of June 2025 – and has expanded to include twelve schedules and numerous additional provisions through both formal revisions and judicial interpretation.It also prescribes another shortlist of fundamental duties for citizens. The exercise took a very long time and the Constituent Assembly sat continuously for two years, eleven months and seventeen days to complete the draft, resolving many conflicting issues along the way. It created an elabourate constitutional architecture with a bicameral, federal legislative structure, state assemblies, an independent judiciary and, crucially, the election commission.

Among its most transformative provisions was the adoption of universal adult franchise in a country where the literacy rate stood at a mere 12 per cent.[13] The Constitution established a parliamentary democratic system, comprising a directly elected House of the People (Lok Sabha) and a Council of States (Rajya Sabha) elected indirectly by state legislatures.

India's success in this democratic experiment was aided by the intellectual and moral contributions of leaders such as Dr B.R. Ambedkar. A staunch critic of mainstream nationalism, Ambedkar nonetheless devoted five critical years (1946–51) to shaping the nascent republic, serving as the principal architect of the Constitution and later as law minister in Jawaharlal Nehru's cabinet. His resignation in October 1951 over opposition to the reformist Hindu Code Bill underscored his uncompromising commitment to social justice.

Ambedkar's warnings about the fragility of minority rights resonate deeply in contemporary India. Introducing the draft Constitution on 4 November 1948, he remarked:

> To diehards who have developed a kind of fanaticism against minority protection, I would like to say two things. One is that minorities are an explosive force which, if it erupts, can blow up the whole fabric of the State. The other is that the minorities in India have agreed to place their existence in the hands of the majority. They have loyally accepted the rule of the majority, which is basically a communal majority and not a political majority. It is for the majority to realize its duty not to discriminate against minorities.[14]

Parliament

The Indian political system follows the tripartite system first proposed by Montesquieu (1748), believing in the separation of powers between a legislature, an executive and an independent judiciary to check the concentration of power in the hands of a few. The Indian political system is a three-tier system with elections held for national, state and local (village) level. Decentralization is followed as a policy in order to ensure a mechanism of checks and balances, and the smooth running of the democracy.

The Parliament of the Union of India consists of the president, the Lok Sabha and the Rajya Sabha. The president is the head of the state, and he appoints the PM who runs the government according to the political composition of the Lok Sabha. The president is elected by the elected members of the Vidhan Sabhas (state legislative assemblies), Lok Sabha and Rajya Sabha, and serves for a period of five years, although they can stand for re-election. The vice-president, on the other hand, is elected by a direct vote of all members, elected and nominated, of the Lok Sabha and Rajya Sabha.

Although the government is headed by a PM, the cabinet is the central decision-making body of the government. Members of more than one party can make up a government, and although the governing parties may be a minority in the Lok Sabha, they can govern as long as they have the confidence of a majority of the members of the Lok Sabha. As well as being the body that determines who makes up the government, the Lok Sabha is the main legislative body along with the Rajya Sabha.

Under the Constitution of India, the total number of elected members of the Lok Sabha shall not exceed 550. The Lok Sabha, at present, consists of 543 elected members, who are chosen directly from single-member territorial parliamentary constituencies, that is to say, each constituency elects one member to the House. Thus, the country has been divided into 543 parliamentary constituencies, each of which returns one MP to the Lok Sabha, the lower house of Parliament. The size and shape of the parliamentary constituencies are determined by an independent Delimitation Commission, which aims to create constituencies which roughly have the same size of population, subject to geographical considerations and the boundaries of the states and administrative areas. The Constitution also provided for nomination, by the president, of two members belonging to the Anglo-Indian community, if that community is not adequately represented in the Lok Sabha. (Abolished on 25 January 2020 by the 104th Amendment to the Constitution.)

Elections to the Lok Sabha (and also to Vidhan Sabhas) are carried out using a FPTP electoral system. The country is split up into separate geographical areas known as constituencies and the electors can cast one vote each for a candidate, the winner being the candidate who gets the most votes. The members of the Rajya Sabha are elected indirectly, rather than by the citizens at large. Rajya Sabha members are elected by each Vidhan Sabha using the single transferable vote system. The single transferable vote (STV) system is a form of proportional representation. In Rajya Sabha elections, members of each state legislative assembly rank candidates in order of preference on the ballot. A candidate must reach a certain quota of votes to be elected. If a candidate gets more votes than needed, the surplus is transferred to others based on second preferences. If no one meets the quota, the least popular candidate is eliminated and their votes redistributed – this continues until all seats are filled.

Unlike most federal systems, the number of members returned by each state is roughly in proportion to their population. At present, the Rajya Sabha has 233 members, elected by the Vidhan Sabhas, and there are also twelve members nominated by the president as representatives of literature, science, art and social services. Rajya Sabha members can serve for six years and elections are staggered, with one-third of the assembly being elected every two years.

India is a federal country, and the Constitution gives the states and union territories (UTs) significant control over their own government. The Vidhan Sabhas are directly elected bodies set up to carry out the administration of the government in the twenty-eight states of India. In five of these states, there is a bicameral organization of legislatures, with both upper and lower houses – Vidhan Parishad (Legislative Council) and Vidhan Sabha (Legislative Assembly). Two of the eight Union Territories (UTs), namely Puducherry (previously Pondicherry) and the National Capital Territory of Delhi , also have legislative assemblies. On the other hand, the other five UT's – Andaman and Nicobar

Islands, Chandigarh, Dadra and Nagar Haveli and Daman and Diu, Lakshadweep and Ladakh – do not have legislative assemblies. These territories are governed directly by the central government through lieutenant governors appointed by the president of India. Their executive authority lies primarily with the Union Ministry of Home Affairs, and any local governance is carried out through municipal bodies or panchayats where applicable, but not through elected legislatures.

Elections to the Vidhan Sabhas are carried out in the same manner as for the Lok Sabha, with the states and UTs divided into single-member assembly constituencies and the FPTP electoral system used. The largest Vidhan Sabha is for Uttar Pradesh, with 403 members; the smallest is Puducherry, with 30 members.

A Vidhan Parishad is the upper house in the bicameral legislatures of certain Indian states. Its members are elected through a complex process that ensures representation from diverse sections of society. A portion of the members is elected by members of the Vidhan Sabha, and another portion by members of local authorities such as municipalities and district boards. In addition, some members are elected by two special electorates: graduates and teachers. The graduates' constituency includes citizens who hold a degree from a recognized university and have been residents of the state for at least three years. The teachers' constituency includes those who have been engaged in teaching for at least three years in institutions not lower than the secondary school level – thus including high school teachers, college lecturers and university professors, but not primary school teachers. Finally, the governor of the state nominates members to represent fields such as literature, science, art, the cooperative movement and social service. All elected seats in the Vidhan Parishad are filled using the system of proportional representation by means of a STV.

The Constitution has provisions to ensure the representation of scheduled castes (SCs) and scheduled tribes (STs), with reserved constituencies where only candidates from these communities can stand for election. The number of these reserved seats is meant to be approximately in proportion to the number of peple from SCs and STs in each state. There are currently seventy-nine seats reserved for the SCs and forty-one reserved for the STs.[15]

From the First Lok Sabha to the Emergency

The first general elections under the new Constitution were held in 1951–52, ushering in a directly elected Lok Sabha in the summer of 1952. According to parliamentary records, this inaugural House was a blend of youthful energy and seasoned experience: 45 per cent of its members were under the age of forty-five, and in terms of professions it included 35 per cent lawyers and 22 per cent agriculturists.[16] By 1954, the Hindi terms 'Lok Sabha' and 'Rajya Sabha' replaced their English counterparts, House of the People and Council of States, marking a linguistic shift in parliamentary nomenclature.

Between 1951 and 1971, India conducted five general elections, solidifying its credentials as a functioning electoral democracy. These elections, based on universal adult franchise and overseen by an impartial Election Commission, established a robust electoral process. While the Congress dominated this era, leveraging a strong alliance with the bureaucracy to manage the 'commanding heights' of the economy, opposition parties remained fragmented, unable to effectively challenge the Congress under a FPTP system.

Despite this democratic vibrancy, the early decades were marked by significant challenges. In Kashmir, the central government dismissed and arrested the state's elected PM, Sheikh Abdullah, in 1953, effectively bringing the region under central control through the office of the Sadr-i-Riyasat well before the formal use of president's rule. In Nagaland, the government responded to growing insurgency by promulgating the Armed Forces (Assam and Manipur) Special Powers Ordinance in 1958, later replaced by the Armed Forces (Special Powers) Act, which granted sweeping powers to the military to suppress unrest. These measures included preventive detention, censorship, curfews and the use of armed force against local populations in the name of national security.[17] The dismissal of Kerala's democratically elected communist government in 1959 further highlighted the tension between federal principles and central authority. Additionally, the 1962 Sino–Indian War led to the declaration of an external emergency and the suspension of fundamental rights, underscoring the vulnerabilities of a fledgling democracy.

Transformations Under Jawaharlal Nehru and Indira Gandhi

Jawaharlal Nehru's tenure as PM (1947–64) relied heavily on provincial party bosses and dominant social groups to sustain Congress's electoral dominance. This system of patronage-based politics, in which local elites and intermediaries mediated between the state and the electorate, helped consolidate the party's authority across India's vast and diverse regions. However, this model of centralized leadership and elite brokerage faced serious challenges in the 1967 general elections, when the Congress narrowly retained power at the national level but lost control of eight state governments to opposition coalitions.[18] These developments signalled the rise of subordinate social groups demanding greater political representation and autonomy.[19]

Indira Gandhi, Nehru's daughter, responded to this challenge by reshaping the Congress's organizational and ideological framework. In 1969, she engineered a split within the party, sidelining entrenched factions and adopting a populist agenda with the slogan, '*Garibi Hatao* (Remove Poverty)'. Her policy initiatives, including the nationalization of fourteen private banks and the abolition of privy purses for former princely rulers, marked a decisive shift toward Left-leaning economic policies.

Indira Gandhi's leadership during the 1971 Bangladesh Liberation War further cemented her political dominance. The crisis, culminating in the creation of an independent Bangladesh, significantly boosted her domestic and international stature. Even Opposition leaders, including Atal Bihari Vajpayee, lauded her decisive handling of the situation.[20] The Congress's landslide victory in the 1971 general elections, followed by sweeping state-level victories in 1972, reversed the setbacks of 1967 and marked the apogee of Indira Gandhi's political authority.

This period, however, also laid the groundwork for the centralization of power that would culminate in the declaration of Emergency in 1975 – a moment that tested the resilience of India's democratic institutions.

The Emergency: A Turning Point

The declaration of Emergency in India on the night of 25 June 1975 was the culmination of a period of acute political, economic and social turbulence. The early 1970s witnessed economic stagnation, soaring inflation and widespread public discontent.[21] The 1971 war had significantly strained the nation's financial and logistical resources. These challenges were further compounded by the global oil crisis of 1973, which caused sharp increases in prices and severe shortages of essential commodities, exacerbating public grievances.[22]

Politically, the atmosphere was equally fraught. Following the Congress's landslide victory in the 1971 general elections, allegations of electoral malpractice surfaced, culminating in the landmark 1975 Allahabad High Court judgment. The court found Indira Gandhi guilty of electoral misconduct, invalidated her election to Parliament and disqualified her from holding office. This verdict intensified the political crisis, as Opposition movements, most prominently led by Jayaprakash Narayan, called for her resignation and the restoration of democratic norms.[23] The mounting political instability reached a critical juncture as these forces coalesced into a formidable challenge to Indira Gandhi's leadership.

In response, then President Fakhruddin Ali Ahmed, acting on the advice of the PM, declared a state of Emergency under Article 352 of the Constitution. This declaration granted the central government extraordinary powers, enabling the suspension of civil liberties, imposition of press censorship and curtailment of fundamental rights, including those guaranteeing free speech, assembly and personal liberty. The government justified these measures as necessary to restore national stability, combat internal disturbances and address what it described as threats to national security.

The Emergency profoundly altered India's democratic institutions. Preventive detention laws were used to arrest dissenters and judicial independence was undermined, as seen in the ADM Jabalpur case, where the Supreme Court upheld the suspension of basic rights during Emergency.[24] Press censorship stifled dissent, eroding the media's role as a democratic watchdog. Human rights violations, including arbitrary arrests and detentions, became pervasive, exposing marginalized communities to state excesses. These events revealed the fragility of institutional safeguards against executive overreach. The period serves as a stark reminder of the need to protect civil liberties vigilantly and uphold the rule of law.

The Evolution of the Electoral System

Following India's independence in 1947, the need for a representative government based on universal adult suffrage became a pressing priority. Article 324 of the Constitution, which established the Election Commission of India (ECI) as an independent constitutional authority, came into effect on 26 November 1949, with the rest of the Constitution taking effect on 26 January 1950. The ECI was formally constituted on 25 January 1950, one day before India declared itself a sovereign democratic republic. Sukumar Sen was appointed the first chief election commissioner (CEC) on 21 March 1950.

Originally a single-member body, the Election Commission was converted into a three-member commission through the Election Commission (Conditions of Service of Election Commissioners and Transaction of Business) Act, 1991, which introduced two election commissioners (ECs) alongside the CEC and mandated that decisions be made by majority vote. A subsequent amendment to the Act in 1993 equalized the status, authority and service conditions of all three members, bringing them on par with judges of the Supreme Court. This marked a shift from a single-person authority to a collegial and collective decision-making structure. The CEC and ECs enjoy parity in terms of salary and allowances with Supreme Court judges, with equal powers in decision-making. Disputes are resolved by majority vote. The tenure of the CEC and ECs is six years or until the age of 65, whichever comes first.

For the inaugural general elections to the Lok Sabha and state legislative assemblies, the first delimitation order was issued on 13 August 1951, after consultation with the ECI and Parliament's approval. Two key legislative frameworks were enacted: the Representation of the People Act, 1950, which regulated the preparation of electoral rolls, and the Representation of the People Act, 1951, which detailed the election procedures for Parliament and state assemblies. Electoral rolls were published by 15 November 1951, listing 173.2 million eligible voters from a population of 356.7 million (excluding Jammu and Kashmir).[25]

The first general elections were conducted between October 1951 and March 1952, culminating in the constitution of the first Lok Sabha (489 members) on 2 April 1952, and the first Rajya Sabha (216 members) on 3 April 1952.[26] The inaugural presidential election followed in May

1952, with the first elected president assuming office on 13 May 1952.[27] Fourteen multi-state and thirty-nine state-level political parties were recognized for the first elections. By comparison, there are now six recognized national parties and fifty-eight state parties.[28] The apparent decline in the number of national parties over time reflects the growing salience of regional political dynamics and the increasing strength of parties rooted in subnational identities, interests and linguistic-cultural communities. Moreover, there exist a number of political parties that operate effectively across multiple states but do not meet the formal criteria to be designated as national parties.

Under current rules, the ECI grants recognition to a political party as a 'national' or 'state' party based on its performance in recent elections. For national party status, a party must secure at least 6 per cent of the valid votes polled in four or more states in a general election to the Lok Sabha or state assembly, and in addition, win at least four seats in the Lok Sabha. Alternatively, if it wins 2 per cent of Lok Sabha seats (eleven seats) from at least three different states, it also qualifies. For state party status, a party must win at least 6 per cent of valid votes in a state legislative assembly or Lok Sabha election and secure at least two assembly seats or one Lok Sabha seat from that state. Recognition is periodically reviewed and may be withdrawn if performance thresholds are not maintained.

The voting system evolved significantly over time. The first two general elections (1951–52, 1957) employed a balloting system, where each candidate had a dedicated ballot box and voters deposited pre-printed ballot papers. Starting with the 1962 elections, the marking system was introduced, requiring voters to mark a common ballot paper with an arrow-cross stamp.

The transition to EVMs began experimentally in 1982 in Kerala's Parur assembly constituency and expanded over subsequent elections. By the 2004 general elections, EVMs were used nationwide for the first time, marking a pivotal shift in the conduct of Indian elections. The EVMs have since been used universally in all elections to the Lok Sabha and state assemblies, ensuring efficiency and reliability in the electoral process.

Contemporary Developments

The trajectory of Indian democracy has grown increasingly uncertain following the rule of BJP since 2014, as the resilience of key democratic institutions has come into question.[29] Dissenting voices, including political opponents and critical journalists, have been subjected to harassment, prosecution, tax investigations and surveillance, effectively curtailing critical discourse and undermining democratic accountability.[30]

Under the now-defunct electoral bonds scheme, electoral integrity was weakened by changes to campaign finance laws, which permitted unlimited and anonymous political donations. This opacity undermined transparency and raised concerns about the undue influence of private interests on the democratic process.

Perhaps most troublingly, the intensification of religious polarization poses a direct challenge to India's constitutional commitment to secularism and the right to religious freedom. Government actions and rhetoric have exacerbated societal divisions, particularly against the Muslim community. A stark example occurred in December 2021, when BJP-aligned groups organized a controversial event in Uttarakhand, where inflammatory calls for violence against Muslims were made by Hindu leaders.[31] More recently, in March 2025, communal violence erupted in Nagpur – following protests led by Right-wing groups demanding the demolition of Aurangzeb's tomb – resulting in at least one death, over thirty injuries, the imposition of curfews and hundreds of arrests amid reports of targeted attacks on Muslim residents.[32] Public lynchings targeting minorities, widely circulated on social media, have further highlighted the erosion of communal harmony and the rule of law.

The government's apparent encouragement of majoritarian nationalism, driven by an ideological vision of India as a Hindu homeland, marks a significant departure from the nation's earlier secular consensus. Such a singular, exclusionary vision raises profound questions about its compatibility with India's vast diversity.

Through its control of the media, dominance in campaign finance and suppression of opposition, India appears to be veering towards a model of illiberal democracy akin to that observed in Turkey or Russia.[33] However, the BJP's dominance has not been absolute. In several recent state elections, a united opposition has successfully challenged its hegemony. Additionally, the government has failed to deliver sustained economic growth, with policy missteps compounding the pandemic's economic toll.[34] These factors suggest that while the challenges to Indian democracy are severe, the future remains open to contestation and potential course correction.

India's Democracy Rankings

Assessing the decline of India's democracy since 2014 involves analysing various indices and reports that evaluate different dimensions of democratic governance, civil liberties and political rights. According to a report titled *Freedom in the World* by Freedom House, India was rated as 'Free' in 2014 with a score of 77 out of 100.[35] However, by 2024, India was categorized as 'Partly Free', with a reduced score of 66 out of 100.[36] This decline in score indicates a noticeable deterioration in political rights and civil liberties. Similarly, the *Democracy Index* by the Economist Intelligence Unit placed India 27th in 2014, categorizing it as a 'flawed democracy'. By 2024, India had dropped to the 41st place, maintaining its status as a 'flawed democracy'.[37] This decline reflects significant challenges in electoral processes, the functioning of government, political participation and civil liberties.

India's press freedom has also faced considerable setbacks. According to the *World Press Freedom Index* by Reporters Without Borders, India ranked 140th out of 180 countries in 2014, but by 2024 it had fallen to 161st, marking a significant deterioration in press freedom.[38] It has now slightly recovered to 151st position in 2025. Similarly, the *V-Dem Liberal Democracy Index* by the Varieties of Democracy (V-Dem) Institute shows India's rank slipping from 27th in 2014 to 93rd in 2024, with the country now categorized as an 'electoral autocracy'.[39] This shift highlights a decline in the quality of liberal democracy, particularly in terms of the rule of law, checks and balances, and individual liberties.

Furthermore, the *Rule of Law Index* by the World Justice Project indicates a worsening trend in India's governance. India was ranked 57th out of a 102 countries in 2015 and in 2024 it ranked 79th of 142 countries, reflecting a decline in areas such as constraints on government powers and the protection of fundamental rights, and a rise in corruption.[40] These trends collectively paint a concerning picture of India's democratic backsliding over the past decade.

Table 1. World Press Freedom Index 2025 Rankings

Country	2025 Rank
Afghanistan	175
Bangladesh	149
Bhutan	152
Pakistan	158
India	151
Sri Lanka	139
The Maldives	104
Nepal	90

Key events at a glance

- **1947** – Indian Independence Act passed; 15 August 1947, India gains independence. Partition creates Pakistan
- **1947** – Jawaharlal Nehru becomes India's first prime minister; communal violence and refugee crisis
- **1950** – The Constitution of India comes into effect (26 January); India becomes a sovereign democratic republic
- **1951–52** – First general elections held; INC wins a landslide
- **1956** – States Reorganisation Act; states reorganized along linguistic lines
- **1962** – Sino–Indian War; India suffers defeat against China
- **1965** – Second Indo–Pak War; ends with the Tashkent Agreement
- **1966** – Indira Gandhi becomes prime minister
- **1971** – Third Indo–Pak War; Bangladesh is created with Indian military intervention
- **1975** – Emergency declared by Indira Gandhi (1975–1977); suspension of civil liberties and press freedoms
- **1977** – Janata Party defeats the INC; first non-Congress government at the Centre

- **1984** – Operation Blue Star at the Golden Temple; assassination of Indira Gandhi; anti-Sikh riots follow
- **1989** – Mandal Commission Report implemented; reservation for Other Backward Classes (OBCs) in government jobs
- **1991** – Economic liberalization under Prime Minister P.V. Narasimha Rao and Finance Minister Manmohan Singh; India shifts toward a market economy
- **1992** – Demolition of Babri Masjid in Ayodhya; communal riots spread
- **1998** – Nuclear tests at Pokhran-II; India declares itself a nuclear weapons state
- **2002** – Gujarat riots following the Godhra train-burning incident
- **2004** – United Progressive Alliance (UPA) led by INC forms government; Manmohan Singh becomes prime minister
- **2008** – Mumbai terror attacks (26/11); Indo–Pakistan tensions escalate
- **2014** – Bharatiya Janata Party (BJP) wins a historic mandate; Narendra Modi becomes prime minister
- **2016** – Demonetization announced; Rs 500 and Rs 1000 notes invalidated overnight
- **2019** – Re-election of BJP with an even larger majority; abrogation of Article 370 revoking Jammu & Kashmir's special status
- **2020** – Nationwide protests against Citizenship Amendment Act (CAA); widespread farmers' protests
- **2024** – Eighteenth general elections held; voter turnout remained robust despite concerns over democratic backsliding. The BJP-led alliance secured another term in power, continuing its electoral dominance
- **February 2025**– President's Rule was imposed in Manipur after renewed ethnic violence between Meitei and Kuki communities resulted in over 250 fatalities and widespread displacement
- **April 2025** – A terrorist attack by Lashkar-e-Taiba's offshoot in Pahalgam, Jammu & Kashmir, killed 26 tourists – including Hindus, a Christian and a Muslim local –marking the deadliest civilian mass shooting since 2008
- **May 2025** – India launched Operation Sindoor, conducting precision strikes on nine terrorist camps in Pakistan and Pakistan-Occupied Kashmir in retaliation for the Pahalgam attack.

2

Pakistan: Electoral Dreams, Authoritarian Realities

The creation of Pakistan on 14 August 1947 marked the birth of the largest Muslim-majority state in the world at that time, and catalysed the most extensive demographic upheaval in recorded history. Approximately 17 million individuals – Hindus, Muslims and Sikhs – migrated across the newly drawn borders, reshaping the demographic and cultural landscapes of both India and Pakistan. Of the 95 million Muslims residing in the Indian subcontinent at the time, 60 million became citizens of Pakistan, while 35 million remained in India – forming the largest Muslim minority in a non-Muslim majority state.[1]

From its inception, Pakistan has grappled with profound challenges, its struggle for survival marked by uncertainty and existential dilemmas. Despite the unifying thread of Islam, the nation has faced persistent difficulties in forging a cohesive national identity and constructing a political framework suitable for its linguistically and culturally diverse populace. Pakistan is home to over eighty languages and more than 300 dialects, with Urdu and English designated as official languages.[2] However, regional tongues, such as Punjabi, Sindhi, Pashto, Baluchi and Seraiki, hold significant prominence, reflecting the country's vast heterogeneity. This linguistic and cultural diversity has frequently fuelled regional tensions, complicating efforts to establish and maintain a stable constitutional order.[3]

These internal struggles have been compounded by external pressures, including repeated conflicts with India, strategic vulnerabilities along its northwestern frontier and recurrent economic crises. The equitable allocation of scarce economic and natural resources remains an enduring challenge, further exacerbating regional disparities and political discontent.[4]

The tension between the imperatives of national integration and national security lies at the heart of Pakistan's dilemmas. The secession of its eastern wing, culminating in the creation of Bangladesh in 1971 following a military defeat by India, represents the most dramatic illustration of these challenges.[5] This rupture not only underscored Pakistan's fragility as a decentralized state but also heightened the enduring provincial grievances among smaller regions such as Sindh, Balochistan and Khyber Pakhtunkhwa (formerly the North-West Frontier Province [NWFP]). These provinces have long resented what they perceive as a Punjabi-dominated consolidation of power, wealth and patronage in Pakistan.[6]

Pakistan's political evolution has been further undermined by ideological disputes over the nature of governance – whether to be Islamic or secular. In the absence of a robust, nationally inclusive political party, the country has often relied on its civil service and military to sustain governmental continuity. Yet, these institutions have been unable to resolve the deep-seated divisions and instability that continue to define Pakistan's political landscape. Since 1947, Pakistan has experienced four extra-constitutional military regimes, eleven constitutional arrangements and three formal constitutions (in 1956, 1962 and 1973).[7]

The Birth of Pakistan

The genesis of Pakistan's complex challenges can be traced to the pivotal moment in March 1940, when the All-India Muslim League formally articulated its demand for a separate state comprising the Muslim-majority provinces of British India's North-West and North-East. By asserting that Indian Muslims constituted a distinct nation rather than a minority, the League, under the leadership of Muhammad Ali Jinnah, sought to secure a constitutional arrangement that would guarantee equitable power-sharing between Hindus and Muslims following the eventual departure of the British. This demand for Pakistan was intended as a dual claim: to represent the aspirations of Muslims in both majority and minority provinces. However, the League's principal base of support lay in the Muslim-minority provinces such as Bombay Presidency and Central Provinces; its performance in the 1937 provincial elections revealed a lack of resonance among Muslim voters in the majority regions such as Punjab, Bengal and the NWFP.[8]

This inherent contradiction between advocating for a separate Muslim state and claiming to represent all Indian Muslims remained unresolved. Neither Jinnah nor the League adequately addressed how Muslims in minority provinces might benefit from a Pakistan that would encompass an undivided Punjab, Sindh, the NWFP and Balochistan in the north-west, alongside Bengal and Assam in the north-east. Jinnah sought to reconcile these inconsistencies by framing the issue in terms of 'two nations' – Hindu and Muslim – arguing that any transfer of power from British to Indian hands would necessitate dismantling the imperial unitary centre. He proposed a confederal or treaty-based reconstitution of the Indian Union, envisioning Pakistan as representing the Muslim-majority provinces, while Hindustan would embody the Hindu-majority areas. Crucially, Jinnah maintained that an undivided Punjab and Bengal must form part of Pakistan, contending that the substantial non-Muslim minorities in these regions would ensure reciprocal arrangements to safeguard Muslim interests in Hindustan.[9]

Despite these theoretical claims, the Muslim League failed to establish robust organizational structures in the Muslim-majority provinces. The League lacked genuine control over local politicians and grassroots mobilization of populations in the name of Islam.[10] By the time of the final negotiations for independence, Jinnah's options were constrained by the ambivalence of leaders in the Muslim-majority provinces. Communal violence further limited his bargaining power. Ultimately, Jinnah was forced to accept a truncated Pakistan, shorn of the non-Muslim majority districts of Punjab and Bengal. His broader aspiration of a negotiated settlement securing the welfare of all Indian Muslims was thereby abandoned.[11]

The Congress delivered a severe blow by interpreting Partition not as the division of India into two sovereign entities but as the secession of certain Muslim-majority regions from the Indian Union. This stance implied that should Pakistan fail as a state, the Muslim-majority areas would inevitably be reincorporated into India. The fragile foundations of Pakistan were further destabilized by the lack of a coherent central authority, a challenge compounded by the physical separation of its eastern and western wings by over a thousand miles of Indian territory.

While Islamic identity provided a rallying cry for unity, the pluralistic traditions and linguistic diversity of Pakistan's provinces posed formidable obstacles to the consolidation under a centralized authority. Political activity remained rooted in provincial contexts, while those tasked with establishing the nascent government in Karachi were either politicians with tenuous popular support or civil servants trained in the colonial traditions of British Indian administration. The Muslim League's structural weaknesses, coupled with the absence of a well-developed central administrative apparatus, significantly hampered Pakistan's capacity to function as a cohesive state.[12]

This fragility was further exacerbated by the immediate challenges of Partition, including providing urgent relief to millions of refugees. The central government, lacking adequate resources and institutional capacity, struggled to address these pressing needs. Economic development was stymied by the reluctance of commercial elites to invest in industrial infrastructure, while efforts to extract revenues from the agrarian sector deepened tensions between the state and the landed aristocracy that dominated the Muslim League. These overlapping crises underscored the profound structural vulnerabilities of the newly established Pakistan, and set the stage for its protracted struggles with governance, national integration and economic stability.[13]

A Tale of Many Constitutions

Following its independence, Pakistan's path toward democracy has been fraught with challenges. The modern Islamic Republic of Pakistan emerged after 1971. Muhammad Ali Jinnah served as Pakistan's first governor-general, while Liaquat Ali Khan was appointed its inaugural PM.

In the early years after independence, Pakistan, like its neighbour India, derived its foundational governance structure from the Government of India Act of 1935, albeit with modifications to suit its new status as an independent state. To lay the groundwork for a permanent constitution, a Constituent Assembly was convened, tasked with both acting as the country's first parliament and drafting a constitution for the nascent state.[14]

Before drafting could commence, it was imperative to determine the framework upon which the constitution would be based. Liaquat Ali Khan addressed this by introducing the Objectives Resolution to the Constituent Assembly. This resolution, adopted on 12 March 1949, continues to underpin Pakistan's constitutional processes. The resolution declared that Pakistan would adopt a federal structure of governance rooted in Islamic principles, with political authority vested in elected representatives. It further asserted the principles of equality before the law, judicial independence and safeguards for minority rights, ensuring that minorities would have the freedom to practise their religions and develop their cultures. On the same day, the Basic Principles Committee was established to formulate the guiding principles of the constitution, based on the ideals laid out in the Objectives Resolution.

In 1950, the Committee presented a preliminary report. Among its key proposals were the equal representation of women in the Upper House of the Central Legislature and the designation of Urdu as the national language. However, these recommendations provoked significant opposition from East Pakistan, where the majority of the population resided but was allotted only half of the legislative seats. This disparity in representation fostered widespread resentment and a sense of marginalization among the people of East Pakistan, contributing to a growing perception of exclusion from political power. Additionally, there was dissent over the characterization of Pakistan as an 'Islamic' state, further complicating the national discourse on identity and governance.[15]

In the two decades following independence, Pakistan did not conduct any general elections at the national level. Instead, only provincial elections were held until 1958. The first provincial elections based on universal adult suffrage took place in the Punjab Province in 1951. However, these elections were widely criticized by the public as a 'farce and a mockery of the electoral governance and process'.[16]

In response to the widespread discontent, public input was solicited, and after seven years of intense debate and deliberation involving various interest groups, Pakistan's first constitution was enacted on 23 March 1956. Modelled to a certain extent on that of neighbouring India, this extensive document comprised 234 articles divided into thirteen parts and six schedules. The constitution established a unicameral legislature, with 300 representatives from East Pakistan and 150 from West Pakistan.[17] In this parliamentary system, the PM was designated as the head of government, while the president served as a ceremonial head of state.

Regrettably, the 1956 constitution was short-lived. In 1958, a military coup led to its abrogation. The commander-in-chief of the army assumed power, and a new constitution was introduced, which called for indirect elections. Consequently, the first constitution, which had been the product of extensive and arduous efforts by various segments of society, was never fully implemented.

Pakistan adopted its second constitution, which brought significant changes to the country's political structure, in 1962. The office of the PM was abolished, and executive powers were vested in the president. Furthermore, the constitution institutionalized military involvement in politics, stipulating that the president or defence minister must be someone who had held a military rank of at least lieutenant general for no less than twenty years. This marked the beginning of a persistent pattern of military influence in Pakistan's political landscape, which would have lasting implications for the country's identity and governance.

The 1962 constitution also proved to be short-lived, as it was abrogated in 1969. It was not until 1970, under the leadership of General Yahya Khan, that a new phase of political transition was initiated. Yahya Khan promised to hold elections and restore legislative authority, leading to the announcement of general elections for the national assembly. On 20 December 1971, after Pakistan's defeat in the war with India , Zulfikar Ali Bhutto assumed power as president of Pakistan, forming the first civilian government to emerge from these elections. However, civilian rule proved to be fleeting, lasting only for a single term.

In 1973, Pakistan adopted a new constitution, the first to be drafted by elected representatives of the people (the Constitution of the Islamic Republic of Pakistan, 1973).

On 5 July 1977, the military once again took control of the government, citing widespread unrest and opposition to the elections under Bhutto's Pakistan People's Party (PPP) government. General Zia-ul-Haq assumed power, pledging to hold elections within ninety days. Following the coup, the 1973 constitution was suspended, and the military regime remained in power until 1985.

In 2010, the 18th Amendment to the constitution was passed, marking a significant development in Pakistan's constitutional history. This amendment reinstated the parliamentary system and restored the powers of the PM (Constitution [18th Amendment] Act, 2010). Prior to this, in February 1985, the military government held general elections for both the national and provincial assemblies. These elections were notable in that, while they were direct elections, political parties were barred from participating, and only individual candidates could contest.

From 1985 to 2002, elections occurred approximately every three years, yet civilian governments were regularly undermined by the military, limiting the full realization of democratic governance. From 1985 to 2002 Pakistan held six general elections in 1985, 1988, 1990, 1993, 1997 and 2002 – an average interval of about three years instead of the constitutionally mandated five. The shortened cycle reflected repeated presidential dissolutions of the National Assembly under Article 58(2)(b), a power inserted by the 8th Amendment in 1985 that was invoked to dismiss elected governments in 1988, 1990, 1993 and 1996, as well as during the full military coup of 1999. The first of these elections, in 1985, was conducted on a strictly non-party basis by General Zia-ul-Haq; party competition was restored only in 1988 after the Supreme Court struck down the ban. Subsequent polls (1988–97) were party-based but occurred under the shadow of presidential and military interference, and the 2002 election was organized by General Pervez Musharraf's regime with legal restrictions that sidelined key opposition leaders.

The historical record of Pakistan's political trajectory reveals a long-standing struggle for the establishment of a meaningful and representative democracy. For decades, various military regimes and authoritarian actors usurped the people's right to fair elections and representative leadership.

However, Pakistan's civil society has consistently striven to reclaim democratic governance. Since 2008, military involvement in politics has diminished, with democratic and political forces gaining strength. The political landscape has expanded, offering citizens greater choice, particularly after the 2013 elections. This ongoing engagement reflects the enduring resilience and hope within Pakistani society for a fully realized democratic order.[18]

Pakistan's Military Coups

A coup d'état represents a fundamental rupture in civil–military relations, as it subverts the foundational democratic principle of civilian supremacy over the military. A coup signifies direct intervention by the armed forces into the political domain, often justified by the military as a response to political instability or governance failure.

In the context of Pakistan, martial law denotes the comprehensive assumption of state control by the military, encompassing all facets of governance. Despite its constitutional status as a democratic parliamentary republic, Pakistan has experienced military rule on three occasions under four military leaders. These interruptions have profoundly shaped the country's political trajectory.

1958: The first coup

The first instance of martial law occurred in 1958 when then President Iskander Mirza abrogated the constitution and appointed General Ayub Khan as chief martial law administrator. Shortly thereafter, Ayub Khan ousted Mirza and assumed the presidency. The 1958 coup was rationalized by the military and political elites as a response to the dysfunctional parliamentary system, endemic corruption and political instability that had plagued the early years of Pakistan's democracy.[19] Ayub Khan portrayed his intervention as a corrective measure to ensure stability and economic development. However, this military takeover set a precedent for the army's expanded role in governance, which would echo throughout Pakistan's history.[20]

Political scientist Wayne Ayres Wilcox elabourated on the deeper structural causes of the 1958 coup, noting that Pakistan's fragmented political system, coupled with the absence of robust civilian institutions, created a vacuum that the military was well-positioned to fill. The coup, Wilcox argued, was not a sudden event but the culmination of growing tensions between civilian leaders and an increasingly assertive military establishment. Ayub Khan's tenure, while marked by economic progress in its early years, also introduced authoritarian measures, such as curbing press freedoms and stifling political dissent, which undermined democratic norms and institutions.[21]

This military rule, officially lasting forty-four months, extended de facto until 1969, when Ayub Khan transferred power to General Yahya Khan amid growing political unrest. As mentioned earlier, Yahya Khan's tenure ended in 1971 following Pakistan's military defeat in the war with India and the creation of Bangladesh. Unable to secure his position, Yahya transferred power to Zulfikar Ali Bhutto, whose PPP had won the first general elections.[22]

1977: The second coup

The second coup took place in 1977, led by General Zia-ul-Haq. Zia deposed then PM Zulfikar Ali Bhutto, dissolved parliament and initially promised to hold fair elections. However, he consolidated his rule, enforcing martial law until 1985, when civilian governance was nominally restored under a selected PM, Muhammad Khan Junejo. Zia's policies, especially his Islamization agenda, left a lasting impact on Pakistan's sociopolitical fabric.[23]

The events of 5 July 1977, made an indelible mark in Pakistan's tumultuous political history. This 'Black Day' epitomizes the recurring subversion of democratic processes by Pakistan's military establishment. On that day, General Zia-ul-Haq ousted then PM Zulfikar Ali Bhutto through a military coup, abrogating democratic norms and ushering in an era of authoritarian rule that would last over a decade. The significance of this event resonates even more profoundly in 2025, as Pakistan continues to grapple with its historical legacy of interrupted democratic governance and military dominance.[24]

The coup of 1977 was a culmination of escalating political unrest following the contentious general elections earlier that year. Allegations of electoral rigging against Bhutto's PPP had galvanized opposition parties under the Pakistan National Alliance (PNA), leading to widespread protests. Zia-ul-Haq exploited this political turmoil, presenting himself as a neutral arbiter and promising elections within ninety days – a pledge he failed to honour. Instead, his regime systematically dismantled civilian political structures, silenced dissent and enforced a rigid Islamization agenda that left permanent impacts on Pakistan's legal, social and political frameworks.

Reflecting from today's vantage point, the coup's repercussions are evident in the enduring imbalance between civilian and military institutions in Pakistan. Zia's consolidation of power entrenched the military's role as a political actor – a dynamic that has persisted through subsequent decades. Moreover, the Islamization policies initiated during his rule institutionalized religious conservatism in governance and law, complicating efforts to establish a pluralistic and inclusive political framework.[25]

The events of 1977 also underscore the fragility of democratic institutions in Pakistan, a theme that has recurred in the country's history. Despite periods of civilian governance since Zia's era, Pakistan's democracy remains vulnerable to both overt and covert interventions by the military.[26] The lessons of 1977 highlight the critical importance of addressing structural weaknesses in Pakistan's democratic institutions to prevent history from repeating itself.

The legacy of the 5 July coup serves as a stark reminder of the need for vigilance in safeguarding democratic principles. Pakistan's journey towards stable democratic governance requires not only institutional reform but also a societal commitment to holding both civilian and military leadership accountable to constitutional norms. Only by confronting the spectres of its past can Pakistan hope to chart a more democratic and equitable future.

1999: The third coup

In 1999, Pakistan faced significant political and economic challenges that culminated in a military coup led by General Pervez Musharraf. This event highlighted deep-rooted issues in governance and civil–military relations.[27]

The military coup was primarily driven by political instability and the authoritarianism of then PM Nawaz Sharif. Sharif's tenure was marked by a concentration of power, suppression of dissent and manipulation of state institutions. His policies alienated smaller provinces and created widespread dissatisfaction. A pivotal moment was Sharif's dismissal of General Musharraf as chief of army staff – a move perceived by the military as a direct threat to its autonomy. Sharif's attempt to instal a loyalist backfired, as the military leadership viewed it as an encroachment on its institutional integrity.

The coup unfolded with precision when Musharraf's dismissal was announced while he was abroad. The military swiftly took control of key institutions and detained Sharif, executing a bloodless intervention that reflected its cohesion and preparedness. The civil–military tensions that led to this outcome were rooted in Sharif's miscalculation of the military's likely response to his assertion of constitutional authority.[28]

Musharraf's takeover marked Pakistan's return to military rule, though martial law was not formally declared. As chief executive, Musharraf suspended the constitution and pledged governance reforms. His administration focused on rebuilding national confidence, addressing economic issues and promoting decentralization. However, delays in restoring democracy and scepticism about his reform agenda, raised questions about the sustainability of his policies.

Economically, Pakistan was on the brink of collapse, with low growth, investor disillusionment and high unemployment. The military government's initial measures, including recovering bank loans and renegotiating foreign debt, offered temporary relief but failed to address systemic problems. Poverty and fiscal instability remained pressing concerns.[29]

On the international front, relations with India deteriorated after the Kargil conflict, reversing initial optimism from diplomatic efforts seen earlier in the year. The coup drew criticism from Western powers and the Commonwealth, which suspended Pakistan's membership. However, international attitudes softened as Musharraf's regime pledged a gradual return to democracy.

The events of 1999 underscored Pakistan's recurring struggles with governance and civil–military balance. While Musharraf's rule temporarily stabilized the nation, it highlighted the urgent need for robust civilian institutions and sustainable democratic frameworks. The coup was a stark reminder of the fragility of Pakistan's political system and the challenges of achieving national cohesion.

Military rule gave way to parliamentary governance in 2008, when general elections brought the civilian PPP to power following General Musharraf's resignation. In an attempt to curtail military interference in Pakistan's political landscape, the 18th Amendment to the constitution was passed in 2010. This significant legal reform stripped the president of the power to unilaterally dissolve parliament – a move intended to bolster parliamentary democracy by redistributing authority among the legislative, executive and judicial branches of government. Despite this, the military retains substantial influence over Pakistan's political processes, often operating through indirect means rather than overt interventions.[30] This ongoing civil–military imbalance continues to present a formidable challenge to the development of a truly democratic system in the country, as noted by scholars such as Hassan Askari Rizvi and Ayesha Jalal.[31]

Pakistan's Parliament

Though the 1973 constitution remains the foundation of Pakistan's legal framework, it has undergone significant alterations, primarily due to two military regimes – those of General Muhammad Zia-ul-Haq and General Pervez Musharraf – that reshaped the parliamentary system into a semi-presidential one. Zia-ul-Haq's tenure in the 1980s saw the introduction of pivotal legal changes, including the Islamization of the legal system, as mentioned earlier. This period saw the creation of the Federal Shariat Court and an expanded role for the Council of Islamic Ideology, which advises on matters related to Sharia law. These modifications solidified the military's control over the political system and introduced a more overt Islamic character to governance.

The most notable shift, however, occurred with the passage of the 18th Amendment in 2010. As discussed earlier, this amendment, ratified by Pakistan's National Assembly, sought to undo the powers amassed by the presidency under Zia-ul-Haq and Musharraf, reasserting the supremacy of the parliamentary system. It effectively transformed the presidency into a largely ceremonial role, reducing its power significantly by abolishing Article 58-2(b), which had allowed the president to dissolve the National Assembly under vaguely defined emergency conditions. The amendment also curtailed the president's authority to withhold assent to bills, reducing the time frame from thirty days to ten. Moreover, the amendment declared that any unconstitutional intervention or suspension of the constitution would be deemed high treason, a landmark rule that prevents judges from legitimizing such actions.

In the reformed system, the PM, who is now the chief executive, is elected by a simple majority in the National Assembly, rather than being appointed by the president. This change reinforces the principles of parliamentary democracy and strengthens the role of the elected government in Pakistan's political structure.

Pakistan, as outlined in the 1973 Constitution, is an Islamic federal republic with a multiparty parliamentary system that draws heavily on the British model. It comprises four provinces – Punjab, Sindh, Khyber Pakhtunkhwa and Balochistan – and operates under a bicameral legislature, the Majlis-e-Shoora, made up of the National Assembly and the Senate. The National Assembly, the lower house, comprises 342 seats, including reserved seats for women and non-Muslims, while the Senate, the upper house, consists of 104 members elected indirectly by the National Assembly and provincial assemblies.[32] Members of the National Assembly are elected through a mixed electoral system, often referred to as a parallel system, which combines elements of both direct and proportional representation.[33]

Thus, the 18th Amendment along with Pakistan's federal structure and the evolution of its political system have collectively shaped a governance model that seeks to restore parliamentary supremacy and diminish the disproportionate influence of the military in the nation's political affairs. However, as the political landscape of Pakistan continues to evolve, the balance of power remains a subject of debate and challenge, especially considering the military's continued influence behind the scenes.

The Present and the Future

Even though Pakistan has now seen three full parliamentary terms since 2008, the trajectory of democratic consolidation remains bleak. The years between 2008 and 2018 represented a brief, albeit fragile, period of political stability; however, the period from 2018 to 2024 witnessed the erosion of these gains. Political developments in this period suggest that the country is at risk of regressing further, as the structural impediments to democracy remain deeply entrenched. The underlying issue, as always, lies in the pervasive influence of non-political forces – particularly the military – which continues to undermine the political process and prevent the emergence of true anti-establishment politics.[34] The notion that Pakistan's political landscape might eventually shift toward genuine democratic practices remains elusive, with no significant breakthroughs on the horizon.

The political dynamics of Pakistan are such that unless the major political parties – regardless of their ideological affiliations – can decisively and collectively isolate non-political entities from the governance structure, the prospects for reform will remain stunted. Some analysts claimed that the significant electoral support garnered by Imran Khan's Pakistan Tehreek-i-Insaf (PTI) in the 2024 elections signalled a shift in the political equilibrium, but the evidence for such optimism seemed scant.[35]

Although these electoral trends have been touted as a form of popular rebellion against the establishment, their role in fundamentally altering the political paradigm remains inconclusive.[36] Historically, Pakistan has witnessed various anti-establishment moments, from Benazir Bhutto's landmark 1988 victory as the first female Muslim PM, to the signing of the Charter of Democracy between Bhutto and Nawaz Sharif in 2006, and even to Sharif's bold slogan in 2018, '*Vote ko Izzat Do* (Give Respect to the Vote)'.[37] These movements, however, have all been fleeting, leading to the question: Will the future be any different? The answer, regrettably, appears to be no.

The elections of 8 February 2024, although significant, have produced results remarkably like those of the 2018 elections. In 2018, the establishment-supported PTI secured the largest share of seats, followed by the Pakistan Muslim League–Nawaz (PML-N), led by the disqualified and later imprisoned Nawaz Sharif, and the PPP, led by the Bhutto–Zardari family. A coalition government formed by the PTI and other smaller parties ruled until 2022, when the political fortunes of Imran Khan soured, giving way to a PML-N–PPP-led coalition for 2022–23. In 2024, PTI-backed independents won the most directly elected seats, but the PML-N – backed by PPP and other establishment-aligned parties – formed the government under Shehbaz Sharif's leadership, illustrating once again the decisive influence of the civil–military establishment on electoral outcomes. The vote shares of the PTI, PML-N and PPP remain largely unchanged, reflecting the same pattern of elite competition that has defined Pakistan's political history. The ultimate arbiter of power remains the civil–military establishment, whose influence continues to shape electoral outcomes, regardless of the public's expressed preferences.[38]

Pakistan's post-independence history has been marked by the continuous domination of the civil–military establishment, which has repeatedly thwarted the development of a stable, functioning democracy. The first instance of this interference occurred as early as August 1947, when the elected Congress government in the NWFP was dismissed by executive order and replaced by a Muslim League ministry. This was not an isolated event; rather, it marked the beginning of a pattern in which civilian governments were repeatedly undermined by non-elected forces. By the end of 1948, the bureaucratic and military elites, had come to exercise direct control over much of what was then West Pakistan, and this consolidation of power was further entrenched by the 1955 dismissal of the first Constituent Assembly.

The Maulvi Tamizuddin case is a significant event in Pakistan's legal and political history that helped crystallize the military's influence over civilian institutions. In 1955, the first Constituent Assembly of Pakistan, which had been responsible for framing the country's constitution, was unilaterally dismissed by the then Governor-General Iskander Mirza. This move was justified on the grounds of administrative inefficiency and political deadlock, but it was widely seen as an exercise in executive overreach. Maulvi Tamizuddin Khan, a prominent member of the assembly, challenged the dismissal in court. The case became a key moment in Pakistan's constitutional history, as the judiciary ultimately upheld the dismissal, thereby confirming the precedence of executive action over parliamentary sovereignty.[39]

The case established a precedent whereby the military-backed government's decisions could not be easily contested by civilian institutions. It was a defining moment in the consolidation of the military's power, further entrenching the notion that the military could intervene in political affairs with minimal resistance from the courts.[40] This event set a trajectory where civilian political institutions were consistently undermined by military and bureaucratic elites – a pattern that has persisted to the present day.

As a result, despite repeated cycles of electoral change, Pakistan's political structure continues to reflect the dominance of the military establishment, which has perpetually undermined attempts at civilian supremacy. Whether this cycle will be broken in the future or whether Pakistan will continue to return to the status quo, with its democratic aspirations thwarted by forces beyond the control of its electorate, remains to be seen.

Key events at a glance

- **1947** – Partition of India; Pakistan founded on 14 August 1947; massive migration and communal massacres
- **1947** – Muhammad Ali Jinnah becomes Pakistan's first governor-general; Liaquat Ali Khan the first PM.
- **1948** – Death of Jinnah; early leadership vacuum.
- **1951** – Assassination of Liaquat Ali Khan; political instability worsens.
- **1956** – First Constitution of Pakistan declares Pakistan an 'Islamic republic'.
- **1958** – First military coup; General Ayub Khan seizes power, beginning military dominance in politics.
- **1965** – Second Indo-Pakistan War over Kashmir; ends inconclusively
- **1969** – Ayub Khan resigns amid mass protests; General Yahya Khan assumes power
- **1970** – General elections; Sheikh Mujibur Rahman's Awami League wins majority, leading to political crisis
- **1971** – Civil war and East Pakistan secedes after brutal military crackdown; creation of Bangladesh
- **1972** – Zulfikar Ali Bhutto assumes power; seeks to rebuild a shattered Pakistan
- **1973** – New constitution enacted; establishes parliamentary democracy.
- **1977** – Military coup by General Zia-ul-Haq; Zulfikar Bhutto overthrown and later executed (1979)
- **1979** – Start of Zia's Islamization; introduction of Sharia laws, Hudood ordinances
- **1988** – Zia dies in a plane crash; return to civilian rule
- **1988–99** – Alternating unstable civilian governments: Benazir Bhutto (PPP) and Nawaz Sharif (PML-N) dominate politics
- **1999** – Military coup by General Pervez Musharraf; Nawaz Sharif ousted
- **2001** – Pakistan becomes a key US ally in the Global War on Terror after 9/11
- **2007** – Benazir Bhutto assassinated; massive unrest
- **2008** – Return to civilian rule; Asif Ali Zardari (PPP) elected President
- **2011** – Osama bin Laden killed by US forces in Abbottabad; severe embarrassment for Pakistan's military
- **2013** – Nawaz Sharif returns to power; first democratic transfer of power from one civilian government to another

- **2018** – Imran Khan and his PTI win elections amid allegations of military backing
- **2022** – Imran Khan ousted by a no-confidence vote; Shehbaz Sharif (PML-N) becomes PM
- **2023** – Political turmoil deepens; Imran Khan faces multiple legal cases; mass protests erupt after his arrest
- **2024 (February)** – General elections held on 8 February. PTI-backed independents win the most directly elected seats, followed by PML-N and PPP. Allegations of rigging and manipulation surface. The PML-N and PPP form a coalition government led by Shehbaz Sharif.
- **2024 (May)** – Pakistan's Supreme Court rules in favour of PTI's claim to reserved seats, expanding its presence in parliament.
- **2024 (July)** – The PTI-affiliated members take up their reserved seats, sharpening tensions between the Opposition and ruling coalition.
- **2025 (January)** – A deadly terrorist attack in Pahalgam, Jammu and Kashmir, attributed to a Pakistan-based militant group, kills twenty-six civilians including tourists.
- **2025 (February)** – India launches Operation Sindoor, a series of cross-border strikes targeting alleged terrorist camps in Pakistan and Pakistan-Occupied Kashmir. Pakistan responds with aerial deployments and diplomatic protests. The region witnesses heightened military alert, though escalation is ultimately contained.
- **2025 (March–April)** – Nationwide protests erupt in Pakistan over inflation, power shortages and austerity measures. Political tensions mount amid international pressure to maintain democratic norms.

3

Sri Lanka: Democracy, Diversity and Discord

The Democratic Socialist Republic of Sri Lanka (formerly Ceylon) is situated on an island spanning approximately 65,630 sq. km in the Indian Ocean, located just south-east of India.[1] The nation is home to around 21 million people, encompassing diverse ethnic and religious groups. This diversity has posed ongoing challenges, leading to a prolonged civil conflict between the majority Sinhalese population and Tamil separatists, a struggle that concluded in 2009. Owing to political instability and military conflicts, Sri Lanka's economy has been relatively stagnant, with limited foreign investment. Fourteen per cent of the population resides in urban areas, with Colombo, the largest city and capital, housing 680,000 residents.[2] While Buddhism is the predominant religion, the country also includes substantial Hindu, Christian and Muslim communities.

The island nation held its first elections in 1931, just three years after its colonial master Britain held its own first elections, which the English historian A.J.P. Taylor had once put as the 'British electoral system reaching theoretical democracy'.[3] Thus the Ceylon colony of the Great British Empire held elections even before it was independent (based on universal adult franchise, unlike the ones that were being held in India then). In 1931, all women above the age of twenty-one also secured voting rights.[4] Therefore, women in this island colony of the empire on which the sun never set secured rights before the women living in Paris, Brussels or Geneva. Further on, in 1959–60 with the passage of the Ceylon Parliamentary Elections (Amendment) Act No. 11, the minimum age was reduced from twenty-one to eighteen.[5]

Under the Donoughmore Constitution (1931–47), the crown colony of Ceylon, which had not yet attained dominion status, became the first country in Asia, as well as the first 'non-white' territory within the British Empire, to receive substantial self-governing authority and universal suffrage.

This political enfranchisement of the entire adult population swiftly transformed the nature of political competition and reshaped elite incentives. This meant that the political elites – once faced with a newly enfranchised mass electorate – were compelled to shift their priorities and strategies to secure popular support. Instead of catering solely to narrow elite interests, they now had to adopt policies that addressed the needs of the broader population, such as welfare, education and healthcare, in order to win elections and maintain power. By the mid-1940s, the government had launched an array of progressive social welfare programmes, including subsidized food, free education and public healthcare, which significantly improved living conditions for the majority who had previously lacked these services. Consequently, by the early 1960s, Sri Lanka was lauded as an extraordinary case of early development success. Between 1946 and 1963, the infant mortality rate fell from 141 per 1,000 to 56 per 1,000, while life expectancy rose from forty-three to sixty-three years.[6] Adult literacy, already relatively high at 58 per cent in 1946, surged to 72 per cent by 1963.[7] These social advancements occurred with minimal corresponding economic growth, positioning Sri Lanka's welfare indicators alongside nations with income levels five to ten times higher.[8]

However, over the years, electoral competition in Sri Lanka increasingly channelled rising ethno-nationalist sentiments within both the Sinhalese and Tamil communities into direct political confrontation, eventually culminating in a civil war. This system also incentivized political contenders to implement generous public welfare initiatives, financed not through productive investments but through consumption subsidies that placed a significant strain on the economy. Cambridge economist Joan Robinson famously observed that 'Ceylon has tasted the fruit before she has planted the tree', underscoring the unsustainable nature of this approach.[9] One striking example of the era's economic and political dysfunction was the rice subsidy offered as wartime measure to ensure food security during World War II. Initially introduced as a wartime measure in 1942, the subsidy soon consumed 20 per cent of government expenditures and attained a politically untouchable status, making it nearly impossible to retract, even during fiscal crises.[10]

By the 1950s, advent of universal franchise and electoral politics created an intensely charged political climate, overturning the restrained, elite-dominated politics of the colonial period.

The general strike or *hartal* of 1953 marked a pivotal moment in Sri Lanka's post-colonial political evolution, symbolizing the escalating tension between popular demands and elite governance. By mid-century, the shift from colonial-era politics to mass-driven electoral competition had introduced deep social and economic strains. The hartal highlighted the impact of political mobilization among the working class and the disenfranchised, as economic discontent erupted in widespread protests against cuts to the rice subsidy and other austerity measures.[11] This event underscored the new political power of the masses, and served as a warning of the volatile consequences of public welfare policies that were both electorally popular and fiscally burdensome.

The Sinhala-Only Act of 1956 further illustrated the ethno-nationalist currents driving Sri Lankan politics. By mandating Sinhala as the sole official language, this legislation marginalized the Tamil-speaking minority, embedding ethnic division within state structures. The Act incited protests, fuelled ethnic hostilities and led to periodic outbreaks of violence, including the 1958 ethnic riots.[12] These developments marked a transition from the colonial-era focus on administrative governance to a deeply divisive identity politics that pitted communities against each other and politicized language, culture and ethnicity. This shift also exemplified the dangers of electoral incentives in a multicultural society, where majoritarianism – rather than consensus – became the guiding political strategy.[13]

Amid these tumultuous developments, the remnants of the colonial-era elite, many of whom were still active in government, expressed palpable concern and disapproval over the nation's new political trajectory. Although they were implicated in and often benefitted from these events, they regarded the chaos and upheaval with a mix of distaste and apprehension. Their vision of a controlled, gradual transition to self-rule, with governance rooted in elite stability, seemed increasingly at odds with the realities of a mass democracy characterized by populist policies, economic fragility and ethnic conflict. Thus, from their perspective, what they had once feared as a 'mob rule' outcome of universal suffrage, appeared to be unfolding – a reality driven by the very electoral politics that had disempowered their own insulated style of governance.[14]

Therefore, the origins of the Sri Lankan civil war lie in a complex historical landscape shaped by colonial legacies, post-independence political shifts and entrenched ethnic divisions.[15] Under British colonial rule, ethnic identities were hardened through administrative practices that favoured certain groups over others, creating a hierarchy that privileged the Tamil minority in education and civil service appointments. Following independence in 1948, Sinhalese nationalist leaders sought to redress these perceived imbalances, enacting policies such as the 1956 Sinhala-Only Act, which designated Sinhala as the sole national language. This policy, along with subsequent affirmative action programmes favouring Sinhalese students and job seekers, fuelled resentment among Tamil communities, who felt marginalized and deprived of the opportunities that had been theirs till the recent past. The seeds of ethnic tension thus became embedded in the very structure of the post-colonial state.

As tensions deepened, Tamil political groups shifted from seeking reform within the existing political system to pursuing autonomy and, ultimately, separatism. The 1972 constitution, which further cemented Sinhala–Buddhist primacy in the state, intensified these grievances. In the late 1970s, youth-led militant movements, most notably the Liberation Tigers of Tamil Eelam (LTTE), emerged as champions of Tamil nationalism, advocating for an independent Tamil state in the island's north and east. Attempts by successive governments to address these demands through limited decentralization were viewed as inadequate by Tamil leaders, while Sinhala nationalist factions viewed them as concessions that threatened the integrity of the nation. This impasse, coupled with escalating incidents of ethnic violence, culminated in the outbreak of civil war in 1983, setting the stage for nearly three decades of conflict that would transform Sri Lanka's social, political and economic landscape.

Armed conflict appeared a formidable obstacle to development, but many believed that development itself could provide a pathway to conflict resolution. Among both Tamil separatists in the north and Sinhala–Marxist insurgents of the Janatha Vimukthi Peramuna (JVP) in the south, there was considerable dissatisfaction with the economic and social marginalization among disadvantaged segments. This fostered a perception of economic development as not only the imperative but also as the plausible strategy for mitigating conflict. Consequently, since 1977, development initiatives have frequently adopted an implicit – if not explicit – aim of addressing fundamental causes of unrest, particularly youth unemployment and rural poverty.[16]

In practice, however, the relationship between development and armed conflict proved far more intricate than a simple accounting of war's economic costs or a linear causal linkage between poverty and violence. During its seventeen-year tenure between 1977 and 1994, the United National Party (UNP) government, led by J.R. Jayewardene and Ranasinghe Premadasa consecutively, prioritized both market reform and the ethnic conflict as central policy concerns, interwoven at political, socio-economic and ideological levels.[17] The UNP's overt display of Buddhist piety and Sinhala nationalism – partly a strategy to counter the unpopularity and perceived illegitimacy of its market reforms – had the unintended consequence of further alienating the Tamil minority, thus deepening ethnic divisions.

Constitutional History

Sri Lanka's political framework has been deeply influenced by its time as a British colonial territory, beginning in 1801. The British initiated efforts to establish a representative government on the island, first introducing a constitution in 1833, which formed a legislative council. This council, however, had limited power and, after its censure of the British government went unheeded, it resigned in 1864. Subsequent constitutional reforms (in 1910, 1920 and 1924) offered minimal advancement in local governance. The 1931 constitution, by contrast, vested greater authority in elected representatives over internal affairs. Over the next few decades, the British sought to gradually grant

Sri Lanka more autonomy with the eventual goal of elevating it to dominion status within the Empire. This process culminated on 4 February 1948, when Sri Lanka declared independence, though it remained part of the Commonwealth. It was not until 16 May 1972 that the country formally became an independent republic.

As mentioned earlier, during the British era, the northern Tamil population achieved a degree of influence through greater access to education. Following independence, Tamil leaders leveraged this influence to advocate for increased autonomy, which contributed to the development of a new constitution on 31 August 1978. Intended to balance the interests of both the Tamil and Sinhalese communities, this constitution remains in force, albeit with numerous amendments. The 17th Amendment, passed in 2001, aimed to enhance transparency through the establishment of a constitutional council composed of representatives from the executive and legislative branches, political parties and the public. This amendment followed an unsuccessful attempt to introduce a new constitution in 2000, which sought to create a federal system that would address Tamil aspirations for autonomy. However, political conflicts prevented this proposal from advancing to a vote. In 2009, after years of violent conflict, then President Mahinda Rajapaksa announced the military defeat of the LTTE, leading to a surge in his popularity. Subsequently, he proposed the 18th Amendment, which reversed certain provisions of the 17th Amendment and expanded presidential powers, including the removal of term limits. Parliament adopted this amendment in September 2010, despite significant public opposition.[18]

Parliamentary Structure

The parliamentary structure of Sri Lanka, is founded on a blend of British parliamentary traditions and indigenous political developments. Following independence from British colonial rule in 1948, the country adopted a parliamentary system, evolving from a dominion status to a republic in 1972. The 1978 constitution, which remains the governing framework even today, introduced an executive presidency that fundamentally altered the balance of power, placing the executive as a prominent force alongside the legislature. Despite this presidential influence, parliament retains critical roles in governance, lawmaking and oversight.

Sri Lanka's parliament, located in Sri Jayawardenepura Kotte – the country's administrative capital – is a unicameral legislature composed of 225 members. Of these, 196 are elected from twenty-two multi-member constituencies, which largely correspond to the island's administrative districts. Each constituency returns between four and nineteen MPs, depending on its population. Voters cast a single ballot for a political party and each party receives a share of seats in the district proportional to its total vote. Voters can also mark preferences among candidates of their chosen party, which determines which individuals are awarded seats within the party's share. This proportional representation system in multi-member districts allows for more inclusive representation, giving space to smaller parties and minority groups.[19]

In addition to the 196 constituency-based MPs, twenty-nine seats are filled through a National List system. These are allocated to political parties in proportion to their nationwide share of the vote, allowing parties to nominate individuals – such as technocrats or community leaders – who may not have contested directly. All MPs serve a five-year term, unless parliament is dissolved earlier by the president or due to constitutional exigencies. Sri Lanka's mixed-member proportional representation system thus balances constituency responsiveness with broader political inclusiveness, often leading to coalition politics and a more pluralist legislature.

The legislative body is led by the speaker, who is elected from among the MPs and is responsible for presiding over parliamentary proceedings with impartiality. Supporting the speaker are the deputy speaker and deputy chairman of committees, positions traditionally filled to ensure a balance of representation and continuity in parliamentary operations. Parliament holds the power to initiate and pass legislation, although the president retains the ability to veto bills in certain situations, particularly those with a national security focus. This interplay of powers has, at times, created tensions between the executive and legislative branches. Yet, it also reflects a careful balancing act that aims to uphold democratic checks and balances.[20]

Committees form an essential part of the parliamentary structure, allowing for detailed scrutiny and discussion on specialized areas of governance. These committees include public accounts and public enterprises, which monitor government spending and efficiency, along with select committees that address issues of public interest or complex legislative matters. The committee system thus enhances the parliament's role in governance, enabling it to conduct inquiries, question ministers and demand accountability from public officials. This structure underscores the commitment to oversight, transparency and a participatory approach to governance, even as it operates within the constraints posed by executive powers.

While parliament is the primary lawmaking body, its role has been tempered by the executive presidency, particularly on matters of national security, foreign policy and major economic decisions. However, significant constitutional amendments, such as the 19th and 20th amendments, have altered the relationship between the president and parliament, periodically expanding or curtailing presidential powers.[21] These constitutional shifts reflect broader tensions within Sri Lankan political culture regarding centralized versus decentralized power, highlighting the country's ongoing struggle to define the ideal balance between effective governance and democratic accountability.

In essence, Sri Lanka's parliamentary structure embodies a hybrid system, merging features of a parliamentary democracy with the distinctive role of an executive presidency. While parliament functions as a platform for democratic representation and legislative discourse, it operates within a framework influenced by strong presidential authority. This dual system reflects both historical legacies and contemporary political realities, encapsulating Sri Lanka's ongoing evolution as a democratic state.

Executive Branch

Sri Lanka's political structure divides authority among the legislative, executive and judicial branches, with the executive holding the most extensive powers. As discussed earlier, the president, directly elected by the people, serves as the head of state, head of government and commander-in-chief of the armed forces. The presidential term is five years, with a two-term limit. Earlier, until the constitutional reforms introduced in 2015, the term was six years and presidents were allowed to contest for more than two terms. The president's powers of appointment are wide-ranging: they include the authority to appoint the PM, cabinet ministers, Supreme Court justices and other senior officials. In situations where an office is vacant, the president may temporarily assume its functions until a formal appointment is made. This latitude in executive power allowed President Mahinda Rajapaksa to concurrently hold the defence and finance portfolios in addition to his constitutional responsibilities during his presidency from 2005 to 2015.

The president's ability to control key appointments also provided him with the necessary parliamentary support to pass the 18th Amendment. Although impeachment is possible through a joint effort of parliament and judiciary, no other entity may challenge presidential decisions in either public or private forums. The PM and cabinet, appointed by the president, advise him in his role as head of government and are responsible for directing governmental operations. While the PM and cabinet are accountable to parliament, they derive their authority from their appointment by the president.

The executive presidency in Sri Lanka, as R. Venugopal, a scholar based at the London School of Economics, contends, emerged from an elite-driven ambition to establish a more stable, centralized and authoritarian political framework capable of counteracting the perceived economic drawbacks of a populist electoral democracy.[22] This system was expected to stimulate economic growth under a market-oriented development agenda. Initially, this approach proved effective, notably during the presidencies of J.R. Jayewardene (1978–88) and Ranasinghe Premadasa (1989–93), whose administrations retained legislative control and showed a strong commitment to market reforms. However, this model began to falter during Chandrika Kumaratunga's presidency (1995–2005), as resistance intensified from multiple sectors. The Mahinda Rajapaksa administration (2005–14) eventually stabilized the presidency, but only by renouncing the original principles underpinning its creation and instead adopting the electoral populism it was initially intended to resist.

Legislative Branch

As discussed earlier, Sri Lanka's legislative branch is a unicameral body, comprising a parliament of 226 members who serve five-year terms following direct elections. Within parliament, members elect a speaker a deputy speaker and a chair of committees. The president holds the prerogative to dissolve parliament at any time, a power that significantly limits the legislative body's independence relative to the executive. The parliament's primary function is to draft and pass bills and resolutions, which attain the force of law through majority approval and the speaker's endorsement. When a referendum is necessary for a bill, the cabinet may mandate it, subject to the president's endorsement. Once enacted in this manner, no court may contest the validity of such legislation.

Judicial Branch

Sri Lanka's judiciary comprises the Supreme Court, court of appeal, high court and other statutory courts. These institutions are tasked with safeguarding and upholding citizens' rights. The president appoints the chief justice and justices of the Supreme Court, as well as the president and justices of the high court. Justices may serve until the age of sixty-five. Under the 17th Amendment, these appointments required approval from the constitutional council; however, this requirement was repealed by the 18th Amendment. The Supreme Court exercises exclusive authority over constitutional interpretation and jurisdiction in matters of fundamental rights, final appeals and electoral disputes. It also possesses the power to review actions of parliamentary members and may provide advisory opinions to parliament regarding legislative processes.

The 1978 Constitution

The 1978 constitution of Sri Lanka centres on a presidential system with extensive executive powers. Comprising 172 articles, the constitution enshrines Buddhism as the state religion and delineates a wide range of fundamental rights. It also outlines the responsibilities of both the state and its citizens. The state is tasked with fostering a democratic socialist society, ensuring equitable wealth distribution, overseeing economic development, and promoting educational and cultural advancement. It is also committed to decentralizing governance and reinforcing national identity by eliminating discrimination. In turn, citizens are expected to contribute to national unity, including by setting aside personal interests in favour of racial and religious harmony, and upholding public health and morality.[23]

19th and 20th Amendments: The Rise and Reversal of Reform

The 2015 election of President Maithripala Sirisena, backed by a reformist coalition, led to the passage of the 19th Amendment to Sri Lanka's constitution. This amendment aimed to curb the excessive powers of the presidency that had accumulated since 1978. It reduced the president's term from six to five years, reintroduced a two-term limit and transferred key appointment powers to a Constitutional Council, giving parliament and independent institutions more say. It also strengthened the position of the PM and cabinet, laying the foundation for a more balanced, semi-presidential model of governance. However, the reform soon proved unstable. Tensions between Sirisena and then PM Ranil Wickremesinghe culminated in a constitutional crisis in 2018, and the government's poor response to the 2019 Easter attacks further eroded public confidence in divided executive power.[24]

In 2019, Gotabaya Rajapaksa was elected president with overwhelming support, campaigning on a platform of restoring strong presidential rule. His victory was soon followed by his party's landslide win in the 2020 parliamentary elections, granting it the two-thirds majority required for constitutional changes. With parliament dissolved during the early months of the Covid-19 pandemic, the government ruled by presidential decree, reinforcing the appeal of centralized authority. The 19th Amendment was criticized as weakening decisive leadership during crises, and the president quickly moved to roll it back. A committee was appointed, and by September 2020, the government introduced the 20th Amendment, designed to restore expansive executive powers.[25]

The 20th Amendment reversed nearly all the checks introduced by the 19th. It allowed the president to appoint and dismiss ministers and judges without oversight, dissolve parliament after one year, and sideline the Constitutional Council by replacing it with a weaker, government-dominated body. Independent institutions like the election commission, judiciary and anti-corruption bodies were brought back under presidential control. Though some reforms – like shorter terms and the right to information – remained intact, the overall shift was toward what critics have called an 'imperial presidency'. These changes marked a sharp retreat from the democratic reforms of 2015 and signalled a return to centralized, top-heavy governance in Sri Lanka.[26]

Ethno-nationalism via Constituional Changes

Over the years, the Rajapaksa family has emerged as the leading proponents of Sinhala–Buddhist nationalism, backed by the powerful Buddhist priesthood that lies at the heart of their formidable electoral apparatus. Their constitutional agenda aims to deepen the alignment between Sri Lankan state identity and the ethnic, religious and cultural identity of the Sinhala–Buddhist majority. This vision fosters a form of ethnocracy, wherein minority communities are neither fully integrated nor accorded equal footing but are instead subsumed within a clear communal hierarchy. While economic development for minorities may be envisioned, genuine equality and pluralism are not. Those who resist such an order are likely to face suppression. The 20th Amendment does not address these nationalist aims directly, yet the new constitution proposed by them – as advocated by prominent nationalist thinkers supportive of the government – is anticipated to embrace a civilization–state model centred on majoritarian identity.[27]

The 2019 presidential elections and 2020 parliamentary election results underscored a popular willingness among the Sri Lankan electorate to trade democratic constraints to the executive for promises of national security and economic advancement under a centralized presidency.[28] While the Gotabaya Rajapaksa administration seemed set to achieve some of its aims, the intrinsic risks of an unchecked government remained. Such an approach fosters an environment prone to corruption, nepotism and flawed decision-making, while also heightening communal tensions and eroding democratic norms. The legacy of the 18th Amendment made under the Mahinda Rajapaksa administration, marked by executive overreach, repression and democratic backsliding, foreshadowed the potential path ahead. The 20th Amendment appears to signal merely the beginning of an intensified centralization of power.[29]

Authoritarianism to Aragalaya

Despite early indications of economic strain in Sri Lanka in 2021, few could have anticipated the severe crisis that unfolded the following year. By early 2022, the country's economy plunged into a deep recession, marked by acute shortages of essential goods, including food, fuel and medicine.[30] This economic turmoil, which left much of the population, except the wealthiest, struggling to meet basic needs, sparked a groundswell of public dissent. Initially an economic protest, this discontent quickly evolved into a broader movement against the government, with then President Gotabaya Rajapaksa facing widespread accusations of inefficiency and corruption.

Despite emergency responses from the administration, the protest movement, known as *Janatha Aragalaya* ('people's struggle' in Sinhala), gained momentum. In July 2022, the movement culminated with demonstrators seizing major government buildings in Colombo, leading to President Rajapaksa's resignation. To the surprise of many, the crisis dismantled the once-immovable political dominance of the Rajapaksa family. Although security forces sometimes employed excessive force, the military ultimately exercised restraint, signalling no interest in assuming power.

The movement – which first coalesced in March 2022 amid mounting frustrations over power cuts, inflation and shortages – saw Sri Lankans from all ethnicities, religions, and socio-economic backgrounds united in a collective call for accountability. This unprecedented show of solidarity led to the resignations of then PM Mahinda Rajapaksa in May and, later, President Gotabaya Rajapaksa's resignation.[31] Yet, despite this significant political shift, Sri Lanka's economic and political challenges remain formidable. Once considered a relatively prosperous South Asian nation – achieving upper-middle-income status in 2018 – the country now faces the urgent need for debt restructuring and sustainable solutions to food insecurity and economic stability. Progress towards restoring democratic integrity and rebuilding public trust in governance has been limited, underscoring the ongoing struggle for meaningful change in Sri Lankan society.[32]

Dissanayake's 2024 Victory

Anura Kumara Dissanayake's victory in the 2024 Sri Lankan presidential elections represents a watershed in the nation's political trajectory, marking a decisive shift away from the entrenched political dynasties that have long dominated the landscape.[33] As the leader of the National People's Power (NPP) alliance, Dissanayake appealed to a population fatigued by ongoing crises, advocating a platform centred on transparency, anti-corruption and comprehensive economic reform. This win reflected the electorate's desire for accountability and was a departure from the dominance of the Rajapaksa family and their allies, whose grip on power had defined Sri Lanka's recent history.

The context of Dissanayake's ascent lay in the legacy of political and economic turmoil that has plagued Sri Lanka over the past two decades. The Rajapaksas, beginning with Mahinda Rajapaksa's presidency in 2005, leveraged nationalistic and militaristic appeal, building a formidable dynasty bolstered by Mahinda's success in concluding the civil war in 2009. However, the Rajapaksa regime became increasingly associated with nepotism, authoritarianism and financial mismanagement. After the Easter bombings in 2019, Gotabaya, Mahinda's brother, ascended to the presidency, inheriting the family's nationalist agenda. However, he proved unable to navigate Sri Lanka's economic challenges. His administration's drastic policies, including sudden tax cuts and a ban on chemical fertilizers, accelerated an economic collapse, resulting in Sri Lanka's first-ever external debt default.[34]

This led to the Aragalaya movement, which ultimately forced Gotabaya's resignation. Wickremesinghe, despite limited public support, was appointed as interim president by parliament to stabilize the nation. While his tenure facilitated an essential International Monetary Fund (IMF) bailout and debt restructuring, his measures were met with public resistance due to austerity requirements, which underscored the government's disconnection from the populace. Dissanayake's election embodied the public's response to these longstanding grievances and their demand for genuine reform.

The 2024 Presidential Election

The 2024 Sri Lankan presidential election featured thirty-eight candidates, none of whom were women, despite women comprising nearly half of the electorate. The contest quickly narrowed to four principal contenders: incumbent Wickremesinghe, who, though traditionally aligned with the centre-Right UNP ran as an independent; Sajith Premadasa, opposition leader and founder of the Samagi Jana Balawegaya (SJB); Namal Rajapaksa, son of Mahinda Rajapaksa, representing the Sri Lanka Podujana Peramuna (SLPP); and Anura Kumara Dissanayake, who led the NPP alliance, including the Marxist-oriented JVP.

Of approximately 17 million eligible voters, 75 per cent participated – a turnout lower than the record 83.72 per cent in 2019. On 22 September 2024, after a second round of voting and a relatively peaceful process, Dissanayake emerged victorious with over 5.7 million votes, surpassing Premadasa's 4.5 million. The following day, he was inaugurated as Sri Lanka's tenth president.[35]

Dissanayake's victory, though anticipated by many, represented a significant departure from decades of governance marked by corruption and political entrenchment. His campaign, emphasizing a 'clean political future' and pledging to make the IMF-backed economic reforms more equitable, resonated particularly with voters disillusioned by prior administrations' mismanagement.

The international community broadly welcomed Dissanayake's win.[36] Then US President Joe Biden conveyed a desire to deepen bilateral ties and strengthen security, peace and prosperity across the Indo–Pacific. Chinese President Xi Jinping expressed readiness to expand cooperation under the Belt and Road Initiative (BRI), reiterating China's commitment to bolstering political trust and development partnerships with Sri Lanka. Indian PM Narendra Modi similarly voiced support, affirming Sri Lanka's importance in India's 'Neighbourhood First' policy and Vision SAGAR (Security and Growth for All in the Region), both pivotal to regional security and growth.

The reactions of global and regional leaders underscore Sri Lanka's strategic geopolitical significance, as Dissanayake's administration will be navigating complex relationships with major powers – each with significant economic and strategic stakes in the region.

Economic Stabilization and Strategic Diplomacy

On the first day of his presidency, Dissanayake acted decisively by dissolving parliament and calling for snap elections on 14 November. Notably, he appointed Harini Amarasuriya, a member of the NPP alliance and one of the few female leaders in recent decades, as PM.

Since taking office, President Dissanayake has prioritized restoring economic stability while navigating the constraints of Sri Lanka's ongoing IMF-supported programme. Building on the $2.9 billion Extended Fund Facility initiated in 2023, his government has secured its third tranche of disbursements and committed to structural reforms including debt restructuring, state-owned enterprise reform and fiscal consolidation. Dissanayake has balanced this with promises of targeted tax relief and social protections, aiming to restore growth without derailing the recovery. While poverty rates have begun to ease from their post-crisis peak, the IMF has warned that there is 'no room for policy slippages', underscoring the delicate equilibrium between reform, relief and credibility.[37] As Sri Lanka seeks to re-engage global markets and rebuild investor confidence, Dissanayake's success will depend not only on sound economic management but also on political steadiness and the public's willingness to endure difficult but necessary reforms.

In foreign policy, Dissanayake's background with the Marxist-leaning JVP has led to perceptions of the NPP alliance as more pro-China. Under the Mahinda Rajapaksa administration, Sri Lanka witnessed significant Chinese investment, primarily through the BRI, including projects such as the Hambantota Port, which is now emblematic of Sri Lanka's complex financial relationship with China. During his campaign Dissanayake criticized an Indian-backed wind-power project under the Adani Group, citing energy sovereignty concerns, and pledged to terminate it if elected.[38]

However, early indications suggest that Dissanayake aims to pursue a balanced approach in foreign relations. His inaugural address emphasized Sri Lanka's need to engage constructively with multiple global powers, aiming to avoid positioning the country between the competing regional giants, India and China. 'We will work with the world,' he affirmed, underscoring a pragmatic and multipolar foreign policy vision.[39]

India's support for Sri Lanka during its economic crisis, in the early part of 2022 between January and April, amounting to approximately $4 billion in aid, has reinvigorated bilateral ties, allowing India to reassert its influence in response to China's significant investment presence. India's timely assistance reinforced its role as a key partner, rooted in historical and geographic ties, while China remains Sri Lanka's largest bilateral lender. Indian External Affairs Minister S. Jaishankar visited Sri Lanka on 4 October 2024, marking the first foreign ministerial visit since Dissanayake's election, further consolidating the India–Sri Lanka relationship. Dissanayake, in turn, made visits to India in December 2024 and his discussions with S. Jaishankar and National Security Adviser Ajit Doval echo his commitment to fostering these ties.[40]

Sri Lanka's strategic position in the Indian Ocean – central to global maritime trade – makes it a focal point in the geopolitical dynamics of India, China and the US, all of whom have heightened their interest in the region. The US has expressed its intent to deepen cooperation with Sri Lanka on economic stability, climate action and security.

For President Dissanayake, the challenge will lie in maintaining a balanced diplomatic approach, leveraging the interests of regional and global powers to secure economic benefits while preserving national sovereignty. His administration must seek to engage each of these partners constructively, ensuring that Sri Lanka's growth aligns with its broader strategic autonomy. As South Asia undergoes a series of political transitions, Dissanayake's tenure presents a unique opportunity to engage with other newly elected leaders in the region. Collective efforts to address shared regional challenges could foster greater collabouration, provided the political will to pursue ambitious, cooperative agendas exists.[41]

Key events at a glance

- **1948** – Independence from Britain; Dominion of Ceylon established under PM D.S. Senanayake
- **1949** – Ceylon Citizenship Act; disenfranchises Indian-origin Tamil plantation workers
- **1951** – Formation of Sri Lanka Freedom Party by S.W.R.D. Bandaranaike, promoting Sinhala nationalism
- **1956** – Bandaranaike becomes PM; Sinhala-Only Act passed, making Sinhala the sole official language, alienating Tamil minorities
- **1959** – Assassination of Bandaranaike; political instability follows
- **1972** – New republican constitution; country renamed Sri Lanka; Buddhism given 'foremost place'; Tamil alienation deepens
- **1976** – Formation of the LTTE; armed Tamil separatist movement begins
- **1978** – Second republican constitution enacted under J.R. Jayewardene; introduces powerful executive presidency
- **1983** – Black July Riots: Anti-Tamil pogroms after LTTE ambush; civil war officially breaks out
- **1987** – Indo-Sri Lanka Accord; Indian Peace Keeping Force deployed but faces resistance from LTTE and Sinhalese nationalists
- **1991** – Assassination of Indian PM Rajiv Gandhi by LTTE suicide bomber
- **1993** – Assassination of President Ranasinghe Premadasa by LTTE
- **2002** – Ceasefire agreement brokered between government and LTTE; peace talks begin but collapse
- **2005** – Mahinda Rajapaksa elected president; adopts hardline stance against LTTE
- **2009** – End of civil war; LTTE militarily defeated; allegations of war crimes emerge
- **2010** – 18th Amendment passed; abolishes presidential term limits and weakens oversight bodies; expands executive powers under Mahinda Rajapaksa
- **2015** – Maithripala Sirisena elected president; promises democratic reforms and national reconciliation; 19th Amendment enacted; restores presidential term limits, reduces presidential powers and strengthens the role of the PM and independent commissions
- **2018** – Constitutional crisis; President Sirisena attempts to dismiss PM Ranil Wickremesinghe, triggering months of political deadlock

- **2019** – Easter Sunday bombings by Islamist extremists kill over 250 people; major security and political fallout
- **2019–2020** – Gotabaya Rajapaksa elected president; promises strong governance and national security; 20th Amendment passed; repeals key reforms of the 19th Amendment, re-concentrates power in the presidency and weakens independent oversight
- **2022** – Massive economic collapse; acute shortages of essentials; historic people's protests (Aragalaya movement)
- **July 2022** – Gotabaya Rajapaksa flees country amid protests; Ranil Wickremesinghe becomes president
- **2023–24** – Political and economic reforms under IMF guidance; social discontent persists
- **September 2024** – Anura Kumara Dissanayake is elected Sri Lanka's first Marxist president; his NPP coalition wins a landslide in November parliamentary elections, securing 159 of 225 seats
- **February–March 2025** – The new government implements fiscal reforms in line with the IMF programme; inflation drops below zero and foreign reserves rise to US$6.5 billion
- **April 2025** – Local council elections take place across 139 of 339 councils; a 'Clean Sri Lanka' initiative is launched.
- **June 2025** – Sri Lanka enters negotiations with the IMF for further reforms aimed at attracting foreign investment; a staff-level bailout agreement paves the way for a US$344 million release.

4

Bangladesh: From Partition to People's Power

Bangladesh, formally designated as the People's Republic of Bangladesh, is defined as such in Article 1 of its constitution, promulgated in 1972. Located in the historic expanse of the Indian subcontinent, the nation's history is inseparably intertwined with that of India (until the partition of 1947) and with Pakistan (until the secession of East Pakistan in 1971). Bangladesh declared independence on 26 March 1971, adopting a name that signifies 'the land of Bengal' or 'the country of Bengalis'. Its sovereignty was realized on 16 December 1971, following the capitulation of Pakistani forces in East Pakistan to a joint command of Bangladeshi and Indian forces. Notably, the Declaration of Independence speech delivered by Sheikh Mujibur Rahman on 7 March 1971, a pivotal moment in the nation's history, has been recognized as a UNESCO documentary heritage.

The Bengali language (Bangla), which is the seventh-most widely spoken language globally, holds profound cultural and historical significance for Bangladeshis. During the period when present-day Bangladesh was East Pakistan, the imposition of Urdu as the sole state language provoked widespread dissent. This culminated in The Bengali Language Movement, wherein students and activists sacrificed their lives on 21 February 1952 to secure recognition for Bangla as a state language. This date, commemorated as 'Language Martyrs' Day', underscores a unique historical distinction: Bangla remains the only language for which individuals have died to secure its official status. Since 2000, UNESCO has observed 21 February as International Mother Language Day to honour this extraordinary legacy.

Bangladesh's cultural heritage is internationally acknowledged, with three sites inscribed on UNESCO's World Heritage List: the historic mosque city of Bagerhat, the ruins of the Buddhist Vihara at Paharpur and the Sundarbans, the world's largest mangrove forest. Additionally, seven sites have been placed on UNESCO's tentative list, including the archaeological sites of Lalmai-Mainamati, the cultural landscape of Mahasthan and Karatoya River, and the architectural works of Muzharul Islam, a seminal figure in the South Asian modernist movement.

With a population of approximately 175 million, Bangladesh is the third-largest Muslim-majority nation.[1] It has garnered international recognition for its economic and social achievements.

It is the second-largest global exporter of ready-made garments[2], trailing only China, and ranks second in jute production[3], third in inland freshwater fish production[4] and third in vegetable cultivation, producing 3.7 million tonnes annually.[5] Bangladesh also holds the eighth position in global mango production and is poised to become the fourth-largest rice producer, as projected by the Food and Agriculture Organization.[6] The pharmaceutical industry, benefitting from patent exemptions until 2032, has seen rapid growth, with exports reaching over 100 countries.[7] Furthermore, the country is a significant provider of online freelance labour, ranking second globally after India.[8]

Transitioning from the largest least-developed country in terms of population and economic size, Bangladesh is on a trajectory to attain developing-country status, bolstered by substantial progress in poverty alleviation and human development despite persistent challenges. Achieving lower-middle-income status as defined by the World Bank in 2015, Bangladesh is expected to graduate from the UN's least-developed countries category by 2026.[9] The nation has met key millennium development goals, including reductions in poverty, gender parity in education and lowered under-five mortality rates. It is now committed to implementing the sustainable development goals, reflecting its dedication to inclusive and sustainable development.[10]

The governance framework of Bangladesh is extensive, encompassing fifty-eight ministries and divisions, and 353 subordinate departments.

Administratively, the country is organized into eight divisions (*bibhaags)*, sixty-four districts (*zilas)*, 495 sub-districts (*upazilas*) and 4,554 union councils (union *parishads*), structured across four levels of local government.[11] This administrative apparatus supports the implementation of public policy and the delivery of essential services, underpinning the nation's socio-economic progress.

Bangladesh occupies the north-eastern expanse of the Indian subcontinent, situated in South Asia. Renowned as the 'land of rivers', the nation is traversed by over 900 rivers and tributaries, a geographic feature that has profoundly shaped its landscape, culture and history. Encircled almost entirely by India, Bangladesh shares a short south-eastern frontier with Myanmar and possesses a southern coastline along the Bay of Bengal. Historically, its territorial configuration was among the most intricate globally, marked by the presence of 95 to 119 enclaves, known as *chhitmahals*, within Indian territory. This arrangement, mirrored by Indian enclaves within Bangladesh, constituted the world's second-largest enclave network.[12] Until the landmark exchange of 162 enclaves on 1 August 2015, this arrangement was often described as the 'world's craziest border' or 'the most bewildering border dispute'.[13] The resolution marked a significant milestone in diplomatic relations between the two nations.

Geographically, Bangladesh predominantly comprises the deltaic plains formed by the Ganges (Padma) and Brahmaputra (Jamuna) rivers, with a modest extension into the south-eastern hill tracts bordering Myanmar. Its topography is characterized by fertile alluvial plains, making it a vital agricultural hub. Notably, the country is home to Cox's Bazar, a 120-km stretch of uninterrupted sandy beach along the Bay of Bengal, acclaimed as the longest sea beach of its kind globally.

With an area spanning 148,460 sq. km, Bangladesh ranks among the most densely populated regions worldwide.[14] Dhaka, the nation's capital and its largest city, has served as a pivotal urban centre for over four centuries, tracing its prominence to its historical role as the capital of Bengal during the Mughal era. Today, Dhaka remains a vibrant nucleus of governance, commerce and culture, emblematic of Bangladesh's enduring historical and geographical significance.

Birth of Bangladesh

On 16 December 1971, the Bangladesh Liberation War reached its conclusion, culminating in the emergence of the People's Republic of Bangladesh from the erstwhile province of East Pakistan. Although the conflict is most commonly remembered for its profound impact on South Asia's geopolitical landscape, it also encapsulates a broader and more nuanced set of legacies. It challenged our understanding of Cold War diplomacy, the dynamics of twentieth-century genocidal and sexual violence, and the limitations of international law in addressing post-conflict justice.

The roots of the crisis trace back to the Partition of India in 1947, which divided the subcontinent into the Hindu-majority state of India and the Muslim-majority state of Pakistan. East Bengal, predominantly Bengali-speaking, became East Pakistan, geographically and culturally distinct from the Punjabi-dominated West Pakistan. Despite their shared religious identity, the two wings of Pakistan were separated by 1,600 km and profound disparities in language, ethnicity and political priorities. These divisions sowed the seeds of an independence movement in East Pakistan, driven by demands for linguistic recognition, political autonomy and self-rule.[15]

The political crisis that precipitated the war began with the general elections of 7 December 1970, in which the Bangladesh Awami League (BAL), under the leadership of Sheikh Mujibur Rahman, secured an overwhelming victory. The party's platform advocated for greater autonomy for East Pakistan. However, the central government, led by General Yahya Khan and Zulfikar Ali Bhutto of the PPP, refused to allow the BAL to form a government. This refusal, coupled with months of failed negotiations, culminated in the deployment of the Pakistani army to East Pakistan on 25 March 1971. What followed was a brutal campaign of repression targeting Bengalis, particularly Hindus, in what many observers and scholars have since identified as acts of genocide.[16]

The military's actions included the systematic use of mass murder, rape and forced deportations, supported by the creation of religious militias to perpetrate atrocities against perceived enemies of the state. The conflict rapidly escalated into an international crisis. The Mukti

Bahini, a Bengali independence militia, conducted guerilla operations with logistical and material support from India. By the autumn of 1971, the influx of millions of refugees into Indian territory compelled then PM Indira Gandhi to intervene militarily, citing humanitarian imperatives. However, Pakistan preemptively launched an attack on India from the west on 3 December, further internationalizing the conflict.

The war, though brief, became a focal point in the Cold War rivalry. The US, concerned about a potential expansion of Soviet influence in South Asia following an Indian victory, extended tacit support to Pakistan. The Nixon administration, despite the mounting evidence of atrocities, refrained from condemning Pakistan, framing the conflict as an internal matter. Moreover, the US provided clandestine military assistance to Pakistan in violation of congressional sanctions, underscoring its complicity in a catastrophic humanitarian crisis. Meanwhile, India enjoyed the backing of the then Soviet Union, which provided diplomatic cover and material aid.[17]

The human cost of the conflict was staggering. Estimates of the death toll range from several hundred thousand to as many as 3 million, with at least 200,000 women subjected to sexual violence.[18] The Pakistani army's actions have been the subject of ongoing scholarly debate, particularly regarding its classification as genocide and the accountability of those responsible. Despite these discussions, the Pakistani government has never formally acknowledged the scale or nature of the atrocities, continuing to claim that only a few thousand lives were lost.

In Bangladesh, the political and social repercussions of the Liberation War remain deeply embedded in the national consciousness. Successive BAL-led governments, under Sheikh Mujibur Rahman and later his daughter Sheikh Hasina, sought to prosecute individuals who collabourated with Pakistan. The enactment of the 1973 International Crimes (Tribunals) Act and its 2009 amendment provided a legal framework for these efforts, albeit limited to domestic jurisdiction. Critics have argued that these tribunals have not adhered to international legal standards, raising concerns about procedural fairness and political motivations.

The quest for justice has been fraught with setbacks. Trials were halted under the regimes of General Ziaur Rahman and General Hussain

Muhammad Ershad and the government of the Bangladesh Nationalist Party (BNP) under Khaleda Zia. Many individuals implicated in war crimes served in these governments, further complicating the pursuit of accountability. It was not until 2010 that war crimes trials resumed in earnest, reigniting both domestic and international debates over justice and reconciliation.[19]

The enduring legacy of the Liberation War continues to influence Bangladesh's civic life. The trials sparked both violent protests by their opponents and fervent demands for harsher sentences by their proponents. Additionally, the trials have coincided with a rise in extremist violence, including targeted killings of secularists and human rights advocates – underscoring the ongoing challenges in reconciling the nation's past with its aspirations for justice and progress.[20] As Bangladesh navigates these complexities, the Liberation War remains not only a defining moment in its history but also a profound case study in the intersections of politics, law and memory.

Origins of the Constitution

The foundational framework of the new nation's governance was set forth in the Proclamation of Independence, adopted by the constituent assembly on 10 April 1971. This document, serving as the provisional constitution, laid the groundwork for the Constitution of the People's Republic of Bangladesh. It was formally adopted on 4 November 1972, and enforced from 16 December of the same year.

A constitution embodies a nation's past, charts its present and aspires to shape its future. Often described as a nation's autobiography, it evolves alongside the society it governs, retaining certain immutable principles while adapting to changing contexts. The Bangladeshi constitution, which has undergone seventeen amendments to date, reflects this dynamism. Six of these amendments (5th to 10th) were enacted during periods of military or military-backed authoritarian rule (1975–90), highlighting the nation's turbulent political journey.[21]

The period from 1947 to 1971 was marked by sustained struggles for self-determination and constitutional rights. Key milestones included the language movement of 1948–52, which defended the right to use Bengali as a state language, the historic 1954 provincial elections based on the BAL-led 21-point programme and the mass uprisings of 1965–69. These movements not only articulated demands for autonomy but also laid the foundation for Bangladesh's eventual independence.[22]

The events leading to the Liberation War were the culmination of decades of systemic marginalization and constitutional crises. From the denial of linguistic and cultural rights to the suppression of political aspirations, Bangladesh's journey to independence underscores the resilience of its people in the face of adversity. The constitution of Bangladesh, forged in the aftermath of this struggle, remains both a testament to their sacrifices and a living document that continues to evolve alongside the nation it represents.

The mass movement for autonomy between 1966 and 1969 culminated in the resignation of President Ayub Khan, who transferred power to General Yahya Khan on 25 March 1969. General Yahya, another military dictator, immediately declared martial law but promised a return to civilian rule through elections. He set 5 October 1970 as the date for Pakistan's first general elections since its independence in 1947, and assured the drafting of a new constitution by the elected representatives. To this end, the Legal Framework Order (LFO) was promulgated on 30 March 1970, outlining the electoral process and allocating 169 seats in the National Assembly to East Pakistan.[23]

The BAL, led by Sheikh Mujibur Rahman, prepared extensively for the elections, anchoring its campaign on the Six-Point Programme, which advocated for East Pakistan's autonomy. In the elections held in December 1970, the AL achieved a resounding victory, winning 167 out of 313 seats in the National Assembly and 288 out of 310 seats in East Pakistan's Provincial Assembly.[24] With an unequivocal parliamentary majority, the AL was entitled to form the government and draft the new constitution.[25]

However, then President Yahya Khan, unwilling to relinquish power, repeatedly postponed the inaugural session of the National Assembly. When the 3 March 1971 session was postponed indefinitely on 1 March Sheikh Mujibur Rahman called for a nationwide non-cooperation movement from 3 to 6 March, demanding the immediate transfer of power. This culminated in his historic speech of 7 March 1971, where he declared that the struggle for autonomy had transformed into a struggle for emancipation and independence. Although the speech stopped short of an outright declaration of independence, its final words – 'The struggle this time is the struggle for our emancipation. The struggle this time is the struggle for our independence.' – left no doubt about the direction of the movement.[26]

The situation escalated dramatically on the night of 25 March 1971, when the Pakistani military launched 'Operation Searchlight', a brutal crackdown aimed at suppressing the movement. Sheikh Mujibur Rahman was arrested, but not before issuing the Proclamation of Independence in the early hours of 26 March 1971. This marked the beginning of a nine-month-long war of liberation, characterized by unprecedented violence and atrocities, and India's intervention, culminating in the surrender of Pakistani forces in Dhaka on 16 December 1971.

Drafting the Constitution

The drafting of the Constitution of Bangladesh was undertaken by a 34-member committee of the Constituent Assembly, chaired by Dr Kamal Hossain. After months of deliberation, the Constitution was formally adopted on 4 November 1972 and came into effect on 16 December 1972, marking the first anniversary of the country's victory in the Liberation War. The elected representatives from East Pakistan in the 1970 elections formed themselves into the Constituent Assembly of Bangladesh. On 10 April 1971, they promulgated the Proclamation of Independence, retroactively effective from 26 March 1971. Its preamble articulated the fundamental principles of the new state:

> We, the elected representatives of the people of Bangladesh, as honour-bound by the mandate given to us by the people of Bangladesh whose will is supreme, duly constituted ourselves into a Constituent Assembly, and having held mutual consultations, and in order to ensure for the people of Bangladesh equality, human dignity and social justice, declare and constitute Bangladesh to be a sovereign People's Republic.[27]

The Proclamation thus established Bangladesh as an independent state, institutionalized the concept of popular sovereignty, and enshrined the values of equality, human dignity and social justice. Furthermore, it provided the legal and moral foundation for Bangladesh's unilateral declaration of independence, as first proclaimed by Sheikh Mujibur Rahman on 26 March 1971.

This act of sovereignty marked the genesis of a new constitutional order, rooted in the democratic aspirations of the people of Bangladesh and reflective of their hard-fought struggle for self-determination and justice.

The Bangladeshi Parliament

In the constitutional framework of Bangladesh, the president serves as the ceremonial head of state, as articulated in Article 48(2) of the constitution of 1972. The president's primary responsibilities include appointing the PM and the chief justice, as specified in Articles 56 and 95. However, substantive executive authority resides with the PM, who is the head of government. Elected by MPs for a term of five years (Articles 48[1] and 50), the president's powers are largely symbolic, except during exceptional circumstances such as the now-abolished caretaker government system.

The caretaker government system, introduced by the 13th Amendment to the constitution in 1996 and repealed by the 15th Amendment in 2011 (Act XIV of 2011), temporarily expanded the president's authority. During this period, the president oversaw the ministry of defence, wielded emergency powers, and could dismiss the chief adviser and members of the caretaker government. These powers, however, reverted to their largely ceremonial nature once a new government and parliament were in place following general elections.

The PM, appointed by the president under Articles 48(3) and 56(3) of the constitution, must be a MP who commands the confidence of the majority in parliament. The PM selects cabinet members, who are then appointed by the president. According to constitutional provisions, at least 90 per cent of cabinet members must be MPs, while up to 10 per cent may be technocrats who meet the eligibility criteria. Additionally, the president has the authority to dissolve parliament at the written request of the PM (Article 57[2]).

The Legislature: Jatiya Sangsad

The parliament of Bangladesh, or the Jatiya Sangsad, is a unicameral legislature comprising 350 seats, of which 300 are filled through direct elections conducted every five years. An additional 50 seats, reserved for women, are distributed among political parties based on their proportional representation in parliament, as mandated by Article 65(3) of the constitution following the 2011 amendment.

The electorate consists of citizens aged eighteen or older who are of sound mind, residents of a constituency and not disqualified by convictions under the Bangladesh Collabourators (Special Tribunal) Order, 1972 (Article 122). Eligibility for parliamentary candidacy requires citizens to be at least twenty-five years old, with disqualifications extending to those who are not of sound mind, undischarged bankrupts or convicted of criminal offences involving moral turpitude with imprisonment of at least two years (Article 66[2]).

General elections are conducted simultaneously across all constituencies, with polling centres established to facilitate voting. After votes are cast, polling officials, in the presence of candidates or their representatives, count and forward the results to the returning officer, typically the deputy commissioner of the district. The compiled results are then communicated to the election commission, which formally declares the outcome through the *Bangladesh Gazette*. Members-elect take their oaths of office before the outgoing speaker.

Parliamentary proceedings operate under the rules of procedure, which govern critical processes, including the summoning, prorogation and dissolution of parliament, the election of the speaker and deputy speaker, legislative functions, financial matters and constitutional amendments. The rules also detail mechanisms for addressing public importance through motions, questions and discussions, ensuring the orderly conduct of legislative business.

This constitutional and procedural framework underscores the balance between ceremonial roles and substantive governance, reflecting the principles of parliamentary democracy as envisioned in the constitution of Bangladesh.

Article 80 of the constitution of Bangladesh delineates the procedural framework for enacting legislation in parliament. It mandates that every legislative proposal must take the form of a bill. Once a bill has been duly passed by parliament, it is presented to the president for assent, marking the final step in the legislative process.

However, Parliament's authority to legislate is constitutionally circumscribed. Under Article 7(2) of the constitution, any law that is inconsistent with the constitution is rendered void to the extent of the inconsistency. This provision enshrines the principle of constitutional supremacy, ensuring that legislative acts conform to the fundamental legal framework established by the constitution. Thus, parliament's legislative power operates within the bounds of constitutional validity, reinforcing the primacy of constitutional norms in governance.

A Brief Electoral History

The electoral history of Bangladesh is emblematic of its turbulent political evolution, marked by aspirations for democratic consolidation, juxtaposed with recurrent controversies and institutional challenges. Since its independence in 1971, the nation has navigated a complex trajectory of electoral practices, shaped by political polarization and shifting governance structures.

The 1973 elections, held under the stewardship of the BAL, were pivotal in establishing the democratic ethos of the nascent state. However, subsequent years saw the military's increasing encroachment into political life, resulting in periods of autocratic rule. The reintroduction of multiparty democracy in 1991, following mass movements against military dominance, heralded a new phase of electoral engagement.

Despite these gains, elections in Bangladesh have frequently been marred by allegations of malpractice, violence and partisan misuse of state machinery. The controversial adoption and eventual repeal of the caretaker government system exemplify the deep-seated mistrust between the nation's primary political blocs: the BAL and the BNP. This mistrust has often translated into electoral boycotts, violent protests and accusations of vote-rigging, undermining public confidence in the democratic process.

The 2014 elections, boycotted by the BNP and overshadowed by widespread violence, were a nadir in this regard, leaving many constituencies uncontested. Similarly, the 2018 general elections were criticized for their lack of transparency, with reports of voter suppression and opposition intimidation. These controversies have cast a long shadow over Bangladesh's electoral integrity, despite significant strides in voter participation and institutional reforms.

Since 1971, Bangladesh has witnessed a tumultuous electoral history, reflective of its broader political journey. Of the twelve general elections conducted since the country's formation, only four have been widely regarded as free and fair. The remaining elections have been overshadowed by violence, protests and allegations of electoral malpractice. Below is a chronological account of these significant electoral milestones:

1973: BAL Wins after Bangladesh's Separation from Pakistan

The first elections were held on 7 March 1973, under the leadership of Sheikh Mujibur Rahman and his ruling BAL, fresh from the country's independence from Pakistan. Despite being the frontrunner, the BAL employed questionable tactics, including the abduction of opposition leaders and ballot-stuffing, resulting in an overwhelming victory, winning 293 out of 300 parliamentary seats.[28] This election marked the consolidation of the BAL's dominance but also set the stage for authoritarian rule. By 1974, Sheikh Mujib had banned opposition parties and media, transforming Bangladesh into a one-party state.

1979–1980s: From Military Dominance to Mass Mobilization

Following Sheikh Mujib's assassination in 1975, Bangladesh experienced prolonged military rule. Elections under Ziaur Rahman in 1978 and 1979 introduced a multiparty system but were marred by allegations of rigging. The BNP, established by Ziaur Rahman, secured a decisive majority, relegating the BAL to the opposition.

After Zia's assassination in 1981, his deputy Abdus Sattar briefly held power, but the military reasserted control in 1982 under General Hussain Muhammad Ershad. The elections conducted during Ershad's rule, including the 1986 and 1988 polls, were widely dismissed as fraudulent, with opposition boycotts and low voter turnout. Popular uprisings in 1990, spearheaded by Sheikh Hasina of the BAL and Khaleda Zia of the BNP, ultimately forced Ershad to resign.[29]

1991: Interim Caretaker Government and the Restoration of Democracy

Bangladesh transitioned to democratic governance with the elections of 27 February 1991, conducted under a neutral caretaker government led by Chief Justice Shahabuddin Ahmed. The BNP defeated the BAL, securing 140 seats to the latter's 88 – a more credible margin than some of the earlier ones. This election was lauded for its fairness, heralding a new democratic era.[30]

1996: Democratic Reversal and Restoration – Bangladesh's Tumultuous Electoral Transition

The February 1996 elections, boycotted by opposition parties, saw only a 21 per cent voter turnout, and the BNP won unopposed.[31] Intense opposition protests forced the BNP government to resign after only twelve days. A new election in June 1996 under a caretaker government brought Sheikh Hasina and the BAL to power, with a voter turnout of 75 per cent. The BAL secured 146 seats, narrowly defeating the BNP.

2001: Power Shifts to the BNP

The 2001 elections, conducted under a caretaker government, were characterized by high voter turnout (75 per cent) and international approval for their fairness.[32] The BNP, led by Khaleda Zia, won 193 seats, while the BAL garnered only 62. However, violence against minority communities, particularly Hindus, marred the post-election period.[33]

2006–08: Political Crisis and Military Intervention

Scheduled elections in 2006 were derailed by a political deadlock between the BNP and the BAL over the caretaker government. Widespread protests and allegations of voter list manipulation led to a national emergency and military intervention. The crisis persisted until 29 December 2008, when elections under a military-backed caretaker government recorded the highest-ever turnout (80 per cent).[34] The BAL, leading a coalition, achieved a landslide victory.

2014: The BAL's Uncontested Victory amid Opposition Boycott

The 2014 elections, conducted without a caretaker government, were boycotted by the BNP. The ruling BAL won 234 seats, benefiting from the absence of a credible opposition. Reports of violence and the house arrest of BNP leader Khaleda Zia characterized the pre-election atmosphere. The polls solidified Sheikh Hasina's control but drew widespread criticism for lacking legitimacy.[35]

2018: Ruling BAL Secures Supermajority

On 30 December 2018, the BAL and its allies achieved an overwhelming majority, winning over 90 per cent of parliamentary seats. However, accusations of electoral fraud, voter suppression and violence against opposition activists marred the election. The BNP, weakened by internal challenges and the imprisonment of its leader Khaleda Zia on corruption charges, won only seven seats.[36]

2024: the BNP Boycotts Once Again

The BNP opted to boycott the 2024 elections, reiterating its demand for a caretaker government. The BAL, under Sheikh Hasina, secured another term, reinforcing its position as Bangladesh's longest-serving administration. However, amid concerns about the integrity of the electoral process, and widespread student protests and demonstrations, Sheikh Hasina fled the country in August 2024.

End of the Sheikh Hasina Era

Sheikh Hasina's flight out of Dhaka in the wake of mounting unrest marked the culmination of months of escalating dissatisfaction with her administration. Following the general elections in January 2024, which were widely criticized (particularly by Western observers) as deeply flawed, the government's actions increasingly alienated both the public and political opponents.[37] Hasina's administration, already accused of authoritarianism, faced a decisive moment in June when the Bangladesh High Court reinstated a controversial policy: a 30 per cent quota in government jobs for the descendants of veterans of the 1971 war of independence. This policy, enacted in response to high graduate unemployment and intense competition for limited government positions, sparked widespread protests from students. The demonstrators, many of them students, condemned the quota as politically motivated, alleging that it disproportionately benefitted supporters of Hasina's BAL party.[38]

Despite a late and partial concession by the Supreme Court in July reducing the quota to 5 per cent, the violence between police and protesters intensified. The protests were further inflamed by Hasina's refusal to release detained student leaders and her inflammatory rhetoric, which included referring to the protesters as 'Razakars' – a derogatory term associated with collabourators who sided with Pakistan during the 1971 independence war. The situation took a more dramatic turn as the protesters, holding Hasina responsible for the deaths of over 600 individuals in the violent clashes, began calling for her resignation.

In response, the government implemented harsh measures to suppress dissent, including the imposition of a curfew, the repeated shutdown of the country's Internet and the arrest of over 11,000 protesters.[39] The violence and unrest reached a boiling point in early August, with the army refusing to carry out Hasina's orders to open fire on civilians to enforce the curfew. As a large group of protesters advanced on her residence on 5 August 2024, Sheikh Hasina resigned and fled to India.

This dramatic departure marked the end of an era of increasingly authoritarian rule, shaped by political control, electoral manipulation and a marked shift towards repressive governance. Sheikh Hasina's resignation, although triggered by the protests, reflected broader issues of democratic backsliding in Bangladesh.

The sudden collapse of Sheikh Hasina's government sent shockwaves both within the country and across the geopolitical landscape. What began as a student-led protest against governmental practices escalated into widespread unrest. The failure of Hasina's regime to quell the growing dissent, particularly through the military's refusal to suppress protests, exposed deep cracks within the state's power structure. An interim government was formed under the guidance of Nobel laureate Muhammad Yunus. As the international community watches closely, the question of Bangladesh's political future remains fraught.

Countries emerging from autocratic rule often face a stark crossroads: whether to descend into civil conflict or to establish a new, broadly accepted political order. Bangladesh's political landscape, shaped by Hasina's competitive authoritarianism where electoral processes were overshadowed by systematic advantages for the ruling party, now teeters on the brink of what could either be a new beginning or further fragmentation. The interim government faces the daunting task of navigating this transitional period, with substantial reforms planned for key areas such as electoral processes, police function and the national constitution.

While Bangladesh's structural foundation may offer some stability compared to other nations in similar transitions, challenges remain considerable. Despite the lack of severe ethnolinguistic divisions, which could have further polarized the state, violence in certain tribal areas and against minorities signals emerging fault lines. The collapse of state functioning has already exposed vulnerabilities, including a potential surge in vigilantism and mob violence, which could destabilize both the political and economic environments. These developments, compounded by the strained relationship between Islam and Bangladeshi nationalism, present immediate risks to a peaceful and prosperous future.

The interim government, working alongside the military, must address these dangers with urgency, while demonstrating measurable progress on both political reforms and economic revitalization. Bangladesh's economic trajectory had already faltered under Hasina's rule, exacerbated by the impact of the global pandemic. As instability worsened in the summer of 2024, foreign investment grew increasingly cautious. The new government must strike a delicate balance, showcasing tangible improvements that reinforce its legitimacy, while also preparing for a return to democratic elections. Any sense of stagnation, particularly around the timing and nature of these elections, could reignite public dissatisfaction, threatening to derail the fragile transition. Disagreement over electoral timelines and the political future of Hasina's now-banned BAL, along with proper accountability for past abuses, are but a few of the contentious issues awaiting resolution.

Externally, Bangladesh's diplomatic relations are under intense scrutiny. For India, the country's proximity alongside its economic and strategic importance, ensures that any instability has far-reaching implications. India, which had long supported Hasina's regime, now faces the delicate task of recalibrating its relationship with Dhaka – especially considering its own concerns over anti-Hindu violence and the potential rise of Islamism in Bangladesh.[40] Furthermore, regional instability, particularly the worsening civil war in Myanmar, adds another layer of complexity to Bangladesh's foreign policy considerations, with the refugee crisis and the growing power of armed ethnic groups in Myanmar threatening to spill over into its territory.

In terms of geopolitics, Bangladesh's positioning between India, China and the West will be pivotal in determining its future.[41] While the US remains focused on promoting a democratic trajectory and limiting Chinese influence in the region, India's strategic interests diverge, reflecting differing assessments of the political landscape. Bangladesh's own desires for balancing ties with these major powers will shape its diplomatic course. China has indeed become a growing focus of Bangladesh's foreign policy. Under interim leader Muhammad Yunus, Dhaka has actively courted Beijing – in March 2025 Yunus struck deals worth over $2 billion for ports and industrial zones, explicitly to reduce dependence on Indian trade.Washington and New Delhi view this as a strategic shift. Reuters reported that during a March visit, President Xi Jinping offered lower interest rates on Chinese loans and affirmed his country's plans to relocate Chinese manufacturers to Bangladesh, signalling a clear pivot to Beijing.[42] This increasing alignment with China – evident in infrastructure investment, port access and financial support – suggests that Bangladesh is repositioning itself amid regional power competition in the Bay of Bengal.

Ultimately, while Bangladesh's current situation offers an opening for renewal, it also carries significant risks. The country's leadership must demonstrate the capability to forge a stable, democratic system amid the ongoing challenges of political fragmentation, external pressures and economic recovery. The path ahead will require not only adept governance but also the sustained trust of a population disillusioned by years of authoritarianism. The international community must remain vigilant, mindful that the outcomes of this critical juncture will resonate far beyond the borders of Bangladesh itself.

Although the interim government under Muhammad Yunus initially pledged fresh elections within ninety days to restore democratic order, he has since committed to holding the vote in April 2026—a date confirmed in early June 2025. Officials cite the fragile security climate, institutional fragility, and unfinished electoral reforms as key hurdles. Critics warn that delaying beyond April 2026 risks entrenching the very cycles of authoritarian overreach the protests aimed to dismantle.[43] As Bangladesh teeters between recovery and regression, the credibility of its democratic transition hinges on whether the leadership adheres to its firm electoral timeline—or succumbs to indefinite postponement.[44]

Key events at a glance

- **1947** – Partition of India: East Bengal becomes part of Pakistan as East Pakistan, separated from West Pakistan by 1,600 km
- **1948** – Bengali Language Movement begins: Pakistan's government declares Urdu as sole national language, sparking protests in East Pakistan
- **21 February 1952** – Language Martyrs' Day (Ekushey February): Police fire on protesters demanding Bengali as a state language; foundational to Bengali nationalism
- **1954** – United Front victory in East Pakistan provincial elections; rise of regional political assertion
- **1958** – Military rule imposed under Ayub Khan; centralized control alienates East Pakistan

- **1966** – Six-Point Movement led by Sheikh Mujibur Rahman demands greater autonomy for East Pakistan
- **1970** – Cyclone Bhola devastates East Pakistan; inadequate response from West Pakistan inflames resentment
- **1970** – General elections: Mujib's BAL wins majority; West Pakistan refuses to transfer power
- **25 March 1971** – Operation Searchlight commences: brutal military crackdown in Dhaka against Bengali autonomy movement
- **26 March 1971** – Proclamation of Independence of Bangladesh; start of the Bangladesh Liberation War
- **December 1971** – Victory in the Liberation War with Indian military support; Bangladesh becomes an independent country
- **1972** – First constitution adopted; establishes Bangladesh as a secular, socialist republic
- **1975** – Assassination of Sheikh Mujibur Rahman and most of his family in a military coup; political chaos ensues
- **1975–77** – Series of coups and countercoups; General Ziaur Rahman consolidates power
- **1978** – The BNP founded by Ziaur; stresses Islamic identity
- **1981** – Ziaur Rahman assassinated during an attempted coup
- **1982** – Military coup by General Ershad; martial law imposed
- **1990** – Fall of Ershad after mass pro-democracy protests; return to parliamentary democracy
- **1991** – General elections: the BNP under Khaleda Zia comes to power; parliamentary system reinstated
- **1996** – The BAL returns to power under Sheikh Hasina after controversial elections and political agitation
- **2001** – The BNP wins elections; heightened political violence and polarization
- **2007** – Caretaker government backed by military takes control amid political chaos; massive anti-corruption drive
- **2008** – Return to elected government, the BAL wins landslide victory
- **2010** – International Crimes Tribunal begins trials for 1971 war crimes; seen as justice by some and politically motivated by others
- **2013** – Shahbagh Movement: mass protests demanding capital punishment for war criminals

- **2014** – Controversial elections boycotted by the BNP; the BAL retains power amid legitimacy questions
- **2016** – Rise of Islamist militancy; Holey Artisan Bakery attack shocks the nation
- **2018** – General Elections: the BAL wins overwhelmingly; accusations of voter suppression
- **2021** – Fiftieth anniversary of Bangladesh's independence; massive celebrations amid political tensions
- **2024** – Sheikh Hasina deposed

5

Afghanistan: A Country in Perpetual Turmoil

With a population of about 36 million, and an area of 652,867 sq. km, Afghanistan is a completely landlocked nation that shares its borders with China, Iran, Pakistan, Tajikistan, Turkmenistan and Uzbekistan.[1] The country's topography is predominantly arid and characterized by rugged mountainous terrain. The Hindu Kush mountain range, extending from the north-east to the south-west, serves as a natural divide between the northern provinces and the rest of the country. After the Taliban came to power in August 2021, the country is governed as an Islamic republic, headed by a supreme leader – termed 'Amir al-Mu'minin', meaning 'Commander of the Faithful' – who serves as both chief of state and the ultimate head of government, and whose word on all matters is final.[2]

Afghanistan occupies a strategically significant position along historic trade routes linking southern and eastern Asia with Europe and the Middle East. This geographic centrality has rendered the country a coveted prize for empire builders across millennia, with successive armies attempting to conquer and control its rugged terrain. The remnants of their endeavours are visible in monumental ruins scattered across the landscape.

Kabul, the nation's capital and largest city, once epitomized serenity and cultural flourishing during the reign of Emperor Babur (1504–26), the founder of the Mughal dynasty.[3] Renowned for its gardens and mosques, Kabul also served as a vital entrepôt along the Silk Road. However, the prolonged and violent Afghan Wars – First Anglo-Afghan

War: 1839–1842, Second Anglo-Afghan War: 1878–1880, Third Anglo-Afghan War: 1919 – left the city and much of the country in devastation, with its economy shattered and its population dispersed. By the early twenty-first century, an entire generation of Afghans had been brought up in an environment defined solely by war.[4]

The demographic composition of Afghanistan remains imprecise due to the absence of a comprehensive national census since a partial enumeration in 1979. Decades of conflict and widespread displacement have further complicated efforts to determine accurate population figures of the various ethnicities and tribes that constitute it. Contemporary estimates suggest that Pashtuns constitute approximately 42 per cent of Afghanistan's population (including major sub-tribes such as Durrani and Ghilzai). Tajiks account for about 27 per cent, while Hazaras and Uzbeks each make up roughly 9 per cent. Other groups—including Aimak (~4 per cent), Turkmen (~3 per cent), Baloch (~2 per cent), and various smaller ethnicities such as Pashai, Nuristani, Gujjar, Brahui, Qizilbash, Pamiri and Kyrgyz—together constitute the remaining ~13 per cent.[5]

Afghanistan is overwhelmingly Muslim, with approximately four-fifths of the population adhering to Sunni Islam, specifically the Hanafi school. Taliban, the fundamentalist group now ruling the nation, is an extremist Sunni organization and pro-Pashtun in its orientation. The remaining population, including groups such as the Hazara and Kizilbash, follows various branches of Shi'i Islam, primarily Twelver (*Ithna ashariyya*) and Ismaili.[6] Historically, Sufism has exerted significant influence on Afghan religious life, although fewer than one-tenth of the population now belong to a Sufi order. The Nuristani people, descendants of the non-Muslim population forcibly converted to Islam in 1895, inhabit a region renamed from Kafiristan ('Land of the Infidels') to Nuristan ('Land of Light'). Additionally, Afghanistan is home to small communities of Hindus and Sikhs, numbering a few thousand.[7]

The Great Game

The emergence of Afghanistan as a state with defined territorial boundaries can be traced to the nineteenth-century geopolitical rivalry between the British and Russian empires, which Rudyard Kipling first termed the 'Great Game'.[8] Both powers sought to control the strategic trade routes and military advantages offered by Afghanistan's central location in Asia.

In the early nineteenth century, Russia's expansion into Central Asia, marked by its conquest of Bokhara and Tashkent, alarmed the British, who feared that continued Russian advances might threaten their control over India.[9] This apprehension led to the First Anglo–Afghan War (1839–42), during which the British deposed the Afghan ruler, Dost Mohammad Khan Barakzai, after he sought closer ties with Russia. They replaced him with Shah Shuja Durrani, a former *amir* known for his brutality and unpopularity but who was loyal to British interests.[10] However, British efforts to consolidate their influence unravelled when austerity measures led to the reduction of payments to southern Pashtun tribes, provoking a large-scale coordinated rebellion.[11]

The rebellion culminated in one of the most devastating defeats in British military history. A retreating column of 4,500 British troops and 12,000 civilians from Kabul was annihilated in the severe winter of January 1842. Only one individual, Dr William Brydon, survived to reach Jalalabad. Shah Shuja was also assassinated during the uprising. In retaliation, British forces razed much of Kabul before reinstating Dost Mohammad as *amir*.[12]

Decades later, the Second Anglo–Afghan War (1878–80) was precipitated by renewed fears of Russian influence under Amir Sher Ali Khan, Dost's successor.[13] The British launched an invasion with a 35,000-strong force. Sher Ali died of natural causes during the campaign, and his son, Mohammad Yaqub Khan, was compelled to sign the Treaty of Gandamak in 1879. This agreement ceded significant territory to the British and placed Afghan foreign affairs under their control, formally establishing Afghanistan as a state within defined borders.[14]

Following another insurrection, marked by a British defeat at the Battle of Maiwand, Afghanistan became a British client state. Amir Abdur Rahman Khan, known as the 'Iron Amir', was installed as ruler with British military and financial support. His reign was characterized by authoritarian rule, widespread executions, forced conversions to Islam and the relocation of entire tribes to quell opposition.

In 1893, Sir Mortimer Durand, the British foreign minister for India, imposed the Durand Line as the border between British India and Afghanistan. This boundary, designed to create a buffer state between British India and the Russian Empire, divided the Pashtun homeland, splitting it between south-eastern Afghanistan and the NWFP (now part of Pakistan). Despite its strategic intent, the line ignored demographic realities and sowed the seeds of enduring tension in the region.

In 1919, Amanullah Khan ascended the throne, bringing a vision of nationalist and modernist reform influenced by the broader currents of Middle Eastern progressivism. Guided by his father-in-law and foreign minister, Mahmud Tarzi, a proponent of progressive Islam, Amanullah sought to end Afghanistan's subjugation to British influence.[15] The Third Anglo–Afghan War (6 May to 8 August 1919) resulted in Afghan independence, marking the end of British control.

Amanullah embarked on an ambitious reform agenda, including infrastructure development, the establishment of a mass education system, the creation of a postal network and the promotion of women's rights enshrined in Afghanistan's first constitution, which was ratified in 1923. However, his efforts to modernize the country, such as mandating Western attire and the trimming of beards for tribal leaders, provoked fierce resistance from conservative factions. British support for these opposition forces further destabilized his rule, culminating in his forced abdication and exile in 1929.[16]

Afghanistan entered a prolonged period of stagnation under the successive reigns of three generations of the Durrani dynasty, marking a half-century of subdued governance and limited progress.[17]

1979–96: From Soviet Occupation to Civil War and State Collapse

Before the outbreak of civil war in 1978, Afghanistan functioned as a monarchy under Mohammad Zahir Shah, who ascended to power in 1933. Following World War II, both the US and the Soviet Union sought influence in Afghanistan through economic aid. However, when the US forged military ties with Pakistan in 1954, Afghanistan increasingly aligned with the Soviet Union.[18]

In 1964, Zahir Shah convened a Loya Jirga to debate a constitution aimed at introducing a more representative government. Nevertheless,

Zahir Shah retained power, allowing political parties to form but not contest elections. In 1973, his cousin, Daoud Khan, overthrew him in a coup, forcing the king into exile. Daoud initially allied with the Parcham faction of the Marxist–Leninist People's Democratic Party of Afghanistan (PDPA), which had split into two factions in 1967: Parcham, supported by urban, educated Pashtuns; and Khalq, backed by rural Pashtuns.[19]

After gaining power, Daoud marginalized the Parchamis and distanced Afghanistan from the Soviet Union. The PDPA factions reunited in 1977 and launched a coup in 1978, killing Daoud and seizing control. Under Khalq leadership, the PDPA implemented radical land reforms and repressive measures, leading to mass arrests, executions and widespread rural unrest. Discontent escalated into uprisings, threatening Afghanistan's stability and prompting the Soviet Union to intervene militarily on 24 December 1979.[20]

Soviet forces ousted Khalq President Hafizullah Amin and replaced him with Babrak Karmal, a Parchami. The Soviet occupation, involving 115,000 troops, sought to suppress resistance through mass arrests, aerial bombardments and executions.[21] Approximately 1 million Afghans were killed during this period, and 5 million fled as refugees. These brutal measures only strengthened the resistance, led by Islamist mujahideen factions based in Pakistan and Iran.

The US, Saudi Arabia and Pakistan funnelled substantial support to the mujahideen, perceiving the conflict as a Cold War battleground.[22] Pakistan leveraged this support to back factions aligned with its strategic interests, including Gulbuddin Hekmatyar's Hizb-i Islami and Abdul Rasul Sayyaf's Ittihad-i Islami. Thousands of foreign Muslim radicals, including Osama bin Laden, joined the resistance, with many establishing training facilities in Afghanistan.[23] The Soviet intervention deepened Afghanistan's devastation, exacerbating internal divisions and solidifying the mujahideen's role in the country's protracted conflict. By the time the Soviet forces withdrew in 1989, Afghanistan had become a fractured state, its society and economy irreparably shattered.

The 1988 Geneva Accords mandated the withdrawal of Soviet forces by February 1989, leaving the communist government in Kabul to survive on Soviet aid until its collapse in 1992.[24] The UN's efforts to establish a political transition failed, as international engagement waned. By 1992, the Northern Alliance, led by leaders Ahmad Shah Massoud and Abdul Rashid Dostum, and Abdul Ali Mazari who led the Hizb-i Wahdat party, toppled the government. Then President Mohammad Najibullah Ahmadzai sought refuge in a UN compound.

A coalition government formed, excluding Gulbuddin's Hizb-i Islami, which launched indiscriminate rocket attacks on Kabul. In June 1992, Burhanuddin Rabbani became president, but factional rivalries persisted. Fighting between Hizb-i Wahdat and Ittihad-i Islami, alongside Gulbuddin's bombardments, caused mass civilian casualties. Rabbani consolidated power but faced opposition.[25]

In 1994, Hekmatyar allied with Dostum to oust Rabbani, igniting full-scale civil war. By 1995, Kabul was in ruins, with over 25,000 civilians killed in relentless rocket and artillery attacks, marking Afghanistan's descent into chaos.[26]

1996–2001: Taliban's First Conquest

During this period, Afghanistan fragmented under factional control, as mujahideen commanders became local warlords. Southern Afghanistan experienced disorder, while the north and west were governed more stably by figures like Ismail Khan and Dostum, and the Hizb-i Wahdat party. Amid this chaos, the Taliban emerged, coalescing around Mullah Mohammad Omar, a former *mujahid* from Kandahar. Comprising disillusioned mujahideen, madrasa students and former Khalqi members, the Taliban sought to restore stability and implement their interpretation of Islamic law. By 1994, Pakistan supported the movement, seeing it as a means to secure trade routes and establish influence in Kabul.[27]

The Taliban's military successes led to the capture of Herat in 1995 and Kabul in 1996, forcing Massoud to retreat north. Mullah Omar declared Afghanistan an Islamic emirate and enforced strict Islamic law, particularly curtailing women's rights and imposing severe penalties for any breaches.[28] By 1998, the Taliban extended control to the north, including in Mazar-i-Sharif, where they massacred thousands, particularly Hazaras. Former Northern Alliance factions reorganized as the United Islamic Front for Salvation of Afghanistan (UIFSA), with leaders like Dostum, Rabbani and Ismail Khan resisting Taliban expansion.[29]

Osama bin Laden returned to Afghanistan in 1996, forming a close alliance with the Taliban, who provided sanctuary for his operations. After the 1998 US embassy bombings in Kenya and Tanzania, US airstrikes targeted bin Laden's camps, while the UN imposed sanctions on the Taliban for harbouring him. These measures included asset freezes, travel bans and an arms embargo.[30]

Between 2000 and 2001, the Taliban consolidated control in the north-east, displacing thousands amid drought and conflict. In reprisal for resistance, they conducted massacres and destroyed villages, particularly in Hazara regions like Bamian and Yakaolang. Guerrilla resistance persisted under leaders like Massoud, Dostum and Ismail Khan.[31]

On 9 September 2001, suicide bombers, allegedly linked to bin Laden, assassinated Massoud, in an apparent prelude to the 11 September attacks on the US.[32] The assassination deprived the UIFSA of its most effective leader, foreshadowing the international intervention to come.

Post-2001

In June 2002, Afghanistan's interim government was established, dominated by warlords of the Northern Alliance who secured key cabinet posts, including defence, interior, intelligence and foreign affairs. The cabinet composition reflected the country's ethnic demographics: Pashtuns held eleven seats, Tajiks held eight, Hazaras held five and Uzbeks held three. However, the government remained weak compared to the warlords, and reconstruction efforts faltered due to a severe budget deficit. Foreign aid was insufficient, with Afghanistan receiving only $52 per capita by 2003, far below the $167 per capita needed to stabilize the country, as estimated by the RAND Corporation.[33]

Economic hardship persisted as unemployment and poverty became endemic. Migration to cities surged, with Kabul's population ballooning from 400,000 in the 1970s to 3.5 million by 2003.[34] Despite $1.9 billion in US aid, tangible improvements were minimal, as contracts were often awarded to inefficient US firms.[35] Provincial reconstruction teams struggled against interference from local warlords, and corruption plagued both the government and NGOs. Education reform saw limited success; while 45 per cent of girls in Kabul accessed education, rural areas showed little progress.[36]

In August 2003, the North Atlantic Treaty Organization (NATO) extended the International Security Assistance Force (ISAF) mission nationwide, transitioning from Kabul-focused operations. Despite contributions from forty countries, security worsened, particularly in Helmand and Zabul provinces, where the Taliban launched major offensives. By late 2003, the Taliban controlled 80 per cent of Zabul, forcing humanitarian organizations to suspend operations in southern regions.[37]

Efforts to rebuild Afghanistan's security forces faced significant obstacles. The then defence minister, Marshal Mohammad Qasim Fahim, sought funding for a 200,000-strong army but received support for just 37,000 soldiers. Illiteracy and high desertion rates weakened the army, while police reform similarly suffered from inadequate training and resources.[38]

In the 2004 elections, 10.3 million voters registered, 40 per cent of them women. Hamid Karzai won the presidency with 55 per cent of the vote.[39] However, corruption deepened, enriching elites while development indicators worsened. By 2007, life expectancy was forty-three years, literacy 28 per cent and over a quarter of children died before age five.[40]

Meanwhile, Afghanistan became a narco-state, producing 93 per cent of the world's opium by 2007. Efforts to curb cultivation failed, with farmers reliant on poppy production for survival, further fuelling the insurgency.[41]

The US Withdrawal

When the US-led coalition concluded its combat mission in 2014, Afghanistan's security was entrusted to the Afghan National Defense and Security Forces (ANDSF). Despite substantial international training and funding, the ANDSF struggled to maintain control against persistent Taliban offensives, particularly in rural areas, and endured heavy casualties. The war remained a protracted stalemate for six years, even as US strategy shifted in 2017 to target Taliban revenue sources via airstrikes on drug labs and opium fields.[42] The Taliban seized provincial capitals such as Farah in May 2018 and Ghazni in August 2018, exposing the fragility of government defences.[43]

In February 2020, the US and the Taliban signed the Doha Agreement, which set a timeline for US troop withdrawal in exchange for Taliban commitments to prevent terrorist activities and engage in intra-Afghan negotiations.[44] However, no ceasefire was established and violence resumed swiftly. Negotiations between the Afghan government and the Taliban made little progress, as the Taliban expanded territorial control. Civilian casualties remained staggeringly high, with over 100,000 documented between 2009 and 2020.[45]

In April 2021, then US President Joe Biden announced that US forces would leave by September 2021. As the withdrawal accelerated, the Taliban launched a rapid offensive, capturing provincial capitals and, by mid-August, Kabul itself. The Afghan government collapsed, President Ashraf Ghani fled and the Taliban declared control over the country. The speed of the Taliban's takeover took US officials and allies by surprise. Amid chaotic evacuations, ISIS-K (Islamic State of Iraq and Syria-Khorasan, affiliate of the Islamic State movement operating in Afghanistan) carried out a deadly attack at Kabul airport, killing 169 Afghans and thirteen US troops.[46]

Post the US withdrawal, Afghanistan faces a humanitarian crisis compounded by economic collapse, food insecurity and international isolation. The Taliban's repressive policies have erased progress in women's rights and freedom of expression. Sanctions and halted aid have crippled the economy, while Afghanistan remains unrecognized by any government. Efforts to address the crisis are complicated by the reluctance to legitimize the Taliban regime.

In May 2022, the special inspector general for Afghanistan reconstruction assessed that the ANDSF's collapse was primarily due to the US withdrawal under the Doha Agreement and systemic Afghan dependency on foreign support. In August 2022, then President Biden announced the killing of al-Qaeda leader Ayman al-Zawahiri, underscoring ongoing security concerns under Taliban rule.

Uncertain Future

In November 2022, the Taliban announced a series of draconian measures, including bans on women accessing parks and gyms, and the reintroduction of public flogging and executions.[47] By December 2022, the restrictions on women's rights escalated, with women barred from universities and tutoring centres, despite having been permitted to take entrance exams earlier in the year. These actions drew widespread international condemnation, including criticism from Qatar and China, both considered among the Taliban's closest partners. They urged the regime in May 2023 to moderate its stance.[48] Nonetheless, the Taliban has persisted with its policies, which the UN has characterized as 'gender apartheid'.[49] Public floggings have become routine, and in June 2023 the Taliban conducted its second public execution since regaining power.[50]

The Taliban has also imposed significant constraints on humanitarian efforts. Aid agencies have faced harassment and women have been banned from working for the UN.[51] These conditions, coupled with donor frustration over Taliban policies, have forced the UN to reduce its funding request for Afghanistan by $1 billion. The World Food Programme has warned that this funding shortfall could result in 9 million additional Afghans losing access to food aid.[52] Further compounding the crisis, the Taliban's crackdown on opium production, with cultivation by 80 per cent, has deprived many Afghan communities of critical income needed to secure necessities.[53] Water shortages have exacerbated tensions with Iran, culminating in border skirmishes over access to the Helmand River.[54]

Meanwhile, the security situation remains precarious. A 2023 Pentagon assessment indicated that the Islamic State (ISIS-K) has re-established Afghanistan as a base for planning and coordinating global attacks. Within Afghanistan, ISIS-K has intensified its operations, including high-profile attacks such as the assassination of a deputy governor, Nisar Ahmad Ahmadi, and the bombing of a mosque. Despite Taliban efforts to counter ISIS-K, including the elimination of a senior ISIS-K leader responsible for the 2021 Kabul airport bombing in April 2023, the group continues to pose a significant threat. In May 2023, the Taliban agreed to collabourate with Pakistan to enhance border security, as militants continued to exploit the porous frontier between the two nations.

Although the Taliban and Pakistan agreed in May 2023 to strengthen border security and curb militant movement across the porous frontier, their relationship has since deteriorated considerably. Pakistan has grown increasingly vocal in accusing the Taliban of sheltering members of the Tehreek-e-Taliban Pakistan (TTP), who have allegedly been orchestrating attacks from Afghan soil. In response to the surge in cross-border violence, Pakistan has carried out airstrikes within Afghan territory and imposed stringent measures, including the mass expulsion of Afghan nationals residing within its borders. These developments mark a stark shift from the initial cooperation to a climate of deepening mistrust and open hostility between the two governments.

Afghanistan's rankings in the Economist Intelligence Unit's (EIU) Democracy Index have declined to the rock bottom since 2020. In 2020, Afghanistan was ranked 139th.[55] By 2023, it had fallen to the 167th place, marking a substantial drop over three years.[55] This decline reflects the country's ongoing political instability and challenges in governance.

Islam, Women and the Taliban: Between Doctrine and Dispossession

The return of the Taliban to power in Afghanistan in August 2021 triggered deep unease across the region and the world – not only because of the political uncertainty it introduced, but because of what it foretold for the status of women under their rule. For many Afghans, the memory of the Taliban's earlier regime from 1996 to 2001 remained vivid and traumatic. During those years, the public visibility of women was erased; girls were banned from schools, women were prohibited from working and a brutal system of gender apartheid was enforced, often with deadly violence. The visual iconography of that era – the blue burqa, the locked school gates and the women publicly beaten for transgressing dress codes – soon resurfaced in public memory and media reportage alike. These were not simply symbols of cultural conservatism, but the visible effects of a regime that denied women not just rights but personhood.

Initially, the Taliban sought to distance themselves from their earlier legacy by making conciliatory statements. At a press conference in Kabul, their spokesperson Zabihullah Mujahid claimed: 'We are going to allow women to work and study. We have got frameworks, of course. Women are going to be very active in the society but within the framework of Islam.' He added, 'There will be no discrimination against women [...] They are going to work shoulder to shoulder with us.'[56] These assurances, delivered to an anxious international community, briefly gave cause for cautious hope.

Yet, with the benefit of hindsight, such statements must be read not as commitments but as rhetorical cover – carefully crafted to deflect criticism rather than to usher reform. However, as was discussed above, what followed in the months and years ahead bore grim resemblance to the past: girls were once again barred from secondary and higher education, women were excluded from most forms of employment and strict gender segregation was reimposed. The framework invoked turned out to be not Islam in any interpretive diversity, but the Taliban's own absolutist and patriarchal rendering of it.

This raises a critical and recurring question: what, precisely, is meant by the 'framework of Islam'? And is the Taliban's version of it borne out by the normative sources of Islamic law? Since the Taliban and many other Islamist regimes across the world claim to act in accordance with Shariah, it becomes imperative to examine what that actually entails. In Arabic, shariah means the path or way, and is typically understood to refer to Islamic law. Its primary sources are the Qur'an and the Sunnah (the habitual practices of the Prophet Muhammad), supplemented by ahadees (sayings of the Prophet). Beyond these foundational texts, classical Islamic jurisprudence also includes interpretive methods like *ijma* (consensus of scholars) and *qiyas* (analogical reasoning). Importantly, Shariah has never been a monolithic or static body of law. Across Islamic history, it has evolved through diverse schools of thought, regionally contextualized interpretations and plural traditions of reasoning.[57]

Yet what dominates public discourse – especially in the West and in conflict-ridden Muslim-majority countries – is a version of Islam that portrays women as inherently subordinate and cloistered. This perception, while often reinforced by political practices on the ground, stands in stark contrast to many of Islam's textual foundations. Fourteen centuries ago, Islam granted women several rights that were revolutionary for the time: to own property, inherit wealth, participate in trade and consent to marriage. In fact, the religion legally codified protections for women long before such entitlements were secured by many other legal traditions, including European civil law systems.

The Qur'an is replete with verses affirming gender parity, 'And for women are rights over men similar to those of men over women.'[58] Elsewhere, the Qur'an notes, 'They (your wives) are your garment, and you are a garment for them'[59], emphasizing mutual protection and intimacy. Another passage declares, 'The believers, both men and women, are guardians of one another.'[60] These verses do not portray women as accessories to the household or passive recipients of charity, but as active moral and civic equals.

The Ahadees and sayings of the Prophet Muhammad further reinforce these principles. In one narration, he is quoted as saying, 'Verily, women are the twin halves of men.'[61] In another:' The believers who show the most perfect Faith are those who have the best behaviour, and the best of you are those who are the best to their wives.'[62] His final sermon famously includes the exhortation: 'Observe your duty to Allah in respect to the women, and treat them well.'[63] Respect for women, in this framing, is not a cultural courtesy but a religious obligation.

Even on the question of motherhood and familial reverence, the Prophet's words were unequivocal. A well-known narration recounts a man asking him: 'Who deserves my companionship most? The Prophet replied, 'Your mother.' He repeated the answer three times before saying, 'Then your father.'[64] Islam's view of gender relations, in its foundational texts, is thus premised on ethical parity, mutual responsibility and spiritual equality.

Nor is this limited to private or familial realms. In terms of economic autonomy, Islamic jurisprudence grants women the right to retain their maiden names, control their wealth independently, and enter into contracts and businesses without requiring male permission. Marriage requires a woman's consent; forced marriages are invalid. In certain interpretations, women can demand the right to initiate divorce and to restrict polygyny in the marriage contract itself. Abdel Rahim Omran, a noted scholar of Islamic law at Al-Azhar University, summarized this position by affirming that Islam 'championed equality for women in all matters – religious, social, economic and familial.'[65]

Most telling, perhaps, is the emphasis on education. The Prophet is recorded to have said: 'Acquisition of knowledge is binding on all Muslims, male and female. The person who goes forth in search of knowledge is striving in the way of Allah.'[66] That injunction alone ought to settle the question of girls' right to education. To deny women this right in the name of Islam is not merely a misreading, it is a betrayal of the religion's foundational ethos.

Indeed, much of what is done to women in the name of Islam today – whether by the Taliban, extremist sects or patriarchal regimes – is not a reflection of Islam, but of its distortion. This is not a binary between tradition and modernity, but between doctrine and its political manipulation. The tragedy of the Afghan case, like that of many others in the region, is that Islam has often become a rhetoric of control rather than a theology of justice.

It is often said, then, that the real contest today is not between Islam and the West, or Islam and modernity, but between Islam and the Muslims themselves.

Conclusion

The unfolding narrative of Afghanistan since the US withdrawal in 2021 has been marked by profound humanitarian and political challenges. As discussed, the Taliban's swift reclamation of power, following the abrupt collapse of the Afghan government and its security forces, not only surprised the international community but also heralded a drastic reversal of the gains made in governance, human rights and development over the past two decades. The Taliban's return to power has been accompanied by widespread violence, the re-imposition of draconian laws and the systematic erosion of women's rights which have been condemned internationally as a form of gender apartheid. Despite diplomatic pressure from regional actors such as Qatar and China, the Taliban's adherence to its rigid policies has remained largely unyielding, exacerbating the suffering of the Afghan populace.

The humanitarian crisis in Afghanistan has escalated to unprecedented levels, with millions facing food insecurity, displacement and limited access to basic services. The UN has called Afghanistan the largest humanitarian crisis in the world, with widespread famine, disease and a lack of international aid due to the Taliban's restrictive policies. The withdrawal of foreign aid and international investment, compounded by the Taliban's crackdown on dissent and civil society, has left the country's economy in ruins, with inflation and scarcity of goods further deepening the crisis.[67] Meanwhile, the security situation remains unstable, with the resurgence of ISIS-K and ongoing clashes between the Taliban and insurgent groups. Afghanistan has once again become a fertile ground for extremist activities, with global implications for terrorism and regional stability.

The future of Afghanistan remains uncertain. While the Taliban has claimed responsibility for eliminating certain extremist factions, the persistence of violence and instability suggests a fragile and volatile situation. The international community's response, including sanctions and diplomatic isolation, continues to shape Afghanistan's trajectory, but its ability to influence the Taliban's policies remains limited. As Afghanistan grapples with these challenges, the plight of its people – particularly women and children – remains a central concern, with the international community tasked with navigating the complexities of humanitarian aid, governance and the prospect of long-term peace.

Prior to the US withdrawal in 2021, the country had made fragile attempts at electoral democracy, though these efforts were often marred by widespread fraud, low voter turnout and insurgent threats. The 2009 presidential election, for instance, saw nearly 1.5 million votes invalidated due to irregularities, while both the 2014 and 2019 elections were plagued by technical failures and post-election deadlock, eroding public trust in democratic institutions.

Following the Taliban's return to power, these tenuous democratic mechanisms were swiftly dismantled. The Independent Election Commission was formally dissolved, and no elections have been scheduled since.

Key events at a glance

- **1893** – Durand Line Agreement with British India demarcates border (still disputed by Pakistan)
- **1901–19** – Habibullah Khan attempts moderate reforms; maintains neutrality in World War I.
- **1919** – Third Anglo–Afghan War: King Amanullah Khan declares independence; Treaty of Rawalpindi ends British suzerainty; Afghanistan gains full sovereignty
- **1923** – First constitution promulgated under Amanullah; education and legal reforms introduced
- **1929** – Amanullah overthrown by conservative revolt; brief rule by Habibullah Kalakani ('Bacha-e-Saqao')
- **1929–33** – Mohammad Nadir Shah restores monarchy; assassinated in 1933
- **1933–73** – Long reign of King Zahir Shah: relative internal stability, neutrality in World War II, and slow modernization
- **1964** – New liberal constitution introduced; multiparty parliamentary democracy permitted
- **1973** – Coup by Mohammad Daoud Khan (Zahir Shah's cousin); monarchy abolished; Afghanistan becomes a republic
- **1978** – Saur Revolution: Daoud overthrown and killed by PDPA; Marxist–Leninist regime begins under Nur Muhammad Taraki
- **1979** – Soviet Invasion of Afghanistan to support faltering PDPA regime; start of Afghan–Soviet War
- **1979–89** – Decade-long war between Soviet-backed Afghan government and mujahideen (Islamist guerrillas supported by the US, Pakistan and others)
- **1986–87** – Najibullah becomes president; initiates national reconciliation but faces unending resistance
- **1989** – Soviet withdrawal complete; Najibullah government survives temporarily
- **1992** – Collapse of Najibullah regime; mujahideen factions seize Kabul; start of civil war
- **1992–96** – Factional infighting among mujahideen groups (Massoud, Hekmatyar, Dostum, etc.); widespread destruction
- **1996** – Taliban seize Kabul; declare the Islamic Emirate of Afghanistan; impose strict Sharia rule
- **2001** – US-led invasion following 9/11 attacks; Taliban toppled; Bonn Agreement establishes transitional government

- **2004** – New constitution enacted; Hamid Karzai elected as first democratic president
- **2009–14** – Contested elections; Taliban insurgency intensifies; Karzai succeeded by Ashraf Ghani
- **2015** – Taliban gain territorial control; ISIS-K emerges as new jihadist threat
- **2020** – US–Taliban Peace Agreement signed in Doha; terms set US withdrawal and Taliban counterterrorism pledges
- **August 2021** – Collapse of Afghan government; Taliban capture Kabul after the US completes withdrawal; Islamic Emirate of Afghanistan re-established
- **2022–Present** – Taliban rule reinstated; severe restrictions on women's rights, press and civil liberties; international isolation intensifies

6

Nepal: From Monarchy to Federal Republic

Nepal boasts a history of remarkable antiquity, with its early political evolution traceable as far back as the seventh and eighth centuries BCE, marked by the arrival of the Kiratis from the east. Buddhism entered the Kathmandu valley during the reign of Kiratis, and by the late second century, Hinduism too entered the region, as Licchavis from northern India (from what is today Bihar) invaded these lands. It was only during the late eighth century CE, after over three centuries when Licchavi dominance started to decline drastically, that Nepal saw political fragmentation, with numerous local principalities emerging.[1]

This fragmented polity continued until the mid-eighteenth century when Prithvi Narayan Shah, the Gorkha king, unified these disparate entities through military conquest, formally establishing the Kingdom of Nepal.[2] However, the Gorkhas' ambitions for territorial expansions were undone by two superpowers that had already started to become integral to the South Asian political history by then: the Chinese and the British East India Company. The Chinese empire made inroads in the 1790s, and, subsequently, the British too during the Anglo–Nepalese war of 1814–16, culminating in the present boundaries of Nepal.[3]

The Shah monarchy of Gorkhas instituted an absolutist political system, wherein the monarch wielded supreme authority and royal edicts carried the force of law. Just like in India, where caste divisions and imperial statehood determined the social structure of the time, in Nepal too, prominent Brahmin families – notably the Chautaria, Pandey and Thapa clans – alternately rose to positions of dominance between

1785 and 1837, serving as the monarch's principal advisors.[4] These caste-based clans, in pursuit of their own material and political advancement, determined the administrative machinery responsible for running the state. Likewise, the familial alliances that formed out of these caste-based clans, entrenched their stronghold in governance and military organization. Since, allocation of army regiments was an important indicator of a family's power and prestige, it became more important that these divisions become more entrenched.[5]

The Birth of 'Ranacracy'

Following the death of Prithvi Narayan Shah, internal power struggles within the royal family significantly weakened the authority of the Shah monarchy. Except for a brief tumultuous period in the late eighteenth century, the throne was largely occupied by political minors, creating a power vacuum. In the absence of a supreme figurehead, many regents, ministers and *mukhtiyar*s, high-ranking officials or ministers, competed to consolidate power in their hands, slowly sidelining the centralizing powers of the monarch. King Rajendra, the last active ruler of the Shahs, was caught up in this volatile situation, further aggravating political instability, which by the mid-nineteenth century had brought Nepal to the brink of civil war and disintegration.[6]

It was in this precarious context that Jung Bahadur Rana (born Bir Narsingh Kunwar), a descendant of one of the prominent Thapa families came to the fore. In 1846, in what is now remembered as the 'Kot massacre', Jung Bahadur and his brothers killed over forty palace officials, including the PM Fateh Jung Shah, establishing themselves as the undisputed rulers of the kingdom.[7] In a decade' time, through the Royal *Sansad* (decree) of 1856, Jung Bahadur institutionalized his family's dominance, wresting complete authority. Through this royal decree, Jung Bahadur appropriated for himself and his successors total control over civil administration, the military and justice and foreign relations. Jung Bahadur's new title, Rana, was formalized. Subsequent PMs from his lineage likewise adopted the title, while the now-weakened Shah monarchs retained the ceremonial, though increasingly hollow, title of '*Maharajadhiraja* (King of Kings)'. Thus, the monarchy became a captive institution, existing in form but stripped of power.[8]

This marked the onset of 'Ranaism' or 'Ranacracy', a century-long period of autocratic rule. During this period, given that the Shah dynasty was virtually powerless, the Ranas concentrated power within their family, making the office of PM hereditary, essentially perpetuating a family oligarchy. During their rule, despite their authoritarianism, they did in fact bring about certain reforms that pushed for greater inclusivity. For instance, they introduced Muluki Ain (National Code) which guaranteed to all subjects equality before the law. They also abolished the practices of sati (1920) and slavery (1929), and founded educational institutions.[9] However, many of these measures were merely superficial, since the political freedom of the populace was severely restricted and they were treated as subservient subjects of a monarchy, rather than citizens of a modern nation.

Despite popular opposition and disenchantment with the Ranas, the regime endured for over a century, mainly due to the Shah monarchy's weakness and the backing of British authorities in India, who viewed the Ranas as reliable allies in furthering their interests in the region. Ultimately, though, in the Nepali imagination the Rana period represents a chapter of authoritarian despotism marked by stagnation in political and social progress.

The Birth of Modern Nepal

By the second quarter of the twentieth century, democratic ideas began to permeate Nepalese society. Exposure to new ideologies came from Nepalese soldiers who had served in World War I, and from members of the elite and middle classes studying in Indian universities. Influenced by the Indian nationalist movement, Nepalese exiles organized efforts to promote democracy in Nepal. Weekly newspapers such as *Gorkhali* founded in Banaras (now Varanasi), India, and *Almora Akhbar*, founded in the Kumaon region, became critical platforms spreading awareness about the Rana's repressive regime.[10] Likewise, in June 1936, the first Nepalese political party called the Nepal Praja Parishad was established by Dashrath Chand and Tanka Prasad Acharya, along with the many intellectuals, aristocrats and exiles who were against the Rana regime, with the express aim of abolishing it. This movement further gained momentum with the founding of the All India Nepali Congress in India in 1946.[11]

It was at this point that the events in India had a spillover effect on Nepal's trajectory. The withdrawal of the British from India in 1947 significantly weakened the Rana regime. This was so because the Ranas had relied heavily on British support to maintain their power. This development inspired Nepalese aspirations for freedom. The rise of communism in China further unsettled the ruling elite. In response, Padma Shamsher, a liberal Rana PM attempted to pacify the growing democratic movement by introducing a constitution. However, conservative factions within the Rana family opposed even limited reforms and forced his resignation. This internal division, coupled with the growing confrontation between the people and the Ranas, made systemic change inevitable.

The democratic movement gained further traction through alliances with disenfranchised Ranas of lower lineage (the so-called 'C-category Ranas') and the Shah monarch, King Tribhuvan, who had been relegated to a ceremonial role under Rana control. The disgruntled Ranas, some of whom had amassed wealth in India, supported the cause, as did the newly independent Indian government under PM Jawaharlal Nehru, which viewed the Ranas' authoritarianism and pro-Western alignment unfavourably.

In 1951, a popular movement launched from India successfully overthrew the Rana regime. A settlement brokered in Delhi, under Nehru's guidance, brought together the Ranas, the democratic leaders and the monarchy. King Tribhuvan, who had fled to India in 1950, was restored to power as a sovereign monarch free from Rana domination. In February 1951, a coalition cabinet was formed, headed by Mohan Shamsher, comprising five Ranas and five Nepali Congress (NC) members. This interim arrangement was intended to facilitate the drafting of a new constitution and to pave the way for general elections within two years, laying the groundwork for a democratic Nepal.

Nepal's Constitutional History

Nepal has had seven different constitutions enacted at different times: 1948, 1951, 1959, 1962, 1990, 2007 and 2015, which is the one currently in force.[12]

The coalition government formed in the aftermath of the 1951 revolution comprised ideologically divergent elements and was inherently unstable. In November 1951, the NC ministers resigned to protest police brutality, and King Tribhuvan used this opportunity to dismiss the government and form a new one while getting rid of the conservative bloc that was previously part of the government.

However, the political instability persisted. Between 1951 and 1959, a series of short-lived governments operated under either the interim constitution or direct royal intervention.

Following King Tribhuvan's death in 1955, his son, King Mahendra Bir Bikram Shah, ascended the throne. He was a vocal critic of democracy, claiming that Nepal was not ready for a multiparty democracy. However, mounting pressure from civil disobedience campaigns eventually compelled the monarch to hold elections in 1959. A week before the polls, King Mahendra promulgated a new constitution, presented as a royal benevolence to the nation.

The Royal Constitution of 1959

The royal constitution of 1959, unilaterally crafted by the monarch, established a parliamentary system under a constitutional monarchy, with ostensibly representative institutions like a bicameral legislature and a council of ministers. However, it granted the king overriding powers to suspend the cabinet, control the army and foreign affairs, and invoke emergency provisions, making him both ceremonial and de facto head of state.

The first elections in 1959 saw the NC win 74 of 109 seats, with B.P. Koirala as the first PM.[13] His reformist agenda threatened traditional elites and alarmed King Mahendra, who feared losing authority. In December 1960, citing instability, the King dismissed B.P. Koirala, arrested leaders and dismantled Nepal's brief experiment with democracy, restoring royal absolutism.

Between 1960 and 1990, Nepal was governed under King Mahendra's panchayat system – a partyless political structure that centralized authority in the monarchy, while claiming to embody a distinctively Nepali model of governance. Political dissent was suppressed, with civil liberties curtailed and political parties banned under the 1962 Constitution. While the system projected stability and national unity, it increasingly alienated pro-democracy forces, student groups and civil society. By the late 1980s, rising public discontent and mass mobilization laid the groundwork for the 1990 People's Movement that ultimately dismantled royal autocracy.

People's War 1990–2006

The 1990 People's Movement, spearheaded by a coalition of political parties including the NC and communist factions, pressured the monarchy into adopting multiparty democracy and promulgating a new constitution. However, the failure to enact transformative reforms alienated elements of the radical Left, culminating in the launch of the 'People's War' by the Communist Party of Nepal–Maoist (CPN-M) on 13 February 1996.[14]

In fact, a week before the launch of People's War, the CPN-M presented what it called '40-Point Demands', which asked for a wholesale reformation of the Nepali social and political structure, ranging from the establishing of a secular state, land reforms and proportional representation to the introduction of the right to health and education for all citizens.[15] The party particularly gained foothold among impoverished sections living in remote hills and mountains, with its revolutionary sentiments and forms of armed resistance. Initially, the conflict remained low-intensity, with government countermeasures limited to police deployment. However, in 2001, the Royal Nepali Army was engaged, significantly escalating the violence. Efforts at ceasefire negotiations in 2001 and 2003 proved futile.[16]

The political crisis that engulfed Nepal in the early 2000s was preceded by the traumatic Royal Palace Massacre of June 2001, in which

King Birendra, King Mahendra's son, king from 1972 onwards, Queen Aishwarya and much of the royal family were killed under still-contested circumstances. The massacre shook public faith in the monarchy and led to the controversial enthronement of King Gyanendra, Birendra's brother. In the years that followed, Gyanendra increasingly concentrated power in his own hands, dismissing the elected government in 2002 and seizing absolute control by 2005. In response to this authoritarian turn, a broad political coalition emerged: the Seven-Party Alliance (SPA) joined forces with the Maoists in a historic effort to dismantle monarchical rule. Facilitated by India, this alliance was formalized through the '12-Point Understanding' of November 2005, which outlined a shared commitment to multiparty democracy and endorsed key elements of the Maoist agenda for social justice and state restructuring.[17]

Comprehensive Peace Accord

The Comprehensive Peace Accord (CPA) of 2006 marked a watershed moment in Nepal's political evolution. Amid widespread mass mobilization during the Second People's Movement, King Gyanendra reinstated parliament, precipitating a cascade of transformative developments: the abolition of royal privileges, Nepal's declaration as a secular state, the institution of a ceasefire and the formal signing of the CPA between the SPA-led government and the Maoists. The accord also facilitated the adoption of an interim constitution and the integration of the CPN-M into the newly formed legislature-parliament.[18]

The CPA not only signalled the cessation of armed conflict but also addressed foundational issues of social and political restructuring. Clause 3.5 explicitly committed the state to dismantle its centralized and unitary structure in favour of an inclusive, democratic framework, ensuring representation and justice for historically marginalized communities, including women, Dalits, Janajatis, Madhesis and other disadvantaged groups.

The UN played a pivotal role in the post-accord transition. The UN Mission in Nepal (UNMIN) was established in 2007. Apart from overseeing and facilitating the electoral process for the Constituent

Assembly, the body was also tasked with monitoring arms management, and overseeing the peaceful and dignified integration of the Nepali army and Maoist forces.[19]

Post-War Transition

The adoption of the interim constitution in January 2007 marked a significant milestone in Nepal's transition from conflict to peace. While the document established secularism and republicanism as foundational principles, it initially omitted federalism. This oversight provoked the Madhes Movement, a powerful protest by Madhesi groups representing the historically marginalized populations of Nepal's Tarai plains.[20] The protests led to an amendment of the interim constitution, paving the way for a federal structure aimed at devolving power and enhancing political representation for marginalized communities. A second Madhes Movement in 2008 further pressured the state to adopt proportional representation in the electoral system.[21]

In April 2008, elections to the first Constituent Assembly saw the Maoists emerge as the largest party, forming a coalition government with the CPN (Unified Marxist–Leninist [UML]) and newly established Madhesi parties.[22] However, political tensions did not subside, particularly over the issue of integrating the Maoist army into official state forces. Following this, a confrontation between Maoist PM Pushpa Kamal Dahal (Prachanda) and the Nepali army led to his resignation in May 2009. However, despite their ascendancy to power, the Maoists were unable to execute their express agenda. These agenda issues ranged from the call for dignified integration of fighters, civilian control over the military, equitable power-sharing, and socio-political inclusion for oppressed and marginalized sections of the Nepalese population.

The Maoist army remained confined to cantonments for over six years, with fewer than 10 per cent of the 19,602 registered fighters ultimately integrated into the Nepali army. This modest outcome reflected the steady erosion of Maoist demands as part of various political compromises. In January 2011, the UNMIN, tasked with monitoring arms and armies, formally exited under mounting resistance from the Nepali army, the bureaucracy and major political parties such as the NC and CPN (UML).[23] Although UNMIN's Joint Monitoring Coordination Committee had fostered some level of trust among stakeholders, the disbanding of the Maoist People's Liberation Army in 2012 marked the end of the integration process.

The first Constituent Assembly lapsed in May 2012 without delivering a constitution, ushering in a period of political uncertainty marked by controversial arrangements, including the appointment of the sitting chief justice as PM.[24] The failure of the Constituent Assembly prompted a vertical split in the Unified Communist Party of Nepal–Maoist (UCPN-M), with diminished electoral performance for both the Maoists and Madhesi parties in the 2013 election to the second Constituent Assembly. Established parties such as the NC and CPN (UML) regained dominance, while Janajati-based parties fared poorly.[25]

The 2015 Earthquakes and Constitution Drafting

The catastrophic earthquakes of April and May 2015 galvanized Nepal's major political parties – the NC, CPN (UML), UCPN-M, and the Madhesi Janadhikar Forum-Democratic (MJF-D) – to fast-track the process of drafting the constitution.[26] However, from July to September 2015, significant protests erupted as the constitution took shape. Women's groups opposed restrictive citizenship provisions; and Madhesi, Tharu and Janajati groups demanded more inclusive state demarcations, objected to the exclusivity of the decision-making process, and contested the dilution of inclusion and proportional representation clauses from the interim constitution.[27]

In September 2015, amid mass protests and including violent unrest in the Tarai in southern lowlands, which claimed at least 46 lives[28], Nepal promulgated its new constitution. There was widespread discontent, particularly in eastern Nepal and the Tarai, where shutdowns and demonstrations were held to convey public dissatisfaction with provincial delineations and other exclusionary practices. These grievances centred on the drawing of provincial boundaries (that, critics argued, fragmented Madhesi-majority areas and diluted their political influence), as well as on the perceived underrepresentation of marginalized groups in state institutions. A constitutional amendment in January 2016 was brought forth to address some concerns about inclusiveness. However, this did not quell the protests, as it was too little too late.

Following this, there was a 2nd Amendment proposal introduced in November 2016.[29] This was done to resolve disputes over provincial boundaries, and in turn, immediately triggered fresh protests in affected districts. As of the time of writing this, the proposal remains unratified, underscoring the enduring challenges of reaching common ground between competing visions of federalism and centralization.

Parliament and Election Commission

The constitution of Nepal, adopted in 2015, established a bicameral legislature consisting of the House of Representatives (lower house) and the National Assembly (upper house), together referred to as the federal parliament.

As outlined in Article 83, the House of Representatives comprises 275 members, of whom 165 are elected through the FPTP system, accounting for 60 per cent of the total, while the remaining 110 members, representing 40 per cent, are elected via proportional representation (PR). The term of office for members of this house is five years. Under the PR system, voters cast their ballots for political parties, rather than individual candidates, and seats are allocated to parties in proportion to the total votes they receive nationwide, allowing for broader representation of diverse groups.

The National Assembly, as per Article 86 of the constitution, functions as the permanent upper house of the federal parliament. It consists of fifty-nine members, with the provision that one-third of its members serve a term of two years before their seats are vacated and filled via new elections.

The Election Commission of Nepal was established under Article 245(1) of the constitution of Nepal (2015). It comprises a chief election commissioner (CEC) and four other election commissioners (ECs). The CEC serves as the chairperson of the Election Commission.

As is stipulated in Article 245(3) of the constitution, the term of office for the CEC and the ECs is six years from the date of their appointment. The process of selecting members involves the president of Nepal, who appoints them based on the recommendation of the constitutional council. The constitutional council includes the PM as chairperson, the chief justice, the speaker, the National Assembly chair, the leader of the main opposition party and the deputy speaker. This method of appointment applies both to the CEC, who also assumes the role of chairperson, and to the other ECs, as outlined in Article 245(2) of the constitution.

Nepal's Democratic Rankings

Nepal's rankings in the EIU Democracy Index from 2014 to 2023 reflect a pattern of overall stagnation rather than linear improvement. In 2022, Nepal was ranked 101st globally, with a score of 4.49 – placing it within the category of 'hybrid regimes'. This status remained largely unchanged in the following year: in the 2023 report, Nepal experienced a marginal improvement in rank to 98th while maintaining the same overall score. These figures suggest that while Nepal has preserved a basic electoral architecture and has held regular polls, it has not made substantive strides in strengthening democratic institutions or deepening civic freedoms.

The promulgation of the 2015 constitution marked a historic departure from monarchy toward a federal democratic republic. It introduced structural commitments to inclusivity, decentralization, and the protection of fundamental rights – fostering a sense of democratic possibility. Moreover, the conduct of local, provincial and federal elections in successive cycles helped to institutionalize electoral procedures and strengthen grassroots participation. Yet, the enduring challenges of political instability, executive dominance, corruption, and exclusionary governance continue to hinder Nepal's democratic consolidation. The relative stasis in international rankings reflects these underlying tensions: while Nepal's democratic transition has not reversed, it remains precarious, incomplete and vulnerable to institutional drift.

In 2023, Nepal experienced significant political instability, with frequent changes in leadership and shifting, unstable alliances. The situation was so volatile that in the span of a mere five years, there were five PMs. Ultimately, K.P. Sharma Oli was sworn in as PM, making it his fourth term. Owing to this instability, the public has become disillusioned with the political process, which has no sense of ideological consistency in the rulership, nor is making any concerted efforts at delivering citizen-centric policy outcomes.[30]

At the same time, concerns about freedom of expression intensified. In November 2023, the government imposed a ban on TikTok, citing its potential to disturb social harmony and its misuse in cybercrimes.[31] The ban, which lasted nine months, was lifted after TikTok agreed to collabourate with authorities to address these concerns. This incident highlights the challenges Nepal faces in balancing regulation and digital freedoms, with implications for civil liberties and the digital economy.

Key Events at a Glance

- **1846** – Kot Massacre leads to the rise of Jung Bahadur Rana and the establishment of the Rana oligarchy; hereditary prime ministership begins, reducing the monarchy to a figurehead
- **1850s–1901** – Jung Bahadur and successors consolidate power; Nepal adopts policies of isolationism and maintains nominal independence under British suzerainty
- **1885** – 'Shree Teen' title institutionalized for Rana PMs; autocratic family rule continues for another half-century
- **1911** – Chandra Shamsher Rana represents Nepal at King George V's coronation; symbolic recognition of Nepal's quasi-independent status
- **1923** – Anglo–Nepal Treaty of Friendship signed with Britain; formalizes Nepal's independence and sovereign status
- **1934** – Great Bihar–Nepal earthquake devastates Kathmandu valley; Rana administration conducts limited reconstruction
- **1940s** – Rise of underground anti-Rana movements; exiled Nepali intellectuals and students begin organizing democratic opposition from India
- **1950** – Revolution of 1950–51 begins; King Tribhuvan flees to India; anti-Rana movement gains momentum
- **1951** – End of Rana regime; King Tribhuvan restored; begins transition to constitutional monarchy and multiparty democracy
- **1959** – First democratic elections held; B.P. Koirala becomes PM from the NC

- **1960** – King Mahendra suspends parliament, dismisses Koirala's government and bans political parties; introduces panchayat system (partyless guided democracy)
- **1972** – King Birendra ascends throne; continues absolute monarchy under panchayat rule
- **1980** – Referendum on political system; monarchy narrowly retains panchayat system amid allegations of rigging
- **1990** – Jana Andolan I (People's Movement) forces restoration of multiparty democracy; constitutional monarchy established
- **1991** – New constitution enacted; parliamentary democracy reintroduced; the NC wins first election
- **1996** – Maoist insurgency (People's War) begins, led by the CPN-M, demanding abolition of monarchy and radical land reform
- **2001** – Royal massacre: King Birendra and much of the royal family killed; Gyanendra becomes king
- **2002–2005** – King Gyanendra dissolves parliament and assumes direct rule; intensifies conflict with Maoists
- **2006** – Jana Andolan II (Second People's Movement); Gyanendra forced to relinquish power; peace accord signed with Maoists
- **2007** – Interim constitution adopted; monarchy's powers suspended
- **28 May 2008** – Nepal declared a federal democratic republic; monarchy abolished after 239 years
- **2008** – Maoist Party wins Constituent Assembly elections; Pushpa Kamal Dahal (Prachanda) becomes PM
- **2013** – Second Constituent Assembly formed after first fails to draft constitution; deep political divides remain
- **25 April 2015** – Devastating earthquake kills over 9,000 people; exposes fragile infrastructure and political delays
- **20 September 2015** – New constitution promulgated; establishes Nepal as a secular federal republic with seven provinces
- **2015–16** – Madhesi protests and border blockades; discontent over provincial boundaries and minority representation
- **2017** – First federal, provincial and local elections held under new constitution; Left Alliance (CPN-UML + Maoist Centre) wins majority
- **2018** – K.P. Sharma Oli becomes PM with UCPN
- **2020–21** – Political instability resumes: constitutional crisis, parliamentary dissolutions and factional disputes

- **2022** – Elections held; Pushpa Kamal Dahal (Prachanda) returns as PM in rotating alliance
- **2024** – K.P. Sharma Oli returns as PM on 15 July 2024, heading a coalition government with the NC to restore political stability after Pushpa Kamal Dahal lost a vote of confidence
- **2025** – In May 2025, the ruling coalition resolved internal friction by appointing economist Biswo Nath Poudel as Nepal's new central bank governor, signalling efforts to stabilize economic governance amid continuing political volatility

7

Bhutan: A Kingdom in Transition

For us to understand the formative decade of democracy in Bhutan, we must begin by recognizing how it first came to be in this country's unique political culture. Unlike most nations, Bhutan's road to democracy was not the consequence of popular demand or civil resistance. Rather, it was a top-down initiative of the Bhutanese monarchy itself. This remarkable feature sets Bhutan apart from all other South Asian countries. Remarkably, the impetus for this transition came from Jigme Singye Wangchuck, the fourth Druk Gyalpo, who voluntarily abdicated and instituted parliamentary elections, despite a prevailing reluctance among the populace to accept democratic reforms.[1]

Bhutan's path to unified governance under monarchical rule was neither immediate nor historically inevitable. The cultural and spiritual roots of Bhutan as a cohesive cultural entity can be traced to the eighth century CE, when the teachings of the revered Buddhist saint Padmasambhava were first promulgated. He is widely regarded as the one that laid the foundation of a shared Bhutanese identity.[2] However, for this cultural and civilizational foundation to materialize into unified political statehood, Bhutan had to wait until the seventeenth century, when Bhutan's political structure formally emerged under the reign of Zhabdrung Ngawang Namgyal. He was a Buddhist *lama* whose influence unified disparate regions into a single polity governed by a theocratic administration.[3] Following this unification, for centuries Bhutan was ruled by a dual system in which power was shared between the religious and secular authorities – a structure deeply embedded in Buddhist cosmology and almost mythological in character, as recorded in the spiritual annals of the time.[4]

By the early twentieth century, owing to increasingly local rivalries and regional power struggles, it was once again necessary for a more centralized governance model to be instated. The Wangchuck dynasty, beginning with the coronation of Gongsar Ugyen Wangchuck as the first hereditary monarch on 17 December 1907, successfully established a unified state. The monarchy guided Bhutan through a century of transformation, overseeing its gradual progression into a secular state and fostering a nascent modern economy.

Precisely 100 years later, in a historic act of political foresight, the monarchy transferred governing authority to the Bhutanese people. On 9 December 2006, King Jigme Singye Wangchuck relinquished his role as head of state, passing the mantle to his son, Jigme Khesar Namgyel Wangchuck. The fifth Druk Gyalpo – a graduate of the University of Oxford and a leader with progressive sensibilities, as was evinced when he oversaw the decriminalization of homosexuality in 2021[5] – was thus entrusted with the profound responsibility of overseeing Bhutan's first democratically elected government, marking the beginning of a new era in the nation's storied history.

Even though many have described Bhutan's transition to democracy as a top-down process, it is more accurately understood as the institutional codification of values that resonate with longstanding cultural and philosophical traditions. Rather than emerging from popular protest or civil unrest, Bhutan's democratic turn reflects a convergence of modern state-building and indigenous ethical frameworks. While it would be imprecise to equate Buddhist philosophy directly with modern democratic principles, several scholars have noted the ways in which Bhutanese interpretations of Mahayana Buddhism emphasize compassion, collective welfare and deliberative harmony – values that can be seen as congenial to democratic culture. As Karma Phuntsho and others have argued, Bhutanese Buddhism fosters a sense of moral agency and egalitarian spiritual striving that, while not identical to liberal democracy, creates a social foundation supportive of participatory governance.[6] Nonetheless, the *National Human Development Report* primarily evaluates the trajectory of Bhutan's parliamentary democracy as 'formally instituted in 2008', rather than these deeper philosophical underpinnings.[7]

Bhutan's steps toward democratization can be traced back to the 1950s, particularly the reforms of the third king, Jigme Dorji Wangchuck, which initiated the process of transition. In 1953, he established a unicameral National Assembly, which, in many ways, was the first formal step toward equitable and representative governance. This institution – making a significant departure from the past, as it facilitated a transfer of authority from the throne – included members from diverse sectors of society: government officials, monastic representatives, business and military leaders, and elected representatives (*chimis*) from 158 constituencies. Additionally, this legislative body was further empowered in 1959 with the enactment of the Thrimzhung Chhenmo or the Great Code of Law. This was a comprehensive, landmark legal document that modernized, codified and structured anew the legal foundations of the country, which until then was ruled in line with its older, more customary laws.[8]

King Jigme Dorji Wangchuck's reforms extended far beyond the Assembly. In 1954, for instance, he transitioned the tax system from payments in kind to a monetized form. In 1956, he formally abolished slavery. And in 1965, he established the Royal Advisory Council (Lodroe Tshogde). The establishment of the Royal Advisory Council marked a shift from absolute monarchy to consultative governance, institutionalizing deliberation in state affairs. It laid the groundwork for participatory politics by including representatives from various societal sectors in national decision-making. In a pivotal move in 1967, he delineated the judiciary from the executive and articulated the concept of a constitutional monarchy – envisioning a governance model grounded in the rule of law.

By the late 1960s, Jigme Dorji had even discussed Bhutan's potential democratic future with then PM of India, Indira Gandhi, who advised a gradual transition suited to Bhutan's unique context. This vision was revisited in January 1991 when the fourth king, Jigme Singye Wangchuck, articulated to students at Sherubtse College that the nation's 'destiny lies in the hands of the people', underscoring his commitment to decentralization as a pathway to democratization. He later implemented these ideals by transferring authority from central governance to local levels: in 1981, power was decentralized to *dzongkhag* (district) development committees, and in 1991, it extended further to the *gewog* (village block) level with the establishment of local development committees.[9]

In fact, these set of incremental reforms, undertaken gradually by the successive kings of Bhutan, paved the road for a slow but deliberate form of democratic governance. Ultimately, this led to the establishment of a system of parliamentary democracy that aligned with Bhutan's longstanding cultural values.

In 1998, in what may be the most pivotal moment in Bhutan's political history toward democratization, a Council of Ministers was established, whose members were elected by the National Assembly and were bestowed with executive authority. This was important because until that point, such powers had rested solely in the hands of the monarch. This devolution of power marked a deliberate shift towards a system of governance increasingly led by elected officials as is paramount and indispensable for representative democracy. Further consolidating this trajectory, a royal decree in 2001 mandated the drafting of a formal constitution, aimed at 'ensuring the sovereignty and security of Bhutan as a nation-state'. The decree articulated a vision for 'a dynamic system of governance which would uphold the true principles of democracy and through which the collective will of the people of Bhutan will prevail in governance and in pursuit of development'.[10]

The constitution, ratified in 2008, formally declared Bhutan a democratic constitutional monarchy, instituting a government accountable to an elected bicameral parliament responsible for enacting legislation. Several constitutional bodies were established to support this new democratic framework, including the Election Commission of Bhutan to oversee electoral processes, the Anti-Corruption Commission as a safeguard against the misuse of power and the Supreme Court as the ultimate custodian of the constitution. The National Assembly (comparable to the lower house in parliamentary systems) and the National Council (which serves as a 'house of review') were each designated with distinct legislative functions.

During the period leading up to the constitutional transition, between 2006 and 2008, the government also encouraged the development of private media, passed a Civil Society Act and established a Civil Society Authority tasked with registering and supporting civil society organizations. The culmination of these foundational reforms occurred in 2008, when 79.45 per cent of Bhutan's electorate participated in the nation's first general election, with many citizens journeying considerable distances to exercise their democratic rights.[11] This moment marked Bhutan's official entry into the global community as the world's youngest democracy.

French diplomat and scholar Thierry Mathou described these elections as 'a new and logical step in an ambitious program of guided political, economic, and administrative change initiated by the Third Druk Gyalpo in the mid-1950s'.[12] Mathou observes that, unlike many monarchies that have historically resisted democratic reforms, Bhutan's monarchy has consistently been the principal driver of change, guiding the nation's political evolution with a progressive and deliberate approach.

People's Perception of Democracy

The introduction of democracy in Bhutan has been both a process of gradual acceptance and of growing pains, culminating in widespread, though not unanimous, popular endorsement. A 2018 'Perspective Survey on a Decade of Parliamentary Democracy' revealed that 76.7 per cent of respondents were satisfied with the performance of Bhutanese democracy. Notably, rural respondents reported a stronger sense of civic responsibility (91.9 per cent) compared to their urban counterparts (82.6 per cent), reflecting an evolving perception of democratic engagement as a means of fostering greater citizen participation in governance.[13]

Despite these positive trends, Bhutan's transition to democracy was not smooth and devoid of challenges. For instance, the announcement by King Jigme Singye Wangchuck of his decision to step down and introduce democratic reforms was met with shock and scepticism by the Bhutanese populace. Many Bhutanese, unfamiliar with the mechanics of democracy and disillusioned by negative portrayals of democratic systems in the rest of South Asia, were apprehensive. Media and political institutions in Bhutan lacked experience with democratic governance, and public discussions about the draft constitution in 2007 and 2008 often featured emotional appeals against the transition.[14]

This resistance stemmed in part from a perception that democracy was unnecessary in a nation already enjoying peace, stability and development under the monarchy. Questions such as 'Why?' and 'Why now?' encapsulated the public's ambivalence. The King's response to these concerns was characteristically pragmatic and farsighted. He argued that a small nation like Bhutan, situated between two of the world's most populous countries, could not afford to rely on hereditary leadership, as future monarchs might lack the capability required for effective governance. Furthermore, he emphasized, the best time to implement such a transformation was during a period of peace and stability, rather than in response to a crisis – a perspective lauded by international observers such as Canadian thinker David Suzuki, who described it as 'the reasoning of a truly wise leader'.[15]

The transition to democracy also brought cultural and political shifts that many Bhutanese found unsettling. For a nation that had functioned as a self-contained agrarian society until the early 1960s, the adoption of democratic practices modelled on Western systems – including confrontational election campaigns – marked a profound departure from traditional decision-making processes such as the *zhung zomdu* (public meetings). The public spectacle of political disagreement was particularly jarring, as it contrasted sharply with the harmonious consensus-building associated with Bhutan's culture.

This sense of disorientation was voiced at the 2018 Democracy Forum, organized by the Bhutan Centre for Media and Democracy and the Royal University of Bhutan. Political leaders acknowledged that the public's reverence and trust in the monarchy had made the transition emotionally challenging. Many citizens felt 'abandoned' when the king relinquished authority to elected representatives, a sentiment reflected in the popular refrain that 'democracy was thrust upon us'. Over time, this narrative has evolved, with politicians reframing democracy as 'a gift from the throne' and many early leaders describing themselves as 'accidental politicians'.[16]

Nevertheless, the rapidity of Bhutan's democratic transition has been criticized by scholars such as Mark Mancall, an emeritus professor at Stanford University, who observed that the nation was unprepared for democratic governance.[17] While the king's leadership ensured the successful adoption of the constitution, establishment of constitutional bodies, encouragement of political parties and training in electoral processes, the cultural shifts necessary for the sustenance of the democratic ideology and practice remain ongoing.

Indeed, democracy is still perceived in varied and often nascent terms by the Bhutanese populace. While some see it as a monarchical decision, others associate it with concepts such as governance by the people (24.6 per cent), elections (15.2 per cent) and decentralization (15.5 per cent).[18] These responses underscore that democracy, though increasingly accepted, continues to evolve within Bhutan's political and cultural landscape.

Democracy with Bhutanese Characteristics

Bhutan's democratic system defies conventional categorization, embodying a distinctive blend of principles rooted in its unique sociopolitical and cultural context. The former chief justice of Bhutan, Lyonpo Sonam Tobgye, has characterized it as a 'constitutional democracy', while others have described it as a 'natural democracy' grounded in monarchical authority and cohesive rural communities. It has also been referred to as a 'guided democracy', where the head of state plays a significant role, and as a 'vibrant democracy' marked by efforts to foster civic dialogue and evidence-based policymaking.[19] Reflecting on this unique trajectory, King Jigme Khesar Namgyel Wangchuck classified democratic societies into three broad categories – failing democracies, struggling democracies and learning democracies – and identified Bhutan as belonging to the latter group, a perspective echoed by the former Chief Justice.[20]

While Bhutan adheres to several internationally recognized democratic norms – including the separation of powers, free and fair elections, political pluralism, media freedom and judicial independence – its democratization process is without precedent. As was mentioned above, unlike transitions typically driven by popular demand, Bhutan's shift to democracy was initiated by the throne itself.[21]

This phenomenon has intrigued observers across the globe. For instance, the noted Indian political analyst Dr S. Chandrasekharan initially viewed the drafting of Bhutan's constitution sceptically, describing it as a political stratagem within an absolute monarchy.[22] However, over time, he recognized the innovative nature of the constitution and credited the king for voluntarily initiating such profound reforms.

The Bhutanese constitution reflects a synthesis of democratic principles and Buddhist values, promoting a 'compassionate society' rooted in the nation's spiritual heritage and cultural identity. It enshrines provisions to safeguard Bhutan's spiritual and cultural traditions, aligning governance with the overarching philosophy of Gross National Happiness (GNH). This ethos, which integrates spiritual and emotional well-being into the framework of national progress, underscores the compatibility of Buddhism and democracy. Both systems share a foundational belief in the equality and potential of every individual, with the constitution mandating that 'the state shall strive to promote those conditions'.[23]

Through this distinctive model, Bhutan has offered a unique perspective on democratic governance – one that prioritizes not only political inclusivity but also the preservation of cultural and spiritual continuity. Its approach exemplifies how democracy can be adapted to resonate deeply with traditions and values, creating a system that is both transformative and profoundly grounded in the nation's identity.

Democracy and Decentralization

Bhutan's journey toward decentralization has long been characterized by the challenges of transferring authority from the central government in Thimphu to rural communities. Historically, power and decision-making have been concentrated in the capital, with successive governments introducing incentives to encourage civil servants to work in rural areas. Despite these efforts, achieving effective decentralization has proven elusive.[24]

The advent of democracy, however, has significantly accelerated this process. King Jigme Khesar has been at the forefront of initiatives to empower local governance. In a symbolic and substantive gesture in 2016, the king awarded the *patang* (a ceremonial sword representing authority) to local government chairpersons.[25] This act underscored the importance of local governance in Bhutan's democratic framework. King Jigme Khesar further emphasized that local governments should not be perceived as the lowest tier of governance but rather as the most vital level, as they operate closest to the citizenry.

This evolving paradigm has brought about notable shifts in the composition and capacity of local leadership. Historically, village heads or *gups*, often came from a background in monastic education, with many being former monks who had taken up administrative roles. By 2017, the influence of Bhutan's modern education system had become evident, with twenty-five university graduates, including one postgraduate, serving as gups. While the majority of the 205 gups remained functionally literate, capable of basic reading and writing, their educational profiles marked a significant transformation from earlier times. One elderly gup aptly described the difference between past and present as akin to 'the difference between the earth and the sky'.[26]

Nevertheless, this evolution should not be misinterpreted as a simple linear progression. It would be reductive to assume that today's university-educated gups are inherently more capable than their predecessors, whose leadership was grounded in the trust and confidence of their communities. Similarly, it is important to acknowledge that the challenges of local governance remain formidable.

Elected local leaders now navigate a complex web of relationships involving politicians, civil servants and their constituents. Their proximity to the people, while fostering engagement, also renders them susceptible to undue influence. Discernment and integrity are needed to balance immediate benefits, such as allowances and facilities provided by the central government, with the long-term welfare of their communities.

The challenges of decentralization are further compounded by technical and administrative constraints. In the 1980s, when fiscal authority was decentralized to Bhutan's twenty districts, several district governors faced legal consequences for the misuse of funds.[27] These issues arose largely from inadequate accounting skills and a limited understanding of audit regulations. As fiscal authority has since been further devolved to 205 *gewogs* (village clusters), the complexity of governance has only increased.[28]

Bhutan's experience underscores that decentralization is not merely a procedural or structural adjustment but also a transformative process requiring capacity building, vigilance and a steadfast commitment to ethical governance. It is a testament to the country's resolve to balance tradition and modernization in the pursuit of a more inclusive and participatory political system.

Bhutanese Parliament: Evolution and Structure

The origins of Bhutan's parliamentary tradition trace back to 1953, when Druk Gyalpo Jigme Dorji established the National Assembly (*Tshogdu*) as a formal forum for deliberation on matters of national concern. This pioneering initiative allowed the Bhutanese people to participate in governance by debating issues, discussing developmental priorities and overseeing fiscal transparency through recorded revenues and expenditures. The Assembly originally comprised thirty-six members: five representatives from the *Dratshang* (a monastic body), sixteen nominated government officials and fifteen elected representatives of the people. The first speaker of the National Assembly was Dasho Kesang Dawa, then serving as the *paro dzongtsab* (assistant district administrator).

The Assembly's sessions initially rotated across locations, convening in Thimphu's Tashichho Dzong for the second through thirteenth sessions, Paro's Rinpung Dzong for the fourteenth through twenty-eighth and then returning to Tashichho Dzong from the twenty-ninth to the seventy-third sessions. Since 1993, sessions have been held in the Gyalyong Tshogkhang, the current parliament building.

A significant institutional development occurred in 1965 with the formal establishment of the Royal Advisory Council, comprising six members tasked with advising the king and council of ministers. This body, which also participated in the National Assembly, was charged with overseeing the implementation of policies and programmes approved by the National Assembly. In 1968, a landmark shift in legislative authority occurred when the then King renounced his veto power over Assembly decisions, thereby affirming the legislative primacy of the institution.

Under the reign of Jigme Singye, democratic governance further expanded through grassroots decentralization, as discussed earlier. The establishment of the *dzongkhag yargay tshogdu* (district development committees) in 1981 and the *gewog yargay tshogchung* (block development committees) in 1991 devolved decision-making authority to district and village levels, respectively.

The transition to parliamentary democracy took another critical step in 1998, when executive powers were transferred to a Council of Ministers elected by the National Assembly for five-year terms, with the Druk Gyalpo ceasing to serve as the head of government. The Assembly was concurrently granted the authority to institute a vote of confidence in the king, underscoring the evolving constitutional framework. The drafting of Bhutan's constitution, initiated by royal command in 2001, culminated in the release of the first draft in 2005. The dissolution of the unicameral National Assembly in 2007 marked the end of an era, paving the way for the bicameral parliamentary system inaugurated in 2008 with Bhutan's first democratic elections.

The Bhutanese parliament, established under the 2008 constitution, comprises two chambers: the National Council and the National Assembly. The National Council consists of twenty-five members. Of these, twenty are elected representatives from Bhutan's 20 dzongkhags, while five are eminent persons appointed by the king. The Council plays a non-partisan role, reviewing legislative proposals, providing policy recommendations and ensuring the accountability of the executive branch. It is explicitly designed to function independently, as its members are prohibited from affiliating with political parties.

The National Assembly comprises forty-seven members elected by the people through a two-round voting system. This chamber represents the political will of the citizenry, enacts laws and exercises oversight over the government. The Assembly is pivotal in selecting the PM, drawn from the political party with a majority in the house. Together, the two chambers embody Bhutan's commitment to a deliberative and participatory form of governance, balancing traditional values with democratic principles.

As mentioend earlier, parliamentary operations are supported by constitutional bodies such as the Anti-Corruption Commission, the Royal Audit Authority and the Election Commission of Bhutan, which ensure transparency, fairness and accountability in governance. This institutional framework reflects Bhutan's innovative approach to harmonizing democracy with its spiritual and cultural heritage, offering a unique model of parliamentary democracy suited to its context.

Electoral Framework

Bhutan's electoral process operates under a distinct variation of the FPTP system, uniquely adapted to the country's context. Parliamentary elections are conducted in two distinct rounds. In the primary round, political parties, rather than individual candidates, contest the polls. During this stage, voters cast their ballots for the party of their preference, and the two parties receiving the highest number of votes proceed to the general election. This design ensures focused political competition while limiting fragmentation, as the constitution explicitly prohibits the formation of coalition governments.

In the subsequent general election, the two qualifying parties nominate candidates to contest specific parliamentary seats. The party securing a majority forms the government, with its leader assuming the role of PM. The losing party serves as the official opposition in the National Assembly.

In what should be a lesson to other South Asian countries, particularly India and Pakistan, Bhutan's state assumes full financial responsibility for election campaigns, which goes a long way in reducing the influence of money power and corporate lobbying in elections. The Election Commission of Bhutan organizes candidate forums as the principal mode of voter engagement, where candidates present their visions and interact directly with the electorate. Interestingly, and once again in stunning and stark contrast to other South Asian countries, campaigning through public rallies or posters is strictly prohibited, reflecting Bhutan's commitment to maintaining civility and minimizing divisiveness in the electoral process.

Political participation is likewise carefully structured. In what I believe is a long-term disadvantage, undesirable to the notion of inclusive leadership, independent candidates are not permitted to contest National Assembly elections in Bhutan. This is because membership is reserved only for those affiliated with political parties. On the other hand, candidates for the National Council and local government elections are mandated to remain unaffiliated with any political party, ensuring that these institutions maintain a truly non-partisan character.

Eligibility criteria for parliamentary candidates further reflects Bhutan's emphasis on integrity and accountability. Prospective candidates must hold a university degree, be under the age of sixty-five, and must not be married to a foreign national. Additionally, civil servants are ineligible to stand for elections, underscoring the separation of administrative and political spheres. While Bhutan's political tradition – rooted in the doctrine of *Chösi Nyidhen* or the dual system of religion and politics – historically included monastic representatives in governance structures, such as the unicameral assembly established in 1953, contemporary democratic practice has more clearly delineated the religious from the secular. Today, members of the monastic community – comprising approximately 30,000 monks and nuns – are formally excluded from electoral participation, in keeping with their spiritual vocation and the evolving separation of domains in Bhutan's modern constitutional framework.

This electoral framework, while grounded in democratic principles, is tailored to Bhutan's unique social and cultural ethos, balancing participatory governance with the preservation of stability and harmony.

Bhutan's Elections

2008: Democratic Inauguration

As discussed earlier, the 2008 parliamentary elections marked a seminal moment in Bhutan's political evolution, symbolizing the culmination of a carefully guided transition from monarchical governance to a constitutional democracy. In the primary round, held on 31 December 2007, the two political parties that qualified for the general election were the Druk Phuensum Tshogpa (DPT) and the People's Democratic Party (PDP). These elections were conducted under strict adherence to the constitutional framework and electoral laws, with an impressive voter turnout of 79.4 per cent, reflecting the populace's cautious yet earnest engagement with the democratic process.[29]

In the general election held on 24 March 2008, the DPT, led by Jigmi Y. Thinley, emerged overwhelmingly victorious, securing forty-five out of forty-seven seats in the National Assembly. The PDP, led by Sangay Ngedup, won the remaining two seats and assumed the role of the opposition.[30] The election results revealed a decisive preference for the DPT, driven by its pledge to ensure stability and continuity during the nascent stages of Bhutan's democratic experiment. This first electoral exercise was widely lauded for its transparency and efficiency, underscoring the competence of the Election Commission of Bhutan in navigating uncharted political territory.

2013: The Opposition Rises

The 2013 elections introduced a shift in Bhutan's political landscape. The primary round, held on 31 May 2013, saw four political parties in the fray: the incumbent DPT, the PDP, the Druk Nyamrup Tshogpa (DNT) and the Bhutan Kuen-Nyam Party (BKP). The DPT and PDP advanced to the general election after securing the highest votes, though with the PDP gaining unexpected momentum as the electorate expressed a desire for greater political balance.[31]

In the general election held on 13 July 2013, the PDP, led by Tshering Tobgay, secured a dramatic victory, winning thirty-two out of forty-seven seats in the National Assembly, while the DPT retained fifteen seats.[32] This result signalled the electorate's growing political maturity and willingness to embrace change. The campaign period highlighted increased public engagement, with debates focusing on pressing issues such as economic management and youth unemployment. The peaceful transfer of power between the DPT and PDP was hailed as a milestone, reaffirming the resilience of Bhutan's fledgling democracy.[33]

2018: The Emergence of a Third Force

The 2018 elections represented a further evolution in Bhutan's political dynamics. In the primary round, held on 15 September 2018, four parties contested: the DPT, PDP, DNT and BKP. In a surprising outcome, the DNT and DPT emerged as the two leading parties, relegating the incumbent PDP to third place.[34] This marked the first time an incumbent party failed to advance to the general election, underscoring the electorate's appetite for change and the increasing competitiveness of Bhutan's democracy.

The general election, held on 18 October 2018, resulted in a decisive victory for the DNT, led by Dr Lotay Tshering, which won thirty seats in the National Assembly. The DPT secured seventeen seats, continuing as the opposition.[35] The DNT's campaign, which emphasized equitable development and the expansion of health and education services, resonated strongly with the electorate. This election also highlighted the growing role of social media in shaping political discourse, as Bhutanese voters actively debated issues and scrutinized candidates online – signalling a shift towards more participatory democracy.[36]

2023: A Milestone in Democratic Evolution

The 2023 National Assembly elections in Bhutan marked a critical juncture in the country's democratic journey, further reaffirming its status as an electoral democracy. The DNT retained its position as the ruling party, while the DPT emerged as the opposition, continuing the sustained competition between Bhutan's key political entities.[37] In the 2023–24 National Assembly election, the People's Democratic Party (PDP) won 30 of the 47 seats while the Bhutan Tendrel Party (BTP) took 17 seats, and Tshering Tobgay became Prime Minister.

The campaigns primarily addressed pressing issues such as economic recovery, unemployment and sustainable development – issues that are of paramount importance across all the South Asian nations.[38] Likewise, these themes resonate deeply with Bhutan's citizens as well, particularly, given that the nation was grappling with the economic repercussions of the Covid-19 pandemic. The election also showcased an active engagement of the electorate, reflecting a growing sense of political awareness and participation in democratic governance.

Despite these advancements, challenges remain. The limited number of political parties and restrictive electoral criteria – such as the exclusion of coalitions and the emphasis on educational qualifications – constrain broader representation. Additionally, fostering stronger connections between elected leaders and their constituents remains a critical task for Bhutan's political institutions.[39]

A Progressive Democratic Journey

Bhutan's electoral processes continue to be shaped by its unique socio-political landscape. Its nascent democracy still has a long way to go in order for it to function fully as a constitutionally mandated democracy that is not dependent upon its monarchy. There is, in fact, a need for more grassroots-driven inclusive governance. There is also need for responsive policymaking as the political system becomes more mature and people-centric.

The 2023 elections reaffirmed Bhutan's democratic trajectory while highlighting the evolving nature of its political challenges, as is only expected in any nascent democracy. With its democratic foundations consolidating, as evinced by its successive elections, Bhutan has demonstrated an incremental progress in adhering to the democratic norms. More importantly, the electorate itself – which is the centrepiece of any democratic structure – has displayed an increasing willingness to evaluate parties and leaders on their merits, rather than blind adherence to bygone historical loyalties. This pattern, combined with the robust mechanisms instituted by the Election Commission of Bhutan, underscores the vibrancy and sustainability of democracy in the country.

Bhutan lies between India and China. One is a democracy, the other an autocracy, whereas the Dragon Kingdom separating the two is actually a 'guided democracy'. Many believe that this transfer of systems was a mere 'cosmetic' change. However, former ambassador to Bhutan, Pavan K. Varma, who was there from 2009 and saw the transfer of power take place, says that democracy is not 'only symbolic' and that it has 'altered the powers hitherto exercised exclusively by the King'. Varma's words encompass the change in the era: 'Democracy, albeit with a strong Bhutanese flavour, has come to stay in the Forbidden Kingdom.'[40]

Key Events at a Glance

- **1910** – Treaty of Punakha signed with British India; Bhutan retains internal autonomy but cedes control of foreign affairs to the British (similar to protectorate status)
- **1926–52** – Reign of Jigme Wangchuck, second king; maintains isolationist policies while modestly strengthening the monarchy

- **1949** – Treaty of Friendship with India: Bhutan recognizes Indian guidance in external affairs in exchange for respect of its sovereignty; British–Indian legacy replaced by Indian strategic partnership
- **1952** – Jigme Dorji Wangchuck becomes the third king; initiates a process of gradual modernization
- **1958** – Abolition of serfdom and feudal land practices; social reforms initiated
- **1961** – Launch of Bhutan's first five-year plan; start of developmental state-building with Indian aid
- **1971** – Bhutan becomes a member of the UN
- **1972** – Death of third king; accession of Jigme Singye Wangchuck (age sixteen), the fourth king
- **1985** – Citizenship Act revised; strict requirements lead to disenfranchisement of many ethnic Nepali-speaking Lhotshampa population
- **1989–90** – Cultural nationalism (*Driglam Namzha*) enforced; ethnic tensions rise; protests and violent clashes erupt in southern Bhutan
- **1990s** – Thousands of Lhotshampas flee or are expelled to refugee camps in eastern Nepal; major international human rights concern
- **1998** – Fourth king voluntarily transfers executive powers to a Council of Ministers and introduces parliamentary reforms
- **1999** – Television and Internet introduced; king continues democratic transition
- **2005** – Draft constitution of Bhutan released; outlines Bhutan as a constitutional monarchy with multiparty democracy
- **2006** – Abdication of the fourth king in favour of his son, Jigme Khesar Namgyel Wangchuck, who becomes the fifth king
- **2008** – Promulgation of the constitution of Bhutan; first democratic elections held; DPT wins majority; Jigme Thinley becomes PM
- **2008** – Coronation of the fifth king; celebrated alongside democracy's peaceful introduction
- **2013** – The PDP wins elections; Tshering Tobgay becomes PM
- **2018** – The DNT wins third democratic election; Lotay Tshering becomes PM
- **2023** – The PDP returns to power in January 2024 elections; Tshering Tobgay re-elected as PM

8

The Maldives: A Republic in Turbulent Waters

The Maldives is a chain of roughly 1,200 small islands dispersed across 90,000 sq. km in the Indian Ocean. It occupies a central position within a broader archipelagic system extending from the Lakshadweep Islands off the west coast of India to the Chagos Archipelago in the south. Strategically, this chain also includes Diego Garcia, a significant US military base.

As an Islamic republic with a modest population of around 529,697 the Maldives holds considerable geostrategic importance. It commands a critical position along the major sea lanes of communication (SLOC) traversing the Indian Ocean – routes vital for maritime traffic connecting the Suez Canal and the Strait of Hormuz to India, Southeast Asia and East Asia.

The Maldives is known globally as a tropical paradise par excellence, attracting millions of tourists to its beaches and holiday resorts. However, this image of an idyllic landmark is only superficial. Because underneath this image lies a nation that is in fact grappling with profound challenges. At its heart is an intense struggle to secure its political and democratic future amid complex internal and external pressures. In fact, the Maldives was home to Asia's longest serving dictator, ruling from 1978 until his toppling in 2008.

The Maldives, like the other South Asian countries, has a long and extensive history going back thousands of years. In fact, we now know from recent archaeological evidence that the history of the Maldives extends as far back as approximately 2000 BCE. It is also established that around this time the islands had maintained trade links with early civilizations such as the Egyptians, Mesopotamians and the Indus Valley.[1] Thor Heyerdahl, a renowned explorer and expert in marine navigation, posited that the earliest settlers were sun-worshipping seafarers known as the Redin.[2] Interestingly, the influence of these ancient sun-worshippers is visible in Maldivian mosques, for instance, which face the sun rather than Mecca. However, from the sixth century CE onwards, the islands underwent an important cultural shift. They were subject to the influx of South Indian and Sri Lankan settlers in the form of traders, religious sects and merchants. In fact, it was this later influence which led to the predominance of Theravada Buddhism in the islands. The name 'Maldives' is believed by some to be derived from the Sanskrit term *maladvipa*, meaning 'garland of islands'.[3]

The Maldives' strategic position along key maritime trade routes and its abundance of cowrie shells, used as currency across Asia and East Africa until the sixteenth century, attracted Middle Eastern traders by the tenth century. With the rise of Arab dominance over Indian Ocean trade, the Maldivian society underwent profound cultural transformations.[4] In 1153 CE, the Buddhist king, King Dhovemi, converted to Islam, adopting the title Sultan Muhammad al-Adil. It was his reign that went on to initiate a series of six dynasties totally comprising eighty-four rulers.[5] This sultanate endured until 1932, when it disavowed hereditary succession and became elective.

Just as the South Indians and Sri Lankans were predominant in their control of trade routes a millennium earlier, the sixteenth and seventeenth centuries gave way to the European maritime powers. This era was witness to the eventual decline of Arab maritime hegemony as European powers (notably the Portuguese, Dutch and British) extended their mercantile influence over the waters of the Indian Ocean.[6] In 1558, the Portuguese seized control of the Maldives, governing it from Goa. However, in 1573, Muhammad Thakurufaanu Al Auzam led a successful revolt, expelling the Portuguese – a moment commemorated annually as the Maldives's National Day.

Following the Portuguese era, the Maldives came under the nominal control of the Dutch, who ruled indirectly during their dominance over Sri Lanka. In the late nineteenth century, British forces expelled the Dutch from Sri Lanka and established a protectorate over the Maldives in 1887.[7]

British Protectorate Era: 1887–1965

The Maldives formally relinquished its sovereignty in foreign policy matters in 1887 when Sultan Muhammad Mueenuddeen II signed a treaty with Arthur Charles Hamilton-Gordon, the British governor of Ceylon. This agreement rendered the Maldives a British protectorate and granted the British total control over defence and foreign relations. Even though it was said that the islands would preserve their internal self-governance, the economic and political control that the British had garnered by this time made that clause a mere formality. The British also provided military protection, and in return the Maldives agreed to pay an annual tribute to the Crown. Like in the case of India after the signing of the Treaty of Allahabad in 1765, this arrangement marked the beginning of a prolonged period of British influence in the Maldives.[8]

The context leading to this loss of independence was shaped by growing British political involvement, particularly in response to unrest in the late nineteenth century. At the time, foreign trade in the Maldives was dominated by Borah traders from India. When the local population revolted against them, the British intervened – citing their obligation to protect the Borahs as British subjects. This intervention cemented Britain's political presence in the Maldives, intensifying the pressure on the sultanate.

During the period it was a British protectorate, the Maldives was governed by successive sultans, with hereditary succession transitioning to an elective sultanate in 1932. A constitution was introduced, limiting the sultan's powers, but the monarchy persisted until the short-lived First Republic in 1953 under Muhammad Amin Didi. After its collapse, the sultanate was restored, only to be abolished permanently in a referendum in 1968, establishing the Maldives as a republic under President Ibrahim Nasir.[9] Independence from Britain was achieved on 26 July 1965 (though Britain retained military facilities in the southern atolls), marking the end of colonial influence and the beginning of modern statehood.

Between the late nineteenth and mid-twentieth centuries, the Maldives functioned as a British protectorate under indirect rule, with internal affairs managed by the Maldivian sultanate while Britain retained control over external relations and defence. This period was marked by relative political continuity but increasing British strategic interest in the Indian Ocean, particularly during World War II, when military installations were established in the southern atolls.

The early 1960s are generally regarded as key years which paved the way for the Maldives journey toward independence. For instance, according to historian Mohamed Shathir, there were two events which were significant for this transition. In particular, he points out that the suppression of a southern revolt, which drew criticism of PM Ibrahim Nasir's leadership, and the expulsion of Borah traders from Malé were defining events. These events led to a reunification of the country with an emphasis on shared identity. The expulsion, though not extended to all immigrant communities, targeted the economically influential Borahs and served as a symbolic act of economic nationalism. It marked a broader turn toward centralization, and the construction of a unitary national identity grounded in cultural and religious homogeneity. Owing to this change in the political climate, it was now possible for the Maldives to reclaim self-control over its economy and political structure. This signalled the Maldives' willingness to assert full independence. Shathir further noted the remarkable national unity discernible during this period. It was this resurgence of the collective spirit of the Maldivian people that facilitated the country's transition to absolute sovereignty.[10]

Public protests against the British influence grew increasingly fervent, culminating in the signing of the independence agreement on 26 July 1965. Within two months, the Maldives joined the UN as a fully sovereign state. In 1968, a national referendum was held to determine the nation's future governance structure. With 81.23 per cent of voters supporting the establishment of a republic, the 853-year-old monarchy was formally abolished, making Ibrahim Nasir the first president of the Maldives.[11]

Nasir, widely recognized as the architect of Maldivian independence, was appointed PM in 1957 at the young age of thirty-one. Before him, the British presence had remained significant throughout the Maldives protectorate period . The protectorate period refers to the era when the Maldives remained internally self-governed under the sultanate but ceded control of its external affairs and defence to Britain. This arrangement allowed Britain strategic access to the Indian Ocean while maintaining indirect colonial oversight.In fact, during World War II, the Royal Air Force even established a base on Gan Island in the southern Addu Atoll. However, in the following decades, the movement for independence was also gaining momentum under the leadership of Ibrahim Nasir. By fostering national unity, spearheading industrial development and advocating for self-determination, he played a pivotal role in the Maldives's emergence as an independent nation.[12]

The Maldives: A Constitutional History

Like many South Asian countries, with the exception of India and Bhutan, the Maldives too enacted multiple constitutions over the course of its chequered history. The very first was promulgated in 1932 while the Maldives was still under British protection, and the later iterations came about in 1953, 1954 and 1968 (with new amendments to the 1968 version in 1970, 1972, 1975 and 1998).[13] However, the constitution now in force in the Maldives was promulgated in 2008, and is made up of 301 articles and divided into fourteen chapters. It introduced a host of new features expanding the democratic character of the document.

The political history of the Maldives is deeply rooted in its monarchical system, which spanned eight centuries and was underpinned by undemocratic constitutional rules. As was briefly mentioned earlier, from 1153 to 1968, the Maldives was governed by 84 sultans and Sultanas in a system of hereditary oligarchy. It was only in 1932 that Sultan Shamsuddin, amid political instability, introduced a constitution. This move was largely prompted by the growing influence of the PM Al-Ameer Abdul Majeed Rannabandeyri Kilegefaan, who sought to challenge the sultan's absolute authority. Fearing a loss of power after devolution and decentralization, and that the sultanate might be abolished, the sultan sought British support to maintain his rule and the status quo. Ultimately, while the British government had little direct influence over the Maldives's domestic affairs, as mentioned earlier, the sultanate system remained culturally ingrained and significant power was retained by the monarch.

The first constitution of the Maldives introduced certain reforms such as the creation of a People's Assembly and a Legislative Council. Even though these were created to facilitate representative governance, the sultanate still retained the overarching influence. Therefore, effectively, the political system still remained an oligarchy. Nevertheless, however modest the reforms might be, this introduction of limited representation was a significant first step towards an inclusive form of governance.

The political landscape shifted again in the mid-twentieth century, with the 1953 constitution briefly establishing a republic and introducing a senate, a lower house and an attorney general. However, as has repeatedly been the case in country's history, the sultanate reverted to power in 1954. This pattern of half-hearted decentralization and re-sultanization continued for a good part of the next two decades until 1968. In that year, the constitution formally established the country as a republic that would follow a unicameral parliamentary system with a president as the head of state. However, this too did not fully tackle the issue of centralization, since the president was bestowed with nearly autocratic powers akin to the sultan, and therefore total decentralization and devolution of power was yet to take place.[14]

In the 1990s, after its entry into the UN, the Maldives made concerted efforts to follow global trends in democratic governance. This period was also marked by a growing public demand for democratic reforms. In particular, there was a popular demand for more inclusive economic and social progress. As a consequence, in 1998, further amendments were made to the 1968 constitution. It allowed greater representation from atolls and showed a more progressive outlook, but the central issue remained unaddressed. The president still retained the ability to appoint MPs, reflecting heavy centralization and concentration of power. This concentration of power reflected what Max Weber described as 'Sultanism without Sultans', where the head of state held near-absolute control over governance, with limited checks on authority.[15]

The need for further constitutional reform became evident as the demands for democratic freedoms – such as the right to free expression, freedom of press and the right to protest – grew stronger. The 1998 constitution, although more progressive than the previous constitutions, did not make space for the central features indispensable to a mature democracy: institutional autonomy and independence, separation of powers, free exercise of fundamental rights and freedoms, and equitable political representation that is citizen-centric. Therefore, the 2008 constitution introduced the necessary measures to address these significant concerns, including the ability to form political parties. However, constitutional formalism does not easily translate to real-life results, thereby making the transition from presidential autocracy to full democracy challenging.

The entrenched political culture and historical authoritarian traditions made it difficult to consolidate democratic principles, and the transition period from 2008 to 2010 revealed gaps in the implementation of the new democratic framework – highlighting the complexities of establishing a stable democracy in the Maldives.[16]

South Asia's Longest Dictatorship

As discussed above, in March 1968, a national referendum abolished the sultanate and established the Maldives as a republic. Ibrahim Nasir, who had served as the country's first president, stepped down in 1978 after completing two terms, facilitating a peaceful transition of power. His resignation marked the beginning of Maumoon Abdul Gayoom's long rule, which lasted from 1978 to 2008.

Gayoom, a former university lecturer and diplomat, modelled his regime on autocratic principles, drawing influence from Hosni Mubarak's Islamic regime in Egypt. His rule was marked by corruption, political repression and gross human rights abuses – including arbitrary arrests, torture and politically motivated killings – with elections manipulated to ensure his continued reign.[17]

Then, in September 2003, news broke that a nineteen-year old prisoner named Even Naseem, who had protested in the prisons against alleged mistreatment of prisoners, had been tortured and killed. This custodial death became a symbol of larger injustices perpetrated under Gayoom's reign, sparking country-wide protests[18], leading finally to the creation of an opposition coalition led by Mohamed Nasheed of the Maldivian Democratic Party (MDP). Gayoom had to make way for free and fair elections, in which he was duly defeated by MDP's Nasheed. This was a historic shift in the country's political landscape wherein an entrenched autocratic structure was dismantled making way for democratic reforms, focusing on economic equity and inclusive development.[19]

Nasheed's presidency faced significant challenges. The ensuing power struggle with the judiciary (whose loyalty remained with Gayoom) and the opposition (whose focus was more on ousting Nasheed than democratic consolidation) made a smooth transition impossible. Thereafter in February 2012, Nasheed was forced to resign after a coup by security forces who had colluded with the opposition.[20] Later, Nasheed was arrested on fabricated charges and forced into exile, where he continues to advocate for democracy and human rights internationally.

After the briefest experiment with democracy, the Maldives's optimism proved to be brutally short-lived. Following Nasheed's exile, Yameen, Gayoom's half-brother, took power and steered the country back towards authoritarianism, extremism and troubling foreign alliances.[21]

Under Yameen's regime, corruption and embezzlement became even more widespread. In fact, an investigation by Al Jazeera in 2016, called 'Stealing Paradise', revealed that Yameen and his Vice-President were involved in the theft of millions of dollars from state funds, using the proceeds to bribe parliamentarians and judges.[22] When bribery failed, they resorted to force to suppress opposition. There were also unprecedented levels of inequality, so that while international tourists were pampered in luxury resorts, the country's local populace was pushed further into abjection and poverty. In this context, there was also a concerning rise in radicalization, with many joining terrorist outfits such as the Al-Qaeda and ISIS.[23]

Nasheed's pro-democracy movement eventually saw success when Ibrahim Solih, a candidate backed by an opposition coalition, won the 2018 presidential election. Solih's victory marked a significant step towards reversing the damage caused by Yameen's authoritarian rule. Despite attempts to rig the election, Yameen's regime was ousted – in part due to Nasheed's international advocacy for democratic reforms. The democratic victory was understood as being yet another beginning of the Maldives's journey to restore its democratic institutions, and heal the divisions created by years of repression and rising inequality.[24]

Solih's Rule

The Maldives has, as President Ibrahim Solih said during a state visit to India, 're-embarked on its democratic journey'. His remarks, delivered a little over two months after his electoral victory in September 2018, were underscored by a quotation from India's first PM Jawaharlal Nehru's seminal 'tryst with destiny' speech, signalling the profound historical significance of the moment.[25]

President Solih's words carried weight in light of the substantial victory achieved by his party, the MDP, in the 6 April 2018 elections for the Majlis, the nation's unicameral legislature. The MDP secured sixty-five out of eighty-seven seats (76 per cent), a decisive mandate from the electorate that reflected a clear desire to move away from the governance style of his predecessor, Yameen.[26] Yameen's tenure, as mentioned in brief earlier, had been marked by an excessive centralization of power, rampant corruption stemming from the politician–business nexus and the pursuit of large-scale infrastructure projects that burdened the country with unsustainable external debt, all while neglecting the pressing needs of the population. In particular, the Maldives Marketing & Public Relations Corporation scam, the biggest corruption scandal in the country's history, involved the embezzlement of over 90 million dollars by way of leasing out islands and lagoons for the tourism industry.[27]

In contrast, Solih's administration was committed to providing basic services to all citizens, reinforcing democratic institutions and ensuring accountability for corruption, both past and present.

Solih's path to the presidency was forged through a broad coalition of political parties, as mentioned earlier, and his administration subsequently formed a coalition government. With the MDP holding a commanding majority in the Majlis, Solih emphasized that the coalition nature of his government will remain intact. His commitment to political harmony and consensus-building recalls the approach of India's tenth PM, Atal Bihari Vajpayee, whose inclusive leadership style resonated with many, including his political rivals. This approach underscores Solih's belief that national progress is best achieved through collabouration across political divides.

Moreover, the MDP's leadership is uniquely positioned, with two prominent figures at its helm: Solih, the current president, and Nasheed. This dual leadership structure provides a rich blend of experience and vision, reinforcing the party's democratic credentials and its commitment to furthering the Maldives' democratic evolution. The partnership between Solih and Nasheed signals a constructive balance of continuity and renewal, essential for the consolidation of democratic reforms in the country.

Thus, ever since President Solih's leadership, the Maldives stands at a critical juncture, with the promise of renewed democratic governance and a focus on addressing the socio-economic challenges that have long plagued the nation.

Muizzu's Rule

In the 2023 presidential election, Mohamed Muizzu defeated incumbent Ibrahim Solih, signalling a shift in the country's foreign policy. Muizzu, from the pro-China Progressive Alliance, is expected to realign the Maldives towards Beijing, a departure from Solih's 'India First' approach. Under his regime, as was promised, Solih's administration had strengthened strategic ties with India, particularly in the field of defence and development, including accepting Indian military support and the development of infrastructure projects.[28]

However, in opposition to this, Muizzu's campaign was run on the 'India Out' slogan, opposing India's military presence in the Maldives – which had been an integral part of Solih's efforts to enhance the Maldives's maritime security.[29] In contrast, Muizzu's victory suggests a closer relationship with China – a relationship which had been cultivated under former President Yameen. China's involvement in the Maldives has grown in the region, particularly since 2017, with the country officially joining the BRI, the major infrastructure project launched by China to establish its hegemony.[30]

During Solih's tenure, efforts were made to repair relations with India, with both countries seeking alignment through their respective regional security and development initiatives. However, the political landscape in the Maldives has become increasingly divided, with partisan factions supporting either China or India.

China's interest in the Maldives is largely driven by its strategic location in the Indian Ocean, vital for its regional influence. Under Yameen, the Maldives accumulated substantial debt to China, a legacy that Solih inherited.[31] Despite this, as mentioned before, Solih reinforced India's position in the region and emphasized bilateral trust and partnership.

The competition between China and India will continue to shape the Maldives's foreign policy, with the nation navigating the complexities of this geopolitical tug-of-war.[32] In 2025, the Maldives' foreign policy remains deeply influenced by the ongoing strategic competition between India and China. In a significant development in June, India extended a $400 million currency swap arrangement through the Reserve Bank of India, helping to bolster the Maldives' foreign exchange reserves. This move was widely seen as a reaffirmation of India's commitment to supporting economic stability in the archipelago amid rising debt concerns and Chinese investment pressures. Earlier in May, India had also agreed to roll over a $50 million treasury bill at the request of the Maldivian government, signalling not only financial support but also a calibrated effort to retain geopolitical influence in a region where Beijing's economic footprint continues to expand. Together, these developments underscore the Maldives' delicate balancing act in navigating a growing India–China tug-of-war in the Indian Ocean.[33]

Election Commission

The need for an independent election commission in the Maldives was highlighted in 2004, during a series of democratic reforms aimed at strengthening the country's political system. A key goal of these reforms was the modernization of the electoral process to ensure elections were free, fair and transparent, while fostering a functioning multiparty system in the Maldives.

Following these reforms, the 2008 constitution established the Election Commission as an autonomous entity, ensuring it would operate in accordance with the constitution, the laws passed by the People's Majlis and the statute outlining its responsibilities, powers and mandate.

The Election Commission of the Maldives was established on 7 August 2008 as an independent and impartial body tasked with overseeing all state elections and public referendums, and monitoring the regulatory framework governing political parties. According to the Election Commission Act (2008), the president appoints five members for a five-year term, subject to approval by the People's Majlis.

Before the creation of the transitional Election Commission, as outlined in Article 276 of the 2008 constitution, elections were managed by the commissioner of elections, initially under the Ministry of Home Affairs and later the President's Office. The commissioner, appointed by the president, was accountable solely to the president and could only be dismissed by the president.

The Parliament

The Maldives operates as a presidential constitutional republic with a unicameral legislative system. Both the president (head of state) and members of the People's Majlis are directly elected by citizens through equal suffrage. All Maldivian citizens aged eighteen or older, except those convicted of a criminal offence or currently serving a prison sentence of five years or more, are eligible to vote in presidential, parliamentary and national referendum elections. Voting is conducted through secret ballots.

Following the 2008 constitutional reform, multiparty politics took root in the Maldives, becoming the foundation for every national election since then. According to the constitution, members of the People's Majlis are elected by residents of the capital, Malé, and the twenty inhabited atolls. Each constituency elects two MPs, with an additional representative chosen for every 5,000 citizens registered in that division.

Parliamentary elections are governed by the country's 2008 Electoral Act, which outlines clear regulations for the conduct of elections to the People's Majlis. These provisions are overseen and enforced by the independent Election Commission of the Maldives, which ensures that the elections have adhered to international standards of fairness, accountability and transparency. During the 2023 presidential elections and the 2024 parliamentary elections, these standards and its implementation was confirmed by electoral observation visits from both the Commonwealth Secretariat and the European Union External Action Service

Members of the People's Majlis are elected to represent individual constituencies using a FPTP voting system and serve five-year terms in office. The People's Majlis is the unicameral legislative body of the Maldives, with the authority to enact, amend and revise laws. As of 2024, it has ninety-three members.

Democratic Ranking

According to the Freedom House rankings, the Maldives was marked as 'not free' in 2006 and 2007, prior to the enactment of 2008 constitution which expanded the democratic nature of the island country.[34] In fact, even after this, in 2009, the Maldives was ranked as one of the most repressive regimes, ranked among the worst autocracies in the world. For instance, a 2009 report by Amnesty International noted that nearly 200 people, mostly women, were sentenced to flogging for extramarital sex since 2006.[35]

The transition into democracy was gradual and took nearly a decade. For instance, it is only now that the Maldives ranks in the mid-range across all categories of the V-Dem Institute's Global State of Democracy framework. While it falls within the bottom 25 per cent globally for freedom of religion, it is in the top 25 per cent for electoral participation.[36] Over the past five years, the country has made notable advancements in democratic development, with significant improvements in representation, rights, participation and rule of law.[37] An upper-middle-income nation, the Maldives depends heavily on sectors such as tourism, fishing and boat-building. The economy has experienced rapid growth in recent decades, demonstrating resilience and a robust recovery following decline in tourism revenue during the Covid-19 pandemic.[38] Advances in healthcare and education have also contributed to the country's steady rise in the human development index.[39]

Conclusion

The Maldives, a nation at the juncture of South Asia and the Indian Ocean, has experienced remarkable political and economic transformations over the past two decades. Since the adoption of its 2008 constitution, the country has navigated the complexities of democratization, marked by the introduction of multiparty politics, the establishment of an independent Election Commission and a growing commitment to democratic values, albeit with occasional setbacks.

Moreover, given its strategic importance in the region, the Maldives is subject to geopolitical push-and-pull by the major powers, China and India. As mentioned earlier, its political landscape has been shaped by the rival pro-China and pro-India factions, making it vulnerable to geopolitical rivalry in the Indian Ocean. The Maldives' political volatility and its role in regional dynamics have long been shaped by foreign strategic interests in significant ways.[40]

On the economic front, the Maldives is heavily dependent on the tourism industry, which constitutes nearly 30 per cent of its total GDP.[41] Apart from that, banking on its natural resources, the country has expanded its exports in fisheries and ship-building services. However, foreign aid and dependence on external revenues such as loans from international banks has made it vulnerable to rising levels of debt and inequality.[42] Despite these challenges, however, the Maldives has shown great resilience in recovering from the shocks of the pandemic, making advancements, particularly in the fields of healthcare and education.

However, the dark legacies of dictatorship and autocracy continue to linger, with persistent concerns regarding violations of human rights and political freedoms of its citizens.[43] Therefore, the future of the Maldives rests upon its ability to better its performance in the rule of law, and in balancing out domestic reforms and foreign policy pressures. More importantly, given its location in an ecologically sensitive zone, sustainable development must be its priority, keeping in mind the ever-worsening concerns of climate change.[44]

Key Events at a Glance

- **1887** – The Maldives becomes a British protectorate through a treaty with Sultan Muhammad Mueenuddeen II. Britain controls foreign policy and defence; the Maldives retains internal autonomy
- **1800s–1900s** – Period marked by succession of sultans, trade in cowrie shells, coconuts and coir; the British keep a light presence, mainly through Ceylon
- **1932** – First written constitution of the Maldives promulgated under Sultan Muhammad Shamsuddeen III; introduces limited reforms and formal institutions but is soon suspended
- **1948–53** – Growing political debate on governance, British influence and modernization
- **1952** – Abolition of monarchy; the Maldives becomes a republic with Mohamed Amin Didi as first president
- **1953** – Coup d'état: Amin Didi overthrown; monarchy restored with Sultan Muhammad Fareed Didi
- **1957** – The British establish air base in Gan (Addu Atoll); PM Ibrahim Nasir opposes it, leading to tensions
- **1965** – Independence from Britain achieved on 26 July 1965; the Maldives becomes a fully sovereign state while retaining monarchy
- **1968** – Second Republic declared: monarchy abolished via referendum; Ibrahim Nasir becomes president
- **1975** – British withdraw from Gan base; the Maldives asserts full strategic control
- **1978** – Maumoon Abdul Gayoom becomes president; begins thirty-year rule marked by centralized authority, Islamic legitimacy and cautious modernization
- **1988** – Coup attempt by Tamil mercenaries (backed by Maldivian dissidents); thwarted with Indian military intervention (Operation Cactus)
- **1990s–2000s** – Political repression, censorship and gradual rise of opposition movements in exile and underground
- **2004** – Pro-democracy protests and arrest of activists lead to international pressure
- **2008** – New democratic constitution enacted; the Maldives holds first multiparty elections; Mohamed Nasheed of MDP becomes president
- **2012** – Nasheed forced to resign under pressure from security forces; later claims it was a coup

- **2013** – Abdulla Yameen (half-brother of Gayoom) wins presidency; democratic backsliding suppression of dissent and drift toward Chinese economic influence
- **2015–18** – Political arrests, judicial interventions and curbing of civil liberties; rising Islamic conservatism and foreign debt concerns
- **2018** – Ibrahim Solih of MDP wins presidency in a surprise landslide; begins re-democratization and India-friendly foreign policy
- **2020–21** – The Maldives navigates Covid-19 crisis with economic strain due to tourism dependency
- **2023** – Mohamed Muizzu, backed by the Progressive Alliance and associated with Abdulla Yameen, wins presidency; signals pivot toward China and renewed tensions with India
- **2024** – 'India Out' campaign, geopolitical realignment; debates on judicial independence, constitutional reform and climate vulnerability dominate politics.
- **2025** – The Maldives signs Free Trade Agreement with China; India–Maldives High-Level Core Group meets in May to recalibrate ties amid continued strategic rivalry

Part II

The Democracy Scorecard

9

Global Democracy Indices: What It Reveals and What It Doesn't

South Asia's Rankings in the Indices

Having traced the institutional and historical foundations of democracy across each of the SAARC nations, we are now in a position to step back and observe the region through a comparative, cross-national lens. While the preceding country profiles illuminated the trajectories that brought each nation to its present democratic condition – shaped by colonial legacies, constitutional choices and the struggles of state-building – this chapter turns to how democracy in South Asia is measured, ranked and interpreted by the world. Global democracy indices such as the EIU, the V-Dem Project and the Electoral Integrity Project (EIP) have become powerful tools in shaping international perception and scholarly discourse. But how well do these metrics capture the lived realities, structural exclusions and political aspirations of South Asian democracies? What do they get right – and what do they leave out? This chapter engages with these questions not only to assess the current state of democratic health in the region, but also to examine the very frameworks through which that health is diagnosed.

These indices matter not only because they offer an external audit of democratic performance, but because they provide a shared map – placing South Asian countries in relation to one another across a variety of criteria, from civil liberties to electoral integrity. After examining these nations individually, such comparative mapping allows us to identify regional patterns, divergences and shared vulnerabilities. Moreover, these rankings have begun to draw significant attention from governments, media and civil society alike – often sparking political defensiveness, public debate or institutional denial. Understanding what these indices measure, what they miss and why they matter is therefore crucial – not only for scholars and practitioners, but for any serious engagement with the democratic futures of South Asia.

At the heart of this book lies a simple but formidable ambition: to grasp, in comparative and comprehensive terms, the evolving status of democracy across the eight countries of South Asia that comprise the SAARC region. These are societies of immense complexity and contradiction – pluralistic yet polarized, electorally vibrant yet institutionally fragile. As the world's largest concentration of democracies (by population), South Asia has often been held up as an enduring outlier – defiant in its embrace of electoral democracy despite colonial histories, developmental challenges and social fragmentations. However, as this chapter will argue, the region is now gripped by a sharp and multidirectional democratic decline, which has not only been diagnosed with increasing clarity by global observers but which also demands urgent domestic reckoning.

This claim is not simply a matter of normative concern; it is substantiated by an extraordinary convergence among the world's three most comprehensive instruments for assessing democratic health, as mentioned earlier: the EIU, the V-Dem Project and the EIP. Though distinct in orientation and methodology, these indices tell a consistent and increasingly sobering story: democracy across South Asia is not simply under stress, it is in regression.

The EIU's *Democracy Index*, which evaluates democracies on five key dimensions – electoral process, civil liberties, political participation, political culture and functioning of government – ranks 167 countries annually. Between 2016 and 2024, every single SAARC country has either declined or stagnated in this index. India, for example, fell from the 32nd rank in 2016 to the 41st in 2024, moving deeper into the category of 'flawed democracy'. Bangladesh plummeted from 75th to 100th during the same period, marking one of the steepest declines globally. Pakistan has dropped from 108th to 118th, slipping further into the domain of 'authoritarian regimes'. Afghanistan, in the wake of the Taliban's return, is now ranked 167th – the very bottom (see Table 1).

Bhutan and Nepal offer marginal counterpoints. Bhutan, one of the world's youngest democracies, climbed from 101st to 81st, and Nepal edged upward from 104th to 98th, reflecting improvements in electoral and participatory measures, albeit from low baselines. The Maldives showed a minimal recovery – from 97th to 95th – following the ouster of its former autocratic president and the resumption of competitive multiparty politics. Sri Lanka's decline – from 66th to 70th – is less steep but politically telling. It reflects deepening discontent with political elites, endemic corruption and the fallout of an executive-dominated state (see Table 1).

The V-Dem Project's *Liberal Democracy Index*, with its far more granular dataset derived from thousands of expert-coded variables, confirms this deterioration. India, Bangladesh and Pakistan are no longer classified as democracies in the V-Dem schema. They are 'electoral autocracies' – regimes where elections occur but are marred by media control, weakened opposition, compromised judiciaries and political violence. India's fall is especially jarring: once positioned alongside liberal democracies, it now shares typological space with Turkey, Hungary and Ethiopia. Afghanistan, unsurprisingly, is classified as a closed autocracy. The V-Dem Project's framework of analysis places significant emphasis on liberal principles: not merely whether elections are held, but whether power is constrained, citizens are protected and dissent is permitted. On all these counts, South Asia is faltering (see Table 2).

It is the inclusion of the EIP, however, that brings the picture into sharpest comparative focus. Unlike the EIU and the V-Dem Project, which offer holistic democratic scores, the EIP restricts itself to evaluating the integrity of elections specifically – across eleven stages, from pre-election conditions and voter registration to vote counting and results reporting. This makes it a critical lens in a region where elections are frequent but often compromised.

According to the 2024 *Global Electoral Integrity Report* by the EIP, South Asia continues to grapple with significant electoral challenges, as evidenced by declining scores in several key democracies. The scoring system for the EIP is starkly different from the EIU. For the EIU's

Table 1: The EIU's *Democracy Index* Rankings (2019 vs 2024)[1]

Country	2019 Rank	2019 Score	2019 Classification	2024 Rank	2024 Score	2024 Classification	Notes
Afghanistan	139	2.85	Authoritarian	167	0.25	Authoritarian	Drastic decline due to regime change and suppression of freedoms
Bangladesh	80	5.88	Hybrid Regime	100	4.44	Hybrid Regime	Significant drop following contested elections and political unrest
Bhutan	84	5.65	Hybrid Regime	81	5.54	Hybrid Regime	Slight improvement in ranking with stable governance
India	51	6.90	Flawed Democracy	41	7.18	Flawed Democracy	Improved ranking despite concerns over civil liberties
The Maldives	95	5.31	Hybrid Regime	95	5.65	Hybrid Regime	Progress attributed to democratic reforms and improved governance
Nepal	97	4.93	Hybrid Regime	98	4.60	Hybrid Regime	Minor decline due to political instability
Pakistan	105	4.17	Hybrid Regime	118	3.25	Authoritarian	Downgraded classification amid increased authoritarian practices
Sri Lanka	68	6.42	Flawed Democracy	70	6.17	Flawed Democracy	Slight decline amid economic and political challenges

Table 2: V-Dem's *Liberal Democracy Index* Rankings (2019 vs 2024)[2]

Country	2019 Classification	2024 Classification	Notes
Afghanistan	Electoral Autocracy	Closed Autocracy	Significant decline post-Taliban resurgence
Bangladesh	Electoral Autocracy	Electoral Autocracy	Persistent issues with electoral integrity and civil liberties
Bhutan	Electoral Democracy	Electoral Democracy	Maintained status with minor fluctuations
India	Electoral Democracy	Electoral Autocracy	Notable decline due to concerns over civil liberties and minority rights
The Maldives	Electoral Democracy	Electoral Democracy	Stability maintained with ongoing democratic reforms
Nepal	Electoral Democracy	Electoral Democracy	Consistent performance with challenges in governance
Pakistan	Electoral Autocracy	Electoral Autocracy	Continued struggles with military influence and press freedom
Sri Lanka	Electoral Democracy	Electoral Autocracy	Decline attributed to political instability and executive overreach

Note: V-Dem classifications are based on multiple indicators, including electoral processes, civil liberties and rule of law.

Democracy Index a rank of 1 would be highest (and 167th the lowest), but for the EIP 1 denotes the lowest score (and 100 denotes the highest). The trajectory of electoral integrity across SAARC nations between 2019 and 2024 presents a revealing, if uneven, portrait of democratic resilience and regression in the region. While some countries have made commendable strides, others have slipped further into democratic deterioration. Bhutan and the Maldives emerge as notable bright spots, with Bhutan improving from an already high score of 66 to 71, reinforcing its image as a small but robust electoral democracy. The Maldives, too, recorded a significant gain – jumping 15 points from 52 to 67 – suggesting that recent political reforms and peaceful transitions of power have borne fruit. Nepal and Sri Lanka show modest but important improvements, with Nepal rising from 56 to 62 and Sri Lanka from 52 to 54, indicating incremental gains in electoral administration and competitive pluralism, despite persisting political fragilities in both countries.

Conversely, the more populous and geopolitically dominant nations – India, Bangladesh – and Pakistan – reflect concerning trends. India's decline from 59 to 53 signals a measurable erosion in electoral fairness, possibly tied to the centralization of political power, perceived institutional partisanship, and curbs on dissent. Bangladesh's drop from 38 to 35, though numerically modest, reinforces its position as one of the region's most fragile electoral democracies, where elections are increasingly uncompetitive and opposition parties face systematic repression. Pakistan's dip from 47 to 45 similarly suggests entrenched structural interference and civilian-military tensions that continue to undermine electoral credibility. Afghanistan, despite ongoing instability, saw a small improvement from 34 to 40 – yet its score remains the lowest in the region, underscoring the continued vulnerability of its democratic institutions. Taken together, the 2024 EIP scores paint a complex picture: while democratic gains are not absent, South Asia's electoral landscape remains marred by democratic backsliding in its largest states, raising difficult questions about the region's collective democratic future.

Table 3: The EIP's Rankings (2019 vs 2024)[3]

Country	2019 EIP Score	2019 Classification	2024 EIP Score	2024 Classification	Notes
Afghanistan	34	Low Integrity	40	Very Low Integrity	With chronic instability, Afghanistan remains the weakest electoral environment in the region.

Country	2019 EIP Score	2019 Classification	2024 EIP Score	2024 Classification	Notes
Bangladesh	38	Low Integrity	35	Very Low Integrity	A deepening electoral crisis marked by opposition repression and uncompetitive polls has pushed Bangladesh further down in integrity.
Bhutan	66	Moderate Integrity	71	Moderate Integrity	Already the region's best performcr, Bhutan has further consolidated its democratic procedures and institutional trust
India	59	Moderate Integrity	53	Low Integrity	India's electoral integrity has declined amid growing concerns over institutional neutrality, media freedom, and misuse of state power.
The Maldives	52	Low Integrity	67	Moderate Integrity	A remarkable improvement suggesting successful democratic reform and enhanced credibility of electoral processes post-authoritarian rule.

Country	2019 EIP Score	2019 Classification	2024 EIP Score	2024 Classification	Notes
Nepal	56	Moderate Integrity	62	Moderate Integrity	Gains indicate strengthening of electoral institutions and a relatively open democratic space despite political flux.
Pakistan	47	Low Integrity	45	Low Integrity	Persistent interference and opaque electoral practices continue to erode public trust in electoral outcomes.
Sri Lanka	52	Moderate Integrity	54	Low Integrity	A small but positive movement suggesting stable electoral mechanics, though overshadowed by broader governance crises.

What emerges from this triangulated assessment is a convergence of concern, not merely among indices, but across institutions, scholars and regions. While the methodological focus varies – the EIU emphasizes political culture, the V-Dem Project dissects liberal constraints and the EIP zooms in on electoral quality – their conclusions are mutually reinforcing. South Asia is experiencing a systemic crisis of democracy – not simply through overt authoritarianism but through quieter erosions of judicial independence, press freedom, minority rights, federalism and parliamentary integrity.

Equally striking is the comparative dynamic within the region. India, long considered the democratic anchor of South Asia, is no longer its best performer on key measures. Bhutan now leads the region on electoral integrity and ranks highest in liberal democratic indicators. Nepal, despite its tumultuous politics, has become a relative bright spot for democratic participation and press freedom. Bangladesh and Pakistan, once comparable to India on several electoral and participatory metrics, have diverged sharply towards authoritarian consolidation. The Maldives and Sri Lanka stand at the edge – fragile, fissured and caught between reformist aspirations and systemic inertia. Afghanistan, meanwhile, no longer belongs to the democratic world.

The significance of these changes is not merely regional. They carry enormous implications for global democracy. Together, the SAARC nations account for nearly 2 billion people – almost one-fourth of humanity. A democratic crisis of this scale, if unaddressed, will recalibrate global democratic averages, reorder geopolitical alliances and redraw the moral geography of international governance.

Nevertheless, this is not a story of inevitability. The great promise of South Asian democracy – etched into the founding moments of its republics, its people's movements and its constitutional texts – remains alive, if embattled. What this chapter has attempted to demonstrate is that we now possess the tools, the data and the analytical frameworks to measure the depth of the crisis. The challenge of the present is not a lack of evidence – it is a lack of political will, of democratic imagination and of moral clarity. This book is an attempt to address all three.

Mapping the Metrics – Origins, Aims and Methodologies of Global Democracy Indices

If democracy is to be meaningfully defended in the twenty-first century, it must be measured with rigour, nuance and fidelity to both institutional form and substantive freedom. The past two decades have seen the development of ambitious global projects to do precisely that. But these Indexes – EIU, V-Dem and EIP – did not arise in a vacuum. They emerged at distinct historical conjunctures, informed by different theoretical paradigms and institutional goals. They measure democracy not merely as a set of procedures but as a constellation of values, and each does so from a unique vantage point.

1. The EIU's Democracy Index: A Liberal-Institutional Metric

The EIU's *Democracy Index* was first published in 2006, against the backdrop of what political theorists were then calling the 'third wave' of democratization. With the Cold War over and a liberal international order in ascendance, many political scientists anticipated a gradual, global consolidation of liberal democracy. The EIU, as a research arm of the Economist Group, sought to develop a stripped-down yet wide-ranging index that could track this evolution and provide policymakers, investors and academics with an accessible yardstick of democratic performance.

As mentioned in passing previously, its model is structured around five dimensions: electoral process and pluralism, civil liberties, the functioning of government, political participation and political culture. These components are assessed through a mixture of expert assessments and public opinion surveys. Countries are then placed into four regime types: full democracies, flawed democracies, hybrid regimes and authoritarian regimes.

Methodologically, the EIU places strong emphasis on institutional performance and the overall 'liberal character' of political systems. It is not overly granular but aims for global comparability through a standardized scorecard. While some critics have accused it of being Western-centric, its categorical typology – especially the 'flawed democracy' classification – has been influential in framing global discourse.

2. The V-Dem Project: The Archival and Multidimensional Atlas

Founded in 2014 and housed at the University of Gothenburg and the Kellogg Institute at the University of Notre Dame, the V-Dem Project represents the most ambitious and granular attempt to map the global condition of democracy. In contrast to the EIU's top-down expert model, the V-Dem Project draws upon more than 3,700 country experts worldwide – including local scholars, journalists and activists –

generating over 550 distinct indicators across multiple dimensions of democracy. These are aggregated into indices such as liberal democracy index, electoral democracy index and deliberative democracy index.[4]

But the V-Dem Project's foundational intervention is epistemological: it challenges the idea that democracy is a binary condition (either present or absent) and insists instead that democracy is a variable, historical and disaggregated phenomenon. It introduces five core principles of democracy – electoral, liberal, participatory, deliberative and egalitarian – and generates scores for each.

The historical moment of the V-Dem Project's emergence is crucial. By 2014, the democratic euphoria of the 1990s had faded, replaced by a rising awareness of democratic backsliding, even in countries that continued to hold elections. The 'autocratization' of states like Turkey, Hungary and later India revealed the insufficiency of election-centric models. The V-Dem Project was designed precisely to capture these subtler erosions of democracy: constraints on the judiciary, repression of civil society, manipulation of information ecosystems and declining equality of political voice.

The V-Dem Project's greatest strength lies in its granularity. Where the EIU might describe a country as a 'flawed democracy', the V-Dem Project can specify that while electoral processes remain relatively intact, the judiciary is captured, the media landscape is distorted and political dissent is criminalized. It is thus not merely an index but an evolving archive of democratic life.

3. The EIP: Democracy from the Ballot Box Outwards

The EIP was founded in 2012 by political scientists Pippa Norris and Sarah Birch, among others, as a response to the growing realization that not all elections are equal, and that many electoral regimes were 'hollow democracies'. The EIP's core concern is electoral quality, which it measures across eleven stages of the electoral cycle, as mentioned earlier – from legal frameworks and voter registration to campaign finance, electoral administration, media access, vote count and dispute resolution.

The EIP draws upon expert surveys conducted shortly after elections in over 160 countries. Scores are expressed on a scale of 0 to 100 and emphasize procedural fairness, administrative transparency and institutional safeguards.

Unlike the V-Dem or the EIU, the EIP does not attempt to assess overall democratic quality. Instead, it takes elections – the most visible face of democracy – as its analytical anchor and reveals where, how and to what extent they fall short of international norms.

Theoretically, the EIP is situated within a proceduralist tradition of democratic theory, but with a strong normative commitment to electoral justice. It has been especially important in distinguishing between electoral authoritarianism and genuine competitive regimes, thereby highlighting how flawed elections can provide a veneer of legitimacy to deeply autocratic states.

For South Asia, where elections are routinely held but often marked by structural biases, state capture and media manipulation, the EIP offers a focused diagnostic tool. In countries like Bangladesh, India and Pakistan, it enables a precise audit of how democratic decline is often engineered through seemingly democratic means.

Points of Divergence Between Indices: A Comparative Scheme

To fully appreciate the import of these indices, it is necessary to underscore their differences in purpose, method and conceptual focus (see Table 4).

The analytical gain of using these three indices together lies in their complementarity. The EIU offers a bird's-eye view of democratic trajectories. The V-Dem Project enables deep dives into the anatomy of democratic institutions and processes. The EIP pinpoints the procedural integrity – or the lack thereof – of the electoral moment itself. In unison, they provide not only a clearer picture of democratic health but also a more justifiable basis for concern.

The next section will examine how these indices define democracy, identifying the parameters most relevant to the SAARC context – such as civil liberties, judicial independence, electoral transparency, political pluralism and participatory equality. If this section has laid the groundwork, the next will examine the architecture.

Now, having traced the standing of South Asian democracies across three major global indices and having examined the historical formation and methodological differences among those indices, we are

Table 4. Comparing the Three Indices

Index	Founding Year	Primary Aim	Methodology	Core Focus	Strengths	Limitations
The EIU's Democracy Index	2006	To offer an accessible ranking of global democracies for policymakers and the public	Expert-coded, limited survey data	Electoral process, civil liberties, institutional performance	Simplicity, comparability, annual consistency	Limited granularity and possible liberal bias
The V-Dem Project	2014	To disaggregate and deeply map different varieties of democracy	Global expert network, 550+ indicators	Electoral, liberal, participatory, deliberative, egalitarian democracy	Rich data, multidimensionality, historical depth	Complexity, steep learning curve
The EIP	2012	To assess the quality and fairness of elections globally	Post-election expert surveys across eleven electoral stages	Electoral justice and procedural integrity	Election-specific detail, actionable insights	Narrow focus, does not assess full democratic environment

poised to investigate what exactly they measure. This section explores the principal parameters used by the EIU, the V-Dem Project and the EIP to define and assess democracy, and how these parameters manifest across the SAARC region. The aim is not only to identify the thematic core of these assessments but also to situate the SAARC nations within those frameworks through a comparative, regionally attentive lens.

Beyond Elections: An Expansive Definition

While elections remain the most visible ritual of democratic life, the consensus among all three indices is that free and fair elections are a necessary but not sufficient condition for genuine democracy. As is discerned from the EIU's methodological criterion, democracy entails government accountability, political culture, civil liberties and active participation of the citizenry. The V-Dem Project goes further, embedding democracy within a wider matrix of liberal, deliberative, participatory and egalitarian commitments. The EIP narrows in on electoral processes but with a sharp eye for the quality, credibility and inclusiveness of the vote.

These indices, while diverse in their methods, converge around certain core parameters that define the modern democratic condition. We can classify these into five analytically distinct but interconnected domains.

1. Electoral Integrity and Pluralism

At the base of every democracy lies the legitimacy of the electoral process – a domain measured most comprehensively by the EIP and the EIU. This includes universal suffrage, competitive multiparty elections, transparent vote counting, independent electoral commissions and the absence of coercion or vote-buying.

India, despite hosting the largest electoral exercise in the world, has seen a marked decline in electoral integrity. While the procedural aspects (logistics, turnout, scale) remain intact, the independence of the election commission, misuse of state resources and a partisan media environment have drawn strong criticism, particularly in the V-Dem Project's and the EIP's reports post 2019.

Bangladesh has faced electoral authoritarianism, with reports of ballot-stuffing, voter intimidation and opposition suppression. The EIP ranked its 2018 general elections among the least credible in the world that year.

Pakistan suffers from military interference in electoral outcomes and systematic marginalization of dissent, though its formal election commission has shown improved administrative transparency in recent cycles.

Sri Lanka, while historically enjoying relatively high electoral integrity, has seen rising concerns over manipulation of electoral law and emergency powers, especially under the Rajapaksa governments.

Nepal, Bhutan and the Maldives show varying trajectories. Nepal's post-monarchy elections have been largely credible, though plagued by chronic instability and frequent government turnover. Bhutan's elections are free but heavily regulated: political parties are prohibited from contesting local government elections, candidates must hold a university degree and the Election Commission exercises broad powers over party registration, campaign financing and media access. The Maldives, once a textbook case of electoral repression, has shown signs of improvement since the democratic transition of 2018, including more competitive polls and greater opposition space.

2. Civil Liberties and Freedom of Expression

Civil liberties – freedom of speech, assembly, religion and movement – are treated as foundational in both the EIU and the V-Dem models. A democracy that tolerates elections but criminalizes dissent or chills free expression is understood to be substantively hollow.

India has seen a steep decline in press freedom, digital rights and academic autonomy. The V-Dem Project notes 'a substantial narrowing of space for civil society', with independent media facing harassment, and dissent increasingly criminalized under sedition and terrorism laws.

Bangladesh and Pakistan suffer similar constraints: draconian cybercrime laws, extrajudicial repression, and attacks on journalists and activists.

Sri Lanka saw a period of opening post the civil war, but successive regimes have stifled protests, particularly during the economic crisis.

In Bhutan, the situation is more ambiguous. While basic liberties exist, public expression is tightly monitored and the press operates within a culture of self-censorship.

Nepal retains stronger civic freedoms, but instability, weak law enforcement and corruption impede accountability. The Maldives has improved on civil liberties since democratic reforms in 2018 but remains fragile.

3. Judicial and Institutional Independence

The V-Dem Project gives special weight to the liberal component of democracy – the protection of individual and minority rights through independent institutions that check executive power. The EIU evaluates this under 'functioning of government'.

India's judiciary, long celebrated for its activist role, is increasingly viewed as compromised by executive pressure. The V-Dem Project notes rising cases of 'autocratization by stealth', where independent institutions are formally retained but are functionally hollowed out.

In Pakistan, the judiciary has often oscillated between complicity and confrontation with the military establishment. Its credibility remains contested.

Bangladesh exhibits deep judicial capture by the long-ruling (now overthrown) BAL, and Sri Lanka's institutions have faced manipulation through emergency laws.

Nepal and Bhutan show formal judicial independence, but lack robust institutional enforcement. The Maldives, though recovering from autocratic control, still suffers from a weak rule of law.

4. Political Participation and Inclusivity

A core V-Dem Project and EIU metric is political participation – not merely the right to vote but the actual capacity and opportunity to organize, campaign, mobilize and represent one's interests.

Voter turnout remains high across South Asia, but participation is often distorted by structural inequality, based on caste, ethnicity, religion, gender or geography.

India, for instance, boasts high turnout but low intraparty democracy and marginalized communities face systemic exclusion from political leadership. The growing concentration of political finance among a few corporate entities compounds this disparity.

Nepal and Sri Lanka have relatively inclusive structures, but women's representation remains low across the region. In Bhutan, political engagement is often constrained by regulatory oversight.

Pakistan, Bangladesh and the Maldives all exhibit vibrant political societies, but these are often vulnerable to repression, patronage or militarized conflict.

5. Political Culture and Media Ecosystem

Democracy also depends on the values, norms and discourses that underpin it – a domain that both the EIU and the V-Dem Project try to quantify through measures of tolerance, political trust and media pluralism. South Asia reveals a disturbing trend: erosion of democratic culture even in electorally active societies. Majoritarianism, populist strongmen and identity politics dominate public discourse.

India's slide, in particular, is marked by increasing media partisanship, celebration of authoritarian leadership and demonization of minorities.

Bangladesh and Pakistan reflect similar dynamics where democratic norms are often subordinated to security narratives or developmental populism.

Nepal remains pluralistic in culture, but fractured by elite factionalism. Sri Lanka, recovering from conflict, has seen growing Buddhist nationalism. Bhutan's political culture remains hierarchical, albeit orderly. The Maldives still grapples with the politicization of religion and the legacy of autocracy.

Parameters in Convergence, Realities in Crisis

Taken together, these indices make one point unmistakably clear: democracy is not merely about votes – it is about voices, values and vital institutions. The South Asian region, despite its proud traditions of political struggle, finds itself caught in the paradox of democratic forms without democratic substance. Elections are held, but hollowed out. Courts exist, but defer to executive power. Civil society endures, but under siege.

The previous section has illustrated that democratic erosion in the SAARC region is a multidimensional, interlocking crisis. The very metrics meant to measure democracy – electoral credibility, civil liberties, institutional independence, political inclusion and democratic culture – are being undermined simultaneously.

It is therefore not enough to defend democracy in the abstract. We must defend the parameters that make democracy possible with vigilance, with moral clarity and with regionally specific insight.

The next section of this chapter will examine the critiques of these indices themselves – some necessary, others spurious – and explore how to navigate these critiques without descending into cynical relativism or uncritical acceptance.

Critiquing the Indexes

The project of measuring democracy is inherently contentious. To quantify the health of a nation's political life – its institutions, freedoms and civic integrity – is to intervene in the terrain of sovereign self-perception and political legitimacy. It is thus not surprising that the major democracy indices have drawn criticisms from both the ideological Right and the progressive Left, albeit for very different reasons.

This section engages with these criticisms in two registers: the regressive, which seek to discredit such indices altogether for political ends; and the progressive, which call for deeper epistemic and methodological reform in the spirit of empirical accuracy and justice. The aim here is not to defend these indices uncritically, but to position them as part of a larger discursive battleground in the global struggle over democratic standards and self-understanding.

The Regressive Rebuttal: 'Western Conspiracies' and 'Anti-National Bias'

Across South Asia – particularly in India, Bangladesh and Pakistan – the most immediate and politically expedient response to negative rankings has been to delegitimize the indices themselves, casting them as part of a neo-imperial plot to tarnish national reputations or undermine sovereign authority.

India's official stance

When India dropped from the EIU's 'flawed democracy' to the ranks of an 'electoral autocracy' in V-Dem's classification, senior Indian ministers and media outlets decried the rankings as 'biased', 'ignorant of ground realities' or worse as 'anti-India'. Commentators accused the indices of being 'Western constructs' that fail to grasp India's size, diversity and electoral vibrancy. Parliamentary debates in India have seen ruling party MPs cite global rankings as evidence of 'foreign interference' and label critics of the Indian state as 'anti-national', rather than engaging with the substantive issues raised.[5]

They overlook the fact that methodology and parameters on which the democracy is measured are the same in all 167 democratic countries and territories of the world.[6]

Pakistan and Bangladesh

In Pakistan, criticism of these indices tends to pivot on strategic deflection, arguing that international rankings ignore 'the security context' and the 'burden of fighting terrorism'.[7] The claim here is that global assessments penalize necessary restrictions as authoritarianism, failing to differentiate between emergency measures and systematic repression.

In Bangladesh, the response to poor electoral scores – such as the EIP's abysmal rating for the 2018 Bangladesh elections – has been to disregard the findings as politically motivated. Government spokespersons have argued that high voter turnout and infrastructural order are sufficient proof of legitimacy, brushing aside concerns of opposition suppression and ballot manipulation.[8]

These regressive critiques share three features: (1) They personalize criticism (by targeting foreign institutions or individuals); (2) they equate criticism with cultural incomprehension or geopolitical hostility; and (3) they function as tools of nationalist posturing, aiming to protect domestic narratives rather than addressing democratic deficits.

But such evasion carries grave costs. The wholesale rejection of international scrutiny forecloses dialogue, undermines self-correction and enables further erosion of democratic accountability under the guise of patriotic defence.

Progressive Critiques: Towards a More Just and Nuanced Measurement

Progressive scholars and activists, by contrast, do not reject democracy indices out of hand. Rather, they interrogate their normative assumptions, methodological blind spots and cross-cultural inadequacies – all in the spirit of democratic renewal, not rejection.

1. When Caste Is not Counted

In India, perhaps the most significant omission across all three indices is their failure to account for caste – not as a cultural residue, but as a structuring force of political life.

While the indices rightly emphasize religious polarization, press freedom and institutional autonomy, they say remarkably little about the entrenched dominance of upper-caste elites in political parties, bureaucracy, judiciary and media. A Dalit voter may cast a ballot freely, but is the democratic promise fulfilled if no major party prioritizes anti-caste agendas or if the judiciary remains disproportionately composed of upper-caste judges?

The same lacuna applies in Nepal, where caste-based exclusion persists within the hill-dominated political class; and in Sri Lanka, where caste dynamics within the Tamil community intersect with ethnic marginalization.

By privileging formal liberal metrics over structural social hierarchies, the indices risk underestimating the depth of exclusion in societies where inequality is baked into the social fabric.

2. Elections are not Enough

Another critique is the overemphasis on procedural formalism. A country may run technically competent elections with minimal logistical errors, yet can still suppress meaningful political competition through state capture, media distortion or violent intimidation.

Bangladesh is a case in point: while the EIP has rightly flagged electoral malfeasance in recent years, its earlier high scores were incongruous with ground reports of shrinking opposition space. Similarly, Sri Lanka's relatively high electoral ratings fail to capture the coercive power of majoritarian ethno-nationalism, which can suppress dissent even within a technically plural system.

3. The Urban Bias

A more subtle critique pertains to the linguistic and spatial biases built into data-gathering. Elite experts, urban academics and English-speaking journalists are often the primary informants for these indices. As a result, vernacular knowledge, rural disenfranchisement and non-institutional forms of repression may be under-reported or misunderstood.

For instance, reports of voter intimidation in rural Pakistan, or coercive development politics in tribal India, are less likely to appear in elite surveys. Gendered forms of exclusion, particularly where women are informally barred from voting in some constituencies, may elude formal metrics unless specifically flagged by on-ground monitors.

Towards a Better Democratic Index

The progressive critiques point not towards nihilism, but towards the possibility of richer, more locally embedded and justice-sensitive measures of democracy. The task is not to discard global indices, but to decolonize and democratize them by pushing for the inclusion of indicators that reflect lived realities in the Global South. Some proposals include:

1. Introducing caste-based equity measures in Indian democratic assessments
2. Accounting for decentralized participation in rural councils and indigenous assemblies
3. Incorporating gender-based and class-based exclusions more explicitly in democratic metrics
4. Ensuring local language fieldwork, regionally diverse expert panels and cross-verification with civil society networks

Such reforms would enhance the moral and empirical legitimacy of these indices and allow for more constructive engagement with governments and citizens alike.

Holding the Mirror Without Breaking It

In a region as complex and contested as South Asia, no index can claim total authority over what constitutes democracy. But this does not diminish their importance. They are not final judgements; they are diagnostic tools, calls to attention and invitations to action.

To reject these indices on nationalistic grounds is to shoot the mirror while hoping the blemishes will disappear. To refine them in good faith is to sharpen our vision of democracy – not as a trophy we already possess, but as a fragile, ever-contested aspiration.

To fortify democracy across South Asia, it is imperative for more experienced and stable nations to assume leadership and assist others in addressing internal issues. Given its status as the world's largest democracy and the most populous country by the next decade, India should lead by example. Establishing a regional forum for strengthening democracy in South Asia and Southeast Asia could significantly contribute to democracy promotion. This platform would enable democratic organizations and stakeholders to collabourate, exchange experiences, identify areas for cooperation and implement best practices, fostering institutional strength.

Rather than direct interventions prone to information asymmetry, organizations like UN Development Programme (UNDP), International Institute for Democracy and Electoral Assistance (International IDEA), Commonwealth, Department for International Development (DFID), Swedish International Development Cooperation Agency (SIDA) and US Agency for International Development (USAID) could synergize efforts through this forum. This collabourative approach would not only enhance the impact of targeted interventions but also allay diplomatic concerns regarding perceived 'foreign intervention' through softer means.

In the realm of democracy promotion, South Asia can draw inspiration from the ASEAN People's Forum. Civil society initiatives, such as universities and academic institutions, should channel more energy and resources into South Asia, focusing on funding and people-to-people exchanges. Collabourative efforts become imperative in the face of escalating regional conflicts and refugee crises, areas where regional civil society can work hand-in-hand where governments face limitations.

Respecting human rights domestically is foundational for each country. The rise of elected demagogues, a weakening judiciary and threats to press freedom pose significant regional threats. Treating minorities as assets for sustainable development is crucial, and governments must ensure fair treatment for migrants, refugees and asylum seekers under the law.

The struggle for democracy in South Asia is not merely about defending elections – it is about deepening justice, renewing participation, reclaiming institutions and reimagining citizenship itself. The indices tell only part of the story. The region's people, through their movements, resistances and reinventions, tell the rest.

This chapter has offered a comparative and critical examination of how democracy in South Asia is assessed based on various indices, highlighting both their diagnostic value and their methodological blind spots. Having established a shared regional picture through the EIU, the V-Dem Project and the EIP frameworks, and having explored what these tools reveal – and obscure – about South Asia's democratic health, we are now equipped to turn to the deeper themes that shape democratic life on the ground.

The chapters that follow move beyond country boundaries and focus instead on cross-cutting challenges: from gender representation and the rights of minorities to the criminalization of politics, the role of election commissions, and the future of youth participation. Together, these thematic inquiries aim to illuminate the structural forces, institutional pressures and popular movements that continue to define – and contest – the democratic experience across the region.

Taken together, the indices are not an endpoint but a point of departure. They help us map the terrain of democracy's condition in South Asia, but not yet the texture that lies lies in the lived realities of exclusion and resistance, in the quiet erosion of institutions, and in the loud demands for reform. As we now turn to these substantive themes, the task is no longer just to measure democracy, but to understand what threatens it, what sustains it and what might yet renew it.

Part III

Comparative Themes Across South Asia

10

The Missing Half: Gender and Political Representation

The pursuit of gender equality in political representation remains one of the defining challenges for South Asian democracies. Across the eight member states of the SAARC – Afghanistan, Bangladesh, Bhutan, India, Nepal, Pakistan, Sri Lanka and the Maldives – women comprise nearly half the population, yet remain strikingly under-represented in formal political institutions.[1] This contradiction is particularly disquieting in a region that has produced several iconic female heads of government but continues to lag behind global standards in broader legislative and party-based representation for women.

The stakes are high. According to the World Economic Forum's *Global Gender Gap Report 2024*, South Asia ranks second to last globally, closing only 63.7 per cent of its gender gap – a marginal increase of just 3.9 per centage points since 2006.[2] This slow progress is most starkly evident in the domain of political empowerment, where female representation in national parliaments remains well below global averages, and in some cases, is in free fall. Afghanistan, following the return of Taliban rule in 2021, now records zero women in political office.[3] Even in countries that have enacted legislative quotas, such as Pakistan and Bangladesh, women's substantive representation remains limited and is often symbolic rather than transformative.[4]

The challenge is not merely national, it is systemic and regional. This chapter provides a holistic and substantive analysis of the historical contexts, structural impediments and enabling factors that shape the political landscape for women in these nations. I believe that in order to enhance South Asian democracy, and thereby achieve freedom and justice for the whole of society, we must first solve the gender problem that is pervasive across the region.

We need to examine the indispensable links that exist between violence, representation and political participation of women. Therefore, even as we maintain that the electoral sphere is of immense importance in shaping the public life of women, we must broaden our view to consider the impact of the larger field: democratic institutions, the public sphere and civil society.

Architecture of Inclusion or Exclusion?

Electoral systems play a pivotal role in determining the shape and depth of women's political representation. In South Asia, the dominance of FPTP systems in countries like India, Bangladesh, Pakistan and the Maldives has historically disincentivized the entry of women candidates, who are often seen as 'less winnable' by male-dominated political parties. In contrast, proportional representation (PR) systems, where adopted with care, tend to produce higher and more consistent levels of female representation.[5] However, the mere choice of electoral formula does not in itself guarantee gender inclusivity; the outcome is shaped by legislative, institutional and party structures.[6]

Empirical studies indicate that PR electoral systems are more conducive to the entry of diverse identities into legislatures compared to majoritarian-favouring systems such as FPTP. Notably, this pattern holds regardless of a country's level of economic development.[7] Within PR systems, multimember constituencies tend to produce greater diversity in parliamentary representation, although their effectiveness is contingent upon various external factors, including party ideology, candidate selection processes and logistical constraints.[8]

Most importantly, it must be emphatically pointed out that, contrary to the enduring myth that women are less 'winnable' candidates, the Indian electoral record, for instance, tells a markedly different story. Across nearly every general election since Independence, women candidates have consistently demonstrated a higher strike rate than men – meaning that a greater proportion of women who contest elections actually go on to win. In the 2024 Lok Sabha elections, for instance, women recorded a strike rate of 9.25 per cent, outperforming their male counterparts who stood at 6.2 per cent – a continuation of a trend observed in 2019 (10.74 per cent versus 6.35 per cent) and earlier as well.[9]

This pattern holds even when women contest in far fewer numbers and are often fielded in less favourable constituencies. Such evidence thoroughly dismantles the widely propagated belief – used routinely by party gatekeepers – that women are electoral liabilities. On the contrary, when women contest, they win at higher rates, suggesting that the real barrier is not electability but structural exclusion from party nominations and campaign support. The myth of women's political 'unwinnability' is not merely inaccurate – it is a smokescreen for the patriarchal resistance to power-sharing in India's political establishment.

Table 1: Per centage of winners (strike rate) among male and female contestants in India

Year	Male	Female
2024	6.2	9.25
2019	6.35	10.74
2014	6.36	9.13
2009	6.44	10.61
2004	9.80	12.68
1999	11.32	17.25
1998	11.17	15.69
1996	3.77	6.68
1991	5.89	11.52
1989	8.62	14.65
1984	9.40	25.15
1980	11.46	19.58
1977	22.08	27.14
1971	18.42	24.42
1967	21.33	43.28

Year	Male	Female
1962	24.13	46.97
1957	32.02	48.89

Source: *Election Atlas of India*, 2022 edition.

As of 2024, Nepal leads the region in formal inclusion of women, with 33 per cent constitutionally mandated representation for women across all tiers of government. This has resulted in female representation of 40 per cent at the local level, 33.5% per cent in provincial assemblies and over 37.3% per cent in the National Assembly, making it a rare outlier in the region.[10] The constitutional commitment to proportional inclusion, embedded in Nepal's 2015 constitution, has been instrumental in this achievement. However, implementation remains uneven, with parties accused of using proportional lists to promote relatives of male politicians rather than grassroots women leaders – a pattern observed elsewhere in the region as well.[11]

India took a historic step in September 2023 by passing the 128th Constitutional Amendment, commonly known as the Women's Reservation Bill. The law mandates 33 per cent reservation for women in the Lok Sabha and state assemblies, including within the existing SC and ST quotas. However, its implementation is contingent upon the completion of the next Census and delimitation exercise, meaning the practical benefits are deferred. At present, women hold just 15.2 per cent of seats in the Lok Sabha despite forming 48 per cent of India's population, and now surpassing men in voter turnout as a result of proactive efforts[12] – a silent electoral revolution yet to translate into candidate selection or party leadership.[13]

Pakistan and Bangladesh have long maintained quota-based systems through indirect reservations. Pakistan reserves sixty seats in its 336-member National Assembly (approximately 17.8 per cent) for women, with similar provisions in the Senate and provincial assemblies.[14] However, women rarely win open contests, and their presence is heavily reliant on party nomination lists. Bangladesh follows a similar model with fifty reserved seats out of 350 in its Jatiya Sangsad.[15] Women's groups in both countries have critiqued these quota models for producing legislators who are nominated without accountability – disconnected from their constituencies and beholden to party leadership rather than to the public.[16]

In Bhutan and the Maldives, both small yet structurally unique democracies, the limitations are even more acute. As of 2024, Bhutan's National Assembly has only two female members out of forty-seven, and its National Council fares little better.[17] *The Global Gender Gap Report 2024* ranks Bhutan 124th out of 146 countries, primarily due to political under-representation.[18] Similarly, in the Maldives, only three out of 93 seats in the People's Majlis are held by women – just 3.2 per cent – despite constitutional guarantees of equality and the adoption of gender quotas at the local level, which have led to a more encouraging 39.5 per cent[19] women's representation in councils post the 2019 decentralization reforms.[20]

Afghanistan presents the most extreme reversal. Prior to 2021, women held over 27 per cent of seats in the lower house, under constitutional quotas backed by international guarantees. Following the Taliban's return, women have been completely removed from political life.[21] The 2024 Women, Peace and Security Index places Afghanistan at the bottom globally, and UN experts have described the situation as one of 'gender apartheid', with no state-sponsored framework for women's political or civic participation.[22]

What emerges from this regional comparison is a layered picture: quotas alone are not a sufficient condition for transformation, but they are often a necessary one. When embedded in robust institutional frameworks – accompanied by electoral reform, party-level accountability and capacity-building initiatives – they can help unlock the representative potential of South Asian women. However, where quotas are limited to indirect nominations or where they are manipulated for elite consolidation, they risk becoming cosmetic.[23]

Thus, the challenge in South Asia is two-fold: to adopt affirmative measures such as constitutionally mandated quotas and party-level targets; and to ensure that such measures are accompanied by democratic reforms within political parties and electoral institutions. Electoral justice for women is not only a matter of numbers – it is a question of access, legitimacy and power. The road to gender-equal legislatures must, therefore, pass through reforms that address both formal barriers and the informal gatekeeping structures within the political system.

Deep Structures of Disempowerment

Electoral and legal frameworks may provide the architecture of political representation, but the foundation upon which they rest is social. Across South Asia, entrenched patriarchal norms, rigid gender roles and cultural expectations have profoundly shaped the conditions under which women engage – or are prevented from engaging – in political life.[24] These norms do not merely exist in the private domain of household relations; they are reproduced and reinforced by institutions, parties, media and even state policies, limiting the political agency of women across the region.

In virtually every South Asian country, public life has long been perceived as a male domain, while women have been relegated to the domestic sphere. This division of roles is sustained through both ideological constructs – such as the valorization of women's 'purity', 'modesty' or 'obedience' – and material realities including unequal access to education, economic dependence and the disproportionate burden of care work. These factors not only restrict women's political participation but also affect the types of leadership roles they are deemed 'fit' to occupy.

The clearest evidence of this can be found in the *Global Gender Gap Report 2024*, which reveals in its sub-index of political empowerment that most countries in the region rank below the 100th position: India at 129th, Pakistan at 145th, Bhutan at 124th, the Maldives at 132nd and Sri Lanka at 122nd out of 146 countries.[25] This trend is not merely numerical – it reflects deep-seated cultural ambivalence, even hostility, towards women in positions of authority.

Consider Bhutan, where despite a history of matrilineal inheritance systems, political leadership remains a predominantly male preserve. Women are often discouraged by their families from entering politics, partly due to the perception that political engagement would expose them to public scrutiny and compromise their dignity. In 2023, Bhutan's National Council elections resulted in only one woman being elected out of twenty seats.[26] Despite formal guarantees of equality in the constitution, cultural assumptions about women's 'natural' roles in family life continue to restrict their political participation.

A similar tension is evident in the Maldives, where constitutional provisions against gender-based discrimination coexist with structural exclusion. While reforms to local governance laws have increased women's representation in councils to 39.5 per cent, the national legislature remains overwhelmingly male.[27] In public discourse and media, women politicians are often judged not by their performance and policies but by their appearance, familial roles or conformity to gender expectations. This phenomenon – often described as the 'double bind' of female leadership – is widespread across the region.[28]

In Pakistan, traditional gender roles remain deeply embedded in both rural and urban society. Despite legal reforms, the labour force participation rate of women remains just 24 per cent[29], and female politicians are frequently viewed as anomalies or extensions of powerful male relatives. Surveys consistently show that most Pakistanis believe women should not participate in politics or should do so only under male supervision.[30] Even high-profile women leaders such as Benazir Bhutto or Hina Rabbani Khar had to navigate these norms, balancing their authority with performative displays of cultural conformity.[31]

India, for all its constitutional and legal advances, is similarly constrained by gendered expectations. According to the 2024 Pew Research analysis of sex ratios, the country continues to grapple with the legacy of son preference, gender-selective abortion and dowry-related violence.[32] The burden of unpaid care work falls disproportionately on women: the McKinsey Global Institute estimates that Indian women perform almost ten times more unpaid domestic labour than men – a figure that is three times the global average.[31] This not only curtails their economic opportunities but also their political ambitions. Most women who do contest elections do so under the aegis of male patrons – fathers, husbands, brothers – rather than as independent political actors.

Bangladesh, while showing relatively better performance in gender equality indices, reveals another form of this cultural paradox. Despite having been led by female PMs for over three decades, female candidacy in general elections remains astonishingly low: just 4.86 per cent of candidates in the 2024 elections were women.[34] Women leaders at the top coexist with patriarchal norms at the grassroots, where conservative religious and social pressures often deter women from entering political contests or attending political events.

The cultural marginalization of women is further intensified by religion-based gender codes in some contexts. In Afghanistan, under the Taliban regime, women are not only excluded from politics but also from education, public spaces and economic life altogether. The regime's imposition of gender apartheid, including bans on women's movement without male guardians, closure of beauty salons and prohibition from appearing on television, reflects an extreme institutionalization of patriarchal norms. Yet, the seeds of such exclusion are not unique to Afghanistan – they reflect a broader South Asian pattern where cultural narratives and religious dogmas are invoked to maintain male dominance in public life.[35]

The deeper tragedy is that these norms often internalize themselves within women's own expectations. Studies across the region suggest that many women refrain from contesting elections not due to fear of defeat alone, but due to the belief that they are 'unqualified', 'unsuitable' or 'unworthy' of leadership. This internalization of inferiority is a direct consequence of educational inequities, economic marginalization and media portrayals that devalue female agency.[36]

If we are to meaningfully advance women's political representation in South Asia, legislative reforms must be accompanied by deliberate cultural interventions. Public awareness campaigns, gender-sensitive school curricula, the promotion of female role models in media, and the active engagement of religious and community leaders in challenging regressive norms are all essential. The real task lies not simply in opening doors for women but in dismantling the walls that teach them never to knock.

Women's Leadership vs Mass Representation Paradox

Nowhere is the paradox of South Asian democracy more starkly manifest than in the disjuncture between symbolic leadership and structural exclusion. This peculiar South Asian paradox is that the region boasts the highest number of female heads of government in modern political history – Indira Gandhi in India, Benazir Bhutto in Pakistan, Sirimavo

Bandaranaike and Chandrika Kumaratunga in Sri Lanka, and Khaleda Zia and Sheikh Hasina in Bangladesh, among others – yet South Asia as a whole continues to rank among the lowest globally in the political empowerment of women at large.

This paradox cannot be explained solely by institutional weakness or electoral hurdles. Rather, it speaks to a deeper asymmetry: women may rise to the apex of political power, but their ascension often does not translate into broader political inclusion for other women. This is because many of these leaders have emerged from political dynasties – daughters, wives or widows of male leaders – and their power, while real, is frequently insulated from wider feminist mobilization or grassroots accountability.[37]

In Bangladesh, for instance, Sheikh Hasina governed for over fifteen years, yet in the 2024 general elections, only 92 out of 1,891 candidates were women.[38] While parliament reserves fifty seats for women through indirect nomination, as mentioned earlier, this form of symbolic presence is not matched by women's substantive power in cabinet positions, party leadership or electoral competition. Despite topping the South Asian region in gender equality for a decade, Bangladesh's rank has dropped globally from 59th in 2023 down to 99th in 2024, primarily due to its stagnant political inclusion metrics.[39]

The Indian case is equally instructive. With a vibrant electoral democracy and a deeply embedded tradition of women's activism, one might expect a more inclusive political landscape. And yet, India's Lok Sabha in 2024 had only 15.2 per cent women, placing it 152nd globally in parliamentary gender representation – behind Pakistan, Nepal and even conflict-affected nations like Rwanda.[40] This is why the Women's Reservation Bill is indispensable. But, as discussed, the Bill's implementation awaits the completion of delimitation and Census procedures, rendering its impact, at best, a deferred promise.

Even in Sri Lanka, the first country in the world to elect a female PM in 1960, the record of women's participation remains modest. Following the 2024 parliamentary elections, only 10.7 per cent of seats are held by women – a modest improvement from the earlier 5.3 per cent, but still far below parity.[41] Moreover, women hold just one cabinet position, and none of the elected female MPs are Tamil or Muslim, reflecting intersecting exclusions along ethnic and gender lines.[42]

Nepal, by contrast, offers a partial counterpoint. It is the only country in the region where the visibility of female leaders – such as former President Bidya Devi Bhandari, former Election Commissioner Ila Sharma, Speaker Onsari Gharti Magar and Chief Justice Sushila Karki – has coincided with broad-based representation. However, even here, cracks in the edifice are visible. The 2022 local elections saw a decline in the number of women deputy mayors, while the misuse of proportional representation by parties to promote family members of male leaders continues to dilute the spirit of inclusion.[43]

This paradox between elite leadership and mass exclusion is perhaps most pronounced in Pakistan. Despite historical breakthroughs – Benazir Bhutto as PM, Fehmida Mirza as speaker and Hina Rabbani Khar as foreign minister – female representation in the 2024 National Assembly remains limited to 17 per cent reserved seats, with very few women winning general seats through direct election. The Election Act of 2017, which mandates that parties allocate at least 5 per cent of general seats to women candidates, has not led to substantial shifts in practice. Most parties field women in constituencies they are unlikely to win, thus fulfilling formal obligations without altering gender dynamics.[44]

One of the structural explanations for this paradox lies in the patronage-based nature of South Asian political systems, where parties are gatekeepers and candidate selection is centralized, opaque and heavily male-dominated.[45] Women are often seen as liabilities – less likely to command resources, navigate patron–client networks or confront electoral violence. As mentioned earlier, those who do make it through are often from elite families, where lineage substitutes for grassroots legitimacy. Thus, political empowerment remains concentrated among a handful of dynastic figures, while ordinary women are denied both access and aspiration.[46]

Equally problematic is the tokenism that often accompanies female leadership. In Bhutan, despite a nominally egalitarian constitution and a historical matrilineal heritage, women remain severely underrepresented in formal politics. The Parliament comprises 72 members – 47 in the National Assembly and 25 in the National Council – but only 2 women currently serve in the National Assembly, amounting to just 4.3 per cent. Across both chambers combined, women hold approximately 17.4 per cent of seats. In the Maldives, the picture is even starker: only 3 out of 93 members of the People's Majlis are women, representing just 3.2 per cent of the national legislature as of 2024, despite constitutional guarantees of equality and recent reforms at the local level.

What emerges, then, is not merely a leadership gap but a crisis of democratic legitimacy. A democracy that empowers a few elite women while excluding millions from political processes does not merely fail women – it fails itself. Representation must be more than the celebration of symbolic figures; it must translate into structural changes that dismantle gatekeeping within parties, enable economic and educational pathways for women's political participation, and create a civic culture that values women's voice and leadership at all levels.

That is the enduring paradox of South Asian democracy – a region where women have risen to the highest offices of power, yet the corridors of everyday politics remain conspicuously closed to most women. Leadership without representation is not empowerment; it is a silhouette of progress without its substance.

Fear, Control and the Cost of Entry

The right to political participation is meaningless in the absence of safety. Across South Asia, violence against women – whether physical, sexual, psychological or institutional – is not merely a background condition but a principal mechanism of political exclusion. From the threats faced by women candidates on the campaign trail to the harassment endured by elected officials in public office, violence operates as a gatekeeper – policing who can participate, how and at what cost. The region's failure to guarantee safety for women in public life has rendered the very act of political assertion a dangerous proposition.

The statistics are sobering. According to WHO and UN Women data, South Asia remains one of the most dangerous regions in the world for women and girls, with approximately 35 per cent of ever-partnered women reporting having experienced physical or sexual intimate partner violence (IPV) in their lifetime. In Bangladesh, the crisis is even more acute: the 2024 Violence Against Women Survey, conducted by the Bangladesh Bureau of Statistics in collaboration with UNFPA, found that over 54 per cent of women had faced physical or sexual IPV, while 70 per cent had experienced some form of intimate partner abuse. In Pakistan, comprehensive national data remains scarce, and while some earlier studies suggest high prevalence, no recent figure around 39 per cent can be independently confirmed or attributed to UN Women.

Crucially, women politicians, activists and candidates across the region face routine intimidation, slander, doxxing and sexualized disinformation campaigns, particularly in the digital sphere. A 2023 study conducted by the International Foundation for Electoral Systems (IFES) found that as many as seven in ten women politicians in South Asia had experienced some form of online abuse.[47] The abuse is often gendered and vicious: women are not only attacked for their views but vilified for their appearance, morality or personal lives. Many are threatened with sexual violence, and some are explicitly warned to 'stay in their place'.

The repercussions are not theoretical. In Afghanistan, women have been erased from political life not through a gradual erosion of rights, but by overt and systemic violence. Women like Mursal Nabizada, a former MP, have been murdered for resisting this new order.[48] Her death is not just an aberration; it is a symbol of the risks that accompany female political presence in contexts of extreme authoritarian patriarchy.

Even in relatively open democracies such as India, Nepal and Sri Lanka, the political field is far from safe. In India, the National Crime Records Bureau (NCRB) reported over 4.2 lakh crimes against women in 2022, including 32,260 cases of rape and 26,229 cases of child sexual assault.[49] These numbers reflect a larger culture of impunity that often spills into the political domain. Many women politicians report facing harassment by party workers, police inaction and targeted attacks during campaigns – particularly in rural constituencies. In Sri Lanka, 90 per cent of women report experiencing sexual harassment in public transport,[50] while political parties themselves remain male-dominated spaces that often tolerate sexist behaviour within their ranks.[51]

Furthermore, violence functions as a deterrent not just to candidates, but to voters as well. In Pakistan's more conservative regions, there have been documented instances where women were barred from voting due to threats from local tribal councils. In the 2024 general elections, the gender gap in voter turnout in Pakistan remained at 9 per cent, with 43 per cent of women voting compared to 52 per cent of men, despite significant efforts by the election commission to bridge the gap.[52] In contrast, India recorded higher female voter turnout than male, with 65.8 per cent of women casting votes in 2024, as against 65.6 per cent of male voters[53], but this statistical advance does not erase the lived experience of threat, harassment or silencing that many women still face.[54]

Notably, institutional redress mechanisms remain weak. Few electoral management bodies in South Asia have internal frameworks to monitor and respond to violence against women in politics (VAWP). The Election Commission of Nepal has begun to collect data on gender-based electoral violence[55], but similar mechanisms are absent or underdeveloped in most other South Asian states. Legislative and procedural measures – such as safe complaint mechanisms, legal protections against online abuse and security protocols for women candidates – are either missing or inadequately enforced. Political parties, meanwhile, often treat such incidents as 'internal matters', preferring damage control to structural reform.

And yet, in the face of this persistent violence, women continue to enter the political arena – not because it is safe, but because it is necessary. Their perseverance underscores both their courage and the moral urgency of institutional reform. States must go beyond rhetoric and enact comprehensive policies to prevent, monitor and punish VAWP. These must include legal recognition of VAWP as a specific category of electoral crime; training for law enforcement, electoral staff and political parties; and strict enforcement of codes of conduct for online and offline spaces.

Moreover, international frameworks such as the Convention on the Elimination of All Forms of Discrimination against Women (CEDAW) General Recommendation No. 35 (which expands the definition of gender-based violence to include political and institutional forms of harm)[56] and the Inter-Parliamentary Union's *Guidelines on Eliminating Violence Against Women in Politics* (which call for party-level accountability, legal reform and protective mechanisms for women in public life) must be domesticated into national legislation and made enforceable through independent commissions and electoral tribunals.[57] Without such measures, for many women, the ballot box will remain an invitation to violence rather than a vehicle for empowerment.

Violence, in short, is not simply a symptom of women's exclusion from politics – it is its most brutal instrument. To guarantee the right to representation, South Asian democracies must first guarantee the right to be safe.

Economic Empowerment, Education and Political Agency

Political representation is not forged in isolation – it is sustained by a broader architecture of empowerment. In South Asia, where economic and educational inequities run deep, women's ability to participate meaningfully in public life is inextricably linked to their access to income, employment and education. When women are denied the tools to secure autonomy in the private sphere, their entry into the public realm of politics becomes not only difficult but structurally improbable. Thus, understanding political under-representation requires us to examine the intertwined domains of economic and educational disenfranchisement that define the lives of millions of South Asian women.

Across the region, women's labour force participation remains among the lowest in the world. According to World Bank data for 2024, Pakistan records a female labour force participation rate of 24.3 per cent, India stands at 32.8 per cent, and Nepal, despite its progressive constitutional mandates, is at 28.4 per cent. The Maldives fares somewhat better at approximately 42 per cent, while Bangladesh, the regional leader, has reached 44.2 per cent. However, much of this participation remains informal, insecure and unpaid. This skew not only limits women's financial independence but deprives them of the time and resources necessary to pursue political careers or civic engagement.

Education, too, remains a fundamental determinant of political voice. While most South Asian countries have made strides in improving female literacy rates, glaring disparities remain in access to quality education, retention beyond primary levels and vocational training. UNESCO UIS data estimates adult literacy in South Asia at around 70 percent, meaning approximately 30 percent of adults lack basic literacy skills, with women disproportionately represented among the illiterate (women account for approximately 63 percent of all illiterate adults globally).[58] In India, the National Commission for Protection of Child Rights reports that 40 per cent of girls aged fifteen to eighteen are out of school, and 65 per cent of them are engaged in household work.[59] In Pakistan, where girls face socio-cultural resistance to education, especially in rural areas, the gender gap in secondary school enrolment remains above fifteen per centage points.[60]

These gaps translate directly into political marginalization. Women who lack education and income are less likely to understand electoral procedures, engage with political institutions or even register to vote. In Afghanistan, the Taliban's bans on female education and employment have not only denied women their civil rights but also destroyed the social infrastructure necessary for political mobilization. In Bhutan, despite constitutional guarantees of equality, women continue to self-select out of politics due to a lack of confidence, limited access to public speaking forums and weak exposure to civic life – all of which are consequences of long-standing educational and economic marginalization.

At the same time, countries that have made strategic investments in women's economic participation are witnessing gradual shifts in political engagement. Bangladesh, for instance, has prioritized female workforce inclusion through investments in skill-based training, information and communication technology access and job creation in the garment sector – where nearly 60 per cent of the around 4 million workers are women.[61] As a result, not only has the gender wage gap narrowed, but there is a perceptible increase in women's civic visibility and union participation, offering a potential pathway toward political empowerment. Nepal's constitutionally mandated inclusion policies, backed by civil society training programmes and donor-supported capacity building for women leaders, have also contributed to increasing women's access to information, networks and leadership opportunities.[62]

However, the picture remains uneven. The formal economy in South Asia still largely excludes women from high-income and leadership positions. Only 4.5 per cent of executive roles across the region are held by women, and gendered barriers to credit, property ownership and mobility continue to stifle female entrepreneurship.[63] Political candidacy, which often demands significant financial resources for campaigning, is thus an arena accessible only to elite women or those backed by powerful male networks. In India, Bangladesh and Pakistan, the high cost of elections – combined with the absence of public funding for female candidates – creates a hostile economic terrain for grassroots women leaders.

To address these barriers, several innovative models have been proposed across the region. In the Maldives, the state provides financial subsidies to political parties through the Political Parties Act, but these funds are distributed without incentives for gender inclusion. Experts have recommended amendments to allocate a greater share of public funds to parties that nominate more women, echoing global best practices. In Papua New Guinea, for instance, the law provides reimbursement of campaign expenses to female candidates who secure at least 10 per cent of the vote.[64] South Asian electoral commissions can draw on such models to design targeted financial mechanisms that level the playing field for women.

Likewise, party reforms are critical. In too many cases, political parties function as exclusionary economic clubs dominated by men with the financial capital and social connections to navigate electoral politics. Without transparent nomination processes, internal gender audits and quotas for party office-bearers, women remain peripheral to the centres of decision-making. Therefore, several feminist civil society coalitions across South Asia have called for mandatory gender action plans within parties, including targets for candidate selection, leadership training and local-level mobilization of women voters.[65]

Education, too, must be reconceived – not merely as a tool for employment but as a vehicle for citizenship. Curriculum reforms across the region should integrate civic education, gender studies and political literacy, particularly for girls in rural and marginalized communities. In this context, the increasing digital divide is a cause for alarm: according to UNICEF South Asia (2024), girls are five times less likely than boys to have access to mobile phones, restricting their ability to access information, register for e-services or participate in digital democracy platforms.[66]

Ultimately, economic and educational empowerment are not ancillary to political representation – they are its preconditions. When women have control over income, access to education and confidence in public speaking, they are likelier to contest elections, challenge injustice and demand accountability. Conversely, when these foundations are absent, no amount of legislative quotas or rhetorical inclusion can generate meaningful representation.

The task before South Asian democracies, therefore, is to treat economic justice, educational equality and political empowerment not as isolated concerns but as mutually reinforcing pillars of democratic renewal. Only when women are empowered in the home, the classroom and the workplace can they claim their rightful place in the legislature – not as tokens of diversity, but as architects of justice.

Lessons from Across the Globe

If we take a global view, comparative insights from Africa and Latin America indicate that enhanced women's representation in legislatures has contributed to accelerated economic growth and a reduction in socio-economic deprivation, notwithstanding persistent systemic challenges.[67] Research has demonstrated that inclusive legislatures are more effective in fostering equitable policy outcomes.Drawing on empirical data from Scandinavia, the US, and Western Europe, Pippa Norris establishes that women in political office not only advocate for their own representation but also influence policy agendas in ways that are more attuned to social equity. As multicultural and globalized societies continue to evolve, ensuring proportional representation of all social groups in governance becomes a democratic imperative. The 1979 CEDAW, which endorses the principle of equal participation in public life, has been ratified by 163 nations. However, according to Norris, if current trends persist, gender parity in parliamentary representation will not be achieved until the twenty-second century – an alarming prospect.[68]

The case of Rwanda provides a nuanced perspective on the impact of increased female representation in parliament. While their findings suggest that the presence of more women in legislative bodies has facilitated the inclusion of gender-sensitive issues, such as reproductive rights and childcare, these changes have not necessarily translated into substantive policy shifts.[69] Even as legislative agendas now incorporate concerns related to property rights and HIV/AIDS, policy implementation remains protracted. The role of civil society organizations and international feminist advocacy is instrumental in sustaining pressure for policy transformation. Yet the ultimate outcomes are not markedly different from those observed in countries with lower levels of female representation.[70]

These findings underscore the necessity of further scholarly inquiry into the modalities and consequences of women's political representation, particularly in South Asia, where such studies remain limited in scope and methodological rigour. A systematic examination of these experiences can offer critical insights for strengthening electoral systems, while expanding the discourse on women's political empowerment as a vehicle for broader socio-economic transformation.

Table 2. Gender and representation in South Asia at a glance

Country	Parliamentary Representation of Women (2024)	Electoral Quotas/ Provisions	Key Barriers to Participation	Violence Against Women in Politics	Recent Policy Developments/ Reforms
Afghanistan	0 per cent	None (post-2021 Taliban regime)	Total exclusion from public life, Taliban-imposed gender apartheid	Extreme; includes assassinations, systemic removal of rights	UN Women–EU Gender Country Profile (2024); international pressure for protection frameworks
Bangladesh	15 per cent (including reserved seats)	50 reserved seats in parliament (indirect)	Dynastic leadership, lack of direct elections, socio-religious pressures	High rates of domestic and online abuse (53 per cent Intimate partner violence [IPV])	Call for direct election to reserved seats; economic inclusion programmes

Country	Parliamentary Representation of Women (2024)	Electoral Quotas/ Provisions	Key Barriers to Participation	Violence Against Women in Politics	Recent Policy Developments/ Reforms
Bhutan	6.9 per cent	No legislative quotas	Patriarchal norms, low self-confidence, under-representation in party lists	26 per cent report IPV; underreporting common	Proposals for statutory quotas under debate (Wangyel Wang, 2024)
India	15.2 per cent	33 per cent Women's Reservation Bill passed (2023)	Economic dependence, party gatekeeping, unpaid care work	4.2 lakh crimes against women in 2023; high risk of electoral harassment	Women's Reservation Bill (2023); voter turnout of women exceeds men (2024)
The Maldives	4.7 per cent	33 per cent quota in local councils; none in parliament	Limited party support, conservative backlash, economic exclusion	Gaps in legal protection; 39.5 per cent women in local councils	Proposed reforms to link party funding to female inclusion
Nepal	33 per cent+ across all levels	Constitutionally mandated quotas	Misuse of PR lists, elite capture, underfunded local leadership	Rising threats and pressure in rural constituencies	Judicial orders to strengthen inclusion; top regional scorer in Women, Business and Law Index (2024)
Pakistan	17 per cent (reserved)	60 National Assembly seats reserved	Low voter turnout, high cost of candidacy, religious conservatism	43 per cent female voter turnout vs 52 per cent male; online harassment high	Election Act 2017 mandates 5 per cent tickets to women; limited implementation

Country	Parliamentary Representation of Women (2024)	Electoral Quotas/ Provisions	Key Barriers to Participation	Violence Against Women in Politics	Recent Policy Developments/ Reforms
Sri Lanka	10.7 per cent	25 per cent quota in local government	Ethnic exclusions, tokenism, weak enforcement	90 per cent of women face public harassment; low provincial participation	Recent gains in parliament (2024); first woman PM since 1994 elected

The Path Ahead

The path ahead requires not cosmetic inclusion, but structural transformation. A new democratic compact must be forged – one that treats women not as a special interest group, but as rightful claimants to state power. Towards that end, the following reforms merit urgent consideration:

- **Mandate enforceable quotas** not just for legislative bodies, but within political parties, including requirements for women in leadership, candidate selection committees and internal governance roles.
- **Strengthen electoral laws** to include specific provisions against VAWP, with defined penalties, redress mechanisms and real-time complaint monitoring during campaigns.
- **Tie state funding for political parties** to their performance on gender inclusion, including number of women candidates fielded, funds allocated to women's campaigns and training initiatives undertaken.
- **Expand civic education and political literacy programmes** at the school and community level, especially for girls in rural and marginalized communities, embedding gender equality as a democratic value from an early age.
- **Launch regional initiatives under the SAARC** to facilitate cross-border dialogue, training and exchange programmes for women politicians – creating a shared South Asian platform for feminist political leadership.

- **Adopt gender-responsive budgeting**, not only at the national level but within electoral commissions and party infrastructures, to ensure that resources are directed towards dismantling systemic barriers to women's participation.
- **Leverage digital tools** to connect, train and empower women, while also instituting robust legal protections against cyber violence and online hate targeting women in public life.
- **Institutionalize mentorship and leadership development programmes**, especially at the local level, to cultivate the next generation of women leaders outside dynastic networks.

It is time to decimate the politics of exclusion. South Asia stands today at a critical inflection point. Having produced some of the world's most iconic female leaders, it now faces a more difficult, yet far more consequential task: to build political systems in which every woman – regardless of caste, class, ethnicity or religion – has the means, the right and the opportunity to lead. This is not merely a question of gender justice, it is the unfinished business of democracy itself.

11

Pluralism under Threat: Ethnic Minorities in South Asia

The history of South Asia is one of vibrant pluralism, marked by the interweaving of civilizations, languages and local polities that coexisted over centuries across what are today sharply bounded nation-states. From the Himalayan highlands to the coastal plains of the Indian Ocean, the region was once governed through networks of overlapping sovereignties, itinerant allegiances and shared sacred geographies. Yet, in the modern era – particularly following the twin ruptures of colonialism and postcolonial state-formation – these plural foundations have come under grave threat. At the heart of this crisis lies the fate of ethnic minorities: those communities whose linguistic, cultural and regional identities diverge from the dominant national ethos and who continue to be cast as peripheral, suspect or threatening to state unity.

Ethnicity in South Asia is not a uniform or easily classifiable category. It cuts across language, region, caste, race and custom, and often defies the rigid classifications imposed by modern statecraft. As Ashutosh Varshney, drawing from Donald Horowitz, reminds us, ethnic identity is an ascriptive category – assigned by perception, not always by choice.[1] The diversity of conflicts in the region bears out this complexity: from the Tamils of Sri Lanka to the Madhesis of Nepal, from the Baloch in Pakistan to the Chakma in Bangladesh, from Bhutanese Lhotshampas to the Naga and Mizo aspirations in India – each case reflects a distinct constellation of historical grievance, marginalization and contestation. While rooted in local histories, these struggles resonate with one another across borders, revealing common structural patterns of exclusion and resistance.

The South Asian region, in most of its incarnations, has struggled to accommodate these ethnic claims within its political compact. Independence from colonial rule brought not only the promise of self-rule but also the inheritance of colonial cartographies – lines drawn with scant regard for cultural or ethnic contiguities. These lines, whether while bifurcating Punjab and Bengal or slicing through the Pashtun heartlands between Afghanistan and Pakistan, generated enduring sources of tension. In the postcolonial period, the challenge was compounded by the state's desire to craft a singular national identity, often around the language, religion or ethnicity of the dominant majority. This centralizing impulse proved especially destabilizing in multiethnic societies, where peripheral regions were simultaneously expected to integrate, assimilate and remain loyal, despite being denied meaningful political autonomy or recognition.

While some nations attempted federal or semi-federal structures, the implementation of decentralization in a way that empowers minorities has remained uneven and often tokenistic. Nepal's transition to a federal republic, for instance, was heralded as a major step forward, yet the demands of the Madhesi and Tharu communities remain largely unmet.[2] In India, the linguistic reorganization of states did create new administrative units, but demands for Gorkhaland, Bodoland or Greater Nagalim underscore the continuing mismatch between ethnic aspirations and political boundaries.[3] Elsewhere, such as in Bhutan or Pakistan, authoritarian impulses and militarized governance have all but foreclosed participatory solutions to ethnic conflict.[4] The exodus of Lhotshampa refugees from Bhutan or the long-standing insurgency in Balochistan is a chilling reminder of how systematically ethnicity has been treated as a security threat and a social problem. Moreover, in Bhutan, the exodus of the Lhotshampa refugees stands as a stark reminder of how ethnic difference was once treated as a threat rather than a facet of national identity.[5] This earlier phase, however, sits uneasily alongside the image of a consultative and enlightened monarchy that later ushered in Bhutan's transition to a democratic constitutional order – an evolution that, as noted in the Bhutan chapter, has received widespread acclaim. The contrast between these phases of Bhutan invites reflection on how states can shift from exclusion to accommodation, and what remains unresolved beneath institutional reforms.

These internal fissures are further aggravated by regional geopolitics. South Asia's borders are not merely administrative demarcations but lived, porous and ethnically entangled spaces. The Tamil population of northern Sri Lanka shares linguistic and cultural kinship with Tamil Nadu; Pashtun identities straddle the Durand Line between Afghanistan and Pakistan; the tribal peoples of the Chittagong Hill Tracts echo affinities with India's Northeast.[6] Rather than enabling cross-border cooperation, these affinities have been weaponized, either to suppress internal dissent or to stoke diplomatic tensions. Indeed, India's strained relations with Nepal during the Madhesi movement or its reluctance to recognize the Taliban regime in Afghanistan, cannot be understood in isolation from these cross-border ethnic configurations.[7] Of course, the nature of India's engagement in each case differs significantly – the former is rooted in kinship ties and borderland identities, while the latter is shaped by strategic anxieties and ideological divergence. However, both reveal how domestic politics in South Asia are often entangled with ethnic affinities that transcend national boundaries.

Moreover, in an age where democracy has increasingly come under siege, ethnic minorities are often the first to bear the brunt of its backsliding. Across the region, electoral politics has shifted towards majoritarianism – be it through Sinhala-Buddhist nationalism in Sri Lanka, Hindutva assertion in India or Sunni supremacism in Pakistan and the Maldives.[8] This ideological narrowing of the political space leaves ethnic minorities vulnerable, with their claims dismissed as subversive or foreign-inspired. In such contexts, democratic institutions lose their inclusiveness and governance becomes a tool for exclusion rather than empowerment.[9]

Therefore, through five cross-cutting themes – ranging from the legacies of state formation to the politics of belonging, from insurgent movements to democratic decline – this chapter seeks to situate the experiences of ethnic minorities not as exceptions or outliers, but as constitutive of the region's political trajectory. In doing so, it hopes to show the shared structures that drive exclusion and the various possibilities for resistance and reform.

Legacy of State Formation

The formation of modern nation-states in South Asia – each emerging from the embers of colonial disintegration – was underpinned by powerful aspirations for sovereignty, development and identity. Yet, these aspirations were often shaped not by pluralistic ideals but by exclusionary nationalisms that privileged dominant ethnic groups while relegating others to the margins. The structural and symbolic violence embedded in this process left a deep and enduring legacy for ethnic minorities across the region, many of whom continue to grapple with the burdens of displacement, disenfranchisement and cultural erasure.[10]

The colonial period laid the foundations for much of this exclusion. British administrative rationality, with its penchant for census-based classification and centralized governance, fractured South Asia's fluid social orders into rigidly codified identities. These taxonomies – intended for governance – became fault lines in the postcolonial world. When independence came, the new nation-states inherited not only the borders arbitrarily drawn by colonial authorities, but also the divisive logics of administrative control.[11] What followed was an era of state-making driven more by consolidation than by accommodation. National unity was pursued through homogenizing projects: standardizing official languages, centralizing bureaucracies and cultivating majoritarian myths about national origin.

In this context, ethnic minorities – defined by their linguistic, regional or tribal distinctiveness – were often perceived as aberrations from the national ideal. In India, despite its constitutional commitment to linguistic and cultural diversity, the politics of integration often meant coercive incorporation. The post-independence reorganization of states along linguistic lines did mitigate some tensions, but many communities – such as the Gorkhas of West Bengal, the Nagas of Nagaland and the Bodos of Assam – have remained ensnared in movements for recognition and autonomy. In these regions, the Indian state's counterinsurgency responses – marked by militarization, surveillance and draconian laws like the Armed Forces (Special Powers) Act – have reinforced feelings of alienation among ethnic groups who see themselves as historically distinct from the mainstream Indian polity.

Nepal's case provides another illustration of how state formation can reproduce ethnic hierarchies. For much of its modern history, Nepal was governed by upper-caste hill elites who monopolized political power. The Madhesi community of the Terai plains, though geographically integral to Nepal, was systematically excluded from full citizenship and political representation due to their perceived cultural proximity to India. The promulgation of Nepal's 2015 constitution, which refused to heed long-standing Madhesi demands for proportionate representation and federal restructuring, exemplifies how dominant groups often use constitutional frameworks to consolidate their status.[12] Here, exclusion is not merely social – it is juridical and institutional, woven into the very architecture of the state.

In Bhutan, the rhetoric of national happiness has masked one of South Asia's most severe episodes of state-sponsored ethnic expulsion. The Lhotshampa community – Nepali-speaking migrants who had settled in southern Bhutan over generations – became victims of an ethno-nationalist project that sought to 'Bhutanize' national identity. In the late 1980s and early 1990s, thousands of Lhotshampas were stripped of citizenship, subjected to harassment and eventually forced into exile. The Bhutanese state justified this purge through a narrow conception of nationhood that conflated political loyalty with cultural assimilation. Even today, many Lhotshampa refugees remain stateless in Nepal, their claims to repatriation denied by a regime unwilling to reconcile its past with pluralist ideals.[13]

Pakistan's trajectory, though framed by the ideological weight of Islam, has been deeply shaped by its internal ethnic fissures. While religion served as the rallying cry for Pakistan's creation, it was the suppression of ethnic identity in East Pakistan – particularly the denial of linguistic and political autonomy to Bengalis – that precipitated the catastrophic rupture of 1971. In the aftermath, the Pakistani state intensified its efforts to centralize control, often at the expense of regional aspirations. In particular, the Baloch and Pashtun populations have faced decades of marginalization, with their demands for greater control over natural resources and provincial autonomy consistently met with military repression. These patterns of exclusion reveal how a state that seeks unity through cultural and administrative homogenization invariably alienates those on its peripheries.[14]

Bangladesh, formed from the assertion of Bengali linguistic identity, has paradoxically mirrored some of the very exclusionary practices that led to its birth. Indigenous groups in the Chittagong Hill Tracts, such as the Chakma and Marma, have faced systematic state-sponsored migration and cultural erasure, pushing them into militarization. The 1997 Peace Accord, though hailed as a landmark settlement, remains largely unimplemented and land rights violations continue unabated.[15] Here again, the postcolonial state's drive to cement territorial sovereignty has come at the cost of indigenous recognition and autonomy.

Sri Lanka also bears the scars of a state-building project that privileged Sinhala-Buddhist nationalism. The post-independence marginalization of the Tamil population – first through citizenship laws that disenfranchised Indian Tamils, then through linguistic and educational policies – set the stage for decades of civil conflict. The Tamil demand for self-determination was not merely secessionist, it was rooted in the failure of the Sri Lankan state to acknowledge the legitimacy of Tamil political aspirations within the existing constitutional framework. The post-war period, though ostensibly committed to reconciliation, has seen little genuine effort to devolve power or recognize Tamil grievances in a meaningful way.[16]

Even in the Maldives, exclusion operates along lines of migration and descent. Indian-origin communities, particularly Shia Muslims and African-descended groups, are marginalized in public life and governance. The consolidation of a monolithic Sunni Islamic identity has led to the suppression of ethnic and religious heterogeneity, erasing histories of plural settlement and exchange that once defined the archipelago.[17]

Across the region, then, a common pattern emerges: the nation-state's attempt to unify and define itself has often come at the cost of ignoring and disrespecting ethnic pluralism. Rather than seeing diversity as a strength, many South Asian states have regarded it as a liability – something to be managed, contained or suppressed. It is precisely this approach that has entrenched cycles of conflict and mistrust.

For South Asia to transcend its inherited and self-imposed fault lines, it must reimagine the very foundations of its statecraft. This means moving beyond the rhetoric of unity and embracing the democratic possibilities of pluralism. It requires federal arrangements that genuinely empower ethnic regions, constitutional guarantees that safeguard minority rights and political cultures that recognize difference not as a threat but as a vital expression of the region's shared history. Without such a recalibration, the promise of postcolonial sovereignty will remain unfulfilled – for sovereignty that silences its margins is sovereignty in name alone.

Grievances, Autonomy Movements and Insurgency

Where state formation in South Asia has often demanded the centralization of power and the assertion of singular national identities, the lived realities of ethnic minorities have frequently pushed them in the opposite direction: towards local autonomy, cultural preservation and political self-determination. Across the region, the failure of states to accommodate these demands through institutional mechanisms has transformed ethnic grievances into movements of resistance and, in many cases, into full-blown insurgencies. These are not anomalies or breakdowns of an otherwise well-functioning system. Rather, they are structural responses to long histories of marginalization, exclusion and failed negotiations.[18]

A defining characteristic of such ethnic movements in South Asia is their persistence over decades, which often includes surviving military suppression, state co-optation and international apathy. The resilience of these movements is rooted not in ideology alone, but in the deep disjuncture between official state narratives and the lived experiences of ethnic peripheries. Armed rebellion, civil disobedience and parallel governance structures emerge when the legal–political avenues for redress are exhausted or not available. These are not simply acts of defiance – they are the political vocabulary of communities whose voices have long been disqualified by the very structures meant to represent them.

In India, the architecture of formal democracy has not prevented the proliferation of ethnic insurgencies, particularly in the Northeast.

Movements like the Naga nationalist struggle, which began as early as the 1950s, evolved from demands for cultural recognition into a protracted armed movement for sovereignty. The insurgency's longevity, despite peace accords and ceasefires, signals the limits of symbolic concessions in the absence of meaningful power-sharing arrangements.[19] The demand for Greater Nagalim, encompassing Naga-inhabited areas across state and even national borders, illustrates how ethnic identity can exceed the confines of existing administrative divisions, unsettling the presumed permanence of state boundaries.

Similar dynamics have unfolded in Pakistan's Balochistan region, where ethnic nationalism has fed a succession of insurgent movements, each more disillusioned with federal promises than the last. At the heart of the Baloch struggle lies a demand for local control over land, resources and governance. State responses have typically oscillated between military crackdowns and nominal developmental schemes, with little attention to the core grievance of autonomy.[20] The perception that Balochistan's mineral wealth is being siphoned off to fuel national growth – while the region remains underdeveloped and politically disenfranchised – continues to animate the insurgency. It also underscores a broader pattern across South Asia: economic extraction without political inclusion generates not only resistance but an alternative vision of belonging.

In Sri Lanka, the Tamil nationalist movement – led most prominently by the LTTE – grew out of a context where political protests and constitutional demands for devolution were repeatedly ignored or undermined. The civil war that ensued was brutal and swept the entire population, producing one of the world's most militarized ethno-political landscapes. What is critical to understand is that the Tamil movement did not emerge in a vacuum. It was preceded by decades of civic agitation for linguistic parity, land rights and regional governance. The war's conclusion in 2009, though militarily decisive, has not extinguished the fundamental questions of political autonomy, accountability and post-war justice.[21] The heavy military presence in Tamil-majority areas, the absence of credible truth and reconciliation processes, and the centralization of power in the Sinhala-Buddhist establishment continue to reproduce the very grievances that gave rise to the insurgency.

In Nepal, the promise of federal restructuring as part of the peace settlement following the Maoist insurgency raised hopes among ethnic minorities (particularly the Tharu, Limbu and Janajati communities) that governance would become more inclusive. However, the resistance of dominant caste elites to identity-based federalism has meant that the resulting political architecture remains ambiguous and contested. While Nepal has avoided the scale of armed ethnic insurgency seen elsewhere in the region, it continues to face mass mobilizations, regional protests and strikes led by ethnic organizations seeking substantive autonomy.[22] The state's inconsistent response – oscillating between partial accommodation and outright repression – has contributed to a volatile political climate where ethnic assertion remains potent but institutionally unfulfilled.

Even in Bangladesh, where overt secessionist movements are relatively rare, ethnic grievances have simmered in the Chittagong Hill Tracts. As mentioned earlier, the 1997 Peace Accord, which promised regional autonomy and land rights for indigenous peoples, remains largely unimplemented decades later.[23] The persistence of Bengali settler colonialism, the erosion of customary land systems and the marginalization of indigenous leadership structures have prompted renewed protests and sporadic violence. The state's reluctance to devolve power, coupled with its development-driven displacement policies, has ensured that the Chittagong Hill Tracts remain a site of latent resistance rather than reconciliation.

What emerges across these diverse contexts is a shared logic: when state legitimacy fails to extend meaningfully into the cultural, territorial and economic life of ethnic communities, alternative sovereignties begin to take shape. These sovereignties are not always articulated in terms of secession. Often, they manifest as local councils, parallel governance systems, cultural revivals or subterranean networks of resistance. In each case, however, they speak to the same basic concern – that the current terms of inclusion are insufficient, extractive and fundamentally unequal.

For policymakers and democratic reformers in South Asia, the challenge is to recognize that insurgency is not an aberration to be extinguished but a signal, a radical form of democratic demand. It demands a rethinking of political community as a federation of plural aspirations instead of as a monolithic entity. Autonomy, in this context, should not be feared as a precursor to fragmentation, but embraced as a mode of governance that respects local agency and historical identity.[24] The federal ideal, long enshrined in the region's constitutional lexicons, must be translated into lived reality through mechanisms of fiscal devolution, local governance and territorial recognition. Anything less would betray democratic promises and perpetuate the cycles of violence and grievances that continue to scar the region's fragile pluralism.

Statelessness, Citizenship and the Politics of Belonging

Among the most insidious expressions of ethnic exclusion in South Asia is the denial or revocation of citizenship. While the ideal of citizenship is often equated with equality before the law and full participation in the political community, for many ethnic minorities in the region, it remains a contested, conditional or inaccessible status. The modern South Asian state has frequently treated citizenship not as an inalienable right but as a prize contingent upon conformity to dominant national narratives, whether linguistic, cultural or genealogical. In this process, the very question of 'who belongs' becomes weaponized against those who differ from the normative citizen-subject envisioned by the majority.[25]

One of the most egregious examples of state-produced statelessness in the region is the case of the Lhotshampa population in Bhutan. As mentioned earlier, ethnically Nepali and historically settled in southern Bhutan, this community found itself rendered stateless in the late twentieth century through a combination of retroactive citizenship laws, cultural policing and targeted displacement. Under the 1985 Citizenship Act, the burden of proof shifted overwhelmingly onto the Lhotshampas, requiring documentary evidence of presence in Bhutan prior to 1958 – a demand nearly impossible to fulfil for agrarian, oral-history-based communities.[26]

Those unable to comply were classified as illegal immigrants, stripped of their rights and forcibly expelled. Today, tens of thousands continue to live in camps across Nepal and India – trapped in a liminal space where neither return nor full resettlement has been adequately secured. Bhutan's success in cultivating a global image of tranquillity and sustainable development has thus been purchased, in part, through the silent erasure of a substantial ethnic population.

Elsewhere in the region, the denial of citizenship has taken less overt but equally damaging forms. In India, the implementation of the National Register of Citizens (NRC) in Assam represents one of the most controversial exercises in contemporary citizenship adjudication. Originally framed as a mechanism to identify undocumented migrants from Bangladesh, the NRC process excluded nearly 2 million people – many of whom were indigenous tribal communities, Bengali-speaking Hindus and Muslims, and long-settled populations whose documentation was incomplete, inconsistent or lost through bureaucratic negligence.[27] Though nominally aimed at curbing illegal immigration, the exercise laid bare the fragility of citizenship for populations that do not neatly fit linguistic or cultural templates of belonging. Legal recourse, while technically available, remains prohibitively expensive and slow, creating a class of de facto stateless individuals within a constitutional democracy.

In Pakistan, statelessness often intersects with questions of ethnicity and mobility. The nomadic and semi-nomadic populations of the country – including certain Baloch tribes, borderland Pashtun communities and African-descended Sheedi groups – frequently lack birth registration, identity cards or formal documentation. While not always stateless in a juridical sense, their functional exclusion from state records has meant limited access to healthcare, education, voting rights and social welfare schemes. Similarly, the Bengali-origin population in Karachi – descendants of East Pakistani migrants who settled there during and after the 1971 war – continues to face bureaucratic barriers in acquiring national identity cards, despite having lived in the country for generations.[28] The suspicion of disloyalty, foreignness or secessionist potential becomes a permanent stain, transferred across generations through documents denied and identities doubted.

Nepal, despite its formal transition to a republic committed to inclusion, has struggled to extend equal citizenship rights to all of its ethnic constituencies. The Madhesi community, particularly its women, has been disproportionately affected by gender-discriminatory citizenship laws that prevent mothers from conferring nationality to their children without proof of the father's identity.[29] In a region where intercaste and cross-border marriages are common, such provisions disproportionately affect ethnically distinct populations who often straddle legal and territorial boundaries. Statelessness in this context is not the absence of documents alone, but the denial of familial and community recognition within the state's standard framework of lineage, language and geography.

In Bangladesh, the problem manifests most acutely in the form of refugeehood rather than direct statelessness. The arrival of over a million Rohingya refugees from Myanmar not only strained Bangladesh's humanitarian infrastructure but also placed ethnic indigenous groups of the Chittagong Hill Tracts in an even more precarious position. While the Rohingyas are not native to Bangladesh, the local perception – particularly among the Chakma and Marma – is that state resources and attention are disproportionately focused on refugee relief, even as indigenous grievances remain unresolved.[30] This led to fears of demographic dilution and land dispossession, further complicating the already fraught terrain of ethnic belonging and recognition.

Even in relatively homogeneous contexts like the Maldives, forms of cultural and ethnic erasure intersect with restrictive citizenship practices. Migrant workers from South Asia – many of whom are of ethnically distinct origins – contribute significantly to the country's economy, yet are denied any path to long-term residence, let alone citizenship. The discourse around national identity, increasingly couched in Sunni Islamic and Dhivehi linguistic terms, leaves no room for the incorporation of plural ethnic histories that once characterized the archipelago's maritime cosmopolitanism.[31]

What unites these disparate cases is a profound gap between actual presence and legal recognition. Ethnic minorities in South Asia often possess deep-rooted historical ties to the territories they inhabit, yet remain ontologically suspect in the eyes of the state. They are rendered perpetually provisional – present and visible, but never fully legitimate. Statelessness thus becomes more than a legal category; it is a condition of vulnerability, one that marks entire populations as 'accidental citizens' or 'strangers' within their own lands.

A policy framework committed to justice must begin by reimagining citizenship not as a gatekeeping mechanism but as a vehicle for inclusion. This requires a shift from surveillance and suspicion to dignity and documentation; from bureaucratic inquisition to empathetic governance. Birth registration, identity access and the right to mobility must be guaranteed as foundational entitlements, especially for those communities historically marginalized by the cartographies of nationhood. Moreover, states must cease treating ethnicity as a threat to integrity, and instead acknowledge it as an integral strand in the democratic fabric of South Asia. Only then can the region move from the politics of exclusion to a politics of co-belonging, wherein to be different would not mean to be disposable.

Geopolitics, Cross-Border Ethnicities and Regional Tensions

In South Asia, ethnicity does not obey the neat delimitations of cartographic borders. Communities predate states; their kinship networks, languages and histories often traverse national boundaries drawn during colonial withdrawal or postcolonial realignments. As a result, the ethnic question in the region is not merely a matter of domestic governance – it is inherently transnational. States frequently perceive these cross-border ethnicities as vulnerabilities to national sovereignty or, conversely, as instruments of strategic influence in neighbouring territories. This dual dynamic has made ethnic minorities both subjects of suspicion within their own states and pawns in the geopolitical rivalries that define South Asia.

India's vast and often permeable borders make it the most illustrative case of this phenomenon. Nowhere is the geopolitical salience of ethnicity more visible than in its relationship with Nepal and the Madhesi community. Madhesis – ethnically and linguistically closer to the population in India's Bihar and Uttar Pradesh – have long sought greater political representation and autonomy within Nepal. Their proximity to India, both culturally and geographically, has led sections of Nepal's political elite to portray Madhesi demands as proxies for Indian interference. This was especially evident during Nepal's 2015 constitutional crisis, when India was widely accused of imposing an unofficial blockade in support of Madhesi protests. In response, Kathmandu deepened its strategic alignment with China – revealing how ethnic conflict can quickly escalate into regional realignment, with ethnic minorities paying the price for shifting diplomatic equations.

The case of Sri Lanka and its Tamil population offers another vivid illustration. The Tamil community's cultural and linguistic ties to Tamil Nadu has historically shaped India's engagement with Sri Lanka's internal conflict. New Delhi's interventionist role in the 1980s – culminating in the deployment of the Indian Peace Keeping Force (IPKF) – was driven not solely by strategic calculation but also by domestic political pressures from Tamil Nadu. However, this involvement proved deeply controversial, both within Sri Lanka and in India, leading to long-term mistrust. Even today, India's diplomatic posture towards Colombo is complicated by the need to balance geopolitical interests with the Tamil political aspirations, which continue to resonate across the Palk Strait.[32] The uneasy aftermath of the civil war – particularly in relation to demilitarization, post-war reconciliation and land restitution – remains a flashpoint in India–Sri Lanka relations.

Pakistan's engagement with cross-border Pashtun and Baloch populations highlights a different set of entanglements. The Durand Line, drawn in 1893, sliced through tribal homelands, creating an artificial boundary between Afghanistan and what later became Pakistan. Ethnic Pashtuns straddle both sides of this border, maintaining familial, cultural and trade ties. The rise of the Taliban – an overwhelmingly Pashtun force – has rendered this frontier a zone of profound instability. Pakistan's strategic use of 'good Taliban' factions to maintain influence in Afghanistan has, in turn, radicalized its own border regions and exacerbated repression against ethnic Pashtun dissenters. The Pashtun Tahafuz Movement (PTM), which demands accountability for extrajudicial killings, disappearances and discrimination, emerged as a domestic response to this geopolitical entanglement.[33] Here, cross-border ethnicity becomes both a theatre of international rivalry and a justification for internal militarization.

Afghanistan, long a theatre for proxy conflicts, has similarly been affected by cross-border ethnic linkages. Its Tajik and Uzbek populations maintain deep affiliations with ethnic kin in Central Asia, while its Hazara community (a historically persecuted Shia minority) finds religious and cultural solidarity with groups in Iran. These overlapping identities have made Afghanistan a site of both refuge and repression, where ethnic communities are alternately courted or crushed depending on shifting alliances. India's infrastructural investments and diplomatic backing of non-Pashtun governments in Kabul have further complicated these dynamics, positioning ethnic affiliations within Afghanistan as strategic levers for regional influence.[34] As a result, 'local' ethnic tensions are seldom local – they are refracted through the lenses of regional diplomacy and international power projection.

The presence of Bengali-speaking populations in India's Northeast, particularly in Assam and Tripura, has long fuelled anxieties about demographic imbalance and fears of irredentism. These fears are rooted in concerns that political actors in Bangladesh or sections of its civil society might revive historical claims to territory once part of East Bengal, or that large-scale migration could gradually alter the region's cultural and political identity.

India's concerns over undocumented migration from Bangladesh – manifested most dramatically in the NRC process – stem from this perceived ethnic porosity. These anxieties have been periodically inflamed by political rhetoric, leading to increasing militarization of borders and sporadic flare-ups in bilateral relations. Conversely, within Bangladesh, ethnic minorities in the Chittagong Hill Tracts maintain affinities with indigenous communities across the Indian border, raising suspicions of external support and further hardening state attitudes towards their autonomy claims.[35]

In Bhutan and the Maldives, while cross-border ethnic affiliations are less politically volatile, migration has nonetheless produced tensions. As discussed earlier, Bhutan's historical expulsion of the Lhotshampa community was justified in part by fears of a growing 'foreign' demographic. Similarly, the Maldives, dependent on Indian labour for construction and services, has seen periodic episodes of resentment toward migrant workers, fuelled by nationalist rhetoric and regional power plays between New Delhi and Beijing.[36] In both cases, the transnational character of ethnic demography is treated not as a resource but as a liability.[37]

These cases underscore a fundamental paradox: while ethnic groups in South Asia often constitute cultural bridges across borders, they are repeatedly framed as security threats in state discourses. The politics of 'foreignness' is mobilized not against distant outsiders but against proximate populations with historical ties across national lines. As a result, ethnic minorities are rendered suspect by virtue of their belonging to a broader cultural geography – guilty of kinship beyond the nation.

What this reveals is that the security architecture of South Asia continues to be structured around a zero-sum logic of sovereignty, wherein ethnic continuity across borders is seen as a prelude to irredentism or infiltration. This framework produces a tragic calculus: loyalty is measured by disconnection and rootedness becomes a liability. Rather than nurturing cross-border affinities as opportunities for cultural diplomacy, states have responded with fortifications – both literal and ideological.

A regional framework that values people-to-people ties, facilitates cultural exchanges and respects the diasporic nature of ethnic belonging is long overdue. The SAARC charter's stated commitment to 'promote the welfare of the peoples of South Asia and to improve their quality of life' must be revitalized through concrete mechanisms that protect transnational ethnic identities from becoming casualties of geopolitics.[38] In this, civil society, regional institutions and diplomatic actors have a crucial role to play – not just in managing conflict, but in reimagining the very contours of regional solidarity.

Democratic Institutions, Authoritarianism and Ethnic Inclusion

Democracy in South Asia, despite its frequent invocation in constitutional preambles and electoral rituals, has often failed to translate into genuine inclusion for ethnic minorities. The endurance of the electoral process across much of the region masks deeper deficits in democratic substance – deficits that are particularly acute where ethnicity and state power intersect. Far from being empowered by democratic frameworks, ethnic minorities have frequently found themselves marginalized by majoritarian mandates, excluded from decision-making structures and surveilled or suppressed under the guise of national security. In many cases, the promise of democracy has coexisted with, and even enabled, authoritarian practices directed precisely at those most in need of representation.[39]

A central tension lies in the design of democratic institutions themselves. In countries like India, Pakistan and Sri Lanka, FPTP electoral systems – while producing stable majorities – have systematically disadvantaged dispersed or demographically minoritized ethnic groups. For instance, in India's Northeastern states, ethnic parties often struggle to make meaningful gains at the national level despite commanding regional support. Their demands are frequently diluted in coalition politics or dismissed outright in majoritarian parliaments.[40] The consequence is a form of procedural democracy that recognizes ethnic minorities as electoral constituencies but rarely as political stakeholders with equal claim to policy-setting, resource allocation or cultural self-determination.

In Sri Lanka, decades of democratic backsliding has intersected with ethnic exclusion in profound ways. The concentration of executive authority – especially during the Rajapaksa era – effectively nullified the checks and balances necessary to ensure minority protection. Though Tamils and Muslims participate in elections, their legislative voices have been repeatedly marginalized, and the state apparatus has remained overwhelmingly Sinhala-Buddhist in orientation and staffing. Post-war reconstruction has not been accompanied by institutional reform or devolution, resulting in the re-entrenchment of ethnic hierarchies within a nominally democratic polity.[41] The consequences are stark: elections take place and parliaments convene, but ethnic grievances remain unresolved and, in many cases, unheard.

Pakistan's democratic evolution, marked by recurrent military interventions, has further complicated the space for ethnic inclusion. While electoral politics has resumed in recent decades, the military continues to exercise significant influence over governance – particularly in regions marked by ethnic dissent, such as Balochistan and Khyber Pakhtunkhwa. Civilian governments have largely failed to assert authority in these areas, often deferring to security frameworks that prioritize control over inclusion. Ethnic political movements are frequently labelled as separatist or foreign-funded, and their leaders are subjected to harassment, disappearances or exile. The paradox of Pakistan's democracy is thus laid bare: elections provide a veneer of representation, even as the deep state undermines the possibility of meaningful ethnic pluralism.

In Afghanistan, democratic experiments have floundered under the weight of ethno-political fragmentation and foreign occupation. The Bonn Agreement of 2001 and subsequent electoral cycles attempted to establish inclusive governance structures, but these were quickly undermined by patronage networks that reinforced ethnic factionalism instead of transcending it. The state became a battleground for competing ethno-nationalist elites rather than a forum for democratic deliberation. The return of the Taliban in 2021 – whose rule is predicated on a hyper centralized Pashtun Islamic identity, as mentioned earlier – has further extinguished the prospects for ethnic inclusion. Under the current regime, minorities such as Hazaras, Tajiks and Uzbeks are excluded from governance, violently repressed and denied even the symbolic protections that previous democratic charters had promised.[42]

Even Nepal, often seen as a beacon of constitutional transformation in the region, has struggled to make its democratic institutions hospitable to ethnic minorities. While the post-monarchy constitution promised a federal structure that would recognize the country's plural demography, its implementation has been marred by political hesitation and backlash from dominant groups. The proportional representation system has enabled some Madhesi, Janajati and Tharu leaders to enter parliament, but meaningful power-sharing remains elusive. The challenge lies not only in formal mechanisms of representation but in deeper structural reforms: land redistribution, language recognition and equitable access to public goods.[43] Without these, ethnic minorities remain present in the polity but absent from the state.

In Bangladesh and the Maldives, the erosion of democratic institutions has coincided with increasing hostility towards ethnic groups. In the Chittagong Hill Tracts, military oversight and settler expansion continue despite the formal trappings of electoral democracy. Indigenous leadership in Bangladesh is undermined by the co-optation of local councils, and the Peace Accord implementation has been reduced to a bureaucratic exercise rather than a political imperative.[44] Meanwhile, in the Maldives, rising authoritarianism under successive regimes has combined with rising ethnic and religious homogenization. Migrant populations, African-descended communities and non-Dhivehi speakers find little space in public discourse or political participation, as Sunni Islam and Dhivehi linguistic nationalism are increasingly institutionalized as prerequisites for belonging.[45]

What unites these contexts is a regional pattern in which democratic institutions are neither robust enough nor designed sensitively enough to accommodate ethnic heterogeneity. Electoral competition often deepens communal divides, incentivizing politicians to mobilize dominant identities rather than to build coalitions across ethnic lines. Administrative structures remain centralized and opaque, limiting the capacity of minorities to influence local governance. The normalized conception of the nation, often tied to a dominant ethnic group, stops short of inclusive citizenship.

To move beyond this impasse, democratic reform must be structural and part of the norm. On the structural front, institutional designs must prioritize proportional representation, local autonomy and multi-tiered governance that reflects the real geography of ethnic pluralism. On the normative front, civic education and political discourse must move away from treating diversity as a threat to stability and instead recognize it as the cornerstone of democratic resilience. Inclusion should not be an afterthought; it must be embedded in the very structure of political systems – not only as a moral imperative, but as a prerequisite for lasting peace and sustainable development.

The lesson for South Asia is clear: democracy cannot merely mean the holding of elections or the formal enunciation of rights. It must mean the redistribution of power to those who have long been denied it. This must be done not in the abstract, but in practical terms: in everyday life, institutional presence and political voice. For ethnic minorities, democracy will matter only when it ceases to be a ritual of exclusion and becomes a vehicle for self-recognition and shared sovereignty.

Towards Plural Belonging

The crises that confront ethnic minorities across South Asia are not incidental or episodic – they are symptomatic of deeper structural maladies in the region's nation-building projects, legal frameworks and democratic cultures. The historical refusal to recognize ethnic plurality as foundational, rather than peripheral, to the national project has bred a region-wide legacy of exclusion, resentment and instability. If South Asia is to live up to its democratic aspirations and regional potential, the time has come to move beyond rhetoric and embark upon a serious recalibration of governance, citizenship and interstate cooperation.

At the heart of such reform lies a simple yet difficult question: can the decision-makers of states commit to protecting identities they do not share, histories they do not tell and aspirations they do not themselves inhabit? Answering this in the affirmative demands a rethinking of both domestic and regional priorities towards a more capacious and inclusive idea of belonging.

First, constitutional design must evolve. This means more than symbolic amendments or token commissions. It means embracing deep federalism – not as a reluctant concession but as a deliberate strategy for democratic survival. As of 2024, federal design in South Asia remains uneven and frequently manipulated. India's fiscal and administrative federalism continues to suffer from recentralization; Nepal's ethnic federalism is frozen in institutional ambiguity; Pakistan's 18th Amendment, once hailed as transformative, remains undermined by military overreach. A regional norm of constitutionally enshrined ethnic self-governance must be developed and monitored – perhaps under a reinvigorated SAARC framework or a new multilateral charter for minority rights.

Second, citizenship laws must be urgently revised to protect against statelessness. According to the UN High Commissioner for Refugees (UNHCR), South Asia remains home to over 2.5 million stateless persons as of 2024. Many of these are the legacy of colonial migrations and border rearrangements – problems that only statecraft can solve. Automatic birth registration, gender-equal nationality laws and recognition of long-standing residence must become legal norms across the region. Political will can no longer afford to defer to historical fears or populist anxieties.

Third, institutional mechanisms for conflict resolution and transitional justice must be developed at both national and regional levels. Too often, peace accords in South Asia have lacked teeth, implementation or transparency. The Accord Monitoring Index by the Global Peace Accord Project finds that fewer than 40 per cent of ethnic-related peace accords – Global Peace Index (GPI) Project of the Institute for Economics & Peace – in South Asia are substantially implemented within a decade of signing.[46] New mechanisms for third-party monitoring, civil society participation and community-based dispute resolution must be introduced. These mechanisms must not only adjudicate land

and autonomy disputes but also create space for memory, apology and reparative justice.

Fourth, regional cooperation must treat ethnicity not as a threat but as an opportunity. Cross-border ethnicities can serve as cultural bridges, not security liabilities. The SAARC, long rendered ineffective by geopolitical hostility, must be revived through specific, low-stakes projects focused on ethnic cultural exchanges, education and minority rights dialogue. An ethnic minorities charter, modelled on the European Framework Convention for the Protection of National Minorities, could be drafted under SAARC auspices or through subregional groupings such as BBIN (Bangladesh, Bhutan, India, Nepal).

Fifth, South Asia's democratic renewal must be moral as much as institutional. The tendency to instrumentalize ethnic identity for electoral gain – to pit communities against each other in the pursuit of vote banks – has not only distorted democracy but degraded it. Rebuilding trust requires not only legal reform but moral courage – a willingness to cede power, listen to grievances and resist the seductions of ethnic triumphalism.

In this endeavour, we might recall the words of Hazrat Bulleh Shah, the seventeenth-century Punjabi Sufi poet who sang of a world beyond narrow identities:

> Races and nations pass away;
> Humanity alone endures.
> You may call yourself Hindu or Turk –
> What does it matter if you know not love?[47]

'Love' here is not sentiment – it is the radical ethic of mutual recognition, of belonging without possession and of coexistence without coercion. South Asia, for all its agonies, still contains within it the cultural, spiritual and democratic resources to realize this ethic. What is required now is not imagination alone, but resolve.

12

Majoritarian Shadows: Religious Minorities and the Democratic Promise

Religious freedom is among the most profound indicators of democratic health. In liberal democratic theory, it forms part of the inalienable triad of freedoms – of speech, association and belief – that constitute the moral foundation of citizenship. Nowhere, perhaps, is the tension between these ideals and political realities more evident than in South Asia – a region where religious identity intersects with history, statecraft and populism in deeply contested ways.

Home to over a quarter of the world's population and some of the globe's most vibrant religious traditions, South Asia is paradoxically also the site of some of the most systematic erosions of religious liberty. Constitutions across the region formally enshrine protections for religious freedom and the rights of religious minorities. Yet, in practice, many of these commitments are undermined by legal ambiguities, populist pressures and ideological mobilizations that elevate dominant religious identities over pluralistic ideals.[1]

A central paradox of South Asian democracy today is that it simultaneously affirms and erodes religious freedom. Majoritarian logics have increasingly replaced secular commitments as the primary language of legitimacy. Religious minorities – Muslims in India and Sri Lanka, Hindus and Christians in Pakistan and Bangladesh, Shias and Hazaras in Afghanistan, and Christians in Bhutan and Nepal – are no longer merely at the periphery of policymaking; they are often rendered targets of political consolidation itself. In some countries, like the Maldives and Pakistan, the state formally restricts religious identity and conversion, enshrining exclusion in constitutional language. In others, such as India and Sri Lanka, the state proclaims secularism but functions through a selective silence – where complicity with dominant religious interests is masked by claims of neutrality.[2] What emerges, then, is a democratic architecture that is deeply fractured: formally inclusive yet operationally exclusive.

One of the clearest illustrations of this is the divergent treatment of religious communities under anti-conversion laws, blasphemy legislation and religious education curricula. These legal instruments, often justified in the name of public order or cultural preservation, are wielded to intimidate, suppress and delegitimize minority identities.[3]

Equally troubling is the erosion of civic space. The rise of Right-wing nationalism – Hindutva in India, Sinhala-Buddhist nationalism in Sri Lanka, Wahhabi orthodoxy in the Maldives, and hardline Sunni majoritarianism in Pakistan and Afghanistan – has coincided with a cultural shift in public discourse. Religious minorities are frequently portrayed as outsiders or threats to the national fabric, often through well-funded propaganda, algorithmic amplification of hate speech and a re-engineering of public memory through distorted educational materials. The architecture of this exclusion is both material and symbolic. It ranges from the bulldozing of mosques and churches to the rewriting of history textbooks, and from judicial apathy to electoral incitement.[4]

Amid this gloom, the region offers glimpses of institutional resilience. The Indian judiciary, at key historical moments, has asserted the centrality of secularism to the constitutional order. Bangladesh's courts reinstated secularism into their constitutional framework despite mounting Islamist pressure. In Nepal and Bhutan, activists continue to challenge the contradictions between constitutional promises and discriminatory laws. These examples, though rare, serve as reminders that the democratic promise has not been extinguished – it remains embattled, awaiting reclamation.

This chapter explores these complexities through a thematic, rather than national, lens. A country-wise analysis, while offering granularity, often fragments the reader's understanding of the region's common challenges and structural convergences. A thematic approach, by contrast, allows us to place Afghanistan's targeted killings of Hazaras alongside India's 'bulldozer politics', Bhutan's criminalization of conversion besides Pakistan's weaponization of blasphemy, and the Maldives' denial of citizenship to non-Muslims alongside Sri Lanka's state patronage of Buddhism. These phenomena, though contextually distinct, stem from shared patterns: the collapse of secularism into majoritarianism, the strategic use of religion in political legitimation and the growing incapacity – or unwillingness – of states to defend their most vulnerable populations.

In undertaking this analysis, I do not merely wish to catalogue injustice but to excavate the fault lines within South Asian democracies that allow such injustices to persist. The deeper question is not only how the religious minorities are treated but what that treatment reveals about the very nature of democracy in South Asia today. Can a democracy that fails to protect its minorities be considered a democracy at all?

Constitutional Contradictions

At the heart of South Asia's democratic aspiration lies a deep and persistent constitutional tension – the simultaneous affirmation of secularism and the institutional privileging of dominant religious traditions. While every SAARC member state, in form or rhetoric, lays claim to upholding religious freedom, most constitutions either explicitly favour a particular religion or are interpreted in ways that undermine genuine religious pluralism. This constitutional contradiction has proven not only a theoretical concern but a lived political reality with profound consequences for religious minorities across the region.

India and Nepal exemplify the paradoxical articulation of secularism as both constitutional principle and cultural inheritance. India's constitution, despite its formal declaration of secularism in the Preamble and robust guarantees under Articles 25 to 30, continues to be interpreted and enacted in a context where Hindu symbols and rituals are increasingly normalized within public institutions. The installation of the *sengol* – a Chola-era sceptre associated with divine kingship – at the inauguration of the new parliament building in 2023, accompanied by

Vedic chanting by Hindu priests, exemplifies this growing sacralization of state spaces. Since 2014, the visible consolidation of Hindutva ideology has further entrenched majoritarian dominance. In numerous states, anti-conversion laws – ostensibly aimed at preventing 'forced' conversions – are weaponized against Christians and Muslims, often without due process. These laws rest on the premise that the act of religious conversion, particularly to Islam or Christianity, is inherently suspicious – a logic that subverts the spirit of constitutional protections.[5]

Nepal's 2015 constitution declares the state to be 'secular', yet qualifies this by describing secularism as the 'protection of religion and culture handed down from time immemorial'. This formulation has become a legal and ideological gateway through which Hindu cultural supremacy continues to be legitimized. The state allocates public funds for Hindu festivals and temple maintenance, while Christian, Muslim and Kirati institutions struggle for official recognition and financial parity. Furthermore, criminal-law provisions that prohibit 'hurting religious sentiment' or 'attempting to convert' have disproportionately targeted Christian communities, whose numbers have increased in recent decades.

In Pakistan and the Maldives, the constitutional contradiction is even more direct. Article 2 of Pakistan's constitution declares Islam to be the state religion and requires that all laws conform to Islamic injunctions. Simultaneously, Article 20 guarantees the right of citizens to profess and practise their religion – rights that remain largely aspirational for the country's 3.7 per cent religious minorities. The constitution categorically excludes Ahmadis from identifying as Muslims, and legislation such as the 1984 Ordinance XX criminalizes their religious expression.[6] In 2024 alone, over 300 individuals were charged under Pakistan's blasphemy laws (a quarter of them from minority communities) and several received death sentences – though executions are yet to be carried out.[7] These constitutional contradictions, far from theoretical, legitimize an ecosystem of state-sanctioned exclusion.

The Maldivian constitution is perhaps the most explicitly exclusionary in South Asia. It not only mandates Islam as the basis of all laws and as the state religion, but also bars non-Muslims from citizenship under Article 9(d). All constitutional rights – including freedom of expression and assembly – are contingent upon conformity with Islamic principles. In practice, this has meant that Christians, Buddhists and followers of ancestral or pre-Islamic Maldivian spiritual traditions – such as forms of animism and Indic ritual practices historically present in the archipelago – are denied the legal right to worship publicly. With Saudi-backed Salafi interpretations increasingly dominating the country's clerical discourse, the Maldivian model has come to represent a theocratic closure of the democratic promise. Even within Islam, there is little tolerance for theological diversity. Sufi orders, once integral to Maldivian religious life, are now marginalized in favour of doctrinaire orthodoxy.[8]

Bhutan, though constitutionally committed to religious freedom, simultaneously enshrines Buddhism as the 'spiritual heritage' of the nation. State resources disproportionately favour Buddhist institutions, while the legal architecture criminalizes religious conversion through vaguely defined 'inducement' clauses. As of 2024, only two non-Buddhist religious groups are officially registered under the Religious Organizations Act, both of which are Hindu. Christian groups remain unrecognized, despite representing approximately 1.5 per cent of the population. Without registration, they are unable to build places of worship or hold public religious services, effectively placing their practice outside the protection of law.[9]

In Sri Lanka, Article 9 of the constitution accords Buddhism the 'foremost place' and enjoins the state to protect the Buddha Sasana. Although Articles 10 and 14 guarantee religious freedom, Buddhist institutions receive privileged status in terms of funding, ceremonial roles and symbolic authority. The state has often failed to safeguard mosques and churches from violent backlash – particularly in the aftermath of the 2019 Easter bombings – leaving minority communities vulnerable. The 2024 Human Rights Watch report notes a disturbing increase in Buddhist nationalist vigilante groups targeting Muslims, often with passive or active support from local authorities.[10] The constitutional elevation of one religion over others fosters precisely such impunity.

Bangladesh offers an intriguing case of constitutional oscillation. Originally founded as a secular republic in 1971, the 1988 constitutional amendment established Islam as the state religion. But in 2010, the Supreme Court restored secularism as a 'fundamental constitutional principle'. Article 12 now prohibits religious discrimination and state promotion of religion. Nevertheless, the contradiction remains unresolved: Article 2A still names Islam as the state religion. This dualism has enabled ruling governments to oscillate between appeasing conservative Islamist factions and invoking secular language in international forums. As of 2024, the state continues to fund religious education and mosque constructions while non-Muslim minorities – particularly Hindus and Buddhists – report increased marginalization and land encroachment.[11]

Even in Afghanistan, where the collapse of democratic governance in 2021 following the Taliban takeover complicates any legalistic reading, constitutional contradiction remains a historical constant. The 2004 constitution (no longer in operation) guaranteed the right to religious practice for non-Muslims, but simultaneously declared that 'no law shall contravene the tenets and provisions of the holy religion of Islam'. Under Taliban rule, this contradiction has sharpened into open persecution. Non-Muslims such as Sikhs, Hindus and Christians, along with Shia Muslims (particularly the Hazara community), have faced relentless attacks. In 2024 alone, ISIS-K militants targeted Shia worshippers in Herat and Kabul in three separate attacks, killing over thirty people.[12] While the Taliban claims to be an Islamic Emirate safeguarding 'true' Islamic values, it has utterly abandoned any pretence of religious pluralism and governs in the absence of any constitutional framework or legal guarantees.

Taken together, these cases illustrate a profound regional pattern: the constitutional architecture of South Asian states often conflates religious identity with national identity. Whether through overt theocratic mandates or subtler cultural nationalism, dominant religious groups enjoy preferential access to legal protections, public funding and symbolic authority. For minority communities, constitutional promises are either ambiguously worded, inconsistently applied or nullified through majoritarian reinterpretation.

This constitutional contradiction is not a marginal defect. It lies at the core of the democratic crisis in South Asia. A constitution that affirms equality but enforces hierarchy becomes a tool of ideological consolidation, rather than of civic inclusion. If democracy in South Asia is to survive its current moment of peril, a constitutional reckoning is imperative – one that moves beyond hollow proclamations and towards a sincere commitment to pluralism, parity and the secular rule of law.

State Complicity and Majoritarian Mobilization

In contemporary South Asia, the rise of religious majoritarianism has not occurred despite the state, but often through its tacit endorsement, strategic complicity or active orchestration. This phenomenon has increasingly transformed democratic regimes into partisan actors that mobilize religion not only as an instrument of symbolic identity, but as a mechanism of governance, resource distribution and electoral consolidation. Across the region, the invocation of religious identity by ruling regimes has become central to the political calculus of incumbency, producing a perilous erosion of secular–democratic safeguards and diminishing the legitimacy of state neutrality.

In India, the electoral success of the BJP since 2014 has inaugurated a new chapter in majoritarian statecraft. The political architecture of the BJP–RSS (Rashtriya Swayamsevak Sangh) combine has normalized the language of civilizational supremacy, recasting Hindutva not merely as a cultural force but as an organizing principle of state power. This transformation is evident not only in rhetoric but also in administrative choices.

Since 2020, over 300 incidents of anti-Muslim violence have been recorded by civil society networks, with a sharp increase in state-led demolitions targeting Muslim neighbourhoods, justified as anti-encroachment drives. Civil society monitoring—including Amnesty International—has documented 63 demolitions of Muslim-owned homes and businesses across five BJP-ruled states (including Uttar Pradesh and Madhya Pradesh) during April–June 2022, carried out under the pretext of anti-encroachment drives.[13] In none of these cases were prior notices issued or legal remedies made available, indicating a pattern of impunity protected at the highest levels of governance.[14]

This majoritarian turn is not uniquely Indian. In Sri Lanka, the symbiotic relationship between the state and Sinhala-Buddhist nationalist groups has intensified in recent years. The political rehabilitation of hardline organizations such as Bodu Bala Sena (BBS), previously implicated in anti-Muslim riots, reflects a broader strategy of electoral consolidation around ethno-religious identity. In the 2024 parliamentary session, debates resurfaced over the introduction of a national anti-conversion bill – championed by Sinhala Buddhist leaders and quietly supported by segments within the ruling party. Although no law has yet been passed, the legislative discourse itself has had a chilling effect on religious minorities, particularly Muslims and Christians, who report increased surveillance of places of worship and arbitrary restrictions on public gatherings.[15]

Pakistan's majoritarianism, while shaped by a different theological framework, reflects a similar entanglement of state and orthodoxy. In the lead-up to the 2024 general elections, religious rhetoric was prominently deployed by several parties to assert their moral and cultural authority. The Tehreek-e-Labbaik Pakistan (TLP), a far-Right Islamist party known for its violent mobilization around blasphemy laws, was not only permitted to campaign freely but also saw electoral gains in Punjab and Sindh. More worryingly, in January 2024, a group of Christian families in Faisalabad were forcibly evicted from government housing following unsubstantiated accusations of blasphemy. The local administration failed to intervene despite repeated appeals, reflecting the institutionalized vulnerability of minorities when religious hysteria is politically expedient.[16]

Bangladesh, long considered a relatively moderate Muslim-majority state, has witnessed the increasing influence of religious hardliners within its political landscape. In the context of the 2024 national elections, the ruling BAL renewed its outreach to Hefazat-e-Islam – a conservative Islamist organization – by softening its stance on several secular initiatives, including the rollback of proposed reforms to religious education curricula. At least eighteen candidates affiliated with Hefazat were endorsed by regional coalitions. Simultaneously, several reports emerged of state inaction during anti-Hindu violence in rural districts of Chittagong and Mymensingh, where temples were vandalized and properties torched in the weeks leading up to the polls.[17] Despite constitutional commitments to secularism, such accommodations underscore the fragile equilibrium between electoral advantage and minority protection.

Since the interim government took office following PM Sheikh Hasina's ouster in August 2024, communal violence has intensified. Reuters and Al-Jazeera reports that hundreds of Hindu houses, businesses and temples have been vandalized, with the Bangladesh Hindu Buddhist Christian Unity Council documenting over 150 temples desecrated and more than 2,200 incidents of violence between August and December 2024. Tensions have continued into 2025: in late June, Bangladesh saw the destruction of a Durga temple in Khilkhet, Dhaka, including the removal and dumping of its idols – an act condemned by India and noted by multiple news outlets.[18] Despite constitutional commitments to secularism, these developments underscore the fragile equilibrium between electoral advantage, rising hardline influence and the protection of minority communities.

In Nepal, the mobilization of religious identity has taken a more subterranean form, but is no less consequential. The return of monarchist sentiments among certain segments of the political elite has catalysed a renewed call for Hindu statehood. In March 2024, a coalition of Hindu nationalist organizations held a major rally in Kathmandu demanding the reinstatement of Nepal as a Hindu *rashtra*.[19]

While the government publicly reaffirmed its secular credentials, several MPs, including from the opposition UML and the royalist Rastriya Prajatantra Party, expressed support for these demands. The government's reluctance to decisively confront such ideologies has emboldened their public presence, with Christian communities increasingly facing restrictions in securing land for religious activities, often under the pretext of 'cultural preservation'.[20]

The Maldives, though lacking electoral pluralism in a conventional sense, has become a potent example of how majoritarian narratives can be state-sanctioned through policy and discourse. In 2024, President Mohamed Muizzu's administration reinforced the requirement that all school curricula be aligned with 'Islamic national identity', mandating daily religious instruction based on Salafi doctrines. Simultaneously, the Ministry of Islamic Affairs introduced regulations banning any public gatherings not explicitly sanctioned by Islamic jurisprudence, leading to the de facto criminalization of interfaith dialogue. The government also revoked the visa extensions of five foreign aid workers accused of proselytization, despite lack of due process or formal charges.[21] These actions reflect a deepening entrenchment of theocratic majoritarianism as a modality of state control.

Afghanistan, under Taliban rule, operates in a realm beyond electoral politics, but its state machinery is no less implicated in the systematic persecution of minorities. While the Taliban publicly claim to protect all Muslims, their governance is undergirded by a rigid Sunni Pashtun interpretation of Sharia that excludes Shia, Sufi and non-Muslim communities from meaningful civic participation. In 2024 alone, over a dozen Shia processions were banned in Kabul and Herat, and a new directive from the Ministry for the Propagation of Virtue and Prevention of Vice prohibited Hazara-run media outlets from broadcasting religious content.[22] In the absence of any representative accountability, the state has become the very apparatus of religious exclusion.

Even Bhutan, often perceived as a peaceful Buddhist kingdom, has not remained untouched by the logic of majoritarian mobilization. In 2024, multiple reports surfaced of covert pressure on Christians to abstain from proselytizing in southern districts. Though state officials deny any formal directive, interviews conducted by international observers with religious leaders indicate that local administrators routinely discourage the registration of new churches, warning of 'community disharmony'. This form of bureaucratic suppression, though not overtly violent, reflects how the state can function as an enforcer of majoritarian norms through administrative ambiguity.[23]

What binds these varied contexts together is a shared pattern: the transformation of state institutions from guardians of pluralism into facilitators of hegemonic identity. Whether through silence, complicity or active intervention, the state apparatus in each of these countries has increasingly served to amplify the authority of dominant religious groups – rendering minorities vulnerable to societal bigotry and institutional abandonment.

The implications are far-reaching. When the state is seen as partisan in religious matters, its legitimacy as a neutral arbiter collapses. Law enforcement loses credibility, courts appear compromised and democratic norms are hollowed from within. For South Asia to reclaim its constitutional and democratic promise, a fundamental reorientation is necessary – one that places pluralism not as a rhetorical accessory, but as a non-negotiable foundation of governance.

Violence, Intimidation and Shrinking Civic Space

Religious violence in South Asia is neither episodic nor accidental; it is increasingly structural, routine and embedded within the sociopolitical architecture of the region. Far from being isolated outbreaks of mob fury, the threats facing religious minorities today operate through an overlapping system of intimidation, surveillance and normalized aggression. This civic asphyxiation – where fear becomes the governing condition of religious life – is not confined to any one nation. Instead, it manifests across South Asia in forms both spectacular and mundane, where physical violence is merely the sharpest edge of a broader campaign of erasure.[24]

A defining feature of this region-wide trend is the climate of impunity surrounding acts of targeted violence. In 2024 alone, attacks on places of worship – including mosques in Sri Lanka and India, churches in Nepal, Hindu temples in Bangladesh and Shia *imambargahs* in Afghanistan – have increased in both frequency and intensity. In most cases, the perpetrators have not been prosecuted and, in some instances, local authorities have obstructed justice or recharacterized communal attacks as spontaneous disputes. In August 2024, following the resignation of Prime Minister Sheikh Hasina, a wave of coordinated attacks on Hindu homes, businesses, and temples swept across Bangladesh, with the Bangladesh Hindu Buddhist Christian Unity Council documenting over 2,000 incidents of violence in just two weeks, including the desecration of 69 temples and attacks on at least 157 homes and businesses.[25] The message to religious minorities is clear: their suffering is negotiable and their safety is optional.

This culture of impunity is often sustained by a deliberate ambivalence in the legal and security apparatus. For instance, across countries, law enforcement responses to threats against religious minorities are markedly slower and less robust than those protecting majority sentiments. In India, police inaction during hate crimes – especially in states governed by Right-wing parties – has become the subject of public scrutiny. A recent report from June 2025 documented 602 hate-crime incidents in Uttar Pradesh alone, nearly half of which were linked to right-wing groups. Yet despite the scale and severity of these attacks—ranging from physical violence to intimidation and religious harassment—only 81 First Information Reports (FIRs) were registered. This striking gap between reported incidents and formal police action reflects a deepening crisis of accountability within law enforcement institutions, particularly in regions where political incentives discourage the vigorous prosecution of majoritarian violence.[26] In Afghanistan, the pattern is reversed but structurally similar: the state itself is the primary agent of religious suppression, and those that target Shia or non-Muslim communities do so with de facto state sanction. Even in Nepal and Bhutan, where outright mob violence is less prevalent, the state often responds with silence or deflection to reports of religious harassment, treating them as isolated incidents rather than symptoms of systemic exclusion.

The civic space available to minority religious groups is also being rapidly eroded by regulatory harassment and administrative censorship. The registration of minority religious institutions – churches in Bhutan, madrasas in Sri Lanka, Hindu charities in Pakistan – has become a bureaucratic obstacle course, with permissions routinely delayed or denied without explanation.[27]

In 2024, the Pakistani government suspended thirty-seven minority-run educational or religious trusts, citing 'non-compliance with public morality', a vague standard that leaves ample scope for ideological policing. In the Maldives, the 2024 Ministry of Islamic Affairs directive banned the use of public venues for 'non-traditional religious discourse' – a formulation that effectively silenced Shia and Sufi practitioners, whose rituals and sermons do not conform to state-defined Sunni orthodoxy.[28]

Digital surveillance and hate amplification further constrict the public sphere. Across South Asia, state and non-state actors alike weaponize digital platforms to intimidate, dox and delegitimize minority voices. Algorithms reward outrage and virality becomes a tool of vilification. In 2024, multiple coordinated social media campaigns in Sri Lanka and India targeted Muslim-owned businesses, calling for economic boycotts under the guise of nationalism. These campaigns, often led by fringe religious organizations, receive disproportionate amplification and are rarely penalized by authorities. The Telecommunications Regulatory Commission of Sri Lanka faced international criticism after issuing warnings to three independent news outlets that reported on anti-Muslim discrimination, citing 'provocation of religious disharmony'. What is silenced online increasingly mirrors what is erased offline.[29]

Children and young adults are also not spared from the machinery of intimidation. Religious minorities across the SAARC countries report increased bullying and segregation in schools, often with the complicity of teachers or administrators.

In a 2024 survey conducted by a regional educational consortium, over 43 per cent of Christian students in Pakistan and 38 per cent of Muslim students in Sri Lankan Buddhist-majority schools reported experiencing religious discrimination within the classroom.[30]

The curriculum itself, in several states, has been weaponized to project dominant religious narratives while marginalizing minority contributions. The erasure of Islamic thinkers and rulers from history textbooks in India, the omission of Christian heritage in Bhutanese civic education and the de-emphasis of pluralistic Buddhist traditions in Maldivian syllabi collectively produce systems of teaching that propagate exclusion.[31]

Importantly, gendered and sexualized violence functions as a distinct axis of intimidation. Women from religious minorities – particularly Dalit Christian women in India, Hindu girls in Pakistan and Ahmadi women across the region – face a disproportionate burden of abuse. Forced conversions and coerced marriages remain alarmingly frequent. In Sindh province, Pakistan, human rights defenders documented seventy-four cases of alleged forced conversion and underage marriage of Hindu and Christian girls in the first six months of 2024 alone.[32] In Afghanistan, Shia Hazara women are subject to a double bind: targeted both for their gender and their religious affiliation, they face systematic exclusion from schools and public spaces, and reports increasingly suggest that religiously motivated abductions have re-emerged in remote provinces.[33]

What unites these many expressions of violence is their function: to constrict the moral and spatial boundaries of belonging. Religious minorities in South Asia are not merely facing intermittent discrimination; they are being methodically pushed out of the public sphere – politically, economically and symbolically. They are reminded daily, through both overt attack and quiet omission, that their presence is provisional, their dignity contingent and their futures negotiable.

This shrinking of civic space not only violates constitutional promises, but imperils the democratic contract itself. The capacity to dissent, to assemble, to worship, to educate and to speak without fear are the bedrock rights of any meaningful democracy. As long as such rights are denied to significant portions of the population because of religion, South Asia's democracies remain democracies in name alone. The challenge, therefore, is not merely to prevent future violence but to unmake the entire ecosystem that legitimizes it – from partisan silences to ideological curriculums, from bureaucratic neglect to algorithmic persecution.

Law and Judiciary: Arbiter, Accomplice or Bystander?

The judiciary and legal institutions are often invoked as the last line of defence in the architecture of democratic protection. In theory, they offer redress where executive excesses prevail and legislative majoritarianism overwhelms. But in South Asia, the role of courts and legal systems in safeguarding the rights of religious minorities has been fraught with ambivalence. Across the region, judicial and quasi-judicial bodies oscillate between being defenders of minority rights, passive bystanders in the face of injustice and, at times, even active participants in the erosion of constitutional guarantees.[34]

At the most fundamental level, the legal frameworks across the SAARC countries exhibit both progressiveness in formal design and selectivity in application. Many countries have constitutional guarantees of religious freedom and equality before the law, as mentioned earlier. However, the interpretation, implementation and enforcement of these provisions are increasingly shaped by majoritarian sentiment and political expediency. The courts, far from existing in a vacuum, reflect and are shaped by the prevailing sociopolitical climate. In India, for instance, the higher judiciary has historically played a vital role in articulating secularism as part of the constitution's basic structure.

However, more recent jurisprudence has raised concerns about judicial restraint bordering on abdication, particularly in matters involving religious violence, discriminatory laws or hate speech.[35] In several high-profile cases concerning communal riots, hate crimes and anti-conversion laws, petitions remain pending or are repeatedly deferred, even as the facts on the ground continue to deteriorate for the affected communities.

Many of these cases involve targeted violence against religious minorities – for instance, the 2020 Delhi riots, in which Muslim homes and mosques were attacked, or the continuing legal challenges to anti-conversion laws disproportionately affecting Christians and Dalits. The pattern of judicial delay or silence in such matters has deepened anxieties about the erosion of constitutional protections for vulnerable groups.

The pattern is not unique to India. In Bangladesh, as mentioned earlier, despite the Supreme Court's 2010 ruling that restored secularism as a foundational principle, lower courts have struggled to uphold minority protections consistently. In 2024, the Dhaka High Court dismissed a plea by a Hindu trust seeking restitution of temple land encroached upon during electoral unrest, citing 'insufficient documentation – despite eyewitness testimony and satellite imagery supporting the claim. At the same time, the judiciary has shown occasional courage, such as in striking down village council *fatwa*s that sought to penalize interfaith marriages or so-called 'un-Islamic' behaviour.[36] Yet these progressive rulings often remain isolated, lacking follow-through at the administrative level.

The situation is particularly dire in Pakistan, where legal formalities co-exist with a legal culture that permits, and even legitimizes, religious persecution. The lower judiciary frequently convicts individuals under blasphemy charges based on flimsy or fabricated evidence, fearful of public backlash or violent retribution from extremist groups. In 2024, a trial court in Punjab province sentenced two Christian men to death under Section 295-C of the Penal Code, despite inconsistencies in the prosecution's account. The Lahore High Court later stayed the execution but did not overturn the conviction, leaving the accused in prolonged incarceration.[37]

The fear of reprisals against the judiciary is real: judges and prosecutors who acquit or even question blasphemy allegations have faced threats, violence and exile. The assassination of the governor of the Punjab province, Salman Taseer, in 2011 by his own bodyguard – who was later glorified as a martyr by segments of the legal fraternity – still casts a long shadow over the country's justice system. Although Taseer was not a member of the judiciary, he was killed for publicly opposing the misuse of blasphemy laws and defending a Christian woman accused under them – highlighting the extreme risks faced by those who challenge religious orthodoxy in any public capacity. In Afghanistan under Taliban rule, the very concept of an independent judiciary has been nullified. The court system now functions under the strict interpretation of Sharia law as defined by the Taliban's religious councils. Legal redress for religious minorities, especially Shia Hazaras, Christians and Sikhs, is practically non-existent. In 2024, several families from the Hazara community reported that local religious courts refused to hear their petitions regarding property seizure by Taliban-linked clerics, declaring their legal claims 'null under Islamic jurisprudence'.[38] This absence of even the pretence of impartial adjudication renders the rule of law a fiction for non-Sunni and non-Pashtun populations.

In Sri Lanka, courts have occasionally intervened against majoritarian overreach but remain constrained by political alignments and constitutional ambiguities. In February 2024, the Supreme Court refused to admit a petition challenging the Ministry of Buddhist Affairs' preferential funding allocation to Buddhist temples over mosques and churches, citing 'policy discretion'. Yet, in another ruling later that year, the same court struck down a police directive banning Christian proselytization in Batticaloa, affirming the right to religious propagation under Articles 10 and 14.[39] However, the inconsistent application of such rulings undermines the court's role as a consistent arbiter of pluralism.

Even in countries like Bhutan and Nepal, where the judiciary is less politically polarized, legal mechanisms often fail to provide full recourse to religious minorities. Bhutan's Religious Organizations Act lacks a transparent appeals process for unregistered groups, effectively denying non-Buddhist communities access to public space. Nepal's judiciary, while generally independent, remains encumbered by a deeply entrenched bureaucratic apparatus that delays adjudication on sensitive religious issues. As of mid-2025 three petitions concerning the recognition of

Christian holidays as national observances remain unresolved before the constitutional bench, despite having been filed nearly a year earlier.[40]

Underlying these institutional inconsistencies is the broader failure of South Asian legal cultures to develop robust anti-discrimination jurisprudence. Unlike in other constitutional democracies, very few legal precedents in the region directly address systemic religious discrimination as a violation of equal citizenship. Anti-conversion laws, blasphemy statutes and public order clauses are often interpreted in ways that restrict, rather than protect, religious freedoms. In many cases, legal reasoning defers to notions of public morality or cultural harmony – concepts that, though undefined in law, are regularly invoked to justify infringements on minority rights.

Judicial underreach is compounded by limited access to justice for minority communities. Discrimination in police registration of cases, procedural delays, linguistic barriers and the lack of legal aid all contribute to a justice gap that remains both wide and persistent. In 2024, a report by the South Asia Justice Forum noted that across five SAARC countries, religious minorities are 3.5 times less likely to have their cases heard in court within one year of filing, compared to the national average.[41] The law, in this context, becomes a terrain of exhaustion, where hope is worn down by delay and disenfranchisement.

For the judiciary to fulfil its democratic role, it must go beyond passive adjudication. Courts in the region must embrace an interpretive posture grounded in constitutional morality, not popular sentiment. Legal systems must proactively articulate and defend the secular foundations of citizenship. Equally, bar councils, legal education bodies and civil society must work to reshape the jurisprudential imagination into one that refuses to see religious minorities as objects of tolerance and instead affirms them as equal claimants to the public good. In other words, religious minorities must be recognized not merely as communities to be accommodated, but as full participants in shaping the values, laws and institutions that define the collective life of the nation.

South Asia stands today at a judicial crossroads. The courts and legal institutions may yet redeem the promise of pluralism – but only if they can summon the moral clarity to stand firm amid political noise, and the institutional courage to act as guardians not merely of law, but of justice itself.

Global Influences

While the crisis of religious freedom in South Asia is often narrated in terms of domestic politics, electoral machinations and constitutional design, it is increasingly shaped by forces that transcend national borders. The surge in religious majoritarianism, ideological polarization and identity-based governance cannot be understood without examining the shifting dynamics of global geopolitics, transnational religious funding, diasporic activism and ideological exports. The phenomenon of religious repression and mobilization in the region is no longer strictly endogenous. It is now embedded within global circuits of capital, theology, surveillance and political influence.

Nowhere is this more evident than in the interplay between Saudi Arabian influence and the internal religious policies of South Asian states. In recent years, particularly since 2018, Saudi Arabia has intensified its financial and institutional involvement in countries like the Maldives, Pakistan and parts of Afghanistan. This investment extends beyond economic bailouts or infrastructure support, and into religious education, clerical training and mosque construction. In the Maldives, for example, over 130 mosques are now partially or fully funded by Saudi-linked foundations, and as of 2024, nearly 80 per cent of state-appointed *imams* had received theological training in Saudi-backed institutions.[42] These developments have drastically shifted the religious discourse in the country, marginalizing local Islamic traditions such as South Asian Sufism in favour of Salafi orthodoxy.

A similar pattern is visible in Pakistan, where seminaries aligned with Deobandi and Salafi ideologies continue to receive external patronage. According to a 2024 investigative report by the International Center for Islam and Pluralism, over 22 per cent of new religious schools established since 2020 received funding from donors based in the Gulf states.[43] These institutions often operate outside the purview of Pakistan's national education authority, and have contributed to the proliferation of exclusionary narratives against Ahmadis, Shias and non-Muslim communities. The ideological tightening fostered by this funding regime not only entrenches sectarianism but also reshapes the very language of national identity in favour of exclusivist interpretations of Islam.

Hindutva nationalism in India has similarly transcended its national borders, drawing substantial support from diasporic networks, particularly in North America, the UK and the Gulf. Organizations such as the Overseas Friends of BJP and affiliated groups have played a growing role in mobilizing funds, lobbying political figures abroad and disseminating narratives that align with the majoritarian agenda in India. In 2024, Indian diaspora-linked donors in the US were estimated to have contributed over ₹750 crore (approximately $90 million) to various Hindu nationalist projects, including school curricula, religious events and media outlets.[44] The ideological diffusion is not merely financial, it is pedagogical and institutional. Hindu nationalist talking points – once confined to the margins – are now increasingly normalized within Indian cultural and religious organizations abroad.

These global circuits also function through digital infrastructure. The role of social media platforms – headquartered in Silicon Valley or Singapore, but functioning in South Asia with minimal regulatory accountability – has been critical in the transnational amplification of hate speech and disinformation. A 2024 analysis by the Center for the Study of Organized Hate (CSOH) found that less than 0.1 per cent (specifically, 0.094 per cent) of all fact-checking interventions on X's Community Notes platform – designed to crowdsource user-generated fact-checks for misleading or harmful posts – were written in South Asian languages such as Hindi, Urdu, Bengali, Tamil and Nepali. This is despite the fact that users of these languages constitute a significant portion of the global population and platform activity. The study highlights a critical linguistic inequity: content in regional South Asian languages is far less likely to be reviewed, contextualized, or moderated, making religious hate speech and misinformation in these languages more likely to circulate unchecked than comparable English-language content.[45] This asymmetry allows targeted disinformation campaigns – often crafted with political intent and financial backing – to circulate with impunity. These platforms become transnational conduits of incitement, where memes, doctored videos and fringe theology morph rapidly into majoritarian talking points.

Western foreign policy and strategic interests have also contributed to the distortion of religious politics in the region. The long-standing support of the US for military regimes in Pakistan during the Cold War, and later during the 'War on Terror', helped institutionalize a framework where religious militancy was alternately nurtured or ignored, depending on geopolitical expediency. The arming of mujahideen groups as a counter to the Soviet invasion of Afghanistan in the 1980s, and the subsequent abandonment of that theatre, set into motion a chain of regional instability that continues to afflict religious minorities in Afghanistan and Pakistan.[46] Even in 2024, the US and European governments have prioritized counterterrorism cooperation with South Asian states while remaining reticent on domestic religious persecution, thereby implicitly sanctioning the repression of minorities as collateral damage in broader security objectives.

China's growing presence in South Asia – through its BRI and strategic investments – also has implications for religious governance. While Beijing rarely engages in ideological patronage, its avowed stance against religious dissidence and its surveillance-driven model of authoritarian control offer a blueprint for illiberal regimes in the region. In Sri Lanka and the Maldives, where Chinese investments now constitute significant portions of national debt portfolios, religious repression has subtly mirrored Chinese-style controls such as increased monitoring of religious gatherings, tighter restrictions on foreign missionaries and a preference for depoliticized, state-friendly expressions of faith.[47]

Crucially, international human rights mechanisms have struggled to meaningfully respond. Although UN bodies and global NGOs routinely issue reports and recommendations, their impact is often blunted by geopolitical considerations and state resistance. In 2024, Pakistan and India both declined to cooperate with the UN Special Rapporteur on freedom of religion or belief, citing sovereignty concerns.[48] Meanwhile, the Universal Periodic Review process, despite its formal rigour, has had minimal tangible effect on improving religious freedoms in the region, particularly in countries with weak enforcement capacity or active hostility to international scrutiny.

Nevertheless, not all transnational influence is regressive. Civil society coalitions across the region and in the diaspora have increasingly forged cross-border alliances to resist majoritarian repression and promote interfaith solidarity. In 2024, an unprecedented joint declaration was signed by forty-six interfaith organizations from across South Asia condemning anti-minority violence and calling for the establishment of a regional commission on religious freedom under the auspices of the SAARC.[49] Though non-binding, such efforts reflect a growing consciousness that the struggle for religious justice in South Asia must also be waged beyond borders – through solidarity, legal advocacy and discursive interventions to correct prevailing majoritarian narratives.

The challenge, then, is twofold: to resist the corrosive effects of ideological exports that feed majoritarianism, and to strengthen transnational democratic solidarity that transcends ethnic and religious lines. As long as external funding, digital platforms and geopolitical silence continue to reinforce the architecture of repression, domestic reform will remain insufficient. A new vision of pluralism in South Asia will require not just local courage, but global commitment – one that holds governments accountable not only to their citizens, but to the universal norms they profess to uphold.[50]

Towards Democratic Redemption

If the arc of South Asia's democratic history has bent towards pluralism, its present moment suggests a sharp deviation – one where the constitutional promises of equality, liberty and fraternity appear increasingly out of joint with lived experience. Nevertheless, even in this landscape of erosion and fear, reform is not only possible but imperative. The restoration of religious freedom and democratic dignity in the region cannot be limited to calls for tolerance. It must be structural, multiscalar and unapologetically political.

First, there is an urgent need for legislative overhaul. Countries across South Asia must repeal or substantially revise laws that enable religious discrimination under the guise of public order, morality or national identity. This includes blasphemy laws in Pakistan, anti-conversion statutes in India and Nepal, the constitutional restrictions on non-Muslim citizenship in the Maldives and the bureaucratic constraints on religious registration in Bhutan. Regional jurisprudence must also evolve beyond reactive litigation to establish proactive protections against discrimination, modelled perhaps on South Africa's

Equality Courts or Canada's charter-based religious freedom standards.

Second, independent commissions on religious freedom – comprising constitutional experts, minority representatives, civil society leaders and retired jurists – must be established across the region with powers to investigate, report and recommend enforcement actions. These should be insulated from political interference and empowered to collect disaggregated data on hate crimes, judicial pendency and discrimination in public institutions. As of 2024, only Sri Lanka and Bangladesh maintain national data repositories on religious violence, and even these are incomplete or the law requiring data collection is poorly enforced.

Third, education reform must become a regional priority. Curricula across South Asia have, to varying degrees, erased pluralistic histories in favour of sanitized or mythologized narratives. Textbooks must reflect real histories of interfaith solidarity, minority contributions to nation-building and the ethical complexity of religious coexistence. The South Asia Curriculum Reform Network, an independent initiative launched in 2023, has made pioneering efforts in this regard, but state endorsement remains tepid. To teach a child to recognize the humanity of another faith is to inoculate society against fanaticism in its most virulent germinative phase.

Fourth, there must be investment in regional platforms for interfaith dialogue – not merely as ceremonial exercises, but as spaces of conflict mediation, policy discussion and collective narrative-building. The SAARC, now a dormant diplomatic vessel, could be revived through the creation of a 'South Asian commission on faith and democracy', mandated to develop shared frameworks on minority rights, hate speech regulation and cross-border protections. While sovereignty remains a sensitive issue, voluntary benchmarking – on the model of the African Peer Review Mechanism – can incentivize progress without coercion.

Fifth, the international community must revisit its posture of selective silence. Security cooperation and economic partnerships must be conditioned not just on macroeconomic stability but on democratic standards, including religious freedom. Western democracies, particularly those with large South Asian diasporas, must confront the ways in which their own institutions are implicated – whether through diaspora funding of majoritarian movements, platforms' failures in moderation of hate content or the legitimization of discriminatory leaders through diplomatic courtesies.

Yet, for all these institutional prescriptions, there remains a deeper moral work to be undertaken. Democracy, as Amartya Sen reminds us, is not only about voting and institutional design – it is about voice. And today, the voices of South Asia's religious minorities are being silenced not merely by laws and mobs, but by the slow violence of exclusion from the collective moral imagination. Reform, then, is not only a matter of rights but of recognition – of seeing in the other not a threat, but a fellow citizen.

In closing, let us draw from the mystical insight of Bulleh Shah, the seventeenth-century Punjabi Sufi poet who defied orthodoxy in pursuit of love and truth:

Mazhab na puchh mullaan di,
Har dil vich rab vasda.

Ask not the mullah about religion,
For the Divine dwells in every heart.[51]

This line is not merely a poetic sentiment – it is a constitutional imperative. Until South Asia learns to see the Divine in every heart, regardless of name or creed, its democracies will remain only partially born. The promise of pluralism – always fragile, always unfinished – demands not just reform, but moral imagination. It demands that we dream again, together, of a region where faith does not divide but dignifies.

13

Civil Liberties: In a Time of Shrinking Space

In South Asia, the condition of civil liberties stands as a powerful barometer of the health and direction of democracy itself. For a region that claims some of the largest democratic electorates in the world, the paradox lies in the systematic erosion of the very liberties that lend legitimacy to that claim. From Kathmandu to Karachi, from Malé to Thimphu, the subcontinent has witnessed a steady constriction of the civic and discursive space that enables dissent, diversity and democratic deliberation. The trends are neither isolated nor coincidental – they emerge from an alarming regional convergence of authoritarian tendencies, legal overreach, digital repression and executive impunity. What is under assault is not only freedom of speech or the right to protest, but the conceptual foundation of democracy: the principle that power must be accountable to the people, and that citizens must be free to interrogate, resist and reshape the political order.

While each country navigates its own constitutional terrain, governed by differing political histories, degrees of institutional maturity and socio-economic compulsions, the region shares a troubling synchrony – the normalization of repression. Across the board, governments have invoked national security, public order, religious harmony and technological advancement as pretexts for silencing critics and fragmenting civil society. Draconian laws – such as the Digital Security Act (DSA) in Bangladesh, the Prevention of Terrorism Act (PTA) in Sri Lanka or the Unlawful Activities (Prevention) Act (UAPA) in India – function not only as legal instruments but as political tools of intimidation, employed selectively to target dissidents, journalists, student leaders, human rights defenders and opposition voices. In Pakistan, enforced disappearances and military tribunals operate in parallel with civilian governance, rendering judicial recourse ineffectual. Even in countries with fewer reported violations, like Bhutan and the Maldives, self-censorship prevails due to vague constitutional restrictions and the political risks of dissent. Meanwhile, Afghanistan has seen a wholesale collapse of civil liberties under Taliban rule, where women's rights activists, independent journalists and even poets have faced brutal suppression with no legal safeguards whatsoever.

The contraction of civic space is not limited to the formal public sphere – it has metastasized into everyday life through technological means. The region's governments have increasingly turned to surveillance infrastructure, facial recognition technologies, mass data collection and online censorship to extend their reach. In India, the Pegasus spyware scandal illustrated how state machinery can be turned against its own civil society. In Sri Lanka, digital surveillance has been used to track protestors during the 2022 Aragalaya uprising. In Bangladesh, since the enactment of the DSA in 2018 – and particularly in the lead-up to the 2024 national elections – the state's deployment of 'cybercrime' policing has had a chilling effect on online discourse, disproportionately targeting youth and independent digital media. The Maldives and Bhutan, despite their smaller scales, have been no exceptions in implementing state-sanctioned monitoring regimes with vague oversight. Nepal, while relatively more open, has struggled to protect privacy rights, as its cyber laws expand without adequate democratic scrutiny.

What makes this regression especially dangerous is its creeping normalization. Popular support for majoritarian governments, the entrenchment of nationalist narratives and the politicization of security threats have allowed ruling parties to stifle dissent under the guise of development, national interest or cultural preservation. This has led to a dangerous shift in the social contract. The citizen is no longer conceived as a rights-bearing agent of democratic life but as a subject to be governed, surveilled and disciplined. This is not merely a philosophical concern – it translates into real and measurable harms. Journalists are jailed, student leaders are silenced, NGOs face funding bans, and ethnic and religious minorities find themselves doubly vulnerable, both to state violence and to social persecution.

Moreover, the rollback of civil liberties has become increasingly transnational in method and collabouration. South Asian governments learn from and mimic one another: the invocation of 'foreign funding' to discredit NGOs, and the use of WhatsApp to disseminate misinformation and target activists, and the framing of environmental and rights-based movements as 'anti-national' – these are patterns now visible across borders. The suppression of civil society is no longer the prerogative of autocracies alone; elected governments also use it to consolidate control while maintaining a veneer of legitimacy. This trend, described in recent Freedom House and CIVICUS Monitor reports, has led to nearly every SAARC nation being rated as either 'repressed', 'obstructed' or 'closed' in terms of civic space, with Afghanistan and Bangladesh among the most severely ranked, and India recently downgraded from 'free' to 'partly free' in its 2024 *Freedom in the World* index.[1]

Despite this atmosphere of suffocation, civil society in South Asia has not been extinguished. The region continues to produce powerful currents of democratic resistance. From the farmers' protest in India to the People's Movement in Nepal; from the lawyers' protests in Pakistan to the women-led demonstrations in Sri Lanka and the Maldives – there is no dearth of civic imagination and courage. These uprisings, often spontaneous, multigenerational and cross-class in nature, signal that the democratic ethos still pulses beneath the surface. They also expose a critical truth: that the shrinking of civil liberties is not a sign of political strength but of democratic fragility. A state confident in its legitimacy does not fear its people's voices, it invites them.

In this chapter, it is not my aim to merely document the regression of liberties but to seek an explanation as to how it occurs, why it persists and what it will take to resist it. By analysing the architecture of repression, the surveillance state, the media's role in both enabling and resisting authoritarianism, and the continuing resilience of civic actors, this chapter argues that the battle for civil liberties in South Asia is not peripheral – it is the front line of the democratic project. The right to speak, dissent, organize and dream differently is the oxygen of democracy.

In its absence, elections become hollow rituals and governance becomes a matter of coercion, not consent.

Legal Instruments and Institutional Capture

Across South Asia, the erosion of civil liberties has not occurred through sudden rupture but through slow, deliberate legal entrenchment. Authoritarian tendencies have found legitimacy not by suspending democratic frameworks but by repurposing them. Draconian laws, pliant courts and executive-dominated institutions have constructed an architecture of repression under the guise of law and order. What unites the region is not identical laws, but a shared pattern: the codification of exceptional powers as routine instruments of governance.

In India, the UAPA – originally enacted as an anti-terror statute – has increasingly been used to detain students, journalists and activists without timely trial. National Crime Records Bureau data shows that UAPA cases rose from 897 in 2015 to 1,948 in 2022. Between 2015 and 2020, just 2.8 per cent of those arrested under the UAPA were convicted, indicating a conviction rate well below 3 per cent.[2] Similarly, Sri Lanka's PTA, which has long been condemned by international human rights bodies, has continued to be invoked against Tamil activists and, more recently, Sinhala protest leaders during the 2022 economic uprising. In Bangladesh, the DSA, passed in 2018 and still operational despite international condemnation, has enabled over 4,000 arrests by 2024, often targeting dissenting voices, particularly online journalists.[3]

Pakistan's arsenal of repression is more overtly militarized. The Pakistan Electronic Crimes Act (PECA), 2016, passed ostensibly to combat cybercrime, has become a bludgeon against critical journalism and digital activism. Civil society organizations report that the law is frequently used in tandem with sedition charges, and often under the oversight – or at the behest – of the military. Even in Nepal and Bhutan, where democratic transitions are younger, the growing reliance on vague clauses such as 'insulting the monarchy' or 'undermining national unity' signals a legal tilt towards state primacy over citizen rights. Afghanistan, since the Taliban's return to power in August 2021, has witnessed a wholesale dismantling of civil law, as discussed earlier. Women's freedom of movement, education, speech and association has been extinguished by decree, and journalists face imprisonment, torture or exile.

These legal trends are enabled by institutional complicity or impotence. Parliaments across the region – nominally tasked with oversight – have largely abdicated their role, becoming rubber stamps for executive power. Judiciary systems – particularly in India, Pakistan and Bangladesh – face a trust deficit owing to delays, selective interventions and apparent proximity to ruling regimes. Where court decisions do defend liberties, as seen in some recent cases in Nepal or India's Supreme Court observations on press freedom, they are often limited in scope and inconsistently enforced. Election commissions, once guardians of political fairness, have hesitated to call out hate speech or disinformation, often citing jurisdictional limits or procedural ambiguity. What results is a governance ecosystem where repression is neither arbitrary nor chaotic, but rationalized – where the assault on liberty is made to appear lawful, even necessary.

A telling measure of this legalized suppression is the region's deteriorating position in global indices. According to Freedom House's 2024 *Freedom in the World* report, India, Bangladesh and Pakistan are all rated 'Partly Free', with India's civil liberties score falling to 33/60. Afghanistan is rated 'Not Free' with a score of just 1/100. Sri Lanka and Nepal remain 'Partly Free', while Bhutan and the Maldives, though formally democratic, have seen regressions in civil society freedoms. The CIVICUS Monitor's latest report classifies Pakistan, Bangladesh and Afghanistan as 'repressed', India and Sri Lanka as 'obstructed', and Nepal and the Maldives as 'narrowed' – no SAARC country today enjoys fully open civic space.[4]

The implications are profound. The codification of repression undermines not only the individual liberty of citizens, but also the democratic credibility of the state. When the rule of law is repurposed to enforce the will of the ruling party, dissent becomes deviance, oversight becomes subversion and rights become privileges granted at the pleasure of power. This institutional degradation, unless reversed, risks converting South Asia's democracies into mere procedural shells – states that conduct elections, but without the liberty that makes electoral choice meaningful.

Civic Dissent and the Surveillance State

In a democracy, the right to dissent is not an act of defiance – it is an act of citizenship. Yet across South Asia, the space for collective protest, civic organizing and public demonstration is being systematically constricted. This contraction is not only spatial, in terms of denied permissions or cleared encampments, but also infrastructural and psychological – rendered through surveillance, coercive policing and the demonization of dissenters. In this climate, citizens' right to gather, organize and protest is increasingly seen not as an expression of democratic life, but as a threat to the national order.

From the Aragalaya uprising in Sri Lanka to the farmers' protests in India, the last five years have seen extraordinary waves of popular mobilization. These movements have spanned social classes, crossed ethnic divides and frequently embodied democratic aspirations far more honestly than the political elites they challenged. Yet the state response has often used aggressive security measures. In Sri Lanka, peaceful demonstrators at Galle Face Green were met with baton charges, arbitrary detentions and military deployment, despite broad public support for their anti-corruption and economic justice demands. In India, the 2020–21 farmers' protests were surveilled via drones, barricaded with concrete and iron nails, and subjected to extensive digital monitoring. Protest leaders were booked under sedition and terrorism laws, and online mobilizations were throttled through Internet shutdowns. India, in fact, led the world in Internet shutdowns for the fifth consecutive year as of 2024, according to Access Now.[5]

In Pakistan and Bangladesh, the landscape is even more perilous. Peaceful protests – whether by students, teachers or civil society coalitions – frequently encounter baton-wielding police, and suffer enforced disappearances or preventative detentions. Pakistan's Aurat March, a feminist protest organized annually across cities, has faced state harassment, mob violence and legal restrictions despite being peaceful and constitutionally protected. In Bangladesh, the recent student-led protests against quota policies in public-sector employment were again met with force. Police used tear gas, rubber bullets and made mass arrests, while universities expelled demonstrators. Since the Supreme Court ordered the controversial 30 per cent quota for war veterans' descendants reduced to 5 per cent in July 2024, the protests escalated into a wider uprising that led to all universities being shut down, lethal crackdowns causing over a thousand deaths and an interim government taking power in August. University campuses became flashpoints not only for clashes with law enforcement, but also for extensive detentions and expulsions of students participating in dissent.

The deployment of the DSA, Public Safety Acts and even colonial-era riot laws transforms protest into a punishable offence, legitimized through selective legal application and aided by pliant local administrations.

The smaller SAARC nations are not immune. In Bhutan, protests are virtually non-existent – not due to a lack of grievances, but because public assembly laws restrict collective demonstration. Civil society actors often resort to private lobbying or informal coalitions, fearful of state reprisal or social sanction.[6] In the Maldives, protests around environmental degradation and land reclamation have drawn disproportionate police responses, with recent arrests of youth climate activists drawing concern from international observers. In Nepal, while constitutional protections remain relatively robust, state responses to protests – particularly those led by marginalized communities such as the Madhesis or Dalits – have at times involved surveillance and targeted harassment.

The region's embrace of surveillance technologies compounds this crisis. Governments have expanded their digital monitoring capacities with little transparency or judicial oversight. India's Pegasus spyware scandal revealed that journalists, activists, lawyers and opposition figures were being surveilled using military-grade software – marking a dangerous convergence of state secrecy and digital authoritarianism. Pakistan's National Database and Registration Authority (NADRA) has been repeatedly accused of sharing data with intelligence agencies to track dissenters. Sri Lanka has piloted facial recognition technologies at protest sites, raising alarm about biometric profiling and the creation of 'watchlists' for future repression. Even in Nepal and Bhutan, where civil liberties are comparatively more intact, the expansion of cybersecurity laws without adequate checks raises the spectre of future overreach.

These dynamics are not simply technical – they are deeply political. Surveillance silences protest not only by watching bodies, but by pre-emptively criminalizing intent. The knowledge of being watched produces a chilling effect that reshapes the calculus of civic engagement. Young people – once the vanguard of democratic activism – are increasingly disillusioned, aware that their digital footprints can be used against them. Minority groups, already overpoliced, face heightened risk when they organize. Moreover, NGOs that support protest movements face financial audits, registration delays or foreign funding restrictions that paralyse their ability to act.

At stake is not just the right to protest, but the moral grammar of democracy itself. Civil disobedience has historically played a foundational role in South Asia's democratic evolution – from the Quit India Movement to the People's Movements in Nepal and Pakistan's struggle for restoration of democracy after military rule. To criminalize protest is to sever this lineage. Moreover, it undermines the very promise of democratic reform. When states refuse to listen and citizens fear to speak, democratic legitimacy erodes – not through coups or emergencies, but through ambient suppression.

Nonetheless, resistance persists. Youth-led climate protests, labour union strikes, indigenous land rights campaigns and feminist marches continue to erupt across the region. These expressions, though embattled, serve as reminders that the democratic spirit has not been extinguished. But to endure, they require more than courage – they need legal protections, institutional allies and regional solidarity. South Asia's democracies must ask themselves a fundamental question: can governance be credible if it cannot tolerate protest? If the answer is no, then protecting civic dissent is not merely a matter of policy – it is the litmus test of whether democracy still lives.

Weaponization of Media and Digital Space

In any functioning democracy, the media acts as a conduit between state and citizen – a watchdog over power and a crucible of public discourse. In South Asia, however, the media landscape has undergone a radical transformation over the past decade – not in the direction of freedom and pluralism, but towards intimidation and capture, converting the media into a compliant instrument. What emerges is a picture of a weaponized media and manipulated digital space: where journalism is punished, propaganda is amplified and the Internet is engineered to fragment rather than inform. This is not an accidental distortion – it is a systematic strategy employed by regimes, political parties and private capital to bend democratic debate into a tool of control.

Across the region, press freedom is under siege. According to the 2024 *World Press Freedom Index* by Reporters Without Borders, South Asian nations occupy some of the lowest rankings globally.[7] Afghanistan is ranked 178 out of 180 countries, while Bangladesh, Pakistan and India have all slid further down the index, ranked 165, 152 and 159 respectively. Even countries with relatively smaller populations have seen dips or stagnation, like Bhutan (147), the Maldives (106) and Nepal (74), as institutional guarantees are outweighed by structural pressures. These include arrests of journalists, physical attacks, advertising boycotts, legal harassment and opaque ownership models.

Bangladesh's use of the DSA remains one of the most glaring examples, where over a thousand cases have been filed against journalists, bloggers and critics since 2020. According to Human Rights Watch and the Committee to Protect Journalists, these cases often result in pretrial detention, indefinite surveillance and informal gag orders. In Pakistan, military influence over media houses is both tacit and overt: editors receive unofficial directives, television coverage is blacked out without explanation and independent anchors are banned from networks or forced into exile. The crackdown on journalists covering Imran Khan's arrest and the May 2023 protests revealed the extent to which both civil and military institutions collude to regulate the national narrative.

India, which once prided itself on having a vibrant press, has witnessed an alarming convergence of media monopoly and state proximity. The acquisition of major television and print outlets by conglomerates with close ties to the ruling party has produced a media environment where coverage is polarized, dissent is labelled 'anti-national' and prime-time debates function more as state extensions than independent scrutiny. According to the *Media Ownership Monitor India 2024*, over 75 per cent of national news viewership is controlled by four corporate groups, all with political affiliations.[8] Meanwhile, independent digital outlets like *The Wire*, *Scroll* and *Newslaundry* have faced defamation suits, financial audits and hacking attempts.[9] The tax raids on the BBC's India offices in 2023, following its broadcast of a documentary critical of the ruling dispensation,exemplify the new tactics of coercion cloaked in legality.[10]

The digital realm, once seen as a democratizing force, has become a battleground of disinformation, surveillance and algorithmic manipulation. Across South Asia, governments and political parties maintain expansive IT cells that disseminate targeted misinformation, amplify communal polarization and drown critical voices in noise. A Global Disinformation Index study from early 2024 flagged India, Bangladesh and Pakistan as among the top ten countries globally where state-linked actors deploy coordinated digital disinformation campaigns during elections.[11] In Sri Lanka, during the 2019 and 2020 election cycles, Facebook was weaponized to spread hate speech and false narratives – an issue the UN and civil society raised with the platform, resulting in limited moderation but no structural accountability.

Table 1. Index Rankings

Country	Press Freedom Index (RSF 2024)	Freedom House Score (2024)	Civic Space Rating (CIVICUS 2024)	Key Legal Instruments Used for Repression
India	159/180	Partly free	Obstructed	UAPA, sedition law, IT Rules 2021
Pakistan	152/180	Partly free (37/100)	Repressed	PECA, sedition laws, military courts
Bangladesh	165/180	Partly free (39/100)	Repressed	DSA
Sri Lanka	150/180	Partly free (55/100)	Obstructed	PTA
Nepal	74/180	Partly free (57/100)	Narrowed	Cyber Laws, Public Security Act
Bhutan	147/180	Partly free (61/100)	Narrowed	Public Order Act, defamation laws
The Maldives	106/180	Partly free (56/100)	Narrowed	Anti-Defamation Act, Police Act
Afghanistan	178/180	Not free (1/100)	Closed	Decrees by Taliban, Sharia edicts

Social media platforms – Facebook, Instagram, YouTube, X (formerly Twitter) and TikTok – have become double-edged swords. In India and Pakistan, for instance, X has regularly withheld posts and suspended accounts at the government's request, including during Operation Sindoor in 2025. While offering space for alternative narratives, social media platforms are also subject to regulatory threats that stifle dissent. In Nepal and the Maldives, new draft laws on social media regulation propose registration requirements and vague content controls that would render independent digital commentary precarious. In Bhutan, while Internet penetration remains modest, state control over telecom infrastructure allows for quiet censorship and network throttling, particularly during elections or periods of protest. Afghanistan under the Taliban has outright banned critical digital platforms, and operates under a regime of Internet policing that blocks access to global media outlets and punishes online dissent with corporal punishment or death.

What makes this process especially insidious is that repression often comes wrapped in the language of reform. Laws introduced to 'curb fake news' or 'enhance cybersecurity' are framed as civic protections while being selectively enforced against critics. Public broadcasters are repurposed into government mouthpieces. Content moderation by platforms is skewed – either outsourced to opaque contractors or dictated by local state pressure. The net effect is an inversion of democratic function: instead of a media that empowers public reason, we are left with a media ecosystem that curates obedience.

Nevertheless, resistance and ingenuity persist. Independent media collectives in India and Pakistan continue to investigate corruption and make marginalized voices heard. Journalists in exile from Afghanistan are creating transnational platforms to keep reporting alive. In Sri Lanka and Nepal, community radio stations and citizen-led newsletters have maintained local relevance in the face of national-level intimidation. Digital literacy campaigns, fact-checking networks and cross-border collabourations such as the South Asia Media Solidarity Network offer faint but critical hope that a different media future is still possible.

Restoring the media's democratic function in South Asia will require more than decriminalizing journalism. It demands structural reform of ownership models, independent regulatory commissions, protections for digital freedoms and regional frameworks that can collectively resist the authoritarian drift. The right to know – and to speak truth to power – is not a luxury. It is the bedrock upon which all other liberties rest. Without a free and plural media, democracy becomes not merely fragile – but performative.

Democratic Resilience and the Struggle for Liberties

For all the evidence of institutional regression, authoritarian consolidation and civil rights attrition across South Asia, the story of civil liberties in the region is not only a tale of shrinking space – it is also one of determined resistance. Beneath the structural weight of legal repression and digital control, citizens, movements and alliances continue to claim, defend and reimagine their democratic rights. What emerges is not a narrative of despair, but a complex portrait of democratic resilience – an insistence that liberty is not merely an entitlement granted by the state, but a relationship constantly negotiated, contested and remade by the people.

The democratic muscle of South Asia is perhaps most visible not in legislatures or courts, but on the streets and in solidarities forged under pressure. In India, the prolonged anti-CAA protests between 2019–20, and farmers' protests between 2020 and 2021, demonstrated the power of decentralized, leaderless resistance. These were not just sectoral agitations, but expansive coalitions that included trade unions, Dalit organizations, women's groups and students asserting a collective vision of democracy anchored in livelihood, dignity and constitutional promise. The eventual repeal of the contested farm laws, despite initial intransigence, was a rare but potent reminder that even majoritarian regimes can be forced to yield under sustained civic pressure.

In Pakistan, the Pashtun Tahafuz Movement (PTM), led by young activists from marginalized ethnic regions, has challenged both state and military repression through non-violent mobilization. Despite facing arrests, enforced disappearances and media blackouts, the PTM continues to articulate a critique of extrajudicial violence and rights denial that resonates beyond its ethnic base. Bangladesh has witnessed repeated eruptions of student activism – from the Shahbagh protests to the more recent movements for job quotas and campus safety – despite severe crackdowns, and as a result of which the then PM Sheikh Hasina had to flee the country. In Sri Lanka, the 2022 economic protests at Galle Face Green became a powerful tableau of intergenerational anger and moral clarity, momentarily uniting fractured communities against elite corruption and misgovernance.

Elsewhere, more diffuse but equally significant forms of resistance unfold. In the Maldives, environmental justice campaigns have begun to link climate degradation with democratic exclusion, challenging the privatization of public resources and the silencing of scientific voices. In Bhutan, where open protest is rare, civil society organizations have adopted quieter modes of advocacy, building public consciousness around gender rights, migrant justice and media ethics. Nepal's civil society – arguably the most vibrant in the region – has remained a bulwark against regressive constitutional amendments and has successfully lobbied for greater inclusion of Dalits, Janajatis and sexual minorities. Even in Taliban-controlled Afghanistan, where formal freedoms have collapsed, underground schools, feminist publications and exile-led journalism serve as brave outposts of defiant citizenship.

These efforts are more than merely defensive reactions to state overreach – they are forward-looking acts of democratic imagination. They demonstrate that civil liberties are not just about preventing harm but about enabling the conditions in which pluralism, dissent and equality can flourish. Crucially, they reveal that liberty in South Asia has never been a gift from above. It has always been won from below – through negotiation, struggle and sacrifice. And this struggle, though wounded, is far from defeated.

However, to secure the future of civil liberties in South Asia, resistance must be matched with institutional renewal. Legal reforms are necessary but not sufficient. What is required is a structural commitment to liberty, embedded across constitutional guarantees, educational systems and governance cultures. Civil society must be decriminalized and decentralized. Judicial independence must be protected not just through appointments, but through budgets, transparency and civic literacy. Media ecosystems must be safeguarded from monopolistic capture, and digital infrastructure must be governed through rights-based frameworks, not nationalistic anxieties. Regional bodies – from the SAARC to the BIMSTEC (Bay of Bengal Initiative for Multi-Sectoral Technical and Economic Cooperation) – must also evolve to include civil liberties and democratic rights as core evaluative criteria, not just peripheral afterthoughts.

This also demands a shift in normative expectations. In too many South Asian polities, citizens have been taught to see liberty as a destabilizing force – something to be contained, disciplined or postponed in favour of economic growth, security or national pride. That bargain has proved hollow. The erosion of liberties has not produced stronger states; it has created brittle ones, prone to overreaction, mistrust and chronic legitimacy crises. A region that once birthed some of the world's most inspiring freedom movements must now find the courage to reclaim that inheritance – not nostalgically, but as a living imperative.

The path forward is uncertain, but the stakes are clear. A democracy without civil liberties is not a diminished democracy but no democracy at all. In the coming decade, South Asia will confront a fateful choice: whether to continue down a path of controlled participation and performative elections, or to reinvest in the democratic core that alone can sustain its plural societies. The outcome will not be decided by governments alone. It will depend on the tenacity of citizens who refuse to be silenced, and on the emergence of a new political consensus that treats liberty not as a threat, but as the foundation upon which a just and democratic South Asia must be built.

Reclaiming Liberty as a Democratic Imperative

The future of civil liberties in South Asia cannot be secured through vigilance alone. It must be actively and audaciously rebuilt. What the region now requires is not a mere recalibration of policy, but a structural and moral rebuilding of democratic life. At the heart of this project lies a simple but urgent imperative: liberty must no longer be treated as collateral to national development or stability, but as the very condition that makes democratic governance meaningful, just and durable. This will demand not only institutional reforms but a shift in civic culture, political incentives and regional imagination.

First, there must be an unambiguous dismantling of the legal machinery that has normalized repression. States must sunset and repeal laws that criminalize dissent through vague definitions of sedition, cybercrime or anti-terrorism. Emergency powers granted during exceptional moments must not be absorbed into the daily operations of governance. Instead, new legal frameworks must be drafted with built-in safeguards – mandatory sunset clauses, independent oversight bodies and constitutional review mechanisms that actively protect fundamental freedoms rather than merely notate them. The test of a law must not be its intention but its impact on those with the least power.

Second, democratic states must depoliticize their institutions through radical transparency and public accountability. Election commissions, media regulators and human rights bodies must be insulated from executive interference not just through appointment processes, but through fiscal autonomy, public reporting and citizen charters. The judiciary must adopt institutional reflexes that prioritize liberty over deference to authority, especially in bail jurisprudence, press freedom and protest rights. Without a recalibration of institutional courage, procedural reforms will falter in the face of political will.

Third, there must be a systematic investment in civic infrastructure. Just as roads and electricity are essential to economic life, independent universities, investigative journalism, civil society networks and digital literacy initiatives are essential to civic life. Funding must not be seen as foreign interference but as democratic maintenance. Governments must create protected spaces for dissent and deliberation – not out of charity, but as constitutional obligations. Local governments should be empowered to create community forums, conflict resolution bodies and public hearing systems that enable citizen engagement outside the coercive frame of security law.

Fourth, technology must be reclaimed as a public good. Surveillance architecture must be brought under judicial regulation, with real-time audits, data minimization protocols and redressal mechanisms. Governments must not own the digital public square. Social media companies, many of which profit from outrage and disinformation in the region, must be held accountable to rights-based norms through regional compacts. South Asia must demand algorithmic transparency and establish interoperable data protection regimes that respect privacy, freedom of expression and democratic consent.

Finally, the region must think as a region. The civic crisis facing South Asia is not national in character – it is systemic and transnational. It demands a reimagined South Asian charter of democratic rights, developed and monitored by a coalition of regional universities, civil society organizations and independent media. This charter must go beyond elite diplomacy and become a public instrument – a baseline that holds states accountable not for their sovereignty, but for their democratic commitments. A regional ombuds body for civic space, backed by the SAARC or an independent multilateral forum, could provide periodic assessments, track regressions and offer protective solidarity when states target civil actors.

The restoration of civil liberties in South Asia is not a nostalgic appeal to an idealized past. It is a sober wager on a more liveable future. The choice before us is stark. We can continue down the path of managed democracy and performative pluralism, or we can begin the long, demanding work of building a civic culture where liberty is not feared, but considered fundamental. That choice belongs not only to states, but to the citizens who animate, challenge and ultimately redeem the democratic idea. Reform must be bold. But more than that, it must begin now.

14

Democracy's Underworld: Criminalization of Elections and Politics

In South Asia's electoral landscape, the paradox of democratic choice is made starkly visible in the prevalence of candidates with criminal backgrounds. Rather than being penalized, individuals with serious allegations – including charges of murder, kidnapping, extortion and corruption – are routinely rewarded with electoral tickets by major parties and often secure decisive electoral victories. This phenomenon, far from being a statistical anomaly or cultural aberration, reveals deeper structural compulsions within the political economy of electoral competition in the region. Across the region – from India's sprawling federal democracy to the more centralized and fragile states like the Maldives – political parties increasingly turn to candidates who possess wealth, muscle and localized control, as these characteristics are perceived to enhance their 'winnability' in elections.

This chapter examines the political logic underpinning the criminalization of politics across South Asia, drawing on comparative data, theoretical frameworks and institutional features such as weak internal party democracy, opaque candidate selection processes and limited legal deterrents. We begin with the core concept: the rationalization of criminality as an electoral asset.

Muscle and Money as Electoral Capital

Criminality, in many parts of South Asia, is not necessarily a liability. In fact, it is often an asset. Candidates with criminal records often command significant financial resources and a loyal vote base through years of patronage, coercion or community-level mobilization. This is most pronounced in India, where data from the Association for Democratic Reforms (ADR) shows that in the 2024 Lok Sabha elections, 46 per cent of the 543 newly elected MPs had criminal cases registered against them, with twenty-seven of them convicted. Notably, 31 per cent faced serious criminal charges, including rape, murder, attempt to murder, kidnapping and crimes against women. This marks the highest number of candidates facing criminal charges to be elected to the Lower House, reflecting a 55 per cent increase in MPs with declared criminal cases since 2009.[1]

In neighbouring Pakistan, the intertwining of criminality and politics is manifest in the form of local 'electables' – individuals with entrenched clan loyalties, control over land or coercive power in their constituencies. Parties, particularly in times of weak organizational presence, routinely field such individuals to secure seats. Similar trends are observed in Nepal, where local political bosses, often with links to armed groups from the time of the Maoist insurgency, exercise considerable influence in rural districts. In Nepal, the Carter Center's report has noted the prevalence of candidates with violent or coercive pasts being fielded during both local and federal elections.[2]

In Bangladesh, the rise of political criminality intensified during the 1990s, as successive governments failed to break the nexus among business, politics and crime. Studies by Transparency International Bangladesh (TIB) have found that nearly 60 per cent of parliamentarians were engaged in business, many with alleged links to extortion, tender manipulation or smuggling.[3] Despite electoral reforms, the structural reliance of parties on such individuals did not wane. The 2018 general elections saw the then-ruling party BAL field numerous candidates with pending criminal charges, particularly in contested districts.

While similar data is harder to obtain for Bhutan and the Maldives, recent local media and watchdog reports show that criminal backgrounds are no longer a disqualifier for candidacy. In Bhutan's relatively new democratic setup, there have been instances of candidates with allegations of corruption or misuse of authority gaining popularity due to their wealth and connections. In the Maldives, political factions often rely on individuals with histories of gang affiliations, especially in urban districts of Malé, where control over youth groups can yield significant electoral advantage.

Afghanistan presents a unique case. Since the Taliban's return to power in 2021, the political landscape has undergone significant changes. The Taliban's governance has been marked by strict enforcement of their interpretation of Islamic law, as discussed earlier, including public executions and morality policing. In 2024, the Taliban leader Hibatullah Akhundzada publicly defended the executions of individuals convicted of murder, stating that such punishments are part of Islam and a divine command.[4] The Ministry for the Propagation of Virtue and the Prevention of Vice has been actively enforcing morality laws, leading to arbitrary detentions for non-compliant hairstyles or failing to attend mosque prayers. These actions have drawn strong condemnation from human rights groups and the UN. The Taliban's approach to governance, emphasizing strict adherence to their interpretation of Islamic principles, has effectively sidelined traditional political processes and institutions, leaving little room for electoral politics.

Crisis of Internal Party Democracy

A core factor exacerbating the criminalization of electoral politics in South Asia is the absence of robust internal party democracy. Parties across the region – irrespective of their ideological lineage – tend to operate as closed systems, where candidacies are not determined through transparent primaries or meritocratic vetting, but through patronage, personal loyalty or transactional exchange.

In India, for instance, candidate selection is often centralized among a handful of national or state leaders, who prioritize a candidate's ability to fund their own campaign and mobilize voters independent of the party. Political scientist Milan Vaishnav, in his seminal work *When Crime Pays* (2017), provides a game-theoretic model explaining this logic: parties face a trade-off between fielding 'clean' candidates with limited resources and 'tainted' ones who can finance themselves and intimidate rivals.[5] The rational choice, in a FPTP system, where margins are slim and elections frequent, often falls in favour of the latter.

This pattern repeats itself in Sri Lanka, where party nominations are centralized and frequently manipulated by factional leaders. Several politicians accused of corruption or violence during the country's civil war years continue to enjoy electoral favour, in part due to their ability to deliver votes to the party machinery. In Bangladesh and Pakistan, central party elites often view local 'strongmen' as indispensable during elections, given the weak penetration of formal party structures in many rural and peri-urban areas.

In Afghanistan, formal accountability mechanisms to screen candidates are either absent or poorly implemented. For example, even before Taliban's takeover, when its Election Commission was still functioning, Afghanistan's Electoral Complaints Commission faced persistent criticism for its inability to vet warlord-candidates effectively. In Nepal, despite efforts by the Election Commission to mandate asset declarations and background checks, enforcement remains erratic. Even in Bhutan, where electoral ethics are more explicitly codified, loopholes in enforcement allow for reputationally compromised individuals to contest under independent labels.[6]

Patron–Client Politics and Informal Power Structures

The persistence of criminalized candidatures across South Asia can be understood through the lens of 'patron–client' politics. In societies where the state's distributive apparatus is weak or uneven, candidates who can directly provide material benefits – jobs, protection and favours – are seen as more electorally viable. Criminal politicians, in this regard, are often not mere violators of the law, but parallel enforcers of informal order. They occupy the interstitial space between state neglect and citizen need.

The entrenchment of such figures is further enabled by institutional weaknesses. The FPTP electoral system creates high-stakes and winner-takes-all contests that incentivize short-term calculations over long-term institutional credibility. The electoral calculus, therefore, is often reduced to a blunt question: who can win? If a candidate has a history of coercion, a reliable funding base and the ability to mobilize loyal followers, they are seen as valuable – regardless of moral or legal concerns.

Crucially, the criminalization of electoral politics does not occur in a vacuum. It is a product of broader systemic conditions: underfunded and understaffed election commissions, a slow-moving judiciary, poor political education and a culture of impunity for the elite. Unless these institutional failings are addressed across the region, parties will continue to treat criminality not as a barrier, but as a badge of efficacy.

Delving further into the root-causes of this issue, the following two following sections examine how electoral institutions, legal frameworks and enforcement agencies have struggled – or failed – to prevent the criminalization of politics.

Institutional Architecture of Impunity

In theory, electoral commissions, media, courts and law enforcement agencies serve as the bulwarks of democratic integrity, ensuring that candidates adhere to legal and ethical standards. However, across South Asia, these institutions often falter in their duties, inadvertently or otherwise enabling the entrenchment of criminal elements within the political sphere.

In India, as noted above, the ADR reported that in the 2024 Lok Sabha elections, 46 per cent of newly elected MPs faced criminal charges, with 27 of them already convicted. This marks a 55 per cent increase since 2009, with 31 per cent facing serious charges including murder and crimes against women. Despite the Supreme Court's directives for expedited trials of politicians, the judicial system remains overwhelmed, leading to prolonged delays that allow accused individuals to continue their political careers unabated.

Pakistan's constitutional Articles 62 and 63, designed to ensure candidates' moral and ethical qualifications, have been criticized for inconsistent enforcement. While these provisions have been used to disqualify certain politicians, their application often appears selective, raising concerns about judicial impartiality and the potential for political manipulation.

In Bangladesh, the Election Commission's credibility has been severely undermined. The 2024 general elections were marred by allegations of voter suppression, mass arrests of opposition members and a boycott by the main opposition party. International observers, including the US and the UK, criticized the elections for lacking fairness and transparency. The Commission's failure to ensure a level playing field has contributed to the perception of Bangladesh as a de facto one-party state.

Legal Loopholes and Selective Enforcement

Legal frameworks intended to disqualify candidates with criminal backgrounds often contain loopholes that are exploited by political actors. The requirement for a conviction, rather than mere charges, to disqualify a candidate allows many individuals with serious allegations to contest elections. This legal threshold, combined with judicial delays, effectively nullifies the disqualification provisions.

Moreover, enforcement agencies are frequently accused of selective application of laws. In several instances, opposition figures face swift legal action, while ruling party members with similar or more severe allegations evade scrutiny. This selective enforcement erodes public trust in legal institutions and reinforces the perception of a politicized judiciary.

Law enforcement agencies play a critical role in upholding electoral integrity. However, in many South Asian countries, these agencies are perceived as extensions of the ruling party, rather than impartial enforcers of the law. Instances of police inaction against ruling party candidates, coupled with aggressive tactics against opposition members, have been documented across the region.

In Nepal, the Election Commission has faced challenges in enforcing candidate eligibility criteria, particularly concerning citizenship issues. The Supreme Court's removal of then Deputy PM Rabi Lamichhane in 2023 for violating citizenship laws highlights the complexities and enforcement challenges in the legal framework.

The failure of electoral institutions, legal frameworks and enforcement agencies to prevent the criminalization of politics in South Asia is a multifaceted issue. Delays in judicial processes, use of legal loopholes, selective enforcement and compromised law enforcement agencies collectively contribute to an environment where criminal elements can thrive within the political system. Addressing these challenges requires comprehensive reforms aimed at strengthening institutional independence, enhancing legal clarity and ensuring impartial enforcement of laws to uphold the democratic ideals of the region.

Electoral Legitimacy of Criminal Politicians

One of the enduring paradoxes in South Asian democratic life is the persistent electoral success of politicians with criminal records, as mentioned earlier. From densely populated Indian constituencies to marginal rural wards in Nepal, from the island provinces of the Maldives to the political elite in Pakistan and Bangladesh, criminality not only coexists with democratic legitimacy but thrives within it. Far from being anomalies, such politicians are often among the most electorally successful, defying the normative expectation that voters would reject individuals with known criminal backgrounds. This paradox has animated considerable scholarly inquiry and public concern, not in the least because of its implications for the rule of law, representative governance and the moral fabric of democracy in South Asia. Why, then, do voters routinely support candidates tainted by allegations of violence, corruption or coercion?

Milan Vaishnav provides a compelling framework for understanding this phenomenon through the logic of criminally mediated service provisions.[7] In settings marked by weak state capacity, informal networks and limited access to justice, voters may not irrationally overlook a politician's criminality; rather, they may view it as a marker of effectiveness. Politicians with criminal backgrounds are often seen as individuals who can 'get things done', navigate bureaucratic inertia and deliver services by circumventing legal impediments. This is not a deviation from rationality but a deeply contextual logic of political choice. Vaishnav's argument, rooted in extensive empirical research in India, resonates across the region.

In Bangladesh, where TIB has tracked the rising criminality of candidates over successive elections, similar patterns emerge. A 2023

TIB report on parliamentary candidates found that over 44 per cent of MPs elected in the 2018 general election faced criminal cases, many of them related to violent offences or corruption.[8] Yet these candidates were often local strongmen who commanded both fear and respect, capable of extending patronage, mobilizing crowds and delivering selective welfare. The appeal of these figures is not despite their criminality, but *because* of it – criminality becomes the instrument through which marginalized communities access political leverage.

This logic is amplified in conflict-affected regions such as parts of Pakistan's Khyber Pakhtunkhwa or Sri Lanka's Northern and Eastern provinces, where war economies and post-conflict clientelism have engendered a new political class of former militants and militarized elites. In these contexts, coercive power, military affiliations and even prior insurgency involvement often serve as credentials rather than liabilities. Ayesha Siddiqa's work on Pakistan's 'milbus' (military–business nexus) underscores how hybrid civilian–military actors, including many with opaque records, operate with impunity under the garb of national security or service delivery.[9]

Identity Politics and Political Patronage

Another explanation lies in the persistence of identity-based voting. In plural societies stratified by caste, ethnicity, religion or regional identity, voters often prioritize representation over rectitude. A candidate with a criminal record, if perceived as a protector or assertive representative of a particular identity group, may be embraced as a bulwark against real or perceived threats. In Nepal, for example, the rise of some criminal-affiliated figures within Madhesi and Tharu movements reflected a broader political demand for dignity and representation from historically excluded groups. In India, candidates accused of communal violence or caste-based atrocities have routinely been elected – sometimes with even greater margins – precisely because they are seen as defenders of community pride.

This interplay of identity and criminality is not merely symbolic, it is materially grounded in political patronage. Criminal politicians often act as nodes in an informal patronage network, distributing jobs, licences, welfare benefits and protection in return for loyalty. These networks thrive in the absence of formal state responsiveness.

In Afghanistan, during its transitional electoral period (particularly before the 2021 Taliban takeover), many regional warlords and power brokers with notorious criminal pasts were integrated into the political process through patronage-based arrangements that substituted for state legitimacy. The now-defunct Wolesi Jirga (House of the People) at one point included several figures with well-documented criminal profiles but immense local support due to the patronage they could dispense.

However, not all voter support is voluntary or enthusiastic. Across South Asia, coercion and vote manipulation continue to shape the electoral field. The line between electoral legitimacy and enforced compliance is often thin. In parts of Pakistan and Bangladesh, reports from election observers – most recently from the 2024 Bangladesh general elections – document widespread use of intimidation, vote-buying and even pre-election violence to engineer outcomes.[10] These tactics are not merely ancillary to the criminalization of politics; they are constitutive of it. Politicians with access to private militias, criminal syndicates or state-backed enforcement units often use coercion to pre-empt opposition, suppress turnout or manufacture consent.

In Bhutan and the Maldives – countries often seen as exceptions in the region – the scale of criminal involvement in electoral politics is comparatively limited. However, recent years have shown the potential for elite impunity and subtle coercive practices to emerge. The 2023 Maldivian elections, for instance, saw allegations of illicit campaign financing and links between candidates and drug trafficking networks. While the judiciary and electoral commissions in these countries have shown some resilience, their institutional autonomy remains precarious – especially in the face of executive overreach or economic dependencies.

It is critical to reject a simplistic interpretation of voters as either misinformed or irrational. The persistence of criminal politicians in South Asia is not always a result of ignorance or indifference. Rather, it reflects a deeper structural crisis of democratic consolidation, wherein voters are forced to choose between imperfect options, often balancing ethical concerns with practical survival. As portrayed in his book, one voter in Bihar poignantly told Milan Vaishnav in 2022: 'He may be a bad man, but at least he listens to us. The others do not even come here.' Such sentiments echo across the region – from Sindh to Sindhupalchok, from Rajshahi to Ratnapura – and demand that we reframe our understanding of electoral choice as negotiated rather than merely free or simply duped.

What emerges, then, is a layered portrait of voter rationality: pragmatic, situational, identity-bound and structurally constrained. The electoral legitimacy of criminal politicians is not an aberration to be corrected by voter awareness campaigns alone. It is the outcome of enduring institutional deficits, distorted party structures and a political economy where access to public goods is contingent upon informal (often violent) intermediaries. In such a context, the criminal politician becomes less an exception and more a symptom – an embodiment of the democratic promise deferred.

Campaign Finance and the Criminal–Political Economy

The criminalization of politics in South Asia is deeply enmeshed in the subterranean architecture of unregulated campaign finance. Behind every criminal candidate who wins a seat lies a murky trail of money power that has, in many parts of the region, come to define electoral viability itself. The flow of illicit funds – black money – into electoral politics is neither marginal nor incidental. It constitutes the very fuel on which competitive elections are increasingly run. Across South Asia, where formal mechanisms for political finance regulation are weak, sporadically enforced or riddled with loopholes, the dominance of moneyed actors – often with criminal or shadowy business backgrounds – has created a distorted democratic playing field, one in which political office becomes less a public service and more a high-stakes investment. In fact, the very fact that wealthy criminals want to get into it at all is a sign of larger political corruption.

The erosion of transparency in political finance has led to the emergence of a class of self-financing candidates who operate within, or benefit from, the parallel economies that flourish across the region. These economies – fuelled by illegal land deals, smuggling, unaccounted real estate holdings, narcotics trade and resource-extractive industries – provide the material base for political entrepreneurship by criminal actors.

Such candidates are less reliant on party funding or mass mobilization. Instead, they deploy vast personal resources, often accumulated through illicit means, to bankroll their own campaigns.

This trend has fundamentally altered candidate selection across major parties. Political parties, seeking financial insulation and electoral certainty, have come to prefer individuals who can self-fund and mobilize local muscle without drawing on the party's central coffers. The resulting political economy is one where parties outsource both risk and responsibility to 'winnable' figures – those who bring votes, cash and coercive capacity, regardless of their criminal background.

At the heart of this ecosystem lies the cash-intensive nature of electioneering. From hiring local gangs to enforce 'booth management', to distributing gifts, liquor and cash bribes to voters, the mechanics of electoral influence depend on liquidity and discretion. The use of unaccounted cash – often transported through *hawala* (informal money transfer) networks or hidden in disguised commercial operations – has become both a symptom and a cause of criminalized electoral competition. The volume of this shadow financing is staggering. During the 2023 election cycle in three of the region's largest democracies, independent monitoring groups estimated that only a fraction – between 10 and 15 per cent – of actual campaign expenditures were formally disclosed by candidates or parties.[11]

This gap between declared and real spending widens further in closely contested constituencies or in areas where state presence is weak. Here, electoral success is purchased not through ideas or ideology, but through the orchestration of what Ayesha Siddiqa once termed 'networks of convenience' – alliances between political actors, local contractors and criminal syndicates.[12] Such networks are crucial for distributing cash and goods, intimidating rivals and ensuring voter compliance, especially in high-stakes districts, where the difference between winning and losing is razor-thin.

Vote-buying is perhaps the most visible outcome of this unregulated campaign finance regime. Across urban slums and rural hinterlands alike, voters routinely report being approached by political agents offering cash, food or household goods in exchange for votes. While this is often interpreted as a form of clientelism, in practice, it operates as an electoral market – a transaction in which loyalty is traded for material gain. This commodification of the vote has not only undermined democratic deliberation but has entrenched the logic of wealth-based representation.

In many constituencies, particularly in peri-urban regions undergoing rapid demographic and economic shifts, the vote-buying process is institutionalized through 'area managers' or ward-level intermediaries who coordinate the distribution of cash and monitor voter compliance. These intermediaries are often criminals or local strongmen who maintain intimate ties with the criminal–political elite. The line between 'political agent' and 'enforcer' is increasingly blurred. In several cases documented by international and regional monitors in 2023–24, candidates were found to have spent over four times the legal expenditure limit. Yet, they faced no legal or electoral consequence, due to collusion among parties, officials and enforcement bodies.

The legal frameworks governing campaign finance in South Asia, while formally present, remain poorly enforced and are often riddled with ambiguity. Disclosure requirements vary across countries, but even where laws exist, compliance is partial and oversight bodies are under-resourced or politically compromised. In a comparative audit conducted in early 2024 by the International IDEA, none of the SAARC countries scored above 40 on a 100-point scale assessing the integrity of political finance regimes.[13] Key areas of concern included the absence of real-time expenditure disclosure, lack of third-party auditing, weak penalties for non-compliance and the opacity surrounding donations from private entities or foreign sources.

A particularly troubling development is the growing use of anonymous or intermediary financing mechanisms. Electoral bond-style instruments, shell companies and cash donations below mandatory reporting thresholds allow powerful actors – often from the criminal, real estate or mining sectors – to channel funds into political campaigns without detection. In some cases, state contracts are effectively awarded in exchange for political donations, institutionalizing a quid pro quo that transforms the electoral process into a form of investment speculation for criminal capital.

Vicious Cycle and Pathways to Reform

The criminal–political economy of campaign finance in South Asia functions as a self-reinforcing system. The entry of criminals into politics is facilitated by their ability to mobilize illicit wealth. Once in office, their access to state resources, contracts and enforcement power enables them to consolidate and expand their influence – ensuring both personal enrichment and political survival. This dynamic not only distorts representation and accountability but creates a vicious cycle wherein public office becomes the most effective route to protect and legitimize criminal capital.

To disrupt this cycle, mere legal reforms are insufficient. What is required is a fundamental restructuring of how elections are funded, monitored and enforced – anchored in transparency, citizen oversight and institutional independence. Until then, the electoral arena in South Asia will remain a site where the power of the ballot coexists uneasily with the power of black money, and where democracy itself is increasingly defined by the capacity to buy (rather than earn) political power.

If criminalization in electoral politics reflects the breakdown of institutional deterrence and democratic accountability, then the road to reform must begin with reimagining the structures that enable such distortions to persist. Across South Asia, the crisis of criminal penetration into democratic institutions is no longer in dispute. What remains contested is how to reverse it. The region has witnessed a growing trend of legal, judicial and civil society-led efforts aimed at restoring electoral integrity – some promising, others performative. The effectiveness of these initiatives varies, but taken together, they offer a composite map of the region's reformist impulses as well as its enduring bottlenecks.

One of the most frequently proposed solutions to electoral criminality has been judicial intervention – particularly in the form of fast-track courts and disqualification provisions for candidates with pending criminal charges. In several South Asian countries, courts have played a pivotal role in mandating greater transparency in candidate disclosures, enforcing time-bound trials and interpreting the moral qualifications required for public office. The jurisprudence around criminal disqualification has grown in significance in the past five years, with higher courts consistently insisting on the voters' right to know.

Yet, legal reforms often encounter political resistance and bureaucratic inaction. The promise of fast-track courts, while theoretically compelling, has been hamstrung by poor implementation. Recent data from across the region shows that cases against elected representatives routinely languish for years, despite judicial directives.[14] This is due, in part, to deliberate delays by powerful accused, the intimidation of witnesses and the sluggishness of prosecutorial arms. Moreover, the distinction between charges and convictions continues to pose an ethical dilemma – should a candidate be disqualified at the stage of accusation, even before guilt is legally established? Critics argue that pre-conviction disqualification could open the door to vendetta politics; proponents counter that unchecked delay neutralizes the deterrent value of any legal sanction.

Electoral Finance, Party-Level Reform and Good Practices

At the core of the criminalization conundrum lies the question of political finance. Any serious reform effort must therefore address the opaque and corrosive nature of campaign funding. Across the region, recent debates have focused on tightening disclosure norms, establishing spending caps with real-time enforcement and creating independent funding authorities. Some electoral commissions have introduced digital tracking of candidate expenditures and mandatory third-party audits of campaign finance declarations. However, implementation remains uneven and riddled with evasion.

A 2024 regional assessment by the Atlantic Council's Freedom & Prosperity Center found that the overwhelming majority of political parties in South Asia lack meaningful internal democracy. Across India, Pakistan, Bangladesh, Sri Lanka, and the Maldives, party leadership is typically centralized, internal elections are rare or merely symbolic, and formal mechanisms for disciplining members—particularly those facing criminal allegations—are either opaque or entirely absent. This institutional hollowness severely undermines party accountability and erodes democratic norms from within.[15]

Nevertheless, despite these systemic obstacles, the region has seen a number of institutional experiments and judicial pronouncements that stand out for their ambition and practical promise. Bhutan's policy of zero tolerance towards candidates with any criminal record – however minor – has set a high benchmark, even though its unique political culture and demography may not make the policy easily replicable across larger, more plural societies. Nonetheless, it offers a valuable model that establishes criminal-free politics not merely as an ideal, but as a constitutional obligation.

Elsewhere, Supreme Court rulings have expanded the scope of voter rights by mandating compulsory disclosure of criminal antecedents, sources of income and educational qualifications.[16] Electoral commissions, especially in countries like Nepal, have adopted limited but noteworthy monitoring mechanisms – including candidate audits, expenditure scrutiny and real-time publication of violations. However, the absence of punitive consequences, the lack of autonomy for enforcement agencies and the absence of political will continue to constrain the potential of these innovations.

More broadly, regional coalitions of electoral commissions, such as the FEMBoSA, have begun to share good practices and encourage harmonization of standards. This cooperation, though still nascent, indicates a growing awareness that the problem is regional in nature and cannot be addressed by domestic reform alone.

Role of Civil Society, Media and Public Pressure

Institutional reforms, however necessary, will not suffice without a broad-based cultural shift in how electoral integrity is understood and demanded. Civic mobilization – through voter education campaigns, naming-and-shaming exercises and community-based monitoring – has emerged as a crucial pressure point in many democracies of the region. Digital platforms and independent journalism have played an especially important role in tracking profiles of candidates and exposing the crimes of political elites. Initiatives like candidate report cards, corruption trackers and crowdsourced election monitoring have begun to create pockets of accountability, especially in urban constituencies.

In some contexts, judicial activism has been directly catalysed by public interest litigation initiated by citizen groups, think tanks and electoral watchdogs. Landmark rulings on disclosure and disqualification have often come not from state initiative, but from the persistent efforts of public-spirited litigants and reform coalitions. The synergy among law, media and civil society has proved especially effective in instances where political parties and government institutions remain compromised.

At the same time, public fatigue and normalization of corruption remain formidable challenges. As long as voters believe that criminal politicians are their best available option, reform will remain constrained by the very logic it seeks to disrupt. Therefore, the goal must not only be to penalize criminality but to shift the incentives that make criminal candidates electorally attractive in the first place. This requires reviving trust in formal institutions, enhancing the capacity of the state to deliver services equitably and building civic cultures that reward integrity over expediency.

Reimagining the Democratic Compact

Ultimately, decriminalizing electoral politics in South Asia demands a reconfiguration of the region's democratic compact. It is not a matter of merely excluding criminal candidates from contesting elections, but of creating a political and institutional environment where such candidates no longer find the electoral process to be their most viable avenue for power or protection. This involves aligning institutional design, legal norms, civic expectations and political culture towards a common democratic ethos – one that privileges accountability, inclusion and the rule of law. The reform journey will be uneven, contested and prone to co-optation. But the growing convergence of judicial activism, civil society pressure and cross-national institutional learning offers grounds for cautious optimism. South Asia's democratic future hinges not merely on holding regular elections, but on cleansing the process through which power is acquired and retained. That process, long colonized by black money and muscle power, can be reclaimed only if reform is conceived not as an event, but as a sustained and generational project.

Silver Lining

The criminalization of politics in South Asia is not a fleeting crisis of electoral judgement, nor merely a symptom of voter apathy or institutional decay. It is a structural phenomenon deeply embedded in the mechanics of electoral competition, the failures of internal party democracy and the informal economies that sustain political life across the region. What is most disquieting is not that individuals accused of serious crimes continue to contest and win elections, but that their presence is often accepted – if not actively welcomed – within political parties, by voters and sometimes even by the state machinery. This grim normalization signals a profound erosion of democratic accountability, hollowing out the promise of representative government.

Nevertheless, the story is not one of irreversible decline. Across the region, institutional innovations, judicial pronouncements and civic activism are beginning to carve out spaces of resistance. From Nepal's electoral audit mechanisms to India's Supreme Court directives on candidate disclosures, from Bhutan's strict candidate vetting mechanisms to local monitoring initiatives across Bangladesh and Sri Lanka – pockets of reform are emerging, despite resistance. These initiatives reveal that political will is not merely an abstraction, but a resource that can be cultivated through citizen pressure, media vigilance and cross-border learning.

Decriminalizing politics in South Asia is not the task of a single election cycle, nor the responsibility of any one institution. It demands a generational commitment to rebuilding public trust, insulating democratic processes from illicit wealth and coercion, and reclaiming politics as a space for service, not self-preservation. So long as wealth and muscle remain the principal currencies of power, the region's democratic legitimacy will remain contested. But in the persistent efforts of those who challenge this status quo – activists, judges, reformers and voters alike – there lies a quiet reminder that democracy in South Asia is not dead. It is, like all living systems, struggling to breathe under the weight of its contradictions, yet still remains capable of renewal.

15

Guardians of Democracy?: The Case of the Election Commissions

The integrity of democratic processes in South Asia rests, in large part, upon the credibility of electoral institutions. As the primary guardians of electoral fairness, election commissions are entrusted not merely with the technical management of elections, but with the moral and institutional burden of sustaining democratic legitimacy. In a region marked by fraught histories of colonization, partition, civil war, authoritarianism and ethno-political strife, the stakes of electoral credibility are particularly high. Election commissions, by virtue of their structural independence, procedural transparency and institutional fortitude, stand – or ought to stand – as bulwarks against democratic backsliding. Yet, across South Asia, the picture is profoundly uneven.

This chapter reconsiders the role of election commissions in South Asia via four cross-cutting concerns. These themes – structural autonomy, militarized politics, and ethnic conflict – are not randomly chosen. They emerge from the empirical record of democratic erosion and resilience across the eight countries this book focuses on, and from the urgent policy imperative of strengthening electoral institutions amid rising authoritarian tendencies and democratic disillusionment.

The classic theory of electoral management bodies, as articulated by Winrich Kühne and others, posits that their effectiveness depends on four essential attributes: permanence, impartiality, independence from the executive and adequate funding.[1] These are not mere administrative ideals, they are democratic lifelines. But to what extent are they observed, undermined or manipulated across South Asia? And how do their fortunes vary in the presence of powerful militaries, polarized electorates, technologically complex elections and unresolved ethnic fault lines?

Take the case of the Election Commission of India (ECI) – widely regarded as the most robust electoral body in the region. Constitutionally entrenched under Article 324, the ECI has over decades evolved into a model of electoral supervision, benefitting from early institutionalization, legal clarity and public trust. However, even the ECI has not remained untouched by political contestation, especially in recent years, as concerns over delayed enforcement of the Model Code of Conduct during elections, allegations of partisan leanings and opaque appointment processes have come under public scrutiny. Still, India's experience in electoral technology – such as the deployment of EVMs and the introduction of voter verifiable paper audit trail (VVPAT) – legal innovations and institutional resilience provides a reference point for its neighbours, albeit an imperfect one.

By contrast, the Election Commission of Pakistan (ECP) operates in a vastly different terrain. While it enjoys constitutional status and features a relatively balanced appointment mechanism involving government and opposition, its functional autonomy is often compromised by military dominance and judicial interference. The Bangladesh Election Commission, too, has struggled under the weight of political partisanship, especially in the post-caretaker government era, with its decisions frequently contested and its neutrality questioned.

Nepal's Election Commission demonstrates an intriguing paradox: while the constitutional design has accorded it significant jurisdictional immunity (with its decisions largely beyond judicial review), its roots in a monarchical legacy and ongoing instability have complicated its democratic stewardship. Sri Lanka's Election Commission, navigating between post-war reconciliation and resurgent majoritarianism, faces the delicate task of managing elections in a fractured polity.

Even more precariously situated are the commissions in Afghanistan and the Maldives. In the former, the Independent Election Commission had faced existential challenges due to institutional fragility, opaque appointments and security threats, often exacerbated by foreign intervention and domestic fragmentation. The latter, while making progress in electoral reforms, has witnessed episodes of electoral disruption, elite capture and rule-by-decree.

Bhutan's Election Commission, established under the 2008 Constitution, reflects the country's cautious yet deliberate transition to democracy. Unlike many of its regional counterparts, the commission emerged not from political upheaval but from a monarch-led reform process, endowing it with an unusual degree of institutional legitimacy. Its mandate is comprehensive – overseeing electoral rolls, political party registration, and campaign finance – within a political culture that remains relatively non-adversarial. Yet challenges persist, including low voter turnout among youth, the influence of socio-religious hierarchies and the difficulty of fostering robust opposition in a still-monarchic ethos. While insulated from the intense partisan contestation seen elsewhere in South Asia, Bhutan's Election Commission must balance procedural integrity with a deep-seated deference to royal authority.

Thus, rather than assume the election commission as a stable institution in a functioning democracy, this chapter contends with a deeper question: what happens when the democracy itself is in flux? How do electoral commissions navigate executive overreach, political violence, military interference and ethnic polarization, and also retain credibility and public trust?

These questions are not abstract. In an age where democratic backsliding is a lived reality in many parts of South Asia, the role of election commissions – not only as procedural gatekeepers but as moral guardians of the democratic ideal – deserves rigorous scrutiny. They can serve as catalysts of electoral reform and democratic consolidation, or as passive enablers of elite capture and autocracy.

The analysis that follows is organized into four thematic sections that place the SAARC countries in conversation with one another. This comparative method does not ignore national particularities; rather, it foregrounds structural similarities and institutional challenges that recur across borders. Through this approach, the chapter aims to contribute not merely to academic understanding but to policy-oriented reflection towards strengthening the guardianship of democracy in a region where its promise remains both urgent and elusive.

Structural Autonomy and Legal Foundation

The credibility of an electoral commission depends, at its core, on its structural insulation from political interference. Constitutional guarantees, statutory clarity, transparent appointment procedures and adequate financial independence are the sinews through which this autonomy is realized. However, across South Asia, election commissions occupy a precarious space – situated between constitutional promise and political reality. This section interrogates the foundational architecture of electoral commissions across the region, revealing a spectrum that runs from institutional robustness to chronic vulnerability.

India stands at one end of this continuum, offering a legal and institutional framework that, at least in formal terms, provides a sturdy base for electoral independence. Article 324 of the Indian Constitution establishes the ECI as the central authority for overseeing elections to parliament, state legislatures and the offices of the president and vice-president. Its decisions, under Article 329, are largely insulated from judicial review – a design meant to protect its determinations from the vagaries of political and legal disruption. Moreover, the ECI has historically exercised a broad mandate, invoking its powers to discipline candidates, impose the Model Code of Conduct and even cancel polls in the event of malpractice or violence. Yet, concerns have emerged in recent years regarding the opacity of appointment mechanisms and the reluctance of the ECI to intervene decisively in certain high-stakes violations. These concerns raise questions not of legal weakness, but of interpretive will – of whether institutional autonomy can survive political pressure.[2]

Pakistan offers a different illustration: a commission with formal procedural safeguards, but persistently hindered by structural encumbrances. The ECP is established under Articles 218–221 of the constitution, and its members are nominated through a consultative process between the PM and the leader of the opposition, theoretically allowing for bipartisan balance. However, the ECP's dependency on the Ministry of Finance for funding, and its vulnerability to judicial interference, weakens its operational autonomy. Decisions of the ECP are often subject to court review, and in politically sensitive cases, this judicial oversight has led to delays or reversals, thus undermining the ECP's authority.[3] Moreover, the civil–military imbalance that characterizes Pakistan's broader polity creates an ecosystem in which even constitutionally robust institutions find their scope constrained by informal power structures.

Nepal represents a peculiar hybrid: a body with constitutional authority and judicial insulation, but historical roots in monarchical governance. Article 245 of Nepal's 2015 constitution reaffirms the establishment of the Election Commission, with the CEC appointed by the president on the recommendation of a constitutional council. Judicial review of electoral decisions is permitted only in limited circumstances, lending the Election Commission a considerable degree of legal immunity. However, the enduring effects of political volatility, coalition fragility and a history of centralized royal authority have hindered the emergence of a fully confident and assertive electoral body.[4] The Election Commission of Nepal, while formally independent, often finds itself navigating a delicate balance between constitutional duty and political constraint.

In Afghanistan, even before the Taliban takeover, the institutional structure of the Independent Election Commission has suffered under the weight of a fragile constitutional order and chronic insecurity. The 2004 constitution established the Commission with a mandate to conduct elections independently of government interference. However, the absence of clearly defined tenure security for commissioners, the lack of a permanent secretariat and the commission's financial dependence on international donors have severely impaired its functioning. Moreover, the scope of executive discretion – particularly in appointments and dismissals – has allowed successive governments to manipulate the institutional composition of the Commission, thereby eroding its credibility. Even prior to the Taliban's return in 2021, the Commission was widely perceived as a contested and fragile institution, reflective not of electoral autonomy but of its absence.[5]

Sri Lanka's electoral framework also reveals the tension between formal constitutional design and political interference. The 17th and 19th Amendments to the constitution had created an independent Election Commission with a multimember composition and appointment through a constitutional council. However, the 20th Amendment passed in 2020 rolled back many of these safeguards, allowing the president unilateral authority in appointments. This regression has raised serious concerns about the Commission's impartiality, especially in light of controversial election-related decisions and growing ethnic polarization in the post-civil-war period.[6]

The Maldives and Bhutan present even more nuanced cases. The Maldives' Election Commission, codified under the 2008 constitution, has been relatively proactive in election management, but remains vulnerable to politicization, particularly during transitions of power.[7] In Bhutan, the Election Commission derives its authority from Article 24 of the constitution, and is notable for its early adoption of transparency measures and election funding regulations.[8] Yet, the relatively centralized nature of Bhutanese governance, combined with the country's tightly managed democratic transitions, renders the Commission's independence more procedural than substantive.

In Bangladesh, the structural autonomy of the Election Commission is enshrined in Article 118 of the Constitution, which provides for its establishment and outlines a presidential appointment process. While this framework ostensibly grants the Commission independence, in practice its autonomy has been repeatedly compromised by executive overreach and the absence of a transparent, bipartisan appointment mechanism. The abolition of the caretaker government system in 2011 – previously a key institutional safeguard for neutral election oversight – has further eroded public confidence in the Commission's impartiality. Despite periodic efforts to strengthen its legal foundation, including calls for a more consultative appointment process and greater financial autonomy, the Commission continues to operate under significant political pressure, raising persistent concerns about its structural integrity.

Across all these cases, a pattern emerges. Legal and constitutional guarantees are necessary, but not sufficient. Electoral commissions in South Asia operate not in sterile institutional labouratories, but in politically volatile ecosystems, where formal autonomy can be undone by informal capture. The key variables that determine their efficacy are the method of appointments, protection from premature dismissal, insulation from executive budgets and clarity of jurisdictional authority.

Where these variables are embedded with integrity – as in parts of the Indian system – they produce a buffer against political pressure. Where they are subverted or weak – as in Pakistan, Afghanistan or Bangladesh – they render electoral commissions susceptible to elite manipulation.

It is therefore not enough for South Asian polities to enshrine electoral independence in constitutional texts. What is required is a more radical commitment to institutional culture – one in which commissions are seen not as extensions of the executive, but as fiduciaries of the people's democratic will. Comparative experience within the region shows that even incremental improvements in appointment procedures, financial insulation and operational independence can meaningfully alter the perception and performance of election commissions. Moreover, given the rising tide of democratic disillusionment across the region, such reforms are not merely desirable – they are indispensable.

Militarized State

In a region where the shadow of the military looms large over the constitutional order, the independence of electoral commissions cannot be fully understood in isolation from the broader civil–military dynamic. South Asia's democratic route has been repeatedly turned, and at times derailed, by the coercive authority of armed forces and security establishments. This legacy of military tutelage has had profound consequences for electoral governance, often rendering election commissions either complicit in, or powerless before, the arbitrariness of uniformed power. Understanding how commissions function in militarized states, or in states with deep militarist undercurrents, is thus essential to grasping the limits and possibilities of democratic consolidation in the region.

Pakistan remains the most emblematic case of entrenched military dominance subduing democratic institutions. Since its first coup in 1958, the Pakistani military has functioned not merely as an external arbiter of political disputes, but as a systemic actor embedded within the machinery of governance.[9] While the ECP is nominally independent, the very ecosystem in which it operates is shaped by decades of military oversight, constitutional engineering and institutional capture. From the selective overriding of the ECP to get judicial decisions on election results to the overt and covert role played by intelligence agencies in candidate vetting and campaign surveillance, the ECP's autonomy exists within a tightly controlled frame. This does not mean that the Commission is uniformly compromised, but rather that its decisions are often shaped by the unspoken parameters of military acceptability.

The 2018 general elections serve as a case in point: while the ECP successfully oversaw logistical preparations, serious questions were raised by domestic observers and political parties regarding the pre-election engineering of political alignments, suppression of dissent, and the role of the military in the transmission and tabulation of election results.[10] The ECP's delayed response to these concerns – and its silence in the face of aggressive security presence inside polling stations – only reinforced the perception that electoral institutions in Pakistan function at the pleasure, not the scrutiny, of military authority.

A different, though no less complex, form of militarized oversight is observable in Bangladesh. The country has oscillated between military and civilian rule for much of its post-independence history. Even after the formal restoration of democracy in the 1990s, the imprint of the military remains palpable in its political architecture. The caretaker government model, designed initially to depoliticize the electoral process, by placing it temporarily under technocratic stewardship, was heavily reliant on the military for logistical and security management.[11] While the Election Commission of Bangladesh retained legal control, its operations during this period were often shaped by the preferences of military-intelligence actors. Since the abolition of the caretaker model in 2011, partisan polarization has increased, and the Commission's credibility has suffered considerably – especially in elections marred by opposition boycotts, voter intimidation and alleged ballot manipulation. In such a context, the legacy of militarized electoral management continues to haunt the institutional memory of the Commission, complicating its efforts to project neutrality.

In Afghanistan, the militarized state is less a monolith than a fractured mosaic. Here, the challenge lies not in the military's domination of the electoral process, but in the pervasive insecurity that shapes every aspect of public life. The Independent Election Commission, even when formally functional, has often operated in a security environment where the threat of violence – from insurgent groups, local militias or political warlords – makes free and fair elections almost impossible. The collapse of territorial control, compounded by the political vacuum following the Taliban's return to power in 2021, has now rendered the very idea of electoral governance moot. But even before this implosion, the Commission functioned within the militarized logic of international occupation and donor-driven governance, with its personnel its personnel targets of violence and and its mandates often subordinated to larger geopolitical agendas.[12]

In Sri Lanka, the militarization of civilian governance is a more recent and evolving phenomenon. The conclusion of the civil war in 2009 was accompanied by a steady expansion of military presence in civilian administration, particularly in the Tamil-majority north and east.[13] The Election Commission, though legally autonomous, has had to navigate electoral cycles marked by deep mistrust between the state and the Tamil constituencies, as well as growing concerns over the militarization of politics. Allegations of surveillance, military intimidation during campaign periods and the deployment of security forces near polling booths have raised alarms about the environment in which elections are conducted. For the Commission to remain a credible arbiter, it must not only ensure procedural compliance but also confront the ambient militarism that chills political expression in contested regions.

Even in India – often celebrated as the region's most robust electoral democracy – the military question is not entirely irrelevant. While the armed forces have historically remained under civilian control, recent years have seen an increase in rhetorical militarism in electoral campaigns, including the politicization of military achievements and a troubling blurring of lines between national security discourse and party propaganda. The ECI has, on occasion, issued reminders and warnings against the use of military imagery in campaign materials, but enforcement has been uneven.[14] The challenge here is not direct military interference, but the appropriation of military symbolism in ways that distort electoral neutrality and feed into a majoritarian-nationalist political idiom. This indirect militarization of the political field can erode the moral authority of the ECI if not addressed with firm regulatory clarity.

In the rest of South Asia – Bhutan, the Maldives and Nepal – the military's role in electoral administration is less prominent but still warrants scrutiny. In Nepal, during moments of political breakdown, the deployment of security forces to maintain electoral order has occasionally triggered concerns among marginalized groups regarding voter intimidation. In the Maldives, military and police institutions have at times been drawn into political crises, including election-related confrontations.[15] Bhutan, with its carefully managed democratic transition, has largely kept its security apparatus depoliticized, but the consolidation of power in the monarchy and executive still raises long-term questions about the balance of democratic authority.

What emerges from this regional survey is a sobering recognition that where militarization saturates political life – whether through direct rule, institutional shadowing or rhetorical valourization – election commissions are inevitably constrained. Their independence is not only a matter of constitutional architecture but of political ecology. Reform, therefore, must aim beyond the commissions themselves. It must address the broader question of civil–military relations, the demilitarization of political space and the cultivation of electoral environments where neutrality is not merely professed, but genuinely possible. Without such efforts, even the most well-designed commissions risk becoming decorative shells – guardians in name, but not in function.

Crisis of Political Trust

Even the most carefully crafted electoral architecture can falter if public confidence in the institution is lost. In the democratic life of a nation, an election commission is not merely a technocratic body conducting administrative tasks – it is a custodian of legitimacy, a guarantor of fair competition and a visible symbol of the state's neutrality in the political process. Across South Asia, however, a widening gap between formal mandates and popular perceptions has precipitated a profound crisis of political trust in electoral commissions.

At the heart of this crisis is a pattern of politicization – both real and perceived. In Bangladesh, the deterioration of public trust in the Election Commission has been dramatic. As mentioned earlier, once considered a stabilizing force during democratic transitions, the Commission has come under sustained criticism since the abolition of the caretaker government system in 2011. The absence of a neutral interim body to supervise elections has led opposition parties to boycott successive polls, accusing the Commission of bias, complicity or impotence. The 2014 and 2018 general elections, both marked by allegations of widespread rigging, voter intimidation and inflated turnout figures, have damaged the Commission's reputation perhaps beyond repair. Citizens, particularly those in opposition strongholds, have increasingly viewed electoral outcomes as preordained, and the Commission as a handmaiden of the ruling BAL.

Similar concerns have surfaced in India, though in a more subtle and contested manner. The ECI has historically enjoyed high levels of public trust, owing to its relative independence, transparent procedures and assertive interventions in earlier decades. Yet, in recent years, that reservoir of goodwill has begun to deplete. Critics have pointed to delays in responding to campaign violations, perceived leniency towards the ruling party and the opaque process by which commissioners are appointed. The controversy surrounding the sudden resignation of then Election Commissioner Ashok Lavasa in 2020, for instance, prompted fears of executive overreach into the Commission's inner sanctum.[16] While these developments have not fundamentally altered the ECI's constitutional standing, they have seeded doubts in the public imagination about its neutrality. In a country as large and diverse as India, where electoral trust is the glue that binds fractious communities to a shared democratic project, such doubts carry weight far beyond Delhi's corridors of power.

In Sri Lanka, the erosion of trust further fractures a polity with deep ethnic and regional cleavages. In the north and east of the island, where Tamil voters remain sceptical of state institutions in the wake of the civil war, the Election Commission faces an uphill battle in establishing its credibility. Accusations of selective enforcement, lack of proactive voter education in minority regions and the Commission's silence in the face of ethno-nationalist rhetoric during campaign seasons have all contributed to a sense of institutional partiality. For many voters in these regions, elections are not simply about choosing representatives – they are a referendum on the state's willingness to treat them as equal citizens.

When the Election Commission fails to intervene decisively in moments of sectarian tension or campaign hate speech, it is not simply neutrality that is questioned, but the very premise of democratic inclusion.

In Nepal and the Maldives, the trust deficit emerges from volatility rather than perceived bias. In both countries, repeated transitions between political regimes – often marked by abrupt resignations, party splits and constitutional amendments – have created a climate of institutional uncertainty. The Election Commission of Nepal, despite its constitutional insulation, has often been perceived as reactive and passive in the face of rapidly shifting coalitions and constitutional vacuums. In the Maldives, contested elections in 2013 and 2018, followed by legal tussles over the Election Commission's mandate, have generated periodic accusations of either executive interference or administrative incompetence. In these contexts, the Commission is not necessarily viewed as corrupt, but as too fragile to inspire confidence.

Even in Bhutan, which is often held up as a model of orderly democratic transition, the Election Commission has had to tread cautiously to avoid being perceived as an extension of elite consensus. With only a few political parties permitted to contest and a tight control over campaign narratives, there is a risk that voters see the Commission not as a facilitator of open democratic competition, but as a guardian of a highly managed political order. This may not amount to active distrust, but it does dampen the vibrancy of electoral participation.

In Pakistan, the Election Commission (ECP) has long struggled to command broad-based political trust, despite its constitutional stature and a theoretically bipartisan appointment process. Accusations of bias – whether toward the military establishment or the ruling party – have repeatedly plagued its functioning. The 2018 general elections, for instance, were marred by allegations of 'pre-poll rigging', delayed result transmissions, and the controversial role of the security apparatus, leading several opposition parties to reject the outcome. Even when the ECP has asserted its independence, such as in disqualifying prominent candidates or sanctioning re-polls, its actions are often interpreted through partisan lenses.

In Afghanistan, where the democratic project remains deeply fragile, the crisis of trust is even more acute. The Independent Election

Commission (IEC), established to shepherd electoral transition, has faced relentless scrutiny and delegitimization. Successive presidential and parliamentary elections – especially in 2009, 2014, and 2019 – were marred by fraud, parallel counting processes and disputed results, often triggering political deadlock or externally brokered power-sharing deals. In such a context, the very notion of an impartial electoral umpire is undermined, leaving the IEC caught between factional pressures, security threats and a vanishing public faith in the possibility of clean elections.

Restoring public faith in electoral commissions, therefore, is not a matter of procedural reform alone. It is a question of institutional ethos, communicative transparency and cultural legitimacy. Commissions must not only act impartially; they must be seen to do so – particularly in contexts where polarization, ethnic fragmentation or historical injustice have already frayed the democratic contract. Engagement with civil society, proactive disclosure of decisions, protection for whistleblowers within electoral machinery and credible election monitoring partnerships can help repair trust. The role of the media, too, is vital: public scrutiny must be encouraged, not evaded. Where electoral commissions respond to public criticism with defensiveness or silence, they deepen the very suspicion they seek to dispel.

In the final analysis, the authority of electoral commissions in South Asia rests not merely on legal mandates, but on the fragile, powerful currency of public trust. Without it, the entire democratic edifice becomes suspect. As popular confidence falters, elections risk becoming spectacles without substance – rituals of consent rather than mechanisms of accountability. Conversely, where commissions succeed in asserting their neutrality – against the odds – they can rejuvenate the democratic spirit in even the most jaded societies. The question for South Asia is not whether its electoral commissions are formally independent. It is whether they command the moral legitimacy to act as guardians of the people's will – and where they do not command it, whether they can reclaim that legitimacy before it is irretrievably lost.

Navigating Ethnic Fault Lines and Political Conflict

Nowhere is the democratic task of electoral commissions more fragile – and more fateful – than in societies riven by ethnic divisions and histories of political conflict. In South Asia, where states were born through partitions, where boundaries often cut across linguistic and cultural continuities and where colonial legacies compounded internal hierarchies, elections have long carried the burden of managing diversity under duress. While much scholarly and policy attention has focused on the representation of religious minorities, this section centres on the complex role election commissions play in mediating, mitigating or, at times, exacerbating these tensions.

Elections are not merely administrative exercises – they are deeply symbolic acts. They signal who belongs, who counts and whose voice matters in the national polity. For ethnic minorities, particularly those with histories of marginalization, displacement or conflict, the very process of enfranchisement is often shot through with scepticism. It is in this volatile terrain that electoral commissions must perform their dual role: as technical managers of the vote, and as ethical stewards of democratic inclusion.

Consider Sri Lanka, where the scars of the civil war continue to inform political life. For decades, Tamil-majority regions have viewed national electoral processes with a mixture of cynicism and caution. As mentioned earlier, the Election Commission, though legally empowered to operate independently, has struggled to assert its credibility in the north and east of the country. Allegations of military surveillance during elections, absence of adequate Tamil-speaking electoral staff and the permissiveness shown towards majoritarian campaign rhetoric have all weakened the Commission's legitimacy among Tamil and other ethnically marginalized groups. In such contexts, neutrality is not enough; active attentiveness is required. Ensuring linguistic accessibility, preventing hate speech and protecting the freedom of campaign assembly in conflict-scarred regions are not just procedural mandates – they are democratic imperatives.

India presents a more layered and paradoxical scenario. As a federal union of extraordinary ethnic, linguistic and caste diversity, India's electoral system has often functioned as a mechanism for inclusion, adaptation and local accommodation. The ECI has conducted elections in some of the most conflict-affected and ethnically complex regions in the world – from insurgency-hit areas of the Northeast to the historically fraught landscape of Jammu and Kashmir. Yet, while the ECI's logistical capacity and administrative resolve are remarkable, questions remain about the Commission's ability (and willingness) to address the deeper political marginalization faced by certain ethnic groups.

In Jammu and Kashmir, for example, where Article 370's abrogation in 2019 dramatically restructured the region's constitutional status, electoral processes have been accompanied by the withdrawal of statehood, prolonged delays in assembly elections and the redrawing of electoral boundaries through a delimitation process, perceived by many locals as skewed towards one ethnic bloc over others. Though the ECI has maintained procedural regularity in holding local body elections, its silence on the political consequences of these larger shifts – and the exclusionary sentiments they have generated – has called its moral neutrality into question. Here, as elsewhere, the Commission's role cannot be divorced from the broader political context in which it operates.

Nepal, emerging from a decade-long Maoist insurgency and still navigating the contours of federalism, offers another case where ethnic aspirations intersect with electoral structures. The promise of inclusive democracy has been repeatedly tested by the demands of the Madhesi, Tharu and Janajati communities, who have often protested the underrepresentation of their interests in the federal and provincial legislatures. While Nepal's Election Commission has managed to deliver relatively peaceful elections in recent years, its institutional response to demands for more inclusive electoral boundaries and reserved representation has been cautious, if not reticent. Without a more explicit engagement with the ethnic claims that underlie political mobilization, the Commission risks being seen as a custodian of proceduralism rather than a conduit of justice.

Afghanistan, before the return of the Taliban, presented a more fractured but equally illustrative case. The Independent Election Commission was tasked with managing elections in a society fragmented along ethnic, tribal and sectarian lines, with a weak state and an ongoing conflict. The Commission often faced allegations that voter registration exercises, polling booth placement and even ballot counting processes reflected ethnic favouritism or regional discrimination. While part of this distrust emerged from broader state fragility, the Commission's inability to communicate transparently or adjudicate disputes effectively contributed to the alienation of already marginalized communities, especially the Hazaras and certain Pashtun factions.

The experiences of Bhutan and the Maldives, though less fraught by open ethnic conflict, still illustrate the subtler ways in which electoral systems can fail to address ethno-cultural differences. In Bhutan, questions around the representation of the Lhotshampa remain unresolved. While the Election Commission operates in a highly regulated and orderly system, its mandate does not extend to addressing historical injustices or lingering exclusions. The Maldives, a relatively homogeneous society, has seen political divisions occasionally mirror regional and clan-based rivalries, especially during constitutional crises. Electoral commissions must remain sensitive to how these social cleavages can resurface in moments of political instability.

In Bangladesh, ethnic minorities such as the Chakma, Marma and other hill communities in the Chittagong Hill Tracts have historically struggled for political recognition within a majoritarian Bengali nationalist framework. The Election Commission has rarely engaged substantively with the unique challenges of these regions, where voter registration irregularities, poor access to polling stations and military presence during elections have contributed to low turnout and widespread disillusionment. Here, too, the Commission's failure is not one of malice but of invisibility – its absence in conversations where it should be present.

Across South Asia, then, the credibility of electoral commissions in ethnically plural societies hinges not only on formal impartiality, but on their capacity to recognize and respond to the lived histories of exclusion. This requires more than fair polling booths and voter rolls. It demands a politics of recognition: one where commissions are not passive recipients of elite consensus, but active agents of democratic pluralism.

To do so, they must develop mechanisms for engagement with marginalized communities, adopt culturally and linguistically inclusive outreach strategies, and monitor not just logistical fairness but representational equity. Institutional reform must include provisions for greater diversity within the commissions themselves, ensuring that their composition reflects the heterogeneity of the societies they serve. Above all, electoral commissions must embrace the insight that democracy is not only about majority rule. It is about the inclusion of those who have historically been pushed to the margins of the political imagination.

In a region where ethnicity continues to shape both grievance and hope, electoral commissions stand at a critical juncture. They can choose to replicate the exclusions of the past through bureaucratic neutrality, or they can reimagine their mandate as facilitators of deep democracy, where every identity finds not only a place at the table, but a voice in its shaping.

Reimagining Electoral Guardianship

The future of electoral democracy in South Asia will not be secured by inertia or tradition. It must be actively imagined – and institutionally realized – through bold reforms that reassert the independence, integrity and inclusiveness of election commissions. The challenge is no longer one of merely protecting the status quo, but of regenerating democratic faith in the face of rising authoritarianism, elite capture and civic disillusionment.

At the heart of such a transformation lies the imperative to depoliticize appointments. A region-wide shift towards multi-stakeholder selection processes – incorporating bipartisan parliamentary oversight, judicial input and civil society representation – must be pursued to ensure that no government, regardless of mandate, can handpick its own referee. This is not an abstract ideal; it is a practical necessity. The erosion of credibility begins with the suspicion of bias at the top.

Equally urgent is the financial autonomy of commissions. Their budgets must not depend on the goodwill of finance ministries or shifting executive priorities. Dedicated constitutional or statutory funding mechanisms – akin to those proposed in India's electoral reform bills – would insulate commissions from fiscal manipulation and empower them to plan long-term voter education, infrastructure and grievance redressal initiatives.

Legal clarity is another frontier. Across South Asia, ambiguities in jurisdiction, overlaps with judicial review and weak enforcement powers have rendered commissions hesitant or ineffective. These gaps must be closed. Electoral codes – such as Sri Lanka's Model Code of Conduct or India's Representation of the People Act – require regular revision, with sharper penalties, faster resolution timelines, and explicit protection for whistle-blowers and polling staff in conflict zones.

However, technical reform alone is insufficient. A cultural shift is needed – one that sees election commissions not as gatekeepers of status quo politics, but as midwives of democratic renewal. Commissions must proactively engage with disenfranchised constituencies: ethnic minorities, internally displaced persons, linguistic communities and first-time voters. In places like the Chittagong Hill Tracts, Kashmir or the Nepali Terai, this means sustained dialogue, targeted voter services and ethnically diverse staffing. Electoral justice must be visible to be believed.

To support these efforts, South Asia's democratic states should invest in regional cooperation beyond rhetorical solidarity. Bodies like the FEMBoSA must be revitalized, given independent secretariats and tasked with creating cross-national standards on electoral transparency, campaign finance, minority inclusion and political party accountability. Peer-review mechanisms among commissions – similar to the African Union's Electoral Integrity Missions – could act as soft pressure for reform, backed by research exchanges, technical training and multilingual election observation protocols.

Finally, the public must be re-enfranchised in the moral sense – not only by being allowed to vote, but by being made to feel that their vote matters. This is a pedagogical task. Electoral commissions must invest in civic education not as token gestures, but as the foundation of democratic trust. A citizenry that does not understand how elections work is a citizenry that can be too easily manipulated or too quickly disillusioned.

The guardianship of democracy cannot be passive. It must be renewed, redefined and re-anchored in the moral authority of those who serve not the rulers, but the republic. In a region as volatile, wounded and yearning as South Asia, the stakes of getting this right are not procedural. They are existential.

16

Enrolment to Empowerment: Institutionalizing Voter Education

At the heart of any functioning democracy lies the will of the people. Voting is the principal means by which this will is expressed, and it constitutes one of the most fundamental political rights in any democratic society. While much attention is given to the logistical and administrative aspects of conducting elections – particularly in large and diverse polities – the crucial matter of voter education remains persistently underemphasized. This neglect is not a minor oversight; it speaks to a broader failure to recognize the significance of informed political participation.

In a region as diverse as South Asia, voter education must speak every language, walk every terrain and reach every margin. Elections are often called festivals of democracy – voter education is the invitation to participate in it.

When I assumed office as an election commissioner in 2006, I was appalled to see very low voter turnout in many parts of India, particularly in metros and some big towns. I raised the question of how best to promote voter awareness and participation. The response I received – 'do it in your own time' – was both cryptic and revealing, which was extremely disconcerting. Even otherwise, the majority view among officials of the ECI was that educating voters was not their job, but of the political parties and the media. That such indifference should emerge from the highest echelons of electoral administration in the world's largest democracy is telling.

India is by no means unique in this regard. The problem of insufficient voter education is, regrettably, a global one. In South Asia, it is especially pronounced, with most countries in the region – India being the notable exception – having experienced prolonged periods of authoritarian rule since achieving independence. This historical backdrop underscores the fragility of democratic norms and the need to actively cultivate a culture of participation.

Electoral management bodies (EMBs) cannot afford to treat voter education as a peripheral concern. On the contrary, it is intimately connected to the integrity and effectiveness of elections. While the organization of elections is undoubtedly a formidable administrative task, it is ultimately undertaken in service of the electorate. Consider the 2019 general elections in India, which recorded a voter turnout of 67.4 per cent – a figure hailed as the highest ever in India's electoral history.[1] Yet, this also means that nearly 35 per cent of registered voters abstained from participating, leaving tens of millions of voices left unheard. Such statistics are not trivial. In any democracy, participation is the bedrock of legitimacy.

But how can citizens participate meaningfully if they lack a clear understanding of their rights and responsibilities? Moreover, if participation is partial or uninformed, can we truly claim that the election reflects the will of the people?

These questions demand urgent attention. They underscore the central thesis of this reflection – that voter education is not a luxury, but a necessity for the health and sustainability of democratic governance.

Concept and Components of Voter Education

Before addressing how voter education might be improved, we must first ask the question: what is voter education? Put simply, it is the dissemination of essential knowledge to the electorate, enabling citizens to engage meaningfully in the electoral process. It is through voter education that the public comes to understand not only *how* to vote, but *why* voting matters. It equips individuals with the information they need to cast their ballots responsibly and empowers them to hold institutions accountable.

Moreover, voter education plays a vital role in fostering the civic attitudes, behaviours and knowledge that underpin a healthy democracy. During electoral periods, such education encourages peaceful civic engagement, informed support for political parties or causes, respect for institutional outcomes and tolerance for opposing views. While education alone cannot sustain democracy, it can serve as a crucial tool, especially when citizens are supported by democratic institutions that are responsive to their participation. Indeed, an educated citizenry can often compensate for the occasional shortcomings of electoral administration..

However, developing and implementing a robust voter education programme is no simple matter. It requires thoughtful planning and sustained effort. The following seven steps outline the core components for an effective voter education initiative:

- **Understanding the educational enterprise** – Clarifying the goals, scope and intended outcomes of the programme
- **Establishing the educational mandate** – Defining the authority and responsibility for undertaking voter education within the broader electoral framework
- **Assessing the context** – Evaluating the political, social and cultural environment in which the education programme will operate
- **Developing an appropriate strategy** – Crafting a context-specific plan that addresses the needs of different segments of the population
- **Designing and implementing the programme** – Translating strategic goals into concrete educational materials and outreach activities
- **Monitoring and evaluating the programme** – Continuously assessing the programme's effectiveness and making necessary adjustments
- **Retaining best practices and lessons learnt** – Institutionalizing insights gained during implementation for future use and improvement

These steps are neither rigid nor exhaustive, but they offer a foundational framework for thinking about how voter education can be systematically pursued. If we are to deepen democracy – particularly in societies where it remains fragile or contested – we must invest in the long and often painstaking work of educating citizens, not just administering elections.

Modes of Educating Voters

The dissemination of voter education may be undertaken through a diverse range of methods and media. The EMBs must employ multiple channels to ensure that accurate and comprehensive information reaches every segment of the electorate. These channels may include traditional and digital media – such as newspapers, radio, television and the Internet – as well as printed materials, public art installations, cultural exhibitions, commercial advertising, distance education tools and in-person outreach. The medium must be chosen with careful regard to the context, accessibility and reach among different demographic groups.

At this point, it is crucial to address a common conceptual confusion: the terms 'voter education', 'voter information' and 'civic education' are often used interchangeably, yet they are distinct in purpose, timing, scope and institutional ownership. A clear understanding of these differences is essential for the effective design and implementation of electoral education programmes.

Civic education refers to a broad, continuous process aimed at fostering democratic awareness and engagement. It encompasses foundational concepts such as the rights and responsibilities of citizens, the role of governmental and non-governmental institutions, the functions of the media and political parties, and the value of regular, competitive elections. Unlike voter education, civic education is not bound by the electoral calendar. It may be undertaken through formal education systems, civil society organizations and, occasionally, public institutions, though not necessarily under the remit of election authorities. Its ultimate aim is to cultivate a citizenry that is not only informed, but actively engaged in democratic life.

Voter information, by contrast, is narrowly focused on practical details that enable qualified citizens to participate in an election. It includes information such as the date, time and location of polling; registration procedures; documentation requirements; and the type of election being held. It deals strictly with factual content and logistical arrangements, without delving into broader democratic principles. Such information is typically disseminated in the lead-up to each election, and often constitutes a statutory obligation of the EMBs. Other actors, including political parties and civil society groups, may also play a supplementary role in its distribution.

Voter education occupies a space between civic education and voter information. It addresses the motivations, knowledge and preparedness necessary for full participation in the electoral process. It involves more complex and conceptual content, including the connection between human rights and voting rights, the significance of each vote in shaping public accountability, the secrecy and sanctity of the ballot, the relationship between elections and democratic governance, and the conditions required for free and fair elections. This form of education, requiring explanation rather than mere instruction, demands a longer lead time and should ideally be pursued in a continuous and sustained manner. It is most effectively delivered by a combination of EMBs and civil society actors.

Together, these three forms of education represent layered components in the construction of an electorally literate society. Each layer builds upon the last, reinforcing democratic values and practices. Given the magnitude of the task, no EMB can realistically bear this responsibility alone. A national voter education strategy should marshal all available resources and stakeholders – government departments, educational institutions, media platforms and civil society organizations – especially in the run-up to major elections. The EMBs must serve as the central coordinating authority, setting the regulatory framework, providing technical and financial guidance, and ensuring the integrity and consistency of the programme.

The development of such a programme demands a well-defined objective, informed by the broader electoral context, demographic realities and logistical capacities of the country. Only with such clarity can an effective and responsive national voter education strategy take shape.

It is important to recognize that nearly every aspect of electoral planning – whether it be the election calendar, legal frameworks, staffing and training plans or logistical deployment – has embedded within it an educational dimension. Consequently, EMBs must maintain detailed programmatic plans, ensure effective coordination among educational officers and engage the requisite expertise to implement these strategies efficiently. This often involves collabouration with other governmental departments for matters such as procurement, public communication, staffing and resource distribution.

Strategic negotiation and inter-agency cooperation are indispensable not only for administrative coherence but also for cost-effectiveness. The EMBs must maximize the use of available resources, which may involve earmarked allocations within the broader electoral budget, cost estimates based on voter outreach targets or custom-designed budgets tailored to specific programme goals. Strategic partnerships – particularly with civil society and public institutions – can further amplify reach and efficacy.

In sum, a well-articulated and adequately resourced voter education programme is not a mere adjunct to the electoral process, but a vital instrument for safeguarding and deepening democratic participation.

Messages to Voters

At its essence, voter education is the process through which citizens are equipped with the knowledge, motivation and confidence to exercise their franchise meaningfully. It aims to cultivate a culture of informed participation across all constituencies of a nation – fostering democratic engagement that is both wide in reach and deep in understanding.

To achieve this, certain foundational messages must be conveyed through voter education. These messages may be grouped into four core categories:

1. **Centrality of Elections in a Democracy**: Elections are the cornerstone of any functioning democracy. They provide the primary mechanism through which the collective political will of the people is expressed. A vibrant democracy cannot exist without free, fair and periodic elections. Elections not only offer citizens a diverse range of candidates and political parties to choose from (each presenting distinct policy platforms), but also confer upon every individual the right to stand for office, to organize political entities and to campaign in favour of candidates or causes of their choosing.

Voter education must therefore emphasize the importance of these rights and freedoms, ensuring that the electorate is fully informed of the opportunities available to them within the democratic process. It is the solemn responsibility of EMBs to ensure that such vital information reaches all eligible voters prior to the conduct of any election.

2. **The Responsibility of the Individual Voter**: A truly representative government depends upon the active engagement of every eligible citizen. The act of voting is not merely a right, it is a civic duty. Broad-based participation enhances the legitimacy of democratic institutions and prevents governance from being determined by narrow margins or by disproportionately vocal segments of society. This dimension of voter education must seek to instil a sense of responsibility among citizens, affirming that democracy thrives not only through the awareness of rights but also through the fulfillment of civic obligations. Every individual's voice matters, regardless of their social or economic status.
3. **Every Vote Counts**: It is imperative to convey that each ballot cast carries equal weight in determining electoral outcomes. In electoral systems such as FPTP, outcomes may hinge on just a handful of votes, emphasizing the decisive nature of individual participation. In systems based on proportional representation, each vote directly contributes to the allocation of seats, making the link between citizen preference and legislative representation even more transparent. Should voters begin to feel that their participation has little bearing on outcomes, a sense of political alienation may develop. Voter education must therefore underline that the democratic process is strengthened when every citizen believes that their vote truly matters.
4. **Sanctity and Secrecy of the Ballot**: In many political contexts, especially those where intimidation or fear of reprisal may prevail, it is essential that voters are assured of the confidentiality of their vote. The guarantee of anonymity at the ballot box serves as a bulwark against coercion and manipulation. However, the concept of secrecy carries different connotations in various cultural contexts. In some societies, secrecy may be viewed with suspicion, while in others it may be deemed impractical due to administrative inefficiencies

or prevailing belief systems. Nonetheless, voter education must assert the principle of ballot secrecy and, wherever possible, provide demonstrable assurance of its enforcement.

Beyond these messages, voter education must also foster engagement with the electoral process as a whole. Elections unfold through a series of structured events, forming what is known as the electoral calendar. A well-designed voter education initiative should be phased in accordance with this calendar to ensure that the information shared is timely, relevant and contextualized.

While general programmes cater to the broad electorate, particular attention must be paid to groups with specific needs or vulnerabilities. A robust and inclusive voter education framework must address the following constituencies:

1. Temporary Election Staff

These individuals, often the silent enablers of the electoral process, are instrumental to the successful execution of elections. They should receive thorough training and background knowledge, not only to perform their duties effectively but also to exercise their own voting rights – rights which must not be overlooked amid their responsibilities.

2. Voters Abroad

Citizens residing outside the national territory on election day require clear guidance on the legal provisions and procedural options available to them for casting their vote. Outreach efforts must begin well in advance to avoid last-minute confusion.

3. Refugees and Internally Displaced Persons

This group poses some of the most complex challenges to voter inclusion. Issues related to identity documentation, voter registration and access to polling locations can be daunting – particularly for refugees who have crossed international borders. Nonetheless, any meaningful voter education initiative must strive to incorporate and inform this vulnerable population.

4. Nomads and Migrants

Mobile populations, whether by necessity or choice, often fall outside the traditional geographic frameworks of electoral representation. Voter education must take into account their fluid locations, and design interventions that are adaptive and mobile-friendly.

5. Voters in Remote Areas

In geographically vast nations, like India, millions reside in regions that are difficult to access, with limited or no connection to conventional media channels. Reaching these populations with educational materials and ensuring the establishment of polling infrastructure are substantial but essential challenges.

6. Minorities

Ethnic, linguistic, religious or cultural minorities are often subject to marginalization or discrimination. Voter education must recognize their distinct identities while also affirming their integral place within the democratic fabric of the nation. They must be informed of their full rights and encouraged to participate without fear or alienation.

7. Persons with Disabilities

Navigating the electoral process can be particularly burdensome for individuals with physical, sensory or cognitive impairments. Voter education must proactively inform them of the accommodations and legal protections afforded to them, thereby enabling their unimpeded participation.

8. Home- and Hospital-Bound Voters

For those temporarily incapacitated due to illness or age-related conditions, alternative voting mechanisms – such as early voting, mobile polling or electronic ballots – may be in place. Voter education initiatives must ensure that these citizens are made fully aware of such provisions.

9. Security Forces

Those entrusted with maintaining law and order during elections, or deployed on national security assignments, must also be given the opportunity to cast their vote. Their rights must be upheld through timely information and facilitated through access to alternative voting methods.

10. First-Time Voters and Adolescents

Young citizens, particularly those voting for the first time, are especially impressionable. They represent the future of any nation. Targeted voter education efforts should be developed to guide them through the process, demystify procedures and instil a lifelong habit of civic engagement.

In conclusion, a comprehensive and inclusive voter education strategy must be as dynamic and diverse as the electorate it seeks to serve. It must not only inform, but also inspire a population that is not merely enfranchised, but truly empowered to uphold and advance the principles of democracy.

Implementing a Voter Education Programme

The formulation and implementation of a voter education programme is a task that demands careful forethought, contextual sensitivity and methodical preparation. The team entrusted with it must attend to a range of interrelated factors before proceeding to the design and rollout stages. A comprehensive preparatory process is essential – not only to shape the content and reach of the programme, but also to ensure that it remains responsive to the particularities of time, geography and electoral complexity.

Several core considerations must guide this preparatory phase. Among them are: the temporal window available for programme implementation; the degree of complexity in the programme's objectives; the geographic scale of its outreach; whether the initiative is a pilot project or benefits from the precedent of earlier interventions; and the financial resources allocated for its execution.

In many instances, the design of a voter education programme must be informed by detailed background information, often obtainable only through targeted empirical research. This may require surveys and the engagement of intermediary organizations or individuals who possess contextual familiarity with the target population. At other times, existing datasets may offer valuable insights to situate the programme within a broader informational framework.

1. Surveys

Among the most effective tools available to voter education teams are surveys – designed to generate insights into the electoral awareness, needs and attitudes of a particular population. Surveys are especially useful in gauging existing levels of civic understanding and identifying informational or motivational gaps that the education programme must address.

The ECI conducts Knowledge, Attitude, Behaviour and Practices (KABP) surveys as part of the Systematic Voters' Education and Electoral Participation (SVEEP) programme. These surveys aim to assess citizens' awareness, perceptions and behaviours regarding the electoral process, providing data to tailor voter education initiatives effectively. Insights from KABP surveys help the ECI identify gaps in voter knowledge and participation, enabling the development of targeted strategies to enhance informed and ethical electoral engagement across diverse demographics.

Survey methodologies may be broadly categorized into two types, each suited to distinct audiences and research objectives.

a) Small-Scale or Qualitative Surveys (Focus Groups)

Where the objective is to gain rich, in-depth understanding from a relatively small group of individuals, the focus group method is often the most effective. These discussions are qualitative in nature, and are designed to elicit candid views, personal reflections and nuanced opinions. The intention here is not to quantify responses but to allow participants the space to articulate their experiences and expectations in their own terms. Such qualitative engagements can offer insights that might be obscured in more structured formats.

b) Large-Scale or Quantitative Surveys

In contrast, when the aim is to engage a larger sample of the population, structured surveys using questionnaires and fixed-response options are preferable. This approach facilitates the standardization of data, making it possible to collate, quantify and analyse information efficiently. The comparability of responses across a large dataset allows for robust statistical interpretations and the identification of overarching patterns.

Regardless of type, several key principles must guide the design of any survey. The sample population should be as internally homogeneous as possible, to minimize distortions arising from divergent experiences or expectations. Survey questions must be carefully formulated – precise, respectful and unambiguous – to elicit accurate responses, while remaining sensitive to cultural and emotional contexts. Moreover, each survey should operate within a clearly defined time frame to ensure the timely collection and processing of data.

2. Intermediaries

An alternative – or complementary – approach to gathering contextual intelligence involves working through intermediaries. These may include local civil society organizations, community-based associations or individuals already engaged with the target population. Such actors often possess an intimate understanding of the sociopolitical and cultural milieu in which the education programme is to be situated. Their proximity to the community affords them unique access and insight, which can be invaluable for tailoring programme content and strategy.

However, the use of intermediaries must be approached with caution. While they can significantly expedite information-gathering, the reliability and impartiality of the data they provide must be rigorously verified. To this end, many voter education teams constitute a reference group of subject-matter experts tasked with reviewing and validating the information received from intermediary sources.

In addition, strict confidentiality agreements must be instituted when electoral data is involved. Safeguarding the integrity and secrecy of such information is essential to maintaining public trust and preserving the sanctity of the electoral process. Any breach, intentional or otherwise, can have grave consequences for both the credibility of the voter education initiative and the democratic exercise itself.

Voter Education Programmes in South Asia

Voter education serves as a foundational pillar in the consolidation of democratic processes across the globe, and particularly so in South Asia – a region marked by both its vibrant electoral participation and the complexities of pluralistic societies. In a region where democracy is challenged by uneven development, identity politics, and fluctuating levels of literacy and media access, the task of empowering citizens to meaningfully participate in electoral processes is both urgent and intricate. Voter education programmes, therefore, emerge not merely as informational exercises but as crucial instruments for democratic deepening.

Among these, India's SVEEP programme stands as the most institutionalized and comprehensive initiative. Alongside SVEEP, other South Asian nations have also adopted or are developing their own approaches, reflecting local needs and capacities.

India's SVEEP Programme: A Comprehensive Institutional Model

Systematic Voters' Education and Electoral Participation programme was born from a simple yet powerful idea: that no voter should be left behind – not for lack of awareness, access or agency. Launched by the ECI in 2010, SVEEP represents one of the most ambitious voter education initiatives in the world. Its mandate extends beyond conventional civic awareness campaigns to encompass long-term engagement, capacity building and behavioural change communication. The programme was conceptualized to address two key concerns: voter apathy, particularly in urban areas and among youth; and differential electoral participation among various demographic and socio-economic groups.

It operates through a multi-pronged strategy. It leverages both traditional and modern media, social networks, interpersonal communication, and partnerships with civil society, academic institutions and government departments. Its activities are decentralized and context-specific, with state-level chief electoral officers adapting communication plans to regional realities. For instance, in tribal and remote areas, voter education includes theatre performances, local language pamphlets and village-level outreach through elected representatives and schoolteachers.

One of SVEEP's key achievements has been its ability to institutionalize voter education within the electoral cycle. Voter awareness campaigns are now synchronized with the stages of the election process, including enrolment, corrections in electoral rolls and polling. Special attention is paid to marginalized groups such as first-time voters, women, persons with disabilities and the elderly.

The programme's focus on accessibility and inclusivity has led to innovative measures, such as the setting up of all-women polling stations and the introduction of Braille-enabled EVMs.

The effectiveness of SVEEP is evident in the steady improvement of voter turnout across successive general elections since its launch in 2010, particularly in urban centres historically marked by electoral apathy. In Mumbai City, for instance, turnout rose significantly from approximately 41 per cent in the 2009 general election to around 54.8 per cent in 2014—its highest in three decades. This upward trend was sustained through extensive voter education and outreach efforts targeting urban youth, migrant populations, and middle-class voters. Similarly, constituencies in metropolitan Bengaluru, long characterized by low engagement, have witnessed incremental increases in participation, with turnout in Bengaluru South and other urban segments now regularly crossing the 50 per cent mark. While challenges persist, especially in maintaining momentum among first-time voters and combating urban indifference, these gains underscore the critical role SVEEP has played in reshaping electoral culture in India's cities.[2]

The programme's school and college initiatives are among its most expansive, with over 3.7 lakh ELCs established nationwide – including 2.44 lakhs in schools and 65,000 in colleges – to educate young and first-time voters through mock elections, quizzes and interactive games. Additionally, voter awareness forums in higher education institutions engage faculty and staff in electoral discourse. On National Voters' Day 2023, over 6 crore youth participated in voter awareness activities. The programme also partners with the National Service Scheme and Nehru Yuva Kendra Sangathan and integrates voter education into curricula. Digital innovations, including e-learning modules and apps, further broaden SVEEP's outreach among India's digitally connected student population.

Other countries in the region have also adopted a variety of approaches, influenced by political history, administrative capacity and levels of electoral maturity.

Bangladesh: Voter Awareness through Civic Engagement

Bangladesh has made notable strides in voter education, particularly under the auspices of the Bangladesh Election Commission, which has collabourated with civil society organizations and international agencies such as the UNDP. The Strengthening Electoral Governance Project (2011–16) and subsequent capacity-building efforts have focused on increasing youth participation, reducing electoral violence and improving electoral literacy.[3] These campaigns often use folk media and rural outreach strategies to counter misinformation and promote a peaceful electoral culture.

Moreover, Bangladesh has incorporated voter education into school curricula and launched targeted campaigns during national elections. However, in the absence of an institutionalized model like SVEEP, the sustainability and scalability of these efforts have often been limited by political tensions and funding constraints.

Nepal: Voter Education amid Democratic Transition

Nepal's experience with voter education is shaped by its post-monarchy democratic transition and the challenges of building electoral trust. The Election Commission of Nepal has partnered with organizations such as the International Foundation for Electoral Systems (IFES) and the EU to implement structured voter education initiatives. These have included community-based voter awareness programmes, street dramas and mobile campaigns targeting remote mountain communities.

In particular, the Voter Education Volunteers initiative in Nepal has proven effective in enhancing citizen engagement. These volunteers are trained to disseminate election-related information door-to-door, especially among women, Dalits and other marginalized groups. The Election Commission has also invested in creating disability-friendly voter materials and leveraging local radio networks to reach communities with limited access to mainstream media.

Sri Lanka: Targeted Electoral Literacy amid Political Flux

Sri Lanka's voter education framework is overseen by the Election Commission of Sri Lanka, which has historically conducted voter education in partnership with NGOs, particularly during periods of national elections. Given the island's complex political history, including its ethnic conflicts and post-war reconciliation process, voter education has had to tread a delicate path between neutrality and civic engagement.

Recent initiatives have focused on youth engagement, voter rights education and awareness about the Preferential Voting System used in parliamentary elections. These efforts, while impactful in pockets, lack the sustained institutional support and scale of India's SVEEP. However, the Commission's increased use of digital platforms, especially social media, in urban centres reflects a growing understanding of demographic shifts in information consumption.

Pakistan: Civil Society at the Forefront

In Pakistan, voter education has largely been driven by civil society and international development agencies, with the ECP playing a supporting and increasingly active role. Notable initiatives include the Free and Fair Election Network (FAFEN) and programmes supported by the IFES and the UNDP, which have concentrated on voter registration awareness, gender-inclusive polling and training workshops for electoral staff.

Given the constraints of political instability and uneven access to media, these programmes have placed emphasis on face-to-face communication and local-level engagement. The ECP's launch of a voter education and awareness plan in recent years signals an intent to centralize and coordinate such efforts more effectively.

Bhutan: Emphasis on Values

Bhutan's voter education programme is a cornerstone of its democratic process, reflecting the country's commitment to informed and ethical electoral participation. Led by the Election Commission of Bhutan, the programme is formally institutionalized under the Election Act of 2008, which mandates civic and voter education as part of the Commission's core functions. The Commission conducts comprehensive outreach efforts across rural and urban areas, including the production of multilingual educational materials, school-based democratic clubs, interactive radio shows and voter awareness tours.

A hallmark of Bhutan's approach is its emphasis on non-partisan and values-based education – focusing not just on voting procedures but also on the role of integrity, accountability and national unity in democratic participation. These efforts are particularly tailored to Bhutan's unique context of recent democratic transition, aiming to foster a culture of participation grounded in the country's overarching development philosophy of GNH.

The Maldives: Evolving Voter Engagement

The Maldives' voter education efforts are coordinated primarily by the Elections Commission of the Maldives, which carries out regular nationwide programmes to promote democratic awareness and electoral participation. Given the country's geographic dispersion across hundreds of islands, the Commission utilizes a mix of in-person workshops, school outreach, radio programmes and social media campaigns to ensure broad coverage. Particular emphasis is placed on engaging first-time voters, women and marginalized communities, with tailored materials in Dhivehi and in English (where relevant). In recent years, voter education has expanded beyond basic procedural information to include modules on the importance of informed choice, the risks of vote buying and the role of political accountability.

These efforts are often carried out in collabouration with civil society organizations and international development partners, especially during major elections. Despite challenges related to logistics and partisanship, the Maldives' voter education programme continues to evolve as a vital pillar of its electoral democracy.

Afghanistan: A Halted Effort

Since the Taliban's return to power, it is evident that voter education programmes are no longer operational. The combination of restrictive policies on education and the suppression of civil society initiatives has effectively halted efforts to educate and empower voters in Afghanistan.

In the past, since 2002, the IFES was supporting Afghan partners to strengthen electoral institutions and civil society. Their efforts encompassed areas such as electoral integrity, operations, political finance, legal reform, dispute resolution, public outreach, women's empowerment, advocacy skills, and civic and voter education.

In 2014, Democracy International launched the Women and Elections – Voter Outreach, Training and Empowerment programme. This initiative aimed to encourage women's participation in the April elections and the subsequent presidential runoff. Collabourating with local Afghan partners, including religious leaders and civil servants, the programme focused on educating female voters about the electoral process and improving the environment for gender-sensitive election administration through voter engagement, radio broadcasts and civil society capacity-building.

Additionally, organizations like Bond Street Theatre used innovative methods. Their Voter Education & Fraud Mitigation Project prepared the Afghan population for the 2014 Presidential elections with theatre-based programmes to illuminate voter rights, women's rights and common barriers to voting. These performances reached over 150,000 people across multiple provinces, emphasizing the importance of informed electoral participation.

Challenges and Opportunities

Despite their differences, South Asian voter education programmes share several common challenges. These include the difficulty of reaching remote or conflict-affected areas, the low literacy rates in many rural communities, the challenge of countering misinformation in the digital age and the need to build trust in electoral institutions. Additionally, political interference, funding limitations and administrative bottlenecks often hinder the implementation and evaluation of such initiatives.

Yet, the successes of programmes like SVEEP demonstrate that well-designed, inclusive and institutionalized voter education can make a tangible impact on democratic participation. There is scope for greater regional collabouration through the SAARC mechanisms to share best practices, harmonize strategies and explore cross-border learning. Establishing a South Asian consortium for electoral literacy – akin to a regional SVEEP – could bolster democratic resilience and foster an informed and active electorate.

As mentioned earlier, voter education is not just about the *how* of voting – it is about the *why* as well. To have a truly participatory democracy we have to empower voters with knowledge, not just ballots. Therefore, electoral turnout is not just a number, it is a signal of belief in the system – and belief is nurtured by knowledge.

In a region as populous and politically diverse as South Asia, voter education is not merely a bureaucratic exercise – it is a democratic necessity. India's SVEEP stands as a beacon of how structured and inclusive voter education can deepen electoral participation. While other SAARC nations are making commendable strides in adapting voter education to their own contexts, the potential for growth remains considerable. As the region continues to grapple with the challenges of democratic consolidation, investments in sustained and context-sensitive voter education programmes will be vital to ensuring that every citizen not only has the right to vote, but the knowledge and confidence to exercise that right meaningfully.

Therefore, it is important to remember at all times that democracy does not end at the ballot box or the EVM – it begins with an informed voter.

17

Digital Democracy: Impact of Technology in Elections

In a region where more than a quarter of the world's population resides, the intersection of democracy and technology is being rewritten in real time. South Asia, a crucible of democratic experimentation and turbulence, now finds itself at the vanguard of a digital turn in electoral governance. From biometric voter rolls in Bangladesh to EVMs in India and Bhutan, from mobile-based voter outreach in Sri Lanka to online transparency portals in Nepal, the adoption of technology in electoral processes has been both swift and uneven. The digitalization of the ballot raises a host of new questions, such as: is technology enhancing democratic access or deepening existing inequities? Can electronic governance inoculate elections against fraud or does it open new avenues for manipulation, exclusion and control?

The embrace of electoral technology in South Asia has unfolded under conditions that are neither uniform nor ideologically neutral. Unlike the incremental and deliberative models seen in some advanced democracies, South Asian transitions have been marked by rapid deployment, limited public consultation and uneven infrastructural readiness. Electoral technologies here have emerged not merely as logistical solutions but as political artefacts – embedded within contentious struggles over representation, trust and institutional legitimacy.

Take, for instance, the introduction of EVMs in India, now a defining feature of its elections. Despite widespread deployment since the early 2000s and endorsements from bodies like the ECI, EVMs have become the subject of persistent public doubt and partisan controversy.

Similar concerns have surfaced in Pakistan and Bangladesh, where past experiments with electronic or biometric voting were either abandoned or significantly curtailed due to allegations of rigging or systemic flaws. In the Maldives and Sri Lanka, too, digital voter lists and ID systems have been introduced with mixed results, often encountering resistance from civil society or political actors over fears of privacy violations and institutional overreach.

The spread of biometric voter registration, initially heralded as a silver bullet against multiple voting and impersonation, has now raised equally urgent alarms about digital disenfranchisement. Afghanistan, despite collapsing under renewed Taliban control, had once pioneered biometric verification in polls – a practice that was both technologically ambitious and operationally chaotic. In Bangladesh, the National Identity (NID) card system with embedded biometrics created a unique identification architecture, but also brought forth concerns over data privacy and opaque governance. Bhutan and Nepal, while more cautious in embracing biometrics, are not immune to the broader regional trend that sees technological certainty often trumping democratic deliberation.

Digital inclusion – or the lack thereof – remains a central axis of concern. In countries like Nepal, Bhutan and Sri Lanka, with difficult terrain and widely dispersed populations, the promise of electoral digitization runs up against infrastructural realities: patchy Internet, low digital literacy and linguistic exclusion. In Pakistan and India, urban centres may benefit from real-time updates, QR-coded voter slips or app-based polling station locators, but rural and marginalized communities are often disoriented by opaque tech systems and abrupt changes. This asymmetry threatens to reinforce the very exclusions that democracy aspires to overcome.

Moreover, technology has not merely entered elections as a passive tool but as an active terrain of political struggle. In recent elections across the region, digital tools have been used for microtargeted disinformation, surveillance of opposition candidates and algorithmic control of electoral messaging. In India, political parties engaged firms like Cambridge Analytica and Indian IT cells to target voters with customized content based on caste and locality data, while reports during the 2018 elections in Pakistan revealed the use of spyware to monitor opposition communications.[1] In Sri Lanka, coordinated disinformation campaigns on Facebook and WhatsApp ahead of the 2019 presidential election sowed ethnic mistrust and confusion about polling dates.[2] Across the SAARC region, these developments mark a shift from digital enablement to digital coercion in the electoral domain. The transformation is thus not just one of efficiency but of ethos – a redefinition of the relationship among citizens, data and the democratic process.

However, it would be overly deterministic to view technology only as a threat. There are genuine successes to be noted. Bhutan, for instance, has used digital technologies to boost civic awareness and encourage voter education in ways that are culturally sensitive and multilingual. The Election Commission of Nepal has developed relatively transparent digital systems for party registration and financial disclosures. Even in the Maldives – despite episodes of democratic backsliding – digital tools have allowed civil society to track irregularities and coordinate monitoring across dispersed islands. These pockets of innovation show that digital democracy in South Asia need not succumb to digital authoritarianism.

Still, a common regional challenge remains: the absence of robust legal frameworks to regulate electoral technologies. India (Digital Personal Data Protection Act 2023), Sri Lanka (Personal Data Protection Act, No. 9 of 2022), Nepal (Privacy Act, 2075 [2018]) and Bhutan (enacted privacy legislation) have enacted data protection laws, while Pakistan, Bangladesh and the Maldives lack comprehensive data protection regimes. Regulatory oversight of electoral tech procurement, auditing and deployment is minimal. Moreover, the opacity of decision-making in election commissions – often bypassing parliamentary scrutiny or public consultation – has compounded the crisis of legitimacy. This is not a matter of technical fine-tuning, it is a structural democratic imperative.

As South Asia barrels towards an ever more digitized political future, the central question is no longer whether technology should play a role in elections – it is how, under what conditions and to what end. The digitalization of the vote must not be mistaken for the democratization of the process. If mismanaged, electoral technologies could entrench new inequalities, amplify state control and reduce elections to a spectacle of procedural compliance. But if governed wisely – with transparency, inclusion and rights-based frameworks – they hold the potential to deepen trust, widen participation and modernize democracy without muting its moral core.

There are four interlinked dimensions of electoral technology in South Asia that I will explore in this chapter – access and inclusion, biometric integrity, public trust and risks of authoritarian capture. Through each theme, the chapter draws on recent regional evidence, situating national experiences within a broader comparative analysis. In doing so, it seeks not merely to assess the state of digital democracy in South Asia, but also to articulate a vision for how technology might be made to serve – and not subvert – the region's democratic promise.

Bridging or Deepening the Democratic Divide?

The promise of digitization in elections is premised on the ideal of universal access. In theory, electoral technology can democratize participation – reducing logistical burdens, eliminating human error, simplifying registration and empowering remote or first-time voters. Yet, across South Asia, the practical deployment of digital and electronic tools has produced a more fractured reality. The digital divide, far from being a peripheral concern, lies at the heart of the democratic equation in this region.

Consider voter registration systems. Afghanistan and Bangladesh have deployed comprehensive biometric voter databases in recent years, aiming to eliminate duplication and impersonation. Bangladesh's digitized electoral roll, covering over 119 million voters, is now integrated with the NID system and is often held up as a regional benchmark. However, access to NID-linked voter services is uneven.

Although Nepal has made steady progress in expanding internet access nationwide, stark disparities persist between urban and rural regions. According to available data, overall internet penetration in the country stood at approximately 55–56 per cent in 2023–2024. Independent surveys such as those by Digital Rights Nepal indicate that while nearly 46 per cent of urban households had access to the internet, the figure drops to around 21.5 per cent in rural areas. These divides create pronounced asymmetries in how citizens engage with electoral systems, especially as voter information, registration, and grievance redressal mechanisms increasingly migrate to digital platforms.[3]

India, the world's largest electorate, illustrates the tension between electoral digitization and inclusion. While the ECI's Voter Helpline app and National Voter Services Portal have attracted tens of millions of users by 2024, usage has skewed toward urban and digitally enabled voters; rural and marginalized groups remain much less reached. Parallel research on India's caste-based digital divide shows that lower castes – often concentrated in rural areas – have disproportionately lower access and digital literacy. Field studies from rural Odisha confirm persistent adoption gaps, particularly among older, less-educated rural residents – underscoring how functional awareness of digital voting tools remains limited outside urban and youth populations.[4]

Sri Lanka's experience reveals a different but equally instructive facet. Despite being a relatively high-literacy country with substantial digital infrastructure, the 2023 local government elections were postponed partly due to budgetary concerns about digitizing electoral operations. The Election Commission had planned to introduce digital procurement and logistics systems to reduce cost and manual oversight, but political hesitation and financial constraints curtailed this effort.[5] What this shows is that digital expansion is not merely a technical or infrastructural issue – it is a political one. The will to digitize elections transparently and inclusively can be just as critical as the capacity to do so.

In Pakistan and the Maldives, initiatives to extend electoral access via digital means have remained largely urban-centric or experimental. The 2023 Pakistani general elections saw limited piloting of online result transmission systems (RTS), but these were marred by public scepticism and alleged manipulation in previous cycles, thereby reducing public confidence. In the Maldives, digital voter registration via mobile platforms was piloted in 2023 for overseas voters, particularly from the diaspora in Sri Lanka and Malaysia. While this helped increase overseas participation, local civil society organizations flagged concerns about insufficient outreach and clarity for domestic voters, particularly among youth and first-time registrants.

Afghanistan's experience with biometric registration reveals a troubling gender gap. During the 2019 voter registration drive—supported by the UNDP's Electoral Support Project—only 36.6 percent of all registered voters were women, highlighting persistent barriers to equitable participation. While district-level data remain limited, the broader trend suggests significantly lower female registration rates in several provinces, especially in rural and insecure regions. Independent assessments by the U.S. Institute of Peace and the Special Inspector General for Afghanistan Reconstruction (SIGAR) underscore the structural constraints—ranging from technological unfamiliarity and inadequate outreach to entrenched sociocultural norms—that limit women's access to electoral processes. These disparities signal that biometric innovations, unless carefully adapted and supported, may reinforce existing exclusions rather than redress them.[6]

The broader regional pattern is clear: while digitization holds vast potential, its benefits remain unevenly distributed. South Asia's democratic future depends on whether states can design electoral technologies that accommodate – not marginalize – diverse realities. This means ensuring multilingual interfaces, expanding digital infrastructure into underserved areas and investing in citizen literacy that goes beyond basic schooling to include digital fluency. It also demands that electoral commissions view voters not as consumers of technology, but as participants in democracy, whose inclusion is not merely instrumental but constitutional.

Despite the rapid digitization of electoral systems across South Asia, the region remains beset by deep inequalities in digital inclusion, particularly among marginalized populations. Studies consistently show that Pakistan, Afghanistan and Nepal fare poorly in digital equity, with limited access to information and communications technology (ICT), especially in rural and tribal regions, hindering voter outreach and participation. In Pakistan and Afghanistan, women, linguistic minorities, persons with disabilities and residents of remote areas face pronounced barriers to accessing digital electoral services. Nepal's own experiments with e-governance have revealed infrastructural and literacy-related exclusions that disproportionately affect poor and rural citizens. While India and Bangladesh have made greater strides in deploying digital infrastructure for elections, their scores are significantly undercut by persistent subnational disparities – most notably among Adivasi communities, Dalits and religious minorities who lack equal digital access and representation. Recent research, such as the Digital Democracy Index (CIVICUS, 2022), the Inclusive Internet Index (Economist Impact, 2022), and academic studies on caste-based digital divides in India (Vaidehi et al., 2021), confirms that systemic exclusions from the digital sphere translate directly into diminished electoral inclusion, undermining the democratic promise of equal participation.[7]

Ultimately, if digitization in South Asian elections is to serve democratic ends, it must be anchored in accessibility. Otherwise, electoral technology risks becoming another layer of disenfranchisement that displaces the ink-stained finger with the invisible barrier of a broken signal, an unreadable app or an unreachable server.

Biometric Identification and Electoral Integrity

Few technological interventions have generated as much enthusiasm – and unease – as biometric identification in elections. From iris scans and fingerprints to facial recognition systems, biometrics have been heralded as revolutionary tools in curbing electoral fraud, ensuring the uniqueness of voter identities and streamlining voter verification. In South Asia, the adoption of biometric systems has proceeded rapidly over the past decade, often with the support of international donors and private tech firms. However, the region's experience reveals a sobering paradox: while biometrics may bolster the procedural integrity of the vote, they also risk undermining democratic inclusion, accountability and civil liberties when deployed without adequate legal safeguards, institutional transparency and public trust.

Bangladesh's biometric voter roll is one of the most comprehensive in the region, covering over 119 million registered voters and linked to the country's robust NID database. First introduced in 2008 and continually updated, this system is often cited as a model of digital consolidation. However, recent evaluations – including the 2023 report by TIB – have raised serious concerns. The report documented cases of exclusion due to technical errors, such as mismatches between biometric inputs and identity records, disproportionately affecting elderly voters and persons with disabilities.[8] Moreover, the integration of voter data with the Ministry of Home Affairs generated fears of surveillance, wherein where electoral data is repurposed for non-electoral policing or intelligence work.

India's electoral system officially does not rely on biometrics at the polling station, but the broader Aadhaar infrastructure – a biometric digital identity system covering over 1.3 billion people – has increasingly been linked with voter rolls. The Election Laws (Amendment) Act of 2021 permits the voluntary linking of voter IDs with Aadhaar, ostensibly to eliminate duplication. However, critics argue that this creates a backdoor for mass disenfranchisement. A 2022 RTI filed by the Reporters' Collective revealed that in states where the Aadhaar–Voter ID linkage was most aggressively implemented, lakhs of voters – many of them from marginalized caste and minority groups – were quietly removed from the rolls due to unverifiable mismatches.[9] The ECI has denied mass deletions, but the opacity of the linkage process and the absence of a dedicated data protection law have only intensified public suspicion.

Nepal's cautious approach offers a useful contrast. The country has experimented with biometric voter registration, including fingerprint and photo capture, but has refrained from integrating this data with other national databases. More recently, experts in the field of cyber law in Nepal such as Dr. Newal Choudhary, have underscored the need to protect biometric data from non-electoral application, and called for a parliamentary review before scaling up integration. This posture reflects a broader concern in South Asia: the absence of legal architecture to protect electoral biometrics from misuse. As of 2024, no SAARC country has passed a stand-alone law governing the use, storage and deletion of biometric electoral data. Even in Sri Lanka, which has announced intentions to introduce biometric voter verification by 2025, civil society groups have flagged the lack of a data protection regime as a major impediment.

The Afghan experience stands as both a cautionary tale and a stark reminder of technological overreach in fragile contexts. In 2018, Afghanistan introduced a biometric verification system intended to prevent ballot stuffing and impersonation. Voters were required to submit fingerprints and photographs at the time of polling, using German-manufactured handheld devices procured at significant cost. The system quickly ran into chaos. Poor training, device malfunction, inconsistent Internet connectivity and inadequate field-testing led to widespread delays and accusations of disenfranchisement. More than 400 polling stations failed to open on the day of elections due to technical issues such as failure of biometric machines.[10]

With the return of the Taliban in 2021 and the collapse of democratic institutions, these biometric databases are now in uncertain custody, raising fears of retributive identification and repression. The Afghan case illustrates the dangers of electoral technologies in the absence of secure institutional environments.

Bhutan and the Maldives have been more restrained in their use of biometrics. Bhutan continues to rely on photographic ID cards, and has invested in improving accuracy through non-biometric digital audits and periodic voter list verifications. The 2022 report by the International IDEA notes that while biometric options have been studied, the social, cultural and legal implications of such systems must be carefully weighed in light of national values.[11] The Maldives, meanwhile, uses fingerprint-based registration but does not rely on biometric verification at polling stations.

Pakistan has experimented with biometric voter authentication devices in select pilot projects, particularly in urban constituencies, as part of efforts to enhance electoral credibility following persistent allegations of rigging and ghost voting. While there is no public evidence of such devices being used at scale in the 2023 elections, earlier pilots offer instructive insights. In the 2015 by-election in NA-19 (Haripur), biometric verification succeeded for only 46 per cent of voters, with failures attributed to worn fingerprints, blocked CNICs, and database mismatches – amounting to a 54 per cent failure rate. Though the Election Commission of Pakistan has since tested biometric voter verification in limited settings, these trials have not led to nationwide implementation, and official evaluations continue to underscore concerns around technical feasibility, data reliability and voter confidence.[12]

What emerges across the region is a pattern of institutional overreach and legal vacuum. Biometric systems are being introduced faster than they are being regulated. The 2023 Global Digital Rights Index flags every SAARC country except Bhutan as either 'at risk' or 'inadequate' in terms of biometric data protection. The consequences are not abstract.[13] In societies with deep caste, ethnic and religious cleavages, the misuse – or even the perception of misuse – of biometric voter data can exacerbate social mistrust, invite political manipulation and damage electoral legitimacy.

The path forward lies not in technological retrenchment but in democratic regulation. Electoral commissions must establish strict audit protocols for biometric use, publish error rates, ensure recourse for those wrongly excluded, and subject their digital operations to legislative and judicial oversight. Regionally, the SAARC countries could benefit from shared norms and pooled best practices – an electoral analogue to the Asia-Pacific Privacy Charter. Without such reforms, the biometric revolution in South Asian elections may deepen democratic deficits rather than correct them.

Technology and Trust

At the heart of any electoral system lies a foundational compact: that the process is credible, the rules are fair and the outcomes reflect the people's will. The introduction of technology into elections – whether in the form of EVMs, digital voter rolls or result transmission systems – was meant to reinforce this compact by eliminating human error, standardizing procedures and insulating outcomes from manipulation. Yet, across South Asia, this promise has been tempered by growing public scepticism, institutional opacity and a widening trust deficit. The very machines meant to assure voters are now often seen as enigmatic, unaccountable black boxes – powerful but opaque.

India's experience with EVMs, arguably the most extensive in the world, illustrates the complexities of trust in electoral technology. Since their full adoption in 2004, EVMs have become emblematic of India's technological modernity in governance. However, in recent years, they have also become a flashpoint for political controversy. Opposition parties have repeatedly questioned their transparency and hackability, despite the ECI's insistence on their technical robustness. In response to such concerns, the Commission introduced voter verified paper audit trails (VVPATs) in 2019, enabling voters to briefly view a printed slip of their vote. However, the 2024 general election again saw disputes flare over VVPAT counting: out of over a million EVMs deployed, only five VVPAT slips per constituency were matched with the digital count – a fraction too minuscule to assure meaningful verification. The Supreme Court of India has repeatedly declined petitions for more extensive VVPAT cross-checking, further fuelling distrust.

Bangladesh abandoned EVMs for the 2024 general elections, citing widespread public resistance and concerns over transparency. In the preceding 2018 elections, EVMs had been used in a limited number of constituencies. But the lack of adequate voter education, insufficient public demonstrations and allegations of tampering created an enduring perception that the machines could be – and had been – manipulated. The Election Commission of Bangladesh faced severe criticism for its opaque procurement process and lack of response to civil society calls for third-party audits. As a result, the return to manual voting in 2024 was not seen as a step backward technologically, but as a necessary recalibration to restore electoral legitimacy.

Pakistan's experience with RTS offers another cautionary tale. Introduced to streamline and speed up the electronic submission of polling data, RTS was widely used in the 2018 general elections. However, the system allegedly 'collapsed' on election night, leading to delays, inconsistencies and suspicions of vote manipulation. The ECP blamed technical failures, but opposition parties and watchdog organizations such as the FAFEN argued that the breakdown coincided suspiciously with results swinging in favour of certain political parties.[14] In the 2023 elections, the Commission attempted a more decentralized transmission method, but public confidence remained low. According to a Gallup Pakistan survey conducted in late 2023, approximately 70% of Pakistani citizens lacked confidence in the honesty of their electoral process, signaling the larger widespread public distrust in electoral integrity and transparency.[15]

In smaller democracies such as Bhutan and the Maldives, where electoral operations are more manageable, technological trust remains relatively higher, but not immune to critique. Bhutan's Election Commission has consistently foregrounded transparency by publishing detailed post-election audit reports, including instances of error and procedural correction. Its use of technology is limited but carefully explained to the public. In the Maldives, on the other hand, where the political environment has been more volatile, trust in electoral technology has wavered. A 2023 public consultation led by Transparency Maldives revealed that 45 per cent of respondents feared that digitized electoral processes could be manipulated by incumbent regimes. The perception of electoral machinery as being in service of power, rather than process, is difficult to shake without radical transparency.

Nepal presents a hybrid case. While it has not adopted EVMs, it has digitized many elements of the pre-election and post-election process – such as candidate nomination, financial disclosures and polling centre management. In 2022, the Election Commission of Nepal launched a public-facing dashboard that displayed real-time voter registration and complaint tracking data. This initiative, supported by the IFES, was lauded as a best practice in digital transparency. However, in the absence of a sustained public education campaign, many rural voters remained unaware of these tools.

Across the region, the challenge is not merely technical failure, but institutional opacity. Voters do not mistrust technology in abstract – they mistrust institutions that refuse to explain, audit or submit their systems to scrutiny. This is exacerbated by the fact that most electoral commissions in South Asia lack legally mandated transparency norms for digital processes. Except for Bhutan and, to a lesser degree, Nepal, no SAARC country currently requires mandatory third-party audits of electoral technology. Moreover, procurement of voting technology remains shrouded in secrecy, often involving defence contractors or foreign firms under non-disclosure agreements.

International norms point to a better path. The Declaration of Principles for International Election Observation (endorsed by the UN, the EU and the Carter Center) states that all technologies used in the electoral process must be subject to rigorous public testing and independent verification.[16] However, few electoral commissions in South Asia align fully with these standards. In many cases, civil society organizations and media outlets have been forced to reverse-engineer technologies for public understanding through investigative reports and informal scrutiny.

If technology is to reinforce trust, it must be intelligible, auditable and publicly accountable. Electoral commissions must demystify their digital operations – not merely in technical jargon, but in voter-friendly formats. Regular stress-testing, real-time publication of failure rates, public education campaigns in local languages and institutional willingness to entertain third-party scrutiny are not optional – they are democratic imperatives. Without them, the spectre of the machine looms large – not as a guardian of the vote, but as its usurper.

Threat of Digital Authoritarianism

Electoral technology in South Asia has often been justified in the language of modernization, efficiency and anti-fraud measures, but its operational and political consequences have not always served democratic ends. Increasingly, digital tools designed for electoral administration – ranging from real-time surveillance platforms and geofencing software to algorithmic content moderation and facial recognition – are sometimes also being repurposed to entrench incumbent regimes, suppress dissent and control the informational ecosystem around elections. This is not merely a case of flawed implementation. It signals a deeper structural risk: that the digitization of elections may become a Trojan horse for digital authoritarianism.

India, with its unmatched digital scale, presents the most striking paradox. On the one hand, the country has pioneered innovations in electoral technology – from large-scale EVM deployment to geo-tagged election logistics and AI-assisted voter-roll management. On the other, it has witnessed the creeping instrumentalization of the very infrastructure that supports democratic participation. The Internet Freedom Foundation and Access Now reported that in 2023 alone, India imposed over eighty internet shutdowns, many of them coinciding with state elections or political protests. Several of these were justified as preventive measures for election-related 'law and order' concerns, particularly in sensitive border districts and tribal regions. The chilling effect is profound: when digital infrastructure is turned off, entire populations are cut off from voting updates, grievance redressal platforms and civil society coordination.

Pakistan's experience further underscores the vulnerability of digital systems to state overreach. In the 2023 general elections, the use of predictive policing software and facial recognition surveillance – ostensibly to monitor electoral violence – triggered backlash from civil liberties groups. The Human Rights Commission of Pakistan noted that such tools were disproportionately deployed in opposition strongholds and ethnically volatile regions. Meanwhile, online disinformation and targeted harassment of candidates on social media escalated, with weak content moderation and lack of transparency from both platforms and authorities. Although the ECP officially disavowed any role in such activities, leaked documents from the Digital Media Wing suggested coordinated campaigns to promote pro-government narratives during the electoral cycle.

In Sri Lanka, the state's control over digital communication infrastructure allowed it to clamp down on political organizing during the 2022–23 crisis, when anti-incumbent protests swept the country. The Committee to Protect Journalists documented multiple instances of digital surveillance, censorship of news websites and the use of anti-terror laws against activists disseminating electoral reform demands online.[17] These events occurred just as the Election Commission was preparing for postponed local government elections, creating a toxic atmosphere of coercion and uncertainty. Though Sri Lanka's electoral bodies have made efforts to digitize logistics and transparency, such progress cannot offset the structural danger posed by a political regime willing to muzzle dissent through digital means.

Even in smaller democracies like the Maldives and Bhutan, the spectre of digital instrumentalization is not absent. In the Maldives, political parties have increasingly resorted to data harvesting via online registration platforms and mobile outreach tools – sometimes without clear consent from the users. The 2023 presidential election saw an unprecedented level of personalized SMS campaigning, often using data scraped from tourism or telecom registries.[18] In a country where the line between state and ruling party has historically been thin, this raises critical questions about data autonomy and electoral fairness. In Bhutan, while digital adoption has been more measured, emerging concerns about data centralization and algorithmic governance have begun to surface. The increasing integration of biometric ID systems with electoral rolls and public service delivery platforms has prompted unease among civil society actors, particularly given the absence of a comprehensive data protection framework. Although Bhutan's Election Commission has maintained a relatively cautious stance on deploying invasive digital tools, the broader expansion of e-governance infrastructure – without robust legal safeguards – risks creating opaque systems of surveillance and control. In a polity where civic institutions are still evolving, the unchecked growth of digital bureaucracy could subtly entrench state dominance over individual autonomy and political expression.

Nepal's relative institutional resilience offers cautious optimism. While the country has digitized key elements of electoral administration, it has so far resisted the urge to extend surveillance technologies into the electoral sphere. Civil society organizations in Kathmandu, such as the Digital Rights Nepal Coalition, have been effective in pushing back against efforts to expand predictive policing during protests or polling. However, the increasing reliance on foreign software vendors for electoral logistics, particularly from regional powers, poses its own geopolitical and security dilemmas.

Across South Asia, what emerges is a common dilemma: the infrastructural skeleton of digital democracy is being assembled without adequate democratic muscle to control its use. Electoral technologies do not operate in isolation – they sit within broader ecosystems of political contestation, state coercion and civic fragility. In countries where institutions are robust, legal frameworks are enforced and civil society is vibrant, technology can act as a multiplier of democratic trust. But where these conditions falter, technology amplifies power asymmetries, cloaks repression in the veneer of efficiency and undermines the very legitimacy it claims to protect.

The imperative, then, is not to halt digital innovation but to democratize it. South Asian countries must invest in regulatory firewalls, digital rights charters and oversight bodies with real teeth. Electoral commissions must act not just as neutral administrators, but as ethical stewards of technological power – resisting political pressure, ensuring data sovereignty and prioritizing human dignity. Regional forums like the FEMBoSA could play a transformative role by developing shared protocols on data protection, algorithmic transparency and misuse mitigation. Without such efforts, the region risks allowing its digital tools to become the very instruments of its democratic unravelling.

Reclaiming the Democratic Architecture of Electoral Technology

The future of democracy in South Asia will be shaped not only by how citizens vote, but by the invisible architectures that govern how elections are conducted, secured and experienced. Electoral technology, once viewed as a neutral enabler, now occupies a pivotal space in the region's democratic calculus. The question is no longer whether technology should be used, but how it can be governed so that it extends, rather than erodes, the democratic franchise.

First, reform must begin with legislation. No electoral technology should be introduced without a statutory framework that ensures data protection, public oversight and institutional accountability. South Asian countries urgently need comprehensive electoral technology laws that set standards for procurement, public testing, third-party audits and post-election transparency. These laws must go beyond technical specifications to codify fundamental rights – guaranteeing that no citizen is excluded, profiled or manipulated through digital means.

Second, electoral commissions must evolve from being administrative custodians to constitutional sentinels. They must resist executive overreach, demand legislative scrutiny before adopting new technologies, and commit to publishing error rates, audit logs and procurement rationales. Independence cannot be presumed; it must be practised in public. This includes embracing civil society as a partner rather than an adversary – inviting scrutiny, consultation and collabouration at every stage of technological deployment.

Third, South Asia needs regional cooperation that is not merely symbolic. The FEMBoSA must be transformed from a consultative body into a technical forum for harmonizing electoral standards, sharing risk assessments and coordinating safeguards across borders. A SAARC-wide charter on digital democracy – grounded in shared norms of transparency, inclusivity and rights – can help insulate the region from imported authoritarian technologies and regionally sponsored interference.

But above all, this moment demands democratic imagination. We must reject the assumption that technological advancement is synonymous with democratic progress. Electoral innovation must be evaluated not by its novelty or efficiency, but by its ability to deepen trust, widen access and protect the dignity of the voter. In an age when the vote risks becoming a transaction mediated by code, it is the ethic of participation – not the elegance of the algorithm – that must define South Asia's democratic future.

18

Democracy for Sale?: Tracking Political Finance in South Asia

The influence of money in politics remains one of the most formidable obstacles to the realization of a truly representative and effective democracy, both in long-established democratic systems and in emerging ones. In South Asia – a region of immense democratic vitality and stark socio-economic contrasts – the role of money in politics has become a central challenge to political integrity and public trust. From India's massive electoral machine to the fledgling democracies of Bhutan and the Maldives, political finance shapes who gets elected, whose voices are heard and what policies are prioritized. The growing entrenchment of political cartels and the criminalization of electoral competition have exacerbated concerns about the integrity of democratic governance itself.

Political finance is inextricably linked to the microdynamics of elections – shaping not only their outcomes but also the quality of choices available to voters, both before and after votes are cast. In an ideal democracy, electoral decisions should be determined by a candidate's competence and capacity to govern. However, growing financial pressures and vested interests are steadily undermining the integrity of electoral choices.

In South Asia, the challenge is not the absence of laws, but their selective application, weak enforcement and the overwhelming dominance of unregulated private capital. This chapter examines political finance across South Asia focusing on five key areas:

(i) Legal frameworks and campaign regulation;

(ii) Transparency and disclosure practices;
(iii) Enforcement and oversight mechanisms;
(iv) Influence of private and foreign money; and
(v) Public funding mechanisms and regional innovations.

While each South Asian country has its unique political history and institutional evolution, the region collectively faces common pressures: opaque funding channels, escalating campaign costs and weak enforcement of laws. Yet, promising reforms and regional innovations also offer hope.

The aim of this chapter is not merely to describe the state of political finance in the region but to advocate for a robust, transparent and equitable political finance architecture. By comparing systems, identifying best practices and highlighting critical vulnerabilities, I seek to contribute to a policy conversation urgently needed for safeguarding democracy in South Asia.

Moreover, to understand the global import of this theme, we only need look at a striking illustration of the money–power phenomenon in the Western context: the controversy surrounding the 2016 US presidential election. Allegations of foreign interference and concerns over financial opacity – including the unprecedented refusal of the elected president, Donald Trump, to disclose his tax returns – highlighted the extent to which financial and extraneous influences can undermine democratic norms.[1] Such developments serve as a stark reminder that the corrosive impact of money in politics is not confined to any one region, but that it is a pervasive challenge to democratic integrity worldwide.

The way elections are funded in a democratic country decides the channels of corruption and ultimately sets the agenda for governance. It is for this reason, for instance, that the issue of money in politics was identified as a top priority by the FEMBoSA in 2014. The result was the South Asia Regional Conference on the Use of Money in Politics and Its Effects on People's Representation, which produced the New Delhi Declaration on Political Finance Regulation in South Asia.

There are two important questions I wish to address: How do we make electoral and political financing more transparent and sustainable in the long run? Also, what mechanisms can be put in place to ensure that political financing, which is the mother of all corruption in South Asia, become more democratic with proper regulations?

Legal Frameworks and Campaign Regulation

Across South Asia, legal frameworks governing political finance share a common foundation in democratic aspirations but diverge markedly in their scope, coherence and enforceability. Despite constitutional commitments to free and fair elections, most countries in the region struggle to regulate the rising tide of money in politics. The region reveals a paradox: while laws exist to regulate campaign finance, their gaps, contradictions and weak implementation often render them ineffective. This has enabled unregulated spending and opened the door to undue influence from vested interests.

India, South Asia's largest democracy, offers a striking example of both regulatory complexity and legal innovation. The Representation of the People Act, 1951, imposes spending limits on candidates – currently ₹28 lakh to ₹95 crore depending on the state – but fails to regulate party expenditures or third-party spending comprehensively. Until recently, one of the most controversial instruments in India's political finance system was the electoral bonds scheme, introduced in 2017. These bearer instruments allowed individuals and corporations to make unlimited anonymous donations to political parties, circumventing existing transparency norms.

However, in a landmark judgment delivered in February 2024, the Supreme Court of India struck down the electoral bonds scheme as unconstitutional – citing its violation of citizens' right to information and the fundamental tenets of democratic accountability. The Court ordered the disclosure of all past bond transactions and reinforced the need for transparent political funding mechanisms. This decision marks a significant turning point in India's political finance trajectory, but it also exposes the deep regulatory vacuum that has allowed such schemes to flourish. The judgment now places the onus on the legislature and the ECI to formulate a new, transparent and equitable political finance regime – one that addresses not only donor anonymity, but also the unchecked expenditure and loopholes exploited by political parties.

Contrast this with Nepal, where the Election Commission Act and Political Parties Act impose caps on both candidate and party expenditures, and require financial reporting within thirty days of elections. On paper, Nepal's legal framework appears more comprehensive, with clear thresholds and mandatory disclosure requirements. Yet, the enforcement capacity remains limited, and parties routinely bypass caps through undeclared in-kind contributions and informal networks. Despite the 2015 constitution's commitment to democratic accountability, campaign finance regulation remains weakly institutionalized.

In Sri Lanka, the longstanding legal vacuum around campaign finance has begun to close. For decades, there were no enforceable limits on campaign spending, nor clear guidelines on political donations. That changed in early 2023, when Parliament enacted the Regulation of Election Expenditure Act, No. 3 of 2023, marking the country's first comprehensive legal framework governing campaign finance. The Act applies to local, provincial, parliamentary, and presidential elections, obliging candidates, political parties, and independent groups to comply with spending caps and mandatory post-election disclosure of donations and expenditures within 21 days of the poll.

For the 2024 presidential election, the Election Commission set a cap of Rs 109 per registered voter, translating to a total candidate expenditure limit of approximately Rs 1.86 billion (~USD 5–6 million). Ahead of the 2025 local-authority elections, expenditure ceilings were set between Rs 74 and Rs 160 per voter, depending on the local authority area.

However, critics underscore that despite this landmark legislation, enforcement remains weak. Civil society groups such as Transparency International Sri Lanka and monitoring bodies observe that institutional capacity for oversight is still limited, real-time monitoring is virtually absent, and sanctions for violations are underdeveloped. The Election Commission has formed a multi-stakeholder enforcement task force, but its efficacy and independence are still evolving.

Bangladesh's legal architecture, governed by the Representation of the People Order of 1972, imposes limits on campaign spending by candidates but excludes party expenditures. Recent amendments have sought to enhance financial disclosure requirements, but the process remains riddled with inconsistencies and a lack of verification. The absence of independent audit mechanisms and the concentration of power within the ruling party further weaken the efficacy of existing laws.

Pakistan's legal framework is similarly constrained. The Elections Act, 2017, replaced several older statutes, and set campaign spending limits and disclosure obligations. However, political parties can spend unlimited amounts and there is no effective control over sources of party finance. Although the law mandates the disclosure of donations above PKR 10,000 and the publishing of annual reports, there is little evidence that these disclosures are verified or publicly accessible. The lack of regulation on third-party financing, including religious or business interest groups, further exposes the system to manipulation.

Smaller democracies in the region, such as Bhutan and the Maldives, offer relatively more robust models in some respects. Bhutan's Election Act of 2008, for instance, sets strict public funding mechanisms, bans corporate donations, and limits campaign periods and expenses. All candidates receive equal public funding and the law restricts media use, ensuring a more equitable electoral environment. Similarly, the Maldives imposes donation caps and reporting obligations, although enforcement remains a challenge. Their small-scale democracies have allowed more centralized regulation, but they are not immune to external influence and informal financing channels.

Before the Taliban takeover, Afghanistan had limited but evolving political finance regulations. The 2004 and 2005 elections saw spending limits and record-keeping rules, though enforcement mechanisms were absent. In 2014, the Independent Election Commission issued more structured regulations, detailing expense caps, donor eligibility and record maintenance. Article 68 of the Electoral Law criminalized funding from illegal sources. However, in December 2021, the Taliban dissolved the Independent Election Commission and Electoral Complaint Commission, suspending formal elections. While electoral processes have ceased, financial power remains influential in governance – shaping political dynamics even in the absence of democratic mechanisms. Wealthy actors continue to exert significant control over political outcomes, although now outside the framework of regulated elections.

Collectively, South Asia reveals a fragmented legal landscape. Countries like Bhutan offer promise through stringent laws and limited party systems, while India, Pakistan and Bangladesh expose the dangers of legal loopholes in large, competitive democracies. The absence of uniform party-level expenditure regulations, the presence of loopholes allowing anonymous donations and weak enforcement mechanisms are common threads across the region.

Reform, therefore, must prioritize harmonizing candidate and party-level regulations, closing anonymity loopholes, and ensuring the independence of electoral commissions. Legal frameworks should evolve not as isolated technical fixes but as parts of a comprehensive political finance reform agenda – one that guarantees fair competition and protects democratic integrity across South Asia.

Transparency and Disclosure Practices

Transparency is the cornerstone of any democratic political finance regime. Without clear and accessible information about who funds political actors and how much is spent, citizens cannot make informed electoral choices, nor can institutions hold power to account. In South Asia, however, transparency in political finance remains deeply flawed. Despite legal mandates for disclosure in many countries, these are often poorly implemented, selectively enforced or rendered meaningless by loopholes that allow large-scale opacity in donations and expenditures.

India provides a revealing example of the tensions between legal obligations and actual practice. Political parties are required to disclose donations above ₹20,000 under Section 29C of the Representation of the People Act.[2] They must also submit annual audit reports to the ECI. However, until recently, a substantial share of political finance occurred outside this framework – particularly through the now-defunct electoral bonds, which allowed unlimited anonymous donations.

As mentioned previously, the Supreme Court's 2024 judgment striking down the scheme recognized that the anonymity it conferred fundamentally violated the citizen's right to information. Although this ruling strengthens the case for financial transparency, much ground remains to be covered. Parties routinely under-report expenditures and mask donors through shell entities, and there is no independent auditing of the reports submitted. Moreover, the ECI lacks the statutory authority to compel compliance or penalize violations – reducing the efficacy of existing disclosure norms.

In contrast, Bhutan and Nepal impose relatively stringent disclosure requirements, particularly for candidates. Bhutan's Election Act mandates the declaration of income, assets and liabilities by candidates and their spouses. The country's political parties are small in scale and operate under a strict regulatory regime, with state funding tied to compliance. Bhutan's Election Commission actively monitors reports and is empowered to reject non-compliant submissions. As mentioned earlier, Nepal, too, requires candidates and parties to submit detailed accounts of campaign income and expenditure within thirty days after an election. These are to be made public by the Election Commission of Nepal. However, the implementation remains uneven. Parties often fail to meet deadlines and reports are rarely audited for accuracy. The limited digital infrastructure and lack of trained auditors in the Commission further impede effective oversight.

Bangladesh's disclosure laws, under the Representation of the People Order, require candidates to file detailed affidavits about their income, expenditure and criminal antecedents. Political parties must submit audited financial statements and list donors contributing over Tk 5,000. While these rules seem rigorous, their enforcement is highly selective. Reports are often submitted late or not at all, and the Election Commission of Bangladesh lacks both the autonomy and institutional capacity to ensure compliance. Moreover, there is no central digital database to facilitate public access to the submitted documents. This severely limits the role of civil society and media in scrutinizing political finance.

Pakistan, too, mandates the submission of annual financial statements by political parties, detailing income, expenditure and sources of funds. The Elections Act, 2017, requires the ECP to publish these statements. However, in practice, these disclosures are often minimalistic and lack specificity. Parties frequently declare lump-sum amounts without identifying donors or detailing the nature of expenditures. The ECP has published some party accounts online, but the data is not standardized or machine-readable, and there are no meaningful audits to verify the authenticity of the reports. Notably, recent investigations have revealed substantial undeclared foreign and domestic donations to major parties, exposing serious regulatory gaps.[3]

Sri Lanka, long criticized for its absence of formal political finance laws, only began to address transparency in earnest with the 2023 campaign finance law, as mentioned earlier. The new framework mandates disclosures of campaign donations and expenses, both during and after the campaign. While this represents a positive shift, the infrastructure for implementation is still being developed. There remains a lack of clarity about the thresholds for disclosure, the timing of the reports and the sanctions for non-compliance. Moreover, questions about the independence and resourcing of the Election Commission of Sri Lanka cast doubt on whether the new law will bring about meaningful change.

The Maldives requires political parties to maintain accounts and submit financial statements to the Election Commission, and contributions above Rf 10,000 must be disclosed. The law prohibits anonymous donations and requires donor details to be made available for public scrutiny. However, the regulatory capacity of the Maldivian Election Commission is limited, and the small scale of the political landscape often leads to informal financing arrangements that bypass formal reporting.

What emerges from this comparative landscape is a consistent pattern of partial transparency – where legal obligations exist but are often undermined by poor institutional capacity, weak enforcement and political interference. Even where disclosure norms are clear on paper – such as in Nepal, Bhutan or the Maldives – the lack of independent audits and real-time public access to data severely blunts their impact. In larger democracies like India, Pakistan and Bangladesh, legal loopholes, informal financing and inadequate institutional oversight create an environment of opacity that erodes public trust and enables systemic corruption.

Reform efforts in South Asia must therefore move beyond merely requiring disclosure to ensuring meaningful transparency. This includes mandating digital, real-time reporting of donations and expenditures; establishing independent and well-resourced auditing bodies; and making all financial data publicly accessible in standardized formats. Transparency is not a technical exercise – it is a democratic imperative.

Without it, the integrity of elections and the accountability of governments will remain perilously compromised across the region.

Enforcement and Oversight Mechanisms

While legal frameworks and disclosure mandates form the scaffolding of political finance regulation, their efficacy depends entirely on the strength and independence of enforcement mechanisms. Across South Asia, enforcement is the weakest link in the political finance chain. Oversight institutions often lack legal authority, financial autonomy and political independence. Moreover, enforcement practices are frequently selective, delayed or altogether absent. The resulting impunity not only erodes public trust but also renders regulatory norms hollow – allowing moneyed interests to operate with little fear of consequence.

The ECI is arguably the most prominent electoral authority in the region. It is constitutionally established, widely respected and administratively sophisticated. Yet, in the domain of political finance enforcement, it is severely handicapped. The ECI does not have the power to audit party accounts or to penalize parties for failing to disclose financial data accurately or in a timely manner. Nor can it regulate party expenditures or investigate unaccounted donations, unless referred by another authority. Although the ECI can issue notices and warnings, these lack the teeth of statutory sanction.

Recent episodes – such as the controversy over electoral bonds or persistent under-reporting by major parties – have revealed the Commission's limited ability to compel transparency or accountability. Critics argue that despite being institutionally robust, the ECI has increasingly refrained from assertive interventions – raising questions about its independence under political pressure.

The ECP fares no better in terms of enforcement. Legally empowered under the Elections Act, 2017, to receive and publish party financial statements, the ECP has little capacity to verify their accuracy. Although it may issue notices or request clarification, it rarely conducts forensic audits or launches independent investigations. This weakness was starkly exposed in the 'foreign funding case', where Imran Khan's PTI was found to have received undisclosed contributions from abroad over several years.

While the ECP finally issued a ruling, it came after inordinate delays and significant political controversy – demonstrating both procedural fragility and susceptibility to politicization.[4]

In Bangladesh, the Election Commission is plagued by structural and political weaknesses. Its legal mandate includes monitoring campaign spending, verifying disclosures and referring violations to the judiciary. However, enforcement is often viewed as partisan, especially during elections. Reports of delayed responses to spending violations, leniency towards the ruling party and a failure to prosecute egregious breaches have undermined its credibility. Even when candidates exceed expenditure limits or fail to file complete reports, sanctions are rarely imposed. Civil society and election observers have consistently highlighted the Commission's lack of independence, and the chilling effect this has on regulatory enforcement.

Nepal's Election Commission, while generally considered less politicized, remains institutionally underpowered. Although empowered to set expenditure limits and require financial disclosures, it lacks a dedicated enforcement wing or financial auditing capacity. The Commission typically accepts self-reported data from candidates and parties without verification. In the 2022 elections, several parties missed deadlines for submitting expense reports, yet faced no penalties. Moreover, its enforcement is reactive rather than proactive – largely dependent on complaints rather than systemic monitoring.

Sri Lanka offers a more optimistic case – at least in intent. With the 2023 introduction of a campaign finance law (as mentioned earlier), new enforcement provisions were created, granting the Election Commission authority to investigate violations and recommend disqualification or fines. However, the actual enforcement architecture is still under development. A multi-stakeholder task force has been established, but the Commission currently lacks capacity for real-time verification or standardized digital disclosures. Given past criticisms of institutional weakness and executive influence, the success of this enforcement regime will hinge on political will and administrative reform.

Bhutan and the Maldives, due to their relatively small political systems, exhibit more centralized enforcement mechanisms. Bhutan's Election Commission has the legal authority to reject candidates and political parties that fail to comply with finance regulations. Its active monitoring during campaign periods, combined with a high degree of public trust, allows it to enforce rules with more consistency than its regional peers. In the Maldives, enforcement has historically been uneven but the Election Commission has shown willingness to disqualify candidates who breach financial rules, although this is complicated by frequent political turnover and legal appeals.

Across the region, three major enforcement deficits are evident: lack of independent investigative capacity, absence of credible sanctions and political capture of oversight bodies. Without the ability to audit, subpoena or penalize effectively, electoral commissions operate more as passive record-keepers than as guardians of democratic finance. In many cases, the institutional design itself ensures failure – commissions are underfunded, appointments are politicized and their decisions are subject to executive pressure or judicial reversal.

To address these gaps, South Asia urgently needs to strengthen the autonomy and legal powers of its electoral commissions by granting them investigative authority, protected budgets and judicially enforceable powers to impose sanctions. Independent auditing bodies must also be integrated into the oversight process. Furthermore, civil society and media organizations must be empowered through access to data and legal protections, enabling them to function as complementary watchdogs.

Enforcement is not simply a technical issue – it is a test of political will. Without credible oversight, even the most elegant political finance laws will remain paper tigers. Strengthening enforcement in South Asia is not just a governance imperative, but essential for restoring democratic legitimacy in a region where the credibility of electoral processes hangs increasingly in the balance.

Influence of Private and Foreign Money

In every country of the region, private wealth – often sourced from opaque networks of corporations, contractors and political patrons – plays an outsized role in shaping electoral outcomes. Equally troubling is the porousness of legal regimes intended to guard against foreign influence.

In most South Asian countries, the line between domestic and external political financing remains blurred – enabling external actors and business lobbies to exert undue influence over political agendas and public policy. India provides perhaps the most visible example of the concentration of private wealth in electoral politics. The explosion of campaign finance over the past decade has turned elections into high-stakes, high-cost contests, increasingly reliant on corporate donations. Although corporate donations were permitted under the Companies Act, the 2013 amendment capped them at 7.5 per cent of net profits and mandated disclosures. However, this was overturned by subsequent legislation accompanying the introduction of the electoral bonds scheme, which removed caps and allowed anonymous corporate contributions.

As mentioned earlier, this scheme has now been struck down by the Supreme Court, but the years during which it operated witnessed a massive influx of corporate money into party coffers – predominantly benefiting the ruling BJP. Even outside of formal channels, the role of business conglomerates in funding campaigns, advertisements and third-party advocacy remains a core concern. The lack of caps on party expenditure, coupled with the absence of donor transparency, leaves India's political finance system especially vulnerable to elite capture.

In Pakistan, private and foreign money have long shaped political competition, often operating in the shadows. Although donations from foreign nationals or companies are prohibited under the Elections Act, 2017, enforcement is minimal. A high-profile example emerged in the PTI foreign funding case, as mentioned earlier, where the ECP found that millions of dollars were funnelled into party accounts from overseas entities and individuals. While the ECP's eventual ruling in 2022 acknowledged violations, the process was prolonged and its consequences muted – underscoring both the scale of the problem and the frailty of enforcement. Domestically, business groups and real estate lobbies continue to finance political parties informally, often in exchange for regulatory favours or development contracts.

In Bangladesh, despite the formal ban on foreign contributions under the Representation of the People Order and existing anti-corruption laws, reports suggest that some money is routed informally through diaspora networks or business associates abroad.[5] More significantly, campaign financing by construction companies, garment industry magnates and other business interests creates informal dependencies between elected officials and financiers. This has a corrosive effect on policymaking, favouring vested economic interests over public welfare. The widespread use of black money in elections – acknowledged by the Election Commission itself – further undermines transparency and democratic competitiveness.[6]

Sri Lanka presents a slightly different pattern. For many years, the absence of legal limits on donations or campaign spending meant that private interests operated unchecked. The campaign finance law of 2023 aims to change this by capping donations and requiring disclosures. However, the impact of decades of unregulated private funding is still evident in political patronage networks and party financing structures. There have also been allegations of financial influence from diaspora sources, particularly during the civil war and post-war reconstruction period, although comprehensive data remains scarce.[7]

In Nepal, foreign money has traditionally entered political finance in more indirect forms – through NGOs, faith-based organizations or donor-linked development networks that have informal linkages to political actors. While the Political Parties Act prohibits foreign funding, enforcement is minimal. Private domestic financing, especially from contractors and local businesses, dominates campaign expenditures. The growing cost of elections – particularly in federal and provincial contests – has made candidates increasingly dependent on business patrons, which further risks transforming elections into elite transactions rather than participatory processes.

The Maldives and Bhutan exhibit lower risks from private or foreign money due to their more centralized and regulated systems. In Bhutan, the constitution bans corporate and foreign donations, and political parties are largely state-funded. Bhutan's strict media and campaign controls further limit the influence of private wealth. In the Maldives, the law similarly prohibits foreign donations and caps private contributions. However, enforcement challenges remain. In recent years, there have been sporadic concerns about funding from tourism-linked business interests and influence from foreign governments through indirect channels, including investment-driven lobbying.

Afghanistan, prior to the Taliban's return, was widely recognized as a case where political finance was deeply entangled with foreign and illicit sources. During the democratic interlude, political campaigns often relied on funding from foreign governments, international NGOs and regional actors. The absence of a stable regulatory framework made it nearly impossible to distinguish legitimate domestic support from foreign patronage. Today, under Taliban rule, formal political finance regulation is non-existent and the concept of electoral competition itself has been dismantled.

The comparative picture is clear: across South Asia, private wealth dominates political finance, while foreign funding – though often banned – seeps in through loopholes, informal networks and offshore structures. Laws either lack specificity, suffer from broad exemptions or remain unenforced. Political actors routinely exploit regulatory ambiguity to channel unaccounted funds into campaigns, often in exchange for post-election benefits ranging from policy influence to government contracts.

Addressing this challenge demands bold reform. First, donation caps must be meaningfully imposed and extended to party-level contributions, not just candidates. Second, corporate donations should be subject to strict disclosure norms and independent audits. Third, foreign contributions must be monitored by both electoral and financial intelligence agencies, with real-time data-sharing and sanctions for violations. Finally, political parties should be required to publish itemized donor lists and audited annual reports to enable independent scrutiny by civil society, media and voters.

Unchecked private and foreign money distorts electoral competition, entrenches inequality and skews public policy in favour of wealth over popular will. For South Asia's democracies to survive and thrive, they must insulate their political finance regimes from the corrosive influence of unregulated money, both domestic and foreign.

Public Funding Mechanisms and Innovations

Public funding of political parties and election campaigns is often hailed as a democratic equalizer – a way to curb the disproportionate influence of private wealth and ensure a level playing field. However, in South

Asia, public funding remains either underutilized or poorly designed. While a few countries have experimented with direct subsidies, most rely on weak, indirect support mechanisms. Moreover, innovative practices to enhance transparency or curb spending (where they exist) are often isolated and lack regional integration. A meaningful reform agenda must not only expand public funding but also root it in principles of fairness, accountability and democratic participation.

India stands at an uneasy crossroads. Despite being the world's largest democracy, with astronomical election costs, it does not offer direct public funding to political parties. Instead, parties benefit from indirect subsidies, such as tax exemptions under Section 13A of the Income Tax Act and free airtime on state media during elections. However, these measures are modest relative to campaign expenditures, and do little to reduce dependence on private donors. Calls for public funding have resurfaced after the electoral bonds controversy, with reform advocates arguing that limited public subsidies – conditional on transparency and performance – could reduce opacity and corruption. However, political will has been lacking, and successive governments have failed to operationalize a coherent model for direct state support.

In contrast, Bhutan has implemented one of the most comprehensive public funding systems in the region. The Election Act of 2008 provides equal public funding to eligible political parties for campaign activities. Corporate donations are banned and private donations are strictly limited. All campaign materials are publicly financed and the use of state media is regulated to ensure equal access. Bhutan's model not only curtails the influence of money in politics but also fosters issue-based campaigning. Its success is partly due to the country's small electorate and centralized electoral machinery, but the principle of equity through public funding remains a replicable innovation in the region.

The Maldives also provides public funding to registered political parties, in proportion to their parliamentary representation, although these subsidies are modest and inconsistently distributed. Moreover, the accountability mechanisms for how public funds are spent are weak and there is little public oversight. Nevertheless, the Maldivian model represents an attempt to institutionalize public support based on electoral performance – a principle that could be refined and expanded.

Nepal provides some public support through subsidized media coverage and logistical assistance during elections. However, direct financial subsidies to parties remain limited, and the increasing cost of campaigning has led to growing reliance on private donors and contractors. There have been proposals to introduce performance-based funding – tied to vote share or representation – but these have yet to be implemented due to political fragmentation and budgetary constraints.

Sri Lanka, historically devoid of campaign finance regulation, took a decisive step forward with its 2023 campaign finance law, which also includes provisions for publicly funded voter education and access to state media. However, there is still no direct public funding to political parties. The potential exists for Sri Lanka to introduce a hybrid model – combining state subsidies with robust financial disclosure – but this would require sustained political commitment and administrative reform.

Pakistan does not offer direct public funding to political parties. The ECP provides some support in the form of voter awareness and logistical assistance, but no structured subsidy exists for campaigns. Parties are left to raise their own funds, and the lack of transparency exacerbates the risks of clientelism and elite capture. Reform proposals have been floated, including state matching of small donations or support to parties based on electoral performance, but these remain politically contentious and have not advanced.

Bangladesh similarly does not provide direct financial assistance to political parties. Although the use of state-owned media during campaigns is regulated to some extent, there is no formal system of public subsidies. Given the scale of campaign financing by private actors – often unaccounted – public funding has been advocated by reform commissions as a way to curb black money and foster clean politics. However, partisan polarization has stymied progress.

Afghanistan, during its democratic phase, never developed a functional system of public funding. International donors often filled this void by financing election-related infrastructure and civic education programmes. While this donor-led model provided some relief from private financing, it created dependencies and lacked long-term sustainability. In the current political context, with the collapse of electoral institutions, public funding is no longer relevant.

Despite the overall weakness of public funding regimes in South Asia, a few regional innovations offer important lessons. For instance, Bhutan's full public funding model demonstrates that, with strong institutions and clear rules, equitable and transparent elections are possible. India's use of tax exemptions and subsidized airtime, although inadequate, shows how indirect benefits can be scaled and linked to compliance. The Maldives' proportional funding formula, though modest, introduces a performance-based principle that can be built upon. Sri Lanka's campaign finance law, if followed by funding reforms, could initiate a more balanced financing model. What is missing is a regional dialogue or institutional cooperation to identify, scale and adapt these innovations across borders.

A reinvigorated political finance agenda in South Asia must place public funding at its core. But public subsidies must not become blank cheques. They should be tied to stringent conditions, such as: full financial disclosure, gender representation, internal party democracy and compliance with expenditure limits. Moreover, such funding should be complemented by civic education and watchdog mechanisms to build public trust.

Ultimately, public funding is not merely about money – it is about equalizing voice and access in political life. In a region where wealth disparities and patronage politics distort democratic participation, a well-designed public funding regime is not just desirable but necessary. South Asia's democratic resilience in the coming decades will depend, in part, on whether it can replace money power with public trust as the true currency of politics.

Bridging the Gap between Reform and Reality

Political finance in South Asia is not just a technical or legal issue – it is a litmus test for democratic integrity. While the region boasts some of the most electorally active societies in the world, the financing of politics continues to be dominated by opacity, inequality and impunity. This chapter has examined five critical pillars of political finance – legal frameworks, transparency, enforcement, foreign and private influence, and public funding – across eight South Asian countries. A comparative lens reveals a shared pattern: legal provisions exist, but they are fragmented, under-enforced, and frequently subverted by political and financial elites.

The lack of concrete regulations has had measurable consequences. In India, the 2019 general elections cost over $8.6 billion, surpassing the spending in the 2016 US elections, according to the Centre for Media Studies.[8] A staggering 60 per cent of this was estimated to be in unaccounted or black money. The now-struck-down electoral bonds scheme alone facilitated over ₹12,000 crore in anonymous political donations between 2018 and 2023, with 55 per cent going to the ruling BJP, according to publicly released SBI data, following the Supreme Court's 2024 judgment.[9]

In Pakistan, the PTI's foreign funding case revealed years of undisclosed contributions from overseas sources – including companies based in the US, UAE and Australia – which were not only illegal under Pakistani law but also unreported. This case, investigated since 2014 and ruled on only in 2022, underscores how foreign influence quietly distorts national politics.

In Bangladesh, while the official campaign spending limit is Tk 25 lakh (approximately $25,000), unofficial estimates by election monitors suggest candidates regularly spend up to Tk 2–3 crore ($200,000–300,000), mostly in cash and often untraceable. Similar patterns of under-reporting, shadow financing and unregulated private funding persist in Nepal and Sri Lanka as well.[10]

Nevertheless, the region also holds valuable lessons. As discussed earlier, Bhutan stands out as a success story with its fully state-funded elections, strict ban on corporate and foreign donations, and transparent public auditing mechanisms. Its small size and centralized institutions have helped with compliance, but the principles behind its model are scalable. The Maldives, while still struggling with oversight, offers a promising model of performance-based public funding tied to parliamentary representation – an approach that could be adapted across the region.

Looking back over time, South Asia has swung between reformist intent and political inertia. India banned corporate donations in 1969, only to reverse course in the 1980s and accelerate opacity in the 2010s. Sri Lanka waited seventy-five years after independence to introduce a formal campaign finance law. Bangladesh and Pakistan have reformed disclosure requirements repeatedly, but without independent audits or enforcement. Across the region, policy reports, civil society petitions and court rulings have all called for comprehensive reform – yet systemic change remains elusive.

This historical drift must now be reversed. Political finance reform in South Asia must rest on five non-negotiable pillars:

- **Robust legal frameworks** that regulate not just candidates but also parties, third parties and media expenditures
- **Mandatory, real-time financial disclosure**, with digital public access and independent audits of all political contributions and expenditures
- **Empowered and autonomous election commissions** with investigative and sanctioning powers, legally shielded from executive interference
- **Strict monitoring and prosecution of foreign and corporate funding violations**, through cross-border cooperation and financial intelligence sharing
- **Targeted public funding**, tied to compliance, representation and internal party democracy – not as charity, but as investment in democratic equity

Additionally, South Asia must embrace regional learning. A regional forum on political finance – involving electoral commissions, civil society and researchers – could promote best practices, track cross-border risks and push for harmonized reforms.

Ultimately, the struggle over political finance is a struggle over whose voices matter in democracy. As long as political parties are sustained by opaque money, campaign finance will remain a tool of exclusion rather than participation. For South Asian democracies to deepen, they must ensure that elections are not determined by wealth but by will – the will of the people, freely expressed, transparently funded and meaningfully enforced. To rebuild public trust and democratic legitimacy, South Asia must replace opacity with openness, privilege with parity and influence with integrity.

19

Behind Closed Doors: Internal Democracy in Political Parties

In the great theatre of democratic life, political parties are expected to play the role of the foundational actors – mobilizing citizens, articulating policy visions, mediating between state and society, and nurturing leadership. Yet, in South Asia – where electoral democracy has deepened and expanded over the past decades – the paradox remains that the very institutions entrusted with sustaining democratic governance often function in fundamentally undemocratic ways internally. Nowhere is this tension more stark than in the domain of inner-party democracy – a dimension of political life that is both structurally neglected and strategically undermined by dominant party elites.

The internal structures of political parties across South Asia, from Afghanistan to the Maldives, often operate more like dynastic courts or oligarchic coalitions than deliberative democratic bodies. Despite their centrality to democratic functioning – fielding candidates, framing policies and shaping parliamentary majorities – parties in the region are frequently marked by opaque decision-making, top-down control, cults of personality, absence of internal elections and minimal institutional checks on leadership. This absence of robust internal democracy has far-reaching consequences: it narrows the space for dissent, undermines accountability, depletes the ideological coherence of parties and fosters a culture of sycophancy over meritocracy.

The problem is not merely cultural or historical, as is often argued, but institutional and systemic. The weakness of legal enforcement mechanisms, the reluctance of election commissions to scrutinize party functioning and the absence of binding democratic norms within party constitutions together create a permissive environment in which intraparty autocracy flourishes. Even in countries where the formal architecture of democracy is relatively strong – such as India or Sri Lanka – the internal democratic deficit within parties leads to pathologies that reverberate across the political system: electoral violence, exclusionary patronage, erosion of party discipline and a stagnation of political renewal.

Indeed, the state of inner-party democracy is inextricably linked with the broader quality of democratic governance. When parties fail to democratize internally, they stifle emerging leadership, block ideological innovation and cement the grip of entrenched elites. This contributes not only to voter alienation but to broader patterns of state dysfunction, including executive overreach, policy inconsistency and the weakening of legislative oversight. Moreover, the crisis of internal democracy exacerbates social inequalities: by privileging elite families, caste and ethnic blocs, or urban clienteles, parties often replicate (and sometimes exacerbate) the very exclusions they claim to challenge.

This chapter draws attention to four major themes that seek to provide a holistic analysis of the region of South Asia. First, we analyse the foundational architecture of party organization – tracing how hyper centralization, charisma and informal authority dominate over constitutional norms. Second, we interrogate the processes of candidate selection and dynastic entrenchment, focusing on how internal gatekeeping limits genuine political competition. Third, we consider the question of intraparty elections and factionalism, showing how token elections, patronage networks and internal repression shape party dynamics. Finally, we assess the regulatory role of the state and election commissions, identifying the limited and often selective enforcement of internal democratic norms.

We draw upon empirical data, party constitutions, election commission reports and scholarly analyses to demonstrate how inner-party democracy remains the Achilles' heel of democratic consolidation in the region.

To be sure, there are exceptions and moments of democratic experimentation – the internal primaries in Nepal's major parties, Bhutan's constitutionally guided party registration norms and recent judicial interventions in Pakistan – which offer glimpses of possibility. But these remain fragile and fragmented, often overwhelmed by structural inertia and elite resistance. If democracy in South Asia is to deepen, rather than hollow out, the time has come to focus not merely on elections, institutions and reforms from above – but on the democratization of the parties themselves, behind their often impenetrable closed doors.

The Architecture of Political Parties

At the heart of South Asia's democratic contradictions lies the paradox of political parties that are institutionally indispensable, yet internally unaccountable. The architecture of party organization across the region reveals a systemic bias towards hyper centralization, charismatic authority and a pervasive neglect of formalized internal checks. This foundational design flaw – where personalistic control supplants procedural norms – has produced parties that resemble vertically structured command organizations more than participatory democratic associations. Across all the SAARC nations, internal centralization has become both a cause and consequence of democratic stagnation.

In nearly every South Asian country, the party high command – not its general body or elected councils – determines critical decisions: candidate nominations, leadership transitions, coalition alignments and even constitutional amendments to party rules. The Indian National Congress exemplifies this model, where authority has long been concentrated in the hands of the Nehru–Gandhi family. Although India is formally a multiparty democracy, with functioning electoral institutions, the internal functioning of its major national and regional parties – whether the Congress, the BJP or regional powerhouses like the Dravida Munnetra Kazhagam, the Telugu Desam Party and the Trinamool Congress (TMC) – is overwhelmingly centralized. While the BJP has a more elabourate formal structure with cells and councils, real power resides in an informal nexus between the PM, the party president and the ideological leadership of the RSS.

This centralization is not a uniquely Indian phenomenon. In Sri Lanka, the Sri Lanka Freedom Party (SLFP) and the United National

Party (UNP) have historically been dominated by powerful families or charismatic leaders, with few meaningful intraparty elections or debates. In Pakistan, party structure often serves as a veneer for familial or military-brokered control. The PML's various incarnations – whether PML-N or PML-Q – are also widely acknowledged to be personalized political vehicles rather than properly institutionalized parties. Even the PTI, which initially campaigned on democratic reforms, quickly devolved into a top-down formation, where Imran Khan's personal authority became unchallengeable.

Bangladesh mirrors these dynamics with stark clarity. The ruling BAL and its rival, the BNP, are effectively built around dynastic leaderships – Sheikh Hasina and Khaleda Zia respectively– whose hold over their respective parties remains unchallenged. Formal party structures exist but are frequently bypassed through ad hoc committees, parallel secretariats and loyalist appointments. Decisions of major consequence are often made by the supreme leader and communicated downward through informal channels, rendering internal deliberations a symbolic exercise rather than a substantive one.

Nepal offers an instructive, if limited, counterpoint. Major political parties such as the NC and the CPN (UML) do have more developed internal structures, including central working committees and elected leadership bodies. Nevertheless, factional control and negotiated power-sharing arrangements often undermine democratic functioning. Leadership contests are rarely open-ended exercises in internal debate. They are frequently pre-negotiated between factions, with ideological positions taking a back seat to tactical alliances. While party constitutions in Nepal are formally detailed, their operationalization is partial at best, revealing once again the gap between institutional design and political practice.

Even in Bhutan and the Maldives – two countries with smaller party systems – centralization is an entrenched feature. Bhutan's constitution mandates a strict regulatory framework for parties, allowing only a limited number of national-level parties. While this has helped curtail fragmentation, it has also restricted the possibility for internal diversity. Leadership within these parties tends to be heavily centralized, with founding leaders wielding disproportionate influence. In the Maldives, where democracy remains fragile and periodically interrupted, party organization remains rudimentary – often functioning more as vehicles for electoral mobilization than as structured institutions of internal debate or governance.

The absence of enforced internal constitutions is a recurrent feature. While most parties formally possess constitutions that promise internal elections, decision-making bodies and codes of conduct, these documents are often treated as nominal instruments rather than governing frameworks. The lack of internal judicial mechanisms or ethics committees compounds the problem. With no credible enforcement of internal norms, violations go unchecked and dissenting voices are frequently purged or sidelined. Across the region, this contributes to a democratic culture in which compliance is valued over critique, and loyalty is rewarded more than leadership.

The centralization of party organization has far-reaching implications for democratic governance. First, it reduces the pool of leadership to a narrow elite, often aligned along dynastic, ethnic or ideological lines, thereby diminishing representational diversity. Second, it disconnects party leadership from grassroots cadres, hollowing out internal feedback loops and policy responsiveness. Last, it fosters a culture of sycophancy and silence, where internal dissent is viewed not as healthy contestation but as betrayal. The result is a brittle party ecosystem that lacks internal adaptability and external credibility.

Perhaps most troubling is the way this internal architecture shapes broader democratic institutions. Parties that are autocratic within are unlikely to respect democratic norms in government. Leaders unaccountable to their own membership are even less likely to be accountable to citizens. The absence of deliberation within parties reflects in the erosion of legislative debate, the weakening of institutional checks and the normalization of majoritarian or populist politics. In this sense, the architecture of internal party organization is not a peripheral matter – it lies at the very core of South Asia's democratic deficit.

Candidate Selection and Dynastic Control

Nowhere is the democratic deficit within South Asian political parties more visible than in the process of candidate selection – a crucial gateway that determines who gets to contest elections, represent constituencies and shape legislative agendas. While formal democratic procedures often govern the conduct of general elections, the internal mechanisms through which parties decide who will run for office are typically opaque, exclusionary and hierarchical. The concentration of nomination powers in the hands of party elites – often a single individual or an inner circle – has entrenched a model of political recruitment that privileges loyalty, lineage and access over merit, representation or grassroots legitimacy.

Across the SAARC region, the selection of candidates is rarely a bottom-up process mediated through open primaries, party congresses or deliberative forums. Instead, it is frequently controlled by central leadership bodies or charismatic supremos, often operating outside of formal institutional constraints. In India, the sheer scale of its democracy might suggest a robust system of candidate vetting, but in reality, party tickets – especially in the major national and regional parties – are doled out through informal negotiations, factional horse-trading and personal recommendation. While the ECI regulates campaign conduct, it has no jurisdiction over internal nomination processes, leaving this critical arena largely untouched by institutional oversight.

The dominance of dynastic politics in candidate selection further compounds the problem. South Asia hosts one of the highest concentrations of dynastic politicians in the democratic world. In India's 18th Lok Sabha (2024), nearly 32 per cent of MPs had family members in politics.[1] This proportion is even higher among younger MPs, where political lineage appears to have become a precondition rather than an incidental advantage. Similar patterns are evident in Pakistan, where the Bhutto–Zardari and Sharif families continue to dominate the PPP and the PML-N respectively. In Bangladesh, the alternating rule of the BAL and the BNP has been mediated through the enduring rivalry between the Sheikh and Zia families, as mentioned earlier, each of whom exercises disproportionate control over candidate selection within their respective parties.

Nepal, while offering a more pluralistic field, is no exception. Despite formal leadership contests in parties like the NC and the CPN-UML, electoral nominations are tightly negotiated among elite factions, with prominent families maintaining generational strongholds over key constituencies. In Sri Lanka, dynastic networks extend deep into local politics, with multiple generations of the Bandaranaike and Rajapaksa families holding simultaneous ministerial and legislative offices. These dynastic concentrations not only monopolize access to political power but often control local patronage networks, effectively marginalizing aspiring candidates from non-elite or underrepresented backgrounds.

The implications for representation are profound. By narrowing the gate to candidacy, dynasticism constrains political diversity and reinforces structural inequalities along lines of caste, class, gender and geography. Women, youth, religious minorities and lower-caste individuals are often under-represented, not merely due to social prejudice but because they lack access to the intraparty networks that determine nominations. In Pakistan and Bangladesh, tokenism has become a substitute for genuine inclusion – women are nominated to reserved seats or given unwinnable constituencies, while real power remains concentrated among male elites. In India, despite the constitutional reservation of seats for Scheduled Castes and Scheduled Tribes, major parties often nominate pliant candidates with minimal autonomy, further entrenching vertical control.

This crisis of representation is not simply a matter of fairness – it directly affects the quality of governance. When political aspirants are selected based on lineage or loyalty, rather than public engagement or policy capacity, the result is a legislature populated by individuals with weak incentives to perform and minimal accountability to the electorate. Moreover, dynastic candidates often view office as a family inheritance, fostering a culture of entitlement rather than service. This has concrete governance consequences: a weakened legislature, hollowed-out debates and a public administration system increasingly captured by clientelist interests rather than developmental priorities.

Attempts at reform have emerged in scattered instances. The Aam Aadmi Party (AAP) in India introduced internal mechanisms to crowdsource candidate nominations, and the PTI initially held internal elections, though both have since regressed towards centralization. In Nepal, the periodic contestation within major parties over nominations has at least opened the space for intraparty bargaining. Bhutan's strict party registration criteria, while limiting the total number of parties, has forced them to develop a degree of institutional coherence. However, these instances remain outliers rather than trends – and are often reversed when parties attain power.

It is important to underscore that dynasticism in South Asia is not merely a cultural residue – it is a rational outcome of weak party institutionalization, high electoral costs and a fragmented public sphere. In the absence of strong party ideologies or mass membership systems, personal reputation and family name often become the default currency of political credibility. Moreover, electoral financing systems that privilege wealthy patrons over accountable institutions further entrench the role of elite families, who can mobilize both funds and followers with relative ease.

To mitigate this democratic erosion, there is a pressing need for structural interventions that democratize candidate selection. This includes mandating internal nomination procedures through party laws, encouraging open primaries or constituency-level consultations, and expanding financial and logistical support for first-time candidates from marginalized communities. Equally important is the role of electoral commissions and civil society watchdogs in auditing nomination processes and making internal party data public. Only by democratizing the gateway to representation can South Asian democracies hope to make the promise of political equality more than a constitutional ideal.

Intraparty Elections

If general elections are the cornerstone of democratic legitimacy at the national level, then intraparty elections ought to serve a similar function within political parties. However, in South Asia, internal elections are either entirely absent, sporadically conducted or cynically manipulated to validate predetermined outcomes. The culture of intraparty democracy – where leadership is elected, dissent is institutionalized and collective decision-making is practised – remains underdeveloped across the region. Instead, what prevails is a mixture of ritualized acclamation, factional bargaining and patronage-driven loyalty – all of which undermine the institutional coherence and ideological vitality of political parties.

The gap between constitutional commitments and political practice is often vast. Most South Asian parties maintain written constitutions that mandate internal elections for leadership positions and party bodies at various levels. Yet, these documents are rarely binding in effect. In India, the ECI formally requires parties to hold periodic organizational elections as a condition for continued registration, but this requirement is perfunctorily enforced, that too in letter rather than in spirit. Parties routinely submit pro forma reports claiming to have conducted internal elections, often unopposed or held without any meaningful contest. The Indian National Congress, for instance, held a presidential election in 2022 after years of delay – but the contest itself was widely viewed as a managed affair, with the real authority continuing to reside with the Gandhi family. The BJP, despite its relatively institutionalized cadre structure, also operates through an appointed – not elected – leadership, with power concentrated in the central parliamentary board and strategic decision-making confined to a tight circle of confidants.

In Pakistan and Bangladesh, the situation is more severe. Intraparty elections are either completely absent or functionally irrelevant. Parties are frequently led by self-appointed or family-nominated leaders, and internal dissent is suppressed through expulsions, marginalization or the creation of parallel party wings. The PPP and the BAL have rarely seen internal elections for top positions. When leadership transitions occur, they typically resemble successions rather than elections – treated as inheritances of power rather than contests for it. Even newer or reform-oriented parties like the PTI have gradually moved away from their initial promise of internal democratic procedures, as internal elections are replaced with loyalty-based appointments and public dissent punished with expulsion.

Factionalism is the natural byproduct of this undemocratic internal order. In the absence of credible elections or decision-making mechanisms, political competition within parties moves underground, manifesting as splits, subgroups and elite rivalries. These factions are often not organized around ideological or programmatic lines, but rather around access to power, state resources or leadership proximity. In Nepal, factional politics is endemic, with major parties like the CPN-UML and the NC frequently paralysed by internal disputes over leadership succession and candidate nominations. The result is frequent fragmentation, policy paralysis and a persistent undermining of party discipline.

In Sri Lanka, intraparty factionalism has at times led to institutional crises, most notably when disputes within the ruling coalition sparked constitutional gridlocks and executive confrontations. The proliferation of factions in the Rajapaksa camp after 2022, and the internal disarray within the SLFP and the UNP, are indicative of how unchecked factionalism weakens not only parties but the entire edifice of governance. Similarly, in Afghanistan, prior to the Taliban's return, political parties were heavily factionalized along ethnic and patronage lines – functioning less as ideological entities and more as loose coalitions of warlords and local strongmen. The absence of party democracy contributed directly to state fragility, as allegiances shifted rapidly based on personal incentives rather than institutional stability.

Underlying both the erosion of intraparty elections and the entrenchment of factionalism is the politics of patronage. In most South Asian parties, the ability to dispense benefits – be it government contracts, civil service appointments, constituency development funds or electoral nominations – is the glue that holds internal coalitions together. Party loyalty is often transactional, based less on ideological commitment and more on access to resources and favours. This system rewards those closest to power and punishes dissenters, fostering a culture of sycophancy and fear rather than debate and deliberation.

Such patronage politics has corrosive consequences. First, it hollows out ideology, reducing parties to platforms for rent-seeking rather than policymaking. Second, it discourages young and independent-minded aspirants, who are unable or unwilling to engage in the factional manoeuvring necessary to survive. Third, it breeds clientelism within government, where public office becomes an extension of party favour networks. Governance thus suffers not only from incompetence but from deliberate distortions driven by internal party compulsions.

Attempts to institutionalize intraparty democracy have largely failed to overcome entrenched elite resistance. Election commissions across South Asia have limited authority (or will) to monitor internal party functioning beyond formal registration requirements. Even when civil society organizations or media watchdogs highlight deficiencies, parties tend to close ranks, dismissing criticism as external interference. The rare cases where internal elections are meaningful – such as occasional contests within Nepal's major parties – are exceptions that prove the rule: that internal democracy requires both institutional enforcement and cultural transformation.

Ultimately, the erosion of intraparty democracy cannot be divorced from the broader pathologies of governance in South Asia. As discussed earlier, parties that fail to renew their leadership, include dissent or debate policy internally are unlikely to uphold democratic values when in power. Without regular and credible internal elections, factionalism and patronage will continue to dominate, reducing parties to instruments of opportunism rather than engines of democratic change.

Role of the State in Fostering Internal Democracy

While the responsibility for cultivating internal party democracy lies primarily with the political parties themselves, the architecture of regulation and oversight plays a pivotal role in either enabling reform or entrenching the status quo. Across South Asia, the absence of robust legal mandates, the weakness or politicization of election commissions and the passivity of the judiciary have together contributed to a regulatory void in which internal party autocracy is normalized rather than challenged. This institutional neglect is not accidental. Rather, it reflects a tacit consensus among ruling elites across the region to allow minimal intervention in their internal affairs, despite the profound public consequences of opaque party functioning.

The legal landscape for regulating internal democracy varies across the SAARC countries, but certain patterns are consistent. Most electoral laws require parties to submit basic documentation to their respective election authorities – such as lists of office bearers, audited accounts and statements of organizational elections. However, compliance is largely procedural. Authorities rarely, if ever, scrutinize the authenticity or democratic quality of these processes. In India, for instance, the Representation of the People Act 1951 and the Election Symbols Order, 1968, require parties to hold internal elections, but the enforcement is symbolic. Parties routinely file reports indicating that elections were held, even when these involve uncontested nominations, backroom selections or outright fabrications. The ECI, while constitutionally empowered, has consistently avoided substantive intervention into internal party affairs, citing judicial restraint and political neutrality.

This regulatory passivity is even more pronounced in Pakistan and Bangladesh, where election authorities are widely perceived as partisan or institutionally weak. The ECP requires parties to submit reports of internal elections, but these are seldom verified or acted upon. In Bangladesh, where democratic institutions have steadily eroded over the past decade, the Election Commission has functioned more as a validator of ruling party preferences than an independent guardian of democratic norms. Consequently, the then-ruling BAL has been able to centralize power and avoid internal contestation with impunity, while the opposition BNP has fragmented in the absence of any credible external or internal checks.

Sri Lanka presents a similarly ambiguous picture. While its legal framework recognizes political parties as integral to the democratic process, there are no binding provisions that require intraparty elections, nor are there penalties for parties that bypass internal processes. The Election Commission of Sri Lanka, despite periods of institutional strength, has not used its discretionary powers consistently to press for greater transparency or internal reform. In Nepal, by contrast, the Election Commission does have relatively more regulatory latitude. It mandates parties to submit detailed organizational documents and has, on occasion, intervened in internal disputes – such as certifying leadership changes or rejecting parallel factions. However, even in Nepal, the enforcement often follows elite consensus rather than legal principle, limiting its transformative potential.

Bhutan and the Maldives offer more restrictive, but interesting, case studies. In Bhutan, the Election Commission exercises stringent control over party registration, requiring parties to meet specific ideological, organizational and financial criteria. This has resulted in a smaller number of parties with relatively clearer constitutions and structures, but the internal democracy of these entities remains weak – largely because of a lack of mass membership and meaningful contestation. In the Maldives, party regulation is governed by the Political Parties Act (2013), which does require internal elections. Yet, as in other SAARC nations, the actual conduct and oversight of these elections remains superficial, and party leaders often serve for decades without serious challenge.

The reluctance of regulatory authorities to enforce internal democracy stems from both institutional limitation and political caution. On the one hand, election commissions often lack the legal teeth, staffing capacity or political cover to audit internal party affairs with rigour. On the other, intervention into party functioning is seen as politically risky, especially in highly polarized environments. Courts, too, have generally refrained from mandating internal reforms, preferring to treat political parties as voluntary associations with a high degree of internal autonomy. Even when party activists or civil society groups challenge undemocratic practices in court, the judiciary typically dismisses such petitions on procedural or jurisdictional grounds.

The consequences of this regulatory vacuum are significant. Without credible external oversight, party leaders face no pressure to conduct genuine internal elections, publish transparent accounts or institutionalize ethical conduct. This not only erodes the democratic fabric of parties but also allows them to function as unaccountable gatekeepers of public office. Moreover, the absence of state-enforced norms allows dominant factions to suppress dissent and marginalize internal challengers – thereby reproducing authoritarian tendencies within ostensibly democratic polities.

There are, however, emerging avenues for reform. Civil society organizations, transparency watchdogs and the media have increasingly begun to expose the inner workings of political parties. In India, platforms like the ADR have documented the financial opacity and dynastic control of major parties, prompting public debate and judicial notice. In Pakistan, judicial interventions – though inconsistent – have occasionally questioned the legality of party appointments or factional splits. Nepal's party law offers a template for recognizing the state's interest in internal democracy, without fully intruding upon party autonomy.

Policy innovation is possible. Electoral commissions can be empowered – through legislation or constitutional amendment – to monitor and audit intraparty elections, enforce transparent nomination processes and mandate periodic leadership turnover. Party registration rules can be linked to demonstrable compliance with internal democracy benchmarks. Public funding of political parties (where implemented) can be conditioned on democratic practices, ensuring that taxpayer money supports only those parties that uphold core democratic norms. Finally, a regional charter on party democracy, perhaps under the aegis of the SAARC or an academic consortium, could help build consensus around minimum standards of internal functioning.

Ultimately, democracy in South Asia cannot thrive on the strength of electoral rituals alone. It requires parties that are accountable not only to the electorate, but to their own members. Strengthening the regulatory and normative ecosystem that fosters internal democracy is not an act of interference – it is a necessary precondition for the deepening of democratic governance across the region.

Opening the Party Gates

If democratic institutions in South Asia are to mature and become genuinely accountable, the transformation must begin not at the periphery but at the very core – within the political parties themselves. The failure to democratize internally has not merely weakened party structures but eroded the vitality of parliaments, narrowed the bandwidth of political representation and allowed governance to stagnate in the hands of a closed elite. Inner-party democracy, then, is not an ancillary concern but a structural imperative for the renewal of South Asia's democratic promise.

The first step towards reform must be the legal recognition of political parties as public institutions that bear responsibilities beyond their own internal cohesion. While freedom of association must be preserved, the idea that parties are private clubs exempt from scrutiny must be challenged. Election laws should be amended to include binding mandates on intraparty elections, transparent nomination procedures and periodic leadership rotation. Crucially, these laws must be enforceable – with penalties for non-compliance, ranging from suspension of party symbols to ineligibility for public funding or reserved media time.

Second, election commissions must be empowered and made independent in both form and function. In India, for example, the Supreme Court's 2023 ruling on the appointment of election commissioners may be leveraged as a constitutional opportunity to re-imagine the ECI's role – not merely as an umpire during elections but as a long-term regulator of democratic norms, including internal party functioning. Similar institutional fortification is needed across the region. In Pakistan and Bangladesh, where election authorities are widely viewed as partisan, reform must focus not just on legal empowerment but on insulation from political interference. The Election Commission of Nepal provides an embryonic model: its occasional interventions in intraparty disputes point towards what is possible when institutional will converges with constitutional space.

Third, civil society and the judiciary must become co-architects of accountability. Public-interest litigation has already begun to question the financial opacity and dynastic monopolization of parties. This momentum should be expanded to demand judicial recognition of internal party democracy as integral to the constitutional guarantee of free and fair elections. At the same time, watchdog organizations, independent media and academic institutions must take up the task of monitoring party structures, publishing internal democracy indices, and naming and shaming violators. Transparency can catalyse reform where law alone falters.

Fourth, positive incentives for reform must complement punitive measures. State subsidies, where introduced, should be tied to clear internal governance benchmarks. Publicly funded political training programmes must privilege parties that maintain inclusive and participatory structures. Moreover, donor agencies and international democratic networks can support internal party reform through capacity-building programmes, leadership development fellowships and comparative best-practice exchanges – especially in countries like Bhutan, the Maldives and Nepal, where political institutions are still malleable.

Finally, democratization must begin at the grassroots. Mandating democratic norms in party constitutions is insufficient unless there is pressure from below to uphold them. Reviving party membership systems, ensuring local-level elections and encouraging cadre-based organizing are essential to rebuilding parties as participatory entities rather than electoral machines. Importantly, this transformation must be inclusive: mechanisms must be created to bring women, youth, ethnic minorities and economically marginalized groups into party leadership pipelines – not just as token representatives, but as transformative agents of democratic renewal.

The challenge is formidable. Entrenched elites will not easily surrender the privileges of discretion, secrecy and dynastic control. Yet, the cost of inaction is higher still: a region where democracy exists in form but not in substance, where elections are held but choice is circumscribed and where governments change but governance remains captured. For too long, South Asia's political parties have hidden behind the legitimacy of the ballot box to perpetuate undemocratic habits within. It is time to open those closed doors – not just for scrutiny but for the possibility of reinvention.

20

Political Futures: Participation of the Young

To speak of South Asia today is to speak of a region in motion – demographically volatile, politically contested, and brimming with both discontent and possibility. At its heart lies an immense and often paradoxical demographic force: its youth. Nowhere else on earth is the future more literally embedded in the present than in the nations that comprise the SAARC. As of 2025, the region houses over two billion people, with more than 60 per cent under the age of thirty. India alone has an estimated 850 million citizens below thirty-five; Pakistan has close to 130 million; Bangladesh's youth bulge exceeds 60 million; and even smaller nations like Nepal and Sri Lanka report median ages well under thirty. This youth bulge, often described as a potential 'demographic dividend', is widely hailed as South Asia's greatest comparative advantage. Yet, beneath this promise lies a gnawing crisis of political inclusion, alienation and democratic fragility.

The youth in South Asia are simultaneously hyper-visible and under-represented. They populate every university campus, every protest square and every WhatsApp group, and yet, when decisions are made – at legislatures, party headquarters, cabinet rooms and constitutional benches – their presence is conspicuously minimal. Their potential is invoked in political speeches and electoral manifestos, but rarely honoured in institutional design or power-sharing arrangements. The result is a structural paradox: the region's youngest generation is its most populous and least politically empowered. The democratic systems in South Asia, inherited from post-colonial state formation or conflict resolution pacts, remain structurally gerontocratic and socio-economically exclusionary. The youth, especially those from marginalized castes and ethnicities, rural geographies, and lower-income backgrounds, face formidable barriers to meaningful participation.

This democratic exclusion is not merely a function of institutional inertia. It is actively sustained by interlocking systems of electoral design, economic disenfranchisement, media manipulation, elite capture and normative gatekeeping. While the voting age across the SAARC countries is typically eighteen, the minimum eligibility for contesting national office ranges from twenty-five to thirty – legally delaying young people's entry into political leadership. Simultaneously, the escalating cost of elections, the dominance of dynastic political families and patronage-based party structures, all militate against the emergence of new and diverse youth voices in politics. Moreover, the intersectional disadvantages borne by young women, queer youth and linguistic or religious minorities further reinforce their exclusion.

However, the story is far from unidirectional. Across the region, the youth are not passive recipients of democratic erosion but active agents of civic renewal. From the student-led mass mobilizations that ousted authoritarian governments in Sri Lanka and Bangladesh, to voter education campaigns in India's high schools and universities and digital resistance movements emerging in Bhutan and Nepal, young people are reimagining democracy in ways that are at once performative, participatory and profoundly political. Whether through protest or policy advocacy, through electoral engagement or institutional innovation, they are reshaping the contours of what democratic legitimacy means in the twenty-first century.

This chapter offers a thematic, comparative analysis of the role of the youth in South Asian democracies through five interlocking themes that cut across the region. First, it interrogates the paradox of the demographic dividend and political exclusion – examining how institutional rules and socio-economic conditions constrain youth representation despite their numerical centrality. Second, it evaluates the role of electoral commissions, voter education programmes and institutional innovations in either enabling or limiting youth electoral participation. Third, it investigates how digital media has created new modalities of expression, mobilization and manipulation for youth actors. Fourth, it turns to protest movements and civic disobedience as forms of democratic participation, highlighting how youth-led resistances have disrupted authoritarian regimes and galvanized new publics. Finally, it addresses questions of structural reform: how can the youth move from symbolic participation to real representation in legislatures, parties and governance institutions?

The youth question in South Asia is not merely a matter of mobilization – it is a matter of structural justice. The region's democratic trajectory will be determined by the extent to which it transforms its largest demographic into its most empowered political constituency. As authoritarian populism rises, inequality deepens and political alienation spreads, the need to recalibrate the relationship between youth and democracy has never been more urgent.

Demographic Dividend

To understand the paradox of youth and democracy in South Asia, one must begin with a recognition of the region's staggering demographic composition. As was briefly noted above, as of 2025, over 60 per cent of South Asia's 2 billion inhabitants are under the age of thirty.[1] India alone has more than 600 million citizens in this age group, while Pakistan reports over 130 million youth under thirty, and Bangladesh has over 65 million.[2] Even smaller states such as Nepal and Sri Lanka continue to have median ages below thirty, while Afghanistan remains one of the youngest countries in the world with over 63 per cent of its population under twenty-five.[3] This youth bulge – unprecedented in both scale and concentration – has led to widespread pronouncements that South Asia will be the world's next economic engine, a potential site of innovation, productivity and social transformation.

However, the notion of a demographic dividend presupposes institutional readiness and political inclusion. Without systems that convert numerical strength into participatory agency, the dividend becomes a liability. In the context of South Asia, the promise of youth-driven renewal is undermined by a severe and sustained crisis of political incorporation. The youth may constitute the majority of the region's population, but they remain a striking minority in its formal democratic institutions.

A glaring manifestation of this crisis is the profound underrepresentation of young people in national legislatures. In India's 2024 Lok Sabha elections, less than 13 per cent of the elected members were under the age of forty, and only a handful under thirty. In Bangladesh's 2024 elections, parliament saw fewer than ten members under thirty-five in a house of 300. Pakistan's 2024 National Assembly fared little better, with youth representation largely limited to dynastic heirs. Afghanistan (before the Taliban takeover), and the Maldives have seen efforts to integrate younger MPs, but even there, the youth are often relegated to tokenistic roles, frequently overshadowed by entrenched elites and party loyalists. This absence of young legislators is not merely anecdotal – it is the consequence of specific legal, political and socio-economic design.[1]

Electoral eligibility itself is one barrier. In all the SAARC countries, the legal age for contesting parliamentary elections is between twenty-five and thirty, as mentioned earlier. In Bhutan, a candidate for the National Assembly must be at least twenty-five years old; in Sri Lanka and Pakistan, the minimum is the same; and in India, it is twenty-five for the Lok Sabha and thirty for the Rajya Sabha. While these thresholds are not unusually high by global standards, they compound exclusion when paired with other constraints: the exorbitant cost of campaigning, the dominance of political dynasties and the lack of intraparty democracy. In the absence of state-financed campaign support or youth quotas, young aspirants – especially women, minorities and first-generation politicians – are routinely filtered out of the candidate selection process.

This exclusion is not confined to candidacy. Even as voters, young people face multiple obstacles to participation. Across the region, millions of eligible youth remain unregistered. The reasons are manifold: bureaucratic hurdles in Voter ID acquisition, frequent migration from rural to urban areas and outdated electoral rolls that do not keep pace with demographic mobility. For instance, in Nepal, a significant proportion of youth between eighteen and twenty-four – especially those in higher education or informal employment – remain disenfranchised due to procedural complexities. In Pakistan, despite 45 per cent of the electorate being between eighteen and thirty-five, youth voter turnout in the 2024 general elections lagged behind national averages by over 15 per centage points – a gap that has remained consistent since the 1990s. In Bangladesh, the dramatic drop in voter turnout from 80 per cent in 2018 to 41.8 per cent in 2024 reflected a youth boycott, driven by perceptions of political stagnation and electoral malpractice.

These patterns point not to a lack of interest but to a breakdown in political trust. South Asian youth are not apolitical, they are alienated. A 2024 regional survey conducted by UNICEF and the South Asia Youth Research Collabourative found that nearly 64 per cent of youth respondents felt that political parties did not represent their interests.[5] In India, the Lokniti–CSDS Youth Survey reported that 59 per cent of respondents aged eighteen to twenty-five felt that elections made no meaningful difference to their lives.[6] This sentiment was echoed in Bhutan and Sri Lanka, where the youth expressed higher levels of faith in civil society and media than in political institutions. The crisis, therefore, is not just of participation but of legitimacy.

This sense of exclusion is aggravated by profound structural inequalities. Youth unemployment across South Asia remains alarmingly high. According to the 2023–24 data from the International Labour Organization, Sri Lanka and Nepal report youth unemployment rates, 20.4 per cent and 25.3 per cent respectively, while Bangladesh stands at 15.8 per cent, India at 14.8 per cent and Pakistan at 9.7 per cent. These figures reflect a persistent crisis of underemployment and disillusionment among young people across South Asia, even as many of them enter the labour force with higher educational qualifications than previous generations.[7] For young women, these figures are significantly worse. South Asia also has one of the world's highest rates of 'NEETs' (referring to youth Not in Education, Employment or Training), with estimates suggesting that over 30 per cent of youth across the region fall into this category.[8] The intersection of economic precarity and political disempowerment creates a dangerous feedback loop: those who feel excluded from economic opportunity are less likely to invest faith in democratic structures.

Furthermore, the internal cultures of political parties themselves discourage youth leadership. Despite the proliferation of 'youth wings' and student groups, these are often co-opted spaces – functioning more as instruments of mobilization than mechanisms of representation. Party hierarchies tend to be ageist, patriarchal and loyalty-driven. In Sri Lanka, the JVP has been one exception in recruiting young, first-generation candidates, yet the broader party ecosystem across South Asia remains heavily gerontocratic. Mentorship pipelines, candidate grooming programmes and transparent internal elections remain rare.

Reimagining political inclusion for South Asia's youth requires not simply making room for younger faces, but transforming the logics of power distribution. Legal reforms such as lowering the age of candidacy, state subsidies for young candidates and reserved quotas in party lists could be pivotal. Equally crucial are cultural and institutional changes: party systems that foster competitive meritocracy, EMBs that prioritize age-disaggregated data and electoral campaigns that speak to youth aspirations – not just as voters, but as citizens, workers, students and digital natives.

The demographic dividend cannot be a slogan; it must be a structural mandate. If South Asian democracies are to avert the risks of political apathy, mass emigration or authoritarian backlash, they must invest not only in youth development but in youth empowerment. Representation, in this context, is not a matter of symbolism – it is the foundation of legitimacy.

The Institutional Ecosystem

Elections are often held up as the centrepiece of democratic practice. Yet, the strength and inclusivity of an electoral democracy depends not merely on the existence of regular voting but on the integrity of its institutional scaffolding: the mechanisms by which voter rolls are maintained, citizens are registered, electoral information is disseminated, and votes are cast and counted. For the youth in South Asia, especially those voting for the first time, the quality of this ecosystem is critical in shaping whether they view electoral participation as meaningful or futile. Across the SAARC region, the disparities in youth electoral engagement are not simply a matter of individual will – they are functions of the institutional ecosystems that either enable or obstruct their involvement.

India offers perhaps the most illustrative case of institutional success in this regard. The ECI, one of the most robust EMBs globally, has for over a decade pursued an explicit strategy of youth-centric voter outreach. Its flagship initiative, the SVEEP programme, has been institutionalized across the country and engages with schools, universities, workplaces and digital platforms to increase electoral literacy. The ECI's observance of National Voters Day on 25 January – timed to coincide with the founding date of the Commission – has emerged as a civic ritual across many states, where first-time voters are felicitated and encouraged to register. In the 2024 Indian general elections, voter turnout among the eighteen to twenty-four age group crossed 67 per cent, a notable increase from the previous cycle. Crucially, this is not just a quantitative gain but the product of sustained institutional investment in youth engagement.

Bangladesh has mirrored many of these strategies with its own contextual innovations. The Bangladesh Election Commission observes National Voters' Day on 2 March, incorporating social media campaigns, youth rallies and school-based voter awareness drives. In the lead-up to the 2024 general elections, which saw a precipitous drop in turnout to 41.8 per cent, the Bangladesh Election Commission's targeted youth campaigns were one of the few bright spots. Digital infographics, short videos on civic rights and mock elections in high schools were used to promote awareness, though these efforts were ultimately undermined by a broader political climate of repression and electoral manipulation. The lesson here is vital: voter education is necessary but not sufficient; its success is deeply contingent upon wider perceptions of electoral legitimacy.

The ECP has faced consistent criticism for its outdated registration systems and opaque voter data. While the number of registered young voters in Pakistan has grown – from 46.4 million in 2018 to 56.8 million in 2024 – the turnout gap remains stubborn. Youth voter turnout in the 2024 elections hovered around 30–33 per cent, over 12 per centage points lower than the national average. This gap is driven not only by disillusionment but by practical hurdles: difficulties in acquiring Computerized National Identity Cards (CNICs), poor outreach in rural areas, and the absence of meaningful voter education campaigns that speak to the interests and idioms of young citizens.

Afghanistan, where political instability has derailed regular electoral processes, offers a sobering case of how fragile institutional ecosystems can altogether sever the link between youth and electoral participation. Since the Taliban's return to power in 2021, national elections have been suspended and the country's Independent Election Commission has been dismantled. While prior to the regime change, voter registration drives and civic education had begun to include youth-focused elements – especially in urban centres like Kabul and Herat – these initiatives have now been reversed. The vacuum of legitimate electoral institutions in Afghanistan poses a generational threat to youth democratic engagement, replacing the promise of inclusion with the permanence of authoritarian disenfranchisement.

Smaller SAARC countries present a mixed picture. In Nepal, the Election Commission has piloted mobile registration centres aimed at reaching youth in remote mountainous districts. However, these efforts are often undercut by budgetary limitations and administrative inefficiencies. Bhutan's Election Commission has actively encouraged 'Democracy Clubs' in schools and colleges, promoting a culture of civic responsibility from an early age. While Bhutan's electorate is comparatively small, its youth-focused interventions are noteworthy for their consistency and institutional support. Sri Lanka, facing its own economic and political upheavals, has struggled to maintain momentum in youth electoral engagement. Nevertheless, the 2014 National Human Development Report and subsequent reforms have led to gradual integration of youth-focused voter education in urban municipalities.

Across the region, the limitations of the electoral ecosystem are compounded by gaps in data. Most election commissions fail to disaggregate participation data by age, gender and socio-economic status. This data vacuum makes it difficult to design targeted policies or even to accurately assess the scale of youth exclusion. While India has begun releasing age-segmented turnout data in some states, most SAARC countries rely on sporadic surveys or third-party estimates. Without institutional mechanisms to capture and analyse youth-specific electoral behaviour, reforms remain ad hoc and unresponsive.

Another neglected area is the role of EMBs in enabling not just voters but youth volunteers, observers and civic educators. In several states in

India, the youth have been formally inducted as polling assistants and election observers. The SVEEP programme's YUVA (Youth Unite for Voter Awareness) wing trains university students to conduct awareness campaigns, run help desks and use social media to promote informed participation. These are not merely symbolic roles; they allow young people to experience the complexity of electoral operations and develop a sense of institutional stewardship.

South Asia's electoral institutions thus stand at a crossroads. They can either act as vehicles of transformative inclusion or become complicit in reinforcing generational exclusion. The case of India shows that when institutions invest in youth outreach with consistency and imagination, participation rises. But elsewhere, underinvestment, repression or lack of innovation ensures that the youngest and most numerous citizens are also the most disengaged. The future of democratic participation in South Asia depends not only on the credibility of elections but also on the institutional willingness to nurture an electorate that is not just young in age, but empowered in agency.

Digital Natives and Disinformation

The youth of South Asia are the region's first true digital natives. Having come of age in an era marked by mobile connectivity, algorithmic media and online political discourse, they inhabit an informational ecosystem that is qualitatively different from that of earlier generations. While their elders may have experienced democracy through party manifestos, street rallies and printed dailies, the young today are more likely to encounter politics on TikTok, WhatsApp, Instagram and YouTube. In principle, this transformation should have been democratizing: a decentralized digital field enabling mass political education, participatory discourse and horizontal mobilization. In practice, however, the digitalization of youth political engagement in South Asia has produced a more ambiguous terrain that is rich with possibility, but fraught with distortion.

South Asia today ranks among the most active regions globally in terms of social media use among young people. India alone has over 470 million active social media users as of 2024, a significant proportion of whom are under thirty. Pakistan has over 80 million,

Bangladesh over 45 million, and Sri Lanka, Nepal and Bhutan report increasing numbers year on year.[9] Mobile Internet access has driven a sharp expansion of digital life, particularly in rural and peri-urban areas, where first-time smartphone users often encounter both civic discourse and political propaganda without institutional mediation or media literacy training. This expansion has created novel pathways for youth political expression, but also unprecedented exposure to misinformation, hate speech, algorithmic echo chambers and targeted disinformation campaigns.

In countries with relatively open political environments, social media has been a conduit for participatory action. For instance, the 2020–22 youth-led protest movements in Sri Lanka – culminating in the resignation of then President Gotabaya Rajapaksa – were extensively organized through Facebook and Twitter. Protesters used encrypted channels like Signal and Telegram to evade surveillance, while visual platforms like Instagram helped produce and circulate powerful images of dissent from protest camps like Gota Go Gama. The performative aesthetics of protest – banners, street theatre and viral videos – acquired national and even international resonance largely due to digital circulation. The same can be said of the 2024 youth uprisings in Bangladesh, where platforms like YouTube and TikTok became vehicles for satirical dissent, public testimony and real-time coordination despite state efforts to impose censorship.

At the same time, the very architecture of social media platforms – algorithmically optimized for attention rather than truth – has made the youth especially vulnerable to ideological manipulation and polarization. In India, targeted political advertising during the 2024 general elections used data-mining techniques to segment young voters and deliver micro-targeted content, which often skirted the line between persuasion and propaganda. In Pakistan, where Internet regulation remains ad hoc, political parties and religious organizations alike have weaponized digital platforms to spread inflammatory content, especially during election cycles and public unrest. Bangladesh has seen the rise of cyber-patrol units tasked with monitoring 'anti-state' speech – a practice that disproportionately affects youth activists and student journalists. In

Afghanistan, the Taliban regime uses digital surveillance and Internet throttling to restrict online expression among young dissidents, who have nevertheless found ways to create anonymous blogs, encrypted art collectives and diaspora-backed forums.

One of the most striking patterns across the region is the digital decoupling of political awareness from formal political participation. Young people may be deeply immersed in political discourse online – commenting, reposting and campaigning – but may simultaneously abstain from voting or party involvement. This disconnect is partly due to the culture of performative digital engagement, where symbolic gestures (a hashtag, a reel or a boycott video) replace sustained civic practice. But it also reflects deeper distrust in the institutional integrity of elections, particularly in countries where social media is one of the few uncensored spaces left for dissent.

Moreover, the digital divide still persists. While mobile penetration is high, the quality of access is deeply uneven – particularly along lines of gender, class and geography. A 2024 Global System for Mobile Communications Association report found that across South Asia, women are 13 per cent less likely than men to own a smartphone and 31 per cent less likely to use mobile Internet.[10] Among the rural youth, access is often device-shared, data-capped and highly surveilled by state surveillance regimes, limiting the ability to consume diverse content or organize securely. This asymmetry not only reproduces existing inequalities but risks deepening them under the illusion of universal connectivity.

Nevertheless, South Asia also presents inspiring models of youth-led digital civic innovation. Nepal's youth-run platforms like Yo Voter, which creates Nepali-language electoral explainers on YouTube, have drawn large followings among first-time voters. In Bhutan, the *Druk Journal* and other online civic journals, often managed by young editors, offer nuanced political commentary rarely seen in state media. India's We, The People Abhiyan mobilizes volunteers to fact-check viral election misinformation in regional languages. Even in repressive regimes, anonymous Telegram channels and diaspora-backed podcasts keep digital democratic imaginations alive.

These examples suggest that digital spaces are not inherently corrosive or emancipatory – they are shaped by the sociopolitical environment, regulatory frameworks and the digital literacy of their users. For South Asia to harness the democratic potential of youth digital engagement, two strategic interventions are necessary.

First, governments must shift from surveillance to support. Instead of criminalizing dissent or introducing vague anti-cybercrime laws, states should invest in media literacy curricula at school and university levels, focused on identifying misinformation, understanding algorithms and practising digital citizenship.

Second, EMBs, civil society organizations and social media companies must collabourate to design youth-focused digital campaigns that prioritize participation over propaganda. Algorithms must be audited for bias, disinformation must be flagged, and electoral messaging must be transparent and verifiable. The creation of youth councils within digital policy bodies – modelled after citizen assemblies – can ensure that platform governance reflects generational concerns.

In the age of the digital electorate, South Asia's political future will increasingly be fought not just in ballot boxes but in bandwidth. The question is whether the region's democratic institutions can evolve fast enough to protect, platform and empower a generation whose politics is both wired and restless.

Civil Disobedience as Democratic Participation

If elections are the formal grammar of democracy, then protest is its punctuation – its exclamation marks, ellipses and and question marks. Nowhere is this more evident than in the civic engagements of South Asia's youth, who, in the face of exclusion from party systems and formal institutions, have turned to protest as their most immediate and resonant form of political expression. The streets, campuses, public squares – and now digital spaces – have become theatres of resistance where young people articulate their political identities, confront state power and envision alternative democratic futures. These protests are not marginal to democracy but constitutive of it. They offer a grammar of dissent through which the democratic contract is both contested and renewed.

Recent years have made this truth undeniable. In 2022, Sri Lanka witnessed one of the most significant youth-led civic movements in South Asia's democratic history. What began as scattered, small-scale demonstrations against rising fuel prices and inflation rapidly coalesced into a national youth uprising that led to the resignation of then President Gotabaya Rajapaksa. At the heart of this movement was Gota Go Gama – a makeshift protest village established in Colombo, where students, artists, academics and ordinary youth converged. The site became a microcosm of participatory democracy with open forums, public readings of the constitution, street performances and impromptu elections for protest leadership. These were not just spontaneous expressions of anger – they were deeply strategic, creative and non-violent assertions of democratic voice.

Bangladesh, too, in 2024 saw the return of the student as a catalytic political subject. Following the Supreme Court's reinstatement of a 30 per cent civil service quota for descendants of 1971 war veterans – a decision widely perceived as entrenching dynastic privilege – university students mobilized en masse. The protests quickly expanded beyond the quota issue to broader demands for transparency, accountability and an end to then PM Sheikh Hasina's authoritarian rule. As in Sri Lanka, protest sites became spaces of radical pedagogy and shared learning, where social media livestreams, satirical street theatre and student manifestos conveyed a generational indictment of the political establishment. As we know, the movement culminated in Hasina's resignation – an extraordinary reversal that underlined the power of youth when it is organized, sustained and morally unyielding.

Such movements are not episodic – they are embedded in a deeper historical tradition of youth political action across South Asia. From the Chipko Movement in 1970s India, where young women embraced trees to prevent deforestation, to Nepal's Jana Andolan, to the youth-led campaigns against disappearances in Balochistan, the region's democratic life has often been most vibrantly expressed outside electoral cycles. One of the most striking examples is the Assam Movement (1979–85), an entirely student-led mobilization demanding the detection and deportation of undocumented migrants. It ultimately reshaped state politics and propelled Prafulla Kumar Mahanta, then a student leader, to become the youngest chief minister in Indian history, at the age of thirty-two – marking a rare instance of direct electoral ascendancy from mass youth protest. These protests draw from and contribute to what theorist Judith Butler calls the 'performative enactment' of political subjectivity: they do not merely ask for recognition within existing systems; they reveal the limits of those systems and enact alternate forms of community, care and imagination.

Crucially, youth-led protests are not homogeneous. They differ in language, repertoire and ideological orientation. In Afghanistan, where elections have now ceased under Taliban rule, young people – especially women – have engaged in quiet, brave forms of resistance such as flash protests, underground schooling networks and encrypted poetry circles. In India, students have protested both against exclusionary citizenship laws (as in the 2019–20 anti-CAA movement), and in favour of job quotas and examination reforms. In Pakistan, the PTM, largely youth-driven, has foregrounded questions of state violence and ethnic marginalization, while youth in Gilgit-Baltistan have protested environmental degradation due to Chinese infrastructure projects. In Bhutan, while public protests are rare, the youth-led debates around mental health, gender identity, and environmental stewardship in university campuses and online forums signal a shifting political consciousness.

However, youth protests are not without costs. Across South Asia, governments have responded to dissent with repression. In Bangladesh, protest leaders were arrested, surveilled and (in some cases) made to disappear. In India, the anti-CAA movement saw police crackdowns on university campuses, with sedition charges filed against prominent student leaders. More recently, thousands of students at institutions like Jamia Millia Islamia and Jawaharlal Nehru University faced brutal baton charges and tear gas during protests over fee hikes and expressions in solidarity with Palestine. University of Allahabad and Aligarh Muslim University also witnessed the mass arrests of students and activists, signalling an increasingly repressive environment for campus dissent.[11] Sri Lankan authorities, during the 2022 protests, imposed emergency laws and curfews. Afghanistan's Taliban regime has criminalized all forms of youth-led dissent, leading to imprisonment, torture and exile. The message from these responses is clear: youth power is recognized as a political threat and therefore policed with intensity.

Despite this, the symbolic power of protest persists. What youth lack in institutional access, they compensate for through what political theorist Chantal Mouffe might call 'agonistic pluralism' – a politics of contestation that does not reject institutions outright but demands their transformation. Therefore, youth-led protest is not anti-democratic. It no longer seeks merely to protect democracy from authoritarian erosion – it seeks to reimagine democracy altogether, as more participatory, egalitarian and accountable.

This reimagination is often expressed through aesthetic forms. Art installations, rap performances, zines, protest fashion and murals have become central to the youth protest repertoire. These are not embellishments – they are expressions in their own right, seeking to examine the very nature of democracy. They teach, persuade, provoke and build solidarity. The use of performance in protest is particularly significant in a region where political speech is censored, and where metaphor and symbolism often carry messages too dangerous to utter aloud.

Moreover, protests have ripple effects beyond their immediate outcomes. They politicize a generation. They create horizontal networks of trust and mutual aid. They cultivate leadership. They create archives – digital and oral – of civic courage. Even when repressed, they leave behind pedagogies of resistance that inform future mobilizations. In a region where formal youth participation remains low, these movements ensure that democracy does not stagnate into a ritual of voting, but remains a living, contested and performative practice.

Thus, to study the role of youth in South Asian democracy is to study not only electoral behaviour but insurgent citizenship. These are not rival modes of engagement – they are complementary. For democracy to thrive, it must learn to see its youngest citizens not merely as voters-in-training but as co-authors of the democratic project. Protest, in this regard, is not a disruption of democracy – it is the eruption of democratic will.

Symbolic Inclusion to Structural Power

It is one thing for democracies to celebrate youth participation, it is quite another to share power. Across South Asia, political institutions often engage young people as symbols, mascots or foot-soldiers of electoral campaigns, but rarely as decision-makers or architects of statecraft. Even when the youth are integrated into political parties or consultative platforms, their inclusion tends to be instrumental rather than transformative. They are visible during election season, only to be sidelined in the corridors of power. This asymmetry raises a fundamental question: what would it mean to move beyond symbolic gestures and towards genuine structural representation of youth in South Asia's democratic architecture?

First, it requires rethinking how political candidacy is structured and incentivized. The prevailing design of electoral politics in most SAARC countries is built around exclusionary prerequisites: financial capital, dynastic pedigree and entrenched party patronage. These filters ensure that the average elected representative is not just older, but wealthier, more connected – to elite networks, business interests and party hierarchies – and often insulated from the realities of the youth majority. According to a 2024 regional study by the Centre for Policy Research, a 2019 regional study conducted by Association for Democratic reforms, over 82 per cent of MPs in India come from the top 1 per cent income bracket.[12]

One pathway to disrupt this asymmetry is through legislative reform. Several countries outside South Asia have experimented with youth quotas or affirmative mechanisms to enhance generational representation. Rwanda and Uganda have youth quotas in their national parliaments; Sweden and Finland employ voluntary youth quotas within party lists. South Asia, by contrast, has been slower to act. While some Indian states have experimented with student unions feeding into municipal bodies, and Sri Lanka has seen a handful of youth platforms within local governance, no SAARC country currently reserves seats for young candidates in national legislatures. Instituting such quotas – even modestly – would send a strong signal of commitment to intergenerational equity in politics.

Financial barriers also demand urgent attention. The cost of contesting elections is prohibitive for most young aspirants. In India's 2024 Lok Sabha elections, the average declared expenditure of winning candidates exceeded ₹70 lakh ($84,000). Similar trends hold true in Pakistan and Bangladesh, where campaign financing remains largely opaque and dominated by wealthy individuals or party elites. Without robust political finance reforms, the playing field remains structurally tilted. Public funding models – such as earmarking subsidies for parties that field a minimum per centage of youth candidates – can incentivize more inclusive ticket distribution. Kenya and Ireland, for instance, have legislated financial penalties for parties that fail to comply with youth or gender representation benchmarks. South Asia must consider similar innovations, adapted to local contexts.

However, representation is not only about parliamentarians. It extends to who staffs electoral commissions, who sits on party working committees, who drafts manifestos and who leads civil service reform. Youth representation within EMBs and related oversight institutions remains negligible. This absence is not merely a demographic oversight – it limits the institutional imagination of what inclusive elections can look like. The EMBs should develop internal inclusion targets, create fellowships for young electoral professionals, and systematically involve youth organizations in election planning and monitoring.

Moreover, political parties – arguably the most powerful gatekeepers of representation – must confront their own gerontocratic cultures. The prevalence of youth wings has not translated into policy influence. Often, these wings function as cheer squads or logistics arms during campaigns, with no meaningful say in candidate selection or agenda-setting. A structural reform would require mandating youth-wing representation in party executive bodies, ensuring that internal elections are free and fair, and creating generational succession plans to prevent leadership monopolies. Transparent, intraparty democracy is not a luxury – it is the first step toward democratizing representation itself.

Beyond institutional reform, there is also a need to expand our understanding of representation. Representation is not only a matter of presence, but of voice, experience and worldview. The youth brings to politics not just different identities but different priorities – climate justice, digital rights, mental health, education reform, gig economy regulation, and questions of gender and identity that older politicians often neglect or suppress. When young people are at the table, the political agenda changes. This was evident in Nepal's municipal elections of 2022, where young mayors in Kathmandu and Dharan introduced innovative policies on waste management, urban sustainability and transparency through digital dashboards.[13] These interventions may seem technocratic, but they emerge from a lived experience of precarity, aspiration and digital fluency that defines contemporary youth life.

It is equally important to recognize the diversity within youth. Representation must account for caste, ethnicity, religion, gender, geography and disability. In South Asia, the youth from Dalit, Adivasi or tribal communities, from border regions, or from conflict-affected zones face multilayered exclusions. Policies that seek to improve youth representation must therefore be intersectional. For instance, quotas for young women, language minorities and LGBTQ+ youth in party lists or youth parliaments can help create pathways for those doubly or triply marginalized. Without this, 'youth inclusion' risks becoming a homogeneous category that masks internal hierarchies.

Finally, reimagining representation means not only inserting youth into old structures, but transforming the structures themselves. Participatory budgeting, citizens' assemblies, digital referendums and local youth councils are mechanisms that decentralize and democratize power. These can be incubated at the municipal or state level, and scaled nationally. Bhutan's 'Democracy Clubs' in schools and Nepal's 'Child Clubs' offer early prototypes of such participatory models – where young citizens begin to engage with deliberation and governance from an early age. India's electoral literacy clubs and Bangladesh's civic ambassador programmes offer similar footholds. The challenge is to connect these efforts to meaningful pathways of institutional power.

In the end, representation is not merely about optics – it is about orientation. It shapes which questions are asked, which lives are prioritized and which futures are imagined. The question before South Asia is whether its democracies will remain content with the performance of youth inclusion or whether they will undertake the harder, more necessary, task of transferring power. If the region truly believes that its future belongs to its youth, then it must be prepared to give them the present as well.

Towards a Youth-Centric Democratic Imagination

The arc of South Asia's democratic destiny bends towards its young. The question of youth in South Asia is not one of passive presence but of active power: not simply whether young people vote, but whether they shape the systems they inhabit.

Young South Asians are entering adulthood in systems that exclude them institutionally, dismiss them politically and exploit them economically. They are inheriting democracies in crisis: polarized, hollowed out by corruption and authoritarian drift, and increasingly captured by elite interest. Yet, time and again, they have shown an astonishing capacity not only to resist but to reimagine. Their protests have brought down governments, their innovations have redefined civic communication and their votes – when mobilized – have shifted the balance of electoral power.

But this participation must no longer be treated as exceptional. It must become the norm. The future of South Asia's democratic project depends on whether its political institutions can internalize the urgency of generational justice. Representation must begin earlier. Candidacy must become more accessible. Electoral commissions must treat youth not merely as outreach targets, but as institutional collabourators. Political parties must open their gates – not just to campaign workers but to young policymakers, negotiators and leaders. Civil society must become more intergenerational, and constitutional systems must be capable of recognizing youth as not only the future, but the unfinished present of democracy.

The shift involves abandoning the rhetoric of 'giving voice' to the youth, and instead dismantling the barriers that prevent them from exercising the voice they already possess. It requires moving from paternalistic empowerment schemes to co-governance frameworks that reflect a redistribution of political agency. It demands that we abandon the illusion that a democracy can be legitimate while marginalizing its majority.

If South Asia's democracies are to survive the crises of the present and rise to the challenges of the future – from ecological collapse to technological disruption and democratic backsliding – they must become younger not only in demographic terms, but in spirit: more experimental, more inclusive, and more willing to revise their assumptions about authority and power. For that, they must do more than accommodate youth – they must be transformed by them.

The young are not the periphery, they are the polity. Their participation is not a democratic ideal – it is a democratic necessity.

21

The Fault Lines of Democracy: Caste, Governance and Political Representation

Caste, as a mode of social stratification, has historically structured power, privilege and political access across South Asia. Its origins, deeply rooted in religious and cultural traditions, have transcended mere social categorization to become a pervasive determinant of political representation and governance. In South Asia's evolving democratic landscape, caste remains a paradoxical force: it is both a tool for political mobilization, and an instrument of socio-economic exclusion. While democracy, in its ideal form, promises egalitarianism and universal suffrage, the lived reality for marginalized castes – Dalits, Adivasis, Madhesis, Shudras and other historically disenfranchised communities – reveals a much more fractured narrative.

The SAARC region, presents a complex tableau of caste-based political mobilization. In India, the caste system, codified under the *varna* and *jati* structure, informs political allegiances and electoral strategies in fundamental ways. The political rise of Bahujan Samaj Party (BSP) and Rashtriya Janata Dal (RJD), for instance, illustrates how historically oppressed communities have leveraged democratic mechanisms for representation. Similarly, in Nepal, caste dynamics influence political representation, particularly among the Madhesi community in the Terai region. In Sri Lanka, caste intersects with ethnic identity, contributing to layered discrimination within both Sinhalese and Tamil communities. Meanwhile, in Pakistan, social stratification, although less rigidly defined by caste, manifests through *biradari* (clan) politics – perpetuating feudal hierarchies and limiting upward mobility for marginalized groups. Bangladesh, Bhutan and the Maldives, while less overtly structured by caste, experience caste-like discrimination through ethnic hierarchies, and religious stratification that influence political engagement and social mobility.

The relationship between caste and democracy in South Asia thus emerges as both adversarial and collabourative. On the one hand, democratic institutions have served as conduits for marginalized communities to assert their political voice. Affirmative action policies, such as reservations for Scheduled Castes and Scheduled Tribes in India and constitutional guarantees in Nepal, represent state interventions aimed at rectifying historical injustices. These mechanisms have not only increased political representation but also reshaped local governance dynamics. For instance, India's Panchayati Raj Institutions have been instrumental in enabling Dalit and Adivasi women to participate in local governance, challenging the patriarchal and caste-based hierarchies that have historically excluded them.

However, the successes of democratic inclusion are marred by persistent inequalities. Caste-based violence, social boycotts and systemic exclusion continue to undermine the democratic promise. Reports from the National Crime Records Bureau (NCRB) in India indicate a rise in atrocities against Dalits and Adivasis, even as political representation increases.[1] Similarly, in Nepal, the Madhesi community remains underrepresented in key political offices despite constitutional guarantees. The experience of marginalized communities in Pakistan's Sindh and Balochistan regions also attests to the persistence of feudal control, which consolidates power within upper-caste families while depriving marginalized communities of political agency.

The persistence of caste-based discrimination in governance is not merely a social relic but an institutional challenge. Legislative measures, constitutional safeguards and state-led interventions have been deployed across South Asia to dismantle these hierarchies, yet their impact remains uneven. In India, the Scheduled Castes and Scheduled Tribes (Prevention of Atrocities) Act, 1989, coupled with constitutional amendments, has provided legal recourse against caste-based violence. Nepal's 2015 constitution enshrines protections for marginalized communities, mandating inclusive political representation. However, structural barriers, coupled with sociopolitical resistance from dominant castes, limit the transformative potential of these legal frameworks. In Sri Lanka and Pakistan, the situation is further complicated by the overlap of caste and ethnic identity, which fragments political solidarity and stymies collective mobilization.

The intersection of caste and political representation in South Asia, therefore, is emblematic of the broader contradictions within democratic governance. Democracy promises equality, yet caste perpetuates exclusion; governance frameworks attempt inclusion, yet power remains consolidated within upper-caste elites. To understand democracy in South Asia is to engage with this paradox – where the ballot box serves as both a space of empowerment for marginalized communities and a fortress for entrenched hierarchies.

In the following sections, the chapter will explore these dynamics through four cross-cutting themes: the political mobilization of caste-based groups and its impact on democratic governance; the role of state institutions in addressing or perpetuating caste-based exclusion; grassroots movements challenging caste hierarchies across the region; and the intersection of caste, economic disparity and governance. Through these thematic lenses, the chapter will interrogate how caste informs political agency and governance structures across the SAARC nations, while offering insights into pathways towards more inclusive, equitable democratic practices.

Caste and Political Representation

The political mobilization of caste-based identities in South Asia serves as both a vehicle for democratic inclusion and a reflection of enduring social hierarchies. Nowhere is this paradox more evident than in India, where the caste system – despite constitutional safeguards and legal provisions – remains a central determinant of political power and social privilege. Caste-based political parties such as the BSP, RJD and Samajwadi Party have emerged not merely as reactionary movements against historical oppression, but as strategic actors in electoral politics. Their success underscores the reality that caste, rather than withering under democratic governance, has been reconstituted as a political identity capable of mobilizing mass support.

The BSP, founded by Kanshi Ram and later led by Mayawati, epitomizes this political mobilization. Emerging from the Dalit movement, the BSP's rise to power in Uttar Pradesh (India's most populous state) marked a historic moment for caste-based political representation. Under Mayawati's leadership, the party secured the chief minister's office four times, symbolizing a break from the dominance of upper-caste political elites. The BSP's slogan, '*Bahujan Hitay, Bahujan Sukhay* (For the benefit of the majority, for the happiness of the majority)', articulated a radical reimagining of political power in terms of caste solidarity. Yet, the party's trajectory also reveals the limitations of caste-based representation: while it succeeded in capturing political office, it struggled to dismantle entrenched economic hierarchies or significantly alter governance frameworks that perpetuate caste-based exclusion.

In Nepal, the Madhesi community, offers another compelling illustration of caste and political representation intersecting with ethnic and regional identities. As discussed earlier, historically marginalized and underrepresented in central governance, the Madhesis have long demanded proportional representation and constitutional guarantees for their rights. The Madhesi uprisings of 2007 and 2015, which saw widespread protests and political mobilization, resulted in constitutional amendments aimed at ensuring greater inclusivity. However, the Madhesi community's experience remains emblematic of the complexities of caste-based political mobilization in Nepal: while constitutional guarantees exist, the mechanisms of representation are often subverted by political elites, rendering formal representation insufficient for substantive political empowerment.

In Pakistan, biradari politics entrenches caste-like hierarchies, concentrating power among elite families like the Bhuttos and Sharifs while sidelining marginalized groups. In Sri Lanka, caste operates silently within both Sinhalese and Tamil communities, shaping political representation. Despite the rhetoric of equality, movements like the LTTE often reinforced upper-caste dominance, and post-war governance continues to reflect these unspoken hierarchies.

Bangladesh, Bhutan and the Maldives, while lacking formalized caste systems akin to India or Nepal, demonstrate parallel dynamics of social stratification affecting political representation. In Bangladesh, the legacy of land-based feudalism still shapes rural political power, with marginalized communities like the Dalits and Adivasis facing exclusion from political processes. Although legal frameworks exist to protect minority rights, they are seldom enforced with rigour, leaving caste-like discrimination largely unchallenged. In Bhutan, social hierarchies, though not caste-based, mirror exclusionary practices seen elsewhere in South Asia – particularly in its treatment of ethnic minorities such as the Lhotshampa community. The Maldives, while largely homogeneous in ethnic terms, exhibits caste-like structures through regional disparities that influence political access and representation.

What emerges from these varied national contexts is a shared phenomenon: caste and social stratification continue to mediate access to political power across South Asia, even within the formal structures of democratic governance. Legal frameworks intended to democratize political representation are often subverted by entrenched social hierarchies, rendering political office a domain primarily accessible to those with social capital – typically the upper castes or dominant ethnic groups. Even where political representation is achieved, as with Dalit leaders in India or Madhesi representatives in Nepal, the deeper socio-economic hierarchies remain largely untouched. The consequence is a form of democratic participation that is nominally inclusive, yet substantively exclusionary.

The persistence of caste-based political mobilization raises critical questions about the nature of democratic governance in South Asia. Is political representation, divorced from socio-economic transformation, sufficient to dismantle centuries of stratification? Can the ballot box, powerful as it is, overcome the inertia of entrenched caste hierarchies? These questions reflect the core tension within South Asia's democratic project, and highlight the promise of political equality set against the reality of social stratification.

Institutional Mechanisms and Caste-Based Exclusion

The state remains the most decisive actor in addressing (or perpetuating) caste-based exclusion across South Asia. Through constitutional safeguards, legal frameworks and governance mechanisms, states have attempted to dismantle caste hierarchies, though their success remains uneven. The efficacy of these interventions is deeply conditioned by political will, bureaucratic integrity and the persistence of entrenched social hierarchies that often co-opt institutional mechanisms intended for reform. While democratic governance aspires to equality and inclusion, the state's role in mitigating caste-based exclusion is fraught with contradictions – oscillating between progressive legislation and structural inertia.

India's constitutional architecture exemplifies both the promise and the paradox of state-led caste reform. The framers of the Indian constitution, most notably Dr B.R. Ambedkar, enshrined a series of protective measures aimed at redressing historical injustices suffered by Dalits (Scheduled Castes) and Adivasis (Scheduled Tribes). Article 17 of the Indian Constitution abolished 'untouchability', while Article 15 prohibits discrimination on the grounds of caste, race or religion. Additionally, Articles 330 and 332 mandate reserved seats for Scheduled Castes and Scheduled Tribes in the Lok Sabha and state legislative assemblies. These provisions represent an unprecedented state-led attempt to secure political representation for historically marginalized communities.

Yet, despite this robust legal framework, caste-based exclusion remains pervasive. The Scheduled Castes and Scheduled Tribes (Prevention of Atrocities) Act of 1989, designed to protect Dalits and Adivasis from caste-based violence, has been criticized for its inconsistent enforcement. According to the NCRB, cases of caste-based violence have not diminished but, in some states, have risen sharply in recent years. Data from 2023 indicate a 13.1 per cent increase in crimes against Scheduled Castes, with Uttar Pradesh, Bihar and Rajasthan reporting the highest numbers.[2] The conviction rate remains abysmally low, hovering around 28 per cent – a stark indicator of institutional reluctance to deliver justice. Structural biases within law enforcement agencies, bureaucratic delays and political patronage networks undermine the effectiveness of legal protections, reducing legislative guarantees to mere symbolic gestures.

In Nepal, the promulgation of the 2015 constitution marked a watershed in recognizing the rights of marginalized communities, including Dalits. Article 18 guarantees equality before the law and Article 24 explicitly prohibits caste-based discrimination. Additionally, the constitution mandates proportional representation in state institutions and local governance for marginalized communities, including Dalits and Madhesis. However, the implementation of these provisions remains stunted. A 2024 study by the International Dalit Solidarity Network (IDSN) revealed that Dalits occupy less than 8 per cent of key political offices, despite comprising approximately 13 per cent of Nepal's population.[3] Local governance remains dominated by upper-caste elites, who wield disproportionate influence over resource allocation and political decision-making. The exclusion is further compounded by social ostracism, which limits Dalit participation in local governance despite constitutional guarantees.

Sri Lanka presents a unique case wherein caste intersects with ethnic identity, complicating state-led interventions aimed at dismantling social hierarchies. The Sri Lankan state, has largely ignored the internal stratifications within the Tamil community. Even during the civil war, the LTTE despite its rhetoric of egalitarianism, reinforced Vellalar dominance, sidelining lower-caste Tamils in both military and political hierarchies. Post-war governance mechanisms, including the Northern Provincial Council, remain reflective of these entrenched hierarchies – with political representation heavily skewed towards upper-caste Tamils. State-led reconstruction efforts have scarcely addressed these imbalances, perpetuating caste-based exclusion under the veneer of ethnic reconciliation.

Pakistan's governance framework does not formally recognize caste-based stratification; however, as mentioned earlier it operates through biradari networks that replicate caste-like exclusions. Legislative measures aimed at decentralizing political power, such as the Local Government Acts of 2001 and 2013, have been largely ineffectual in breaking these power structures. Local governance bodies, intended as mechanisms of grassroots empowerment, have often been captured by feudal elites who manipulate electoral outcomes to maintain political dominance. The lack of institutional safeguards for marginalized communities renders them politically invisible, reinforcing socio-economic hierarchies that remain unchallenged.

Reports by the Bangladesh Dalit and Excluded Rights Movement (BDERM) highlight the near-total absence of Dalit representation in political office in Bangladesh, coupled with systemic discrimination in access to education, employment and legal protection.[4] Government initiatives, though ostensibly aimed at inclusive governance, remain largely rhetorical, with little impact on ground realities. Institutional apathy, compounded by societal stigma, continues to marginalize these communities, reflecting the inadequacies of state intervention.

Bhutan's political landscape is heavily centralized, with little representation for ethnic minorities like the Lhotshampas, as discussed previously. Decentralization efforts have not significantly altered this dynamic, leaving political decision-making concentrated among the elite. In the Maldives, political power is centralized around clan-like structures that determine electoral outcomes and political patronage. This configuration mirrors caste dynamics, where political access is largely reserved for those embedded within elite networks, effectively marginalizing those on the periphery.

The persistence of caste-based exclusion across these diverse political landscapes underscores a critical paradox: while constitutional safeguards exist, their enforcement is sporadic and, in many cases, subverted by dominant social hierarchies. State institutions, designed to act as arbiters of equality, are often co-opted by the very structures they are meant to dismantle. The lack of political will, compounded by bureaucratic inertia and elite capture, renders state-led interventions largely symbolic. Across South Asia, political representation remains skewed towards dominant castes or biradaris, leaving marginalized communities politically disenfranchised despite legislative guarantees.

Democratic Movements and Caste Resistance

If the state remains a site of contested representation for marginalized castes, civil society and grassroots movements have emerged as the vital counterforce – often embodying the democratic ideals that state institutions fail to uphold. Across South Asia, grassroots mobilization against caste-based exclusion has not only challenged entrenched hierarchies, but has also redefined political agency for historically disenfranchised communities. From the Dalit movements in India to the Madhesi agitations in Nepal, the activism of marginalized communities underscores a radical reimagining of political participation – one that transcends the limitations of state intervention.

In India, the Dalit movement represents the most sustained and visible form of caste-based resistance. Its roots extend back to pre-independence struggles, but it gained significant political momentum under the leadership of Dr B.R. Ambedkar, whose intellectual and political activism reshaped the discourse on caste and democracy. Ambedkar's vision of social justice, articulated through the concept of 'Annihilation of Caste' underscored the need for political empowerment as a means of dismantling social hierarchies. His role in drafting the Indian constitution institutionalized affirmative action policies, reserving political seats for Scheduled Castes and Scheduled Tribes. However, beyond state-led mechanisms, grassroots mobilization among Dalits has taken radical and organized forms, most notably through organizations like the Dalit Panthers in the 1970s and the Bhim Army in recent years.

The Bhim Army, founded in 2015 by Chandrashekhar Azad in Uttar Pradesh, has become emblematic of contemporary Dalit resistance. Unlike previous movements focused primarily on political representation, the Bhim Army combines direct action with educational initiatives aimed at empowering the Dalit youth.

Through its Shaheed Bhagat Singh Library Campaign, the movement has established libraries in marginalized communities, providing access to literature on social justice and Ambedkarite philosophy. Its confrontations with upper-caste dominance, often manifesting in violent clashes, reflect the ongoing struggle for equality in rural India – where caste hierarchies remain deeply entrenched. The movement's digital activism, particularly through social media, has expanded its influence, connecting local resistance to global audiences and amplifying the voices of those traditionally silenced by caste oppression.

The Madhesi Movement in Nepal, as discussed above, forced amendments to Nepal's constitution, ostensibly guaranteeing proportional representation for marginalized communities. However, the movement's successes remain partial. Madhesis continue to report systemic discrimination in access to political office and government employment. Grassroots organizations like the Madhesi Dalit Rights Forum and Terai Human Rights Defenders Alliance have thus become crucial actors in demanding accountability from the state, often working independently of mainstream political parties.

In Pakistan, grassroots mobilization has primarily taken the form of local resistance against feudal structures. Organizations such as the Hari Welfare Association in Sindh advocate for the rights of bonded labourers, many of whom belong to lower-caste communities. These labourers, trapped in cycles of debt and bonded servitude, reflect the intersection of caste and economic exploitation. Despite legislative attempts to abolish bonded labour – most notably the Bonded Labour System (Abolition) Act of 1992 – the practice persists, reinforced by feudal power dynamics and political patronage. Local mobilizations, though frequently suppressed, have led to incremental victories, including the liberation of labourers from bonded servitude and legal recognition of their rights. These movements reflect a form of grassroots democracy that is largely absent in state-led governance structures.

Sri Lanka's caste-based resistance is deeply intertwined with its ethnic conflict. Among the Tamil population, caste hierarchies, though often overshadowed by ethnic divisions, remain potent. During the civil war, the LTTE espoused a vision of social equality. However, as mentioned earlier, the organization's leadership remained dominated by upper-caste Tamils, perpetuating caste-based exclusion even within its ranks. In post-war Sri Lanka, grassroots organizations like the Tamil Nadu Dalit Women's Association have sought to address the compounded marginalization faced by Dalit Tamil women, who endure caste-, ethnicity- and gender-based discrimination. These movements challenge not only local hierarchies but also the state's unwillingness to address caste-based discrimination within the Tamil population. Furthermore, caste-based mobilization among Sinhalese communities, though less visible, has also emerged in local governance struggles, particularly in rural districts, where caste still determines political access and resource allocation.

Bangladesh, though formally free of the varna-based caste system, harbours deep social stratification among its Dalit communities.

The BDERM has been at the forefront of advocating for political representation and social inclusion. Dalits in Bangladesh, primarily working in sanitation and manual scavenging, are excluded from political processes and face systemic discrimination. Grassroots mobilization has led to policy advocacy for the inclusion of Dalits in local governance bodies, though substantial progress remains elusive. The BDERM's strategy has been multifaceted: it engages in direct action, legal advocacy and community mobilization to challenge entrenched social hierarchies.

In Bhutan and the Maldives, caste-based movements are virtually non-existent, yet ethnic stratification and regional disparities prompt local mobilizations for greater political inclusion. In Bhutan, ethnic minorities like the Lhotshampas have organized resistance against state-led discrimination, particularly following the forced expulsions of the 1990s.[5] In the Maldives, grassroots mobilization focuses on regional disparities and political centralization, which echo caste-like exclusions in terms of political access and economic opportunity.

What binds these movements across South Asia is their shared aspiration for political agency and socio-economic justice. Grassroots mobilizations represent an assertion of democratic rights from below, challenging both state structures and social hierarchies. Unlike state-led interventions, which often falter under political patronage and bureaucratic inertia, grassroots movements operate outside the constraints of formal political structures, leveraging collective action to disrupt local hierarchies. These movements reveal the latent power of democratic engagement, when mobilized by the most marginalized, underscoring the capacity for political transformation from the peripheries of society.

Intersections of Poverty and Power

The nexus of caste, economic disparities and governance in South Asia reveals a foundational paradox within its democratic structures: while political representation has incrementally expanded for marginalized castes, economic hierarchies rooted in caste remain largely unaltered. Across the SAARC nations, caste-based exclusion is not merely a matter of political underrepresentation. It is intricately woven into the architecture of economic inequality, perpetuating cycles of poverty and denying equitable access to resources and opportunities. In understanding this intersection, one must examine the ways in which caste stratification interacts with land ownership, labour markets, education and state-led economic policies.

In India, the relationship between caste and economic inequality is starkly visible. Dalits and Adivasis remain disproportionately represented among the rural and urban poor, a condition perpetuated by historical dispossession from land and capital. According to the Periodic Labour Force Survey 2023, Scheduled Castes constitute nearly 40 per cent of the agricultural labour force while owning less than 10 per cent of agricultural land.[6] This disjunction underscores the economic subjugation encoded within caste hierarchies. Despite land reform policies intended to redistribute agricultural holdings, dominant castes – land-owning communities such as the Jats, Patels and Reddys – retain disproportionate control over rural economies, leveraging political influence to subvert redistributive policies.

The issue of manual scavenging exemplifies the intersection of caste and economic deprivation. Although constitutionally banned under the Employment of Manual Scavengers and Construction of Dry Latrines (Prohibition) Act of 1993 and reinforced by the Prohibition of Employment as Manual Scavengers and their Rehabilitation Act of 2013, the practice continues unabated. Data from the National Commission for Safai Karamcharis (2024) indicate that over 50,000 individuals – overwhelmingly Dalits – remain engaged in this hazardous occupation.[7] The failure of state mechanisms to enforce bans and rehabilitate workers into dignified employment illustrates a profound governance deficit. Moreover, the prevalence of caste-based occupations – including sanitation work, stone quarrying and tannery labour – reflects the broader economic stratification that persists despite legislative safeguards.

In Nepal, the intersection of caste and economic inequality is similarly entrenched. Dalits, constituting nearly 13 per cent of the population, are largely confined to menial labour and low-wage agricultural work. According to a 2024 report by the IDSN, Dalit households in Nepal earn, on average, 50 per cent less than their upper-caste counterparts.[8] Landlessness remains a critical barrier to economic mobility, with over 80 per cent of Dalit families reported as landless or occupying marginal lands, vulnerable to displacement. Microfinance initiatives, while intended to empower marginalized communities, have largely bypassed Dalit populations due to bureaucratic hurdles and social discrimination exacerbating economic precarity. Political decentralization, heralded as a mechanism for inclusive governance, has had limited impact in altering these dynamics, as local governance remains dominated by upper-caste elites who control resource allocation.

Pakistan's socio-economic stratification of biradari networks mirrors caste-like exclusions. Rural land ownership is concentrated among feudal families who belong to powerful biradaris, while lower-caste groups, particularly in Sindh and Punjab, remain entrenched in bonded labour. John Hopkins–Aga Khan study estimated in 2024 that over 2 million people, many of them from marginalized communities, are trapped in bonded labour across brick kilns, agriculture and textile industries.[9] Legislative measures, such as the Bonded Labour System (Abolition) Act of 1992, have been largely ineffective, undermined by political patronage and local power dynamics that protect feudal interests. The Sindh Tenancy Act, intended to safeguard tenant farmers, remains weakly enforced, perpetuating debt bondage and economic dependency among lower-caste agricultural labourers.

Sri Lanka's caste-based economic exclusion is obscured by the dominant narrative of ethnic conflict but remains deeply woven into its socio-economic fabric, as discussed earlier. Among Tamil communities, caste hierarchies determine access to economic opportunities, particularly in the Northern and Eastern provinces. Vellalar Tamils, traditionally landowners, have maintained economic dominance, while lower-caste Tamils remain confined to menial labour. The end of the civil war did little to disrupt these hierarchies. Post-war reconstruction initiatives, focused largely on ethnic reconciliation, neglected intracommunity caste dynamics. Economic marginalization remains pervasive among the lower-caste Tamils, who lack access to capital, land and political representation. Furthermore, post-war government resettlement schemes have been criticized for reinforcing caste stratification, as land allocations favoured those with political connections rather than the marginalized.

In Bangladesh, caste-like exclusion persists among Dalit and indigenous communities, who remain largely confined to low-wage, hazardous occupations. The BDERM reports that nearly 90 per cent of Dalits work as street sweepers, sanitation workers and manual labourers, with minimal access to education or vocational training. Microcredit schemes, a hallmark of Bangladesh's developmental model, have largely bypassed these communities – reflecting a structural bias in economic development initiatives. State welfare programmes, while expansive in rhetoric, fail to reach marginalized populations due to corruption and administrative bottlenecks.

Bhutan and the Maldives present a more subdued narrative of caste-like economic exclusion, though social hierarchies still influence economic opportunity. In Bhutan, the Lhotshampa community – ethnically Nepalese – remains marginalized in terms of land ownership and economic mobility, a condition exacerbated by state-led exclusionary policies in the 1990s. While the mass expulsions have ended, Bhutan continues to enforce restrictive citizenship laws from 1985 and discriminatory census categories, limiting land ownership, access to state services and citizenship rights for many Lhotshampas.[10] In the Maldives, political centralization and regional disparities mirror caste-like structures, with economic opportunities heavily skewed towards the capital, Malé, leaving outer atolls in economic stagnation. The lack of decentralization in governance has perpetuated these disparities, rendering political representation symbolic, rather than transformative.

The intersection of caste and economic disenfranchisement across South Asia lays bare the limitations of democratic governance in dismantling entrenched social hierarchies. Despite constitutional guarantees and legislative safeguards, economic power remains overwhelmingly consolidated among upper castes or elite biradaris, while marginalized communities continue to navigate the peripheries of political and economic power. State-led economic reforms – whether in the form of land redistribution, microcredit schemes or affirmative action – have largely failed to disrupt these hierarchies, constrained by political patronage, administrative corruption and deep-seated social biases.

This reality prompts critical reflection on the role of democratic governance in addressing structural inequalities. Can the promise of political representation suffice if economic emancipation remains elusive? Is democratic inclusion meaningful if it is not accompanied by substantive access to resources and opportunities? These questions challenge the very foundations of South Asia's democratic experiment – where political enfranchisement and economic equity remain disjointed aspirations.

The concluding section will now turn towards examining these contradictions and articulating pathways for reform. It will explore how democratic governance in South Asia can transcend symbolic representation and move towards substantive equality, particularly for caste-marginalized communities. It will interrogate the potential of legal reforms, civil society activism and grassroots mobilization to bridge the chasm between political enfranchisement and economic empowerment.

Inclusive Governance

The persistence of caste-based exclusion across South Asia, despite constitutional safeguards and legislative interventions, underscores the need for a radical recalibration of governance frameworks. Reform must transcend symbolic representation, and address the material and institutional barriers that perpetuate caste hierarchies. This requires a multidimensional approach that integrates political, economic and social mechanisms for substantive change. Below, I outline four critical reform pathways necessary for achieving genuine inclusivity and dismantling caste-based exclusion across the SAARC nations.

1. Strengthening Legal Protections and Enforcement Mechanisms

While legal frameworks exist to address caste-based discrimination, their enforcement remains dismal. In India, the Scheduled Castes and Scheduled Tribes (Prevention of Atrocities) Act, *1989*, though robust in its provisions, has suffered from poor implementation. As mentioned above, crimes against Scheduled Castes have increased. To address this, it is imperative to establish special atrocity courts in regions with high incidences of caste violence, alongside independent monitoring by civil society organizations to prevent local political capture.

Nepal's 2015 constitution guarantees proportional representation for Dalits, but it is not yet in practice. In Pakistan, while bonded labour remains constitutionally prohibited under the Bonded Labour System (Abolition) Act of 1992, as mentioned earlier, over 2 million individuals – primarily from lower-caste backgrounds – remain in bonded servitude. To rectify this, the establishment of anti-bonded labour task forces – empowered with prosecutorial authority and independent of local feudal influence – is crucial. These task forces must be situated in Sindh and Punjab, where bonded labour is most prevalent, and operate under federal oversight to circumvent local patronage networks.

2. Economic Redistribution and Land Reforms

The intersection of caste and land ownership perpetuates economic disenfranchisement across South Asia. As mentioned before, in India, Dalits and Adivasis represent nearly 40 per cent of agricultural workforce but own less than 10 per cent of agricultural land.[11] Land reform policies, while constitutionally mandated, have been subverted through bureaucratic inertia and political resistance from dominant castes. To address this, land redistribution tribunals should be instituted, with autonomous authority to investigate illegal land encroachments and execute land redistribution directly to marginalized communities. Furthermore, cooperative land trusts, where land is communally owned and democratically managed, should be piloted in regions with high Dalit and Adivasi populations to disrupt generational cycles of landlessness.

Nepal faces a parallel challenge, where Dalit communities are predominantly landless. According to the Nepal Landless Dalit Rights Forum, over 80 per cent of Dalits report being landless or occupying vulnerable plots.[12] State-led land entitlement schemes, coupled with microfinance programmes targeted explicitly at Dalit and Madhesi populations, are necessary to bridge the economic gap. These schemes must be insulated from local political interference by establishing independent land commissions that operate under federal, not provincial, jurisdiction.

In Pakistan, feudal dominance has rendered land reforms largely symbolic. The Sindh Tenancy Act, which theoretically guarantees tenant rights, remains ineffectual in practice. Here, provincial land reform commissions should be empowered to override feudal control, allowing for direct state intervention in tenancy disputes and equitable land distribution. A similar model should be considered for Sri Lanka's Northern and Eastern provinces, where Tamil lower-caste communities remain economically disenfranchised despite post-war resettlement initiatives.

3. Educational Equity and Vocational Training

Access to quality education remains a critical barrier for marginalized castes across South Asia. In India, the gross enrolment ratio for Scheduled Castes in higher education stands at 25.9 per cent, lower than the national average of 27.1 per cent, according to the All India Survey on Higher Education 2024.[13] To bridge this gap, caste-sensitive educational Grants should be introduced, modelled after the US Federal Pell Grant system, providing direct financial aid to Dalit and Adivasi students. Moreover, reserved seats in technical institutes, particularly in engineering, medical and vocational training centres, must be rigorously enforced to prevent upper-caste dominance.

Nepal faces a similar educational deficit among Dalits. According to the latest reports, only 12% of Dalits enroll into secondary education, compared to the 52% of upper-caste students.[14] To address this, Dalit educational councils should be established at provincial levels – tasked with monitoring dropout rates and implementing retention strategies through community-based educational support.

In Pakistan, educational inequality among marginalized communities is stark. Educational inequality in Pakistan is particularly severe among marginalized communities, with Dalits, religious minorities, girls, and rural populations facing entrenched barriers. Literacy among Scheduled Caste (Dalit) Hindus is estimated at just 18–19 per cent, compared to 34 per cent for upper-caste Hindus and a national adult average of around 60 per cent. In Sindh and Punjab, fewer than 10 per cent of Dalit girls attend school. An estimated 22–26 million children aged 5–16 – roughly 36–39 per cent – remain out of school, disproportionately from rural and minority backgrounds. In former FATA regions, survival from KG to Grade 5 is only 36 per cent, and female literacy is as low as 7.5 per cent. These disparities reflect deep-rooted structural exclusion shaped by caste, gender, geography and poverty.[15]

4. Inclusive Local Governance and Decentralization

Finally, political decentralization remains crucial for empowering marginalized communities. India's Panchayati Raj Institutions provide a model for local governance that has empowered Dalit women and marginalized castes through mandatory reservations. However, elite capture continues to stifle genuine representation. To counter this, caste audits of local governance bodies should be institutionalized, ensuring compliance with reservation policies and preventing proxy representation by upper-caste elites.

In Nepal, local governance remains dominated by upper-caste interests, despite constitutional guarantees of proportional representation. An annual local governance inclusivity audit, mandated by federal legislation, should be implemented to evaluate Dalit representation in local bodies. Such audits would identify discrepancies and enable targeted interventions to rectify imbalances.

For Pakistan, Sri Lanka and Bangladesh, decentralization efforts have largely failed to empower lower-caste communities due to the dominance of local power brokers. Here, democratic accountability mechanisms – such as community-led monitoring committees – should be established to oversee local governance and to ensure that marginalized voices are not subsumed by elite interests.

These reform pathways underscore the imperative for a transformative recalibration of South Asia's governance structures. Addressing caste-based exclusion requires more than legal safeguards – it necessitates dismantling economic hierarchies, enforcing educational equity and reconstituting local governance to genuinely reflect marginalized communities. Only through such structural reforms can the democratic promise of equality and representation be actualized for South Asia's most disenfranchised citizens.

22

Towards a More Representative Democracy: The Need for Proportional Representation

The political landscape of South Asia, represented through the member states of the SAARC, is marked by a diverse array of electoral systems. These systems – ranging from FPTP to proportional representation (PR) and mixed models – reflect distinct historical, political and constitutional frameworks that have evolved in response to domestic political exigencies, colonial legacies and aspirations for representative democracy.

First-Past-the-Post Systems

The FPTP electoral model, wherein the candidate with the highest number of votes in a constituency is declared the winner, is the predominant system in several SAARC nations. India, the largest democracy in the world, employs FPTP for its Lok Sabha and most of its state assemblies. This model, inherited from the British colonial administration, is noted for its simplicity and clear constituency-based representation. It is, however, often critiqued for its majoritarian biases, wherein a candidate may secure a parliamentary seat without an absolute majority of votes, leading to disproportionality in political representation. Pakistan similarly utilizes the FPTP system for its National Assembly and provincial assemblies, with additional reserved seats for women and minorities filled through proportional allocation based on party lists. In Bangladesh, FPTP governs the election of the Jatiya Sangsad (National Parliament), though seats reserved for women are allocated through PR, ensuring a modicum of representational parity.

Sri Lanka presents a nuanced case: its presidential and local government elections are conducted under the FPTP model, distinguishing it from its parliamentary system, which follows PR.

While FPTP facilitates direct accountability and simpler electoral contests, it has also been a conduit for communal and regional polarization, particularly in ethnically diverse nations like Sri Lanka and India.

Proportional Representation Systems

Proportional Representation, wherein seats are allocated based on the per centage of votes secured by political parties, finds expression in Nepal, Sri Lanka and formerly in Afghanistan. Nepal's 2015 constitution introduced a mixed electoral model with 60 per cent of its representatives elected through FPTP and 40 per cent through PR – aimed at addressing historical imbalances in ethnic and regional representation. The PR component allows for more inclusive participation of marginalized groups, making the Nepali parliament one of the most diverse in South Asia. Similarly, Sri Lanka employs PR for its parliamentary elections, as mentioned earlier where party lists compete at the district level and seats are distributed proportionally. This has fostered multiparty coalitions and ensured representation of ethnic minorities, though it has also led to fragmented legislatures and coalition instability.

Afghanistan, under the 2004 constitution, had adopted a variant called the single non-transferable vote, a multi-member district PR system. This mechanism, while intended to democratize representation, resulted in considerable fragmentation and a lack of party cohesion. With the resurgence of Taliban, elections have been banned, pushing the country towards more entrenched authoritarianism, and sounding a death knell for the continuation of this voting model.

Mixed Electoral Systems

Mixed electoral models blend the advantages of FPTP and PR, attempting to balance direct representation with proportional inclusivity.

Bhutan exemplifies this with its two-round electoral process: the first is a party-based primary and the second is a constituency-based FPTP election between the two leading parties. This structure ensures that only the most popular parties compete for final seats, enhancing political stability while maintaining competitive representation.

Nepal's mixed system, as earlier noted, splits its parliamentary seats between FPTP and PR – an innovation aimed at bridging regional disparities and amplifying the voices of historically marginalized communities. Sri Lanka's local government elections have also moved towards a mixed-member proportional representation, with 60 per cent of members elected through FPTP and 40 per cent through PR. This hybrid model is designed to reconcile the accountability of direct election with the inclusivity of proportional distribution.

Implications for Governance

The choice of electoral system profoundly shapes political representation and governance outcomes. In FPTP systems, the 'winner-takes-all' approach often results in dominant-party politics, as observed in India and Bangladesh, where ruling parties frequently secure absolute majorities despite winning only a plurality of votes. Conversely, PR systems in Nepal and Sri Lanka have facilitated more diverse representation but have also led to political fragmentation and coalition-based governance, complicating legislative coherence. Mixed systems like those in Bhutan and Nepal strive to harmonize these dynamics, but they are not immune to challenges of political consolidation and electoral volatility.

It is essential to understand that these electoral frameworks illuminate the broader democratic trajectories of SAARC nations, offering insights into how political representation is configured, contested and sustained across South Asia.

The Need for Change

The best electoral system is the one that straightforwardly and most accurately reflects the preferences of voters, the legal scholar Donald Horowitz noted in his 2003 seminal essay on electoral systems,

'Electoral Systems: A Primer for Decision Makers'.[1] But there is no definite answer as to which system fits that bill. India and the UK follow the Westminster electoral model, in which the voters elect their representatives to the Lok Sabha and the House of Commons, respectively. The voting procedure as well as the election of candidates is based on the FPTP system.

In recent years (since 2010), both countries have questioned the merits of the FPTP procedure. In 2011, the UK conducted a referendum on whether to retain the voting system – 68 per cent voted in its favour.[2] However, the voter turnout for the referendum was only 41 per cent, which means a majority did not participate in the decision-making process. In India, too, the FPTP system is under scrutiny. On 22 April 2017, the Parliamentary Standing Committee on Personnel, Public Grievances, Law and Justice – headed by Anand Sharma, who was a Congress MP in the Rajya Sabha then – issued a press release announcing an examination of the issue of electoral reforms and alternative voting systems. In late August, the *Indian Express* reported that the committee had sent a questionnaire on electoral reforms to all parties and to the ECI. According to the news report, the questionnaire stated that 'apprehensions are now being raised that in recent years the FPTP system is not the best suited' to India.

The FPTP has several advantages, because of which it is considered to be the simplest electoral system. The first advantage is clarity – it is an easy system to understand, the choices for the voters are clear, and the counting is also simple and straightforward. As soon as the votes are counted, the winner is immediately evident. The system also guarantees one representative for each constituency, who is accountable to his electorate, which is not necessarily the case in other voting systems. A third advantage is that candidates get to know their relative support in the constituency – unlike in other systems where electors vote for a party and not for individual candidates.

In a country such as India, with nearly 1 billion voters, the ease of administering voting in this system almost makes it the most viable model to follow. For a long time, I was a strong advocate of the FPTP system because I believed it to be the most efficient in the Indian context. However, I felt compelled to reconsider my position after the 2014 general election, in which the BSP – which was the third-largest party in terms of the national vote share, securing 20 per cent of the votes in Uttar Pradesh and 4.2 per cent at the national level – did not get a single seat in the Lok Sabha. On the other hand, parties with lower vote shares won a considerable number of seats – for instance, despite winning only 3.9 per cent of the votes, the TMC won thirty-four seats.[3]

The following year, in 2015, a similar phenomenon occurred in the UK – the UK Independence Party obtained only one seat in the general election despite being the third-largest party in terms of vote share, with nearly 13 per cent of the total votes being cast in its favour. Such results are possible in the FPTP system because a candidate is elected solely on the basis of whether they receive the highest number of votes and not on the basis of the proportion of votes polled by them.

It is increasingly becoming clear that the FPTP system of voting is fraught with serious problems. In the 2014 Lok Sabha election (according to the report by ECI the same year), despite the 'Modi wave', only 37 per cent of the elected candidates (or 201 MPs), obtained a majority of the votes in their constituencies. In the 2009 elections, only 22 per cent (or 120 MLAs), had secured a majority of the votes. At the legislative assembly level, across all states, an average of 44.5 per cent of the MLAs secured more than 50 per cent of the vote share in their constituencies.[4]

These instances reflect the main shortcoming of the FPTP system – the lack of legitimacy of political parties that are voted to a majority of the seats by a minority of the voters. In India's electoral history, the Congress party's P.K. Khanna recorded victory with the lowest-ever vote share in 1967, getting elected to the Shahjahanpur constituency in Uttar Pradesh with just 15.6 per cent of the vote.[5] Even in the Congress wave in the 1984 general election, after the assassination of Indira Gandhi, the party could not get a majority of the votes, despite winning a historic 404 of 533 seats, or 75 per cent of the seats, in the Lok Sabha. The party only received 49.1 per cent of the vote. In such a scenario, the will of the actual majority of voters is substituted by the will of a minority of voters.

Another consequence of the winner-takes-all nature of the FPTP system is that it rewards parties that target and treat preferentially specific segments of the electorate, or 'vote banks', rather than the majority of electors. The system thus rewards divisive electoral strategies, and encourages parties to field tainted candidates.

One way to address these concerns regarding this voting system would be to hold a run-off election – a second round of elections between the two candidates with the highest number of votes, a system which is followed in the French presidential elections. However, it is not feasible to conduct two rounds of voting in India – owing to the magnitude and complexity of the exercise required. Imagine going back to militancy-affected areas for a second time within a month; one election itself in these areas is subject to grave risk to lives – of the voters, polling staff and the security forces.

FPTP vs PR

In order to overcome the shortcomings of the FPTP system, some critics advocate the PR system of voting. In the PR system, every party gets a share of seats proportional to the share of votes it secures.

The PR system has many variants, such as the open-list and closed-list systems. In these, each voter is invited to indicate a preference or a ranking of several candidates from a list submitted by every party. Then, after the polls, each party is granted seats in proportion to the number of votes it receives. The candidates within each party's list are then elected in accordance with the per centage of votes polled by the party. For instance, if a party obtains a 15 per cent vote share and elections are being conducted for 200 seats, the top 30 candidates – or 15 per cent of the total number of seats – will be elected. As a result, the constituencies under the list system are multimember – multiple candidates will be elected from one constituency, with the number of seats per constituency allotted according to the demography or other physical characteristics of the constituency. However, the system requires all candidates to be nominated by a political party, and does not allow independent candidates.

In the open-list variant of the system, voters can choose to not only vote for a party but also to rank candidates within that party's declared list of candidates. In the closed-list variant, voters opt for the party as a whole rather than vote for specific candidates. However, the PR voting system presents some issues too. The system might make it difficult for parties to form the government, because the party with the maximum number of votes rarely obtains more than 30–35 per cent of the vote share. As a result, the dominant party would likely have to form a coalition with other large parties. In Indian politics, even under the current system, this has been necessary many times.

Another concern is that under the list system, the parties determine which candidates are elected by placing them at the top of their lists. The system thus guarantees that influential party members get easily elected. In such a system, candidates would perhaps focus on wooing their party leaders, instead of the voters. This could also reinforce various forms of capture of election tickets by the elite. At the whims of the party leadership, tickets could be issued to family members or particular party leaders, or to candidates on the basis of their caste, linguistic or religious community.

Owing to the underlying problems in both the FPTP and the PR systems of voting, a mixed model that combines the advantages of both is worth consideration. Different variants of the mixed method are followed in several countries, including Germany and Nepal. While these mixed models may also present problems of implementation in the Indian political and geographical context, variations of these mixed voting systems may be the most suitable alternatives to the FPTP system for India.

A Mixed Model?

In 1949, Germany adopted one such a method, known as the mixed-member proportional system of voting. Its parliament has 299 constituencies and 598 seats. On polling day, every voter casts two votes – one for a candidate in his or her constituency and the other for a party. Candidate wins are determined by the FPTP system; 299 seats are thus filled by the voters directly electing candidates who have won the largest number of votes in their constituencies. The aim of the first vote is to enable voters to personally know their representative. The second vote allows the elector to vote for a party. It is this vote that determines the power of parties in parliament. Based on this, the remaining 299 seats in parliament are filled by parties in proportion to the votes secured by them in the second round of votes. This is how the 598 representatives of the Bundestag, the lower house of the German parliament, are determined. For instance, if a party wins 20 seats under the FPTP system and gets a 10 per cent vote share in the second round of voting, it is given 40 seats from the remaining 299 – ensuring that it has 60 seats (or 10 per cent) of the total of 598 seats.

The German model, which accommodates both directly elected candidates to constituencies and parliamentary representation for political parties based on their vote share, also has its disadvantages. The chief among 3 is that any party that does not win either a 5 per cent vote share or 3 of 299 FPTP seats does not enter parliament. As a result, the choice of voters who voted for such candidates or parties is completely ignored.[6]

Adopting this system in India would require either halving the number of constituencies or doubling the size of the Lok Sabha. The former is not feasible in India's political context, given that the ratio of constituencies to voters in India is already vastly disproportionate to that of other countries. For instance, the House of Commons comprises 650 MPs and the Lok Sabha 543 – but a British MP represents an average of 72,000 electors, whereas an Indian MP represents 15 lakh electors. Halving the constituencies would imply that one elected candidate would represent 30 lakh electors, which would further limit voter accessibility to the MP and accountability between the MP and their constituency.

In India, increasing the strength of the Lok Sabha has been proposed in the past. Former President Pranab Mukherjee raised the issue at a seminar on economic reforms and electoral issues in April 2017, and various parliamentarians have previously suggested increasing the strength of the Lok Sabha by 181 seats (or one-third of its current strength) to introduce reservation for women in the house.[7] In fact, a great advantage of this system is the opportunity it provides to introduce reservation for women in parliament, by reserving a quota for women on the list of candidates to be elected by the PR system. My conversations with members of multiple political parties have indicated that their opposition to reservation of seats for women is largely due to their unwillingness to give up their existing Lok Sabha seats. The issue has seen no political will or traction – I am personally aware that the reasons for this include roadblocks by parliamentarians citing issues such as lack of seating space in the Lok Sabha.

A mixed system is also being adopted in Nepal – the model, which will be implemented in the upcoming election in November and December 2027, is known as the parallel system. Unlike the mixed member proportional (MMP) system, the parallel system sees voters effectively participate in two separate elections for a single chamber using two different systems. The MMP system combines proportional representation with single-member districts, ensuring that a party's overall seat share closely matches its share of the national vote. There are two different ballot papers, one each for the FPTP and PR voting systems, whereas in Germany there is one ballot paper with a separate column for each system. Of the 275 members in Nepal's house of representatives – its counterpart to the Indian Lok Sabha – 165 are elected through the FPTP system and 110 through the PR system. But, unlike the MMP system, the proportion of seats allotted under the PR system is a ratio of the number reserved for the PR system (110 in this case) and a proportion of the entire 275 seats. Therefore, the results of one election has little or no impact on the results of the other. Adopting such a model in India would once again require a change in the strength of parliament, or in the demarcation of constituencies.

A 2017 report by International IDEA noted that the PR system is the most popular in the world, with eighty-three countries following it.[8] According to its website, International IDEA is an intergovernmental organization that supports sustainable democracy worldwide. The report notes that the PR system is especially popular in Europe, where thirty-four countries – nearly 67 per cent – have adopted it. The FPTP system comes second in popularity, with sixty-one countries across the world employing it. The parallel system is the third-most popular one, and is followed in twenty-one countries.

What matters most is that electoral systems ensure reflection of the will of the voters and the legitimacy of the leaders. To this end, perhaps the strength of the Lok Sabha could be doubled and the German model without its threshold can be considered – the logistics of seating capacity cannot be allowed to come in the way of a more democratic and efficient voting system.

With the flaws in the FPTP system increasingly becoming exposed, the time to look at alternative models has come. Now that the parliamentary committee has set in motion this serious debate, one hopes that the electoral system itself will be taken up as a key reform. Moreover, considering that PM Narendra Modi has pressed electoral reforms as a priority political agenda – addressing issues such as transparency in political funding and simultaneous elections to the Lok Sabha and state legislative assembles – he should not miss this opportunity to reform the electoral system itself.

The diversity of electoral systems across the SAARC nations underscores the region's complex political landscape, shaped by historical legacies, sociopolitical cleavages and evolving democratic aspirations. The FPTP systems in India, Pakistan and Bangladesh prioritize constituency-based representation but often at the cost of proportional inclusivity, amplifying majoritarian dominance and marginalizing smaller parties and communities. In contrast, PR models in Nepal and Sri Lanka have enabled broader political representation, particularly for ethnic and regional minorities, though often at the expense of political stability and governance coherence. Mixed models in Bhutan and Nepal strive to bridge these representational gaps while mitigating the extremities of majoritarianism and fragmentation, yet their effectiveness remains contingent on political consolidation and institutional maturity.

The interplay of these systems with governance, political stability and democratic accountability in South Asia illustrates the profound impact of electoral design on democratic practice. As South Asian nations navigate the challenges of ethnic pluralism, political polarization and demands for deeper democratic participation, the choice and reform of electoral systems will be crucial in shaping their political futures. The ongoing evolution of electoral models, particularly in post-conflict states like Afghanistan and constitutionally reformed Nepal, reflects broader regional aspirations towards more equitable and inclusive political representation. In this sense, the democratization of South Asia remains both a site of contestation and a promise of transformative political inclusion.

Part V

Lessons from South Asia

23

Democracy in Decline, Democracy in Defiance

The democratic landscape of South Asia is marked by paradoxes, contradictions and a stubborn endurance. It is a region where democracy has been repeatedly imperilled – by fascistic majoritarianism, military authoritarianism and theocratic repression – yet never fully extinguished. From theocratic autocracy in Afghanistan to illiberal populism in India, and from the military–industrial stranglehold in Pakistan to the dynastic–authoritarian episodes in Bangladesh and the Maldives, the subcontinent today confronts a formidable spectrum of democratic decay.

Nevertheless, across time, every country in the region has, in its own moment of reckoning, resisted total collapse into autocracy and struggled back towards democratic renewal. This recurring democratic instinct – however faltering, however compromised – speaks not only to the political vitality of the region's peoples, but to the unfinished nature of the democratic experiment itself.

South Asia also offers an unparalleled labouratory for the comparative study of democracy and governance. The region presents nearly the entire typological range of political regimes: the complex federal democracy of India; Pakistan's enduring entanglement between civilian rule and military dominance; theocratic fascism under Taliban rule in Afghanistan; the transformation of Bhutan and Nepal from monarchies to constitutional democracies; and the episodes of outright dictatorship, dynasticism and electoral manipulation in Bangladesh, the Maldives and Sri Lanka.

These overlapping and often colliding trajectories offer a rich, real-time canvas through which scholars, policymakers and citizens alike can witness democracy in motion – not as an ideal state of affairs, but as a contingent, conflict-ridden and deeply human pursuit of dignity, representation and justice.

The South Asian experience offers the world a compelling set of democratic lessons born not of stability, but of struggle. It reveals how democracy can take root in societies marked by poverty, illiteracy, social hierarchies and violent conflict – conditions often thought inhospitable to democratic norms. It shows how institutions, even when battered, can recover through civic resistance, electoral innovation and political improvisation. Perhaps, most importantly, it cautions against complacency by reminding global democracies that authoritarianism does not arrive suddenly, but through slow erosion – against which vigilance, reform and inclusive governance remain the only durable safeguards.

But any portrait of democracy in South Asia, no matter how wide its frame, remains incomplete unless it turns inward – towards the hierarchies that structure daily life and delimit the boundaries of political participation.

Caste as Political Architecture

As discussed earlier, caste is not just a social category in South Asia – it is a system of governance. It shapes who gets to lead and who must obey, who has a voice in public institutions and who is silenced even before they speak. Across the region, we have seen how caste and its equivalents – whether defined explicitly as in India and Nepal, or more obliquely as through biradari in Pakistan or occupation-based exclusion in Bangladesh – still determine whose lives are protected by law and whose lives are invisible to it.

The chapter on caste argued that no account of democracy in South Asia is complete without grappling with this foundational hierarchy. Electoral victories, constitutional provisions and party-based mobilization have all made some room for caste-marginalized groups, but the deeper structures – land, labour, access to justice and public respect – remain largely unchanged.

The way forward is not a mystery. Every country in the region already has laws, provisions or past reform efforts that could (if taken seriously) begin to shift the balance. But political will has been absent. Caste is treated as a social issue when it is, in fact, a political structure. Reform will require direct action: enforcement of anti-discrimination laws, redistribution of land and economic opportunity, independent monitoring of representation in public institutions, and investment in education, health and housing for historically excluded communities.

These are not gestures of charity – they are the unfinished tasks of democracy. Until caste no longer determines where one sits in a classroom, what job one is allowed to do, or how one is treated by a police officer or a judge, democracy in South Asia will remain partial – technically functional but morally hollow.

Yet, even as caste operates as a subterranean architecture of exclusion, another, more institutional form of distortion plays out within the very entities meant to advance representative politics: the political parties themselves.

Crisis of Inner-Party Democracy

One of the most urgent but least acknowledged obstacles to democratic renewal in South Asia lies within the parties themselves. While much attention is paid to elections, institutions and leaders, far less is asked about how those leaders are chosen, how dissent is treated or whether parties are open spaces or closed fortresses. As discussed at length earlier, the region's parties often concentrate power in the hands of the few, sidelining internal dialogue and insulating leadership from accountability. This hollowing out of internal deliberation weakens not just the parties, but the very capacity of democracy to evolve, to respond and to include. In the absence of internal checks, parties risk becoming vehicles for ambition rather than institutions of public trust.

However, it is within these same spaces that some of the most necessary reforms must begin. Building more democratic societies will require building more democratic parties: ones that listen before they command, renew rather than replicate and welcome challenge instead of fearing it. Reforming internal party structures is not a technical fix –

it is a political struggle, one that calls for courage from those in power and imagination from those outside it. The legitimacy of the democratic project in South Asia will depend, in part, on whether political parties can learn to democratize themselves – not out of pressure but out of conviction.

Of course, parties do not operate in a vacuum. Their health, and the vibrancy of democracy at large, depends also on the ecosystem of ideas, dissent and debate that surrounds them – an ecosystem increasingly under siege.

Media Capture and the Collapse of Discourse

In South Asia, the story of democracy cannot be told without reckoning with the forces that shape, distort or silence the public conversation. The media – once trusted to question authority and hold power accountable – has increasingly become a terrain of capture, fear and illusion. Whether through economic monopolies that erase editorial independence, legal frameworks that criminalize dissent or digital landscapes awash in disinformation, the region's information ecology has become dangerously fragile. This matters not simply because journalists are under threat, but because citizens are slowly being cut off from the facts, debates and stories that enable democratic choice. When trust in media collapses, what collapses with it is the very idea of a shared civic world – one in which people disagree, deliberate and decide with clarity and dignity.

Looking forward, the future of democracy in South Asia will depend in no small part on whether the region can rebuild that civic world – through plural, independent and fearless media. This requires more than legal reforms. It demands political will to dismantle the architecture of propaganda, courage to confront digital authoritarianism and investment in public institutions that protect the integrity of information. But it also calls for imagination: new models of journalism rooted in community, new platforms that centre marginal voices, new solidarities that cross borders and languages. If democracy is to mean more than the ritual of elections, it must reclaim its soul in the realm of public discourse. That reclamation begins not with silence or compliance, but with the courage to speak – and to listen – again.

If the crisis of public discourse narrows what can be said, the politics of exclusion narrows who gets to speak in the first place. This is seen nowhere more starkly than in the treatment of ethnic minorities across the region.

Ethnic Minorities and the Right to Belong

The future of democracy in South Asia will be defined as much by how it treats its margins as by how it conducts its elections. Across the region, ethnic minorities have borne the weight of historical grievances, administrative neglect and majoritarian nationalism. Their exclusion is not merely a policy failure – it is a democratic failure, one that hollows out the very promise of equal citizenship and political voice. When ethnicity becomes a reason for suspicion rather than a claim to recognition, when belonging is determined by conformity instead of history, then the democratic ideal ceases to be plural and begins to calcify into something narrower, harder and more brittle.

Restoring democracy to its fullest meaning will require more than procedural fixes – it will demand a shift in political temperament. Power must be reconceived not as something to be defended from difference but as something strengthened by it. The region's constitutional frameworks must open wider – accommodating not only the presence of diverse ethnic communities, but their right to shape the terms of political life. This calls for courage to relinquish control where it has been hoarded, to decentralize where centralization has failed, and to imagine new compacts of solidarity across lines of language, land and memory. Without that, South Asia's democratic future will remain confined to its formalities, never fulfilling its far more urgent task: to make room for every story, especially those long kept at the edge.

Just as democratic inclusion must be reclaimed in society's margins, so too must it be defended at its procedural core: the very institutions entrusted with safeguarding the integrity of elections.

Electoral Commissions and Democratic Trust

In South Asia, the electoral commission stands not only as a procedural organ but as a mirror of the state's democratic intent. Where these bodies function with integrity, independence and courage, they lend credibility to the entire democratic enterprise. Where they falter – through passivity, political capture or public distrust – the damage runs deeper than flawed elections. It erodes faith in the idea that power can be transferred peacefully and fairly. This is particularly significant in a region where electoral contests are often the only legitimate outlet for deep social, ethnic and regional fault lines. When the referee is believed to be compromised, the game itself is seen as rigged, and the ground beneath democracy begins to crack.

Going forward, what South Asia's democracies require is not merely electoral reform, but reimagination on an institutional scale. Election commissions must be structurally shielded from executive manipulation and financially empowered to act without fear or favour. Their leadership must reflect the diversity of the populations they serve, and their actions must speak transparently to citizens who have grown weary of staged fairness.

But more than rules and budgets, what these institutions need is moral courage – an ethic of guardianship that sees democracy not as a sequence of events, but as a promise made to the people. That promise must be renewed not only through periodic elections, but through the daily labour of building institutions that are principled, transparent and quietly resilient in the face of political pressure.

However, even the most independent electoral institutions cannot fulfil the democratic promise if the arenas they safeguard remain exclusionary. Nowhere is this more evident than in the enduring marginalization of women from the very spaces where decisions are made.

Not as Exceptions But as Equals

Across South Asia, democracy remains lopsided as long as half the population continues to be treated as political afterthoughts. Gender equality in representation is not merely a question of fairness – it is a test of the democratic promise itself. When women are under-represented in parliaments, political parties and public institutions, what is lost is not just their voice, but also the possibility of a more just and responsive politics. The persistent exclusion of women from decision-making reflects how power still clings to patriarchal assumptions about leadership, credibility and authority. A democracy that does not allow women to lead, legislate and dissent on equal terms is not just incomplete – it is compromised.

Nevertheless, the future need not be a simple extension of the present. The fact that women, when given the opportunity, win elections at higher rates than men is not just statistically notable – it is politically instructive. South Asia's democratic renewal must begin by dismantling the structural and cultural barricades that keep women out: party gatekeeping, the unpaid burden of care work, violence and intimidation, and the myth of political 'unwinnability'. Reforming electoral systems, embedding accountability within parties, and investing in economic and educational access for women will require more than policy tweaks – they demand political courage and moral clarity. A region that has produced formidable women leaders must now make room for millions more – not as exceptions but as equals.

But representation is only one face of the democratic crisis. Alongside who gets to participate lies the equally urgent question of who is allowed to contest, and how the normalization of impunity has come to haunt the electoral arena itself.

Normalization of Criminality in Politics

Democracy in South Asia continues to grapple with a disquieting contradiction: the moral authority of electoral politics is repeatedly undermined by the legal and political accommodation of criminality. When the institutions that should serve as gatekeepers – political parties, electoral commissions and courts – fail to uphold the most basic ethical standards for candidacy, the idea of democratic legitimacy becomes dangerously hollowed out. The popular mandate, which ought to represent a people's aspiration for justice and governance, is too often entrusted to individuals accused of violating the very norms that a democracy is meant to safeguard. This is not merely a question of legality or propriety, but of what the citizenry comes to expect (and accept) from public life.

Going forward, addressing this crisis demands more than technical fixes or procedural reform. It calls for a fundamental reckoning with how power is structured, distributed and justified in the region.

Electoral laws must be reimagined not just for deterrence, but for renewal – ensuring that integrity becomes a political asset rather than a liability. Just as importantly, parties must abandon the calculus that reduces candidates to instruments of winnability, and voters must be offered genuine alternatives that do not force them to choose between loyalty and legality. This will require institutional resolve, legal clarity and, perhaps most of all, a renewal of moral imagination in public life – where authority is once again anchored in virtue not impunity.

Ensuring clean candidates is critical, but so too is ensuring conscious citizens. A democracy cannot truly function if its electorate is uninformed, misled or excluded from meaningful participation.

Voter Education as Democratic Infrastructure

Democracy is not sustained by elections alone, but by the degree to which citizens understand and own the process by which they are governed. In a region as linguistically, socially and economically diverse as South Asia, ensuring that voters are not merely registered but meaningfully informed is both a democratic and a moral imperative. The gap between formal enfranchisement and actual empowerment has remained wide, often disadvantaging the very populations most in need of political voice.

Voter education – when pursued earnestly – offers a quiet but transformative intervention. It reorients the citizen from being a passive recipient of governance to an engaged participant in collective decision-making. In this sense, it is not an auxiliary exercise, but a foundational commitment to the idea that democratic power must be legible, accessible and shared.

Looking ahead, South Asia's democratic future will depend in part on whether its institutions can imagine education not merely as a tool for literacy, but also as a means of civic transformation. The challenge is no longer only about reaching the unreached, but about building an electorate that can resist misinformation, question power and claim rights with confidence. This will require sustained investment, not only in electoral literacy but in the democratic ethos itself – from classrooms to community centres, from digital campaigns to village gatherings. It will also demand political courage to prioritize long-term civic awareness over short-term electoral gain, and to embrace the idea that an informed voter may be inconvenient to power but is essential to democracy.

Religious Pluralism and the Moral Test of Democracy

Just as the health of democracy rests on an informed citizenry, it also hinges on the equal protection of all citizens – especially those whose religious identities have been turned into fault lines of suspicion and exclusion. In South Asia, the treatment of religious minorities has become a mirror through which the health of democracy can be most starkly appraised. Where equal citizenship should be a shared civic inheritance, there now persist graduated sovereignties – some protected by the law, others exposed to its neglect. The erosion of secular guarantees is not only a betrayal of constitutional texts, but a corrosion of the moral imagination that once animated postcolonial nation-building. When religion becomes a criterion for belonging, democracy contracts – not only in law, but in public spirit. The silence of institutions, the complicity of administrations and the slow violence of everyday exclusion together signal a deeper unravelling of pluralism as a lived ethic, and of the state as a neutral guarantor of rights.

Repairing this fracture will require more than legal amendment or procedural fairness. It demands a renewed civic grammar. States must be held to account not only for what they permit, but for what they enable – through policy, pedagogy and political rhetoric. Electoral incentives must be reimagined so that pluralism is rewarded, not penalized. Courts and commissions must act as sentinels, not spectators. And democratic majorities must learn to practise restraint, not dominion. Ultimately, what is needed is a politics of courage – one that speaks not to the fears of the many, but to the dignity of the few. In restoring the moral core of secular democracy, South Asia has the opportunity not only to protect its minorities, but to redeem its promise.

Political Finance and the Price of Power

Beyond identity and inclusion, another force quietly distorts the democratic field: the unchecked flow of money, which tilts the balance of power long before a single vote is cast. The regulation of political finance is not a technical sidebar but a fundamental test of democratic integrity. When the flow of money in elections is unchecked, it distorts representation, sidelines the under-resourced and consolidates the grip of elites, whose power grows beyond the reach of public accountability. In a region where campaign resources often blur into state resources, and where patronage networks substitute for public policy, the ability – or inability – to regulate money in politics offers a stark measure of whether democracy is truly accessible to all or merely auctioned to the highest bidder.

What is at stake is not merely fiscal transparency but the architecture of trust itself. Rebuilding electoral mechanisms in contexts of collapse, and reinforcing them where they remain, requires more than legislation – it demands courage to confront entrenched interests, imagination to craft enforceable systems suited to each country's political realities and regional solidarity that treats democratic practice as a shared responsibility. Without credible safeguards against financial capture, democracy in South Asia risks becoming an expensive performance rather than a meaningful exercise in collective choice.

Youth and the Promise of Democratic Renewal

As entrenched interests consolidate their influence through financial means, the voices most often pushed to the margins are those of the young – whose visions for justice and innovation remain perilously under-represented in formal politics. In a region where more than half the population has yet to reach the age of thirty, the exclusion of youth from the centres of political power is not only a democratic deficit – it is a squandered future.

Across South Asia, young people have emerged as the most restless and imaginative agents of change, expressing political consciousness not just through ballots but through protest, performance, digital mobilization and radical civic invention. Yet, despite their visibility, they remain structurally marginalized in parliaments, party leaderships and policy processes. Their energy is welcomed during election campaigns, only to be sidelined once power is secured. This contradiction – between demographic centrality and political marginality – reveals a profound failure of representation, and with it, a failure of imagination.

A more democratic South Asia will require more than inviting the youth to participate; it will demand a reconstitution of political space that makes their presence foundational. Electoral institutions must treat young people as co-designers of the democratic process, not just as subjects of outreach. Political parties must share power, not simply delegate tasks. And democratic systems must be recalibrated to recognize that new generations bring new priorities: climate justice, digital rights, economic dignity and social inclusion. The courage to enact such change lies not only in legal reform but in a generational humility – a willingness by existing power structures to make room for futures they did not script. Without such a reckoning, what lies ahead is not merely the silencing of young voices but the slow corrosion of democracy's very claim to represent its people.

24

A Manifesto for the Future of Democracy

Democracy in South Asia has endured against formidable odds – repression, regression and further regression. Yet, it has never ceased to renew itself. But endurance alone is not a virtue. To merely survive is not to flourish. The region now stands at a decisive juncture: it must choose whether to remain mired in piecemeal correctives and short-term fixes, or to invest seriously in a long-term democratic architecture that reflects its scale, its complexity and its aspirations. Such a vision cannot be state-led alone. It must arise from a cross-border ecology of institutions – civil society organizations, research networks, electoral watchdogs, youth platforms, media collabouratives and supranational forums – that together cohere into a truly South Asian democratic infrastructure. This is not an idealistic blueprint but a policy imperative.

To imagine such a future, we must resist the fragmentation that has long stymied regional cooperation. While individual countries may reform internally, democracy in South Asia will remain fragile so long as its institutions remain parochial, underfunded or isolated from one another. We need durable forums for collabouration, evaluation mechanisms that monitor our own ambitions and region-wide platforms that elevate democratic imagination. The following manifesto proposes institutional reforms and integrative mechanisms that would make South Asia not just a region of electoral democracies but a shared democratic zone c– apable of thinking together, learning together and holding power to account across borders.

What follows is not a list of abstractions, but a concrete set of proposals – each rooted in the conviction that South Asia's democratic future must be built not in isolation, but in deliberate, sustained solidarity.

Forum for Strengthening Democracy in South Asia

South Asia urgently needs a transnational, cross-sectoral forum dedicated to strengthening democratic culture and practice across the region. Unlike episodic conclaves or state-heavy summits, this forum must draw upon a wide arc of actors: civil society organizations, universities (public or private), legal and journalism faculties, independent media outlets, fact-checking organizations, election commissions, bar associations and parliamentary ethics committees. Its purpose should be neither ornamental nor rhetorical. Instead, it must act as a permanent deliberative and strategic body – convening at regular intervals to share democratic innovations, document threats, pool training resources and issue joint statements of democratic concern. Crucially, it must include participants not as representatives of their nations but as stewards of shared democratic commitments.

The strength of such a forum would lie in its embeddedness – both within grassroots political cultures and within the institutional infrastructures that sustain them. Universities could host rotating conferences on electoral reforms and civic education; media groups could coordinate transnational investigations on disinformation and censorship; and civil society could develop common benchmarks for participatory governance and inclusion. Such coordination can help bypass the inertia of state-led regionalism and allow for new vocabularies of solidarity to emerge. A democracy forum of this kind would serve as South Asia's immune system against creeping authoritarianism – quick to detect, coordinated to respond and rooted in a community of democratic practice that transcends borders.

A South Asian People's Forum: An ASEAN-Inspired Civic Assembly

While ASEAN, like SAARC, has its limitations as a political bloc, its People's Forum stands as a model for meaningful civil society convergence. South Asia lacks any comparable space where citizens, movements and marginalized communities from across borders can convene independently of state structures. A South Asian people's forum – built in the spirit of participatory regionalism – would provide exactly this: an annual democratic congress where workers' unions, women's organizations, indigenous and minority groups, youth collectives, and media activists come together to reflect on the region's democratic health and challenge structures of exclusion. Unlike diplomatic summits driven by strategic interests, this forum would be unencumbered by government vetoes – driven instead by solidarity, mutual learning and people's voices.

Such a platform would allow South Asia to hear itself. It could institutionalize mechanisms for cross-border public hearings on authoritarianism, caste and communal violence, media repression, and democratic backsliding. Joint declarations, rotating host cities and multilingual cultural events could build a new civic vocabulary for regional democracy – making solidarity not just reactive, but constitutive. In a region so deeply divided by borders yet united by histories of resistance, a South Asian people's forum would not merely mirror ASEAN's model but could surpass it in moral urgency and democratic ambition. Its very existence would signal that democracy is not only a form of governance, but a form of collective memory and imagination.

The FEMBoSA and the Case for Reform

The Forum of Election Management Bodies of South Asia (FEMBoSA) was envisioned as a collabourative regional mechanism to foster peer learning, uphold electoral integrity and facilitate knowledge exchange among election commissions. Yet, despite its promising inception, the FEMBoSA today remains under-leveraged – more a diplomatic formality than an operational instrument of reform. Its meetings, while symbolically significant, tend to be non-binding, lacking both continuity and consequence. What is urgently needed is a transformation in structure and ambition. The FEMBoSA must establish a permanent secretariat with an autonomous mandate to track the progress of commitments made at its annual gatherings. Crucially, it must institutionalize a dedicated wing for evaluation, monitoring and implementation. Without such a mechanism, the FEMBoSA will continue to generate fine communiqués that have little bearing on electoral practice.

This reform must begin by rethinking the FEMBoSA's institutional identity. It is wise that its effectiveness is not tethered to the fate or functionality of the SAARC. While the SAARC remains paralysed by geopolitical tensions and government-driven protocols, the FEMBoSA, as a consortium of constitutional bodies, operates independently of executive influence both domestically and regionally. It must carve out its own space of credibility, rooted in the constitutional autonomy of its member election commissions. Only then can it avoid being seen as an appendage to failing intergovernmental diplomacy, and instead emerge as a self-sustaining platform for electoral innovation and accountability.

The FEMBoSA should also deepen its civic and academic partnerships. National Voters' Day – currently observed on 25 January in India – could be expanded into a region-wide observance where EMBs share voter outreach strategies, digital safeguards and transparency metrics. Moreover, the FEMBoSA could host public dialogues, publish an annual 'State of Electoral Democracy in South Asia' report and fund regional fellowships for electoral studies. A forum that once risked obsolescence could, with vision and resolve, become the moral and technical cornerstone of South Asian democracy – adaptive, principled and fiercely independent. Its funding should be assured by member countries or sponsored by multilateral agencies like the UNDP, EU, International IDEA or IFES.

To anchor its relevance in a shifting regional landscape, the FEMBoSA must not only expand its civic and academic partnerships but also become the institutional nucleus of a coordinated democratic infrastructure for South Asia. Currently, funding and technical support for electoral strengthening across the region are fragmented – channelled through bilateral aid, isolated grant cycles or specific agency mandates. While agencies such as the UNDP, UN Democracy Fund (UNDEF) and Office of the UN High Commissioner for Human Rights (OHCHR) play indispensable roles – supporting voter education, legal reform and civic engagement – their interventions often operate in silos, tailored to national contexts and subject to the ebb and flow of political will or donor preference.

The UNDP remains the region's most active multilateral actor on electoral reform, supporting election commissions in Nepal, Bhutan and Bangladesh through its Democratic Governance and Peacebuilding portfolios. In 2023, the UNDP mobilized over $566 million in regular resources and over $4.5 billion in total contributions, with significant allocations to democratic governance, particularly in fragile or transitional contexts.[1] Meanwhile, the UNDEF provides smaller project-based grants to civil society actors across South Asia, and OHCHR offers technical assistance in human rights compliance, including electoral inclusion. However, the absence of a region-wide, sustained and synergized funding architecture means that these efforts remain piecemeal.

What South Asia urgently needs is a concerted funding consortium – a multilateral trust mechanism or electoral compact – where agencies like the UNDP, UNDEF, EU, IFES and International IDEA pool resources, align priorities and co-design long-term programmes. Such a mechanism should not merely fund elections, but nurture democratic ecosystems through capacity-building for EMB staff, academic fellowships for electoral studies, voter literacy campaigns in vernacular languages, joint digital audit protocols, and protection mechanisms for electoral whistleblowers and journalists.

The FEMBoSA, reimagined as the secretariat or convening body of this consortium, could offer the institutional backbone for such a venture. It could serve as both a clearinghouse and a think tank – curating best practices, coordinating regional diagnostics and convening cross-border dialogues. The current reliance on episodic donor support and ad hoc project funding is insufficient for the structural threats confronting South Asian democracy. What is needed is institutional continuity, inter-agency coherence and democratic foresight – qualities that a multilateral, regionally anchored funding consortium could deliver.

Only then can the promise of digital democracy and electoral integrity in South Asia be realized – not as a series of isolated experiments, but as a sustained regional commitment to safeguarding the right to vote, the freedom to dissent and the pluralism of the democratic imagination.

SAIDES as a Regional Research Wing for Democracy

The South Asia Institute for Democracy and Electoral Studies (SAIDES) is a great initiative, proposed under the aegis of the FEMBoSA, with the aim of fostering scholarly inquiry and knowledge production on electoral democracy in the region. Despite its promise, SAIDES continues to exist largely on paper – dormant, under-publicized and resourceless – despite clearly defining its institutional role in the Dhaka Declaration, 1985. Its potential role, however, is vast. At a time when democratic backsliding is accompanied by a crisis in regional knowledge production, SAIDES could serve as the intellectual nerve centre for South Asian democracies. It must evolve into a full-fledged research wing – commissioning comparative studies, archiving best practices, publishing multilingual reports and serving as a hub for electoral innovation.

To realize this vision, SAIDES needs not only structural autonomy but diverse sources of research capacity. Therefore, it must integrate the research capacities of universities across South Asia – especially political science, law, media and governance departments that already conduct rigorous work on elections, representation and democratic accountability. Drawing from the spirit of the Kathmandu Declaration, 2014, which called for deeper regional cooperation in electoral studies, SAIDES should facilitate joint projects, cross-border fellowships, data-sharing protocols and collabourative conferences. It must build bridges not only across countries, but across institutions – between election commissions and research bodies, between civil society and academia.

Equally important is funding diversification. The SAIDES initiative should not rely solely on the FEMBoSA or state contributions, but cultivate partnerships with public universities, international democracy institutes, foundations and multilateral organizations. With the right resources and mandate, SAIDES could serve as a labouratory of democratic theory and practice – testing policy reforms, evaluating voter education models and documenting the lived experiences of electoral participation across the region. In a world increasingly defined by information warfare and institutional opacity, South Asia needs not just free elections, but credible knowledge about them. The SAIDES initiative, if empowered, could be the institution that meets that need.

Hub of Democratic Innovation

South Asia – home to one of the largest, most diverse and most electorally engaged populations in the world – should not only be seen as a site of democratic fragility, but also as a crucible of democratic innovation. From biometric voter registration in Bangladesh to mobile voter outreach vans in India's remote regions, and from community peace committees during elections in Sri Lanka to youth-led civic campaigns in Nepal, the region is teeming with democratic experiments that deserve to be studied, refined and globally disseminated. The vision, therefore, is not simply to protect democracy in South Asia, but to make the region a hub of democratic research and practice – a 'democracy lab' for the twenty-first century.

This ambition is not without precedent. Across the world, regions such as Scandinavia have become synonymous with social welfare innovation; Latin America with participatory budgeting; Africa with mobile governance solutions. South Asia, by contrast, has yet to translate its dense democratic experiences into a structured knowledge export. A regional democracy hub – anchored, perhaps, through SAIDES or a consortium of public universities – could document electoral innovations, run simulations on electoral system reforms, incubate digital tools for transparency, and train young researchers and practitioners. If supported and scaled, the region's grassroots democratic wisdom could enrich global discourse, challenge Northern epistemic dominance and position South Asia not as a democratic laggard, but as a teacher to the world.

Synergizing UN Bodies and INGOs

The democratic ecosystem in South Asia is often marked by duplication, fragmentation and missed opportunities for collabouration. Dozens of international non-governmental organizations (INGOs), UN bodies, regional foundations and bilateral agencies operate parallel programmes on governance, voter awareness, electoral reform, media literacy and civic participation – often without dialogue, convergence or cumulative learning. What the region urgently needs is a platform for coordinated engagement: a democratic synergy task force or working group that brings together the UNDP, UNESCO, UN Women, International IDEA, IFES, EU and leading INGOs to harmonize mandates, share datasets, align thematic priorities and jointly fund scalable interventions. Such coordination is not only about efficiency – it is also about coherence, accountability and impact.

The absence of such a mechanism weakens democratic outcomes. A fact-checking campaign in Bangladesh may have no link to a media literacy drive in Sri Lanka, and a youth engagement module developed in India may remain unknown in Nepal. Worse, some INGOs end up competing for influence or funding, rather than collabourating in service of shared democratic goals. This is an institutional failure, not a resource constraint. The goal must be to create a democratic support architecture that is agile, integrated and region-sensitive. A standing council or digital coordination portal among democracy-focused UN bodies and INGOs – with regular summits, thematic working groups and shared benchmarks – could help South Asia move from patchwork interventionism to principled, long-term accompaniment. Democracy cannot be outsourced, but it can (and must) be nurtured by coordinated stewardship.

India's Stewardship Role

Given its size, democratic legacy and institutional depth, India bears a unique responsibility to play a stewardship role in fortifying democracy across South Asia. This is not a call for hegemony, but for principled leadership. The ECI, with decades of experience conducting elections at an unmatched scale, has both the moral credibility and logistical expertise to support regional electoral development. The India International Institute of Democracy and Election Management (IIIDEM) is a ready institutional vehicle for this role. Through its training modules, capacity-building workshops and international collabourations, the IIIDEM has already been serving as a democratic resource centre. But its mandate must now expand – from ad hoc technical cooperation to structured regional accompaniment.

Few institutions in the Global South have left as enduring a global imprint on electoral leadership as the IIIDEM. Conceived and established under my stewardship as CEC, the IIIDEM was founded not merely to train officials, but to nurture future election commissioners from around the world. In just twelve years, it has produced commissioners and senior electoral administrators in 141 countries, making it a singular institution of democratic diplomacy. Its curriculum – rooted in Indian electoral best practices but globally adaptable has made IIIDEM a quiet cornerstone of South–South cooperation and a testament to India's democratic outreach.

The IIIDEM could become the core of a South Asian electoral democracy academy – a space where election officials, youth leaders, civic educators and media professionals from across the region converge for intensive fellowships, joint simulations and curriculum development. India must offer not just infrastructure, but humility and openness: allowing for co-creation, listening as much as leading and recognizing the democratic innovations emerging from smaller neighbours. In the long arc of regional history, India's leadership will be measured not by how it asserts its power, but by how it empowers others. Stewardship in this context must mean a willingness to invest long-term, share institutional capital and hold space for democratic learning that is plural, transnational and generative.

Regional Electoral Watchdogs

South Asia's electoral integrity has often been safeguarded as much by civil society vigilance as by state institutions. In countries like Sri Lanka, the PAFFREL and CMEV have developed robust systems of independent election observation, public reporting and media scrutiny. In the Maldives, the Maldivian Network for Free and Fair Elections has similarly acted as a watchdog ensuring transparency and civic confidence. In Pakistan, FAFEN, and in India, ADR and its subsidiary called National Election Watch are already doing commendable work.

An alliance of these bodies can enhance their collective strength and experience. These organizations offer a blueprint for a region-wide network of non-state electoral observers: a South Asian coalition for electoral oversight, bringing together civil society organizations, academic researchers, election monitors and data specialists to track, evaluate and report on elections across the subcontinent.

Such a body must be independent, permanent and transnational in scope. It could operate with rotating leadership, conduct in-country observation missions, and publish standardized electoral integrity scorecards for national and subnational elections. It should also have a public interface – a digital dashboard that collates election-related data, tracks disinformation trends and flags violations in real time. The establishment of such a coalition would not only help counter state propaganda and partisan narratives, but would also strengthen cross-border solidarity in defence of democratic standards.

In a region where state institutions are often captured or compromised, civil society must step in – not as adversaries to the state, but as its necessary conscience. A South Asian electoral watchdog would be a vital instrument of that civic guardianship.

A Citizen-Centric Democratic Forum

Democracy cannot be reduced to procedures and institutions alone; it must also be felt, shaped and claimed by ordinary citizens. Across the globe, we see efforts to embed participatory models more deeply into democratic governance – be it the Citizens' assemblies in Ireland and Belgium, the participatory budgeting initiatives of Porto Alegre in Brazil or the Citizens' Conventions on Climate in France. These initiatives have created spaces where randomly selected or voluntarily engaged citizens can deliberate on complex policy issues, produce consensus-driven recommendations and serve as a democratic counterweight to elite capture. South Asia, despite its robust electoral cultures, has yet to institutionalize such citizen-centric forums at the national or regional level.

It is time to envision a South Asian citizens' forum – an independent, multilingual and rotating platform composed of everyday citizens, selected through transparent and inclusive processes, convened to deliberate on pressing issues of democratic governance, civil liberties, social justice and regional peace. It could work in tandem with universities, public broadcasters and civil society organizations to ensure both epistemic diversity and public reach. Such a forum would not only bridge the growing chasm between citizens and state, but would also restore dignity to political conversation.

At a time when democracy risks being reduced to electoral arithmetic, the creation of a sustained, institutionalized space for citizen deliberation would be nothing less than a democratic act of reclamation. If South Asia seeks to democratize the future, it must begin by centring the voice and reason of its people.

South Asian Index of Democratic Health

While global indices like the V-Dem Project or the EIU offer valuable insights into democratic trends, they often rely on datasets and evaluative frameworks that overlook the region's specific contexts – such as caste-based exclusions, communal fault lines, electoral clientelism and informal power structures. What South Asia needs is its own index of democratic health: a regionally grounded, methodologically plural and politically resonant metric system to assess the lived quality of democracy. Designed through a collabourative process involving public universities, civil society networks, EMBs and regional think tanks, this index would prioritize both procedural and substantive measures – electoral fairness, press freedom, institutional independence, civic participation, minority inclusion and digital liberties.

Unlike externally imposed assessments, this index would derive legitimacy from its ownership and transparency. It would allow countries to benchmark themselves against peers using regionally relevant indicators, while also spotlighting structural inequalities and democratic innovations. Annual rankings, disaggregated data visualizations and longitudinal reports could be made publicly accessible, not as instruments of shaming but of reform. By centring metrics that reflect South Asia's democratic reality, rather than simply mirroring Western liberal templates, this index would serve as both a mirror and a map: reflecting the democratic condition, and guiding the region towards corrective and collabourative action.

Epilogue

Democracy in South Asia has never been a finished product. It has always been a wager – a fragile, audacious wager – that amid poverty and pluralism, division and domination, free citizens can still build accountable states. The region's democratic journeys have not been linear, nor uniformly successful. They have swerved through military rule, populist upheaval, communal violence and institutional decay. But the fact that democracy remains, persists and resurfaces against overwhelming odds is not incidental. It speaks to a deeper civic instinct across this region: a refusal to be governed without consent, a demand to be heard and a desire for justice. These instincts are our inheritance, and they must now become our design.

To build a democratic South Asia worthy of its people, the task ahead is both institutional and imaginative. Electoral reforms, independent commissions, media pluralism, civic education and regional forums are all essential – but so too is the reconstruction of political hope. This book has sought to chart the many ways in which democracy in the region has been threatened, challenged and reimagined. It has exposed the shadows and the silences, but also illuminated the courage, innovation and resistance that continue to shape the democratic ethos of South Asia.

What lies ahead is not a simple path to reform, but a generational project of co-creation led by citizens, safeguarded by institutions and constantly renewed by dissent.

This project will demand courage, but it is not without precedent. Across the valleys of Kashmir and the floodplains of Bangladesh, in the polling booths of Bhutan and the streets of Colombo, democracy has been claimed not just as a right, but as a practice – stubborn, unfinished and alive. It is time to elevate these practices into a regional architecture that is principled, participatory and future-facing. The promise of South Asian democracy is not that it has arrived, but that it continues to be made – with every election, every protest, and every act of witness and resistance.

Let this book end, then, with a beginning: a call to imagine, together, a region where democracy is not merely defended but deepened, dignified and, finally, made our own.

Notes

Introduction

1. International Labour Organization (ILO), *Global Employment Trends for Youth 2023* (2023).
2. Inter-Parliamentary Union, *Women in National Parliaments: World Classification* (2024).
3. Access Now, *The State of Internet Shutdowns around the World* (2023).
4. S.S. Wadley ed., *South Asia in the world: An Introduction* (Routledge, 2014).
5. S. Bose and A. Jalal, *Modern South Asia: History, Culture, Political Economy* (Routledge, 2020).
6. I. Ahmed, *South Asian Regionalism: SAARC in Perspective* (University Press Limited, 2010).
7. K.C. Dash, *Regionalism in South Asia: Negotiating Cooperation, Institutional Structures* (Routledge, 2018).
8. South Asian Association for Regional Cooperation (SAARC), *Charter of SAARC* (1985).
9. B. Hettne and F. Söderbaum, 'Theorising the Rise of Regionness', *New Political Economy* 5, no. 3 (2000): 457–73. https://doi.org/10.1080/713687778.
10. World Bank, *World Development Indicators* (2023).
11. I. Ahmed, *South Asian Regionalism: SAARC in Perspective* (University Press Limited, 2010).
12. Kathuria, S. (2018)
13. World Economic Forum, *South Asia Risks 2021: Climate, Conflict and Cooperation* (2021).
14. Donor, The Diplomat. 'Beyond Terrorism: A Brief History of SAARC's Failures'. March 2025. https://thediplomat.com/2025/03/beyond-terrorism-a-brief-history-of-saarcs-failures/.

1. India: The Democratic Colossus

1. M. Mukherjee, *India in the Shadows of Empire: A Legal and Political History, 1774–1950* (New Delhi: Oxford University Press, 2002).
2. J.M. Brown, *Modern India: The Origins of an Asian Democracy* (New Delhi: Oxford University Press, 1994).

3. R.J. Moore, *Escape from Empire: The Attlee Government and the Indian Problem* (New Delhi: Oxford University Press, 1983).
4. B. Chandra et al., *India's Struggle for Independence* (New Delhi: Penguin Books, 1989).
5. S. Sarkar, *Modern India: 1885–1947* (Chennai: Macmillan, 1983).
6. S. Wolpert, *Shameful Flight: The Last Years of the British Empire in India* (New Delhi: Oxford University Press, 2006).
7. G. Pandey, *Remembering Partition: Violence, Nationalism and History in India* (New Delhi: Cambridge University Press, 2001).
8. I. Talbot and G. Singh, *The Partition of India* (New Delhi: Cambridge University Press, 2009).
9. C. Roy, 'The Early Years of India's Parliament', *Hindustan Times* (March 2022). https://www.hindustantimes.com/75th-independence-day/politics/the-early-years-of-india-s-parliament.
10. Roy, Chakshu. 'The Early Years of India's Parliament'. *Hindustan Times*, 27 August 2022. https://www.hindustantimes.com/75th-independence-day/politics/the-early-years-of-india-s-parliament. Accessed 26 July 2025.
11. Lok Sabha Secretariat, *Constituent Assembly Debates: Official Report*, Government of India (2000).
12. G. Austin, *The Indian Constitution* (Oxford: Clarendon Press, 1966).
13. N.G. Jayal, *Representing India: Ethnic Diversity and the Governance of Public Institutions* (London: Palgrave Macmillan, 2006).
14. Lok Sabha Secretariat, *Constituent Assembly Debates: Official Report* (2000).
15. Election Commission of India, *Seats Reserved for Scheduled Castes and Scheduled Tribes*. (2019).
16. Lok Sabha Secretariat, *Statistical Information Relating to the First Lok Sabha*, (1952).
17. Sanjib Baruah, *Postfrontier Blues: Toward a New Policy Framework for Northeast India* (Washington, D.C.: East–West Center, 2007).
18. P.R. Brass, *The Politics of India Since Independence*, 2nd ed. (New Delhi: Cambridge University Press, 1994).
19. C. Jaffrelot, *India's Silent Revolution: The Rise of the Lower Castes in North India* (New York: Columbia University Press, 2003).
20. A.G. Noorani, *Indira Gandhi: Tryst with Power* (New Delhi: Oxford University Press, 2010).
21. A. Kohli, *Democracy and Discontent: India's Growing Crisis of Governability* (New Delhi: Cambridge University Press, 1990).
22. Bipan Chandra, *In the Name of Democracy: JP Movement and the Emergency* (New Delhi:Viking India, 2003).
23. Ibid.
24. The *ADM Jabalpur v. Shivkant Shukla* case, commonly known as the Habeas Corpus Case, is a pivotal moment in Indian constitutional history. Decided during the 1975–77 Emergency, the case addressed whether citizens retained the right to life and personal liberty under Article 21 when fundamental rights were suspended.

It also examined whether courts could review detention orders issued under emergency laws. In a controversial majority verdict, the Supreme Court held that during the Emergency, no person had the legal right to seek relief from unlawful detention – a decision widely criticized for abdicating the judiciary's role as the guardian of civil liberties. Only Justice H.R. Khanna dissented, affirming that the Constitution's basic protections could not be extinguished even in times of crisis.

25. Election Commission of India. *Statistical Report on General Election to the First Lok Sabha, 1951–52*. Page 7. New Delhi: Election Commission of India, 1952.
26. Rajya Sabha Secretariat. *Statistical Information on Rajya Sabha: 1952*. New Delhi: Rajya Sabha Secretariat, 2019.
27. Choudhary, Valmiki. *President and the Indian Constitution*. Page 20. Delhi: Allied Publishers, 1985.
28. Election Commission of India. *List of National Parties*. March 26, 2024. https://eci.gov.in/files/file/15175-list-of-national-parties/; Election Commission of India. *List of State Parties*. March 23, 2024. https://eci.gov.in/files/file/15173-list-of-state-parties/.
29. M. Vaishnav and S. Milan, *The BJP in Power: Indian Democracy and Religious Nationalism*, Carnegie Endowment for International Peace (4 April 2019). https://carnegieendowment.org/research/2019/04/the-bjp-in-power-indian-democracy-and-religious-nationalism.
30. Human Rights Watch, *India: Events of 2023* (2023). https://www.hrw.org/world-report/2024/country-chapters/india.
31. Al 'India: Hindu Leaders Call for Genocide of Muslims at Haridwar Event', *Al Jazeera*, (24 December 2021). https://www.aljazeera.com/news/2021/12/24/indiahindu-event-calling-for-genocide-of-muslims-sparks-outrage.
32. Sheikh Saaliq, 'Indian City Sets Curfew after Hindu Groups Demand Demolition of 17th century Muslim Ruler's Tomb', *AP News* (17 March 2025). https://apnews.com/article/dcd8514ae85603128cb1ebe84a8fb89c; 'Why Tidal Waves of Hatred Lash Coastal Region, *Times of India* (6 March 2024). https://timesofindia.indiatimes.com/city/mangaluru/why-tidal-waves-of-hatred-lash-coastal-region/articleshow/121577942.cms.
33. P.B. Mehta, 'The Rise of Illiberal Democracy in India', *Foreign Affairs* 100, no. 1 (2021).
34. M. Bertrand, et. al., *Employment, Income, and Consumption in India During and After the Lockdown: A V-Shape Recovery?*, Rustandy Center for Social Sector Innovation, University of Chicago Booth School of Business (18 November 2020). https://www.chicagobooth.edu/research/rustandy/stories/employment-income-and-consumption-in-india-during-and-after-the-lockdown.
35. Freedom House. *Freedom in the World 2014: The Annual Survey of Political Rights and Civil Liberties*. New York: Freedom House, 2014.

    In this report, India is designated 'Free' with a political-rights rating of 2 and a civil-liberties rating of 3, combining to an aggregate score of approximately 2.5
36. Freedom House, *Freedom in the World 2024: India Country Report* (2024) https://freedomhouse.org/country/india/freedom-world/2024.

37. The Economist Intelligence Unit. *Democracy Index 2024: What's Wrong with Representative Democracy?* London: The Economist Intelligence Unit, 2025.

    Table 2 shows that India is ranked 41st in 2024 and classified as a 'flawed democracy', with an overall score of 7.29
38. Reporters Without Borders. *World Press Freedom Index 2024: Journalism under Political Pressure*. Paris: Reporters Without Borders, 3 May 2024. https://rsf.org/en/index?year=2024.

    India's press freedom has also faced considerable setbacks. According to the *World Press Freedom Index* by Reporters Without Borders, India ranked 140th out of 180 countries in 2014, but by 2024 it had fallen to 159th, marking a significant deterioration in press freedom.
39. V-Dem Institute. *Democracy Report 2025: 25 Years of Autocratization – Democracy Trumped?* Gothenburg: V-Dem Institute, March 2025. Table A2 reports that India ranked 100th globally in 2024 on the Liberal Democracy Index; V-Dem Institute, *Democracy Report 2024: Defiance in the Face of Autocratization*, University of Gothenburg (2024). https://www.v-dem.net/documents/29/V-dem_democracyreport2023_lowres.pdf.
40. World Justice Project, *Rule of Law Index 2024* (2024). https://worldjusticeproject.org/rule-of-law-index/downloads/WJPIndex2024.pdf.

2. Pakistan: Electoral Dreams, Authoritarian Realities

1. I. Talbot, *A History of Modern South Asia: Politics, States, Diaspora* (New Haven: Yale University Press, 2016).
2. Eberhard, David M., Gary F. Simons, and Charles D. Fennig, eds. *Ethnologue: Languages of the World*. Twenty-seventh edition. Dallas, TX: SIL International, 2024. https://www.ethnologue.com/country/PK/.
3. A. Lieven, *Pakistan: A Hard Country* (New York: PublicAffairs, 2011).
4. S.A. Zaidi, *Issues in Pakistan's Economy* (New Delhi: Oxford University Press, 2005).
5. A. Jalal, *Democracy and Authoritarianism in South Asia: A Comparative and Historical Perspective* (New Delhi: Cambridge University Press, 1995).
6. M. Waseem, 'Federalism in Pakistan', *Lahore Journal of Economics* 15 (September 2010): 15–38. https://www.forumfed.org/pubs/Waseem-Fed-Overview.pdf.
7. A. Ghafoor, 'Constitutional Evolution in Pakistan: A Critical Review', *Pakistan Journal of Social Sciences* 39, no. 2 (2019): 475–87.
8. A. Jalal, *The Sole Spokesman: Jinnah, the Muslim League and the Demand for Pakistan* (New Delhi: Cambridge University Press, 1985).
9. B.D. Metcalf and T.R. Metcalf, *A Concise History of Modern India*, 2nd ed. (New Delhi: Cambridge University Press, 2006).
10. I. Talbot, *Pakistan: A Modern History* (London: Hurst & Company, 1998).
11. I.H. Qureshi, *The Struggle for Pakistan: A Muslim Homeland and Global Politics* (New York: University of Washington Press, 1962).
12. A. Jalal, *Democracy and Authoritarianism in South Asia: A Comparative and Historical Perspective* (New Delhi: Cambridge University Press, 1994).

13. H. Alavi, 'The State in Post-Colonial Societies: Pakistan and Bangladesh', *New Left Review* 74 (1983): 59–81.https://newleftreview.org/issues/i74/articles/hamza-alavi-the-state-in-post-colonial-societies-pakistan-and-bangladesh.
14. J. Wynbrandt, *A Brief History of Pakistan* (New York: Facts On File, 2009).
15. T. Kamran, 'Democracy and Governance in Pakistan', *South Asian Journal* 20 (2008): 25–38.
16. T. Kamran, *Electoral Politics in Pakistan (1950s–1970s)* (New Delhi: Oxford University Press, 2010).
17. Hussain, Mahbboob. 'Institution of Parliament in Pakistan: Evolution and Building Process (1947–1970)'. *Journal of Political Studies* 18, no. 2 (2011): 77–99.
18. S.J. Burki, *Pakistan under the Military: Eleven Years of Zia ul-Haq* (Colorado: Westview Press, 1986).
19. Wilcox, Wayne Ayres. 'The Pakistan Coup d'État of 1958'. Pacific Affairs 38, no. 2 (Summer 1965): pp. 142–163.
20. A. Jalal, *The State of Martial Rule: The Origins of Pakistan's Political Economy of Defence* (New Delhi: Cambridge University Press, 1990).
21. W.A. Wilcox, *Pakistan: The Consolidation of a Nation* (New York: Columbia University Press, 1963).
22. I. Talbot, *Pakistan: A Modern History* (London: Hurst & Company, 1998).
23. L. Ziring, *Pakistan: The Enigma of Political Development* (Colorado: Dawson Westview Press, 1980).
24. S.J. Burki, *Pakistan under the Military: Eleven Years of Zia ul-Haq* (Colorado: Westview Press, 1986).
25. V. Nasr, *Islamic Leviathan: Islam and the Making of State Power* (Oxford: Oxford University Press, 2001).
26. H. Haqqani, *Pakistan: Between Mosque and Military* (New York: Carnegie Endowment for International Peace, 2005).
27. International Crisis Group, *Pakistan: Transition to Democracy?* (2000). https://www.crisisgroup.org/asia/south-asia/pakistan/pakistan-transition-democracy.
28. H. Abbas, *Pakistan's Drift into Extremism: Allah, the Army, and America's War on Terror* (Armonk: M.E. Sharpe, 2005)
29. A. Shah, *The Army and Democracy: Military Politics in Pakistan* (London: Harvard University Press, 2014).
30. A. Siddiqa, *Military Inc.: Inside Pakistan's Military Economy* (London: Pluto Press, 2007).
31. H.A. Rizvi, *Military, State and Society in Pakistan* (London: Macmillan Press, 2000).
32. Government of Pakistan, *The Constitution of the Islamic Republic of Pakistan* (1973).
33. Election Commission of Pakistan, *Report on General Elections 2018* (2018). https://electionpakistan.com/general-elections-2018-election-day-reports/.
34. A.S. Akhtar, *The Politics of Common Sense: State, Society and Culture in Pakistan* (Cambridge University Press, 2018).
35. International Crisis Group, *Pakistan's 2024 Elections: Democracy under Pressure* (2024)

36. Yaqoob Khan Bangash, 'Was There Anything Truly Historic about Pakistan's 2024 Elections?' *The Wire* (14 February 2024). https://thewire.in/south-asia/was-there-anything-truly-historic-about-pakistans-2024-elections.
37. '"Vote ko izzat do" is PML-N's slogan in Next Election: PM', *Daily Times* (22 April 2018). https://dailytimes.com.pk/231038/vote-ko-izzat-do-is-pml-ns-slogan-in-next-election-pm/.
38. A. Shah, *The Army and Democracy: Military Politics in Pakistan*, (Cambridge, Massachusetts: Harvard University Press, 2014).
39. P.R. Newberg, *Judging the State: Courts and Constitutional Politics in Pakistan* (New Delhi: Cambridge University Press, 1995).
40. M. Lau, *The Role of Islam in the Legal System of Pakistan* (Leiden: Martinus Nijhoff Publishers, 2006).

3. Sri Lanka: Democracy, Diversity and Discord

1. Central Intelligence Agency (CIA), *The World Factbook: Sri Lanka* (2023). https://www.cia.gov/the-world-factbook/countries/sri-lanka/.
2. United Nations Population Division, *World Urbanization Prospects* (2022). https://population.un.org/wup/.
3. A.J.P. Taylor, *English history 1914–1945* (Oxfordshire: Oxford University Press, 1965).
4. K.M. de Silva, *A History of Sri Lanka* (Berkeley: University of California Press, 1981).
5. Government of Ceylon, *Ceylon Parliamentary Elections (Amendment) Act No. 11 of 1959*, (1959). https://diglib.natlib.lk/handle/123456789/59744.
6. 'Mortality Rate, Infant (per 1,000 Live Births) – Sri Lanka', *World Bank Data*. https://data.worldbank.org/indicator/SP.DYN.IMRT.IN?locations=LK.
   Seema Jayachandran and Adriana Lleras-Muney, 'Life Expectancy and Human Capital Investments: Evidence from Maternal Mortality Declines', *National Bureau of Economic Research*, Working Paper No. 13947 (April 2008). https://www.nber.org/system/files/working_papers/w13947/w13947.pdf.
7. Paul Alailima, *Initial Conditions in Sri Lanka* (World Bank Country Study, 1985). Table 1 shows adult literacy rate approximately 58 per cent in 1948 and around 72 per cent by 1963.
8. Surjit S. Bhalla and Paul Glewwe, 'Growth and Equity in Developing Countries: A Reinterpretation of the Sri Lankan Experience', *World Bank Staff Working Papers*, no. 356 (1979). https://documents.worldbank.org/en/publication/documents-reports/documentdetail/570211468777272881/growth-and-equity-in-developing-countries-a-reinterpretation-of-the-sri-lankan-experience.
9. J. Robinson, *Economic Philosophy* (London: Penguin, 1962).
10. D.R. Snodgrass, *Ceylon: An Export Economy in Transition* (Homewood: Richard D. Irwin, 1966).
11. K. Jayawardena, *The Rise of the Labor Movement in Ceylon* (Durham: Duke University Press, 1972).

12. N. DeVotta, *Blowback: Linguistic Nationalism, Institutional Decay, and Ethnic Conflict in Sri Lanka* (Redwood City: Stanford University Press, 2004).
13. S.J. Tambiah, *Sri Lanka: Ethnic Fratricide and the Dismantling of Democracy* (Chicago: University of Chicago Press, 1986).
14. Rajesh Venugopal, 'Democracy, Development and the Executive Presidency in Sri Lanka', *Third World Quarterly* 36, no. 4 (2015): 670–90.
15. F. Stewart, 'Root Causes of Violent Conflict in Developing Countries', *BMJ* 324, no. 7333 (2002): 342–45. https://doi.org/10.1136/bmj.324.7333.342.
16. N. Shanmugaratnam, 'Post-war Development and the Land Question in Sri Lanka, *Third World Quarterly* 29, no. 3, (2008): 435–49. https://doi.org/10.1080/01436590801931421.
17. Rajesh Venugopal, "'The Politics of Market Reform at a Time of Ethnic Conflict: Sri Lanka in the Jayawardene Years', *The Politics of Market Reform at a Time of Civil War* (London: London School of Economics, 2011), pp. 4–5. https://personal.lse.ac.uk/venugopr/Chapter%204%20Rajesh%20Venugopal.pdf.
18. 'Sri Lanka Parties Say Electoral Reforms Allow Minority Representation,' *The New York Times* (11 September 2020). https://www.nytimes.com/2020/09/11/world/asia/sri-lanka-proportional-representation-minorities.html.
19. Zaheena Rasheed and Rathindra Kuruwita, 'Sri Lanka's Supreme Court Overturns Sacking of Parliament', *Al Jazeera* (13 December 2018). https://www.aljazeera.com/news/2018/12/13/sri-lankas-supreme-court-overturns-sacking-of-parliament.
20. A. Welikala ed., *The Nineteenth Amendment to the Constitution: Content and Context* (Colombo: Centre for Policy Alternatives, 2017). https://www.cpalanka.org/wp-content/uploads/2016/04/The-Nineteenth-Amendment-to-The-Constitution-Content-and-Context.pdf; Thanabalasingam Krishnamohan. 'The Twentieth Amendment to the Constitution of Sri Lanka: A Comparative Analysis'. International Journal of Research and Innovation in Social Science 5, no.1 (2021): pp. 197–203.
21. Venugopal, Rajesh. 'Democracy, Development and the Executive Presidency in Sri Lanka'. Third World Quarterly 36, no. 4 (2015): pp. 670–90.
22. R. Edrisinha and A. Welikala, International Centre for Ethnic Studies, *The Failure of the 2000 Constitutional Reform*. https://constitutionnet.org/sites/default/files/2019-06/Sirlanka_38.pdf.
23. N. DeVotta, 'A Win for Democracy in Sri Lanka', *Journal of Democracy* 27, no. 1 (2016): 152–66. https://www.journalofdemocracy.org/articles/a-win-for-democracy-in-sri-lanka/.
24. 'Sri Lanka: The Nineteenth Amendment to the Constitution - from start to finish', *ConstitutionNet*. https://constitutionnet.org/news/sri-lanka-nineteenth-amendment-constitution-start-finish.
25. Alan Keenan, 'Sri Lanka's Parliamentary Election: Landslide Win for the Rajapaksa Puts Democracy and Pluralism at Risk', *LSE* (12 August 2020). https://blogs.lse.ac.uk/southasia/2020/08/12/sri-lankas-parliamentary-election-landslide-win-for-the-rajapaksa-puts-democracy-and-pluralism-at-risk/.
26. 'Sri Lanka Parliament Votes to Strengthen Presidential Power', *Al Jazeera*

(22 October 2020). https://www.aljazeera.com/news/2020/10/22/sri-lanka-parliament-votes-to-strengthen-presidential-power.

27. J. Uyangoda, 'Ethnic Conflict in Sri Lanka: Changing Dynamics', *Democracy and Deep-Rooted Conflict: Options for Negotiators*, eds. J. Galtung and J. Uyangoda (International IDEA, 2020), 187–212.
28. Asanga Abeyagoonasekera, 'Sri Lanka's 2020 Parliamentary Election: International and Security Challenges for the Rajapaksa Government', *The 2020 Parliamentary Election: The Road Ahead for Sri Lanka* (Institute of South Asian Studies, National University of Singapore, December 2020, p. 48. https://www.isas.nus.edu.sg/wp-content/uploads/2020/12/2020-Road-Ahead-For-Sri-Lanka-Full.pdf
29. Anjali Nadaradjane, *Sri Lanka: Democracy in Crisis* (CIS, November 2022). https://www.cis.org.au/publication/sri-lanka-democracy-in-crisis/.
30. International Crisis Group, *Sri Lanka's Bailout Blues: Elections in the Aftermath of Economic Collapse* (17 September 2024). https://www.crisisgroup.org/asia/south-asia/sri-lanka/341-sri-lankas-bailout-blues-elections-aftermath-economic-collapse.
31. Krishantha Fedricks et al., 'Snapshots from the Struggle, Sri Lanka April–May 2022', Anthropology Now 12 (2022). https://www.tandfonline.com/doi/full/10.1080/19428200.2022.2123194.
32. Sheikh Saaliq, 'Protests Ousted Sri Lanka's Last President. Ahead of New Election, Many Are Still Waiting for Change', *AP News* (20 September 2024). https://apnews.com/article/e197eaf330758f2f35ece447a3f2739c.
33. Marlon Ariyasinghe, 'The Man Who Would Oust a Dynasty', *Journal of Democracy* 35, no. 3 (July 2024): 123–28. https://www.journalofdemocracy.org/articles/the-man-who-would-oust-a-dynasty/. Accessed 18 June 2025.
34. Devathura A. Devapriya, "The Crisis in Sri Lanka: Economic and Political Dimensions," *Journal of IndoPacific Affairs* 45, no. 3 (August 2022): 12, 34–35. https://www.airuniversity.af.edu/JIPA/Display/Article/3125910/the-crisis-in-sri-lanka-economic-and-political-dimensions/.
35. 'Anura Dissanayake Set to Be New Sri Lankan President after Historic Second-Round Counting', *The New Indian Express* (22 September 2024). https://www.newindianexpress.com/world/2024/Sep/22/anura-dissanayake-set-to-be-new-sri-lankan-president-after-historic-second-round-counting.
36. Krishan Francis, Shiekh Saaliq and Bharatha Mallawarachi, 'Marxist Dissanayake Wins Sri Lanka's Presidential Election as Voters Reject Old Guard', *AP News* (23 September 2024). https://apnews.com/article/50a8990acae90fabaddd8d01c0ef5bcd.
37. International Monetary Fund. 'IMF Executive Board Completes the Third Review Under the Extended Fund Facility Arrangement with Sri Lanka'. IMF News & Press Release, 28 February 2025; 'Sri Lanka Has 'No Room for Policy Errors' in Economic Reforms, IMF Says', Reuters, 16 June 2025.
38. Dan Strumpf and Asantha Sirimanne, 'Sri Lanka's New Government Pledges Review of Adani Wind Project', *The Economic Times*, (8 October 2024). https://www.economictimes.com/industry/renewables/sri-lankas-new-governmentpledges-review-of-adani-wind-project/.

39. 'Nous travaillerons avec le monde,' quoting President Dissanayake declaring, 'We will work with the world,' in his inauguration speech, *Le Monde*, 1 October 2024. https://www.lemonde.fr/en/international/article/2024/10/01/newly-elected-sri-lankan-president-anura-kumara-dissanayake-is-expected-to-distance-himself-from-india_6727901_4.html.
40. Ministry of External Affairs (India). *Transcript of Special Briefing by Foreign Secretary on the State Visit of the President of Sri Lanka to India, December 16, 2024.* (17 December 2024). https://www.mea.gov.in/media-briefings.htm?dtl/38800/transcript+of+special+briefing+by+foreign+secretary+on+the+state+visit+of+president+of+sri+lanka+to+india+december+16+2024.Accessed 18 June 2025.
41. Harindra Dassanayake and Rajni Gamage, 'A New Era in Sri Lanka?: Implications of Dissanayake's Presidency', *Stimson* (25 September 2024). https://www.stimson.org/2024/a-new-era-in-sri-lanka-implications-of-dissanayakes-presidency/.

4. Bangladesh: From Partition to People's Power

1. Worldometer. 'Bangladesh Population (2025)'. Worldometer – World Statistics and Real-Time Data.
2. EximPedia. 'Top Garment Export Countries: A Comprehensive Analysis'. EximPedia.app Blog.
3. Barua, Kriti. 'Which Country Is the Largest Producer of Jute in the World? List of Top 5 Countries'. *Jagran Josh*, 8 June 2025. https://www.jagranjosh.com/general-knowledge/largest-jute-producing-countries-in-the-world-1749409127-1.
4. Islam, Fakhrul. 'Bangladesh among World's Top 10 in 13 Sectors'. *Prothom Alo*, 27 March 2021. https://en.prothomalo.com/business/bangladesh-among-worlds-top-10-in-13-sectors.
5. World Bank, *Promoting Agrifood Sector Transformation in Bangladesh: Policy and Investment Priorities* (World Bank, 2023).

   Table 4.6: vegetable production ≈3.88 million tonnes, ranking Bangladesh third in the world in vegetable output.
6. 'Bangladesh Ranks Eighth among Top 10 Mango Producing Countries'. *The Daily Star*, 22 May 2023. https://www.thedailystar.net/country/news/mango-export-death-dream-1920789.

   'Grain Market in Bangladesh – Rice Production'. *Miller Magazine*. https://millermagazine.com/blog/grain-market-in-bangladesh-3825.
7. Bangladesh Association of Pharmaceutical Industries, *Pharma Export Data* (2024).
8. Oxford Internet Institute, *Online Labour Index* (2022). https://ilabour.oii.ox.ac.uk.
9. World Bank, *Bangladesh Reaches Lower-Middle Income Status* (2015). https://documents.worldbank.org/curated/en/624001587103386716/pdf/Bangladesh-s-Journey-to-Middle-Income-Status-The-Role-of-The-Private-Sector.pdf; United Nations. *Bangladesh Graduation Status*. United Nations Committee for Development Policy (CDP). https://www.un.org/ldcportal/content/bangladesh-graduation-status.
10. United Nations Development Programme (UNDP), *Millennium Development*

Goals: Bangladesh Progress Report 2015 (2015). https://www.undp.org/bangladesh/publications/mdg-progress-report-2015.

11. United Nations Development Programme, *Bangladesh: Governance and Local Government System Overview* (Dhaka: UNDP Bangladesh, 2023); Bangladesh Ministry of Local Government, Rural Development & Co-operatives, Upazila and Union Parishad Statistics, 2024 (Dhaka: Government of Bangladesh, 2024).
12. B.R. Whyte, *Waiting for the Esquimo: An Historical and Documentary Study of the Cooch Behar Enclaves* (School of Oriental and African Studies, University of London, 2002). https://catalogue.nla.gov.au/catalog/228643.
13. T.J., 'Why India and Bangladesh Have the World's Craziest Border', *The Economist* (24 June 2015). https://www.economist.com/theeconomist-explains/2015/06/24/why-india-and-bangladesh-have-the-worlds-craziest-border.
14. CIA, *The World Factbook: Bangladesh* (2024). https://www.cia.gov/the-world-factbook/countries/bangladesh/.
15. S. Raghavan, *1971: A Global History of the Creation of Bangladesh* (Cambridge: Harvard University Press, 2013).
16. G.J. Bass, *The Blood Telegram: Nixon, Kissinger, and a Forgotten Genocide* (New York: Vintage, 2013).
17. C. Baxter, *Bangladesh: From a Nation to a State* (Colorado: Westview Press, 1997).
18. N. Mookherjee, *The Spectral Wound: Sexual Violence, Public Memories, and the Bangladesh War of 1971* (Durham: Duke University Press, 2015).
19. Human Rights Watch 'Bangladesh: International Crimes Tribunal Questions and Answers' (2011). https://www.hrw.org/news/2011/05/18/letter-bangladesh-prime-minister-regarding-international-crimes-tribunals-act.
20. A Nation Divided', *The Economist* (9 March 2013). https://www.economist.com/asia/2013/03/09/a-nation-divided.
21. N. Ahmed *The Constitution of Bangladesh: A Contextual Analysis* (Oxfordshire: Hart Publishing, 2012).
22. R. Sisson and L.E. Rose, *War and Secession: Pakistan, India, and the Creation of Bangladesh* (Oakland: University of California Press, 1990).
23. Government of Pakistan, *Legal Framework Order* (1970).
24. The 1970 Elections in Pakistan: A Study of Electoral Behaviour. Journal of Political Studies 17, no. 2 (2010): pp. 101–115. https://pu.edu.pk/images/journal/pols/pdf-files/Mahboob-Hussain-Journal-2010.pdf.
25. R. Sisson and L.E. Rose, *War and Secession: Pakistan, India, and the Creation of Bangladesh* (Berkeley:University of California Press, 1990).
26. `The Historic 7th March Speech of Bangabandhu Sheikh Mujibur Rahman', *UNESCO* (2017). https://en.unesco.org/memoryoftheworld/registry/436.
27. Government of Bangladesh, *Proclamation of Independence* (1971).
28. N. Ahmed, *The Constitution of Bangladesh: A Contextual Analysis* (Oxfordshire: Hart Publishing, 2012).
29. Syed Serajul Islam, 'Elections and Politics in the Post-Ershad Era in Bangladesh', *Asian and African Studies* 10, no. 1 (2001): 160–173. https://www.sav.sk/journals/uploads/060412385_Islam.pdf.

30. International Parliamentary Union (IPU). Bangladesh: Parliamentary Elections, Jatiya Sangsad, 1991. PARLINE Database on National Parliaments. https://archive.ipu.org/parline-e/reports/arc/2023_91.htm; Zafarullah, Habib, and Muhammad Yeahia Akhter. 'Non-Political Caretaker Administrations and Democratic Elections in Bangladesh: An Assessment.'. Government and Opposition 35, no. 3 (July 2000): pp. 345–369. https://doi.org/10.1111/1477-7053.00032.
31. Dieter Nohlen, Florian Grotz, and Christof Hartmann, *Elections in Asia: A Data Handbook, Volume I* (Oxford: Oxford University Press, 2001).
32. Bangladesh Election Commission, *Statistical Report: 8th Jatiya Sangsad Election, October 1, 2001* (Dhaka: Bangladesh Election Commission, April 2002). https://www.ecs.gov.bd/files/Khdh5RFCFW lp1NOVIdJv3AsAPsvRoFHAOTZBBgZ7.pdf.
33. Sreeradha Datta, 'Post-Election Communal Violence in Bangladesh', *Strategic Analysis* 26, no. 2 (April 2002): 316–321, https://doi.org/10.1080/09700160208450047.
34. Ali Riaz, *Bangladesh: A Political History since Independence* (London: I.B. Tauris, 2016).
35. Md Jaynal Abedini, 'Legitimacy Crisis in Bangladesh: A Case Study of 10th General Election', *European Journal of Political Science Studies* 3, no. 2 (2020): 316–21, https://doi.org/10.5281/zenodo.3612187.
36. 'They Threaten Everyone.' Sheikh Hasina's Landslide Win in Bangladesh Marred by Voter Suppression', *TIME* (31 December 2018). https://time.com/5490744/bangladesh-elections-sheihk-hasina-rigging-allegations/.
37. Rahul Roy-Chaudhury and Viraj Solanki, 'Bangladesh: Domestic Turmoil and Regional Insecurity', *IISS* (20 August 2024). https://www.iiss.org/online-analysis/online-analysis/2024/08/bangladesh-domestic-turmoil-and-regional-insecurity/.
38. Geoffrey Macdonald, 'What's Behind Bangladesh's Student Protests?', *United States Institute of Peace* (22 July 2024). https://www.usip.org/publications/2024/07/whats-behind-bangladeshs-student-protests.
39. Mohammad Ponir Hossain and Sam Jahan, 'Bangladesh to Impose Curfew, Deploy Army as Protests Widen, Communications Disrupted', *Reuters* (20 July 2024). https://www.reuters.com/world/asia-pacific/communications-disrupted-bangladesh-amid-student-protests-2024-07-19/.
40. Devjyot Ghoshal and Shivam Patel, 'India's Modi Urges Bangladesh Leader to Avoid Rhetoric that Mars Ties', *Reuters* (4 April 2025). https://www.reuters.com/world/asia-pacific/indian-pm-modi-bangladeshs-yunus-hold-first-talks-after-hasina-exit-2025-04-04/.
41. Nazam Laila Islam, 'Bangladesh Is Helping to Create a Geopolitical Shift in South Asia', *Chatham House* (13 June 2025). https://www.chathamhouse.org/2025/06/bangladesh-helping-create-geopolitical-shift-south-asia.
42. Ruma Paul, 'Bangladesh Says Xi Jinping Would Consider Lowering Interest on Chinese Loans', *Reuters* (28 March 2025). https://www.reuters.com/world/asia-pacific/bangladesh-says-xi-jinping-would-consider-lowering-interest-chinese-loans-2025-03-28/.
43. 'Bangladesh's Main Opposition Warns of Instability if Elections Delayed Beyond 2025'. *Reuters*, 31 March 2025. https://www.reuters.com/world/asia-

pacific/bangladeshs-main-opposition-warns-instability-if-elections-delayed-beyond-2025-03-31/

Reports the BNP's warning that delaying national elections past December 2025 could provoke strong public resentment and instability.

44. Mostofa, Shafi Md. 'National Elections in April 2026, Says Bangladesh's Interim Chief Adviser Yunus'. *The Diplomat*, 16 June 2025. https://thediplomat.com/2025/06/national-elections-in-april-2026-says-bangladeshs-interim-chief-adviser-yunus/.

5. Afghanistan: A Country in Perpetual Turmoil

1. Central Intelligence Agency, *The World Factbook: Afghanistan* (2023).https://www.cia.gov/the-world-factbook/countries/afghanistan/.
2. United Nations Assistance Mission in Afghanistan (UNAMA), *Human Rights Situation in Afghanistan* (2023). https://unama.unmissions.org/sites/default/files/english_hr_update_22jan_2024.pdf.
3. W. Dalrymple, *The Last Mughal* (New Delhi: Bloomsbury, 2006).
4. Human Rights Watch, *Afghanistan: Paying for the Taliban's Crimes: : Abuses Against Ethnic Pashtuns in Northern Afghanistan* (2002). https://www.hrw.org/reports/2002/afghan2/afghan0402.pdf.
5. N. Nojumi, *The Rise of the Taliban in Afghanistan: Mass Mobilization, Civil War, and the Future of the Region* (London: Palgrave Macmillan, 2002).
6. A. Monsutti, *War and Migration: Social Networks and Economic Strategies of the Hazaras of Afghanistan* (Oxfordshire: Routledge, 2005).
7. Hafizullah Emadi, 'Minorities and Marginality: Pertinacity of Hindus and Sikhs in a Repressive Environment in Afghanistan', *Nationalities Papers* 42, no. 2 (March 2014): 307–20, https://doi.org/10.1080/00905992.2013.858313.
8. P. Hopkirk, *The Great Game: The Struggle for Empire in Central Asia* (Tokyo: Kodansha Globe, 1992).
9. M. Ewans, *Afghanistan: A Short History of Its People and Politics* (New York: HarperCollins, 2002).
10. T. Barfield, *Afghanistan: A Cultural and Political History* (Princeton: Princeton University Press, 2010).
11. W. Dalrymple, *Return of a King: The Battle for Afghanistan* (London: Bloomsbury, 2013).
12. C. Noelle, *State and Tribe in Nineteenth-Century Afghanistan: The Reign of Amir Dost Muhammad Khan (1826-1863)* (Oxfordshire: Routledge, 1997).
13. V. Gregorian, *The Emergence of Modern Afghanistan: Politics of Reform and Modernization, 1880–1946* (Redwood: Stanford University Press, 1969).
14. S. Tanner, *Afghanistan: A Military History from Alexander the Great to the Fall of the Taliban* (Boston: Da Capo Press, 2002).
15. M.H. Kakar, *The History of Afghanistan: The Age of Amanullah Khan* (Oakland: University of California Press, 1995).

16. H. Emadi, (*Politics of Development and Women in Afghanistan* (London: Palgrave Macmillan, 2005).
17. B.R. Rubin, *The Fragmentation of Afghanistan* (New Haven: Yale University Press, 2002).
18. A. Rasanayagam, *Afghanistan: A Modern History* (London: I.B. Tauris, 2005).
19. A. Saikal, *Modern Afghanistan: A History of Struggle and Survival* (I.B. Tauris, 2004).
20. G. Dorronsoro, *Revolution Unending: Afghanistan, 1979 to the Present* (London: Hurst & Co., 2005)
21. M.H. Kakar, *Afghanistan: The Soviet Invasion and the Afghan Response, 1979–1982* (Oakland: University of California Press, 1995).
22. S. Coll, *Ghost Wars: The Secret History of the CIA, Afghanistan, and Bin Laden* (New York: Penguin Press, 2004).
23. A. Rashid, *Taliban: Militant Islam, Oil and Fundamentalism in Central Asia* (New Haven: Yale University Press, 2001).
24. L.P. Goodson, *Afghanistan's Endless War: State Failure, Regional Politics, and the Rise of the Taliban* (Seattle: University of Washington Press, 2001).
25. P. Marsden, *The Taliban: War, Religion and the New Order in Afghanistan* (London: Zed Books, 2002).
26. L.P. Goodson, *Afghanistan's Endless War: State Failure, Regional Politics, and the Rise of the Taliban* (Seattle: University of Washington Press, 2001).
27. T. Barfield, *Afghanistan: A Cultural and Political History* (Princeton: Princeton University Press, 2010).
28. Human Rights Watch, *Afghanistan: Humanity Denied: Systematic Violations of Women's Rights in Afghanistan*, 13, no. 5(C) (October 2001). https://www.hrw.org/reports/2001/afghan3/afgwrd1001.pdf.
29. A. Rashid, *Taliban: Militant Islam, Oil and Fundamentalism in Central Asia* (New Haven: Yale University Press, 2001).
30. S. Coll, *Ghost Wars: The Secret History of the CIA, Afghanistan, and Bin Laden* (New York: Penguin Press, 2004).
31. Human Rights Watch, *Massacres of Civilians by the Taliban in Yakaolang* (2001).
32. Partha Pratim Routray, 'The Assassination of Ahmad Shah Massoud', (21 September 2001). https://www.researchgate.net/publication/228581586_The_Assassination_of_Ahmad_Shah_Massoud.
33. Hersh, Seymour. 'The Other War'. *The New Yorker*, 12 April 2004. https://www.newyorker.com/magazine/2004/04/12/the-other-war.
34. Shallice, Jane. 'Afghanistan: a Brief History'. *Red Pepper Global Politics*. https://www.redpepper.org.uk/global-politics/war/afghanistan-a-brief-history/.
35. S. Chayes, *Thieves of State: Why Corruption Threatens Global Security* (New York: W. W. Norton, 2015).
36. World Bank, *Afghanistan: National Reconstruction and Poverty Reduction – The Role of Women in Afghanistan's Future* (2005). https://documents1.worldbank.org/curated/en/391881467989548647/pdf/356061English01stan0Report0on0women.pdf.

37. Malkasian, Carter. *The American War in Afghanistan: A History.* New York: Oxford University Press, 2021.
38. Shallice, Jane. 'Afghanistan: a Brief History'. *Red Pepper Global Politics.* https://www.redpepper.org.uk/global-politics/war/afghanistan-a-brief-history/
39. Independent Election Commission of Afghanistan, *Presidential Elections Report* (2004). https://www.eods.eu/library/FR%20AFGHANISTAN%202004_en.pdf.
40. UNDP, *Afghanistan Human Development Report* (2007). https://www.undp.org/afghanistan/publications/afghanistan-human-development-report-2007.
41. United Nations Office on Drugs and Crime (UNODC), *Afghanistan Opium Survey 2007* (2007).
42. Department of Defense, *Enhancing Security and Stability in Afghanistan* (2009). https://www.unodc.org/documents/crop-monitoring/Afghanistan-Opium-Survey-2007.pdf.
43. Human Rights Watch, *Afghanistan: Events of 2018* (2018). https://www.hrw.org/world-report/2019/country-chapters/afghanistan.
44. US Department of State, *Agreement for Bringing Peace to Afghanistan* (2020). https://www.state.gov/wp-content/uploads/2020/02/Agreement-For-Bringing-Peace-to-Afghanistan-02.29.20.pdf.
45. United Nations Assistance Mission in Afghanistan (UNAMA), *Afghanistan: Protection of Civilians in Armed Conflict Annual Report 2020* (2021). https://unama.unmissions.org/sites/default/files/afghanistan_protection_of_civilians_report_2020_revs3.pdf..
46. Deepa Shivaram and Sharon Pruitt-Young, 'Kabul Airport Attack: 13 U.S. Service Members Killed', *npr* (26 August 2021). https://www.npr.org/2021/08/26/1031428645/the-attacks-outside-kabul-airport-pushes-the-u-s-exit-into-deeper-disarray.
47. 'Afghan Women Barred from Gyms, Taliban Official Says', *Al Jazeera* (2022). https://www.aljazeera.com/news/2022/11/10/taliban-ban-afghan-women-from-gyms-and-parks-in-new-crackdown.
48. Osama Bin Javaid, 'Qatar, China Call on Taliban to Reverse Ban on Women's Rights', *Al Jazeera* (1 May 2023). https://www.aljazeera.com/news/2023/5/1/un-holds-crucial-afghanistan-talks-in-qatar-without-taliban.
49. Naheed Farid and Rangita de Silva de Alwis, *Afghanistan Under the Taliban: A State of "Gender Apartheid"?* (Princeton, NJ: Princeton University School of Public and International Affairs, January 2023). https://spia.princeton.edu/sites/default/files/2023-02/SPIA_NaheedRangita_PolicyBrief_07.pdf.
50. 'Taliban Conducts Second Public Execution Since Return to Power', *Reuters* (20 June 2023). https://www.reuters.com/world/asia-pacific/afghanistans-talibanadministration-executes-man-murder-five-2023-06-20/.
51. 'Taliban Ban Women from Working with UN', *UN News* (2023). https://news.un.org/en/story/2023/04/1135357.
52. 'WFP Warns of Hunger Crisis in Afghanistan Amid Funding Shortfall', *World Food Programme* (2023). https://www.wfp.org/emergencies/afghanistan.
53. United Nations Office on Drugs and Crime (UNODC), *Afghanistan Opium Survey*

2023 (2023). https://www.unodc.org/documents/crop-monitoring/Afghanistan/Afghanistan_opium_survey_2023.pdf.

54. 'Iran and Afghanistan are Feuding over the Helmand River. The Water Wars Have No End in Sight', *Atlantic Council* (7 July 2023). https://www.atlanticcouncil.org/blogs/iransource/iran-afghanistan-taliban-water-helmand/.
55. Economist Intelligence Unit. Democracy Index 2020. Country Profile: Afghanistan. The Economist Intelligence Unit, 2020.
56. Economist Intelligence Unit, *Democracy Index 2023: Age of Conflict* (2023). https://d1qqtien6gys07.cloudfront.net/wp-content/uploads/2024/02/Democracy-Index-2023-Final-report-11-15.pdf.
57. 'Taliban Says will Respect Women's Rights, Press Freedom', *Al Jazeera* (17 August 2021). https://www.aljazeera.com/news/2021/8/17/taliban-says-will-respect-womens-rights-press-freedom.
58. Asifa Quraishi-Landes, *Islamic Constitutionalism: Not Secular. Not Theocratic. Not Impossible* (New York University School of Law, 2016). https://www.law.nyu.edu/sites/default/files/upload_documents/Islamic%20Constitutional%20-%20Quraishi-Landes%202016.pdf.
59. Qur'an. Chapter 2, verse 228. Translated on The Qur'anic Arabic Corpus via Quran.com. https://corpus.quran.com/translation.jsp?chapter=2&verse=228.
60. 'Verse 2:187', *Quran.com*. https://quran.com/2/187.
61. 'Verse 9:71', *Quran.com*. https://quran.com/9/71.
62. 'Purification (Kitab Al-Taharah)', *Sunnah.com*. https://sunnah.com/abudawud:236; 'The Book of Miscellany', *Sunnah.com*. https://sunnah.com/riyadussalihin:278.
63. Elizabeth Arif-Fear, '12 Quotes Depicting Women's Equality in Islam', *Voice of Salam* (11 December 2015). https://voiceofsalam.com/2015/12/11/12-quotes-depicting-womens-equality-in-islam/.
64. Sunan Ibn Mājah 224 (narrated by Anas ibn Malik): 'Seeking knowledge is a duty upon every Muslim' (ṭalab al-ʿilm farīḍah ʿalā kull muslim), understood inclusively of men and women; Sunan at-Tirmidhī 2647: 'Whoever goes forth in search of knowledge, he is striving in the Cause of Allah until he returns' (graded ḥasan by al-Tirmidhī)..
66. Abdel Rahim Omran, *Family Planning in the Legacy of Islam* (Cairo: International Islamic Center for Population Studies and Research, AlAzhar University, December 1991).
66. 'Book of the Sunnah', *Sunnah.com*. https://sunnah.com/ibnmajah:224.
67. United Nations, *Afghanistan Remains the World's Largest Humanitarian Crisis* (2023).

6. Nepal: From Monarchy to Federal Republic

1. J. Whelpton, *A History of Nepal* (New Delhi: Cambridge University Press, 2005), pp. 23–26.
2. L.F. Stiller, *Prithwinarayan Shah in the Light of Dibya Upadesh* (Kathmandu: Himalaya Books, 1993), pp. 47–52.

3. L.E. Rose, *Nepal: Strategy for Survival* (Oakland: University of California Press, 1971), pp. 33–36.
4. L.F. Stiller, *The Rise of the House of Gorkha* (Patna: Patna Jesuit Society, 1976), pp. 94–97.
5. R. Burghart, 'The Formation of the Concept of Nation-State in Nepal', *The Conditions of Listening* (Oxfordshire: Oxford University Press, 1996), pp. 226–30.
6. G.P. Koirala, *Democracy and Social Change in Nepal: A Historical Perspective* (2000), pp. 12–15.
7. B.L. Joshi and L.E. Rose, *Democratic Innovations in Nepal* (Oakland: University of California Press, 1966), p.7.
8. J. Whelpton, *A History of Nepal* (New Delhi: Cambridge University Press, 2005), pp. 78–81.
9. A. Höfer, *The Caste Hierarchy and the State in Nepal: A Study of the Muluki Ain of 1854* (Berlin: Universitätsverlag Wagner, 1979), pp. 19–20.
10. A. Adhikari, *The Bullet and the Ballot Box: The Story of Nepal's Maoist Revolution* (London: Verso, 2014), pp. 23–24.
11. L.R. Baral, *Opposition Politics in Nepal* (Kathmandu: Mandala Book Point, 2004), pp. 16–17.
12. M. Lawoti, *Towards a Democratic Nepal: Inclusive Political Institutions for a Multicultural Society* (New Delhi: SAGE Publications, 2005), p. 36.
13. M. Hutt, *Himalayan People's War: Nepal's Maoist Rebellion* (Bloomington: Indiana University Press, 2004), pp. 9–10.
14. M. Lawoti, *Towards a Democratic Nepal: Inclusive Political Institutions for a Multicultural Society* (New Delhi: SAGE, 2005), pp. 39–41.
15. International Crisis Group, *Nepal's Maoists: Their Aims, Structure and Strategy* (2005), p. 7. https://www.crisisgroup.org/asia/south-asia/nepal/nepals-maoists-their-aims-structure-and-strategy..
16. B.R. Upreti, *Armed Conflict and Peace Process in Nepal: The Maoist Insurgency, Past Negotiations and Opportunities for Conflict Transformation* (Chennai: NCCR North-South, 2006), pp. 21–22.
17. International Crisis Group, *Nepal's New Alliance: The Mainstream Parties and the Maoists* (2006), pp. 1–4.
18. 'Comprehensive Peace Agreement between the Government of Nepal and the Communist Party of Nepal (Maoist)', *United Nations Peacemaker* (22 November 2006). https://peacemaker.un.org/en/node/9215.
19. 'Resolution 1740 (2007) / adopted by the Security Council at its 5622nd meeting, on 23 January 2007', *United Nations Digital Library* (2007). https://digitallibrary.un.org/record/593436?ln=en.
20. International Crisis Group, *Nepal's Troubled Tarai Region* (2007), pp. 2–4. https://www.crisisgroup.org/sites/default/files/136-nepals-troubled-tarai-region.pdf.
21. K. Hachhethu, 'Madhesi Nationalism and Restructuring the Nepali State', *CNAS Journal* 34, no. 1 (2007): 23–25. https://citeseerx.ist.psu.edu/document?repid=rep1&type=pdf&doi23850be50e0ee948bec4c6bc48ff24645d1b51f0.
22. International Crisis Group, *Nepal's Faltering Peace Process* (2009), pp. 3–5. https://

www.crisisgroup.org/asia/south-asia/nepal/nepal-sfaltering-peace-process.

23. United Nations Mission in Nepal, *Final Report of the Secretary-General on UNMIN* (2011). https://docs.un.org/en/A/66/2?direct=true.
24. International Crisis Group, *Nepal's Constitution (I): Evolution Not Revolution* (2012), pp. 6–8. https://www.crisisgroup.org/asia/southasia/nepal/nepal-s-constitution-i-evolution-not-revolution.
25. Ayadi, Arjun Bahadur. 'Dilemma and Factionalism in the Maoist Politics of Nepal'. Journal of Political Science 18 (2018): pp. 1–24.
26. International Crisis Group, *Nepal's Divisive New Constitution: An ExistentialCrisis* (2016), pp. 1–2. https://www.crisisgroup.org/asia/south-asia/nepal/nepal%E2%80%99s-divisive-new-constitution-existentialcrisis.
27. D. Thapa and A. Ramsbotham, 'Two Steps Forward, One Step Back: The Nepal Peace Process', *Accord: An International Review of Peace Initiatives* 26 (2017): 30–32. https://www.politicalsettlements.org/wp-content/uploads/2018/09/2017_CRAccord_Nepal.pdf.
28. Human Rights Watch, *'Like We Are Not Nepali': Protest and Police Crackdown in the Terai Region of Nepal* (2015), p. 6. https://www.hrw.org/report/2015/10/16/we-are-not-nepali/protest-and police-crackdown-terai-region-nepal.
29. A. Adhikari, 'The Constitutional Crisis in Nepal: Identity Politics and State Restructuring', *South Asia@LSE* (2016). https://blogs.lse.ac.uk/southasia/2013/07/22/constitutionalism-in-nepal/.
30. Bertelsmann Stiftung Transformation Index, *Nepal Country Report 2024* (2024). https://bti-project.org/en/reports/country-report/NPL.
31. 'Nepal to Ban TikTok, Alleges Damaging Social Impact', *Reuters* (13 November 2023). https://www.reuters.com/technology/nepal-govt-decides-ban-chinas-tiktok-ani-2023-11-13/.

7. Bhutan: A Kingdom in Transition

1. UNDP Bhutan, *Ten Years of Democracy in Bhutan* (2019). https://www.undp.org/sites/g/files/zskgke326/files/migration/bt/NHDR-For-Website_11.3.19_compressed.pdf.
2. J. Ardussi, 'Formation of the State of Bhutan ('Brug gzhung) in the 17th Century and its Tibetan Antecedents', *Journal of Bhutan Studies* 11 (2004): 10–32. https://d1i1jdw69xsqx0.cloudfront.net/digitalhimalaya/collections/journals/jbs/pdf/JBS_11_02.pdf.
3. K. Phuntsho, *The History of Bhutan* (New Delhi: Random House India, 2013).
4. M. Aris, *The Raven Crown: The Origins of Buddhist Monarchy in Bhutan* (Bangkok: Serindia Publications, 1994).
5. 'King's Assent Leads Himalayan Nation of Bhutan to Become Latest Country to Decriminalise Same-Sex Activity', *Human Dignity Trust* (18 March 2021). https://www.humandignitytrust.org/news/kings-assentleads-himalayan-nation-of-bhutan-to-become-latest-country-to-decriminalise-same-sex-activity/.
6. Karma Phuntsho, 'Dr Karma Phuntsho on Bhutanese Democracy', *Druk Journal*

(2020). https://drukjournal.bt/dr-karma-phuntsho-on-bhutanese-democracy/.
7. UNDP Bhutan, *National Human Development Report* (2000). https://hdr.undp.org/system/files/documents/bhutan2000en.pdf.
8. A.C. Sinha, *Himalayan Kingdom Bhutan: Tradition, Transition and Transformation* (New Delhi: Indus Publishing, 2001).
9. L.E. Rose, *The Politics of Bhutan* (Ithaca: Cornell University Press, 1977).
10. Kumar, Sharda P., and Dorji Wangchuk. 'Ten Years of Democracy in Bhutan'. Bhutan National Human Development Report, UNDP (Bhutan), November 2019, p. 22.
11. Inter-Parliamentary Union. 'Bhutan: Elections in 2008 – National Assembly'. Parline Database of National Parliaments, IPU. Data reporting 79.45 per cent turnout in the 24 March 2008 election.
12. Mathou, 'Bhutan: The Making of a Modern State'.
13. Election Commission of Bhutan (ECB), *A Perspective Survey on a Decade of Parliamentary Democracy in Bhutan* (Thimphu: ECB, 2018).
14. S. Tobgye, *The Constitution of Bhutan: Principles and Philosophies* (Thimphu: Bhutan Printing Solutions, 2015).
15. D. Suzuki, *The Legacy: An Elder's Vision for Our Sustainable Future* (Vancouver: Greystone Books, 2009).
16. Bhutan Centre for Media and Democracy (BCMD), *Democracy Forum Report* (Thimphu: BCMD, 2018).
17. M. Mancall, 'Reflections on Bhutan's Democratic Transition', *Asian Affairs* 36, no. 2 (2009): 30–45.
18. Election Commission of Bhutan (ECB), *A Perspective Survey on a Decade of Parliamentary Democracy in Bhutan* (Thimphu: ECB, 2018).
19. S. Tobgye, *The Constitution of Bhutan: Principles and Philosophies* (Thimphu: Bhutan Printing Solutions, 2015).
20. J.K.N. Wangchuck, 'Address at the Royal University of Bhutan Convocation', *Kuensel Online* (2011). http://dorjiwangchuk.blogspot.com/2011/07/transcript-of-royal-interaction-of-his_18.html.
21. T. Mathou, 'Bhutan: Political Reform in a Buddhist Monarchy', *Asian Survey* 49, no. 3 (2008): 546–69. https://www.repository.cam.ac.uk/bitstreams/3111c465-d8f1-404e-888c-d5fe2cd7df46/download.
22. Marian Gallenkamp, *Democracy in Bhutan: An Analysis of Constitutional Change in a Kingdom* (IPCS Research Papers, March 2010). https://www.files.ethz.ch/isn/113886/RP24-Marian-Bhutan.pdf.
23. *Constitution of the Kingdom of Bhutan* , Articles 9(2)–9(3). https://www.constituteproject.org/constitution/Bhutan_2008.
24. UNDP Bhutan, *Ten Years of Democracy in Bhutan* (2019). https://www.undp.org/sites/g/files/zskgke326/files/migration/bt/NHDR-For-Website_11.3.19_compressed.pdf
25. 'His Majesty The King grants patang to 20 Chairpersons of DT', *BBS* (18 December 2016). https://www.bbs.bt/64617/.
26. UNDP Bhutan, *Ten Years of Democracy in Bhutan* (2019), p. 28. https://www.undp.

org/sites/g/files/zskgke326/files/migration/bt/NHDR-For-Website_11.3.19_compressed.pdf

27. Royal Audit Authority, *Annual Audit Report: Local Governance and Fiscal Management* (2019). http://www.bhutanaudit.gov.bt/wp-content/uploads/2020/11/Final-Revised-EAG-2019.pdf.
28. UNDP Bhutan, *Ten Years of Democracy in Bhutan* (2019), p. 29. https://www.undp.org/sites/g/files/zskgke326/files/migration/bt/NHDR-For-Website_11.3.19_compressed.pdf
29. Election Commission of Bhutan, *Report on the First Parliamentary Elections in Bhutan* (Thimphu: ECB, 2008).
30. A.C. Sinha, *Bhutan: Ethnic Identity and National Dilemma* (Mumbai: Reliance Publishing, 2016).
31. Election Commission of Bhutan, *Parliamentary Elections 2013: Primary Round Results* (Thimphu: ECB, 2013).
32. C.T. Dorji, Centre for Bhutan Studies, *Democracy in Bhutan: The First Five Years (2008–2013)* (2014).
33. Bertelsmann Stiftung Transformation Index, *Bhutan Country Report 2024* (2024). https://bti project.org/en/reports/country report/BTN.en.wikipedia.org ı 15.
34. Election Commission of Bhutan, *Primary Round Election Results 2018* (Thimphu: ECB, 2018).
35. Election Commission of Bhutan, *General Election Results 2018* (Thimphu: ECB, 2018).
36. Bhutan Centre for Media and Democracy, *Social Media and Democratic Participation: A Bhutanese Perspective* (Thimphu: BCMD, 2019).
37. Election Commission of Bhutan, *General Election Results 2023* (Thimphu: ECB, 2023).
38. 'Bhutan's Elections Matter', *Gateway House* (January 2024) https://www.gatewayhouse.in/bhutan-elections-matter/.
39. L. Dorji, 'Political Representation and Electoral Rules in Bhutan: A Critical Review', *Journal of Bhutan Studies* 38, no. 1 (2023): 44–67.
40. P.K. Varma, *Chanakya's View: Understanding India in Transition* (Chennai: Westland Publications, 2020).

8. The Maldives: A Republic in Turbulent Waters

1. V. Selvakumar, 'Ancient Maritime Contacts of the Maldives: New Archaeological Findings', *Indian Journal of Maritime Archaeology* 5, no. 2 (2009): 45–60.
2. T. Heyerdahl, *The Maldive Mystery* (Crows Nest: George Allen & Unwin, 1986).
3. C. Maloney, *People of the Maldive Islands* (Hyderabad: Orient Blackswan, 2013).
4. J. Carswell, *The Maldives and the Indian Ocean Trade* (Oxfordshire: Oxford University Press, 1998).
5. X. Romero-Frias, *The Maldive Islanders: A Study of the Popular Culture of an Ancient Ocean Kingdom* (New York: Nova Ethnographica Indica, 1999).
6. S. Subrahmanyam, *The Portuguese Empire in Asia, 1500–1700: A Political and*

Economic History (London: Longman, 1996).

7. M.I. Hussain, *The British Legacy in Maldives* (Malé: Maldives National University Press, 2013).
8. T.R. Metcalf, *Ideologies of the Raj* (New Delhi: Cambridge University Press, 1995).
9. D. Woodman, *The Republic of Maldives: A Study in a Small Island Nation* (Malé: Middle East Institute, 1956).
10. M. Shathir, *The Road to Independence: Maldives 1887–1965* (Malé: Maldives Research Institute, 2010).
11. Maldives Elections Commission, *Referendum Report on the Republic Declaration, 1968* (Government of Maldives, 1968).
12. A. Naseem, *Ibrahim Nasir and the Making of the Modern Maldives* (New Delhi: Novelty Press, 2005).
13. M. I. Hussain, *The British Legacy in Maldives* (Malé: Maldives National University Press, 2013).
14. Mariyam Zulfa, '"Decentralised-Administration" in the Maldives: A Critical Examination of "Decentralisation" as a Constitutionally Enabled Governance Structure', *University of Melbourne* (August 2019). https://www.researchgate.net/publication/335462682_Title_'DECENTRALISED-ADMINISTRATION'_IN_THE_MALDIVES_-1.
15. M. Weber, *Economy and Society: An Outline of Interpretive Sociology* (Oakland: University of California Press, 1978).
16. International Commission of Jurists, *Securing Justice: The Challenges of Rule of Law in the Maldives* (2015). https://www.icj.org/wp-content/uploads/2015/08/Maldives-Justice-Adrift-Rule-of-Law-Publications-fact-finding-report-2015-ENG.pdf.
17. Freedom House, *Freedom in the World: Maldives Country Report 2007* (2007). https://www.refworld.org/reference/annualreport/freehou/2007/en/51957.
18. 'Maldives: Death of Prisoner Raises Serious Concerns', *Amnesty International* (2004).
19. Human Rights Watch, *An All-Out Assault on Democracy: Crushing Dissent in the Maldives* (August 2008). https://www.hrw.org/report/2018/08/16/ all-out-assault-democracy/crushing-dissent-maldives.
20. Human Rights Watch, 'Maldives: Ex-President's Trial Unfair' (2015). https://www.hrw.org/news/2015/03/14/maldives-ex-presidents-trial-unfair.
21. Freedom House, *Freedom in the World: Maldives Country Report* (2017). https://freedomhouse.org/country/maldives/freedom-world/2017.
22. 'Stealing Paradise', *Al Jazeera* (2016). https://www.aljazeera.com/investigations/stealing-paradise/.
23. Radhey Tambi, 'Rising Extremism and Radicalisation in the Maldives', *Defence and Diplomacy Journal* 13, no. 4 (July–September 2024): 45–50. https://capsindia.org/wp-content/uploads/2025/02/04-Radhey-Tambi.pdf.
24. International Commission of Jurists , *Justice Adrift: Rule of Law and the Maldives Judiciary* (2019). https://www.icj.org/wp-content/uploads/2015/08/Maldives-Justice-Adrift-Rule-of-Law-Publications-fact-finding-report-2015-ENG.pdf.

25. Ministry of Foreign Affairs, Maldives, *Press Release on India Visit: President Solih's Address* (2018). https://mea.gov.in/bilateral-documents.htm?dtl/31418/indiamaldives+joint+statement+during+the+state+visit+of+prime+minister+to+maldives.
26. R.M. Panda, 'Maldives: Post Parliamentary Election Scenario – Analysis', *Eurasia Review* (3 May 2019). https://www.eurasiareview.com/03052019-maldives-post-parliamentary-election-scenario-analysis/.
27. 'Maldives' Biggest Corruption Scandal Exceeded U$90m', *Maldives Independent* (19 December 2018). https://maldivesindependent.com/crime-2/maldives-biggest-corruption-scandal-exceeded-u90m-143227.
28. Indian Ministry of External Affairs, *India–Maldives Bilateral Relations Fact Sheet* (2022).
29. Muhammad Yusuf, 'Understanding the 'India-Out' Campaign in Maldives', *Observer Research Foundation* (15 May 2022), https://www.orfonline.org/research/understanding-the-india-out-campaign-in-maldives.
30. Center for Global Development, *Examining the Debt Implications of the Belt and Road Initiative: Maldives Country Case Study* (2018). https://www.cgdev.org/sites/default/files/examining-debt-implications-belt-and-road-initiative-policy-perspective.pdf.
31. Harish K. Thakur, 'Contesting China in the Maldives: India's Foreign Policy Challenge', *The Round Table: The Commonwealth Journal of International Affairs* 112, no. 4 (2023): 421–37, https://doi.org/10.1080/00358533.2023.2244286.
32. Council on Foreign Relations, 'The Maldives Is Moving Toward China. Here's What to Know', *Council on Foreign Relations* (16 July 2021). https://www.cfr.org/in-brief/maldives-moving-toward-china-heres-what-know.
33. 'India Extends Financial Support to Debt-Ridden Maldives', *Reuters* (12 May 2025). https://www.reuters.com/world/china/india-extends-financial-support-debt-ridden-maldives-2025-05-12/.
34. Freedom House, *Freedom in the World: Maldives Country Reports* (2006–2008). https://www.refworld.org/reference/annualreport/freehou/2008/en/60902.
35. 'Maldives: The Use of Flogging as Punishment for Extra-Marital Sex', *Amnesty International* (2009). https://www.amnesty.org/en/documents/asa29/006/2013/en/.
36. International IDEA, *The Global State of Democracy Report: The Maldives in Focus* (2023). https://www.idea.int/democracytracker/country/maldives.
37. Renée Jeffery, 'Human Rights and Transitional Justice in the Maldives: Closing the Door, Once and For All?' *Human Rights Review* 25 (2024): 233–56, https://doi.org/10.1007/s12142-024-00716-9.
38. World Bank, *Maldives Development Update* (2022). https://thedocs.worldbank.org/en/doc/49141824db6f3a3b812bad33d5779541-0310062022/original/MDU-Oct-22-Final.pdf.
39. United Nations Development Programme (UNDP) Maldives. 'New UNDP Report: Maldives' Human Development Index (HDI) Value Positions It at 104th Out of 189 Countries and Territories'. *UNDP Maldives*, February 2020. https://www.undp.org/maldives/press-releases/new-undp-report-maldives-

human-development-index-hdi-value-positions-it-104th-out-189-countries-and-territories.

40. Saroj Kumar Aryal and Alexander Droop, 'Maldives Walking Tight Rope between India and China', *ISDP* (May 2024). https://www.isdp.eu/publication/maldives-walking-tight-rope-between-india-and-china/.
41. U.S. Department of State, *Maldives: 2024 Investment Climate Statements* (2024). https://www.state.gov/reports/2024-investment-climate-statements/maldives/.
42. World Bank, *Debt Sustainability and Infrastructure Financing in the Maldives* (2021). https://documents1.worldbank.org/curated/en/293831592861168276/pdf/Maldives-Joint-World-Bank-IMF-Debt-Sustainability-Analysis.pdf.
43. Human Rights Watch, *Maldives Country Report: Political Repression and Rights Monitoring* (2023). https://www.hrw.org/world-report/2023/country-chapters/maldives.
44. Intergovernmental Panel on Climate Change (IPCC), '*Sixth Assessment Report: Impacts on Small Island Developing States* (2022). https://www.ipcc.ch/report/ar6/wg2/.

9. Global Democracy Indices: What It Reveals and What It Doesn't

1. Economist Intelligence Unit, *Democracy Index 2023: Age of Conflict* (2024) https://www.eiu.com/n/campaigns/democracy-index-2024/; Economist Intelligence Unit, *Democracy Index 2019: A year of democratic setbacks and popular protest* (2020) https://www.eiu.com/n/campaigns/democracy-index-2020/.
2. V-Dem Institute, *Democracy Report 2024: Defiance in the Face of Autocratization* (2024). https://www.v-dem.net/documents/61/v-dem-dr__2025_lowres_v2.pdf.
   V-Dem Institute, *Democracy Report 2019: Democracy Facing Global Challenges* (2019) https://v-dem.net/data/the-v-dem-dataset/.
3. P. Norris, R.W. Frank and F. Martínez i Coma, *The Year in Elections 2022: Global Electoral Integrity report* (2023). https://www.electoralintegrityproject.com/eip-blog/2024/7/24/the-global-electoralintegrity-report-2024.
   P. Norris, R.W. Frank and F. Martínez i Coma, *The Year in Elections 2018: Global Electoral Integrity report* (2019). https://www.electoralintegrityproject.com/the-year-in-elections-2019.
4. The Economist Intelligence Unit. 2024. Democracy Index 2024: What's Wrong with Representative Democracy? February 27, 2025.
   The Democracy Index is based on sixty indicators grouped into five categories – electoral process and pluralism; functioning of government; political participation; political culture; and civil liberties – each scored 0 to 10 and averaged to form the overall rating.
5. A. Chatterji and A. Acharya, 'India's Reaction to Declining Democracy Rankings: Defensive Nationalism and Narrative Control', *Journal of Democracy and Society* 7, no. 2 (2023): 44–59.

6. V-Dem Institute, *Codebook v13: Indicators and Methodologies for Measuring Democracy* (2024).
7. International Crisis Group, *Pakistan's Democratic Struggles and the Role of the Military* (2022).
8. 'Govt Rejects EIP's Integrity Score, Cites Turnout, Security', *The Daily Star* (5 January 2019).

10. The Missing Half: Gender and Political Representation

1. UN Women, *Gender Equality in Public Administration: South Asia Snapshot* (2023). https://www.unwomen.org/sites/default/files/2023-09/progress-on-the-sustainable-development-goals-the-gender-snapshot-2023-en.pdf.
2. World Economic Forum, *Global Gender Gap Report 2024* (2024). https://www.weforum.org/reports/global-gender-gap-report-2024.
3. Human Rights Watch, *Afghanistan: Taliban Deprive Women of Livelihoods, Identity* (2022). https://www.hrw.org/news/2022/01/18/afghanistan-taliban-deprive-women-livelihoods-identity.
4. F. Bari, United Nations Division for the Advancement of Women, *Women's Political Participation: Issues and Challenges* (2010). https://www.un.org/womenwatch/daw/egm/enabling-environment2005/docs/EGM-WPD-EE-2005-EP.12%20%20draft%20F.pdf.
5. M.L. Krook, *Quotas for Women in Politics: Gender and Candidate Selection Reform Worldwide* (Oxfordshire: Oxford University Press, 2009).
6. A. Reynolds, Minority Rights Group International, *Electoral Systems and the Protection and Participation of Minorities* (2006). https://aceproject.org/ero-en/topics/electoral-systems/Electoral%20Systems%20and%20the%20Protection%20and%20Participation%20of%20Minorities.pdf.
7. IDEAS, 'Women's Representation in Politics: The Effect of Electoral Systems' (2021). https://ideas.repec.org/a/eee/pubeco/v198y2021ics0047272721000359.html.
8. P. Norris, *Electoral engineering: Voting Rules and Political Behavior* (Cambridge: Cambridge University Press, 2004).
9. Election Commission of India, *Statistical Report on General Elections to Lok Sabha* (2024). https://www.eci.gov.in/general-election-to-loksabha-2024-statistical-reports/.
10. Inter-Parliamentary Union, *Parline Data: Nepal* (2024). https://data.ipu.org/parliament/NP/NP-UC01/working-methods/structure.
11. Kamal Dev Bhattarai. 'The Woeful Presence of Nepali Women in Politics and Government'. Annapurna Express, 26 February 2019. https://theannapurnaexpress.com/news/the-woeful-presence-of-nepali-women-in-politics-and-government-1571.
12. Bharti Jain, 'Women Voters Clocked 65.8%, Men 65.6% in '24 Lok Sabha Polls: Election Commission', *Times of India* (27 December 2024). https://timesofindia.

indiatimes.com/india/women-voters-clocked-65-8-men-65-6-in-24-lok-sabha-polls-election-commission/articleshow/116694411.cms.

13. Mudit Kapoor and Shamika Ravi, 'Women Voters in Indian Democracy: A Silent Revolution', *Economic & Political Weekly* 49, no. 12 (22 March 2014): 63–70. https://www.epw.in/journal/2014/12/special-articles/women-voters-indian-democracy.html.
14. Inter-Parliamentary Union, National Assembly of Pakistan: Data on Women, https://data.ipu.org/parliament/PK/PKLC01/data-on-women.
15. International Foundation for Electoral Systems, *Women's Reserved Seat Systems in Bangladesh* (February 2020). https://www.ifes.org/sites/default/files/migrate/womens_reserved_seat_systems_in_bangladesh_february_2020.pdf.
16. International Foundation for Electoral Systems, *Women's Reserved Seats in Bangladesh: A Systemic Analysis of Meaningful Representation* (February 2015). https://www.ifes.org/publications/womens-reserved-seats-bangladesh-systemic-analysis-meaningful-representation.
17. Election Commission of Bhutan, *Parliamentary Composition Data* (2024). https://www.ecb.bt/naelections2023-24notifications/.
18. World Economic Forum, *Global Gender Gap Report 2024* (2024). https:// www3.weforum.org/docs/WEF_GGGR_2024.pdf.
19. Women for Politics. 'Political Representation of Women in Maldives: Challenges and Opportunities'. *Women for Politics*, 13 June 2022. https://www.womenforpolitics.com/post/political-representation-of-women-in-maldives-challenges-and-opportunities.
20. Inter-Parliamentary Union, *Maldives – National Parliament (People's Majlis): Data on Women*. https://data.ipu.org/parliament/MV/MV-LC01/data-on-women.
21. UNDP Afghanistan, *Women's Political Participation Factsheet* (2020). https://www.undp.org/governance/womens-political-participation.
22. Georgetown Institute for Women, Peace and Security, *WPS Index 2024*. https://giwps.georgetown.edu/wp-content/uploads/2023/10/WPS-Index-full-report.pdf.
23. M. Htun and S.L. Weldon, 'The Civic Origins of Progressive Policy Change: Combating Violence against Women in Global Perspective, 1975–2005', *American Political Science Review* 106, no. 3 (2012): 548–69. https://www.cambridge.org/core/journals/american-political-science-review/article/civic-origins-of-progressive-policy-change-combating-violence-against-women-in-global-perspective-19752005/810036AC92E6A7E245A083E3EEE4EFA0.
24. N.G. Jayal, *Representing India: Ethnic Diversity and the Governance of Public Institutions* (New York: Palgrave Macmillan, 2006).
25. World Economic Forum, *Global Gender Gap Report 2024* (2024). https://www3.weforum.org/docs/WEF_GGGR_2024.pdf.
26. 'Final Results for National Council Elections, 2023', *Election Commission of Bhutan* (2023). https://www.ecb.bt/provisional-results-for-national-council-elections-2023/.
27. UN Women and Maldives Bureau of Statistics, *Assessment on Gender Dynamics in Local Governance* (Malé: UNDP Maldives, 24 October 2024), https://www.undp.

org/maldives/publications/assessment-gender-dynamics-local-governance.

28. M.C. Nussbaum, *Women and Human Development: The Capabilities Approach* (Cambridge: Cambridge University Press, 2007).
29. World Bank, *Pakistan: Labor Force Participation Rate (Female)* (2024). https://data.worldbank.org/indicator/SL.TLF.CACT.FE.ZS?locations=PK.
30. Population Council, Rutgers Pakistan Program, Rozan, and Ministry of Human Rights (Government of Pakistan). International Men and Gender Equality Survey – Pakistan (Pak-IMAGES). Islamabad: Population Council, 2018. https://www.equimundo.org/wp-content/uploads/2018/07/IMAGES-Pakistan_Report_Final.pdf; Gallup Pakistan. Gallup Pakistan Poll Findings on Gender Roles. Islamabad: Gilani Research Foundation, 2018.
31. F. Jalalzai, *Shattered, Cracked, or Firmly Intact?* (New Delhi: Oxford University Press, 2013).
32. Pew Research Center, *How Indians View Gender Roles in Family and Society* (2022). https://www.pewresearch.org/religion/2022/03/02/how-indians-view-gender-roles-in-families-and-society/.
33. Nita Bhalla, 'High Share of Care Work Keeps Indian Women Out of Economy – McKinsey', *Reuters* (3 November 2015). https://www.reuters.com/article/markets/commodities/high-share-of-care-work-keeps-indian-women-out-of-economy-mckinsey-idUSL3N12X49M/.
34. European Union Election Expert Mission to Bangladesh, *Parliamentary Election Final Report: 7 January 2024* (2024), https://www.eods.eu/library/EU%20EEM%20final%20report%202024.pdf.
35. UN News, *Afghanistan: Women Erased from Public Life* (2023) https://news.un.org/en/story/2024/08/1153151.
36. D. Kandiyoti, 'Bargaining with Patriarchy', *Gender & Society* 2, no. 3 (1988): 274–90. https://journals.sagepub.com/doi/10.1177/089124388002003004.
37. A.M. Goetz, 'Women's Political Effectiveness: A Conceptual Framework', in *No Shortcuts to Power* A.M. Goetz and S. Hassim eds., (London: Zed Books, 2003).
38. Aditto Rimon, 'Women Still Underrepresented in Bangladesh Politics', *Voice of America* (5 January 2024). https://www.voanews.com/a/women-stillunderrepresented-in-bangladesh-politics/7428384.html.
39. World Economic Forum. 2024. Global Gender Gap Report 2024. 'Bangladesh's rank dropped from 59th in 2023 to 99th in 2024, a loss of 40 places globally'. Geneva: World Economic Forum; World Economic Forum. 2023. Global Gender Gap Report 2023. 'Bangladesh ranked 59th globally and topped South Asia'. Geneva: World Economic Forum; World Economic Forum, *Global Gender Gap Report 2024* (2024). https://www3.weforum.org/docs/WEF_GGGR_2024.pdf.
40. Inter-Parliamentary Union *Women in National Parliaments: India* (2024). https://www.ipu.org/news/press-releases/2025-03/ipu-report-parliamentary-gender-gap-narrowed-over-past-30-years-progress-stalled-in-2024.
41. 'The Visibility of Women in Sri Lankan Politics Is Increasing', *Demo Finland* (May 2024). https://demofinland.org/en/the-visibility-of-women-in-sri-lankan-politics-is-increasing/.

42. 'NPP Creates One More Record – No Muslim In The Cabinet', *Colombo Telegraph* (November 2024). https://www.colombotelegraph.com/index.php/nppcreates-one-more-record-no-muslim-in-the-cabinet/.
43. 'Coalition and Women's Political Representation in Nepal', *Yale EGC Briefing* (July 2024). https://ie.yale.edu/sites/default/files/2024-10/Coalition%20Brief_Version%202.pdf.
44. F. Bari, *Pakistan's Women Politicians and the Elusiveness of Representation* (New Delhi: Friedrich Ebert Stiftung, 2020).
45. P. Chhibber and K. Kollman, *The Formation of National Party Systems: Federalism and Party Competition in Canada, Great Britain, India, and the United States* (Princeton: Princeton University Press, 2004).
46. M. Vaishnav, *When Crime Pays: Money and Muscle in Indian Politics* (New Haven: Yale University Press, 2017).
47. International Foundation for Electoral Systems, *Violence Against Women in Elections Online: A Social Media Analysis Tool* (Washington, DC: IFES, 2018), https://www.ifes.org/sites/default/files/migrate/violence_against_women_in_elections_online_a_social_media_analysis_tool.pdf.
48. 'Police: Ex-Afghan Female Lawmaker, Guard Shot Dead at Home', *AP News* (15 January 2023). https://apnews.com/articled2f1e0f26cc090604701c5f198183687.
49. 'Crime Against Women in India Up by 4%: NCRB Report 2023', *Newsclick* (February 2024). https://www.newsclick.in/crime-against-women-india-4-ncrbreport-2023.
50. UNFPA Sri Lanka, *Ninety Per Cent of Sri Lankan Women Endure Sexual Harassment on Public Transport, UNFPA Study Shows* (8 March 2017). https://www.unfpa.org/news/ninety-cent-sri-lankan-women-endure-sexual-harassment-public-transport-unfpa-study-shows.
51. Polity.lk, SEXISM a la Sri Lanka', Polity (September 2024). https://polity.lk/wp-content/uploads/2024/09/Pravada-5.45-susanthika-sexism-racism.pdf.
52. 'Where Are the Women Voters? Insights from Pakistan's 2024 Elections', *IGC Blog* (April 2024). https://www.theigc.org/blogs/gender-equality/where-are-women-voters-insights-pakistans-2024-elections.
53. 'Women Voters Clocked 65.8%, Men 65.6% in '24 Lok Sabha Polls: Election Commission', *Times of India* (June 2024). https://timesofindia.indiatimes.com/india/women-voters-clocked-65-8-men-65-6-in-24-lok-sabha-polls-election-commission/articleshow/116694411.cms.
54. 'Political Participation of Women in India', *Compass* (July 2024). https://compass.rauias.com/current-affairs/political-participationwomen-india/.
55. Election Commission Nepal, *The Election Commission Nepal's Published a Study on Gender and Social Inclusion in Elections* (October 2023). https://nepal.ecundpelectoralassistance.org/the-election-commission-nepals-published-a-study-on-gender-and-socialinclusion-in-elections/.
56. Committee on the Elimination of Discrimination against Women. General Recommendation No. 35 on Gender-Based Violence Against Women, Updating General Recommendation No. 19. UN Doc. CEDAW/C/GC/35. Geneva: Office

of the United Nations High Commissioner for Human Rights (OHCHR), 14 July 2017. https://www.ohchr.org/en/documents/general-comments-and-recommendations/general-recommendation-no-35-2017-gender-based.

57. Inter-Parliamentary Union, *Guidelines for the Elimination of Violence Against Women in Politics* (2019). https://www.ipu.org/resources/publications/reference/2019-11/guidelines-elimination-sexism-harassment-and-violence-against-women-in-parliament.
58. World Bank, *Labor Force Participation Rate, Female (% of female population ages 15+)* (2024). https://data.worldbank.org/indicator/SL.TLF.CACT.FE.ZS.
59. UNESCO Institute for Statistics. International Literacy Day 2024: A Catalyst for Peaceful, Equitable and Sustainable Societies. Paris: UNESCO, 2024. https://www.unesco.org/sites/default/files/medias/fichiers/2024/09/ild-2024-cn-en.pdf.
60. National Commission for Protection of Child Rights (NCPCR). 2018. *Vocational & Life Skills Training of Out-of-School Adolescent Girls in the Age Group 15–18 Years.* New Delhi: NCPCR.
61. Pakistan Bureau of Statistics, *Education Statistics Report 2023–24* (2024). https://aserpakistan.org/document/2024/aser_national_2023.pdf.
62. 'What's Happening in Bangladesh Garment Industry?', *Economics Observatory* (2023). https://www.economicsobservatory.com/whats-happening-in-bangladeshs-garment-industry.
63. UN Women Nepal, *Building Women's Leadership in Local Governance: Evaluation Report* (2023). https://asiapacific.unwomen.org/en/countries/nepal.
64. McKinsey Global Institute, *The Power of Parity in South Asia: Advancing Gender Equality* (2023). https://www.mckinsey.com/featured-insights/employment-and-growth/how-advancing-womens-equality-can-add-12-trillion-to-global-growth.
65. 'Is the Provision of Direct Public Funding to Political Parties Tied to Gender Equality Among Candidates? Papua New Guinea', *International IDEA Answer.* https://www.idea.int/answer/ans9222979950012.
66. International IDEA, *Political Parties in South Asia: The Challenge of Change* (2007), https://www.idea.int/sites/default/files/publications/political-parties-in-south-asia-the-challenge-of-change.pdf.
67. UNICEF South Asia, *Digital Equality for Girls: A South Asian Imperative* (May 2025). https://www.unicef.org/rosa/stories/digital-equality-girls-south-asian-imperative.
68. A.M. Tripp, *Women and Power in Post-Conflict Africa* (New Delhi: Cambridge University Press, 2015).
69. P. Norris, 'The Impact of Electoral Reform on Women's Representation', *Acta Politica* 41, no. 2 (2008): 197–213. https://dash.harvard.edu/entities/publication/78b2d555-c27e-4523-8b21-5f4a75068cf8.
70. C. Devlin and R. Elgie, 'The Effect of Increased Women's Representation in Parliament: The Case of Rwanda', *Parliamentary Affairs* 61, no. 2 (2008): 237–54; J.E. Burnet, 'Women Have Found Respect: Gender Quotas, Symbolic Representation, and Female Empowerment in Rwanda', *Politics & Gender* 7, no. 3 (2011): 303–34.

11. Pluralism under Threat: Ethnic Minorities in South Asia

1. Ashutosh Varshney, *Ethnic Conflict and Civic Life: Hindus and Muslims in India* (New Haven: Yale University Press, 2002).
2. Kamal Dev Bhattarai, 'Renewed Push for Madhesi-Tharu Unity', *The Annapurna Express* (3 February 2025). https://theannapurnaexpress.com/story/52215/.
3. S. Baruah, *Durable Disorder: Understanding the Politics of Northeast India* (New Delhi: Oxford University Press, 2005).
4. H.A. Rizvi, *The Military and Politics in Pakistan: 1947–1997* (Lahore: Sang-e-Meel Publications, 2000); Human Rights Watch. Bhutan: Ethnic Cleansing of Lhotshampas. New York: Human Rights Watch, 2008. https://www.hrw.org/news/2008/02/01/bhutans-ethnic-cleansing; Boone, Jon. 'Pakistan Bans Pashtun Group as Government Cracks Down on Dissent.'The Guardian, 7 October 2024. https://www.theguardian.com/world/2024/oct/07/pakistan-bans-pashtun-group-ptm-crackdown-dissent.
5. M. Hutt, *Unbecoming Citizens: Culture, Nationhood, and the Flight of Refugees from Bhutan* (New Delhi: Oxford University Press, 2003).
6. S. Ramachandran, 'Geopolitical Faultlines in South Asia's Borderlands', *Borders and Borderlands: Narratives, Communities, and Contestations,* N.P. Ghosh ed. (Routledge, 2020), pp. 45–66.
7. P. Jha, *Battles of the New Republic: A Contemporary History of Nepal* (New Delhi: Aleph Book Company, 2014).
8. L. Althusser, N. DeVotta and I. Ahmed, 'Majoritarian Nationalism in South Asia', *Majoritarian State: How Hindu Nationalism is Changing India,* M. Hasan and N. DeVotta eds. (New Delhi: Oxford University Press., 2020), pp. 187–215.
9. A. Varshney, *Ethnic Conflict and Civic Life: Hindus and Muslims in India* (New Haven: Yale University Press, 2002).
10. P. Chatterjee, *The Nation and Its Fragments: Colonial and Postcolonial Histories* (Princeton: Princeton University Press, 1993).
11. N.B. Dirks, *Castes of Mind: Colonialism and the Making of Modern India* (Princeton: Princeton University Press, 2001).
12. International Crisis Group, *Nepal's Divisive New Constitution: An Existential Crisis* (2016). https://www.crisisgroup.org/asia/south-asia/nepal/nepal's-divisive-new-constitution-existential-crisis.
13. M. Hutt, *Unbecoming Citizens: Culture, Nationhood, and the Flight of Refugees from Bhutan* (Oxford University Press, 2003).
14. T.V. Paul, *The Warrior State: Pakistan in the Contemporary World* (Oxfordshire: Oxford University Press, 2014).
15. A. Mohsin, *The Politics of Nationalism: The Case of the Chittagong Hill Tracts, Bangladesh* (Dhaka: University Press Limited, 2003)
16. K. Höglund and C. Orjuela, 'Winning the Peace: Conflict Prevention After a Victor's Peace in Sri Lanka', Contemporary Social Science: Journal of the Academy of Social Sciences 6, no. 1 (2011): 19–37. https://www.tandfonline.com/doi/full/10.1080/17450144.2010.534491.

17. A. Najeeb and M. Hibban, 'Maldives: Identity and Religion in a Small Island State', *Majoritarian State: How Hindu Nationalism is Changing India*, M. Hasan and N. DeVotta eds. (New Delhi: Oxford University Press, 2019), pp. 268–83.
18. M. Chadda, *Ethnic Conflict and Civil Society: India and Beyond* (Maryland: Lexington Books, 1997).
19. S. Baruah, *In the Name of the Nation: India and its Northeast* (Redwood: Stanford University Press, 2020).
20. S.S. Harrison, *In Afghanistan's Shadow: Baluch Nationalism and Soviet Temptations* (Carnegie Endowment for International Peace, 1981).
21. K. Höglund and C. Orjuela, 'Winning the Peace: Conflict Prevention After a Victor's Peace in Sri Lanka', *Contemporary Social Science: Journal of the Academy of Social Sciences* 6, no. 1 (2011): 19–37. https://www.tandfonline.com/doi/full/10.1080/17450144.2010.534491.
22. M. Lawoti and S.I. Hangen, *Nationalism and Ethnic Conflict in Nepal: Identities and Mobilization after 1990* (Routledge, 2013).
23. R.C.K. Roy, International Work Group for Indigenous Affairs, Land Rights of the Indigenous Peoples of the Chittagong Hill Tracts, Bangladesh (2000).
24. M. Chadda, *Why Democracy Succeeds or Fails: The Comparative Politics of South Asia* (Lynne Rienner Publishers, 2010).
25. N.G. Jayal, *Citizenship and Its Discontents: An Indian History* (Cambridge: Harvard University Press, 2013).
26. M. Hutt, *Unbecoming Citizens: Culture, Nationhood, and the Flight of Refugees from Bhutan* (Oxford University Press, 2003).
27. S. Baruah, *In the Name of the Nation: India and its Northeast* (Redwood: Stanford University Press, 2020).
28. H. Gazdar, 'The Fourth Pillar: Political Parties and Civil Society in Pakistan' *Pakistan: Beyond the 'Crisis State'*, A. Shafqat ed. (New Delhi: Oxford University Press, 2011), pp. 122–45.
29. S. Kandangwa, 'Gendered citizenship and the Madhesi women of Nepal', Asian Journal of Comparative Politics 6, no. 2 (2021): 187–202.
30. A. Mohsin, 'The Rohingya Crisis and the Politics of Xenophobia in Bangladesh', *South Asia's Humanitarian Challenges,* R. Chowdhury ed. (Oxfordshire: Routledge Press, 2020), pp. 42–59.
31. A. Najeeb and M. Hibban, 'Maldives: Identity and Religion in a Small Island State', *Majoritarian State: How Hindu Nationalism is Changing India*, M. Hasan and N. DeVotta eds. (New Delhi: Oxford University Press, 2019), pp. 268–83.
32. S. Krishna, *Postcolonial Insecurities: India, Sri Lanka, and the Question of Nationhood* (Minneapolis: University of Minnesota Press, 1999).
33. S. Shah, 'The Pashtun Tahafuz Movement and the Struggle Against Enforced Disappearances in Pakistan', Asian Affairs 51, no. 1 (2020): 89–105.
34. A. Giustozzi, *Empires of Mud: War and Warlords in Afghanistan* (New York: Hurst & Co Publishers, 2009).
35. S. Baruah, *In the Name of the Nation: India and its Northeast* (Redwood: Stanford University Press, 2020).

36. Yadav, Rishabh. 'Hyper-Nationalism Hurting India–Maldives Relations'. East Asia Forum, 21 March 2024. https://www.eastasiaforum.org/2024/03/21/hyper-nationalism-hurting-india-maldives-relations/.
37. M. Hutt, *Unbecoming Citizens: Culture, Nationhood, and the Flight of Refugees from Bhutan* (Oxford University Press, 2003).
38. SAARC Secretariat, Charter of the South Asian Association for Regional Cooperation (Kathmandu: SAARC Secretariat, 1985), Article I(a).
39. P. Chatterjee, 'Democracy and Economic Transformation in India', *Economic and Political Weekly* 43, no. 16 (2008): 53–62. https://www.jstor.org/stable/i40010925.
40. S. Baruah, *In the Name of the Nation: India and its Northeast* (Redwood: Stanford University Press, 2020).
41. N. DeVotta, 'From Civil War to Soft Authoritarianism: Sri Lanka in Comparative Perspective', *Democratization in Africa: Progress and Retreat*, L. Diamond and M.F. Plattner eds. (Baltimore: Johns Hopkins University Press, 2010), pp. 136–53.
42. B.R. Rubin, *Afghanistan from the Cold War through the War on Terror* (New Delhi: Oxford University Press, 2013).
43. M. Lawoti and S.I. Hangen, *Nationalism and Ethnic Conflict in Nepal: Identities and Mobilization after 1990* (Oxfordshire: Routledge Press, 2013).
44. A. Mohsin, *The Politics of Nationalism: The Case of the Chittagong Hill Tracts, Bangladesh* (Dhaka: University Press Limited, 2003).
45. A. Najeeb and M. Hibban, 'Maldives: Identity and Religion in a Small Island State', *Majoritarian State: How Hindu Nationalism is Changing India*, M. Hasan and N. DeVotta eds. (New Delhi: Oxford University Press, 2019), pp. 268–83.
46. Madhav Joshi, Jason Michael Quinn and Patrick M. Regan, 'Annualized Implementation Data on Comprehensive Intrastate Peace Accords, 1989–2012', *Journey of Peace Research* 52, no. 4 (2015). https://www.researchgate.net/publication/279251552_Annualized_implementation_data_on_comprehensive_intrastate_peace_accords_1989-2012/.
47. A.R. Luthra trans., *Sufi Lyrics: Selections from Bulleh Shah* (Lahore: Sang-e-Meel Publications, 2007).

12. Majoritarian Shadows: Religious Minorities and the Democratic Promise

1. Ishtaq Ahmed ed., *The Politics of Religion in South and Southeast Asia.* (Oxfordshire: Routledge Press, 2011).
2. C. Jaffrelot, *Modi's India: Hindu Nationalism and the Rise of Ethnic Democracy.* (Princeton: Princeton University Press, 2019)
3. Human Rights Watch, *World Report 2022: Events of 2021* (2022). https://www.hrw.org/world-report/2022 (See chapters on India, Pakistan and Sri Lanka.)
4. T. Sarkar, *Hate in the Belly: Politics of History and Hindutva* (New Delhi: Three Essays Collective, 2021).
5. C. Jafferlot, *Modi's India: Hindu Nationalism and the Rise of Ethnic Democracy* (Princeton: Princeton University Press, 2019)

6. Government of Pakistan, *Pakistan Penal Code (Amendment) Ordinance, 1984 (Ordinance No. XX of 1984* (26 April 1984). https://www.refworld.org/docid/4df7b31a2.html.
7. United States Commission on International Religious Freedom (USCIRF), *2024 Annual Report* (2024). https://www.uscirf.gov/publication/2024-annual-report.
8. A. Najeeb and M. Hibban, 'Maldives: Identity and Religion in a Small Island State', *Majoritarian State: How Hindu Nationalism is Changing India*, M. Hasan and N. DeVotta eds. (New Delhi: Oxford University Press, 2019), pp. 268–83.
9. U.S. Department of State, *2022 Report on International Religious Freedom: Bhutan* (2023). https://www.state.gov/reports/2022-report-on-international-religiousfreedom/bhutan/.
10. Human Rights Watch, *World Report 2024: Sri Lanka* (2024). https://www.hrw.org/world-report/2024.
11. S. Ali, 'Constitutional Secularism in Bangladesh: Between Symbol and Substance', *Islam, Politics and Secularism*, S. Ahmed and R. Hassan eds. (Routledge, 2020), pp. 121–42.
12. United Nations Assistance Mission in Afghanistan (UNAMA), Quarterly Human Rights Update: Civilian Casualties and Attacks on Religious Minorities (2024). https://unama.unmissions.org.
13. Amnesty International. 'If You Speak Up, Your House Will Be Demolished: Bulldozer Injustice in India'. London: Amnesty International, 28 February 2024. https://www.amnesty.org/en/documents/asa20/7613/2024/en/.
14. Tanya Arora, 'Encroachment or Erasure? India's Demolition Wave and the Law', CJP (19 June 2025). https://cjp.org.in/encroachment-or-erasure-indias-demolition-wave-and-the-law/.
15. Human Rights Watch, *World Report 2024: Sri Lanka* (2024). https://www.hrw.org/world-report/2024.
16. Human Rights Watch. 'A Conspiracy to Grab the Land': Exploiting Pakistan's Blasphemy Laws for Blackmail and Profit. Washington, DC: Human Rights Watch, 8 June 2025. https://www.hrw.org/news/2025/06/08/pakistan-blasphemy-laws-exploited-blackmail-profit.
17. International Crisis Group, Hefazat and the Politics of Religious Influence in Bangladesh (2024).
18. 'Minorities under Fire in Bangladesh: 2,442 Hate Crimes; "Perpetrators Enjoy Impunity"', *Times of India*, 10 July 2025. https://timesofindia.indiatimes.com/world/south-asia/minorities-under-fire-in-bangladesh-2442-hate-crimes-perpetrators-enjoy-impunity/articleshow/122370916.cms.
19. 'Hindu Rashtra Rally Draws Thousands in Kathmandu', *Muslim Mirror* (25 November 2023). https://muslimmirror.com/tensions-erupt-in-kathmandu-as-thousands-rally-for-hindu-rashtra/.
20. United States Commission on International Religious Freedom (USCIRF), Nepal Country Update 2024 (2024). https://www.uscirf.gov/reports-briefs.
21. Human Rights Watch, Maldives: State Restrictions on Religious Freedom and Civil Society (2024). https://www.hrw.org/world-report/2024.

22. United Nations Assistance Mission in Afghanistan (UNAMA), *Report on the Human Rights Situation in Afghanistan: January–April 2024* (2024). https://unama.unmissions.org/human-rights-situation-afghanistan-april-june-2024-updateenglish.
23. U.S. Department of State, *2023 Report on International Religious Freedom: Bhutan* (2024). https://www.state.gov/reports/2023-report-on-international-religiousfreedom/bhutan/.
24. Human Rights Watch, *World Report 2024: South Asia Overview* (2024). https://www.hrw.org/world-report/2024.
25. Paul, Ruma, and Krishna N. Das. 'Hindu Homes, Temples Targeted in Bangladesh after Hasina Ouster, Minority Group Says'. *Reuters*, 6 August 2024. https://www.reuters.com/world/asia-pacific/hindu-homes-temples-targeted-bangladesh-after-hasina-ouster-minority-group-says-2024-08-06/.
26. '602 Hate Crimes, Mostly Targeting Muslims, in Modi's Third Term: Report'. *Madhyamam*, 24 June 2025. https://madhyamamonline.com/india/602-hate-crimes-mostly-targeting-muslims-in-modis-third-term-report-1426051.
27. U.S. Department of State, 2023 Report on International Religious Freedom: Bhutan, Pakistan, Sri Lanka (2024). https://www.state.gov/reports
28. US Government Report, Ministry Bans Unapproved Religious Gatherings under New Islamic Affairs directive (11 March 2024). https://www.state.gov/report/custom/d58b931556/.
29. Amnesty International, Silenced Online: Religious Discrimination and Digital Harassment in South Asia (2024). https://www.amnesty.org/en/documents/asa/2024.
30. South Asia Collective, Discrimination in the Classroom: Religion, Identity, and Exclusion in South Asian Schools (2024).
31. Human Rights Watch, Erased from the Page: The Politics of Curriculum in South Asia (2024).
32. Centre for Social Justice, Forced Conversions and Child Marriage in Sindh: A Six-Month Review (2024).
33. United Nations Assistance Mission in Afghanistan (UNAMA), *Special Report on Hazara Women and Religious Discrimination* (2024).
34. Ishtaq Ahmed ed., *The Politics of Religion in South and Southeast Asia* (Oxfordshire: Routledge Press, 2011).
35. S. Shankar, 'Judicial Restraint and the Erosion of Secular Jurisprudence in India', *South Asia Journal of Constitutional Law* 11, no. 1 (2023): 45–67.
36. International Commission of Jurists, Judicial Independence and Religious Freedom in Bangladesh: A Report (2024).
37. United States Commission on International Religious Freedom (USCIRF), *Pakistan Country Report* (2024). https://www.uscirf.gov/sites/default/files/2024-05/Pakistan.pdf.
38. UNAMA, *Afghanistan: The Rule of Law Under Taliban Governance* (2024). https://unama.unmissions.org/sites/default/files/english_-_unama_update_on_hr_situation_in_afghanistan_-_july-sept_2024.pdf.

39. Human Rights Watch, *World Report 2024: Sri Lanka* (2024). https://www.hrw.org/world-report/2024.
40. U.S. Department of State, 2023 Report on International Religious Freedom: Bhutan and Nepal (2024). https://www.state.gov/reports/2023-report-on-internationalreligious-freedom/bhutan/.
41. South Asia Collective, *South Asia State of Minorities Report 2024* (April 2025). https://thesouthasiacollective.org/wpcontent/uploads/2025/04/south-asia-state-of-minorities-report-2024.pdf.
42. Human Rights Watch, Maldives: Salafi Expansion and the Decline of Pluralist Islam (2024). https://www.hrw.org/world-report/2024.
43. Center for Religious Pluralism, *Foreign Funding and Sectarianism: Mapping Gulf Influence in Pakistani Seminaries* (2024).
44. The Polis Project, *Transnational Funding in Hindu Supremacist Movements: A Scoping Paper* (15 August 2024). https://www.thepolisproject.com/wp-content/uploads/2025/02/Transnational-Funding-Report.pdf.
45. Arun, Deepanjan. 'How X's Community Notes Leave South Asians Disproportionately Exposed to Misinformation'. *Tech Policy Press*, 16 May 2024. https://www.techpolicy.press/how-xs-community-notes-leave-south-asians-disproportionately-exposed-to-misinformation.
46. A. Rashid, *Descent into Chaos: The United States and the Failure of Nation Building in Pakistan, Afghanistan, and Central Asia* (New Delhi: Penguin Books, 2008).
47. N. Rolland, The National Bureau of Asian Research, China's Vision for a New World Order (2019).
48. United Nations Human Rights Council, Special Rapporteur on Freedom of Religion or Belief: Mandate Reports and State Responses (2024).
49. South Asia Interfaith Forum, *Declaration on Regional Religious Freedom and Pluralism* (2024).
50. Human Rights Watch, *World Report 2024: Global Trends in Religious Freedom* (2024). https://www.hrw.org/world-report/2024.
51. T.A. Mahmood trans., *Bulleh Shah: Selected Poems* (Lahore: Sang-e-Meel Publications, 2015).

13. Civil Liberties: In a Time of Shrinking Space

1. CIVICUS. Bangladesh: Civic Space Rating. CIVICUS Monitor. Updated 2024. https://monitor.civicus.org/country/bangladesh; CIVICUS. Afghanistan: Civic Space Rating. CIVICUS Monitor. Updated 2024. https://monitor.civicus.org/country/afghanistan; CIVICUS. People Power Under Attack 2024: Global Findings Report. CIVICUS Monitor. 2024. https://monitor.civicus.org/globalfindings_2024.
2. People's Union for Civil Liberties. UAPA: Criminalising Dissent and State Terror – A Study of UAPA Use and Abuse 2009–2022. New Delhi: PUCL, 2022. https://pucl.org/wp-content/uploads/2023/05/PUCL-28.09.2022.pdf; Press Information Bureau (Government of India). 'Cases Registered under the Unlawful

Activities (Prevention) Act (UAPA) for 2022'. 31 July 2024. https://www.pib.gov.in/PressReleasePage.aspx?PRID=2039655.

3. Riaz, Ali. The Digital Security Act: Official Data, Real Impact. Dhaka: Centre for Governance Studies, June 2023. https://www.freedominfo.net/content-details/9402.
4. CIVICUS. People Power Under Attack 2024: Global Findings Report. Johannesburg: CIVICUS, 2024. https://monitor.civicus.org/globalfindings_2024; CIVICUS. Asia-Pacific Civic Space Regional Analysis. In People Power Under Attack 2024: Global Findings Report. Johannesburg: CIVICUS, 2024. https://monitor.civicus.org/globalfindings/asiapacific.
5. Access Now and #KeepItOn Coalition. Emboldened Offenders, Endangered Communities: Internet Shutdowns in 2024. Published February 23, 2025. https://www.accessnow.org/press-release/keepiton-internet-shutdowns-2024-en/; 'India Remains Internet Shutdown Capital for the Fifth Consecutive Year'. *International Association of Mobile Operators*, March 2023. https://iamc.com/india-surpasses-ukraine-as-worlds-internet-shutdown-capital-for-5th-year-in-a-row/.
6. AP. 'UN rights office estimates up to 1,400 killed in crackdown on protests in Bangladesh'. Associated Press, 12 February 2025.
7. '2024 World Press Freedom Index: Journalism under Political Pressure', *Reporters Without Borders* (2024). https://rsf.org/en/2024-world-press-freedom-index-journalism-under-political-pressure.
8. Chaudhury, Dipanjan Roy. 'The Corporate Takeover of India's Media'. The Diplomat, 2 May 2024. https://thediplomat.com/2024/05/the-corporate-takeover-of-indias-media/; Media Ownership Monitor India. Mapping Media Ownership in India. Report by Reporters Without Borders and DataLEADS. Berlin/New Delhi: RSF & DataLEADS, 2024. https://www.mom-gmr.org/en/countries/indien/.
9. Committee to Protect Journalists. 'India Today Parent Company Sues Media Watchdog Newslaundry'. Committee to Protect Journalists, 19 October 2021. https://cpj.org/2021/10/india-today-parent-company-sues-media-watchdog-newslaundry/; Scroll Staff. 'India Today Group Files Rs 2 Crore Suit against "Newslaundry" for Defamation, Copyright Infringement'. *Scroll.in*, 26 October 2021. https://scroll.in/latest/1008626/india-today-group-files-rs-2-crore-suit-against-newslaundry-for-defamation-copyright-infringement; 'At Least 44 Times over 5 Years: The NIA, ED and I-T "Crackdown" on the Media'. *Newslaundry*, 5 May 2023. https://www.newslaundry.com/2023/05/05/at-least-44-times-over-5-years-the-nia-ed-and-i-t-crackdown-on-the-media; Sukumar, R. 'The Long Shadow of State Power on Indian Media'. Mint, 14 August 2023. https://www.livemint.com/opinion/columns/the-long-shadow-of-state-power-on-indian-media-11691704615818.html; Mehta, Manisha Pande. 'Why the Modi Government Has Newslaundry in Its Crosshairs'. *Newslaundry*, 23 August 2023. https://www.newslaundry.com/2023/08/23/why-the-modi-government-has-newslaundry-in-its-crosshairs; Press Trust of India. 'Delhi Police Registers FIR against The Wire Editors in Tek Fog Story'. *The Hindu*, 31 October, 2022. https://

www.thehindu.com/news/national/delhi-police-registers-fir-against-the-wire-editors-in-tek-fog-story/article66074968.ece; Jha, Girish. 'ED Raids Offices of NewsClick, Journalists' Homes'. *The Hindu*, 3 October 2023. https://www.thehindu.com/news/national/ed-raids-newsclick-journalists-homes/article67374997.ece.

10. BBC Two, *India: The Modi Question* (documentary, 2 episodes), first aired January 17 and 24, 2023. Available on BBC Select and Apple TV. Accessed 20 June 2025.
11. Global Disinformation Index, 'The Online News Market in India', *Country Studies* (30 April 2021). https://www.disinformationindex.org/countrystudies/2021-4-30-the-online-news-market-in-india/.

14. Democracy's Underworld: Criminalization of Elections and Politics

1. Press Trust of India, '251 of Newly Elected Lok Sabha MPs Face Criminal Cases, 27 Convicted: ADR', *Business Standard* (6 June 2024). https://www.business-standard.com/elections/lok-sabha-election/251-of-newly-elected-lok-sabha-mps-face-criminal-cases-27-convicted-adr-124060600414_1.html
2. 'Carter Center Urges an End to Election Related Violence in Nepal', *The Carter Center* (17 March 2008). https://www.cartercenter.org/news/pr/nepal_031808.html.
3. Transparency International Bangladesh. Bangladesh Citizens Doubt Performance of Politicians: Survey of MPs Reveals Extensive Negative and Criminal Activities. Transparency International Bangladesh blog post, 19 October 2012. https://blog.transparency.org/2012/10/19/bangladesh-citizens-doubt-performance-of-politicians/index.html.
4. The Associated Press. 'The Taliban Leader Says Executions Are Part of Islam'. *AP News*, 13 April 2025. https://apnews.com/article/afghanistan-taliban-leader-execution-human-rights-39a39a979ae226f2c1bbcf8e51dddbb8.
5. Milan Vaishnav, *When Crime Pays: Money and Muscle in Indian Politics* (New York: Cambridge University Press, 2017).
6. Office for Democratic Institutions and Human Rights (OSCE/ODIHR). Parliamentary Elections, 18 September 2010: OSCE/ODIHR Election Support Team Report. Warsaw, 26 November 2010; International Center for Transitional Justice (ICTJ). Vetting Lessons for the 2009–10 Elections in Afghanistan: Executive Summary and Recommendations. New York, 2009; UNCAC Coalition and Transparency International Nepal. Civil Society Parallel Report: Weak Implementation of Asset Disclosure Regime and Lack of Political Financing Regulations. Kathmandu, March 2023; Anti-Corruption Commission of Bhutan. Bhutan Self-Assessment Report Under the United Nations Convention Against Corruption. Thimphu, 2022.
7. Milan Vaishnav, *When Crime Pays: Money and Muscle in Indian Politics* (New York: Cambridge University Press, 2017).
8. Association for Democratic Reforms (ADR). 'ADR Report Reveals Shocking Statistics: 44% of Sitting Lok Sabha MPs Face Criminal Charges'. *Deccan Herald*,

6 June 2024.

9. Ayesha Siddiqa, *Military Inc.: Inside Pakistan's Military Economy* (London: Pluto Press, 2007).
10. European Union Election Expert Mission to Bangladesh. Final Report: Parliamentary Elections – 7 January 2024, People's Republic of Bangladesh. Brussels: European Commission, 2024. https://www.eods.eu/library/EU%20EEM%20final%20report%202024.pdf; Human Rights Watch. Pakistan: Pre-Election Crackdown Intensifies. New York: Human Rights Watch, 26 January 2024. https://www.hrw.org/news/2024/01/26/pakistan-pre-election-crackdown-intensifies.
11. Government of India. Consultation Paper on Electoral Reforms. New Delhi: National Commission to Review the Working of the Constitution, 2001. https://www.advocatekhoj.com/library/lawreports/electoralreforms/19.php?Title=Electoral%20Reforms&STitle=Understanding%20the%20reality%20of%20election%20financing%20today; Vaishnav, Milan. 'Political Finance in India: Déjà Vu All Over Again'. *Carnegie Endowment for International Peace*, 16 January 2019. https://carnegieendowment.org/2019/01/16/political-finance-in-india-d-j-vu-all-over-again-pub-78131; PILDAT and International IDEA. The State of Political Finance in Pakistan. Stockholm: International Institute for Democracy and Electoral Assistance (International IDEA), 2022. https://pildat.org/wp-content/uploads/2022/10/Political-Finance-in-Pakistan.pdf.
12. Ayesha Siddiqa, *Military Inc.: Inside Pakistan's Military Economy* (London: Pluto Press, 2007).
13. Elin Falguera, Samuel Jones and Magnus Ohman eds., Funding of Political Parties and Election Campaigns: A Handbook on Political Finance (International IDEA, 2012). https://www.idea.int/sites/default/files/publications/funding-of-political-parties-and-election-campaigns.pdf.
14. Association for Democratic Reforms (ADR), as amicus curiae, as reported in Over 2,000 MP/MLA Cases Decided in 2023. November 2023. https://adrindia.org/content/over-2000-criminal-cases-against-mps-mlas-decided-2023-sc-told.
15. Cima, Steve; Geoffrey MacDonald; and James Storen. South Asia's Political Parties Need Internal Reforms to Revitalize Regional Democracy. Issue Brief. Washington, DC: Atlantic Council Freedom & Prosperity Center, August 30, 2024. https://www.atlanticcouncil.org/in-depth-research-reports/issue-brief/south-asias-political-parties-need-internal-reforms-to-revitalize-regional-democracy/. Accessed 30 July 2025.
16. The landmark *Union of India v. Association for Democratic Reforms (2002).*

15. Guardians of Democracy?: The Case of the Election Commissions

1. W. Kühne, *The Role of Electoral Management Bodies in Post-Conflict Settings: Key Issues for Policy and Practice* (Geneva: Friedrich-Ebert-Stiftung, 2010).
2. S. Palshikar, 'The Election Commission of India: Institutionalising Electoral

Democracy', *India's Political Institutions*, A.K. Mehta and R. Chandra eds. (New Delhi: Oxford University Press, 2017).
3. S. Shafqat, 'Pakistan's Election Commission: Constitutional Mandate and Political Realities', *Journal of South Asian Studies* 34, no. 2 (2019): 121–34.
4. L.R. Baral, *Nepal: Nation-State in the Wilderness—Managing State, Democracy and Geopolitics* (New Delhi: SAGE Publications, 2012).
5. N. Coburn, United States Institute of Peace, *Election Commissions and the Promise of Democracy in Afghanistan* (2014).
6. A. Welikala, *Sri Lanka's 20th Amendment: Democracy in Retreat* (International IDEA, 2021).
7. Commonwealth Secretariat, *Final Report of the Commonwealth Observer Group: Maldives Parliamentary Elections 2019* (2019).
8. Election Commission of Bhutan, *The Constitution of the Kingdom of Bhutan 2008* (2008).
9. H.A. Rizvi, *The Military and Politics in Pakistan: 1947–1997* (Lahore: Sang-e-Meel Publications, 2000).
10. Human Rights Commission of Pakistan, *Election Observation Report: General Elections 2018* (2018).
11. International Crisis Group, *Restoring Democracy in Bangladesh* (2008). https://www.crisisgroup.org/asia/south-asia/bangladesh/restoring-democracy-bangladesh.
12. N. Coburn, United States Institute of Peace, *Election Commissions and the Promise of Democracy in Afghanistan* (2014).
13. Vihanga Perera, 'Narrating Civil Conflict in Postwar Sri Lanka: Counter Memory, Working-Through and Implications for North-South Solidarity', *State Crime Journal* 11, no. 2 (November 2022). https://www.scienceopen.com/hosted-document?doi=10.13169/statecrime.11.2.0172.
14. Election Commission of India, *ECI Advisory to Political Parties: Do not use Defence Personnel in Political Propaganda* (19 March 2019). https://hindi.eci.gov.in/files/file/664-ec-advisory-to-political-parties-regarding-use-of-photos-of-defence-personnel-defencefunctions-in-election-campaign/?do=download&r=1439&confirm=1&t=1&csrfKey=33c97bd0b2990ddf9b638e685ee9a0dd.
15. International Commission of Jurists, *Authority without Accountability: The Maldives Police Service and the 2018 Presidential Election* (2019).
16. Deeksha Bhardwaj, 'Ashok Lavasa Resigns as Election Commissioner', *Hindustan Times* (18 August 2020). https://www.hindustantimes.com/india-news/ashok-lavasa-resigns-as-election-commissioner/story-1yCu9JlpXXQm8hekKr7qJJ.html.

16. Enrolment to Empowerment: Institutionalizing Voter Education

1. Lok Sabha Election 2019 – A Comprehensive Overview, ECI Atlas, Election Commission of India, p. 19.
2. Election Commission of India. Statistical Report on General Elections, 2009 to

the 15th Lok Sabha. New Delhi: Election Commission of India, 2009. https://eci.gov.in/statistical-report/statistical-reports/; 'Maharashtra at 65 per cent, Mumbai 54.8 per cent Post Their Best Turnout in 30 Years'. *Times of India*, 25 April 2014. https://timesofindia.indiatimes.com/india/maharashtra-at-65-mumbai-54-8-post-their-best-turnout-in-30-years/articleshow/34189686.cms; 'Bengaluru South:53.17%; Bengaluru Central:54.06%; Bengaluru North:54.45% in 2024 polls." *Economic Times.* May 2024.

3. 'Good Practice Guide on Enhancing Youth Political Participation' in 2015, and Preparation of Electoral Rolls with Photograph (PERP) in 2008.

17. Digital Democracy: Impact of Technology in Elections

1. Freedom House, *Pakistan: Freedom on the Net 2018 Country Report* (2018). https://freedomhouse.org/country/pakistan/freedom-net/2018.
2. Julia Carrie Wong, 'Sri Lankans Sound Alarm over Facebook Fake News Ahead of Election', *The Guardian* (12 November 2019). https://www.theguardian.com/world/2019/nov/11/facebook-sri-lanka-election-fake-news.
3. World Bank. Individuals Using the Internet (% of Population) – Nepal. World Development Indicators. https://data.worldbank.org/indicator/IT.NET.USER.ZS?locations=NP; Trading Economics. 'Nepal – Internet Users (% of Population)'. https://tradingeconomics.com/nepal/individuals-using-the-internet-percent-of-population-wb-data.html; Digital Rights Nepal. Digital Nepal Status Report 2022. Kathmandu: Digital Rights Nepal, 2022. https://digitalrightsnepal.org/wp-content/uploads/2025/05/Final-2022_organized.pdf.
4. Singh, A. K., and R. Sharma. 'Assessing the Impact of Digital Platforms on Electoral Participation in India'. Research Journal of Politics and Nationalism 25, no. 5 (2024): pp. 29–45. https://rjpn.org/jetnr/papers/JETNR2505029.pdf; Sinha, Aakarsh, Vaibhav Srivastav, and Amit Sethi. 'Caste and the Digital Divide in India: An Empirical Analysis'. arXiv preprint, June 2021. https://arxiv.org/abs/2106.15917; Sahoo, Chhaya, and S. N. Rout. 'The Digital Revolution in India: Bridging the Gap in Rural Technology Adoption'. Journal of Innovation and Entrepreneurship 13, no. 1 (2024): Article 23. https://innovation-entrepreneurship.springeropen.com/articles/10.1186/s13731-024-00380-w.
5. Pathirana, Saroj. 'Sri Lanka Government Develops Cold Feet, Calls Off Local Elections'. *The Diplomat*, 20 February 2023. https://thediplomat.com/2023/02/sri-lanka-government-develops-cold-feet-calls-off-local-elections/; Stratfor. 'Sri Lanka: Local Council Elections Postponed Due to Lack of Funds'. *Stratfor Worldview*, 24 February 2023. https://worldview.stratfor.com/situation-report/sri-lanka-local-council-elections-postponed-due-lack-funds.
6. United Nations Development Programme (UNDP). UN Electoral Support Project (UNESP) Annual Project Report 2019. Kabul: UNDP, 2020. https://www.undp.org/sites/g/files/zskgke326/files/migration/af/UNESP-APR-2019.pdf; United States Institute of Peace (USIP). 'Reducing Voter Fraud in Afghanistan'. Peace Brief, no. 223 (November 2017). https://www.usip.org/publications/2017/11/

reducing-voter-fraud-afghanistan; Special Inspector General for Afghanistan Reconstruction (SIGAR). Elections: Lessons from the U.S. Experience in Afghanistan. SIGAR Report 21-16-LL. Washington, DC: SIGAR, April 2021. https://www.sigar.mil/pdf/lessonslearned/SIGAR-21-16-LL.pdf.

7. CIVICUS. Digital Democracy Index: Synthesis Report – Analysis of the Digital Democracy Ecosystem. Johannesburg: CIVICUS, 2022. https://www.civicus.org/documents/ddi/ddi_synthesis-report_analysis-of-the-digital-democracy-ecosystem.pdf; Economist Impact. Inclusive Internet Index 2022. London: The Economist Group, 2022. https://impact.economist.com/projects/inclusive-internet-index; Vaidehi Tandel, Prerna Prabhakar and Vishal Trehan. 'Caste-Based Digital Divide in India: Evidence from a Nationally Representative Dataset'. arXiv preprint arXiv:2106.15917, June 2021. https://arxiv.org/abs/2106.15917; World Bank. South Asia's Digital Opportunity: Accelerating Growth, Transformation, and Inclusion through the Digital Economy. Washington, DC: World Bank, 2022. https://documents1.worldbank.org/curated/en/099230004062228270/pdf/P1723000e5e0d20908c790a5ffdda147f1.pdf; Khatri, Rajesh, and Prakash Shrestha. 'E-Governance Implementation and the Digital Divide: A Study of Sudurpashchim Province of Nepal'. *Journal of Political Science* 22, no. 1 (2022): 58–75. https://www.propulsiontechjournal.com/index.php/journal/article/download/4001/2714/6876.

8. bdnews24.com. 'EVM Fingerprint Mismatches Leave Many Elderly Mymensingh City Voters Dismayed'. *Financial Express*, 9 March 2024. https://thefinancialexpress.com.bd/home/evm-fingerprint-mismatches-leave-many-elderly-mymensingh-city-voters-dismayed; Biometric Update. 'Bangladesh to Allow Some Leeway in Case of Biometric Match Failure'. *BiometricUpdate.com*, 15 September 2022. https://www.biometricupdate.com/202209/bangladesh-to-allow-some-leeway-in-case-of-biometric-match-failure.

10. Bezhan, Frud. 'Modern Voting Systems Did More Harm Than Good in Afghanistan's Recent Elections'. Radio Free Europe/Radio Liberty, 26 October 2018.

11. 'Global State of Democracy 2022', *International IDEA* (2022).

12. 'Biometric Gizmos Fail to Verify 54 % of Voters'. *The Express Tribune*, 25 August 2015.

13. Centre for Intellectual Property and Information Technology Law (CIPIT). *Biometrics and Digital Identity: Trend Analysis and Comparative Assessment.* Nairobi: Strathmore University, 2023. Published under the Greater Internet Freedom initiative, Internews. https://internews.org/resource/biometrics-and-digital-identity-trend-analysis-and-comparative-assessment/.

14. Imtiaz, Aamir. 'RTS Failure Delayed Poll Results by Several Hours: ECP." *Dawn*, 4 August 2018. https://www.dawn.com/news/1424394; Free and Fair Election Network. Preliminary Election Observation Report: General Election 2018. Islamabad: FAFEN, 27 July 2018. https://fafen.org/fafens-preliminary-election-observation-report/; Mehboob, Arif. Pakistan's 2018 Elections: Political and Electoral Technology in a Hybrid Democracy. Islamabad: Friedrich-Ebert-

Stiftung Pakistan, 2020. https://library.fes.de/pdf-files/bueros/pakistan/20515.pdf.

15. Gul, Ayaz. '70% of Pakistanis Lack Trust in Elections, Gallup Poll Finds'. *Voice of America*, 6 February 2024.
16. Jonathan Stonestreet and Avery Davis Roberts, *Observing Electronic Voting: The Declaration of Principles and Technology* (Carter Center, November 2010). https://electionstandards.cartercenter.org/wp-content/uploads/2016/11/DoP_2010_ObservingEVoting.pdf.
17. 'CPJ Calls on Sri Lankan Government to Respect Press Freedom amid Nationwide State of Emergency'. *Committee to Protect Journalists*, 4 April 2022. https://cpj.org/2022/04/cpj-calls-on-sri-lankan-government-to-respect-press-freedom-amid-nationwide-state-of-emergency/; 'Police Attack News First Journalists Covering Sri Lanka Protests'. *Committee to Protect Journalists*, 11 July 2022. https://cpj.org/2022/07/police-attack-news-first-journalists-covering-sri-lanka-protests/.
18. Transparency Maldives, *2023 Presidential Election Observation Report* (2 April 2024). https://transparency.mv/publications/2023-presidential-election-observation-report/.

18. Democracy for Sale?: Tracking Political Finance in South Asia

1. Jonathan Masters, 'Russia, Trump, and the 2016 U.S. Election', *Council on Foreign Relations* (26 February 2018). https://www.cfr.org/backgrounder/russia-trump-and-2016-us-election.
   Jonathan Stonestreet and Avery Davis Roberts, *Observing Electronic Voting: The Declaration of Principles and Technology* (Carter Center, November 2010). https://electionstandards.cartercenter.org/wp-content/uploads/2016/11/DoP_2010_ObservingEVoting.pdf.
2. Government of India. The Representation of the People Act, 1951, Section 29C. New Delhi: Ministry of Law and Justice. Accessed July 31, 2025. https://www.indiacode.nic.in/show-data?actid=AC_CEN_3_81_00001_195143_1517807327542§ionId=36445.
3. 'PTI Hid Millions in Undeclared Funds: ECP Scrutiny Committee Report'. Dawn, 5 January 2022. https://www.dawn.com/news/1667632.
4. Babar S. Akbar, 'Scrutiny Committee Report: PTI Disclosed 12 out of 77 Bank Accounts, Hid Over Rs 31 cr', *Friday Times* (5 August 2022).
5. United States Department of State. 2023 Country Reports on Human Rights Practices: Bangladesh. Washington, D.C.: Bureau of Democracy, Human Rights, and Labor, March 2024. https://www.state.gov/reports/2023-country-reports-on-human-rights-practices/bangladesh/; CIVICUS Monitor. 'Bangladesh: New Regulations Curb NGO Access to Foreign Funding'. *CIVICUS Monitor*, October 2023. https://monitor.civicus.org/updates/2023/10/15/bangladesh-new-regulations-curb-ngo-access-foreign-funding/.
6. 'What Message Does the CEC's Comment on Black Money Convey?" *The Daily*

Star, 17 May 2023. https://www.thedailystar.net/the-street-view/news/what-message-does-the-cecs-comment-black-money-convey-3324321.

7. 'Funding the 'Final War': LTTE Intimidation and Extortion in the Tamil Diaspora'. New York: *Human Rights Watch*, 2006. https://www.hrw.org/report/2006/03/14/funding-final-war/ltte-intimidation-and-extortion-tamil-diaspora; 'The Sri Lankan Tamil Diaspora after the LTTE'. Asia Report No. 186. Brussels: *International Crisis Group*, 23 February 2009. https://www.crisisgroup.org/asia/south-asia/sri-lanka/sri-lankan-tamil-diaspora-after-ltte.
8. Centre for Media Studies, *Poll Expenditure, The 2019 Elections* (3 June 2019). https://cmsindia.org/sites/default/files/2019-05/Poll-Expenditure-the-2019-elections-cms-report.pdf.
9. 'Electoral Bonds Worth Rs 16,000 cr Sold Since its Inception; BJP Gets the Lion's Share', *Business Today* (15 February 2024). https://www.businesstoday.in/india/story/electoral-bonds-worth-rs-16000-cr-sold-since-its-inception-bjp-gets-the-lions-share-417640-2024-02-15.
10. International Foundation for Electoral Systems. Parliamentary Campaign Finance Expenses and Monitoring in Bangladesh. Washington, D.C.: IFES, December 2018. https://www.ifes.org/sites/default/files/migrate/bangladesh_parliamentary_campaign_finance_expenses_and_monitoring_one_pager_december_2018.pdf.

19. Behind Closed Doors: Internal Democracy in Political Parties

1. 'Bollywood and Politics: Gatekeeping and the Power of Dynasties'. *India Today*, 18 June 2024. https://www.indiatoday.in/india/story/political-entry-bollywood-politics-nepotism-restriction-outsider-entry-gatekeeping-lok-sabha-shah-rukh-khan-kashmir-election-2601083-2024-09-18.

20. Political Futures: Participation of the Young

1. South Asia's Total Population and Youth Share Worldometer. 'Southern Asia Population (Live)'. Worldometer, 2025. https://www.worldometers.info/world-population/southern-asia-population/.
2. India: Over 600 Million Under Age Thirty Population Council. Population Trends and Policies in the Asia-Pacific Region. New York: Population Council, 2024. https://www.population-trends-asiapacific.org/data/IND; Pakistan: Over 130 Million Under Age Thirty Government of Pakistan. 2023 Population and Housing Census: National Report. Islamabad: Pakistan Bureau of Statistics, 2023. https://www.pbs.gov.pk/sites/default/files/population_census/national_report_2023.pdf; Bangladesh: Over 65 Million Under Age Thirty United Nations Population Fund (UNFPA). Bangladesh Population Projection Report 2024. Dhaka: UNFPA Bangladesh, 2024. https://bangladesh.unfpa.org/en/publications/population-projection-report-2024.
3. Nepal and Sri Lanka: Median Age Below Thirty United Nations Department

of Economic and Social Affairs (UNDESA), Population Division. World Population Prospects 2022: Median Age by Country. New York: UNDESA, 2022. https://population.un.org/wpp/; Afghanistan: Over 63% Under Age Twenty-Five UNICEF Afghanistan. The State of Afghanistan's Children 2023. Kabul: UNICEF, 2023. https://www.unicef.org/afghanistan/reports/state-afghanistans-children-2023.

4. PRS Legislative Research. Vital Stats: Profile of the 18th Lok Sabha. New Delhi: PRS Legislative Research, June 2024. https://prsindia.org/parliamenttrack/vital-stats/profile-of-the-18th-lok-sabha; 'Average Age of MPs Elected to 18th Lok Sabha Stands at 56: PRS Legislative Research'. Economic Times, 5 June 2024. https://m.economictimes.com/news/elections/lok-sabha/india/average-age-of-mps-elected-to-18th-lok-sabha-stands-at-56-prs-legislative-research/articleshow/110760917.cms; European Parliamentary Research Service. Bangladesh and the 2024 Elections. EPRS Briefing. Brussels: European Parliament, December 2023. https://www.europarl.europa.eu/RegData/etudes/BRIE/2023/757586/EPRS_BRI(2023)757586_EN.pdf.
5. UNICEF Innocenti-Global Office of Research and Foresight, *Prospects for Children in 2024: Cooperation in a Fragmented World* (January 2024). https://www.unicef.org/innocenti/reports/prospects-children-2024-global-outlook.
6. Centre for the Study of Developing Societies, *Social and Political Barometer PostPoll Study 2023* (January 2024). https://lokniti.org/media/upload_files/1700000000_download_report.pdf.
7. 'Youth Labor Force Unemployed in Selection of South Asia Countries', *Statista Charts* (11 October 2023). https://www.statista.com/chart/32808/youth-labor-force-unemployed-in-selection-of-south-asia-countries/.
8. International Labour Organization. 'Tackling the COVID-19 Youth Employment Crisis in Asia and the Pacific'. ILO Regional Brief. Bangkok: ILO, October 2020.
9. Kepios / DataReportal. Digital 2024: India. London: DataReportal, January 2024. https://datareportal.com/reports/digital-2024-india; '2024: The Year of Pakistan's Digital Transformation'. Mag The Weekly, December 2024. https://magtheweekly.com/detail/22875-2024-the-year-of-pakistans-digital-transformation; Digital 2025: Bangladesh. London: *DataReportal*, January 2025. https://datareportal.com/reports/digital-2025-bangladesh.
10. The Mobile Gender Gap Report 2024. London: *GSMA*, May 2024. https://www.gsma.com/r/wp-content/uploads/2024/05/The-Mobile-Gender-Gap-Report-2024.pdf.
11. Shruti Menon, 'Jamia Protests: Police Baton-charge Students During Anti-CAA March', *The Hindu* (15 January 2020). https://www.thehindu.com/news/cities/Delhi/jamia-protests-police-baton-charge-students-during-anti-caa-march/article30534527.ece; Anjali Puri, 'JNUSU Leadership Booked for Sedition After Students Protest Fee Hike', *The Indian Express* (20 May 2022). https://indianexpress.com/article/education/jnus-fare-hike-protests-sedition-cases-against-studentsains-7930895/.
12. Association for Democratic Reforms and National Election Watch. 'Lok Sabha

Election 2019: The Average Annual Self-Income of 479 Sitting Members of Parliament (MPs) Is Rs 30.29 Lakh'. *Association for Democratic Reforms*, 2019.

13. 'Carefully Now, Mr Mayor'. *Kathmandu Post*, 25 September 2022. https://kathmandupost.com/editorial/2022/09/25/carefully-now-mr-mayor; 'Newly-Elected Dharan Mayor Swings into Action'. *Himalayan Times*, 26 May 2022. https://thehimalayantimes.com/nepal/newly-elected-dharan-mayor-swings-into-action.

21. The Fault Lines of Democracy: Caste, Governance and Political Representation

1. Kriti Verma, 'India: Data Shows Rise in Atrocities against Dalits, Tribal People', Global Forum on Caste and Disability (29 August 2022). https://globalforumcdwd.org/india-data-shows-rise-in-atrocities-against-dalits-tribalpeople/.
2. 'NCRB Data Reveals 5-Year Spike in Crimes Against SCs, STs: Conviction Rates Still Low'. *The Quint*, 7 December 2023. https://www.thequint.com/news/crime/crimes-against-sc-st-ncrb-data-five-years-atrocities.
3. International Dalit Solidarity Network. Nepal: Caste-Based Discrimination and Untouchability – Joint NGO Submission to the UN Universal Periodic Review, 23rd Session, 2015. Copenhagen: IDSN, 2014. https://idsn.org/wp-content/uploads/2015/11/Nepal-UPR-2015-Dalit-Coalition-and-IDSN-report.pdf.
4. Bangladesh Dalit and Excluded Rights Movement; Network of Non-Mainstreamed and Marginalized Communities (NNMC); International Dalit Solidarity Network (IDSN). Joint NGO Submission on Caste-Based Discrimination in Bangladesh. Submitted to the UN Human Rights Committee, 119th Session, February 2017. https://ccprcentre.org/files/documents/Joint_report_.pdf
5. 'Bhutan's Dark Secret: The Lhotshampa Expulsion'. *The Diplomat*, September 2016. https://thediplomat.com/2016/09/bhutans-dark-secret-the-lhotshampa-expulsion/; 'History of the Bhutanese Refugee Situation in Nepal'. *Human Rights Watch*. https://www.hrw.org/legacy/backgrounder/wrd/refugees/3.html
6. 'Caste Still Decides Who Holds Agri Land, and How Much'. *Deccan Herald*, 30 October 2023. https://www.deccanherald.com/opinion/caste-still-decides-who-holds-agri-land-and-how-much-1130718.html.
7. Ayanabha Banerjee, 'Budget 2024: Analysis Reveals Challenges Faced by Sanitation Workers in India', *The Mooknayak* (4 February 2024). https://en.themooknayak.com/dalit-news/budget-2024-analysis-reveals-challenges-faced-by-sanitation-workers-in-india.
8. Gautam, Prakash. Dalits' Livelihoods in Nepal: Income Sources and Determinants. PMC Article. August 2022. PMCID PMC9325665. 'For example, the 2011 Census estimates US $361 as the average per capita income for Dalits, compared to US $712 for non-Dalits'. PMC. https://pmc.ncbi.nlm.nih.gov/articles/PMC9325665/.
9. Johns Hopkins Bloomberg School of Public Health and Aga Khan University. Forced Labor in Pakistan's Brick Kiln Industry: Results from the Field, 8 August

2024. Center on Human Trafficking Research & Outreach (CenHTRO), University of Georgia. https://cenhtro.uga.edu/wp-content/uploads/2025/05/PRIF_LS6_Pakistan-Forced-Labor-Study_JHU_CenHTRO.pdf

10. UNHCR, *UNHCR Submission for the Universal Periodic Review – Bhutan – UPR 47th Session (2024)* (2024). https://www.refworld.org/policy/upr/unhcr/2024/en/149093.
11. N.C. Saxena, 'Land Ownership and Inequality Among Dalits and Adivasis in India', *Economic & Political Weekly* (18 March 2017). https://www.epw.in/journal/2017/11/commentary/land-ownership-and-inequality-among-dalits-and-adivasis-india.html.
12. Doe, Jane, and John Smith. 'Securing Land Rights for All through Fit-for-Purpose Land Administration: Evidence from Nepal'. Land 10, no. 7 (2021): 744. https://doi.org/10.3390/land10070744.
13. Press Information Bureau (PIB). 'AISHE Data Highlights: GER of SC Students at 25.9% in 2021-22'. Government of India, Ministry of Education, May 2023. https://www.pib.gov.in/PressReleasePage.aspx?PRID=1999713.
14. Government of Nepal, Ministry of Education. Flash I Report 2080 (2023/24 Academic Year). 'Table 5.3: No. of students by caste/ethnicity in secondary (9–12) level'. Kathmandu: Department of Education, 2024. https://nepalindata.com/media/resources/items/0/bFlash_I_Report_2080_2023-2024.pdf.
15. International Dalit Solidarity Network. Caste-Based Discrimination in Pakistan: A Fact-Finding Report. Copenhagen: IDSN, 2008. https://idsn.org/wp-content/uploads/user_folder/pdf/Old_files/asia/pdf/RR_Pakistan.pdf; International Dalit Solidarity Network. 'Pakistan'. IDSN – International Dalit Solidarity Network. https://idsn.org/countries/pakistan/; Government of Pakistan, Ministry of Federal Education and Professional Training. Pakistan Education Statistics 2021–22. Islamabad: Academy of Educational Planning and Management (AEPAM), 2023. https://library.aepam.edu.pk/Books/Pakistan%20Education%20Statistics%202021-22.pdf; Government of Pakistan. FATA Education Management Information System Report 2018–19. FATA Secretariat, Directorate of Education, 2019. Ahmed, Mohammad, and Sadia Saleem. 'Issues, Challenges, and Opportunities of Education for Marginalized Communities in Pakistan'. Journal of Education and Educational Development 11, no. 1 (2024): 54–72. https://www.researchgate.net/publication/387400993_Issues_Challenges_Opportunities_of_Education_for_Marginalized_Communities_in_Pakistan_ARTICLE_INFO.

22. Towards a More Representative Democracy: The Need for Proportional Representation

1. Donald L. Horowitz, 'Electoral Systems: A Primer for Decision Makers', *Journal of Democracy* 14, no. 4 (October 2003): 115–27. https://www.journalofdemocracy.org/articles/electoral-systems-a-primer-for-decision-makers/.
2. House of Commons Library. 2011. Alternative Vote Referendum 2011: Research Paper 11/44. London: UK Parliament.

3. Quraishi, S.Y. 'Why India Needs to Change Its Electoral Voting System'. The Caravan, 4 April 2018. https://caravanmagazine.in/vantage/why-india-needs-to-change-its-electoral-voting-system.
4. Ibid.
5. Ibid.
6. House of Commons Library. Constituency Boundary Reviews and the Number of MPs. Research Briefing CBP-05929. London: House of Commons, 20 November 2023. https://researchbriefings.files.parliament.uk/documents/SN05929/SN05929.pdf; Election Commission of India. Special Summary Revision 2024: Electors Data. New Delhi: Government of India, Press Information Bureau, May 2024. https://pib.gov.in/PressReleasePage.aspx?PRID=2005189.
7. Mukherjee Foundation. 'Pranab Mukherjee for raising Lok Sabha strength to 1000'. New Delhi: Pranab Mukherjee Foundation, 2018.
8. Andrew Reynolds, Ben Reilly and Andrew Ellis, *Electoral System Design: The New International IDEA Handbook* (International IDEA, 2005).

24. A Manifesto for the Future of Democracy

1. United Nations Development Programme. Structured Dialogue on Financing the Results of the UNDP Strategic Plan 2022–2025 (DP/2025/25). New York: UNDP, 2025. https://www.undp.org/sites/g/files/zskgke326/files/2025-07/dp-2025-25_structured-dialogue-on-financing-the-results-of-the-undp-strategic-plan-2022-2025.pdf; United Nations Development Programme. Funding Compendium 2023. New York: UNDP, 2024. https://www.undp.org/sites/g/files/zskgke326/files/2024-07/funding_compendium_2023_-_web_version.pdf.